The VES Handbook
of Visual Effects

The VES Handbook of Visual Effects

Industry Standard VFX Practices and Procedures

Edited By
Jeffrey A. Okun
Susan Zwerman

Co-Editors:
Scott Squires
Toni Pace Carstensen
Kevin Rafferty

ELSEVIER

AMSTERDAM • BOSTON • HEIDELBERG • LONDON
NEW YORK • OXFORD • PARIS • SAN DIEGO • SAN FRANCISCO
SINGAPORE • SYDNEY • TOKYO

Focal Press is an imprint of Elsevier

Focal
Press

Focal Press is an imprint of Elsevier
30 Corporate Drive, Suite 400, Burlington, MA 01803, USA
The Boulevard, Langford Lane, Kidlington, Oxford, OX5 1GB, UK

Notices

Knowledge and best practice in this field are constantly changing. As new research and experience broaden our understanding, changes in research methods, professional practices, or medical treatment may become necessary.

Practitioners and researchers must always rely on their own experience and knowledge in evaluating and using any information, methods, compounds, or experiments described herein. In using such information or methods they should be mindful of their own safety and the safety of others, including parties for whom they have a professional responsibility.

To the fullest extent of the law, neither the Publisher nor the authors, contributors, or editors, assume any liability for any injury and/or damage to persons or property as a matter of product liability, negligence or otherwise, or from any use or operation of any methods, products, instructions, or ideas contained in the material herein.

Library of Congress Cataloging-in-Publication Data
The VES handbook of visual effects: industry standard VFX practices and procedures/edited by Jeffrey A. Okun, Susan Zwerman; co-editors, Scott Squires, Toni Pace Carstensen, Kevin Rafferty.
    p. cm.
 Includes bibliographical references and index.
 ISBN 978-0-240-81242-7 (pbk. : alk. paper) 1. Cinematography—Special effects—Handbooks, manuals, etc.
2. Digital video—Handbooks, manuals, etc. 3. Digital cinematography—Handbooks, manuals, etc. I. Okun, Jeffrey A.
II. Zwerman, Susan. III. Visual Effects Society. IV. Title: Handbook of visual effects.
 TR858.V47 2010
 778.5'345—dc22

2010008415

British Library Cataloguing-in-Publication Data
A catalogue record for this book is available from the British Library.

ISBN: 978-0-240-81242-7

For information on all Focal Press publications
visit our website at www.elsevierdirect.com

10 11 12 13 5 4 3 2 1

Printed in China.

Typeset by: diacriTech, Chennai, India

CONTENTS

ABOUT THE VES

The Visual Effects Society (VES) is a nonprofit professional, honorary society dedicated to advancing and promoting the art and science of visual effects and to foster and strive for excellence and knowledge in all matters pertaining to visual effects. Further, the VES strives to actively cultivate talented individuals in this discipline; to educate and develop public awareness and understanding; to support and encourage technological advancements in the field of visual effects; and to establish a collective organization that recognizes, advances, and honors visual effects as an art form, in order to promote the interests of its membership.

FOREWORD

It became apparent to the Visual Effects Society that a need for exposing, and thereby standardizing, best practices in the creation of visual effects and the associated processes to the industry and others has long been overdue. This is especially true now, when one considers that our art is currently involved in virtually every moving image project regardless of medium—sometimes having a larger budget and creative impact on the final product than any other aspect of the industry today. The Society therefore made it a priority to create this book.

The VES Handbook of VFX has been written by artists and technologists who have helped create literally millions upon millions of shots, images, scenes, and visuals for television, movies, commercials, animation, games, and visual media worldwide. Every one of the 88 contributors to this effort is an experienced, highly qualified professional who can be classified as a leader in the field. Their contributions, their opinions, and their understanding come at the price of hard-won lessons taught by that best teacher of all: *experience*. And each has selflessly given his or her time, knowledge, and expertise to the creation of this book. Our intention is for *The VES Handbook of VFX* to set an industry standard for visual effects practices and procedures.

The book is meant to guide and inform as well as to enlighten, share, and educate. But it is far from being a *complete* explanation and discussion of *all* aspects of visual effects. As detailed as it might appear, every shot is different from every other one, and no set of rules, beliefs, opinions, or suggestions will be applicable to all. There is no substitute for experience, and this book should not be taken as such.

Everyone in the business of imagery has the same goal, or at least similar goals. Whether a visual effects producer, supervisor, pyrotechnics expert, miniature builder, cinematographer, plate supervisor, CG god, software engineer, rotoscoper, production coordinator, studio executive, compositor, matte artist, illustrator, color timer, etc., all will be, and should be, seeking the highest quality imagery at a reasonable cost. It is never an easy task to achieve this goal. But by being better informed, by learning from others' successes and mistakes, it will make achieving that goal at least a bit easier.

We hope that as you read this book, you will begin to understand the steps, experiments, processes, software, hardware, relationships, politics, and tasks that lead to the successful creation of visual effects. And as you gain that knowledge and begin to test, create, and invent, you will be able to add to that knowledge.

An online companion site (www.VESHandbookofVFX.com) accompanies this book. It is populated by more in-depth discussions of the material contained herein. But more importantly, this is where you will be able to add to this wealth of information, as your experience dictates.

One thing of utmost importance that this book does not address directly is *story*. As visual effects artists, we always need to keep in mind that our purpose is to tell the story. Visual effects is a very powerful and effective art to that end. And it is fast rising to be the most important and flexible art in the moving image industry. We have enabled directors and writers to tell stories that have never been told before in ways that have never been seen before! Consider what the stories of George Lucas, Steven Spielberg, and James Cameron, to name but a few, would have been like without the work of the visual effects artists and technologies. Where would Pixar be without our art? But, as Spiderman's Uncle Ben[1] said to him, "With great power comes great responsibility." And so it is with visual effects. We have a responsibility to the art, to each other, and most importantly, to the story. We must never lose sight of the fact that the best visual effects in the world are pointless if they cannot advance the story.

So to you, the reader, the student, the artist, the professional, we applaud you for wanting to know more, for reading and digesting the information contained in this book. We hope that after reading it, you will feel better prepared to go out into the world armed with greater knowledge and a more powerful tool set than you had before that will help you create the images you need to tell your story.

Jeffrey A. Okun
Editor
Susan Zwerman
Editor

---

[1] *Spider-Man* (2002)

INTRODUCTION

Michael Fink, Jacquelyn Ford Morie

The art of visual effects involves nothing less than making words into pictures, technology into art, and magic into reality. Artists and technicians who create this magic have labored throughout the history of moving imagery, always working in service of the story, the director's vision, and the cinematographer's art. This book, and its accompanying online version, is meant to be an exhaustive source that clearly describes and explains the techniques we use in the incredibly creative process of visual effects.

It is important to keep in mind that film may have been the first moving image medium that employed visual effects, but as new technologies developed—animation, video, games, the Internet—visual effects were there. From the early video tricks of Ernie Kovacs, to YouTube, to your local cineplex, visual effects have been employed to help the creators of all moving media tell their stories. So to the reader, we stress that when you read the word "film," we mean by implication all moving media. As technology improves—and video games start to look like film, and film's visual effects are created like video games, and all are done at the same resolution, and they look photoreal in animated films as well as live-action films—visual effects will merge into a shared technology.

Visual Effects and Special Effects

Although in this book we will use almost entirely the term *visual effects*, we hope the reader will always understand that creating effects for moving images requires the skills of both visual effects artists and special effects artists. The public at large often confuses which techniques relate to special effects and which to visual effects, and often calls our work *special effects*

The VES Handbook of Visual Effects. DOI: 10.1016/B978-0-240-81242-7.00001-6

regardless of how the effect is accomplished. This section explains the differences and how the two disciplines are often inextricably linked.

Visual Effects

Visual effects is the term used to describe any imagery created, altered, or enhanced for a film or other moving media that cannot be accomplished during live-action shooting. In other words, much of the art of visual effects takes place in post-production, after primary image capture is complete. Visual effects can be added to live-action capture through techniques such as matte painting; rear- and front-screen projection; miniature or forced perspective sets; computer graphic objects, characters, and environments; and compositing of disparate images recorded in any number of ways. The recent explosion in digital tools that make flawless compositing, digital sets, and fully computer-generated characters possible and accessible to moving image makers at all levels has made visual effects a standard part of every moving image maker's tool kit.

Special Effects

Special effects are generally described as effects that can be done while the scene is being captured and are commonly called *practical effects*. Special effects go hand in hand with visual effects in current methodology, such that it is often difficult to determine what was a special effect and what was a visual effect. This collaboration has been enhanced by digital technology. For instance, the early acceptance of digital rig removal allowed more freedom for special effects artists to create more elaborate flying rigs on set while greatly increasing safety for all involved. Examples of more typical special effects are bullet hits, practical explosions, rain, fire, car gags of all sorts, flying rigs, motion rigs that shake sets or props or vehicles, gimbals to mimic the motion of boats or planes, and artificial ocean waves and spray.

Why Use Visual Effects?

There are three reasons to use visual effects in a film: The first is when there is absolutely no practical way to film the scenes described by the script or required by the director. The astronauts' perilous trip around the moon in *Apollo 13* (1995) and the transition of Mystique into Logan in *X-Men* (2000) are examples of this.

The second reason to use visual effects comes to fore when you *could* do the scene practically, but doing so might place someone's life at risk. In the very first visual effect done in a narrative film, *The Execution of Mary, Queen of Scots* (1895), it probably would have been a bad idea to actually behead the actor portraying Mary. The 1926 silent film *Fire Brigade* contains a scene where a toddler gets left behind in a burning building. It is clear she is surrounded by flames and must be rescued by the heroic fireman. The little girl, however, could never be exposed to real fire. She was shot separately from the fire and the two shots were optically composited so the girl really appeared to be threatened by the flames. This technique allowed for some hair-raising scenes without risking anyone's safety.

The third reason arises when it is more cost effective or practical to utilize a visual effect than to film a scene for real, due to issues of scale or location (or both). Examples of this are the huge crowds of Orcs attacking in the *Lord of the Rings* films (2001–2003), the little girl among the bears in Svalbard in *The Golden Compass* (2007), and Russell Crowe commanding his ship midstorm in *Master and Commander* (2003), or even the much simpler work done for *Tropic Thunder* (2008), with added shots of Ben Stiller having a phone conversation with his agent, long after the location was lost to the production.

The Creation of Visual Effects

Visual effects, if they are done well, are not obvious. At their best, they work to further the story being told, becoming an integral part of what makes us willing to suspend disbelief. We know when we see a film depicting fantasy places or characters, such as the distant planets in the film *Star Wars* (1977) or the Na'vi in *Avatar* (2009), that such places or people don't really exist, but we believe in them nonetheless. Visual effects at their most powerful seamlessly combine different aspects of the story in each frame, in essence packing ever more story into the scene. The history of moving imagery is filled with examples, many of which are presented in this book.

From the earliest times, artists have been technologists. The progression from painting with crude dyes to painting with plaster (frescoes) to painting with oil paints; the invention of mathematical perspective; modern uses for lenses and mirrors; and the development of cameras, lenses, emulsions, and film itself were all advances driven by artists. These advances were all developed to create a more real, more believable, more fantastical visual effect, and above all, to tell a better story.

A Bit of Visual Effects History

In the very first years of commercial filmmaking, 1895 to 1905, any visual effect was limited to what could be done in-camera, which included fairly rudimentary effects such as substitution shots (stopping the camera and changing the scene before starting it again) or simple frame splits. In this latter technique, the first part of the effect would be shot, during which hand-drawn mattes[1] would be slipped into the light path before the film plane, placed in front of the camera on stands, or even attached directly to the lens of the camera. The film was wound back to the starting point of the scene and the second element then exposed onto the film in the area that had no exposure from the black matte (thus the term *matte box* for the square fixture in front of a camera, which in current use holds filters in front of the lens). In these early days, the camera was always locked down, which made such effects possible.

The first widely acknowledged visual effect was in the 1895 film *The Execution of Mary, Queen of Scots*, a historic dramatization shot at Thomas Edison's studio in New Jersey. Alfred Clark, who had recently joined Edison's crew as a director-producer, devised a technique of stopping the camera so he could replace the actor portraying the queen with a dummy whose head could safely be detached from its body. One year later in France a magician named George Méliès discovered the same technique while filming a Paris street. His camera jammed, and when he got it going again, just seconds later, it was enough time for a bus in the street to seemingly transform into a hearse. Méliès went on to use such tricks in hundreds of short films over the next 15 years.

Edwin S. Porter, a member of Thomas Edison's production team, drew on these techniques, and more, in his 12-minute film *The Great Train Robbery* (1903). The film was considered a breakthrough work, making a huge impression on the public and future filmmakers. One scene, inside the station ticket office, showed a moving train outside the office windows. The office was shot on a set, making sure it was black outside the windows so that there was no exposure on the film in those areas. The filmmakers, using a black matte to hold out the previously exposed region, then filmed a moving train into the black, unexposed area. Today we can see that the perspective doesn't match and the scale is incorrect, but in 1903, this was an amazing *tour de force*.

The decade of the 1920s was also witness to movies enhanced by increasingly sophisticated matte paintings used for backgrounds

---

[1]Mattes: usually a black or opaque shape used to block the exposure in part of an image so that another image can be exposed into the matted, unexposed area.

that extended the depth of the screen image and created extraordinary scale. Painters such as Norman Dawn, in California, and Percy Day, in England, invented and refined matte painting techniques that were in continual use until the development of digital tools for matte paintings and composites. Norman Dawn is often credited with inventing matte painting for films with his use of glass paintings in *California Missions* in 1907. Percy Day, who was Peter Ellenshaw's stepfather and Albert Whitlock's teacher, began his career in 1919 and was very well known by the time he painted the matte paints for *Thief of Baghdad* in 1940 and *Black Narcissus* in 1947.

Early on, nearly all visual effects shots required a locked-off camera. By the 1930s, filmmakers had started experimenting with nodal pans and tilts. By moving the camera such that the horizontal or vertical rotation occurred around the nodal point[2] of the lens, the filmmakers removed parallax[3] and made possible the photography of matte paintings on glass and hanging miniatures, combined with live-action pans and tilts.

Borrowing technology from developments in sound in the late 1940s and early 1950s, visual effects artists adapted the use of synchronous motors to control pans, tilts, and dolly moves. This allowed for accurately duplicating a camera move shot on one set or location with a matching move back on the lot in the visual effects department. The gear was clumsy, and true-frame accurate recording and playback of moves was not always possible or consistent, but this precursor to motion control of film cameras provided visual effects artists with another tool to meet the growing demands of directors and camera people for more innovative shots.

Process photography, the rephotographing of previously shot footage projected on a screen in combination with a live-action scene, became a powerful tool by the 1930s, allowing actors to be placed in what appeared to be moving vehicles, airplanes, dogsleds, and ships, and on what appeared to be precipitous cliffs, mountainsides, and building tops. Process photography needed the convergence of the development of pin-registered camera movements, fine-grain film stocks, and synchronous motors before it could become practical. Benefitting from the seemingly nonstop progress in image capture and projection technology, process photography became more and more commonplace

[2]Nodal point: the point at which the light entering the lens converges before it spreads again to form an image at the film plane.
[3]Parallax: visible shifting of objects at different distances, in this case due to panning or tilting a camera that is not rotating around the point where the image converges in the lens (nodal point). Essentially equivalent to a very tiny crane or dolly move—the off-nodal mount of the camera creates a small translation of the lens through space.

through the 1930s and 1940s. It was in heavy use until the advent of digital compositing allowed for the creation of flawless bluescreen and greenscreen composites.

In addition to projecting backgrounds onto large screens behind actors, process photography allowed live-action images to be projected onto tiny screens placed in miniature sets, and by way of careful blending of the projected image with the set, the actors appeared to be in some very difficult circumstances. Fay Wray, when projected into a small screen at the top of the Empire State Building miniature in *King Kong* (1933), made the 18-inch Kong into a mighty beast.

The famous airplane chase scene in *North by Northwest* (1959) with Cary Grant is an excellent example of process photography in its heyday. The plane buzzing Grant's character was rear projected, while Grant ran on dirt on the set, which also served to form a false horizon in front of the screen. The final shots are completely convincing.

The first film to effectively use front projection was Stanley Kubrick's *2001* in 1966. Front projection had many advantages over rear projection—particularly color clarity of the projected image. Even so, it was nearly always used with static cameras, or limited to pans and tilts, because of the inability to create a camera move that was separate from the projection. In the late 1970s, Zoran Perisic introduced the Zoptic front projection system, which coupled zoom lenses on the camera and the projector. Used initially on Richard Donner's *Superman* (1978), the system allowed for what appeared to be camera motion when in fact the motion was driven by the changing image size from the zooms.

Another development in process projection technology was further refined in the early 1980s by Jon Erland and John Dykstra at Apogee. In an attempt to create flawless bluescreen photography for photochemical compositing, Erland worked on a frontprojected bluescreen technique, building on a technology first developed by L.B. "Bud" Abbott for the film *Tora! Tora! Tora!* in 1970. The result was the Blue Max system. In this technique the blue projected field is not very bright, but the screen's retroreflective material is so directionally reflective that it returns nearly all of the projected light back to the camera lens. People or objects in the scene, lit in a normal fashion, reflect so little of the blue light that you don't see blue on them—only on the screen. This was a major advantage for the time: There is virtually no blue spill on the actors or shiny objects.

It might surprise some to know that blue screens were used as far back as the 1930s in black-and-white films. In the 1933 film *King Kong*, the scene where Kong comes pounding through the gates was shot with blue behind the set. Because of the black-and-white film's color sensitivity, it was possible to add filters so that the blue area did not receive any exposure. Thus, it was "simple" to reexpose the blue-screened parts of the film with the stop-motion of Kong.

Other systems besides bluescreen systems were developed to create traveling mattes for films. Like many of the techniques to create color images on film, and the many film formats, most of these now lie in obscurity. Systems that used ultraviolet light or infrared-sensitive emulsions in two-strip motion picture cameras were experimented with and even used but eventually were abandoned due to technical hurdles in their implementation. A very successful technique, used with great success by the Walt Disney Studio in the 1950s and into the 1960s and 1970s, was the "sodium vapor" process (named for the lamp used to light the screen). This method generated mattes by simultaneously exposing, through prisms in modified Technicolor three-strip cameras, both the live-action footage and footage on a second strip of film that had an exposure only where it captured light from the yellow screen. The filmmakers were able to generate first-generation mattes for much of their work using this technique. Disney used this process to great result in films such as *Mary Poppins* (1964) and *Bedknobs and Broomsticks* (1971). In the 1980s, modification of older techniques mentioned above using ultraviolet lights to expose some or all portions of the subject (by now, miniatures painted with ultraviolet-sensitive paint) came into use. These techniques were used with success on films such as *FireFox* (1982).

It was the groundbreaking work by Petro Vlahos in developing technology for creating color difference mattes that made all of these advances possible.

Optical Printers

By the late 1920s, in-camera effects had become very elaborate, and a new tool had appeared to create more complicated effects. The first optical printers made it possible to combine images shot in multiple locations into one shot without having to risk the original negative in an irreversible process. The early history of optical printers is not well documented. One of the first commercial versions, sold in the 1920s by the Dupue Company in Chicago, was fairly remarkable. It was able to handle both 16mm and 35mm film in 1000-foot loads and appears from illustrations to be able to carry bi-pack mattes. But from the 1920s and into the 1930s and 1940s, optical printers generally were custom made by camera people and technicians as the need arose. Whether driven by the demands of a particular scenario (i.e., 1941's *Citizen Kane*) or by the creativity and endless experimentation of effects camera people (Linwood Dunn being the premiere example), optical printers increased in sophistication and capabilities, but they remained a "cottage industry" until the government got involved.

Linwood Dunn is widely acknowledged to have built the first modern optical printer during his work for the U.S. military during World War II. The military was actively involved in creating films for training and propaganda around the world. They wanted a printer that would use common parts available everywhere. With Cecil Love, Dunn created a very sophisticated version of the optical printer that could be mass produced, called the Acme-Dunn Special Effects Optical Printer.[4] Visual effects created by use of the optical printer enabled directors like Orson Welles, Fritz Lang, Alfred Hitchcock, and Cecil B. DeMille to take us beyond our previous experience and show us exciting scenes in ways that were extraordinary.

In *Citizen Kane* (1941), Orson Welles worked with Dunn to create a large number of composites that were needed to complete Welles' vision. The Thatcher Library statue shot from *Citizen Kane* was originally filmed to include only the base of the statue and the plaque. Welles, however, asked for a much richer shot. In what became one of the first matchmoves, Dunn's crew built a miniature of the statue, as well as the dome and the ceiling of the room it is "in." The miniature elements were photographed at an angle to match the live-action photography. Dunn then carefully matched the camera move frame by frame in the optical printer. We see the camera tilt down from the extreme up angle on the statue and onto the live-action scene, and there is nothing to give the effect away.

Electronics for Camera Control

Early experiments in controlling the motion of cameras were conducted in Thomas Edison's studio in 1914, but these were mechanical connections linking cameras, and they were clumsy and impractical. Electronic control of camera motion was first seen in the 1940s, with a system devised by O.L. Dupy, a sound engineer at MGM. The Dupy Duplicator was a system that drew on the same technology used to synchronize sound recorders with motion picture cameras. It was used on films such as *Samson and Delilah* in 1949 to provide identical camera moves that allowed actors to appear truly threatened by a crumbling temple, and *An American in Paris* in 1951 to combine location footage with matte paintings and stage photography. The use of such synchronous motor controls continued well into the 1960s.

---

[4]This advancement was important enough to be recognized in 1945 with an Academy Award for technical achievement.

Stanley Kubrick's *2001: A Space Odyssey* in 1968 was a groundbreaking film in terms of both the visual storytelling used by Kubrick and the technology and artistry used by Doug Trumbull, Con Pederson, Wally Veevers, Tom Howard, Bruce Logan, and others to create those visuals. Cameras moved past miniature spaceships, driven by motors actuated by electrical timers, allowing precise control and multiple passes, of all elements in the shot. Timers and synchronized motors were employed to drive camera motors and art in pursuit of the famous, mesmerizing "slit-scan" images running toward the climax of the film.

By the mid-1970s, basic digital control of electronic stepper motors had been introduced for controlling the motion of industrial machines. Visual effects and special effects artists realized the potential of this technology and adapted digitally controlled motors to precisely control the motion of cameras and miniatures in multiple axes. The film *Star Wars* (now *Star Wars Episode IV, A New Hope*), released in 1977, brought audiences exciting and complicated sequences that would not have been possible without the innovations of John Dykstra, Don Trumbull, Jerry Jeffress, Alvah Miller, and a number of others.

During this same period, for *Close Encounters of the Third Kind* (1977), Jerry Jeffress and Alvah Miller built a system similar to the *Star Wars* system, but one that could record live-action pan, tilt, and focus on location in Alabama and then play that move back—now scaled to capture a matching move on a miniature—in California.

Star Trek: The Motion Picture (1979) followed on this technology with systems that controlled more axes simultaneously. Innovations by Paul Johnson at Apogee, Fred Iguchi at the Maxella facility supervised by Doug Trumbull, and others, provided simultaneous computer control of motion and camera, allowing shooting speeds that reduced demands on lighting, and allowed the recording of real-motion blur. Pan, tilt, roll, camera speed, aperture, dolly (east/west and north/south), boom, and swing were all available for camera motion, and the miniatures, lights, projectors, or other objects could be moved with purpose-built "model movers" that had the capability of roll, pitch, yaw, dolly (e/w and n/s), boom, and swing. When combined, the relative motion of the camera and the objects being photographed allowed for some thrilling choreography that audiences had never before seen.

Live-action motion control requires systems that are reliable, fast, quiet, and quick to set up and program. A number of individuals and companies have contributed to the ongoing development of this technology and have found ways to continue innovating so that the technology remains a powerful tool in filmmaking.

A very important recent development in motion control has given us the ability to integrate previsualized computer graphic scenes with live-action cameras. This technique allows directors to see dimensionally accurate real-time composites of digital backgrounds and characters with the actors who are being photographed. This provides confidence that the camera will not be moving through the digital set, or that the giant robot will have room for itself between the actor and the virtual set's wall. It gives the director of photography confidence that the lighting will work with the digital set yet to be built, and that the camera moves and lenses are proper for the scale of the digital environment, which is invisible outside the camera monitor. Taking this technology a step forward, there are now systems, such as the system used by James Cameron for *Avatar* (2009), to capture manual camera moves using virtual camera devices on previsualized virtual sets with motion captured characters. Cameron and his visual effects team could plan and execute fully digital shots that achieved all the look and feel of physical photography, seamlessly integrating the language of live action camera work into fully digital scenes.

The Digital Age

In the late 1950s and into the 1960s, John Whitney, Sr., began creating intricate and involving images using surplus analog military equipment. He photographed moving patterns of light and lit objects that were moved by these analog computers. The patterns recorded by a camera synchronized to the motion were intricate and complex. This work was the inspiration for the slit-scan technique used to create the stargate sequence in the film *2001* (1968). John Whitney's techniques and images attracted much attention, and after establishing his company, Motion Graphics, Inc., in 1960, he created the animated graphics for Hitchcock's *Vertigo* (1961) opening.

In 1962 Ivan Sutherland's MIT dissertation introduced the concept of the interactive graphic interface for a computer. From Sutherland's original work flowed the work of many famous computer scientists who were driven to find ways to create images with a computer: Alvy Ray Smith, Jim Blinn, Ed Catmull, Steven Coons (who actually inspired Sutherland; d. 1979), Pierre Bezier (d. 1999), Henri Gouraud, Bui Thuong Phong (d. 1975), Turner Whitted, and the list goes on. Looking up any one of these names is a great adventure in the origins of digital computer graphics.

In the early 1970s John Whitney, Jr., and Gary Demos were working at Information International, Inc. (also known as Triple-I), a company that produced high-resolution scanning and image processing equipment. While at Triple-I, Whitney and Demos formed the Motion Picture Products Group and began creating computer graphic images to provide filmmakers with a tool for storytelling that up until then had been in the realm of academic researchers. Triple-I did tests for films such as *Close Encounters of the Third Kind* (1977) and *The Empire Strikes Back* (1980), in addition to creating some very early CG animation for commercials. They went on to contribute seminal computer graphic work for *Westworld* in 1973 and *Futureworld* in 1976, which had the first shaded 3D objects (a hand and Peter Fonda's head) seen in film. Triple-I also created motion picture's first fully shaded 3D computer graphic images and a full 3D digital body for the film *Looker* in 1981. Of course, the most famous film at Triple-I was 1982's *Tron*, which used the talents of some of the most creative artists in motion pictures and computer science to create its imagery. In fact, it took the four major existing computer graphics companies to make the amazing visuals for *Tron*: Triple-I, MAGI, Robert Abel & Associates, and Digital Effects—an unprecedented effort.

Star Wars (1977) showed a scene in which pilots were training to fly through the Death Star trench, leading to the destruction of the Death Star. This graphic was created by Larry Cuba while still at the University of Chicago. In 1979, the film *Aliens* also had a small sequence displaying a vector graphic[5] terrain flyover. In 1982, Pixar, then a division of ILM, created the "Genesis effect" for *Star Trek: The Wrath of Khan*. The effect was the first use of particles in a film to re-create the appearance of natural phenomena. Although not photorealistic, the effect was entirely convincing because it helped tell the story in a very strong visual sequence.

Whitney and Demos formed Digital Productions in 1983, with the acquisition of a Cray X-MP (the most powerful supercomputer of the day) and support from Control Data with a number of VAX computers. In 1983, Digital Productions undertook the task of creating hundreds of shots for the film *The Last Starfighter* (1984). This was a groundbreaking event in visual effects history, and the group created stunning computer graphic images at a far higher level of complexity than ever seen before, setting the stage for the future of computer graphics in film. From this point on, CG could be used to create images that were not just seen as a computer display, but as an original image in the story. Digital Productions went on to record a number of firsts for digital storytelling—the first fluid dynamics, the first attempt at

---

[5]Vector graphics: images created with lines drawn by a deflected electron beam hitting the phosphor coating on the inside of a CRT. Unlike raster graphics, which contain solid areas of color or texture, vectors are just lines drawn on a screen. Vector graphic displays, although computationally friendly and amazing for their time, were incapable of creating shaded objects.

a photoreal animal, and entirely new techniques in digital film scanning and compositing.

In 1985, Pixar, under the supervision of Dennis Muren, created arguably the first CG-animated character in a motion picture—the stained glass man in *Young Sherlock Holmes*.[6] Yet less than 30 years later, we see the successors of this pioneering work in amazingly believable characters such as Gollum in *The Lord of the Rings: The Two Towers* (2002) and the Na'vi in *Avatar* (2009).

deGraf/Wahrman, formed by Brad deGraf and Michael Wahrman, opened the 1988 Electronic Theater showcase at SIGGRAPH[7] with a low-resolution animated opera singer, remarkable for being rendered and displayed in real time. Using technology that has since been adapted for motion capture and performance capture, this was a stunning indication of the direction of computer games, video, and film animation in coming years. Trey Stokes, a puppeteer, now CG artist, manipulated a "Waldo"[8] with his fingers. His motions drove the motion of the CG opera singer in sync with the prerecorded music. Devices based on this technology continue to be used in film, video, games, and even brain surgery.

Major advancements in computing speed, power, and storage led to the creation of tools to record and then film out scenes captured by motion picture cameras. Visual effects facilities and visual effects and special effects artists and scientists used imagination, technical knowledge, and an amazing amount of creativity to invent and create these first tools. In the late 1980s Kodak, with collaboration from ILM, developed the technology for the first (more or less) practical film resolution scanner. Along with this invention came the development of the Cineon digital film format, which became the standard format for motion picture image recording and filming across the world.

In 1988 audiences were excited by the use of digital "morphs" in *Willow*. *The Abyss*, with its water character, was released in 1989, and *Terminator 2*, featuring a fully CG leading man, opened in 1991. In 1992 the first attempt was made to replicate real, recognizable creatures in a feature film—the penguins and bats in *Batman Returns*. These films revealed to audiences amazing

[6]The argument comes from those who think the character Bit in *Tron* (1982) was the first.

[7]SIGGRAPH stands for Special Interest Group on Computer Graphics and Interactive Techniques, which is part of the international Association for Computing Machinery. SIGGRAPH holds an annual conference that highlights the most innovative work in computer graphics and typically attracts attendance of up to 40,000 computer artists, scientists, filmmakers, and other CG enthusiasts.

[8]Waldo: mechanical device that has encoders attached to its axes of motion such that any motion of the device will translate to a series of numbers that are read by the computer as locations or rotations in 3D space.

new characters and story moments that could not have been created in a convincing way without the developments in computer graphics. *Jurassic Park*, in 1993, finally showed the power of digital visual effects to help tell a compelling story.

The years since 1993, it can be argued, included as much innovation as the previous 100 years of visual effects. Everything was open, and a legion of incredibly clever visual effects artists, scientists, and engineers redrew the landscape such that no effect was beyond our reach. We saw the world of optical printing fade from common use faster than any of us would have believed possible as digital scanners and printers, augmented by new compositing, 2D software, and fantastic developments in 3D camera and object tracking came to the fore. We have seen tremendous work done in graphical user interfaces tailored to the needs of artists; improvements in animation, modeling, and rigging; the application of physiological attributes to characters; improved motion capture; physical simulation; and—absolutely essential to our current state of accomplishment—huge advances in lighting and rendering.

Paralleling the progress in visual effects for film has been the exponential increase in the power and complexity of computer games and web-based media, with stunning real-time graphics. As expectations rise with improved technology, visual effects techniques will disseminate through all aspects of visual storytelling done with moving images.

Unintended Consequences: Where Does Creativity End?

All of the improvements and progress in visual effects during the past 100+ years—the changes from the original hand-cranked camera, to optical printing, to digital compositing, to computer graphics imagery—have had one major impact: They have opened creative options well into the post-production process, virtually until the last possible moment.

When the techniques available to us were photochemical, visual effects artists knew exactly what had to be done to finish the film. Shots were not easily changeable, and filmmakers had long settled on what they expected from a given visual effect. You had to get the *Millennium Falcon* to fly between the asteroids, and you knew exactly what everything had to do. It was an intense exercise to get it done, to come up with a creative technical solution that looked good on screen. Now, after extraordinary progress in the power to create visual effects, everything can be constantly manipulated and changed—although often with extraordinary effort. Because of this, filmmakers are no longer disciplined to make critical creative decisions up front and often postpone them as long as they can. In essence, the creative process only ends when time runs out and the film, game, or other project must be released.

What does all this mean for the future? Very shortly, with digital distribution employed across the world, films will be directly downloaded into servers at theaters. Filmmakers will be able to change scenes even while the movie is playing! Many of the technologies that make online game playing, and changes to games, possible could fuel changes in the exhibition of feature films. Films can be altered for specific demographics. They can "play in Peoria" … or in San Francisco, or Alaska, or for different countries or groups. Visual effects may never be done.

Conclusion

Visual effects have allowed filmmakers to take us on journeys to places that have ceased to exist or that have never existed, and to see things that we could only imagine. With the magic of visual effects, we have witnessed stories set on imaginary planets; embraced rich fictional worlds; come to know beasts, devils and angels, robots, and talking apes; and brought dinosaurs back to life, not from insect DNA trapped in ancient amber but from the magical plasticity of digital imagery created by talented visual effects artists.

It is important to emphasize the word *artist*. As our predecessors Masaccio, Piero della Francesca, Leonardo da Vinci, Muybridge, Maret, and Méliès drove their technologies forward, they created great art. So it is with visual effects artists. Computers today provide artists with a powerful tool to create fantastic images, but computers alone cannot make those images. It is the eyes of the artists—their imaginative and innovative use of these new tools—that create the wonderful new worlds we see in games, on television, on the web, and at the cinema. The magic is really and truly from the artist's vision.

The art of visual effects can serve to change our perspectives and instill new understandings of our relationship with the universe. An amazing example of this is the opening scene from the 1997 film *Contact*, where we zoom out from earth's atmosphere through bands of electromagnetic signals we have sent into space … defining our small corner of the universe … out past exceedingly distant galaxies where our signals will take countless millennia to penetrate—vast, unfathomable distances … at last coming back to the blue eye of a little girl just discovering the wonders of this earth and the "small moves" it takes not to miss anything.

We, the visual effects artists and technologists of the Visual Effects Society whose daily lives are dedicated to making magic real, hope you will enjoy this book and that it serves in some way to enable you to see things in a new light, exercise your imaginative powers, perhaps even join us on this journey to make stories that engage, astonish, and captivate. We are proud of the work we have helped create as makers of movie magic, and we are glad to share our ideas, history, and techniques with you in this book.

2

PRE-PRODUCTION/ PREPARATION

OVERVIEW
Scott Squires

The making of a film, commercial, or television show is broken into three main phases:

Pre-production: where all the design, construction, and preparation occurs before any filming is done.

Production: the actual filming of the live action that occurs on a set or location.

Post-production: all the work to complete the project after the filming. This includes editing, sound, music, and visual effects.

Even though the majority of visual effects are done in post-production to augment the shots that were filmed, all of these phases are important to visual effects. During production a visual effects supervisor or plate supervisor is on the set to make sure the live action is shot in a way that visual effects can be added correctly in post-production.

This chapter covers pre-production relative to visual effects. This includes the budgeting of the visual effects and the decisions about what company and visual effects team will work on the show. More importantly, it covers the designs and the techniques that will be used and that will ultimately determine much of the success of the visual effects. Pre-production is also a good time to develop new techniques, test ideas, and start the building of models when possible. Although this chapter approaches many of these areas from a feature film standpoint, the same steps apply to commercials and television production, just in a smaller number of shots and shorter time schedules. Each production is unique, so the issues covered in this chapter are meant as a starting point for a typical production. Budgeting requirements may be a bit different from studio to studio, and some areas, such as previs, are continuing to develop and change.

The VES Handbook of Visual Effects. DOI: 10.1016/B978-0-240-81242-7.00004-2

Production (producer, director, studio) may be reluctant to spend much time on visual effects pre-production, but this can have a huge impact on the cost and quality of the visual effects and the time required. A VFX Supervisor is able to work with the director, producer, and production departments to determine trade-offs for different approaches. This may prevent the construction of large elaborate sets that could be replaced by matte paintings or the use of digital doubles for stunts that could be impractical on the location. The choice of techniques in pre-production will also determine what steps are required during shooting and what can be done to shoot as efficiently as possible. Pre-production costs are relatively small since a smaller team is involved. If design decisions are not locked in before filming, then it is possible the live action may be shot in a manner that will need to be completely changed in post-production when the designs are locked in place. This is not only very expensive but is unlikely to provide the best-quality shots.

BREAKING DOWN A SCRIPT—BUDGETING
Scott Squires

Budgeting visual effects is a difficult and ongoing process because of the number of unknowns associated with visual effects shots. Any assumptions should be listed on any bid, along with the date of the script and any additional materials (storyboards, etc.). Shots will have an average length assigned by default (usually 5 to 8 seconds).

To balance the flexibility of editing with the costs associated for animating and rendering visual effects, a "handle" length is usually assigned on a project. These are the number of extra frames at the start and end of each shot (typically 4 to 8). This allows the director and editor some slight adjustment in editing even after a visual effects shot is completed. Without this handle, many shots would have to be redone, which would cost more time and money.

The creative aspect of film production plays a major role in the ultimate costs of the shots. The design and style of the shots along with the decisions by the director will shape the budget requirements. Changes later tend to be much more costly than if the shots were designed and shot as planned.

Visual effects companies do the majority of visual effects work on feature films as fixed bids. Any miscalculation can be very costly to them. It is important to be as specific as possible and to budget a certain amount of creative freedom for the director. Change orders are created by the visual effects company when a shot changes so much that the costs have increased, but there should be some built-in budget tolerance to avoid having to issue a new change order on every shot daily.

Some small films may be done on a time-and-materials basis. The visual effects company provides an estimated budget but the actual cost will depend on the actual time required to complete the work.

Ballpark Budget

The first visual effects budget (ballpark, rough, or initial budget) is likely to be done before a director is even assigned to the film. The studio will have a script that it would like to get a rough budget for. A VFX Producer at the studio or an independent VFX Producer may do this initial budget.

The VFX Producer reads the script and notes any scenes that would seem to require a visual effects shot. In visual effects, each shot is custom done. The first step to breaking down a script is to determine the numbers and types of shots. A script, however, does not provide this information. Even a production script will be broken down only per scene, not per shot.[1]

If a director is not yet involved in the project, then the VFX Producer will have to make guesstimates about the rough number of shots required in any given scene. This will be based on the VFX Producer's experience and knowledge of film. A single scene can be one shot or a dozen shots. A rough rule of thumb might be a shot per sentence in the scene or per action verb, but once again this is very dependent on the writer and director.

A simple ballpark budget may be arrived at merely by taking the number of total visual effects shots and multiplying this by a shot average cost for this type of film. This figure could be based on the experience of the VFX Producer. Since unions do not cover most visual effects positions, there are no set salary levels. Actual rates will depend on the location and company hiring. A slightly more accurate approach is to assign shots to easy, medium, and hard ratings with corresponding costs associated with each. Another approach is to break shots into basic shot types (2D composites, 3D animation, matte painting, etc.) and related costs for each. Note that each of these costs would include all direct costs, overhead, and profit to provide the final figures.

The VFX Producer typically uses a spreadsheet or a database program to list the shots, with a brief description and the costs and totals of each. Any assumptions are listed in the final budget (i.e., "car crash assumed as stunt, with only rig removal required").

---

[1] Scene: a progression of shots taking place in one location. Shot: a continuous and uninterrupted action on film. Cut: the edited footage. Sequence: a collection of scenes that make up a section in a film.

More Detailed Budgets

Once a director is assigned to the project, the VFX Producer and VFX Supervisor will review the script and adjust the shot count and shot types based on the director's thoughts. In some cases shots that were deemed to be visual effects may be able to be accomplished by other means on the live-action shoot (such as stunts or special effects[2]).

It is important for the other department heads to be realistic about what they will be able to achieve on the set or location. Anytime something does not work during the live action, it is likely to be added to the visual effects list of work to be done.

As the sequences are designed, they are assigned a two- or three-letter abbreviation per sequence. Shots are then assigned as three or four numbers within the sequence and frequently incremented by 10 to allow new shots to be added between planned shots. For example, RL010, RL020, and RL030 may refer to three shots in the rocket launch sequence. If a shot is added between RL010 and RL020, it might be designated RL015. These numbers are assigned to storyboards and previs so there is a one-to-one correspondence.

As sequences are storyboarded or prevised, they will be rebudgeted based on these. Rebudgeting is also required if there is a rewrite on the script that involves visual effects. A dozen or more revised budgets may be required over the course of a film.

Cost and time requirements are taken into account when determining techniques to be used. Any change in technique will require adjustment to the budget.

Bidding

At some point in pre-production, a package of identical material is sent out to various visual effects companies. This will include the script, any storyboards and previs completed, and a breakdown provided by the VFX Producer. The breakdown will list the shots, their description, and a defined technique, if any. The same information is supplied to all of the companies with the hope that the bids received can be compared directly to one another.

Depending on the show, bid packages may be prepared for specific sequences or types of shots and assigned to different companies that specialize in a particular type of effect. Some film projects are awarded to one visual effects company and some are split up among a number of visual effects companies. The

---

[2] *Special effects* covers effects work done live on the set, such as fire and breaking props. *Visual effects* covers effects done in post-production.

latter approach is used when schedules are limited or production quality and costs are best deemed to be split among a few visual effects companies, with each doing a specific sequence or type of visual effect.

The choice of which visual effects companies will bid on a show depends on their availability and the studio's experience with them. Location of the company is no longer the issue it once was.

The visual effects company has its own VFX Producer and VFX Supervisor review the material and create a detailed bid. This is usually done with the various department heads or leads when accuracy is desired. Each shot may be discussed and assigned a number of man-days per task (matchmoving, roto, compositing, etc.). Each of these estimates is placed into a spreadsheet and cost calculations are based on each particular task. By default, a profit margin and a small amount of padding are added to the total. These types of details, however, are not usually turned over to the studio; only the costs for the shots.

All model building, model shooting, element shooting, and other assets will need to be calculated based on time-and-materials estimates. The length of research and development (R&D) and the number of people involved will need to be noted as well.

Plate Photography[3]

Typically, a small team of visual effects artists is sent to cover the live-action shoot to make sure the shots are correct for visual effects use. This team usually consists of the VFX Supervisor, coordinator, and data collectors. These costs are billed on a time-and-materials basis to the studio.

The overhead or non-shot-specific costs (operating costs, support people, equipment usage, etc.) and assets (CG models, physical models, etc.) are usually broken out separately from the shots. If asset costs were folded into shot costs, then a change in the number of shots would be incorrectly budgeted.

It is important when bidding to make sure realistic numbers are gathered. Pressure from the studio and competition may produce a bid below the actual cost, which may get the project awarded but cause problems later if the work cannot actually be done for that amount.

Another problem in bidding is being too optimistic. Nothing will go as well as expected and even simple shots will take more time than anticipated. Do not budget for the best-case scenario.

---

[3] Plates: filmed shots to be used for visual effects. *Plate photography* refers to filming those shots.

When department heads bid a specific function, they should provide estimates based on their average team member and not themselves. Whenever possible, costs and times required for recent projects should be compared to the new bid as a reality check.

While bidding the costs, the VFX Producer lays out a linear timeline based on the amount of work. Visual effects production usually ramps up with the modelers and texture-painting artists starting first, along with the key department leads. Any R&D will have to ramp up as well. If the time required to complete the visual effects is longer than the production allows, then the visual effects company has to consider adding additional artists and workstations or they have to budget for overtime. The other option is to tell the studio that the company will be able to do only certain sequences in the time provided.

Live-action filming usually involves a 12-hour workday, 5 or 6 days a week. Visual effects production can be as low as 8 hours a day but is much more likely to be 10- to 12-hour workdays. Toward the end of the visual effects work, the amount of time required can skyrocket. The release date of a film is usually considered unchangeable, so time lost anywhere in the production has to be made up in visual effects. Ideally, the number of shots completed each week would remain constant, but usually there is a slow ramp-up. Concept or editorial changes can also pile up, requiring a lot of overtime work (90-hour workweeks or even longer) to complete the film. This is hard on the artists and provides the lowest quality at the highest cost. Unfortunately, this seldom is in the full control of the visual effects company, and those costs will have to be factored into the bid at some point.

Temp Screenings

For efficiency, shots are usually worked on in a preplanned schedule based on the turnovers[4] and delivery schedule as well as resources and assets. The studios may have temp screenings and ask for temp versions of all shots or marketing materials for trailers, which causes a reschedule. This should be discussed with the studio before production begins and should be included in any contracts.

Reviewing Bids

Final selection of the companies will depend on the costs, experience, and quality of previous work. Tax incentives may also play a role in the decision. The size of the company will be taken into account since an expansion of shots could be problematic.

---

[4] Turnovers: edited and locked sequences that are delivered to the visual effects company to work on.

Contracts

The studio will draw up contracts with the selected visual effects companies. These should document the final bid along with the date/version number of any storyboards. The contract should also have specific dates for turnovers, the sequence completion dates, and the completion date. The completion date is known as the *finals deadline*. Due to time constraints, it is not unusual for large visual effects shows to edit and lock sequences for visual effects to begin even before the entire movie is finished being shot. So there may be multiple turnovers even while filming continues. Any key discussions or agreements should be put in writing if they will affect the cost or schedule.

Rebidding during Shooting

During live-action filming, changes are usually made that will have an impact on the visual effects. The visual effects team on the set should flag these, and it is likely the studio will want to rebid a sequence based on this new information.

Rebidding in Post

Once the film has been edited and the work is turned over to the visual effects companies, it will be reviewed based on the initial bid. Any changes from the original bid will require a change order from the visual effects company and a possible renegotiation of costs.

Monitoring the Budget and Schedule

During post-production the time each artist spends on a specific shot is recorded so the VFX Producer can flag when a shot is about to go over budget. The visual effects team needs to reevaluate the approach if a number of shots in a sequence are running over the original bids.

Typically, the number of visual effects shots for the film is divided by the number of post-production weeks available. This provides the average number of finals that need to be completed each week. This number is recalculated every week to reflect how many shots were actually completed the previous week.

Keeping the Budget Down

Creating visual effects is a complex task, with thousands of technical and creative decisions being made. It is a very time-consuming and labor-intensive process, which is the main reason for the high cost of visual effects. The number of people working on the visual effects can easily eclipse the number of live-action crew members. On a live-action shoot, the crew is visible and it is clear to the director and the producer that timely decisions are required. In post-production it is easy to lose sight of the fact that expenses are accumulating every day since the visual effects artists are busy working away at a different location from the director and producer. Here are some good practices to keep in mind:

- Simplify techniques whenever possible.
- Time and budget should be considered when determining techniques.
- Avoid working on coming up with the ultimate universal solution if a simpler, faster solution can be applied to the shots in hand.
- Work out any kinks in the pipeline before production begins.
- Avoid miscommunication. Try to be as clear with the director and visual effects artists as possible to avoid wasted work.
- Make large changes or adjustments to a shot early on. It is better to go too far and come back a bit than to do a dozen small takes to get to that same point. In many cases it may be necessary to go too far in order to determine the correct selection.
- Start with the larger issues in a shot and progress to the finer details.
- Do not wait until the shot is polished before showing it to the director. If there are changes to be made, it is better to make them early on. The exact point when a shot can be shown will depend on the specific director.
- Get clean plates[5] and as much data as possible during live-action photography.
- Try to cast your visual effects artists to take advantage of their strengths on specific shots and sequences.
- Keep an eye on the schedule. Avoid large bottlenecks in the workflow.
- Try to keep the workflow moving and to anticipate and schedule elements and tasks accordingly.
- Review shots in a cut sequence. Rather than looping a shot over and over again on a computer monitor, it is better to see it in the context of surrounding shots. This will avoid fixating on a small detail that will not make a difference in the final film.
- Be clever with the number of visual effects shots and angles required to tell the story.
- Avoid big changes when possible. Some change is expected in the creative process of making a film, but a big change can be costly.

[5] Clean plates: filmed versions of shots without actors or major action. These are used to make any rig removal easier in post-production.

- Lock designs before the start of production. If a key design is not locked before shooting, it is possible the shots will need major rework.
- Avoid unnecessary visual effects. If something can be done live or on a normal set, then do it.
- Avoid "fix-its." Visual effects are used more and more as a catch-all to cover problems on the set that could have been avoided. These may not be major work, but they can add up quickly.

WORKING WITH THE DIRECTOR AND PRODUCER
Scott Squires

Before meeting with the director and the producer, the VFX Supervisor or VFX Producer should prepare by obtaining as much information about the project as possible. Is a script available? Who are the key people involved? What were their other projects? What is the project based on? Has the project been greenlit?[6] A supervisor may be working for a visual effects company or may be freelance. Becoming familiar with past projects and any additional source material will make it easier to discuss the project requirements using these as references. If a script is available, it is best to read through it and make notes and questions in terms of the director's vision and how the various sequences will be approached. The VFX Supervisor will have to consider some of the techniques required to accomplish what is described in the script.

Demo Reel

Before the meeting a demo reel and resume/credit list should be submitted if there is time. The supervisor should bring the same reel and multiple copies of the resume to the meeting. The following information applies to other visual effects artists as well. The demo reel should include only the best work and should be on a DVD that is no longer than 5 minutes (2 to 3 minutes may be a more useful maximum). The DVD case cover should include the artist's name, position, and phone number. The inside flap of the DVD case should list the scenes or films in order and what the artist did or what their job role was. The DVD itself should also include the name and contact information since it may become separated from the case. A supervisor can usually just include the finished shots. A visual effects artist should include the before and after versions of key shots. Normally, this is done by showing the

---

[6] Greenlit: approved for full production with funding.

finished shot, then the original plate, and then the finished shot again. It's not necessary to show a before and after for every shot. Customize it based on your job type (i.e., an animator may want to show an animation test for a shot). The DVD should include the name (and possibly contact info) on the main menu. Avoid showing running footage in the DVD menu screen so that when the reviewers see the shots, the images are full screen. Consider using movie music as a basic soundtrack, which the reviewers can listen to or not. Any music that is considered grating should be avoided. Do not take credit for work you did not do and do not falsify anything on your resume. The facts will be uncovered during the project and will make things very difficult moving forward.

The Meeting

The meeting with the director and producer is both a job interview and, it is hoped, a meeting of the minds. They will want to determine if the VFX Supervisor can provide the creative and technical expertise needed for the project and whether they feel they can work with this person for 6 months to 2 years, depending on the scope of the project. Does the director feel that he or she can speak in creative film terms and not be caught up in the technical requirements? Does the producer feel that the supervisor has the experience and organizational skills to oversee other artists and companies? They will also be evaluating how passionate the supervisor is about the project.

The supervisor needs to be confident and part salesperson, as with any job interview. One of the first questions will likely be how they can do a particular type of effect for a sequence in the film. The exact answer to this may be very dependent on learning other details of the project, but they will want to know the supervisor has answers and can work with them on determining the best solution for their needs. The supervisor will want to determine the scope of the work, the general look and approach the director is planning, and as many details as are reasonable in an hour meeting. The supervisor needs to evaluate the director and producer and the project as a whole to determine whether it is a project that the supervisor wants to commit to for the next year or two. There is no guarantee when the next potential project will be offered to the supervisor, so that will have to be considered as well.

Moving Forward

Once the supervisor is selected, the first issue will be determining the true scope of the work with the director, producer, and VFX Producer. A detailed breakdown will have to be done for budgeting, and this budget will have to be adjusted as storyboards and previs are completed. These breakdowns may be sent out to multiple visual effects companies to bid. The supervisor should work with production to make use of as much pre-production time as possible. There will never be enough pre-production time, so it is important to schedule storyboards, previs, designs, and tests to be done. The supervisor needs to be able to communicate clearly to both the director and to others what will be required and how they can strike the right balance of creative design, time, and budget to accomplish the visual effects. The supervisor may have to do mock-ups and work with other artists who can produce designs and mock-ups to try to refine the specifics.

If the director has worked with visual effects before, then the supervisor will have to explain any differences from other approaches that were used on the director's previous projects. If the director has not done visual effects, then the supervisor will have to explain the basics of the process and what the director will need to know (without getting tied up in the technical details).

The supervisor needs to support the director with creative suggestions on shot design, creature design, and other visual effects creative issues. The approach many directors take for their visual effects shots differs from that taken for their other shots, but it is important to design the shots to match as if the objects and scene actually existed during the shoot. The supervisor will work with the director and producer to determine the best approach needed for the visual effects. This includes how to dovetail the visual effects into the design and execution of the film to achieve the best results within the budget. Planning how the elements will need to be filmed during production will be one of many issues the supervisor will have to convey to the director and the key production departments. When the director and supervisor work together well during pre-production, they develop a shorthand for communication, and the supervisor can use their understanding of the direction to guide decisions in production and post-production.

It is important for the director to look at visual effects as a required art, not something to be feared or ignored. The supervisor should be looked on as a key part of the creative production team, the same as the director of photography. The director's and producer's support of the supervisor will go a long way toward making the filming of the visual effects elements easier and more productive. The first assistant director and the production manager will take their cues from the director and producer, and if plate photography is rushed to the point of compromise, then the finished visual effects will be compromised as well.

PRODUCTION DEPARTMENTS
Scott Squires

Production Design

The *production designer* works closely with the director, director of photography, and VFX Supervisor to develop the overall look of the film. The production designer oversees the art department. An *art director* supervises the construction of sets and modifying locations. The *set decorator* is responsible for the decoration of the sets, and the *property master* deals with all things that the actor will have to handle. The art department also includes production illustrators, concept artists, and storyboard artists. Vehicle design falls under the art department. Creature and character design is usually done by specialists brought in by the art department.

The design and the look of the film have a large impact on the approach and techniques employed for visual effects. The production designer and VFX Supervisor will work closely to determine the trade-offs of set construction or location modification versus using visual effects (matte paintings, models, etc.). Cost plays the largest role but time, stage space, and interaction requirements are also considered. Note that production may have production costs in a different budget than visual effects, so it may not be a direct correlation between the two. In some cases just a small area will be constructed that covers the majority of the shots in a sequence. Anything beyond this would be done with visual effects extending the set or location.

The art department creates a number of concept art studies in pre-production for the director and the studio to review. Once this concept art is refined and approved, it will be used by the visual effects artists as both a reference and a guide. This applies to matte paintings and virtual shots (shots created entirely in the computer or as a miniature) as well. If a visual effects company has its own art department, that group will work closely with the production designer in addition to the director and VFX Supervisor.

The visual effects team gathers additional references of the sets and props that will have to be matched or re-created in computer graphics or as miniatures. That includes specific photos for texture mapping, photos for reference, and measurements of the set. Blueprints are gathered for any sets and props, but be aware that changes can happen during the construction that are not reflected in the blueprints. These days, the art department also uses 3D graphics programs that facilitate the transfer of CG models between the art department and the visual effects team. These may be used as a starting point for the fully rendered models to be used in post-production.

Many of the same CG models of sets, locations, and props from the art department can be imported and used for previs. In this case the scenes and camera placement can be much more accurate and will reflect the final shot very closely. The art department plays a pivotal role in storyboarding and previs. More specifics on storyboards and previs appear later in this chapter.

Camera

The camera department consists of the director of photography[7] (DP[8]) and a crew of camera operators and camera assistants. The DP is in charge of all photography, including lighting and composition. The gaffer, head of the electrical department, works very closely with the DP on the lighting. Whatever is captured by the camera system (film or digital) will be used as the basis for the visual effects plates and will also be used as a look reference for any virtual shots. The VFX Supervisor should work with the DP, director, and production designer regarding the format and look desired since these will have a direct impact on the visual effects and post-production pipeline. With the use of previs in pre-production, some DPs are starting to rough-in lighting designs even at this stage. These designs provide them with a guide for lighting the real sets. This information will be useful in the post-production phase if the lighting design remains consistent.

The VFX Supervisor should discuss a number of issues with the DP. Some of the issues include film format, capture media (film/digital), color correction, and special equipment requirements (repeatable heads, etc.). The overall look of the images and any required VFX shooting tests should also be discussed.

Camera Operator

The VFX Supervisor will work with the DP and camera operator on the set to let them know the framing requirements for the shot since there may be creatures or objects that will be added later.

Camera Assistant

The VFX Data Collectors will work with the camera assistant on the set to record the lens and exposure information for each shot and take.

---

[7] Also known as *cinematographer*.
[8] Another abbreviation is DOP.

Special Effects

The layman frequently uses the term *special effects* to refer to both visual effects and special effects, but these are distinct areas in filmmaking. The SFX Department handles special requirements on the set, including effects such as fire, rain, snow, explosions, breaking glass, and special props or set pieces such as a boat mounted to a motorized gimbal on a stage. Special effects are dealt with on the set during production, whereas visual effects are usually done to the images in post-production. Special effects are sometimes referred to as *practical effects* or *mechanical effects*.

The visual effects team needs to work very closely with the special effects team. In some cases the finished shot could be done either way. In those instances a number of factors will determine which approach should be used. Using special effects on set has the advantage of interacting naturally with the sets, actors, and lighting. Once it's been shot and approved on set, the shot is finished. There are times, however, when safety issues, timing issues, or just on-set time are limited to accomplishing these types of shots at the time of shooting.

A more common requirement is for the special effects team to work together with the visual effects team. Special effects provides what it can on set for interaction, and visual effects adds to it with CG or other methods in post-production.

In pre-production the VFX Supervisor would work closely with the special effects lead and discuss the requirements on a shot-by-shot basis. This allows the SFX Department to build and test any special devices or rigs. A rig may have to mimic the shape and size of an object that will be added later with visual effects. This is known as a *mandrill* and could be an object covered in blue or green if it involves screen work. In some cases it may be something as simple as supplying a fan to produce a slight breeze to blow an actress's hair in front of a green screen.

Visual effects frequently need additional photographic elements to add to shots. These may be torch fires for a matte painting, an explosion to replace a spaceship, or a puff of dust used to represent a large creature stepping in dirt. All of these involve the SFX Department and may be done some time during production or post-production as a second unit or separate visual effects element shoot.

Stunts

The stunt department is in charge of any risky action that would involve an actor or stunt person. Some shots could be done either with stunts or visual effects. A man being thrown across the street or a truck being flipped over could be done on the set by the stunt department or could be done by visual effects as digital animation or, as in the case of the truck, optionally as a physical model. In pre-production the director and production team will discuss the shot requirements with stunts and visual effects to determine the best solution. All shots that involve stunts will be reviewed. There may be certain physical limits on a real stunt that require a visual effect or at least completion of part of the shot as a visual effect. When it is possible to do the stunt on the set safely and in the way the director desires, that is usually the first choice. In many cases it may be a mix of techniques for a sequence, with some shots being done totally with stunts on set intercut with digital stunt people animated in other shots. Visual effects may have to create a total digital stunt double or may just do a replacement of the real actor's face over the stuntperson's face.

Flying people or animals in front of a green screen will require the stunts and special effects departments to provide the harnesses and wire work required to move them around.

Even simple stunts may require rigs that will need to be removed by visual effects in post-production. These may be wire rigs, ramps for cars, or small trampolines for stunt people.

Wardrobe

The wardrobe department is in charge of designing, creating, or obtaining costumes for all actors. Visual effects and wardrobe will discuss any costume issue that may affect the other department. The choice of bluescreen or greenscreen photography is mainly influenced by the colors needed for the costumes and wardrobe of the actors.

The VFX Supervisor will want to check any of the costumes that may need rotoscoping or keying against a colored screen. Thin veils, small tassels, and extra-shiny material such as foil could present problems in the compositing stage. These issues are discussed with the intention of coming up with a solution that will balance the creative choices with the cost, time, and quality required in visual effects.

If a digital version of an actor is required, the actor will likely need to be scanned in the specific costumes, so this will need to be scheduled accordingly. When possible, another copy of the costume is sent to the visual effects company so the modelers and the texture painters can use it as a reference instead of relying only on photos. A digital version may present some challenges of its own. If a costume has numerous dangling strings, these will have to be built and will require simulations to re-create the correct motion when the digital actor is animated. This will have to be taken into account when budgeting. In some cases the costume may be augmented with visual effects such as adding flapping wings or animated gadgets. In this case the wardrobe department would work with the director and VFX Supervisor (and likely the art department) to determine the look and requirements.

Occasionally the wardrobe department may create specific costumes for visual effects use, such as a motion-tracking suit or greenscreen suit. If an actor will be flown on wires or rigged to a special device, wardrobe will need to modify a costume to accommodate the harness by making parts of it slightly larger or by cutting the costume at specific points.

Makeup

The makeup department handles the hair and makeup for the actors. Specific makeup people may be assigned to specific actors. For elaborate prosthetics or unique makeup, a specialist may be brought in. If visual effects is required to augment existing makeup, then visual effects will need to work closely with the makeup department to determine how and where the visual effect will be added. It is likely tracking markers will have to be applied to the actor's face using self-adhesive dots or by applying a spot of colored makeup. This will aid in the process of making sure the computer graphic face augmentation or face replacement will look like it is locked to the actor.

If a digital version of the actor needs to be created, the hairstyle chosen will have an impact on the shots. Special software tools may have to be written to style the CG version of the hair to match and simulate the motion of the hair, especially if it is an elaborate or long hairstyle.

Special contact lenses may be used for the actor, or production may ask for any special eye changes (different colors, simulated blind eye, animal eye, etc.) to be done as a visual effect. These types of shots can add up quickly and do take some work to do correctly.

The supervisor will ask the makeup department to keep an eye on visible tattoos that the director doesn't want to see in the final film and any other cosmetic issues, such as wig netting, that can be dealt with on the set rather than in costly paint-out later.

Production

The production department includes the producer(s) and a number of support people. There may be line producers, production managers, and executive producers, depending on the film. Directors and their support teams are also covered under this department. When changes occur during the course of the production, it will be important to notify the producer so that adjustments can be made and to obtain permission to make such changes. This is very important if the changes have an impact on time or budget.

One of the other key production people who will interact with visual effects is the first assistant director.[9] The 1st AD is very much involved in the scheduling of the daily shooting calendar and in keeping production shooting on the set. The VFX Supervisor will want to check the shooting schedule for any visual effects conflicts. The 1st AD is a key link in making sure that visual effects has the time necessary to get what it needs on the set, so it is important for the VFX Supervisor to work closely with that person and to have them as an ally. All visual effects shooting requirements should be made clear in pre-production so that the 1st AD can consider the extra time required and can help facilitate the shooting of references and data gathering when the shoot starts. Without the support of the 1st AD, shooting visual effects shots will be problematic and could ultimately have a large impact on the cost and time required to do the visual effects.

Visual Effects

While the various departments are getting prepared for production, the visual effects team should take as much advantage of this time as possible and be proceeding with their own pre-production. The intention is to lock as many of the concepts as possible and to accomplish any work that does not require the team to have finished footage in hand.

Planning

During pre-production the VFX Supervisor should be getting a better idea of what the director is looking for in the completed film and how the director likes to work. That, along with the concept art, storyboards, and budget, will influence the techniques chosen by the supervisor. It is important to reevaluate the approach to make sure it follows any changes in the design and look of the shots.

Testing

During pre-production tests often need to be done to resolve a problem or check a technique or look before filming starts. This needs to be scheduled and budgeted since it could have a large impact in the coming production phase.

---

[9] The first assistant director is also known as the 1st AD.

R&D

A film project may require developing new techniques, software, or pipelines. That work should begin in pre-production since it can be time consuming to develop. If it is to be used to create a special look for the film, the director and studio may need to see it before moving forward with the project. The VFX Supervisor may need to work out a new technique before shooting begins to confirm it will work as expected, to fine-tune the process, and to determine the requirements for filming.

Reference Materials

Footage and images should be gathered as reference for the visual effects artists. This might be videotaping an animal at the zoo or reviewing other movies or photos. Reference material can be used as a starting point for animation, modeling, matte paintings, and lighting. The material is also useful to share with the director and other department heads such as the production designer and the director of photography. With clear imagery and references, it is possible to narrow down what works visually for the show and what does not.

Direct references will also be required. This includes shooting both reference photos and texture photos for any props, sets, and costumes that will need to be re-created in computer graphics. It also includes scanning the actors and props for 3D models. Once shooting starts it can be difficult to schedule the actors, and any delay in getting this information will delay the construction of the models. Note that the actual props or costumes may be modified in the first week of shooting since everything will be reevaluated on set.

Modeling

As soon as designs are approved by the director, physical and computer graphics models may be started. If these need to tie in with actual production (such as a set), they may need to be delayed or at least be done with enough flexibility to change based on the live action. As modeling proceeds the director will be shown the work at different stages to get his approval and adjustments. If the model is to be used for animation, a rough version may be used to start experimenting with the animation and exploring the character.

Editorial

An editor works with the director to take the raw footage that has been shot and assemble it into the finished film. A film that has a large number of visual effects shots will likely have a VFX Editor or Assistant Editor. The VFX Editor will be writing up the information shot sheets for the visual effects companies and cutting in shots in progress during post-production.

Although most of the editorial work will be done in post-production, the editor may actually start during pre-production. The storyboards can be scanned and assembled to provide a rough sense of the action and timing. As previs becomes available, it will replace the storyboards. The editor may also assemble rough sequences of "scrap" material made up of action sequences from other films to use as a template.

Scheduling may require the editor and director to complete the editing of specific scenes even while still shooting others so that the visual effects can be started. The visual effects editor and visual effects company may both be doing mock-ups to be cut in as the edit proceeds.

One of the issues to be discussed with the editor is the choice of format for the visual effects footage delivered for review. This may require the visual effects company to output a specific file with an applied color correction so that it works in the sequence on the editing system.

The editor will also work with the post-production supervisor and the VFX Supervisor to determine the requirements for the visual effects delivery. Some of these issues would be
- film or digital or both,
- format for delivery,
- method of delivery,
- digital intermediate (DI) requirements,
- any alternate deliveries (versions for television framing, etc.),
- schedule for DI or lab color correction,
- schedule required for temp screenings,
- schedule required for music and sound work that might require finished shots, and
- schedule for final deliveries and in what order of sequences.

Locations

Location Scout

During pre-production the production department and the production designer will have a location scout[10] searching for appropriate locations. The VFX Supervisor will want to discuss the requirements for visual effects at these locations. If they have a large impact on the visual effects, the VFX Supervisor may be asked to review the actual location or to review multiple locations to determine which may be best for the particular

---

[10] Refers to both the person who scouts the locations and the process of visiting the locations.

sequence. Which things will need to be added or removed in post-production to get the shots required? The VFX Supervisor will need to flag things that are not an issue (such as an area to the side that will be replaced in post-production by a matte painting). Light, shadows, hours of daylight, and light direction will also need to be considered and noted. Since a location scout may take place months before filming in that area, it is important to consider the expected weather and hours of daylight in the future. If the locations are locked early, some of the features or layout may be incorporated into the storyboards or previs. Some photos of the locations may be used for creating mock-ups or as lighting and rendering environments for CG models.

Tech Scout

Once the basic locations are decided on, the production department usually schedules a tech scout or multiple tech scouts. The primary purpose of a tech scout is to allow each department to see the locations and sets directly and review them for technical issues. The director, producer, and production designer usually take the key department heads to check out the approved locations and sets in progress. This includes the VFX Supervisor and VFX Producer or other support persons. Typically, a handout of drawings, layouts with basic measurements, and concept artwork is provided.

At each location the director describes the sequence that will take place and specifics about how he or she wants to use the location. The production designer describes what changes or additions will be done. They may be modifying the location or constructing a set on the location. In some cases the production designer may have artwork or a design miniature to help explain the layout. Storyboards and previs may be shown on the location. Armed with this information, the group then discusses any issues regarding the location. Any problems for a department are flagged and an attempt is made to solve potential problems.

From a visual effects standpoint, the VFX Supervisor has to see how the location or set will work for the visual effects shots. The same issues covered by the location scout will need to be reviewed, with more details. How different are the locations and sets compared to the storyboards or previs? Will this require a revised budget or a rethinking of the techniques? Are there items at the location that can or should be used for interactivity? The VFX Supervisor needs to visualize the shots currently designed for this location or set and determine what post work will be required to complete the intended scene.

Production Meeting

Many meetings are held throughout the pre-production phase, but at some point close to shooting, a full production meeting is held. All department heads attend, along with the director and producer. This is meant to provide the big picture to all departments and to cover enough details so that surprises on the day of the shoot are minimized. The storyboards are usually displayed around the room and passed out to each person as a book. If previs exists for a sequence, it will be presented on a large screen if possible. The 1st AD usually runs the meeting and steps through the sequences. For complex sequences each shot may be quickly stepped through, with a representative from each key department discussing what they will be doing for the shot (i.e., stunts will be handling the driving car, special effects will be knocking over the hydrant, and visual effects will add the rainbow in post).

Various department heads raise any special requirements. Visual effects will need to discuss the unique requirements they have, along with a quick rundown of the process.

Visual effects should flag any new issues raised in the meeting that would affect or alter the visual effects.

DESIGNING VISUAL EFFECTS SHOTS
Scott Squires

One of the key elements to a successful visual effects shot is the design. With today's technology most of the technical issues can be resolved (even if problematic), but there is little point in doing an elaborate and costly visual effects shot if the design is unsuccessful. Some suggested guidelines follow, but as with any art form, there are no absolute rules.

Visual effects shots require the same eye for composition as standard live-action shots, but there are a number of issues that directly relate to visual effects shots.

The costs and planning required for visual effects may lead the director to avoid dealing with the visual effects and the VFX Supervisor. This approach tends to lead to a more painful process during production and post-production. It also increases the costs and, more importantly, decreases the quality of the final shots if the visual effects team is second-guessing the director. The VFX Supervisor should be looked at as a creative collaborator and be relied on along with the director of photography and production designer to help design the film. The VFX Supervisor is there to serve the director and the film to create the appropriate effects in the most efficient way possible.

The main objective of any shot is to help communicate the story the filmmaker is trying to tell. It is easy to lose sight of this and have a visual effects shot become just eye candy with no intrinsic storytelling value. Visual effects are tools for the filmmaker that open up an almost unlimited range of stories that can be told on film. Locations, time periods, sets, props, and even the characters can all be changed or rendered from scratch. It is very easy to abuse such powerful tools and get caught up in the technique and pure visuals created. When anything becomes possible, including during post-production, there may not be as much care and design as there should be in pre-production. When an audience complains about too much CGI, this usually means there are too many unnecessary shots or that the shots have been pushed beyond the level expected for the type of movie.

Guidelines for Directors

1. Work with the VFX Supervisor and his or her team. Don't make the mistake of thinking that they just bring technical knowledge to your project. They bring a creative eye and experience that can help design the best visual effects for your project.
2. Assume everything is real and exists on the set. How would this scene be shot if everything were really on the set or location? This mind-set avoids treating visual effects shots differently.
3. Design for the finished shots. The VFX Supervisor will have to work out the techniques required and determine the different pieces to be shot.
4. Do the first pass of the storyboards without limitations. What visuals are needed? These may need to be pared back as the storyboards are reviewed, but sometimes shots are neutered to try to make a budget based on incorrect assumptions about the costs for the visual effects or what the technical requirements may be.
5. Design the shots necessary to tell the story well. If a particular story point can be made in two simple shots, then it may not be necessary to turn it into a 30-shot extravaganza. This is something to consider in the large scope of the film. Use the visual effects shot budget where it counts.

Storyboards

On a traditional live-action film, the director is unlikely to have storyboards. The director creates a shot list and then works with the director of photography and the camera operator to determine how best to visually capture the action that has been blocked out with the actors. Some directors are focused entirely on the actors and allow the director of photography to lay out the visuals. If storyboards are done for a live-action film, they are typically used as a rough starting point to be revised on the set with the director of photography.

Storyboards for visual effects are used to make budgets and to plan the multiple elements that need to be shot or created. They are usually critical for determining the visual effects techniques and assets required. There is still some flexibility when shooting, but it will be dependent on the specific shot.

A director typically works closely with a storyboard artist. Directors have varying degrees of visual design sense. If the director doesn't have much of a visual sense, then the first pass at shot design falls into the hands of the storyboard artist.

Because some directors want to shoot without planning, they avoid storyboards or simply do a pass to appease the studio and then ignore them in production. This approach has multiple problems. The budget may not take into account what the director really wants. It may be necessary to tell a director on the set that it's not possible to do what is now being asked. The stunt team and special effects crew may have to build special rigs and set them up for the shot being described. Additional plates for the scene may have already been shot for different camera setups.

This isn't much different from a director walking on set and wanting to shoot in a direction where there is no set. When the physical limits are obvious, concessions are more likely to be made. Since the visual effects costs and limits aren't quite as obvious, there's a danger that shots will be done anyway with the intention of working it out later. When "later" means in post-production, it's likely there will have to be even larger compromises to the shots, and it becomes a difficult situation for the supervisors caught between the director and studio. With proper planning and storyboards, the odds of success are much higher, the final shot quality will likely be better, and the shooting time will probably be less. All of this is very dependent on the director and the specifics of the shot.

Previs

The next step up from storyboards is previs. Details of previs are covered in the main previs section later in this chapter. The moving imagery in the previs provides directors with an even more precise method to convey their vision. This allows design of not only the basic composition but the timing and camera motion as well. By editing the previs together, it's possible to create a sense of the design for the whole sequence. Storyboards and previs will then be used on the set to help maintain the design and consistencies of the shots.

Objective of the Shot

If the primary design goal of the shot is to make it cool and awesome rather than to advance the story, then it will likely fail. The reality these days is that it's very difficult, if not impossible, to wow the audience. There was a time at the start of digital visual effects when it was possible to show something totally new and different by technique alone. With the sheer volume of moving images these days, however, it's hard to amaze the audience even with something original. The best solution to creating compelling images is to design shots that enhance the story and then have the director work with the production designer, director of photography, and VFX Supervisor to come up with the best possible visuals for the film.

Even with the best intentions, the original concept of a shot may veer off course. The original storyboard is sketched up with the director and a storyboard artist. This is then reinterpreted by a previs artist, and then reinterpreted by a DP. Finally, in post, the animator, technical director, lighting artist, and compositor working on the shot may enhance it. In many cases this collaboration improves the shot, but there are times when the changes are at cross-purposes with the original intent of the shot.

Concept Art

It helps, of course, to have finished concept art when doing the storyboards and designing the shots. The design of the creature or scenes being painting as concept art can then be included in the storyboards and more accurately represent the final shots. Ideally, concept art is done in the same aspect ratio as the film and represents a frame in the sequence. As the concept art, storyboards, and previs progress, they sometimes inspire the director and writer to incorporate ideas from the various artists into the story and script.

Continuity

One of the largest issues with visual effects occurs when the visual effects shots are treated and designed differently from their surrounding shots. Sometimes the director and storyboard artist design the shots differently by making them simple and typical. An example might be when a sequence starts with a number of handheld shots for the live action, followed by a locked-off shot of a building matte painting, and then back to handheld shots. The inverse is also true (the visual effects camera turns into a super-crane that does impossible moves). The film should flow smoothly and the visual effects shots should integrate with the surrounding live-action shots without calling attention to themselves.

Photorealism

Directors are keen on photorealism but this, of course, is very dependent on the subject matter. A scene may include objects or images that have no foundation in reality. In these cases not only does the execution have to be great, but the narrative of the film also has to convince the audience to suspend their disbelief. If photorealism is the aim, then anything that breaks that goal will break the shot. Non-photoreal camera moves and exaggerated color timing are two things that can easily change the shot from being photoreal to being very stylized. Stylized imagery can pull the audience out of the shot (depending on the style and the film) and lose any sense of photorealism, which is a creative call. Photoreal and stylized images usually work at cross-purposes.

If a shot ignores standard physics, such as a CG jet that does an impossible maneuver, the realism of the shot may be ruined. As with other aspects of filmmaking, the director and VFX Supervisor will have to work out the balance of realism versus cinematic impact. These are the same issues the production designer and the director of photography have to deal with.

Original Concepts

At times the director will request something totally different, and the VFX Supervisor may be able to suggest certain new techniques or creative approaches. Tests should be scheduled and budgeted to explore new concepts. Some alternating of concept art and tests might happen as the ideas and results are refined. Sometimes the request to have something unique may actually mean to have an interesting shot, just like one already featured in another film. It is best to get this clarified before a lot of time and effort are put into developing something that is not actually original.

Budget

A script might have a simple shot description: *Only a wood fence separates the hero from the monster*. The VFX Supervisor envisions a shot with a solid fence and the hero below the line of the fence so that a simple matte can be created. The director may be envisioning five shots of a dilapidated fence with vines that the camera swoops up and over to a reverse of an over-the-shoulder from the monster. This is where storyboards and previs help clarify the director's vision. This will provide a much more accurate budget as well as help determine the best techniques available.

By reflex many supervisors may try to steer the shots to something simple and less expensive (based on studio pressure and past projects). Care should be taken to avoid sacrificing the film design and making adjustments too early.

Reality and Magic

Sometimes a secondary purpose of a shot is to sell the audience on its reality. Care has to be taken that this is subtle. For example, in *Forrest Gump* (1994), one of the characters has lost his legs. This is treated in a realistic manner, and since the audience knows that this can happen in real life, they tend to accept it in context and not focus on the visual effects. There is no need to "sell" the visual effect. Later, there is a shot where the character swings his partial legs in a way his real legs would not be able to move. This is a subtle hint to the audience to keep believing.

Some other directors may have approached this in a different way, with the intention of showing the audience that it's all real in much the same way a magician does. Focusing on the visual effect and trying hard to prove it's real has the unfortunate consequence of causing the audience to look at the shot as a visual effects shot and not an emotional shot helping to tell the story. A magician wants to point out his accomplishment to the audience, but a visual effects artist wants the shot to work in context.

Camera Angles

Most film shots are done from the approximate height of a person. To create the sense of an object of great height, the camera can be lower and tilted up. This is very useful for something like a giant. Looking down typically gives the sense of smaller objects. This is one of the reasons why, when shooting physical miniatures, the camera is kept at the model's eye level (6 feet scaled to model scale) when possible. When the camera looks down on a model, this tends to emphasize the model aspect. If the camera is to move over the model, mimicking an aerial shot in real life, it is best to replicate the motion and speed of a scaled helicopter. If the camera moves too quickly or in a manner not possible in real life at that scale, the illusion will be broken and the miniatures will look like what they are—miniatures.

For initial storyboards the director may select pure profiles or straight-on designs to get their ideas across. When it comes to actual shooting, though, it is usually better to shoot a bit off axis, such as at a ¾ angle, to provide more of a sense of depth and dynamics. This will also make the pure profile or straight-on shots stand out for more impact.

Framing

In addition to standard composition guidelines (such as designing the shot so it leads the eye to specific areas), the framing should be considered for its clarity and impact. Is this the best angle to make the story point the shot is trying to tell? If the framing is too tight or the angle is too abstract, the audience may be confused or may miss the point of the shot.

Scale

Visual effects are frequently called on to create creatures or objects that don't exist in real life. One of the issues that needs to be solved in such a case is to indicate to the audience the scale of these types of items. Sensing the scale of a smooth metallic cube in space is very difficult. It could be 1 inch or 1000 miles across. Everyone working on the film knows the scale it's supposed to be, so it is easy to forget to convey even this type of basic information to the audience in a visual form.

The best way to indicate scale is to show a comparison to a known object that overlaps it. If two fingers reach into the frame and grab the cube, then instantly the audience knows its scale. If the cube is behind the earth, then its scale is now known to be gigantic. In the example of the cube, it would also be possible to attach a ladder or door or some known frame of reference to the model to indicate scale.

Detail

Most man-made objects will be judged based on their complexity. A smooth object will be considered to be small, and an object with a lot of detail will typically be assumed to be large unless otherwise indicated. Physical model spaceships may be covered with detailed items such as parts from commercial models. Smooth-sided physical spaceships may be dabbed in cosmic crud—an affectionate term for a mix of modeling paste that provides a sense of organic texture. These same approaches can be used on CG models. If a CG model lacks detail, it looks either very small or, more likely, fake. Lack of detail and varied texture in CG models is what usually gives them away. Note that in nature even microscopic objects can be very complex.

Speed

The speed at which an object moves also tends to convey its sense of size. The faster it moves, the smaller it will seem to be, especially if it shows no sense of momentum and weight. This becomes problematic when the director wants a very large creature or character to move very fast and to change direction on a dime. Since the scale is likely to have been established, the creature just looks artificially lightweight, and this in turn makes the creature less real and does the opposite of what the director actually wanted to achieve.

Scaled Images

Creating large or small versions of people and props is fairly common. Shooting full-size objects (person, animal, etc.) and merely rescaling them in the compositing software is fairly straightforward. The problem is that they tend to look exactly like what they are. Just as fire and water are tough to scale realistically, so are many images. When possible, adjust the object as much as feasible to help sell the scale. This may include things such as clothing made out of thicker cloth that will look natural when scaled smaller in the composite. In this example, since thread and cloth thickness are a known size, if they are compensated for in the original costume, they will look correct when scaled in the shots.

Depth of Field

Depth of field can be useful when trying to keep the audience focused on a character or object. Anything in front of or behind the depth of field will be out of focus and blurred. This is one of the many optical effects from standard photography that can help create a convincing shot. When shooting scaled images (such as a person who's supposed to be 3 inches tall), re-creating the shallow depth of field that is common for macro photography will help this match the audience's expectations. When shooting a miniature you want to have as much depth of field as possible to replicate a full size set or object. Virtual shots and animated features tend to simply set the depth of field to whatever is desired without considering the focal length or lighting. A sunny outdoor scene shot with a wide-angle lens would look odd with a shallow depth of field. These are the types of things that people subconsciously notice as being a bit off. Try to base the design on what would be reasonable if the object were really being filmed.

Sequence of Shots

Shots need to be designed with the sequence and surrounding shots in mind. If each shot is designed independently, then each may be great individually, but when viewed as a sequence, redundancies and missed opportunities may arise. Shots should flow from one to another and be used to build an emotional impact.

Camera Motion

Visual effects allows a camera to perform unlimited moves between scenes or within a virtual scene. This can be used to create very stylized scenes, but as previously noted, this can cause problems if the intent is to be as photoreal as possible. Sometimes if the actor is doing a complex action, it's best to keep the camera motion subdued so that the audience can view the action clearly. A complex and quick camera on top of action in the scene can be confusing to the audience and lose the point of the shot. The balance is trying to create a visceral experience that maintains the story points.

Less Is More

Sometimes the most powerful shots are the simplest ones. In many cases there is a desire to increase the number of extras, space ships, creatures, etc., within a scene or to keep layering element after element in an attempt to "amp up" the action. An example is a fight between two characters. If the audience knows the two characters, then it can become both an emotional and an action scene. If the same shot were done with thousands of people, then the end result is likely to be a dilution of interest instead of the desired increase in impact. The same thing applies to the number of spaceships in a scene. Layering a number of fighting creatures, thrown objects, smoke, and dust may result in a muddle instead of a dramatic scene.

With visual effects there can be a tendency to overdesign a shot and try to include everything including the kitchen sink. Spending a lot of time and money on a shot that becomes a 2-second quick cut or is so full of things that the audience has no idea what they are looking at is a waste.

Action Pacing

If an action scene goes on too long, especially with "in your face" visual effects, the audience is likely to get bored. It is important for the action to vary much as a roller coaster has a rise and fall of action. The impact of a shot has much to do with the surrounding shots. A steady stream of action doesn't provide a relative difference for the audience and doesn't allow for any suspense or anticipation.

CG Characters

It takes a great script, direction, and animation to make the audience care about a CG character. This is especially true in a visual effects film where the CG character exists in a real world. If the CG character defies natural physics and anything is possible, then it can easily turn into a cartoon where any violence doesn't mean anything.

Creatures and Character Design

The design of creatures and characters can play a major role in the film. It will have an impact on the creative success and the technical approaches used. Much effort should be spent testing and refining the designs.

In *District 9* (2009), the aliens worked very well for the visuals and yet had some design aspects that aided the technical approach. By keeping the aliens close to human size, actors could be used to stand in for the aliens and compositions with humans and aliens could easily work. The hard shells reduced the costs and difficulties of dealing with flexible skin, hair, and feathers. The alien language eliminated the need for precise lip syncing.

Avatar (2009) used character design to its advantage. The humanoid characters were similar enough to humans to allow the audience to connect and made it easier to utilize motion capture of actors. The differences (blue skin, facial structure, etc.) avoided the issue of the "uncanny valley." The uncanny valley refers to the result that occurs when an attempt is made to mimic humans in look and action but the closer it gets to matching a human, the more creepy it can be for the audience if it does not succeed exactly. This has been an issue with some motion capture animated films.

Powers of 10 Shots

It's not unusual for a director to want a *powers of 10* shot. The camera starts at a vast distance, usually in space, and then moves down to finally end up at the reflection in a person's eye, or the reverse. These shots have been done [*Contact* (1997), *The 'Burbs* (1989), etc.], so they are not as original as they might appear. They also tend to be difficult, expensive, and questionable as to how much impact they have on an audience who has already seen these types of shots in other films and commercials.

Oner

Oner is the term for doing one long shot instead of breaking it into multiple shots with different angles or cutaways. This may serve the narrative well but at other times it's devised to prove the shot is real (not cheating by cutting away) or to try to reduce costs. Since visual effects are budgeted per shot, some thought can be given to combining multiple shots into one to reduce the budget. However, any long and complex shot is likely to cost more time and money than if it were split up. Depending on the scene, cutaways can show the details and reactions, which may help create more of an emotional impact than holding on a single shot for an extended length of time.

Summary

When designing shots and sequences, it is worth coming at it from the viewpoint of an artist. Any reference material of great art, photos, and scenes from other films can be viewed as inspiration. If photorealism is key, then reference documentary photos and films. Base all aspects of the shot on as much reality as possible. If a stylized look is desired, then it may be necessary to take it to a level such that it doesn't appear to be poorly done photoreal images. Take advantage of all the parameters that visual effects provide—the lighting, color, composition, camera motion, and object motion—as long as it works with the surrounding live action and helps to tell the story.

VISUAL EFFECTS TECHNIQUES
Scott Squires

Many factors can influence the exact technique used for a visual effects shot or sequence. In most cases it is not a matter of figuring out how to do a visual effect but of determining which technique will work best for this particular project. Each chosen technique will have some type of trade-off between cost, time, quality, and flexibility. Some of the main issues to consider are discussed next.

Technique Considerations

Budget

This is one of the largest issues to consider when selecting techniques. There is never enough money in the budget. On low-budget productions it may be necessary to select less expensive techniques by rethinking the problem and reviewing all options. It is usually best to consider reducing the number of shots and the complexity of shots to a minimum to tell the story but still keep within the budget. It is better to have 100 well-done shots rather than 200 poorly done shots. This will require working closely with the director and editor to make clever design decisions that make the most of the budget. Lower budget productions also have to be even more careful about time and changes.

Time

The supervisor has to make it clear that enough time has to be allocated in all stages of production (including pre-production). Too little time will result in much higher budgets and, more importantly, reduce the quality of work. Visual effects shots can usually be roughed in fairly quickly, but raising them to the level where they hold up on the big screen takes time. To make them great takes even longer.

Number of Shots

A large number of similar shots can support more R&D and assets than a single shot. A large number of shots will make an automated solution more useful. With a single one-off shot, it would be overkill to spend months developing a special computer script. If there are a number of similar shots, then the learning curve on the first shots likely will make the later shots more efficient.

Length of Shots

A 1-second shot is easier to create as a quick illusion, even if hand done, than a 30-second shot. The longer shots will require even more care in selecting a technique.

Complexity

A large number of running creatures moving through an elaborate environment will certainly require more techniques (collision avoidance, crowd animation, etc.) than a simple object moving through a scene.

Flexibility and Time on a Live-Action Set

Some techniques take more time or special rigging on set to accomplish (motion control, multiple elements, etc.). If circumstances change or for some reason the technique is not possible to schedule, then a different technique will have to be considered.

Flexibility in Post

Some techniques allow more flexibility in post-production, which can be necessary for films that are in flux or when a director and studio want to make a number of adjustments after the edit. Examples would be the choice between a CG building (which can be changed or rendered late in post-production) and a physical miniature building (which is what it is when filmed). Shooting separate elements also allows more flexibility in post-production.

Camera Motion

A locked-off camera is simpler to work with than a large crane or a handheld camera. A moving camera may dictate special techniques (such as matchmoving) that a locked-off shot would not.

Look

Most productions request images that are photoreal, but even in these cases the realism will be adjusted to make the images cinematic. Those involved want the *sense* of realism but not necessarily realism (the same applies to photographic lighting). Some productions will require very stylized imagery, which will require approaches different from a photoreal approach in both original photography and post-production.

Additional Suggestions for Determining Techniques

The Actual Shot Requirements

Communicate with the director to find out specifically what he or she requires. Also be sure to consult with other departments to see how they can help with a solution. A communication error can have the visual effects crew trying to accomplish a different shot from what is actually requested. Note that this can change at any point and needs to be confirmed before starting the shot(s).

Breaking It Down to the Simplest Requirements

Do not become overwhelmed by the complexity and number of shots. If there's a choice between a complex and a simple solution, the simple solution is usually the better option if everything else is equal.

Review Other Films and Alternative Techniques

Review other films that have achieved anything similar. Do research on how they were done. Use the Internet, SIGGRAPH[11] notes, behind-the-scene supplements on DVDs, *Cinefex*,[12] and other sources of information.

Think Outside the Box

Consider other techniques: practical special effects, reverse action, shooting upside down, in-camera effects, or approaches a stage magician might take.

Think Pre-Digital

Not every visual effects shot needs to be done using digital techniques. The trailer for *Close Encounters of the Third Kind* (1977) had the camera moving down a road at night with a glow beyond the mountains. This was a motion control shot done in smoke. The road was 2 feet across, with forced perspective. The mountains were 3-foot-tall cardboard. Someone lay behind the "mountains" and adjusted the brightness of the glow by slowly turning a dimmer up and down. This same shot in CG could be turned into a very elaborate and complex shot. There are many examples of this from the pre-digital era.

---

[11] Special Interest Group on Graphics and Interactive Techniques.
[12] *Cinefex* is a magazine devoted to visual effects.

Budget Time and Money for Testing

This is especially true for new techniques and for major sequences. Budget both photography and post-production work on test shots.

Research and Development

Experimenting with software and other digital techniques will be required. Explore the options or develop new ones.

Keep the End Result in Sight

It is easy to get sidetracked on solving the problem while losing sight of what the final results need to be. Remember: All that matters is the final results.

Hand Versus Automated Work

Sometimes doing something by hand or even frame by frame is a faster, cheaper, and easier solution. An example would be spending a week on a complex green screen with problems that could have been solved with a rotoscope and standard composite in a couple of days. The same thing applies to computer scripts and simulations. Painting out a rendering error on a couple of frames is faster than rerendering the shot.

Try Not to Solve Every Permutation

Software engineers and visual effects artists sometimes try to cover every possible variation on a problem. Just solve what needs to be solved.

Balance Techniques

Try to use the same technique for a number of shots. This will tend to make it faster and easier since the crew will get up to speed and be able to apply what they have learned to new shots. However, there are times when a shot may be unique and require a different approach from the rest of the sequence. Balance the best technique for each shot with the efficiencies of sequence techniques.

Cheating

If the same effect can be achieved in front of the camera by any other means, do it. Theatrical movies are created from illusions. The front of a house may only be a facade and contain no actual rooms or even sides. The marble floors you see are likely the work of a gifted painter using a sponge to paint pieces of Masonite. If you can do something simple that provides the effect, then it probably doesn't matter that it is technically incorrect.

One on-set example of this was a shot for *The Mask* (1994). In the wide shot large items were going to be pulled out of Jim Carrey's pants pockets, so computer graphics pants were planned to show the objects stretching the pants. On the day of the shoot, the director wanted the shot tighter and Carrey was wearing baggy pants. The pants were turned into shorts with scissors and holes were made in the pockets that allowed props to be pushed up by assistants. This saved the cost of a visual effects shot and allowed them to do it live.

Examples

Here are a few examples of trade-offs to be made when determining the techniques to use:

* *Create a castle on a hill where none exists.* One shot. Add flags and people to add life to it. Matte painting will likely be the simplest and most cost-effective approach. Part of the painting could be based on photos of real castles. Painting would allow the image to exactly match the lighting and the angle required.

  Flags on the castle could be done by shooting real flags against a green screen. If these are small in the frame they could be shot on 24p[13] standard or HD consumer video. People could be shot on a green screen from the correct perspective using a similar type of video if they are small enough in frame. Both the flags and the people could be done with computer graphics, but for most companies, simulating them, preparing the models, and making them look real would likely take more time and effort than filming them.

  Closer coverage could be done with the actors in front of a castle set piece consisting of a section of one or two walls. These would be fully live-action shots and require no visual effects.

* *Same shot but with a simple camera move.* If the castle is far enough away and the camera move is small, then a matte painting could still be used since the perspective change would not be enough to show a problem. 2D[14] tracking software could be used.

  If the camera move is large enough that a perspective change is visible, then this could be done as a 2.5D[15] matte painting solution. In a 3D program the matte painting is projected onto a simple 3D model. 3D tracking would be done to

---

[13] 24p: video shot at 24 frames per second (fps), the same as film. Most NTSC video is 60i (approximately 60 fields per second). PAL video is 50i (50 fields per second).

[14] 2D is represented with only height and width (as in a still image). XY tracking is sufficient for 2D motion tracking.

[15] 2.5D is a cross between 2D and 3D. It provides the illusion of 3D without being fully 3D and is usually done in CG by projecting images onto very simple 3D shapes.

match the camera motion. The simple model would provide enough sense of perspective change without requiring a fully detailed 3D model.

- *Static camera but multiple shots.* If the shots are all from the same camera setup, then a single matte painting could be used, with minor changes for lighting as necessary. If many different views are required, then it may be more cost effective to do it as a model (CG or physical) than to create a matte painting for each shot.
- *Complex camera move*, such as flying from the ground and over the castle. Note that the camera move should mimic a real camera move (such as a helicopter) in terms of speed and motion unless the desire is for it to be stylized. This would be done as a physical or computer graphic model of the castle.

In this case it may be worth doing the flags and people as computer graphics so the perspective would be easier to match.

There are trade-offs to both of these:

Computer Graphics Advantages:
- If the castle or part of the castle needs to transform.
- If a CG character or creature is interacting with the castle.
- Easier to re-do the shot later if there was a change. With a physical model once the model was shot it would require a full reshoot if there was a major model change or different view required.
- Unlimited number of takes and lighting variations.
- Unlimited number of dynamic simulations for breaking or falling. Downside can be hard to control.
- If the visual effects company is already doing 3D visual effects and doesn't want to subcontract the model construction and photography.

Physical Model Advantages:
- Relatively easy to do organic shapes including things like flowering vines on buildings.
- Real interaction. Breaking models can be built to break at specific points and to crush based on a design.
- Being physical makes it more tangible to work with in terms of shot angles.
  Here are a few techniques to composite a person in front of a background:
1. *Blue or green screen.* Some video formats work better with green screens due to color response, but most of the time the choice of screen color is dictated by the dominant color of the costumes. Blue costumes would require a green screen.

Fine detail such as hair, glass, water, and shadows can be extracted. These may require extra work such as creating garbage mattes and specific key settings.

2. *Rotoscoping*. If it is not possible to shoot with a colored screen or if a decision is made later to use just the foreground, then rotoscoping the foreground image is typically a reasonable way to create a matte.

     If the live action shot against a colored screen has too many problems (a lot of contamination, very unevenly lit, etc.), then rotoscoping may be faster and better than just a straight key.

     If the main issue is to put something in the middle ground (e.g., a creature or object between the actor and the background), then rotoscoping is usually preferred. This allows the subject and the background to be shot at the same time and with the same lighting and camera move. This could be done as a blue or green screen, but that would require shooting the actor in front of the screen, removing the screen, and then shooting just the background. This would take more time on location or the set.

Summary

Don't rush to assign the first technique that seems to apply. Give some thought to the implications and the trade-offs of various approaches. Expand your knowledge and thinking so you have more options from which to select. Keep in mind the final results as your target. Keep the technique as simple as possible for the desired effect. The technique chosen will have a large impact on the final results and difficulty getting there.

WHAT IS PREVIS?
Mat Beck[16]

Previs, which is an abbreviation of *previsualization*, has been around since the first director framed a shot with his thumbs and forefingers and the first pencil sketch illustrated a proposed set. It is a natural function of the need to figure out the visual story to be told and how best to tell it. Previs can be simply described as a visual rough draft of a shot, sequence, or show. But that would underestimate its power. It often represents not only the best way to develop a sequence but the best way to collaboratively link the variety of departments, technologies, and points of view that have to come together in a modern production to bring the sequence to life.

---

[16] With substantial help and input from Marty Kline and John Scheele in original drafts.

As the technology and scope of previs have grown, it has become more challenging to precisely define exactly what qualifies as previs and what does not. A previs sequence can be composed of anything from animated storyboards to video shot with stand-ins to CG motion-captured characters rendered in a real-time virtual environment. Regardless of technique or practitioner, it seems that any definition would include certain key concepts:

- Previs is *visual*. It is a collection of images (generally moving) that can be viewed, manipulated, and discussed.
- Previs comes *before* a larger and more complex production effort, thereby conserving resources. Even postvis (discussed later), which comes after main production, still comes before the significant effort of more complex visual effects work.
- Because the techniques are more economical and have quick turnaround, they can be used for *experimentation and exploration* of images, ideas, etc.
- It is a tool for *communication and collaboration*. The images promote a common understanding of what is intended.
- It provides *guidance* for the larger effort down the road.

Here are the definitions proposed by the Joint Technology Subcommittee on Previsualization, a collaboration between the Visual Effects Society (VES), the Art Director's Guild (ADG), and the American Society of Cinematographers (ASC)[17]:

Previs is a collaborative process that generates preliminary versions of shots or sequences, predominantly using 3D animation tools and a virtual environment. It enables filmmakers to visually explore creative ideas, plan technical solutions, and communicate a shared vision for efficient production.

The reference to filmmakers includes anyone performing visual storytelling for movies, television, games, and other related media.

The same committee recognized a number of subgenres of previs in current practice:

- *Pitchvis* illustrates the potential of a project before it has been fully funded or greenlit. As part of development, these sequences are conceptual, to be refined or replaced during pre-production. (Although pitchvis is not part of the main production process, it allows people like executives and investors to take a first look at the potential result.)
- *Technical previs* incorporates and generates accurate camera, lighting, design, and scene layout information to help define production requirements. This often takes the form of dimensional diagrams that illustrate how particular shots can

---

[17] Curtis Clark ASC, Chris Edwards, Ron Frankel, Colin Green, Joel Hynek, Marty Kline, Alex McDowell, Jeff Okun, and John Scheele all had critical input in generating and refining the definitions of previs.

be accomplished, using real-world terms and measurements. (In good practice, even preliminary previs is most often based on accurate real-world data, allowing technical data to be more easily derived.)

- ***On-set previs*** creates real-time (or near-real-time) visualizations on location to help the director, VFX Supervisor, and crew quickly evaluate captured imagery. This includes the use of techniques that can synchronize and composite live photography with 2D or 3D virtual elements for immediate visual feedback.
- ***Postvis*** combines digital elements and production photography to validate footage selection, provide placeholder shots for editorial, and refine effects designs. Edits incorporating postvis sequences are often shown to test audiences for feedback and to producers and visual effects vendors for planning and budgeting.
- ***D-vis*** (design visualization) utilizes a virtual framework in pre-production that allows for early in-depth design collaboration between the filmmakers. Before shots are developed, d-vis provides a preliminary, accurate virtual design space within which production requirements can be tested, and locations can be scouted. Approved design assets are created and made available to other previs processes.

In recent years, digital previs (in virtual 3D space) is playing a more and more dominant role. It offers a path to new forms of filmmaking (see later section on advanced techniques). But traditional practical previs techniques also continue to provide economical ways to communicate desired action and imagery. Regardless of the technique chosen, the principal goal has always remained the same. By developing and then expressing the intention of a sequence in an accessible visual format, successful previs increases the likelihood that that intention will eventually be realized.

DEVELOPMENT OF PREVIS TECHNIQUES
Mat Beck, Stephanie Argy

History and Background

Over the years, movies have been previsualized using a variety of techniques, including storyboards, story reels, live-action tests, photography using foam-core or dime store models, "proof-of-concept" work, and editorial precomposites—all of which relate to visual effects and the broader concept of visualizing a film.

There is no requirement that storyboards or previs be used in pre-production. Although prominent directors like Alfred Hitchcock and Orson Welles were renowned for meticulously planning out their films ahead of time, other filmmakers have relied more on improvisation, but storyboards and previs have become standard tools for clarifying difficult issues in advance.

In animation, story reels were a filmed assembly of story-boards (or other key frames), put together to give an early feel for the look and pacing of the final film. This has been a key production step at Disney since their earliest feature films.

Some illustrators became specialists at rendering detailed "exploded" images to deconstruct complex visual effects sequences—which were similar to the images now generated in technical previsualization using digital tools. Other art department staff became expert at projecting lens angle information and determining how much practical set would need to be constructed for anticipated camera views—and where matte paintings might be required.

Editors and VFX Designers have used (and continue to use) preexisting footage to help refine visual effects while they are still in the planning phase. Such "rip-o-matics" are another method of previsualization, which can be cut together well in advance of principal photography. The most famous example of this may be George Lucas' use of World War II fighter plane footage for *Star Wars* (1977), which enabled him to plan out his space battles.

Later, for *Return of the Jedi* (1983), Lucas used toy figures shot with a lipstick video camera to plan out the sequence in which speeder bikes race through a forest.

In the 1980s, computer-generated imagery first began to be used for previs. For 1982's *Tron*, Bill Kroyer and Jerry Reese used a combination of drawn storyboards and vector-line CG graphics for crucial scenes such as the lightcycle chase and the solar sailor.

Another of the earliest instances was in the film *The Boy Who Could Fly* (1986). To figure out how to stage an elaborate sequence in which two children fly over a school carnival, production designer Jim Bissell turned to the computer graphics company Omnibus, which created a virtual representation of the scene that enabled Bissell to see where he could place towers to support the actors on wires, as well as the Skycam that would cover their flight. James Cameron also used video cameras and miniatures to plan out sequences for the *Abyss* (1989).

Two groups made a significant contribution to the development of digital previs: On the East Coast, in the early to mid-1990s, Douglas Trumbull hired students from the Harvard Graduate School of Design, Yale, and the Massachusetts Institute of Technology to work at his company, Ride Film, doing what he called *image engineering*. Using CAD systems, the group began by working on a project called *Luxor Live* (1996) and then went on to do the movie *Judge Dredd* (1995).

Meanwhile, on the West Coast, Industrial Light and Magic formed a previs division called JAK Films, which created its first full sequences for the movie *Mission: Impossible* (1996). The group then went on to work on all three *Star Wars* prequels: *The Phantom Menace* (1999), *Attack of the Clones* (2002), and *Revenge of the Sith* (2005).

As previs evolved, it became clear that it could be used to provide some very useful technical information to the production crew. On *Starship Troopers* (1997), for example, the motion control rigs (crane, track, etc.) were modeled along with spaceships in virtual space so that not only spaceship animations but model and camera data could be handed off to the motion control unit for subsequent shooting. Information generated this way reportedly increased throughput by more than 10 times.

Other studios and film projects applied virtual previs in ways suited to the specialized needs of their projects. Disney built on its tradition of previsualizing animations, using digital tools to figure out how to combine computer-generated characters with live-action plates in the movie *Dinosaur* (2000). In the Fox animated film *Titan AE* (2000), previs elements became the basis for final shots. And *Panic Room* (2002) offered one of the first uses of previs for straight-up filmmaking, as opposed to visual effects, allowing David Fincher to use virtual cranes, the camera, and the environment to take best advantage of the movie's elaborate set.

In current practice, previs most commonly takes the form of 3D animation within a virtual environment, but traditional techniques remain an efficient and economical tool. Storyboards and live-action footage may be incorporated with CG elements. As in all visual effects work, previs can be a hybrid composite technique, taking advantage of whatever works to refine, convey, and implement an idea.

THE APPLICATIONS OF PREVIS: WHO BENEFITS FROM IT AND HOW?
Mat Beck

At its best, previs allows the making of the show before production begins—it is a form of rehearsal for an entire production. Every department can benefit, both in its internal operation and in its myriad communications with the other departments. Not every previs will be suitable for every application in scope or level of detail, but the arena of possible influence is broad—assuming, of course, that the work of the previs is carried forward into the later stages of production.

The following is a list of possible benefits/applications for the previs process, organized by department.

Writers can use previs to:
- Work out story concepts as part of development. Seeing a story even roughly put together on screen can be as beneficial as a script read-through to experience written words coming to life.

Directors can use previs to:
- Engage in blue-sky concept building initially unencumbered by implementation considerations. Before previs has to settle down and be responsible to the realities of production, it can sow its wild oats in the space of whatever is imaginable.
- Build compelling sequences through experimentation at a low burn rate (lower rate of expenditure).
- Limit excessive coverage by predetermining what angles are necessary and which are not (see the section titled *Camera and Art Departments: A Special Case* below for savings resulting from shooting and building only what is necessary).
- Take storyboards to the next level, by making them move.
- Bypass storyboarding entirely in some cases by building the world of the story and finding the best shots with a virtual camera within that world [sequences from the movie *2012* (2009) provide a recent example].
- Bypassing conventional production entirely and making the movie in a virtual studio (by using previs techniques with motion capture in a virtual space with virtual cameras, a process available to more advanced practitioners; see more about this in the section titled *The Future of Previs: Advanced Techniques* below). In those cases, ironically, simple filming of actors or stand-ins is sometimes used to previs the motion capture sessions—like the old-time Warner Brothers animators acting out scenes before animating them.

Producers can use previs to:
- Sell the movie. The special subcategory pitchvis allows demonstration pieces of key sequences to convince distributors/investors/studios of the potential of a project. More than one movie has been greenlit based on a previs alone. This is an example of previs that is pre-script, pre-director, pre-anything but a concept.
- Generate a more accurate estimation of the scope of a job—thereby reducing costs for overbuilding, lighting, shooting, etc.
- Allow more accurate cost estimation for the individual departments and overall project.
- Achieve an earlier determination of the division of labor between departments—for example, between practical effects and visual effects, between visual effects and set construction, etc.

- Often working with a VFX Producer, prepare apples-to-apples bidding packages for visual effects vendors.
- Control the process by making informed decisions earlier, without engaging the full production.
- Get every department on the same page—or image sequence, if you will.

Camera and Art Departments: A Special Case

The previs process has a special relationship with the camera and art departments for the obvious reason that it is occupied so intimately with movement of the camera within the set. The creative decisions that are embodied in previs need to heavily involve these two departments, not only for the best input, but so that those decisions have the approval of the individual who is charged with executing them.

The relationship of previs with the art department is especially critical because it has primary responsibility for designing the world of the story. It is critical that the two departments maintain clear and easy communication and share a common data space so that designs from the art department are efficiently used in the previs and results from the previs—that is, camera views, compositions, and changes in set requirements—can be easily communicated to the art department.

The concept of a *virtual production space* has been proposed by the production designer Alex McDowell. The basic idea is the creation of a common data space that accurately represents the world of the production and that informs the production all the way through post-production and beyond (e.g., game design). The term *d-vis* (design visualization) has been proposed as the name of the process.

Undoubtedly creative responsibilities will evolve as evolving technology blurs some of the boundaries between traditional creative categories and gives different departments a strong interest in the results of a previs, as well as the ability to generate or change it.

Regardless of any changes that occur, three principles seem likely to prevail:
- the necessity of a common data format that allows clear communication in both directions between the production designer/art department and the previs process,
- the necessity of early involvement of people with the greatest creative stake in executing the vision, and
- the necessity of disseminating the common data to all the sectors of the film production that can make use of it.

Art Department involvement with previs, other examples:
- 2D paintings done on top of still images rendered out of 3D CG previs scenes can convey tone, texture, lighting, set extensions, etc., to set dressing, props, SFX, etc.

- Dimensionally accurate set information, used to set up technical previs, can then be bounced back to the art department along with approved shots and angles so that they can modify sets based on the new information.
- The determination of how much to build practically, how much to generate digitally, how much greenscreen work is needed, etc., can be derived from technical previs.
- Needs of special lighting and camera equipment can have an early influence on set design.
- Previs can help with location issues, defining requirements in advance. For example, time-of-day analyses can be used to figure sun angles, etc.

Directors of photography can use previs to:
- Help to drive the process by providing critical input on camera moves, lens choice, and composition.
- Pre-determine equipment needs (including special rigs) early enough to figure budget implications and build what is deemed necessary.
- Predetermine the size of a green screen.
- Design or modify a lighting scheme once lens choices and fields of view are known.
- Perform a virtual prelight, in more advanced systems, using physically accurate models for individual lighting instruments and other main components of the scene.
- Get a sense of the rhythm and coverage of a scene, based on a preliminary previs cut put together by the editorial department.

Assistant directors can best use previs to:
- Plan a schedule based on anticipated coverage.
- Calculate the number of extras (both real and virtual).
- Help with planning and the consideration of safety issues by using exploded views of complex scenes.
- Predetermine equipment needs (including special rigs) early enough to figure out a budget.

Actors can use previs to:
- Understand the flow of scenes.
- React more convincingly to a yet-to-be-realized CG monster, tidal wave, etc.

Special effects coordinators and **stunt coordinators** can use previs to:
- Coordinate with visual effects for division of labor.
- Determine the size and scope of an effect.
- Determine the basic timing requirements for their effects or stunts—and coordinate with visual effects and camera to determine whether to shoot high speed or regular speed.

- Allow early consideration of rigging and safety issues, including keeping rigging and camera from fouling each other.

Editors can use previs to:
- Precut a scene so that the process of visual storytelling can take place before production begins.
- Give the director an opportunity to fine-tune what coverage is needed and what is not.
- Recut a scene, once production has started, with actual photographed elements incorporated into previs, or possible subsequent postvis (see the section titled *Postvis* below).
- Stand in for final visual effects in screenings. (Postvis may also be used for this when applicable.)

Editors can also generate simple postvis internally for coordinating with the visual effects department. Any postvis is a useful tool for validating the choice and length of plates to be used in the final visual effects.

And, of course,

VFX Supervisors—when they are not generating or supervising previs—use it in all the ways listed above, including to:
- Ensure that the shots conceived and the elements shot are in line with the anticipated visual effects production.
- Provide a clear and inspirational reference on set. There is a lot of power in everyone viewing the gag before shooting it.
- Ensure a continuum between an original idea and its final screen realization that is as smooth as possible.
- Tweak visual effects methods based on actual assets that have become available (working with editorial and postvis).
- Create or influence suitable previs to nudge the production in a direction that serves the director's vision in a way that is more feasible within the restrictions of schedule, budget, etc.

VFX Producers—working in concert with VFX Supervisors—use the previs to address many of the same concerns of the supervisor as well as the producers, including to:
- Provide a basis for dialogue, ensuring that the visual effects department is getting and disseminating all necessary information.
- As mentioned above with the overall producer, achieve an earlier determination of the division of labor between departments—another example is the boundary between real and digital stuntman in a sequence or shot.
- Again, in concert with the overall producer, provide clear guidance and uniform bidding packages for visual effcts vendors.

POSTVIS
Karen Goulekas

Postvis, like previs, is used to plan and visualize scenes in a production. However, although previs is most often a full-CG approach to planning scenes before filming begins, postvis visualizes scenes after the film is shot using any combination of live-action plates, miniatures, and CG.

Unlike the previs stage, wherein the director and visual effects team can experiment with an open canvas in terms of camera placement and motion, postvis, for the most part, is constrained by the live-action camera moves shot on set during filming. (Full-CG shots can still be visualized without limitation.) Even though these constraints can be somewhat manipulated and/or overridden with 2D compositing techniques, it is important that the basic shooting style already established for the film be respected and adhered to when making these adjustments.

The use of postvis has become an essential part of films, both small and large, that require visual effects to create the final shots. When dealing with a CG character or effect that is critical to the storytelling, it can be difficult for the director and editor to cut together a sequence of live-action plates without the ability to visualize the cut with its CG components. For example, how large will the CG character or effect be in frame? Where will it be positioned in frame, and how fast will it move? Will the camera angle and motion of the plate allow the CG character or effect to perform the required action? Even scenes featuring live actors shot against a blue or green screen can benefit from postvis as a means of ensuring the match between the actors and the live-action, miniature, or full-CG environment they need to interact with.

Therefore, once the first pass of the edit using the various live-action and miniature plates is available, the postvis can be used to determine whether the various elements and their corresponding CG will work together correctly.

Unlike previs, where the cost of each shot is simply a percentage of the artist and equipment weekly rate, postvis incurs additional hard costs. These costs include, but are not limited to, film scanning (unless the project has been shot digitally), camera tracking, and, for some shots, roto and paint work. Because the edit is only a "best guess," the postvis work may show that different plates or action is required. This will mean that a new postvis will need to be created using the new material, resulting in added costs.

However, in the long run, this is money well spent because the costs of camera tracking, roto, paint, and possibly complete redos are far less expensive than the money spent with the visual effects vendor moving too far ahead into animation and effects work on a plate before discovering that a different plate needs to be selected to best serve the shot.

Postvis, like previs, can be accomplished with the facility that will be doing the final shots or with a separate team of artists who work on site with the production team and whose sole purpose is to create the previs and postvis for the project. A combination of the two, using the inherent strengths of both the off-site facility and the in-house team, will usually be most effective.

For example, because previs is generally a full-CG creation, most previs artists don't specialize in the tasks associated with live-action plates such as camera tracking, roto, and paint work. As a result, it makes good sense to send the plates selected for postvis to the visual effects facilities that will be doing the final work. And, if the postvis plates end up in the final cut, this gets the facility way ahead of the game by addressing these tasks early in the post process.

Additionally, because the visual effects facilities have artists who specialize in these types of tasks, they will be much faster at producing camera tracking curves and getting that data back into the hands of the postvis team working on site with the production team. This, in turn, allows the postvis artists to concentrate on the postvis tasks they specialize in, such as modeling, texturing, rigging, and animation.

Because of the very iterative nature of previs and postvis, full-time artists specializing in them tend to be very fast and are able to turn out multiple iterations of shots routinely. For this reason, it is quite beneficial to have the previs and postvis teams on location in the production offices, where they can work closely with the VFX Supervisor, the editor, and quite often, the director to get fast and direct feedback.

Some visual effects facilities have full-time previs/postvis units as well, but if they are supervised by the facility's internal team rather than directly by the production team, there can be, by its very nature, a longer lag in getting shots for review to production and, in turn, getting their feedback to the artists at the facility. The result is an unnecessary slowdown of the process.

In the case of an off-site team doing the previs/postvis, some effective solutions to meeting the requirements of a fast feedback loop include daily in-person visits from the production VFX Supervisor and a high-bandwidth link between the off-site previs/postvis unit and production so that editorial can cut in the daily shot updates for the production team to review.

Another effective technique features the use of a parallel mini-cut that tracks with editorial's main cut but lives within the facility doing the previs/postvis. Using the mini-cut, new versions of the shots can be reviewed in context at the facility without waiting for editorial to process it. These techniques, combined with the use of real-time playback video conferencing sessions, such as Cinesync, can greatly enhance the lines of communication and shorten the feedback loop time.

However, the visual effects facility could choose to send its own previs/postvis artists to work on site with production, thus removing any significant differences between using an independent team or the vendor's team. It is all about getting a great many iterations and fast feedback to get the most value for your time and money!

Sometimes very rough postvis is performed by the editorial department using the tools available in their nonlinear editing system, such as Avid or Final Cut. This has the advantage of being fast and tied directly to the editor, so it will be clear what they have in mind for the shot(s). However, the disadvantage of this type of postvis is that it can be extremely rough, and more importantly, it is separated from the realities and technical requirements of a final visual effects shot, meaning that it may not be reproducible in the real world of visual effects or may require a great deal more frame-by-frame work to create it. Because of these disadvantages, this form of postvis should be used with restraint. It is important not to fall in love with a shot that may look promising in its rough form but that will not work at the higher quality levels necessary for the final film.

The differences between postvis and formal animation blocking might appear to be small at first glance, but they are, in reality, quite significant in terms of the time and attention to detail spent on each shot. When doing postvis, it is common to have an extremely simple and light animation rig[18] as a means of increasing animation speed. However, sometimes a visual effects facility will tend to use a lighter version of a very complex and tricked out animation rig to carry them all the way through to final animation, which can slow down the speed of animator iterations and eat up valuable time.

Animation blocking for the real visual effects shot needs to deal with the technical issues related to the animation, such as feet being planted firmly on the ground and ensuring that neither the feet nor any other part of a character's body passes through any objects found in the live-action plates. By contrast, the only technical issues associated with postvis are using the correct camera lens and object scale and fixing small technical issues such as animation pops and large-scale sliding that are jarring enough to take the viewer out of the edit/story when viewing the sequence.

In general, for postvis, if it doesn't disrupt the storytelling, leave it alone and move on to the next shot. This luxury does not exist for animation blocking, and as a result, that takes more time and care to create.

---

[18] Animation rig: CG structure built for the model and used by the animator as a type of skeleton to pose the animation model. A light rig would be a simple rig, without extras, that would make moving the animation model fast.

Another benefit of the formal postvis stage is that it gives the director, editor, and studio a complete version of all of the visual effects shots to cut into the film at a relatively early stage in the post-production process. This, in turn, may be used for studio and audience screenings as well. Additionally, it provides continuity across each sequence for the look of the models, textures, and lighting, which is an extremely important issue to keep the viewers focused on the storytelling rather than the progress of the visual effects work!

For example, when viewing the most updated version of the facility's work in the edited project on any given day, there might be a grayscale animation cut next to a shot with first pass of lighting, which is cut next to a shot of a particle test, and so on. This is jarring and will interrupt the story being told. Therefore, it might be better to use the postvis material at this stage to help smooth over the visual effects and allow the story to be told without interruption. Of course, even though it is important to be reviewing and commenting on all the latest visual effects work in context, this is not conducive to screenings where the story must be judged. In fact, even if there was a version of all the first passes of lighting for a particular CG character in each shot, this could be more jarring to the viewer if the work is not yet photoreal than it would be to use the postvis look—which the viewer will immediately accept as a work in progress. The worst thing is to have the studio or test audience think that the early and in-progress visual effects shots are what the characters will actually look like in the final film!

Naturally, as the cut progresses, shots will continue to be omitted, added, or changed in terms of length, speed ramps, and framing. With a dedicated postvis team, it doesn't take very long to add or change shots to keep the cut up-to-date, whereas with a visual effects facility team, it can be quite disrupting to try to reschedule the artists from their already assigned shots to go and fix a postvis shot every time a shot changes.

Figure 2.1 presents an example from *10,000 BC* (2008) of a frame from a shot, showing its progress from previs to postvis to final.

Figure 2.1 Previs, postvis, and final from *10,000 BC* (2008). (*10,000 BC* © Warner Bros. Entertainment Inc. All rights reserved.)

CAUTIONS AND SUGGESTIONS FOR GOOD PRACTICE
Mat Beck

The Perils of Previs!

For all that previs has to offer, its very power makes the process vulnerable to misuse. There are a number of problem areas to be aware of—but, fortunately, they can generally be avoided by observing certain standard practices. Below is a list of possible perils—with each followed by a suggested rule to help those using and creating previs to evade that particular trap.

Some of the following rules apply to the consumers of previs— the directors, writers, and other collaborators who use the previs to help them tell their story. Other rules apply more to the artists and companies that actually create the previs. However, everyone involved should understand both sides of the process so that previs can serve the story and the movie as effectively as possible.

Peril #1: Excessive Cost for the Previs Itself

Often, a principal goal of previs is to find ways to budget and schedule more efficiently. But as with any process that has limitless possibilities, previs can lead to too many hours spent noodling and refining. Therefore, one pitfall to watch out for is excessive expenditures (of both time and money) on the previs itself.

One of the principal ways to control those expenditures is to think carefully about which sequences in a film will benefit the most from previs. The larger the scope of the production effort necessary to capture a shot or sequence, the greater the value in prevising it. Also, the longer it will take to produce the final version of a shot or sequence, the greater the benefit of previs, because it will not only guide the subsequent work but can serve as a stand-in for purposes of editing, test screening, and so on. Choose your battles and work on areas with the biggest implications for savings in visual effects, set construction, production time, and so on.

It is also critically important to define exactly what is desired from previs. Is it being used as a sales tool (as in pitchvis)? Is it a tool to develop broad ideas? Is it meant to generate very specific technical information? Different purposes call for different approaches. For example, when previs is being used only to develop ideas, it doesn't have to be as concerned with exact technical accuracy, but if the shots or sequences are meant to evaluate feasibility or to help various departments prepare to execute a sequence, then it is essential to be technically accurate.

With a specific goal in mind, it's then possible to choose the right tool for doing the previs. Although computer-generated previs is the most powerful and current tool, it is important to remember that traditional techniques are still valid and can be extremely efficient. Storyboards or animated storyboards can show framing action and timing issues and can also serve as a precursor to more elaborate techniques. Rough "saddle-back" previs that can happen on a scout or stage walk can be extremely useful: A director, director of photography, or VFX Supervisor can use a video camera—or a digital still camera that records video— to perform a rough move that matches the director's description. A camera with readable lens markings is useful for this, because the previs lens can be translated to the production lens with a calculation that adjusts for the difference in the sizes of the taking apertures. The goal is to use a focal length for the previs lens that has the same field of view as the selected production lens. Numerous computer and smartphone apps (e.g., pCAM) can perform the lens conversion; it is most helpful to concentrate on the width of the format when converting. It is convenient when a previs camera has virtually the same aperture width as the production camera (e.g., Nikon D300s versus Super 35mm) because the lens focal lengths will correspond almost exactly.

If lens markings are not available, it is possible to make a simple calibration of the field of view by setting a frame with a director's finder corresponding to the final camera, noting two landmarks at either side of the frame, and then matching that field of view with the previs camera.

From there, it is a simple process to insert a few props (paper plates and toy store ants served in a recent scout) or stand-ins to get a sense of the rhythm and scope of a scene. Other forms of previsualization in the recent past have featured the director and DP acting out a fight scene on the set while being photographed by the VFX Supervisor. The point is that previs does not always have to be a computer-generated version of the shot or sequence.

Finally, previs software packages are available for the do-it-yourself previs artist/filmmaker. However, it is beyond the scope of this chapter to evaluate them.

Rule #1: *Predetermine the scope and goals of the previs, as well as the appropriate tools and techniques for the task.*

Peril #2: Too Many Choices—Stalling Out on the Details

Previs is a powerful tool, but with the exception of virtual production (described below), doing previs is not the same thing as making the movie. Just because you have the power to explore every choice doesn't mean you should. It's the bones of a sequence that are important. Excessive refinement of shot subtleties can get seductive—and expensive. For example, although the movements of a virtual character in a previs can be extensively tweaked for an acting performance, a real actor on set is going to do something different—and most often should be allowed to.

Rule #2: *Use previs to set up the general structure of a sequence, not to tighten every nut and bolt.*

Peril #3: Personnel Disconnects

One of the great powers of previs is the way in which it can facilitate clear communication. Partly, that means that effective previs has to be grounded in the technically correct world of the production. But it also means that previs should be grounded in the expertise of those who will be employed to make the movie. Besides the director, the most important people in this process are the director of photography, the production designer, the VFX Supervisor, and the editor. Previs that doesn't include their input runs the risk that shots and sequences will be created that break the laws of physics—basic reality—or exceed the capability of the equipment and that therefore will not be achievable by those key departments, and it also risks the possibility that talented members of the production will feel alienated and resentful that their years of experience are being ignored.

Rule #3: *Involve key department heads early.*

Peril #4: Financial Disconnects

A script can be written so that it vastly exceeds the available budget for a movie, and a previs sequence can sometimes do the same. It is important for the previs process to include constant input from key department heads, including the VFX Producer and VFX Supervisor, as well as the Producer, Production Manager, etc., so that feedback about estimated costs is gained. Prevising a sequence that is unaffordable within the project's budget is no more effective than writing such a sequence.

Rule #4: *Use the previs to control the budget, not inflate it.*

Peril #5: Practical and Technical Disconnects

Not all previs has to be technical previs, where every measurement is perfectly accurate. But previs that does not conform to the world of production well enough to be doable in the real world is a recipe for disaster.

Technically, accurate previs simply means that the virtual space matches the real world. At the risk of stressing the obvious, remember that even if previs is purely animated in a computer, it must by definition anticipate a real production. Any disconnect between the virtual world of the previs and the actual world of production can result in serious problems. In the real world, buildings are not 6 inches tall. Cars don't drive 500 mph. Cameras have real dimensions and cannot be mounted inside a bridge abutment (without a lot of additional expense). This is one reason why it is so useful to model actual camera, grip, and other production equipment and use those models when working in virtual space. A cool-looking previs move that requires a 500-foot Technocrane moving 1000 feet per second is a move toward major disappointment on set.

If you want to cheat physics for greater impact in the final composite, that is fine, but do not cheat the physics of the things that will really be on set, such as cameras, cranes, cars, people, etc. A corollary: *Do not animate the world.* This means that a virtual environment should match the real world in camera motion as well. A camera and/or a person may fly down a street, but don't keep the camera static and make the street fly past the camera.

Rule #5: *Base your previs on real-world dimensions, with real-world parameters of camera movement.*

Rule #5A: *Don't cheat on what is possible to make a shot more exciting.*

Rule #5B: *Make sure the image parameters are accurate as well.* Keep in mind your final output format. Things like aspect ratio, frame rate, shutter angle, dimensions of camera back, etc., should match the real image-gathering equipment. (In the newer generation of video, the problem of the nonsquare pixel should not rear its head, but be sure to avoid it.) Similarly, it is always a time-saver to use the package of lenses anticipated by the camera department. This in turn is connected to rule #5C:

Rule #5C: *Make the modeled camera-support equipment accurate.* It is extremely useful for the hierarchy of pan, tilt, and roll embodied in the real camera head to be matched in the virtual previs. It is optimal to model the crane, dollies, etc., that will move the camera.

Peril #6: Not Enough Room for Creativity

The power of previs is its ability to anticipate the possibilities of production—that is, to define a shot or sequence from the millions of possible options. Ironically, in doing previs it is also important to remain open to possibilities that may present themselves on the set when the real crew, equipment, and actors are there. Don't fall in love with the previs to the extent that possible improvements are rejected during production or post-production.

This is related to rule #2 above, but it is slightly different in that the cost is not financial but creative. Here, the restraint should be psychological: The structure of the previs should ideally leave some room for serendipity.

In addition, conditions on set may change the aesthetic of the shot. For instance, a point of view (POV) from a car that seems too slow at a low-resolution render can seem quite a bit faster with more visual information from the high-resolution real world, or even a higher resolution rendering.

Rule #6: *Don't fall in love with the temp—it's only a previs.* Don't be so worried about implementation that you foreclose options.

Rule #6A: *Leave room for iterations.* Often the greatest creativity comes from the ability to try different versions. Make sure that your previs system and/or previs provider is nimble enough to turn out a number of iterations if needed. If working in 3D animation, use artists sufficiently skilled to come up with solutions quickly.

Peril #7: Not Using the Previs to Its Potential

Having been warned about excessive reliance on every aspect of the previs, also be warned about not using it *enough*. In the heat of production, many plans can go awry. Previs represents an exceptionally powerful form of planning—and a previs that ultimately is not used represents a plan wasted; and to the extent that other people have relied on it, it represents work that is wasted.

Rule #7: *Don't spend time, money, and energy on previs if you are ultimately going to ignore it.* Plans are often meant to be broken—and sometimes thrown out—but don't junk this one without good reason.

Passing the Work On

Quite often—although not always—shots that are prevised are visual effects shots as well. Keep in mind that previs may be created by separate companies, a separate department, or just separate personnel or even the same personnel at a different time. They do not always come from the visual effects team, company, or individuals. Regardless, it is important that good communication between these companies or individuals be maintained so that preliminary stages of the work and the later high-resolution completed shots can flow through the pipeline without creating confusion. So, there are rules that help preserve the work that was done and build on it through the process. Many of these rules come from the ASC/ADG/VES Joint Technology Subcommittee on Previsualization and reflect the concerns of the people who are exclusively practitioners of the previs art:

1. If the previs team can build an environment using low-res assets that can be replaced with high-res versions later on, significant benefits will be gained by preserving the original animation.
2. Maintain a library of assets that the production and subsequent visual effects vendors can use.

3. Preserve key frames if possible—that is, do not bake out[19] animation. This allows changes to be made to the previsualized action without starting over from scratch—saving time and frustration.
4. If possible, use the same rigs for characters that will be used later in final animation. This is difficult to achieve, but it's not impossible and the benefits are obvious. Animation files from the previs become useful in the final action. [However, do not do this if the resultant animation is so expensive (render intensive) that it reduces the ability to do multiple iterations.]
5. When doing previs, use a software package that can carry over to subsequent visual effects production work.

Important caveat: There are two values that are often in conflict in previs: preservability versus disposability.

It is useful to pass on work that has been done to avoid reinventing the wheel in later stages. It is also important, in the effort to preserve what has been done, not to weigh down the process so much that it excessively constrains creativity or the number of iterations. Sometimes it is just better to start over, and one should allow for that possibility.

For practitioners of previs, the following 14 "commandments" of previs are offered. These were originally presented by the joint ASC/ADG/VES Subcommittee at the 5D Design Conference in October 2008[20]:

1. Always use real-world scale.
2. Know your final output format.
3. Match your DP's lens package.
4. Work within real-world constraints (if applicable).
5. Establish and enforce a set of organizational standards and workflow procedures.
6. Foster interdepartmental communication.
7. Play "nice" with others.
8. Do *not* animate the world.
9. Understand film language.
10. Be open to constructive criticism.
11. Always remember the end product.
12. Create shots with sufficient heads and tails.
13. Know how to work within a given time frame.
14. Understand budgetary factors.

The Role of the VFX Supervisor in Previs

The glory and curse of VFX Supervisors is that they are always in the middle: balanced between the horns of multiple technical and creative dilemmas—between solving the right now and

---

[19] Bake out: to build in, lock, or render certain settings that make it impossible to make adjustments later.
[20] List of commandments supplied courtesy of Peter Nofz.

anticipating the future, between what can be imagined and what can be done in time, between good enough and tantalizingly close to perfect, between what can be saved and what must be thrown away—between the magic that can be controlled and the magic that just happens.

The challenge and fun and misery and triumph are in finding the balance between all those competing values. It is one of the great challenges of film (and life). Previs can be the vessel that allows exploration of the space between those extremes without committing too soon to one lesser solution—thereby expanding our creative universe.

THE FUTURE OF PREVIS: ADVANCED TECHNIQUES
Mat Beck

As with most of filmmaking, the state of the art in previs is a moving target. The advancing technology is likely to increase the speed and power of the process at the same time that it broadens its reach into new areas.

One area advancing rapidly is in the technology of data input. The techniques for gathering data for the performance, for the environment, and for camera movement are all advancing rapidly.

Environment Input

The technology for inputting data for creation of virtual space is already well established. Photogrammetry employs photographs of a real-world object from a variety of vantage points to create a 3D computer-generated image of, for example, a building or room. A scan of a room or neighborhood using an automatic laser rangefinder can generate a point cloud, which can be converted into a 3D space that accurately represents a set or location. Exterior scans are commonly linked up with satellite data to help build the large space. As the technology becomes more powerful, expect a broader use of it, including more application to such processes as virtual scouting.

Character Input

Motion capture (MoCap) is effective and broadly used as an input technique, and it is becoming more so. MoCap tracks the movements of real-life performers through the use of electronic or, more commonly, optical reference points on key parts of their bodies. The data that is gathered can then be applied to computer-generated characters existing in the virtual world.

This results in animation that is not only less labor intensive to create but also potentially more realistic. Although many effects and previs companies have their own proprietary tools for doing motion capture, there are also third-party companies that sell motion capture suits, cameras, and software.

The combination of a premodeled virtual space and real-time rendering means it is possible to get feedback as the performer moves through the virtual world. On the MoCap stage, scaffolding or steps can stand in for architecture or terrain that can be climbed in virtual space.

The addition of props with tracking markers on the MoCap stage allows the performer to interact with elements of that space. For example, a cardboard tube identified by the software as a tree can be picked up by the performer, and a display will show, in real time, a beast uprooting that tree in a virtual city street. It is not a high-res city street, but the resolution is only going to increase with time. This is the technology used in *The Adventures of Tintin* (2011) and *Avatar* (2009) to direct action.

Sometimes performance can be captured through the fingers of an experienced puppeteer. The Jim Henson Company has a system that uses MoCap performers to drive characters' body movements, while their facial expressions are driven by puppeteers controlling Waldo rigs that capture subtle movements of their fingers and hands. (Waldos were named after a Robert Heinlein short story character with a handicap who uses devices to extend his own physical abilities.)

Camera Input

The characters in the scene are not the only performers whose movements can be captured. A virtual camera can also be tracked and moved through the scene, either contemporaneously with a performance or after the scene is created. This removes the creative barrier that a director may feel while driving a camera through mouse clicks. The director can carry a video camera, a display monitor, or even just a box with tracking markers through a MoCap space to create the movement desired. The software tracks the stand-in camera through the real MoCap volume of space and then flies a virtual camera through the virtual space, displaying the result either on a monitor or on the display in the director's hand. The software can smooth movements or scale them, such that a gesture of the operator's arm becomes a 30-foot crane move or an aerial flyover. Directors will often program one master camera along with the scene as it is being recorded and then later go to a smaller, cheaper MoCap stage to record coverage of additional camera angles as the established scene is played back.

It is also possible to track a real camera's motion on a real set. Traditionally, this was done using encoders on heads, cranes, and/or dollies. Newer techniques have had success employing sensors on the camera that report angle and movement and that track on-set markers for position. More advanced techniques using MoCap or gaming techniques can be expected.

Gaming Techniques

As noted earlier, faster previs is better previs, because quality and creativity go up with the number of iterations. And game engines (which rely heavily on accelerated graphics hardware processing rather than a main CPU) continue to get faster. Many companies (e.g., ILM) are making great strides applying game engines to previs. The most successful implementations of this require the ability to transfer the data generated—geometry, texture, lighting, and movement—to high-end CG programs for high-res rendering.

Beyond faster processing time, a gaming-based system allows for camera control through the gaming console or wand—a fast and economical use of existing—and advancing—technology.

On-Set Previs

The ability to render previs composites in real time, combined with on-set data on camera position and attitude, allows for on-set previs, while still making it possible for the sequences to later be finished using high-end renderers for polished final versions. The speed of this kind of work—made possible by faster processors, more powerful software, and optimized use of graphics hardware—offers directors more on-set feedback on the interaction between practical and virtual elements. It allows a scene to be framed for the 20-foot monster that will appear in the final film. It is previs and postvis at the same time. As systems get even faster, there will be more of what has already started to appear: simple composites being declared final as they are generated on stage.

Lighting Previs

Another challenge in previs—and a particular concern for cinematographers—is that the lights available in the computer-generated world of previs have been unrelated to those in the real world. In the past, with more primitive graphics, previs was more about composition and action. As previs becomes more powerful, it can include more attention to look. Because of this, cinematographers may worry that once lighting is set in the previs world, they could be tied into a look that is impossible to realize in real life. However, with increased power comes increased flexibility. Software is already available that previsualizes lighting for concert venues; as the software evolves and becomes capable of simulating the variety of lighting instruments available on set and as the power of processors allows for more and more detail on the figures being lit, expect that lighting previs will have an increasing impact—and that cinematographers will play a greater role in the previs process.

3D Stereo Previs

In a 3D stereo project, the sense of depth is controlled largely by two variables: (1) the interocular distance—the distance between the two cameras or "eyes" looking at the scene, and (2) the point of convergence—that is, the point in Z space (distance from the viewer) where the images from the two cameras overlap exactly. At the risk of some oversimplification, the interocular determines the overall depth of the scene, whereas altering the point of convergence determines how close the scene appears to the viewer. The viewer's eyes are constantly adjusting their amount of toe-in to resolve the scene and place the elements in space. When the eyes are forced to make too many radical adjustments too quickly, it can lead to eyestrain and headache—and eventually to the belief that 3D movies just aren't any fun to watch. Although images can be right/left offset in post-production to help finesse convergence, the interocular distance set on stage cannot be changed. The use of true 3D previs for 3D movies means that it is possible to pre-edit such sequences and ensure that there is maximum continuity of those depth cues.

Besides giving depth cues, the convergence is also (much like focus) a cue to the audience as to what the filmmaker wants them to look at in a scene. Previs can allow experimentation so that 3D stereo is a storytelling aid, not a distraction.

Virtual Production

If the movie never actually involves real shooting on a stage or set but goes directly from previs to CG rendering with virtual sets and characters, then the question presents itself: Is the previs still previs, or is it making the movie?

Such projects as James Cameron's *Avatar* (2009) and Steven Spielberg's *The Adventures of Tintin* (2011) use virtually every advanced previs technique. They employ full-on virtual production sets with MoCap tracking for characters, for set pieces, and for the camera as well as on-set rendering of the entire scene. In many cases these sessions become part of the production process. All of this technology is so expensive that it is important to go in with a plan of what is going to be shot. So, ironically, the filmmakers often "previs" the virtual production day. Cameron calls it *precap*. Peter Jackson has videotaped real people acting out scenes before using motion capture to drive animated characters. So, ironically, humans are now sometimes used to stand in for computer characters instead of the other way around.

This is another example of how advancing technology is altering the traditional definitions and job categories in modern production. The techniques of previs, which were once confined to pre-production, now sometimes begin before greenlight and continue until a week before the premiere, and sometimes replace the entire traditional production cycle.

One unifying aspect is the concept of a virtual production space, originally suggested by Alex McDowell, which serves as a common meeting ground for many of the crafts. This space—and the data contained in it—could begin to be built at the very inception of the ideas and persevere past release into marketing and merchandising.

The most dramatic possibilities for previs may involve grander visions that go well beyond how most people are using the technology these days—ways of creating a vision of production with new jobs, less obvious boundaries between crafts, and a whole new philosophy of filmmaking.

For example, as games become more like movies and movies become more like games, it is easy to imagine more blurring of lines. Perhaps as the tools for visualization become more powerful, they will continue to spread from planning to production to becoming a part of the actual enjoyment of the movie/ride/game. The visualization process will no longer be pre or post; it will have become part of the interactive entertainment experience.

Whatever new developments arrive, anything that previs techniques can do to facilitate the creative process of imaginative people and then transmit their visions to an engaged audience is likely to be a hit with everyone on both sides of the screen— whether a screen is involved or not.

CAMERA ANGLE PROJECTION
Steven D. Katz
Introduction by Bill Taylor

Drawing What the Lens Sees

Steven Katz describes techniques devised by Harold Michelson, a top production designer who worked on many important visual effects films—*The Birds* (1963) and *Star Trek: The Motion Picture* (1979), to name only two. Only simple drafting tools are required. The article is available on *The VES Handbook of Visual Effects*' companion website (www.VESHandbookofVFX.com)

and shows, step by step, how to use plan and view drawings of a set to create a two-point perspective drawing that shows what the camera will see from any given distance, with any lens. Katz also demonstrates Michelson's inverse procedure: how to find the camera position and lens focal length from a still photograph or a frame enlargement of any subject (such as a room or building) where two perspective vanishing points can be discovered. The inverse procedure is particularly valuable when visual effects must be incorporated into a scene for which camera data was not recorded or was lost.

The demands on art department personnel sometimes exceed the available time, so it is quite valuable to be able to derive these answers simply—for example, when the visual effects team needs to know exactly where to put their cameras to match a storyboard or rendering or how big a green screen must be to cover the action. Knowledge of these basic projection techniques will prove invaluable to the VFX Supervisor or VFX DP, if only to better communicate with the production designer and his or her team.

This section is reprinted from the book *Film Directing Shot by Shot: Visualizing from Concept to Screen*[21] with the permission of the author, Steven D. Katz, and the publisher, Michael Wiese. The illustrations were redrawn for *The VES Handbook* website through the generosity of Mr. Katz. Visit www.VESHandbookofVFX.com for the complete article and its illustrations.

---

[21] Reprinted from *Film Directing Shot by Shot*, © 1991 Steven D. Katz, Published by Michael Wiese Productions, www.mwp.com

ACQUISITION/SHOOTING

WORKING ON SET
Scott Squires

A small group of the visual effects team works on set during the production to make sure that all of the shots that will require visual effects are shot correctly and to obtain the necessary data and references.

The visual effects crew can consist of the following:

- The VFX Supervisor or plate supervisor works with the director and key production departments to make sure visual effects shots are correct creatively and technically.

- An animation supervisor may be on set if there is a lot of complex animation to be added.

- A VFX Producer may be on set to help organize and schedule the visual effects crew and to flag issues that may affect the budget.

- A coordinator takes notes, logs visual effects shots, helps to communicate with the different departments, and can fill in for the VFX Producer.

- Other visual effects production personnel handle the reference items (chrome sphere, monster sticks[1], etc.), take reference photos, and handle other miscellaneous reference gathering.

- Data collectors (sometimes called data wranglers or match-movers; the terms vary from company to company) document all camera and lens information and take measurements of the set.

It is not unusual for members of this crew to fill multiple positions, and on a small show this may all be handled by the VFX Supervisor. Additional visual effects personnel may come to the set for short durations, such as modelers to help scan and photograph the actors, sets, and props for later modeling. Shooting can

---

[1] See the section *Monster Sticks* in this chapter for more details.

The VES Handbook of Visual Effects. DOI: 10.116/B978-0-240-81242-7.00003-X

be a single day for small projects or up to 6 months or longer for a large film.

Working on the set is much different from working at a visual effects facility. It tends to alternate between boredom and terror—waiting for the crew to get to the visual effects shot(s) and rushing around to actually film the shot (sometimes under adverse conditions). There can be a lot of pressure on the set due to the time limits of getting everything shot and the costs of shooting. Depending on the show, the visual effects crew may be involved in just one shot that day or may be required to work on every shot. Being on a set and observing are very good experiences for any visual effects artist. It will do a lot to explain why visual effects plates are not always perfect.

Shooting may take place on a sound stage or outside for exterior shots. A live-action shooting day is usually 12 hours long. Locations may require a good deal of climbing or walking, so physical fitness is called for. Exterior shooting will require standing outside from sunrise to sunset in sun, rain (natural or made by the special effects team), cold, or snow. Night scenes require working from sunset to sunrise. Dress appropriately for the given weather—good walking shoes, socks, hat, layered clothing, sunscreen, sunglasses, or full rain gear (including rain pants) for rain and very heavy boots for cold weather. Have a small flashlight. Think of it as camping with 100 to 200 other people.

The visual effects crew will have to work hand in hand with the other departments, so it is important to keep a good relationship with them. (See Chapter 2 for a discussion of the basic departments.)

Typical Process

Call sheets are handed out the night before. These list the scenes to be shot the next day and include the actors and crew members to be on the set and their call times (time to arrive on set). They will also note any special instructions for transportation or shooting that day.

The Director will arrive and meet with the 1st Assistant Director (1st AD) and Director of Photography (DP) to discuss the order of the day and the first shot. The VFX Supervisor should be involved in this to help plan the visual effects needs. Sometimes this is done at the end of a shooting day to prepare for the next day.

The Director works with the actors to block out a scene with the 1st Assistant Director and Director of Photography. If the blocking of the scene has a large impact on the visual effects (e.g., an animated character is to be added), the VFX Supervisor should be involved as well. A stand-in or creature reference may be required to block[2] the scene. The VFX Supervisor should have a reduced set of storyboards (to fit in a coat pocket) to refer to. It is best to supply these to the DP and Director as well. A laptop with a DVD or video file of the previs is also useful to play back for the Director and actors to get a sense of the scene. A handheld device (iPod, iPhone, etc.) can also be useful for referencing previs material on set.

The Director of Photography and VFX Supervisor may discuss camera placement as it relates to visual effects. A model or other visual reference may be placed in front of the camera to help determine final framing. If the shot is to be matched to another element already shot, such as a background plate, then that should be referenced with the DP as well so that the lighting and angle can be matched. The DP works with the gaffer (head of the electrical department) to set the lighting and with the camera operator to set up the camera equipment and the camera move required. This may take a few minutes or several hours, depending on the complexity of the scene.

The VFX Supervisor should discuss the shot and requirements with the visual effects crew ahead of time. This will enable them to set up any special equipment (i.e., transit,[3] witness cameras,[4] etc.) so that they are prepared. Any tracking markers or other visual aids should be set up as soon as possible so that this doesn't slow down the current setup, the crew, or the progress of the director's day. Any measurements that won't change (such as a building or street) should be done as soon as is feasible. The visual effects crew has to work as efficiently as possible as a team to make sure everything gets done. On a large show there may be an office for visual effects near the stages and a trailer for location work. The equipment is usually stored in these areas and moved to the location by modified carts to handle rough terrain. Production should provide the visual effects crew with production walkie-talkies to keep in communication. A channel is usually assigned to each department.

Once the shot is ready, the visual effects references may be shot at the start or end of the sequence of takes. Someone from the visual effects crew holds up the gray sphere, chrome sphere,

---

[2] Block a scene: when a director works with the actors to determine their action during the scene. Once done, the camera positions are determined.
[3] Transit: surveyor's tool to measure positions and distances; used for large sets and exteriors.
[4] Witness cameras: video cameras used to record the scene for matchmoving purposes.

or other references while the camera rolls. (See *On-Set Data Acquisition* in this chapter for details.) It is common practice to add a "V" to the slate to indicate it is a visual effects shot. All of this should be discussed with the production department (1st AD, script supervisor, etc.) before production begins because they may require different slating regimens.

An actor may be given an eye-line reference for anything that will be added later (e.g., the window of a building, a CG creature). This will help the actor look at the correct place even if the object will be added later in post-production. A reference take may also be shot of an actor standing in for a CG creature, or a monster stick may also be used for a large creature to be added. This provides the actors with an eye-line and timing reference. It helps the director to visualize the shot, and it helps the operator to know what the action is. It is also useful in post-production for the animators to see the action and timing.

The Director, Director of Photography, and VFX Supervisor usually gather at the video village to watch the shot. *Video village* is the name given to the sitting area where the video monitor (or multiple monitors) is set up. The video assist operator handles this. The video comes from a video tap (camera) on a film camera or may be from a digital camera. Each take is recorded for referencing by the Director for performance. Normally, directors' chairs are assigned to all key personnel at the video village. For a show that is heavy with visual effects, this should include the VFX Supervisor to make sure the video is always visible to them.

The VFX Supervisor watches each performance carefully and monitors a number of things, including the eye lines of the actors and extras, any crossing of the matte lines, the locations of the actors, and the timing of the special effects, camera move, and actors. The VFX Supervisor has to keep in mind where the creature or any additional objects will be added and their timing relative to what the actor does. It is also necessary to keep an eye on things that should not be in the shot (microphone, crew member, tattoos on the actor, etc.). If there are issues regarding the actors, the VFX Supervisor should discuss these with the Director, who in turn will discuss them with the actors. The VFX Supervisor should avoid giving direction to the actors to avoid confusion. Other issues may be flagged to the 1st Assistant Director or the DP, depending on the specifics.

The VFX Supervisor has to weigh the cost and time to make an adjustment on the set against fixing the problem or making the change in post-production. In some cases it will be less expensive and faster to make the adjustment in post, but if it is critical, the VFX Supervisors will have to stand their ground to make sure the shot is done correctly. Complaining about it months later in post will not be of any value. Any issues that will have a large cost impact should be flagged to the VFX Producer (or, if unavailable, the film producer).

After each take someone from the visual effects crew records information from the camera assistant with regard to camera settings (lens, tilt angle, *f*-stop, focus, etc.) for the start and end of the camera move. Multiple cameras may be used that will need to be monitored and recorded. Some camera views may not require visual effects. In some cases a splinter unit will take another camera and shoot a totally separate shot at the same time off to the side. It is necessary to monitor that camera as well if it is being used for visual effects shots.

This process repeats itself throughout the day. Lunch is provided and craft services sets out snacks during shooting. Restrooms on location are at the honeywagon (a truck with built-in restrooms for the crew).

The crew filming the key live action with principal actors is considered the 1st unit (or main unit). On large productions a 2nd unit may be filming different scenes on different sets or locations, such as inserts, scenes with secondary actors, or action scenes that production has determined will be more efficient to shoot with a separate crew. If these scenes require visual effects and are being shot the same day as the 1st unit shooting, then another VFX Supervisor and visual effects crew will be required for this unit.

Guidelines for On-Set Work

- Be professional in actions, with words, and when working with others.
- Be quick and efficient at the tasks you have been assigned. Avoid holding up or slowing down the production any more than is absolutely necessary.
- Be quiet when the camera is rolling.
- Do not enter a stage when the red light outside the door is flashing.
- Avoid being in the shot. There may be a number of cameras shooting, with very large camera moves. Check to see where the cameras are set and how much they will cover during the shot. Ask the supervisor and check the video if necessary.
- Avoid getting in the actor's eye line. The actor will be focused and looking at another actor or looking off the set at something or someone who is supposed to be off-screen. Any movement where they are looking will be distracting and cause them to lose focus.
- Do not move, touch, or borrow items controlled by other departments (C-stand, light, etc.). Ask someone from the appropriate department for permission to do so.

- If you need to add markers to an actor's wardrobe, talk to the head of the wardrobe department. Check with the 1st AD first since this may affect other cameras, including non-visual effects shots.
- If you need to add markers to an actor, talk to the makeup person. Check with the 1st AD since this will affect other cameras, including non-visual effects shots.
- Prepare and gather data ahead of time when possible. Measure the sets, gather blueprints, set bluescreen markers, etc. Construct reference objects and transportation carts before production begins.
- Take care of the visual effects equipment. All equipment should be protected from the elements (plastic covers for transits, protective bag for the chrome sphere, etc.). All equipment should be locked up or watched by a crew member or security guard when not in use. Losing or damaging a critical and expensive piece of equipment on set will be a real problem. In cold weather watch for condensation on equipment.
- Always carry a small notebook and pen for notes.
- Monitor the areas you are covering and adjust accordingly (camera move changed, another camera added, etc.).
- Be alert. The shot could be changed significantly between takes, or plans may be changed without much notice. Be ready for a call from the VFX Supervisor.
- If anything is preventing the visual effects task from being completed (obtaining camera data, taking measurements, etc.), it should be flagged to the VFX Supervisor immediately. The VFX Supervisor may need to hold production for a moment to obtain the necessary element or reference data.
- If there is a visual effects question or any confusion regarding the requirements, check with the VFX Supervisor immediately.
- If the only time to take texture photographs or measurements is during lunch, check with the VFX Supervisor or VFX Producer, who will in turn discuss it with the 1st AD and the DP. Lights may have to be left on, and all crew members must be given their full lunchtime.
- If you are leaving the set for any reason, notify the VFX Supervisor *before* you leave.
- Avoid hanging out at the video village if you do not need to be there.
- Always be on the set on time as per the call sheet.
- If actors need to be scheduled for scanning, check with the VFX Supervisor so they can work with the 1st AD.
- Keep an eye on production. It's not unusual for them to try to shoot a visual effects shot without supervision (if the VFX Supervisor is unavailable). This is always problematic.

- Be alert to safety issues on the set and location. There can be cables, equipment, and moving vehicles that need to be avoided. The temporary and constantly changing nature of the environment can lead to trouble if a crew member is not paying attention.

COMMON TYPES OF SPECIAL EFFECTS
Gene Rizzardi

What Are Special Effects?

Special effects are the on-set mechanical and in-camera optical effects, which are created in front of the camera—also referred to as *SFX*. Special effects include, but are not limited to, pyrotechnics, specially rigged props and cars, breakaway doors or walls, on-set models and miniatures, makeup effects, and atmospheric effects such as wind, rain, snow, fire, and smoke.

A Brief History of Special Effects

The quest to suspend reality has been the challenge of special effects since the beginning of film history. Special Effects progressed from simple in-camera tricks at the turn of the century to increasingly complicated works of the '60s, '70s and '80s (when special effects miniatures and optical printers were the norm) to the complex and seamless effects of today (digital cameras, CGI, digital pipelines, and digitally projected films). Special Effects still plays an important role today as a cost-effective means of creating reality and by helping the filmmaker create his vision.

The Special Effects Supervisor

As the digital and physical worlds merge in film and television, the work of the SFX Supervisor and VFX Supervisor must also change to accommodate the demands of the project. Cooperation between these two individuals is of the utmost importance to create seamless and convincing visual effects. Understanding and communicating the components of each visual effects shot is critical for the successful completion of the effect. This begins in pre-production, when the VFX Supervisor and SFX Supervisor determine what techniques and which shots will use a blend of visual and special effects. Storyboards and previs are quite helpful in this process. Some shots may be all visual effects with special effects providing only a separately photographed element to be composited later. Others might be more special effects with visual effects enhancing them or providing rig removal.

Working with the Visual Effects

In many instances the SFX Supervisor's skills will complement those of the VFX Supervisor to create or complete the action of a shot:

- *Elements:* The SFX Supervisor can provide flame, smoke, water, pyrotechnics, dust, snow, and other elements as raw material to composite into the shot.
- *Greenscreen:* The SFX Supervisor can work with the VFX Supervisor and the DP to position and move actors and/or props to provide direct active elements for compositing.
- *Interactivity:* The SFX Supervisor can provide interactivity during principal photography or 2nd unit shots to complement digital or composited elements.

Visual Effects in Service to SFX

Visual effects can be most useful to the needs of special effects by performing the following:

- *Rig removal*, such as removing cables, support arms, or safety equipment from the shot.
- *Face replacements*, which allow stunt performers to stand in for principal actors.
- *Effect enhancement*, such as adding more flame, rain, water, dust, smoke, or other elements to the shot.
- *Compositing*, where logistically complicated and expensive shots can be shot as elements by a visual effects, special effects, and stunt unit and composited into plates shot at a principal location.

In the end, seamless, realistic, and cost-effective visual effects are the result of careful planning involving visual effects, special effects, stunts, miniatures, and the art department to ultimately realize the director's vision.

Special Effects Design and Planning

It all starts with the script. The experienced SFX Supervisor will break down the script by the various effects and elements required. Once a list of atmospheric and physical elements is created, discussions about the budget and schedule can begin. This process may go through many versions before it is completed. It is a valuable period of discovery before the construction begins and the cameras roll.

Storyboards and Previs

Storyboards tell a visual story of the film. They give the key elements in the scene for the Director and Production Designer to plan the film action, construction, and scheduling. This visual reference is also a valuable tool for the SFX Supervisor, who can use it to visualize the plan of action, such as where the atmospheric effects are needed and where the mechanical, pyrotechnic, or physical effects are needed, in order to plan and achieve the desired shot(s). This valuable tool, along with a location and technical scout, will give the SFX Supervisor invaluable information on how to achieve production goals.

The Elements: Rain, Wind, and Snow and Ice

Rain

The ability to make rain indoors or outdoors is part of the movie magic that adds convincing realism to any movie. Rain bars 60 and 100 feet long with specially designed sprinkler heads can cover wide areas, but the most important part of rain making is to place the rain above the actors using the "over-the-camera" effect.

- By adjusting the water pressure, rain can be made to appear as a fine mist (high pressure) or heavy droplets (low pressure).
- Backlighting rain will make it more visible; frontlighting it will make it almost disappear.
- To make rain appear to be falling straight down, one must move the rain bars or rain towers to a higher position to eliminate the effect of crossing rain.
- Rain rigs can be used with traveling cars to extend the effect from the driver's point of view.
- Rain windows are devices that create reflections for lighting effects to simulate rain.
- Indoor or outdoor sets can be rigged with rain bars to make rain appear to be falling outside a window. Rain mats or hog hair can control the noise made by the rain falling in the drip pans.

Wind Effects

Wind is another effect an SFX Supervisor can use, creating anything from the soft rustling of the leaves on the foliage outside a set window to raging tornadoes. The devices used range from small electric fans to large electric or gas-powered machines that can move air at over 100 mph.

- E-fans are a staple of any special effects kit. Their use varies from the soft blowing of leaves to moving smoke on set to add atmosphere. The E-fan is well suited to this work because its flow is very directional.
- Ritter fans are large electric fans that can be placed on gimbals or platforms and are capable of moving air in excess of 100 mph. They can be fitted with rain bars to make driving rain for raging storms.

- Jet-powered fans are used for tornado effects, large dust clouds, and destructive winds. They also emit a lot of heat, so great care must be used when they are working.

Snow and Ice

Snow and ice can be made from real ice for the foreground areas or where actors may want to interact with it and get a wet effect. Snow is usually made from paper products since this does not melt, and if applied properly, it is easy to clean up. Paper snow is also good for extended snow scenes because ice would melt after the first day and make everything wet and muddy.

- Effective snow scenes must be planned properly. Failure to apply snow in an orderly process will make for an extended and messy cleanup.
- A white underlay will create a good surface that will protect the ground or surface below. The underlay will also give you a white base to apply the snow on. Snow will then be sprayed over this underlay to achieve the desired effect. The snow can be made to appear deeper or undulating by placing sandbags or bales of hay beneath the underlay before the snow is sprayed.
- Falling snow, water dripping from icicles, and frost on windows are routinely created by the SFX Supervisor.
- Frosty breath can be created in a refrigerated set or with cigarette smoke and will be more convincing and cost effective than CGI replacements.
- Frozen pond or lake surfaces can be created with heated paraffin wax that is carefully flowed onto the surface.

The SFX Supervisor will work with the VFX Supervisor, Director, and location manager to get the right snow look for the scene. Permits are required to make snow in state or federal parks, and cleanup procedures must be strictly followed so as to not endanger the local plant and wildlife.

Smoke, Fire, and Pyrotechnics

Pyrotechnics covers a wide and impressive range of effects, from simple sparks and smoke to squibs used for bullet hits to the fiery destruction of whole city blocks.

Pyrotechnic special effects are generally designed to produce a great visual and audio effect without the massive destruction associated with commercial blasting and military explosives. Filming these types of explosions is difficult at best: Safety concerns prevent filming in close proximity, and explosions happen too quickly for effective filming. The special effects pyrotechnic explosions enable more effective filming, allowing stunt players to be relatively close. The film crew can be close enough to shoot it, and the explosion itself is slow enough to be captured on film as a progression of events, with fire and smoke, while anything that may fly off and injure someone is safely tied with cable. Every aspect of the pyrotechnic is designed to create a great and breathtaking visual.

All pyrotechnic effects must be performed with constant consideration for safety, because all pyrotechnic materials can cause harm. These materials, and the pyrotechnic operator as well, are tightly regulated by a host of government agencies, starting with the Bureau of Alcohol, Tobacco, Firearms and Explosives (BATF&E) and extending down to local jurisdictions, usually the local fire department. Each use must be licensed and permitted by these agencies.

A few examples of the wide range of pyrotechnics (and this just scratches the surface) are as follows:

- *Pyrotechnic smoke:* This includes colored smokes, smoke that can be set off at a distance, or smoke in conjunction with explosions or fire.
- *Squibs:* Squibs are small electrically detonated explosive devices used for bullet hits on props, buildings, water, and cars. Squibs are used inside special shields in conjunction with small bags of movie blood on actors and stunt performers to create horrifying body hits. There are even tiny 1:32 size squibs for use with makeup effects to attach onto prostheses for close-up effects. Squibs are used to operate quick releases, trunnion guns,[5] and glass poppers. Squibs are also used to initiate detonating of primer cord[6] and black powder lifters.
- *Spark effects:* A wide range of spark effects are available, from the tiny Z-16 squib to giant Omnis that can fill a room. In addition, there is an entire range of stage-specialized spark effects that come in colors and have a set duration, spray, or fall.

---

[5] Trunnion gun: small device used to create bullet holes in car windows or to break glass; also known as a *trunnion launcher*. Trunnion guns have the appearance of a small cannon mounted to a small heavy metal plate with a swivel arm, and they can be adjusted to various angles. They have a removable end cap with a small hole in it. A squib is placed inside the end cap with the wires passing through the hole. A small projectile made from epoxy putty or a ball bearing is then placed in the tube. When the squib is triggered, the projectile will exit the barrel and create a hole in the glass it was aimed at. They are commonly used in autos with actors to achieve the effect of bullet holes in the car windows. A protective shield of Lexan must be used between the window and the actor to prevent injury because the projectile may ricochet or the tempered glass may disintegrate.

[6] Detonating cord: waterproof explosive that has the appearance of a cord; also known as *det cord* or *primer cord*. It is available in different diameters that relate directly to the explosive power of this product. All det cord has a white core of powerful explosive that detonates at about 4 miles per second. It is commonly used in special effects work to destroy something quickly, such as to vaporize a building facade on a miniature or to create the effect of a traveling shock wave when buried just below a dirt surface.

- *Display fireworks:* Public display–type fireworks are occasionally used by special effects teams. These include all manner of aerials and set pieces.
- *Specialized effects rockets:* These will send a rocket down a wire and produce flame and smoke. These devices fit in the mouth of a cannon barrel and mimic the firing of the cannon. Custom pyrotechnics can also be designed for specific gags.
- *Explosions:* A staple of special effects, these include car explosions, where the car blows up and flies through the air; blowing up of buildings; and huge dust explosions far away to simulate artillery fire. Explosions can be created with or without flame and with stunt performers in or very close to them.
- *Car effects:* Rollover cannons for stunt-driven picture cars[7] are frequently operated by pyrotechnics. Car crashes, explosions, and fires are some of the many car effects that are written into today's scripts.
- *Miniature pyrotechnics:* This is an entire specialized art in itself. The pyrotechnics must match the miniature in scale, and the timing is frequently measured in milliseconds due to high-speed photography.
- *Fire effects:* Burning houses, fireplaces, bonfires, candles, campfires, burning bushes, lightning strikes, and many other fire effects are the responsibility of the SFX Supervisor.

All special effects equipment can cause serious injury when used improperly. Hire a trained professional to use such equipment.

Mechanical Effects

Mechanical effects are an integral part of the special effects department's responsibility and cover a wide range of rigging, building action props, creating specialized elemental effects, and providing mechanical help for other departments. Examples include the following:

- *Action props:* props that do something on set, such as mechanical bulls, clock workings, gadgets with blinking lights, retractable knives, trees that fall on cue, or self-growing plants. These may include all manner of working mechanisms, either built from scratch or existing items modified to work on set in a film-friendly manner.
- *Breakaways:* balsa furniture, windows, walls, door panels, hand props, floors, glass of all sorts, concrete, or handrails.
- *Crashing cars:* roll cages to protect stunt performers, rollover cannons, cars with self-contained traveling flames and other effects, cables pulling cars in stunts too dangerous for

[7] A picture car is a vehicle that is featured in the production, or any vehicle that is involved in a stunt or special effect.

even stunt drivers to perform, on-cue tire blowouts, special picture cars, cars ratcheted or launched by pneumatic cannon through the air. Other requirements may include wheels that come off, cars breaking in half, or cars that appear to drive backward at high speed.

- *Bullet hits and blood effects:* on walls, cars, people, water, plants, concrete, or windows. Bullet hits can be sparks or dust puffs or, for hits on wardrobe, can spew blood. Other blood effects are blood running down the walls, blood sprayed on the walls, or props that bleed—red blood, clear vampire slime, or green goo—as well as pipes that burst and gush blood, slime, and goo.
- *Action set pieces:* sets on gimbals, elevator doors and elevators themselves, trapdoors, guillotine doors, tilting floors, water tanks, floods, avalanches, collapsing buildings.
- *Set rigging:* fireplaces, showers, tubs, stoves, heating swimming pools or any water that crew and actors have to work in, or moving on-stage greenery with monofilament or wire to simulate wind.
- *Flying effects:* flying and moving people and objects on cable, synthetic rope, wire cranes, parallelogram rigs, hydraulic gimbals and overhead, floor, subfloor, and through-the-wall tracks, or arrows and rockets on wires.
- *Greenscreen work:* rigging actors, props, and models to fly in front of the green screen. With today's digital wire removal, this job has become much easier and safer than in days past when actors were flown on fine music wire that was more likely to break than the thicker, safer wires of today.
- *Set effects:* stoves, kitchen sets, and working faucets, showers, or bathrooms.

Flying Wire Rigs and Stunts

Wire flying is one of the oldest forms of illusion. Several basic systems are used in the creation of flying effects as well as countless variations of them based on the requirements of the job and the SFX Supervisor's imagination.

Flying rigs are either controlled by overhead track systems or, in certain instances, by cranes used to hold the flying rigs.

- *Overhead track system:* This system can be set up to fly a person or object in either a two-direction system, where the actor or object moves either left to right or front to back on stage at a fixed height, or a four-direction system, which allows the actor or object to move left to right and up and down at the same time. A third variation involves an overhead cab that contains a special effects technician who operates a device that allows the actor or object to spin.
- *Pendulum or Peter Pan rig:* This is the most complicated flying device to rig and work because it demands a comprehensive

rehearsal and coordination between the actor and the effects person to make the actor fly on stage and land in an exact location.

- *Cable overhead flying rigs:* These are similar to the overhead track system and can also be used outdoors, with the traveler mounted on an overhead cable system that may span 1000 feet or more. They can have all the same features as the overhead track system. An example of this is the camera systems used in football and soccer that follow the actors down the field, or when the shot involves a character like Spider-Man who travels along the street by leaps and bounds. CGI and greenscreen effects can be used in conjunction with this rig to place an actor or character anywhere the director imagines.
- *Levitation:* As opposed to flying, this method of flying actors or objects uses lifting mechanisms such as parallelograms or vertical traveling lifts. The device can be as simple as a forklift or as complex as a counterweighted lift machine. Although typically stationary, it can be mounted on a track to give a left-to-right motion. It also can be used with miniatures.
- *Descenders:* These are used to control the fall of a stuntperson who leaps from a tall building or cliff when the terminal velocity can exceed the ability of the airbag safety system or when an actor needs to stop inches from the floor, as in *Mission: Impossible* (1996).

Flying effects and stunts involving actors are the shared responsibility of the SFX Supervisor and the Stunt Coordinator. They work as a team to provide the proper rigging and equipment to achieve a safe and desired result that is repeatable.

Safety

The most important aspect of special effects is ensuring that all effects and rigs are executed in a manner that maximizes safety and minimizes risk. This is a tall task in that many effects are designed to produce the appearance of great danger, with the cast and crew close enough to film, but must at the same time protect them from harm. The SFX Supervisor must not only operate all effects safely but must also take precautions for the unnoticed hazards of special effects:

- noise,
- tripping and slipping,
- dust,
- smoke,
- moving machinery,
- flammables,

- high-pressure gases and liquids,
- toxic substances, and
- wind effects and flying debris.

Careful planning goes into each effect or gag, including consultation with the stunt coordinator, the 1st AD, the VFX Supervisor, and anyone else concerned. If pyrotechnics or fire is involved, the fire department having jurisdiction must issue a permit. Immediately prior to the filming of the special effect, the 1st AD will call a safety meeting, where it is ensured that everyone knows what to do and all contingencies are addressed.

The VFX Supervisor can frequently help out with safety by providing rig removal for safety devices, by adding or enhancing elements to increase the feeling of jeopardy, and by compositing actors and stunt performers into shots in which their physical presence would expose them to too much risk.

When working on set, it is important to be aware of your surroundings, pay attention, and work safely. Look out for your coworkers and keep your eyes open for anything that could be a potential hazard. If you have a doubt, ask the proper personnel to have a look at the condition you are concerned about. Safety is everyone's responsibility.

FRONT AND REAR PROJECTION SYSTEMS FOR VISUAL EFFECTS
Bill Mesa and John Coats

In the pre-digital era of visual effects, front projection, rear-screen projection, and "side-screen" projection were processes used for creating large-scale sets and new environments as well as for moving images out the windows of cars and planes. Although the techniques for using these tools have changed a great deal, the mechanics of the tools are basically the same, except for the new digital projection systems. In the past the background plates had to be created prior to on-set shooting, and once the on-set shooting was done, there was no fixing it in post, but it did and still does allow one to shoot many versions of the action with the subjects to give the director a variety of takes from which to choose. Experimentation can be done on the set with lighting and other smoke and debris elements to blend the subjects together. A good example of this is a shot from *The Fugitive* (1993), in which dust and debris shot from an air cannon landed on top of Harrison Ford just as a train crashed into the hillside. This was done using a front projection system that tied in all of the dust and debris on top of Harrison with the plate for integration of the elements.

Rear Projection

Advantages

Rear projection holds fine edge detail because no mattes are involved, since the background and the object in front of the screen are being shot as one. The object or person in front of the screen acts as an interactive light source because the two objects are together. One obstacle to overcome when backlighting a person or object is to make sure the bounce light from that person doesn't contaminate the screen and cause a loss of black detail or make the image look low in contrast. Adding black velvet to the back of the person to cut down on the spill light works well for this issue, as long as the person isn't rotating. The more the ambient light spill can be blocked, the better the results.

Rear projection can be cost effective, especially when there are similar shots that just require a change of backgrounds—allowing many shots to be done at one time or a whole scene to be played out from that angle. Since the shots are finished on stage, no post-production costs are associated with rear projection and results can be seen immediately—thus providing the ability to make eye-line, position, and other corrections in real time.

Disadvantages

Heavy expenses can be involved if large screens are used, which would require a move-in day, a setup and test day for testing background plate colors, plus however many actual shoot days, and then a wrap day. They also require a large space. For a shot out the front window of a car, an 18-foot screen is required—with little to no camera movement. Additionally, 50 to 60 feet of space would be required behind the screen for the projector. That is a lot of space. Getting high-resolution images for backgrounds requires shooting in VistaVision or using a high-resolution digital system. Even then it is difficult to get black detail. It also requires all of the backgrounds to be registered and color-corrected plates to be made prior to filming on stage. In many of today's big visual effects movies, it is impossible to generate backgrounds with all the necessary elements. Shooting this way can be limiting because the background timings can't be changed in post.

Front Projection (Blue or Green Screens and Picture Imagery)

Advantages

There are still good reasons to use blue or green screens. *The Poseidon Adventure* (2006) had an all–stainless steel kitchen. Some tests were shot using traditional blue screens, but the blue contamination was so great that it couldn't be removed. Using a front projection blue screen eliminated the blue reflection because the screen doesn't put out any blue light. One light source can light up a 20- by 40-foot screen with an even light field. This can provide much higher light intensity for working at higher *f*-stops. It is easy to change out blue or green screens for whatever color is needed. The space needed is a lot smaller than with rear projection. Although front projection with picture imagery is not used much anymore due to the quality of the final image, it could be used when a scene has many of the same shots or shots that go on for long periods of time.

Disadvantages

The screen material is quite expensive and must be kept in optimum condition for continued use. It requires a special camera projector or light source setup.

If the alignment of the camera projector is not 100% correct, fringing may appear around the actors. This requires setup time to get the projector and camera lined up, depending on how close or far away the actor is from the camera. There are also issues with haloing, depending on how dark the projected image is and how much light is on the actor or foreground object. Again, haloing can be reduced by putting black velvet on the actor's backside, as long as the actor doesn't rotate during the shot.

Rear Projection Equipment

Digital DLP and LCD Projectors

Considerations in using digital projectors are the limitation of resolution, contrast ratio, and the light output of the projectors. The size of the projected image needs to be known before determining the required projector light output. Also, different screens react differently to the camera being off center. There are 50/50 screens that allow camera moves of up to 50% off center. These screens need higher light output from the projectors. There are also synchronization issues, depending on what type of projector is used—especially when shooting with 24-frame cameras. This must be tested prior to shooting. Sometimes flickering will occur. It is always good practice to start with the best quality image possible and then diffuse or soften on the set. Special equipment might be needed for soundproofing the projector system.

Film Projectors

These can give greater light output but require registered film plates.

Front Projection Equipment

Characteristics of the Retroreflective Material

The material needs to be mounted in a pattern that will not show up when an image is projected on it. Hexagonal and diamond patterns have been used successfully. On small screens, the straight 3-foot widths with back-beveled cut edges to allow seamless overlap have been used successfully. This needs to be done in completely clean conditions, with white gloves and no oil.

Set Lighting Conditions

Although small projection systems on cranes have been used, they need to stay parallel to the screen axis or the image will start to fade. In the lighting setup of the actors or objects, all lights need to be blocked from hitting the screen or they will gray the image.

Camera-Mounted Light Source

Various light sources, including LED (light-emitting diode) rings, can be placed around the camera lens to light up (with a blue or green source of light) a screen. If using a projector source, this requires a beamsplitter, generally 50/50 in transparency, with antireflection coatings. If there is any camera movement, the projector and beamsplitters must all move together and stay parallel to the screen.

Large-Area Emissive Displays (LCD, Plasma, and Jumbotron Screens)

These types of screens are often used just to reflect imagery on windows or reflective objects, but they can also be used as backgrounds in place of rear projection. As these screens continue to get better due to their great light output, they will take over the projection systems for smaller backgrounds. Because of their high output and low contamination threshold, the Jumbotron and others can provide some great flexibility for various uses. Have fun trying all the new technology.

GREENSCREEN AND BLUESCREEN PHOTOGRAPHY

Bill Taylor, ASC

Overview

Greenscreen and bluescreen composites begin with foreground action photographed against a plain backing of a single primary color. In a digital post-production process, the foreground action is combined with a new background. The new background can be live action, digital or traditional models, artwork or animation, or any combination.

For the sake of simplicity, we'll refer to "greenscreen" shots, with the understanding that the screen or backing can instead be blue or even red.

These composites (and others using related technology) are also called *traveling matte* shots because they depend on creating an alpha-channel silhouette "mask" or matte image of the foreground action that changes and travels within the frame.

The final composite is usually created in post-production, although real-time, full-resolution on-set compositing[8] is possible in HD video.

Function of the Backing—Green, Blue, or Red

The purpose of the blue or green backing is to provide an unambiguous means by which software can distinguish between the color hues and values in the foreground and the monochromatic backing. White and black backgrounds are used in special circumstances to create luminance masks or "luma keys," but since it is likely that similar luminance values will be found in the foreground, these backings have limited use.

The degree to which the compositing software "sees" the backing determines the degree of transparency of the foreground in the final composite. Where the backing value is zero, the foreground is completely opaque; where the backing value is 50%, the foreground will be partly transparent, and so forth for all values to 100%, the areas of the frame where the foreground image is either not present or completely transparent. The goal is to retain the foreground subjects' edge transitions (including motion blur), color, and transparency in the final composite.

Fabric and Paint

The best materials currently available are the result of years of research to optimize lamp phosphors, fabric dyes, and paint for film purposes.

Fabrics

When using fabric backings, minimize the seams and avoid folds. Stretch the fabric to minimize wrinkles.

---

[8] In live composites, full-bandwidth HD video is fed to an HD Ultimatte hardware device with a second camera, an HD deck, or a digital workstation providing the background.

Even an indifferent backing can give good results if it is lit evenly with narrowband tubes to the proper level (within plus-or-minus 1/3 *f*-stop). Spill from set lighting remains a concern.

Composite Components Co.[9] offers a fabric that is highly efficient, very light, stretchy, and easy to hang. It must be backed by opaque material when there is light behind it. The green fabric is fluorescent, so it is even more efficient under UV-rich sources like skylight. CCC also makes a darker material for use in direct sunlight.

Following Composite Components' lead, many suppliers now provide "digital-type" backings of similar colors. Although similar in appearance, some of these materials are substantially less efficient, which can have a great cost impact when lighting large screens. Dazian Tempo fabric, a fuzzy, stretchy material, has a low green or blue saturation when lit with white light, so it isn't recommended for that application. Dazian's Lakota Green Matte material is a better choice for white-light applications like floor coverings; it is resistant to fading and creasing and can be laundered.

Paint

Composite Components' Digital Green or Digital Blue paint is the preferred choice for large painted backings. As with fabrics, there are other paint brands with similar names that may not have the same efficiency. Paints intended for video use, such as Ultimatte Chroma Key paints, can also be used with good illuminators (lights). A test of a small swatch is worthwhile for materials whose performance is unknown.

Backing Uniformity and Screen Correction

Since the luminance level and saturation of the backing determine the level of the background scene, it is important to light the backing as uniformly as is practical, ideally within plus-or-minus 1/3 *f*-stop.

Although a perfectly uniform backing is desirable, it may not be achievable in the real world. (Please refer to the *Illuminators* section in this chapter.) If the backing itself is blotchy, the background image will become equally blotchy in the composite.

It is possible to clean up the alpha channel by increasing the contrast (gamma) in the blotchy areas until all the nonuniform values are pushed (clipped) to 1.0. Although clipping the alpha

---

[9] A noted researcher and pioneer in the field, Jonathan Erland of Composite Components Co. in Los Angeles, won an Academy Award for CCC's line of patented Digital Green and Digital Blue lamps, fabric, and paint.

values eliminates the nonuniformity in the backing, the same values on the subject's silhouette are clipped too, resulting in the subject's edges becoming hard and shadows and transparencies starting to disappear.

Figure 3.1 Alpha clipping. (Image courtesy of Ultimatte Corporation.)

In Figure 3.1, frame A shows the actor shot against an uneven blue screen. Frame B shows the alpha "cleaned up" by boosting the contrast. Note that fine detail in the transparent shawl and the hair has been lost in the alpha and in the composite, frame C.

Virtual shooting sets are even more troublesome. They often contain green set pieces that correspond to objects in the final background so that the actor can climb stairs, lean against a doorway, and so forth. The props all cast shadows on themselves and the green floor, and the actor casts shadows on everything. With lighting alone it's impossible to eliminate set piece shadows without washing out the actor's shadow.

Several software packages have features to cope with nonuniform backings. Ultimatte Screen Correction software can compensate for backing luminance variations as great as two stops.

Screen correction is easy to use: After lighting the set, shoot a few seconds before the actors enter. This footage is called the *clean plate* or *reference plate*. All the backing and lighting imperfections are recorded on those few frames. Now shoot the actors as usual.

In the composite, the artist selects a well-lit reference point near the subject. Software derives a correction value by comparison with the clean plate and corrects the rest of the backing to the measured level. Software compares the clean frames pixel by pixel with the action frames and inhibits the correction process in the subject area (the actor) and proportionately inhibits the correction in transparencies. In the example shown in Figure 3.2, frame D shows the clean plate without the actor. The backing has a wide variation in color and brightness, simulating a virtual set. Frame E shows the alpha with screen correction. Note that the fine hair detail and the full range of transparencies in the shawl have been retained in the alpha and in the composite, frame F. This demonstration frame is an extreme example; very dark and desaturated backing colors such as those at the right and top right should be avoided in the real world!

Figure 3.2 Screen correction before and after. (Image courtesy of Ultimatte Corporation.)

Backing defects, scuffed floors, set piece shadows, uneven illumination, and color variations in the backing and lens vignetting all disappear. The actors' shadows reproduce normally, even where they cross shadows already on the backing.

There is a significant limitation: If the camera moves during the shot, the identical camera move must be photographed on the empty set for the length of the scene. Although it is reasonably quick and simple to repeat pan-tilt-focus camera moves with small, portable motion control equipment, skilled matchmovers can bring a "wild" clean pass into useful conformance around the actor and remove discrepancies with rotoscoping. Some matchmovers prefer the clean footage to be shot at a slower tempo to improve the chances that more wild frames will closely match the takes with the actors.

Ultimatte AdvantEdge software can semiautomatically generate synthetic clean frames. The software can detect the edges of the foreground image, interpolate screen values inward to cover the foreground, and then create an alpha using that synthetic clean frame. Ultimatte Roto Screen Correction, which predated AdvantEdge, uses a loosely drawn outline to assist software in distinguishing foreground subject matter. There are some limitations; it's always best to shoot a clean plate if possible.

Illuminators

The best screen illuminators are banks of narrowband green or blue fluorescent tubes driven by high-frequency flickerless electronic ballasts.[10] These tubes can be filmed at any camera speed. The tube phosphors are formulated to produce sharply cut wavelengths that will expose only the desired negative layer while not exposing the other two layers to a harmful degree. These nearly perfect sources allow the use of the lowest possible matte

---

[10] Flickerless electronic ballasts prevent the light from being unevenly exposed on film at speeds that are faster or slower than 24 frames per second. If one does not use them and shoots at any other speed than 24 frames per second, the image will appear to flicker.

contrast (gamma) for best results in reproducing smoke, transparencies, blowing hair, reflections, and so forth.

Kino Flo four- and eight-tube units are the most widely used lamps. They are available for rent with Super Green or Super Blue tubes from Kino Flo in Sun Valley, California, and lighting suppliers worldwide. The originators of narrowband tubes, Composite Components, supplies Digital Green and Digital Blue tubes tailored specifically to film response.

All of these lamps have very high output and can be set up quickly. The light from the tubes is almost perfectly monochromatic; there is almost no contamination. Flickerless, high-frequency ballasts power the units. Some high-frequency ballasts can be dimmed, a great convenience in adjusting backing brightness. Fluorescent sources like Kino Flo make it easy to evenly illuminate large backings, and the doors built into most units simplify cutting the colored light off the acting area.

A good scheme for frontlit backings is to place arrays of green fluorescents above and below the backing at a distance in front equal to approximately 1/2 the backing height. The units may be separated by the length of the tubes or brought together as needed to build brightness. The lamps must overlap the outer margins of the screen. Keep the subjects at least 15 feet from the screen. Figure 3.3 shows side and top views of an actor standing on a platform that serves to hide the bottom row of lights. If the actor's feet and shadow are to be in the shot, the platform may be painted green or covered with green cloth or plastic material.

Note that if a platform is not practical, mirror Plexiglas or Mylar on the floor can bridge the gap from the acting area to the screen, extending the screen downward by reflection.

A backing can be evenly lit entirely from above by placing a second row of lamps about 30% farther away from the screen and below the top row. The advantage of lighting from above is that the floor is clear of green lamps. Lighting from above requires careful adjustment to achieve even illumination. The overhead-only rig requires about 50% more tubes and spills substantial green light onto the foreground in front of the screen. To film 180-degree pan-around shots on Universal's *The Fast and the Furious* (2001), the ace rigging crew lit a three-sided backing 30 feet high and more than 180 feet long, entirely from above.

The number of tubes required depends on backing efficiency, the film speed, and the desired *f*-stop. As an example, six 4-tube green lamps are sufficient to light a 20-by-20-foot Composite Components green backing to a level of *f*4 with 200-speed film. Eight 4-tube blue lamps yield *f*4 with a 20-by-20-foot blue backing from the same maker.

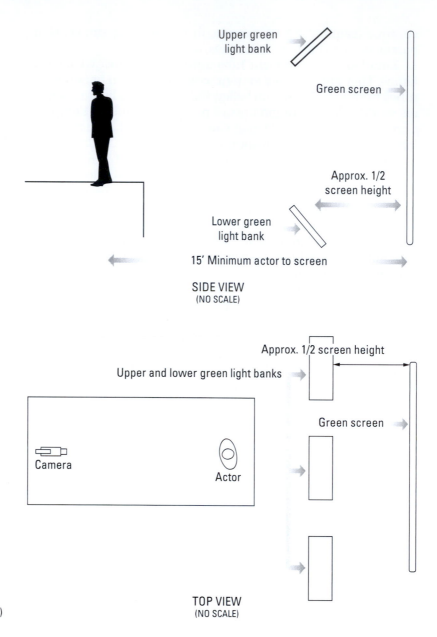

Upper green
light bank

Green screen

Approx. 1/2
screen height

Lower green
light bank

15' Minimum actor to screen

SIDE VIEW
(NO SCALE)

Approx. 1/2 screen height

Upper and lower green light banks

Green screen

Camera

Actor

Figure 3.3 Diagram of screen
lit with six fluorescent banks.
(Image courtesy of Bill Taylor, ASC)

TOP VIEW
(NO SCALE)

Alternative Light Sources

In a pinch, commercial daylight fluorescent tubes or Kino Flo white tubes wrapped with primary green or primary blue filter sheets can produce good results. The downside is great loss of efficiency; it takes about four filtered daylight tubes to equal the output from one special-purpose tube.

Regular 60-Hz ballasts can be used with commercial tubes at the cost of weight and power efficiency. As with any 60-Hz fluorescent lamps, 24-fps filming must be speed-locked (non-locked cameras are fortunately rare) to avoid pulsating brightness changes, and any high-speed work must be at crystal-controlled multiples of 30 fps. These tubes are somewhat forgiving of off-speed filming because of the "lag" of the phosphors.

Backings can also be frontlit with primary green- or primary blue-filtered HMI lamps. The only advantage is that the equipment is usually already "on the truck" when a shot must be improvised. Getting even illumination over a large area is time consuming, and filters must be carefully watched for fading. Heat shield filter material is helpful. Because of high levels of the two unwanted colors, HMI is not an ideal source.

In an emergency, filtered incandescent lamps can do the job. They are an inefficient source of green light and much worse for blue (less than 10% of the output of fluorescents), so they are a poor choice for lighting large screens. Watch for filter fading as above.

A green or blue surface illuminated with white light is the most challenging, least desirable backing from a compositing standpoint. White light, however, is required for floor shots and virtual sets when the full figure of the actor and the actor's shadow must appear in the background scene. Advanced software can get good results from white-lit backings with the aid of screen correction and a clean plate as described above. Difficult subjects may require assistance with hand paintwork.

Eye Protection

A word about eye protection is necessary here: Many high-output tubes produce enough ultraviolet light to be uncomfortable and even damaging to the eyes. Crew members should not work around lit banks of these fixtures without UV eye protection. It is good practice to turn the tubes off when they are not in use. The past practice of using commercial blueprint tubes was dangerous because of their sunburn-level UV output.

How to Expose a Greenscreen Shot and Why

Balancing Screen (Backing) Brightness to the Shooting Stop

Let's assume that the camera choices are optimal, screen materials and lighting are ideal, and the foreground lighting matches the background lighting perfectly.

A common misconception is that backing brightness should be adjusted to match the level of foreground illumination. *In fact, the optimum backing brightness depends only on the* f-*stop at which the scene is shot.* Thus, normally lit day scenes and low-key night scenes require the same backing brightness if the appropriate *f*-stop is the same for both scenes. The goal is to achieve the same blue or green density on the negative, or at the sensor, in the backing area for every shot at any *f*-stop.

The ideal blue or green density is toward the upper end of the straight-line portion of the H&D curve (in the 90% range in video) but not on the shoulder of this curve, where the values are compressed. Figure 3.4 presents an idealized H&D curve, a graph that shows how the color negative responds to increasing exposure. Each color record has a linear section, where density increases in direct proportion to exposure, and a "toe" and a "shoulder" where shadows and highlights, respectively, can still be distinguished but are compressed. Eight stops of exposure range can comfortably fit on the H&D curve, a range as yet unmatched by digital cameras. The "white point"—the density of a fully exposed white shirt that still has detail—is shown for all three records.

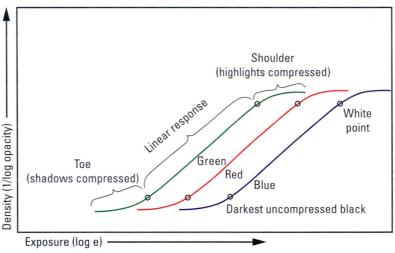

Figure 3.4 Schematic H&D curve. (Image courtesy of Bill Taylor, ASC)

Imagine a plume of black smoke shot against a white background (Figure 3.5). It's a perfect white: The measured brightness is the same in red, green, and blue records. The density of the smoke in the left-hand image ranges from dead black to just a whisper. What exposure of that white backing will capture the full range of transparencies of that smoke plume?

Obviously, it's the best compromise exposure that lands the white backing at the white point toward the top of the straight-line portion of the H&D curve in film (a white-shirt white), or a level of 90% in video, and brings most dark values in the smoke up off the toe. If the backing was overexposed, the thin wisps would be pushed onto the shoulder and compressed (or clipped in video) and pinched out by lens flare. If the backing was underexposed (reproduced as a shade of gray), detail in the darkest areas would fall on the toe to be compressed or lost entirely.

Figure 3.5 Normal and under-exposed smoke plumes. (Image courtesy of Bill Taylor, ASC)

You could make up for underexposure by boosting the image contrast. As the right-hand image in Figure 3.5 shows, this makes the backing white (clear) again, but tonal range is lost (the dark tones block up), the edges of the smoke become harder, and the noise is exaggerated.

Now imagine that instead of a white screen, we're shooting the smoke plume against a green screen and that the measured green brightness is the same as before. What's the best exposure for the green screen? Obviously, it's the same as before. The only difference is that the red- and blue-sensitive layers aren't exposed.

Just like in the smoke plume, greenscreen foregrounds potentially contain a full range of transparencies, from completely opaque to barely there. Transparent subject matter can include motion blur, smoke, glassware, reflections in glass windows, wispy hair, gauzy cloth, and shadows.

To reproduce the full range of transparency, the green screen should be fully exposed but not overexposed. In other words, its brightness should match the green component of a well-exposed white object like a white shirt, roughly defined as the whitest white in the foreground that still has detail. (It's not desirable to expose that white shirt as top white, because it's necessary to leave some headroom for specular reflections, on the shoulder in film, 100% and over in video.)

Setting Screen Brightness

Meter readings of blue and green screens can be misleading. Some exposure meters respond inconsistently to monochrome color, especially blue, and some are affected by the high levels of UV coming from green and blue tubes. The most reliable method for balancing a blue or green screen is still by eye, with the white card method, as discussed next.

White Card Method for Screen Balancing

1. Choose the *f*-stop at which the scene is to be shot. Let's say it is *f*4. Position a 90% reflectance white card in the acting area (Figure 3.6) and light it to an *incident light* reading[11] of *f*4, keeping the spill light off the backing. The white card is now lit to the brightest tone that still has detail (white-shirt white) even though the actual set lighting may not reach that level.

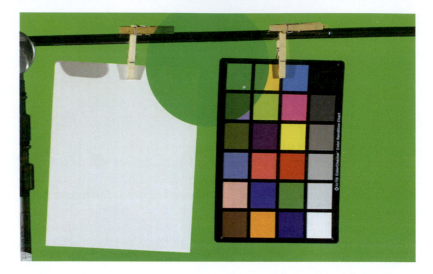

Figure 3.6 White card in set, lit to shooting stop (incident reading). (Image courtesy of Bill Taylor, ASC)

2. View the white card against the screen through a Wratten No. 99 green filter. (Use a Wratten No. 98 blue filter for a blue backing.) In a pinch, primary green or primary blue lighting gels, folded to several thicknesses, will serve.

3. Adjust the backing brightness so that the white card blends into the backing. The overlay in Figure 3.6 shows the view through the filter. *When the edges of the card are invisible or nearly invisible, the green light coming from the screen is now the same brightness as the green light component coming from the* f4 *white card.* (If you were to photograph the white card now, the red, blue, and green components coming from the card would reproduce near the top of the straight-line portion of the curve. Since the green screen matches the brightness of the green component coming from the white card, the green layer will also be exposed near the top of the straight-line portion of the curve, without overexposure.) The backing will now expose properly at *f*4.

---

[11] Incident light reading is usually measured with a light meter. The meter measures the light that is illuminating or falling on the subject. It also takes into account the angle, or geometry, of the light—what direction it is coming from—and averages these two things together into a single reading.

If it is easier to adjust set lighting than backing brightness, the procedure can be reversed. Adjust the white card's light until the card blends in, and then take an incident reading. Light the set to that f-stop.

Once the backing brightness is set, a spot meter may be calibrated for use with the appropriate color filter to read f-stops directly: Wratten No. 98 (or 47B + 2B) for blue, and Wratten No. 99 + 2B for green. [The UV filters (built into the No. 98) ensure that UV from the tubes does not affect the reading.] Simply adjust the meter's ISO speed setting until the reading from the screen yields the target f-stop ($f4$ in the example above).

Just as in the smoke plume example, more exposure is counterproductive; it pinches out fine detail due to image spread and pushes the backing values into the nonlinear range of the film or video sensor. Less exposure is also counterproductive; it would then be necessary to make up matte density by boosting contrast.

Levels for Digital Original Photography

Most of the same considerations apply as in film photography. It's particularly important that none of the color channels be driven into highlight nonlinearity or "clip," allowing some headroom for specular highlights. If the screen lighting can be adjusted independently of the set, light the screen to a video level of about 90% in the appropriate channel.

Choosing the Backing Color

The choice of backing color is determined by the costume or subject color. The range of permissible foreground colors is wider when the backing can be lit separately from the actor, rather than when the actor must be photographed in a white-lit green set (a *floor shot*), for example.

A blue backing is satisfactory for most colors except saturated blue. Pastel blues (blue eyes, faded blue jeans, etc.) reproduce well. The color threshold can be adjusted to allow some colors containing more blue than green (such as magenta/purple) into the foreground. If too much blue is allowed back into the foreground, some of the blue bounce light will return. Therefore, if magenta costumes must be reproduced, it is prudent to take extra care to avoid blue bounce and flare. Keep the actors away from the backing, and mask off as much of the backing as possible with neutral flats or curtains. Saturated yellows may produce a dark outline that requires an additional step in post to eliminate. Pastel yellows cause no problems.

A green backing is satisfactory for most colors except saturated green. Pastel greens are acceptable. Saturated yellow will turn red in the composite unless green is allowed back into the subject, along with some of the green bounce or flare from the original photography. The same precautions as above should be taken to minimize bounce and flare. Pastel yellow is acceptable. Figure 3.7 shows a test of green car paint against a green screen. The hue and saturation of the "hero" swatch was sufficiently distinct from the screen color to pose no difficulties in matting or reproduction, and there is no green spill. Note that none of the colors in the Macbeth chart is affected except for the more saturated green patches.

Figure 3.7 Green and blue paint swatches test against a green screen, before and after. (Image courtesy of Bill Taylor, ASC)

Because bounce is unavoidable where the actor is surrounded by a green floor or virtual set, one should not expect to reproduce saturated magenta or saturated yellow on a green floor without assistance in post.

If the foreground subject contains neither saturated green nor saturated blue, then either backing color may be used. However, the grain noise of the green emulsion layer on color negative and the green sensor in a digital camera is generally much lower than the grain noise of the blue layer. Using a green backing will therefore result in less noise in shadows and in semitransparent subjects. Black smoke in particular reproduces better against a green backing.

Obviously, it is important for the VFX Supervisor to be aware of wardrobe and props to be used in traveling matte scenes. Sometimes a difficult color can be slightly changed without losing visual impact, thus saving much trouble and expense in post.

If in doubt, a test is always worthwhile. The Ultimatte previewer (see later section titled On-Set Preview) can be invaluable.

Some visual effects experts prefer blue backings for scenes with Caucasian and Asian actors because it is easier to achieve a pleasing flesh tone without allowing the backing color into the foreground. For dark-skinned actors, either backing color seems to work equally well.

In extreme cases (for example, if the foreground contains both a saturated green and a saturated blue), troublesome foreground colors can be isolated (with rotoscoping if necessary) and color corrected separately.

Backing Types and Lighting

The color and illumination of the backing are crucial to a good result. A perfect green backing would expose only the green-sensitive element of the color negative or digital sensor. Cross-color sensitivity in the negative or sensor, imperfect illuminators, and spill light from the set all compromise this ideal. It's no surprise that the best combinations of backing, illuminators, and camera type yield the best-quality composites.

Backlit Backings

Backings can be backlit (translucent) or frontlit. Translucent backings are almost extinct due to their high cost, limited size, and relative fragility. Translucent Stewart blue backings gave nearly ideal results and required no foreground stage space for lighting. Due to lack of demand, Stewart has never made translucent green screens. Frontlit backings are more susceptible to spill light, but with careful flagging they can produce a result every bit as good as backlit screens.

Translucent cloth screens can be backlit effectively, but seams limit the usable size.

Frontlit Backings

If the actor's feet and/or shadow do not enter the background scene, then a simple vertical green or blue surface is all that is needed. The screen can be either a colored fabric or a painted surface. Any smooth surface that can be painted, including flats, canvas backings, and so forth, can be used. Fabrics are easy to hang, tie to frames, spread over stunt air bags, and so on. Please see the *Illuminators* section above for spacing and positioning of lamps.

Day-Lit Green and Blue Backings

For big exterior scenes, authentic sunlight makes a very believable composite that can only be approximated with stage lighting.

Daylight is the ultimate challenge, requiring the best quality backings and screen correction compositing for good results. Thanks to those advances, there are no limits to the size of a traveling matte foreground, aside from the size of the backing.

Figure 3.8 Daylight greenscreen composite from *Greedy*. (Image courtesy © 1994 Universal Studios Licensing, LLLP. All rights reserved.)

Coves as shown in Figure 3.8 (the first daylight greenscreen shot made for a feature film) are to be avoided; there is usually a wide band of glare in the cove. Later experience has shown that a clean, straight line is much easier to deal with in post. A raised platform, painted or covered with backing material, with a separate vertical backing well behind it is ideal. The cinematographer of *Journey to the Center of the Earth* (2008), Chuck Schuman, recommends a flat 45-degree join between green floors and walls.

Limits of Day-Lit Backings

Because the green backing set must be oriented to achieve the sun direction matching the background plates, one can shoot relatively few setups in a day. At some times of year, the sun on the set may never get high enough to match the background sun, thus requiring a replacement source.

Floor Shots, Virtual Sets

If the actor must be composited head-to-toe into the background scene, as in Figure 3.8, then the floor must also be the color of the backing. (Green is preferred for floor shooting since the shadows will be less noisy.) The same type of white light and lighting fixtures that light the actor are also used to light the floor and backing. A shadow cast on a green-painted wall or floor by the subject can be transferred (when desired) into the background scene together with the subject.

Floors may be painted or covered with fabric. Fabric can be hazardous if loose underfoot. Painted floors scuff easily and quickly show shoe marks and dusty footprints.

Pro-Cyc's Pro Matte plastic material is a good alternative for floors. The material is a good match to Digital Green and Digital Blue paint and fabric. It is tough, scuff resistant, and washable. It is available in sheets, preformed coves, and vertical corners in several radii. Permanent sets are good candidates for this material, due to cost.

Lighting uniformity problems (within plus-or-minus one *f*-stop), color contamination of the floor, scuff marks, and green set piece shadows can be dealt with in compositing when screen correction frames are available.

Sheets of 4-by-8-foot mirrored Mylar or mirrored Plexiglas may also be used as a walking surface. (Please see section titled *Illumination and Reflections from the Backing* below). Of course, no shadow is cast on a mirror surface, and the reflection must be dealt with.

The choice of fabric and paint affects not only the quality of the composite but also the lighting costs. Some screen materials are much more efficient than others, requiring many fewer lamps to light to the correct level. In general, green screens and tubes are more efficient than blue screens and tubes. *Savings on lamp rentals can amount to tens of thousands of dollars per week on large backings.*

Limitations of Floor Shots and Virtual Sets

Floor shots and virtual sets are both difficult and rewarding, because the actor can walk or sit on objects in the background, climb stairs, and walk through doorways, even when the background scene is a miniature. When the actor's shadow appears in the background scene, it adds believability to the shot.

Alpha channel (matte) contrast must be high in a floor shot to achieve separation from the contaminated color of the floor. Even the finest green pigment or dye reflects significant quantities of red and green. The problem is often compounded by glare from backlighting. Since the matte is created by the difference between the backing color and the colors in the subject, and since there is inherently less difference because of white light contamination, the alpha values must be multiplied by some factor to yield an opaque matte that will prevent the background from showing through. This multiplication raises the gamma (contrast) of the matte image.

If the real shadow can't be reproduced, it can be simulated within limits with a distorted copy of the alpha channel. If necessary, the shadow can be hand animated.

Foreground Lighting

Creating the Illusion: Lighting to Match the Background

Inappropriate lighting compromises a shot the instant it appears on screen, whereas an imperfect compositing technique may be noticeable only to experts.

Obviously, the foreground photography must match the background lens and camera positions, but lighting considerations are just as important. This is why it is generally preferable to shoot live-action backgrounds first. (If the background hasn't been shot yet, the job depends on everything from careful map reading to educated guesswork! Even the best guesses can be defeated by unexpected weather.)

Foreground lighting must match the background in direction, shadow hardness, and key-to-fill ratio. True sunlight has nearly parallel rays coming from a single point at a distance that's optically equivalent to infinity. To simulate the sun, use the hardest source available, as far away as the shooting space will allow. Multiple sources cast multiple shadows—an instant giveaway. Sometimes folding the light path with a mirror will allow the hard source to be farther away, a better representation of the parallel rays of the sun. Skylight fill and environmental bounce light must be shadowless. Therefore, surrounding the actors with the biggest, broadest sources of light available is preferable. The perfect skylight source would be a dome like the real sky, which can be approximated on stage by tenting the set with big silks or white bounces.

Environmental Bounce Light

Since the software drops out the backing and the backing reflections from the foreground object, the subject is "virtually" surrounded by black. The black surroundings cause no problem if the composite background is an essentially dark night scene.

However, if the eventual background is a light day scene, and if the subject had really been in that day environment, the environmental light would light up the hair and provide the normal edge brightness along arms, sides of the face, and so forth. The cinematographer must light the back and sides of the subject to provide about the same amount and direction of lighting the environment would have provided. Large, white bounces are useful in creating back cross-reflection sources just outside the frame. Otherwise, edges of arms, legs, and faces will go dark, causing the foreground to look like a cutout.

Simulated light from the environment can be added digitally to replace the suppressed screen color with color derived from the background. It's a slight glow around the edges that can look good when tastefully applied. The real thing is preferred, though.

High levels of fill light in wide day exteriors, although sometimes desirable for aesthetic reasons, hurt the believability of day exterior composites. Movie audiences are accustomed to seeing more fill in close-ups, a common practice in daylight photography.

Local Color

Skylight is intensely blue, so fill light supposedly coming from the sky should be blue relative to the key. Likewise, if actors and buildings in the background are standing on grass, much green light is reflected upward into their shadows. If the actor matted into the shot does not have a similar greenish fill, he will not look like he belongs in the shot. Careful observation is the key. In a green-screen shot, the bounce light from grass is low in both brightness and saturation compared to the screen color, so that color cast can be allowed in the composite foreground while still suppressing the screen. The same is true of sky bounce in a bluescreen shot.

Shooting Aperture

A day exterior shot will often be shot in the f5.6 to f11 range or with an even deeper f-stop. Fortunately, efficient lighting and high ASA ratings on films and sensors permit matching these deep f-stops on the stage. In a day car shot, for example, holding focus in depth from the front to the rear of the car contributes greatly to the illusion.

Figure 3.9 Green screen lit to f11 with fluorescent lamps. (Image courtesy of Bill Taylor, ASC)

Figure 3.9 shows a 28-foot-wide screen lit with 16 four-tube Kino Flo lamps, plus two HMI helper lamps with green filters on the sides. This combination made it possible to film at $f11$ with a 200 ASA Vision 2 negative. Curtains at left, right, and top made it easy to mask off unwanted portions of the screen.

Color Bias in Foreground Lighting

In the past, some cinematographers used an overall yellow or magenta color bias in foreground lighting to help the composite, with the intent that the bias be timed out later. This practice is counterproductive, resulting in false color in blurs and transparencies. If an *overall* bias is desired, it's easy to achieve in post-production.

Illumination and Reflections from the Backing

Colored illumination and reflections from the backing on the subject must be minimized for top-quality results. *Illumination and reflection are separate issues!*

Blue illumination from the backing can be made negligible by keeping the actors away from the backing (at least 15 feet, but 25 feet is better) and by masking off all the backing area *at the backing* that is not actually needed behind the actors. Use black flags and curtains. (The rest of the frame can be filled in with window mattes in compositing.) Any remaining color cast is eliminated by the software.

Reflections are best controlled by reducing the backing size and by tenting the subject with flats or fabric of a color appropriate to the background. In a common worst case, a wet actor in a black wetsuit, the best one can do is to shoot the actor as far from the screen as possible, mask the screen off as tightly as possible, and bring the environmental bounce sources fully around to the actor's off-camera side, without, of course, blocking the screen. A back cross-light will of course wipe out any screen reflection but will look false if it's not justified by the background lighting.

Big chrome props and costumes present similar challenges. Since they also present the cinematographer with a huge headache (every light shows, and sometimes the camera crew as well), it is usually not too difficult to arrange modifications to these items. When the visual effects team is brought in early on, problems like these can be headed off in the design stage.

A common reflection challenge is a Plexiglas aircraft canopy, which can show every lamp and bounce source, depending on the lighting angle and camera position. A bounce source for a canopy shot must be uniform and surround the canopy 180 degrees on the camera side. Sometimes the best solution is to shoot without the canopy and track a CG model canopy back in, in the composite. An advantage to a CG canopy is that it can reflect the moving composited background.

Some reflections can be disguised with dulling spray, but sometimes they cannot be eliminated. In the worst case, reflections make holes in the matte that must be filled in digitally in post. Pay particular attention to the faces of perspiring actors, which can be very reflective. Of course, when the actor must stand in the middle of a blue-painted virtual set, some blue contamination is unavoidable; it will be removed by the compositing software.

Sometimes reflections are desirable! Sheets of mirror Mylar or Plexiglas can extend a screen by reflection, even below the stage floor. Actors can walk on mirror Plexiglas to be surrounded by the screen's reflection. (Of course, their own reflection must be dealt with.)

In a scheme devised by the late Disney effects wizard Art Cruickshank, ASC, an actor on a raft in a water tank was shot against a sodium matte backing. The backing and the actor reflected strongly in the water. This enabled the Disney optical department to matte the actor and his reflection into ocean backgrounds. Cruickshank's method was revived and used effectively in bluescreen shots in *Daylight* (1996) (Figure 3.10) and more recently in greenscreen shots in *Bruce Almighty* (2003), where Jim Carrey and Morgan Freeman seem to be walking on Lake Erie while actually standing in shallow water tanks on the back lot (Figure 3.11).

In Figure 3.10, which shows a diagram of the swimming tank setup for *Daylight* (1996), the spillway in front of the screen makes a seamless transition from the screen reflection in the water to the screen itself.

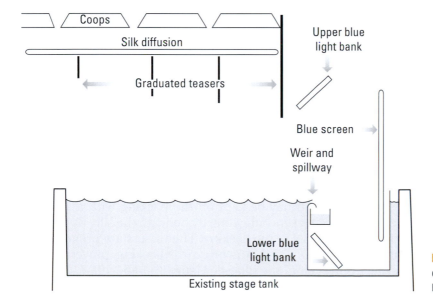

Figure 3.10 Water tank diagram. (Image courtesy of Bill Taylor, ASC)

Figure 3.11 *Bruce Almighty* (2003) water tank composite. (Image courtesy © 2003 Universal Studios Licensing, LLLP. All rights reserved.)

Controlling Spill Light

Attentive use of flags and teasers on set lighting and black cloth on light-reflecting surfaces outside the frame will eliminate most spill light on the backing. (Even concrete stage floors reflect a surprising amount of light. To see spill light when the backing is lit, look through a red filter.) A small amount of white spill light from the set inevitably hits the backing. It often comes from the large, almost unflaggable soft sources that simulate skylight. Since the skylight is typically two or three stops down from the key light, the spill has little effect on the backing. Realistic lighting should be the paramount concern.

If white light is contaminating an area of the backing, a higher level of the alpha channel can be applied in post to darken it. Since there is no difference in color between, say, transparent white smoke or mist and white light of the same brightness falling on the backing, it's clear that the less white light contamination there is to be cleaned up, the better. Otherwise, as the contamination disappears, so do all the transparent foreground pixels of the same color. Screen correction is invaluable in extracting the maximum detail from smoke and spray shot against white-lit backings.

If the foreground must be flat lit to simulate overcast conditions, a good approach is to bring most of the light in from overhead through a large, translucent silk. On stage, much of the overhead soft light may be kept off the backing with a series of horizontal black teasers hung directly beneath the silk, running its entire width parallel to the backing. The teasers are progressively longer top to bottom as they get near the backing, preventing the backing from "seeing" the silk (see Figure 3.11 above).

Lighting Virtual Sets

Inescapably, if one is lighting an actor and the surrounding floor with white light, there is no way to control the floor brightness independently of the actor, other than changing the floor paint or floor fabric. The only control available is the balance between the actor's shadow and the rest of the floor and backing.

Lighting Procedure for Holding the Shadow (Petro Vlahos Technique)

1. Turn on the key light to cast the desired shadow.
2. Measure the brightness on the floor just outside the shadow (use a spot brightness meter and green filter, assuming that it's a green floor).
3. Light all the rest of the green floor to this measured brightness while adding as little light as possible to the shadow area.
4. Light the green walls to achieve the same brightness as the floor.
5. Shadow density may be increased by blocking fill light from the shadow area or lightened by adding fill light to the shadow area.

Shadow density is controlled by adjusting the fill light, not by adjusting the key light. Outside the shadow, the entire green set should appear to have equal and uniform intensity as seen from the camera position. Strive to stay within plus-or-minus 1/3 f-stop; screen correction can deal with brightness variations as great as plus or minus one f-stop.

The human eye quickly compensates for small light changes; it is not a good absolute measuring device. (It is, however, superb at comparisons.) It is necessary to use a spot brightness meter and green filter to check for uniform brightness. A digital camera with a computer display is also useful for making a quick check of lighting uniformity in the three-color channels.

In backlight, because of the shallow angle between the camera and floor, the floor will not appear as green as the back wall. A diffused, polarized white-light glare component is reflected by the floor because of the shallow angle. For holding good shadows in backlight, it is essential to use a polarizing filter over the camera lens. The HN38 is recommended. Rotate the filter until the floor glare is canceled. Ideally, the backlights should be polarized too, but it is rarely done. Large sheets of polarizing plastic are available up to about 19 feet wide; they can be protected against heat with heat shield reflecting filter material. Of course, HMIs emit less heat than tungsten lamps to begin with.

Lighting to Eliminate the Shadow (Vlahos Technique)

1. Light the entire green set uniformly with large-area diffused light sources.

2. Check uniformity as noted above.
3. Place the actor in position. If he casts a shadow, add additional low-level lighting to return the light level in the shadow to its original level.
4. Add a modest key light to create the desired modeling, and ignore the shadow it casts. The added key light will cause a shadow to be visible to the eye, but because the key light did not affect the green intensity of the floor in the shadow it has created, the shadow can be made to drop out in compositing.

Tracking Marks on the Screen

When the foreground camera moves, the background must move appropriately. Unless the foreground and/or background can be photographed with a motion control camera, tracking data must be extracted from the foreground image and applied to the background during compositing. This process is called *matchmoving*.

Tracking marks applied to the otherwise featureless screen give the matchmovers fixed points to track. These marks must obviously show in the photographed scene, but ideally they should clear the foreground actors, or at least avoid their heads, since they must be removed in the composite. Marks are typically laid out in a rectangular pattern, with about 3 to 5 feet between them, depending on the lens used, the action, and the distance to the backing. Black or white tape pieces or crosses will usually suffice, though uniquely identifiable markers are very helpful if there is much tracking to do.

If camera shake or other sudden motion is required in the foreground photography, motion blur can obliterate the tracking marks. The Aerocrane Strobe Tracking System created by Alvah Miller provides target arrays of LED lamps that strobe in sync with the camera shutter, giving well-defined marks on every frame even if they are not in focus. Cylindrical LEDs have uniform brightness even when viewed off-axis.

Sometimes it is desirable to light the tracking LEDs continuously, allowing them to blur in motion. Valuable tracking information can be derived from the length of the blur. Consult the tracking team for their preference.

On-Set Preview

On-set preview composites made with a still camera and calibrated monitor, like the Kodak/Panavision Preview System, or a live composite made with a hardware Ultimatte device will alert the crew to problems before they are committed to film. A few video assist companies provide this specialized service.

Using the digital Ultimatte previewer (hardware device or software on a computer) on the motion picture set eliminates much guesswork and uncertainty. It provides great assistance when photographing actors who must be realistically integrated with people and objects in the background scene. Previewing with Ultimatte also immediately identifies the acceptable limits in lighting irregularities and wardrobe color.

If it's a digital shoot, an output video stream must be available that's compatible with the Ultimatte. An outboard processor may be needed. This yields the best preview available with all the foreground–background relationships visible at full quality.

For film shoots, a small, outboard color camera feeds the previewer. (Film camera color taps, even when they can be switched to 100% video, are so starved for light that they usually cannot make good composites, although if their geometry is properly adjusted, they are fine for alignment purposes.) Playback from disk or tape provides the background scene.

Camera for Bluescreen or Greenscreen Photography

Film Photography: Choosing a Camera Negative

Some camera negatives are better suited to composite work than others. Ideally, one would choose the finest grained, sharpest film available. It is also important to have low cross-sensitivity between the color layers. Foreground and background film stocks do not have to match, but of course it's helpful if they have similar grain and color characteristics.

Kodak Vision 2, 100T and 200T (tungsten balance), films are ideal for green and blue backing work. The dye clouds are very tight and well defined. Vision 3, 500T, the latest in a series of remarkably fine-grain high-speed films, as one would expect, is still grainier than the lower speed films. Although the 500T film is not ideal, a well-exposed 500T negative is much better than a marginally exposed 200T negative!

An interlayer effect in these films produces a dark line around bright foreground objects (such as white shirts) when they are photographed against a green screen. Software can deal with this effect.

Kodak Vision 2, 50-speed daylight film and Fuji 64 daylight film produce superb results in sunlight, with very low shadow noise, but require high light levels on stage.

If these 100T and 200T films cannot be used for aesthetic reasons, one should still pick the finest grain emulsion compatible with lighting requirements. Be aware that additional image processing (and cost) may be required. A few negative emulsions have so much cross-sensitivity between the color layers that they should not be used.

Film emulsions are constantly evolving. As an example, recent improvements in red sensitivity in some emulsions have been accompanied by more sensitivity to infrared reflected from costumes, altering their color noticeably. This effect is easily dealt with by filtration—if you know it's there! A quick test of actors and costumes is always worthwhile.

Choosing a Digital Camera

Since all three-color channels are used in creating the composite, an ideal camera would have high resolution and uncompressed color (bandwidth).

Three major factors affect color recording:
1. spatial resolution,
2. captured bit depth, and
3. recorded bit depth and compression.

Spatial Resolution

Spatial resolution is broadly related to the number of photosites (light-sensitive elements) available for each color. In the commonly used Bayer array there are half as many blue photosites as there are green photosites. Likewise, there are half as many red photosites as green photosites. The missing values are derived through interpolation from adjacent pixels in the de-Bayering operation. Because human visual acuity is greatest in the green wavelengths, Bayer's array gives excellent visual results from an optimally small number of photosites. Although they are not ideal for the purpose, Bayer array cameras can yield good composites with care in original photography and in post.

However, the blue and red image is still half the resolution of the green image, which limits the resolution and fine detail of the mask image.[12] To address this and other image quality issues, a few high-end cameras like Panavision's Genesis and Sony's F35 (same sensor as the Genesis) have full resolution in all three colors. These cameras are ideal for composite work.

Color Bandwidth and Compression

Assuming your camera can produce a full-bandwidth, uncompressed RGB signal, much information can be lost when that signal is compressed and recorded. Many HD VCRs are limited to 4:2:2 recording, which includes rolling off the green channel's high

---

[12] It should be noted that film builders use a roughly equivalent compromise: Green- and red-sensitive negative layers have more grain and less resolution than the green layer.

frequencies and applying half-bandwidth MPEG compression to blue and red.

The designation 4:2:2 does not refer directly to RGB bandwidth but rather to YUV. The Y channel carries the luma or brightness information, while U and V are the channels from which the color information is derived (similar to LAB color space in Photoshop). In a 4:4:4 recording, every channel is recorded at the full color depth. (The designation 4:4:4 is actually a misnomer, carried over from standard definition D1 digital video. Because it's well understood to mean full bandwidth in all three channels, its use has continued into the high-definition and higher digital cinema world.)

Just as the classic Bayer array has a negligible effect on images intended for viewing but adversely affects composite quality, well-compressed images designed to look good on screen can have serious limitations when composited. Good software engineering can recover some of the lost bandwidth, but edge detail (fine hair and so forth) and shadow noise still suffer from compression artifacts. A laundry list of compression artifacts includes dark or light lines trailing or leading moving objects, banding in dark areas, and so forth. These problems are even more pronounced in "DV" and "SD" format cameras. With new cameras coming on line every day, testing on the actual subject matter is always worthwhile.

Edge Enhancement/Sharpening/Detail Settings

Camera edge enhancement/sharpening should be turned off! The artificial edges that sharpening produces will otherwise carry into the composite. If sharpening is needed, it can be done during compositing.

Recording

Recording in data mode gives maximum flexibility and best quality in post. Data mode records the uncompressed data (as directly off the camera sensor as the camera's design allows) to a hard disk. This is often called *raw mode*, but beware: At least one camera's (Red) raw mode is in fact compressed. Since raw mode data cannot be viewed directly, a separate viewing conversion path is required to feed on-set monitors.

If recording in data mode is not possible, shoot material intended for post-compositing as uncompressed 4:4:4 full-bandwidth HD (or better) video onto a hard drive or use a full-bandwidth VCR, such as Sony's 4:4:4 SR format machines.

To sum up, resolution numbers are not the whole story, since some cameras trade off resolution for color depth. Test your available camera and recorder choices.

Because this is an imperfect world, you may have no choice but to shoot or record with 4:2:2 equipment. Although 4:2:2 is not ideal, don't forget that the last two *Star Wars* films, which included thousands of greenscreen, were shot with 2/3-inch 4:2:2 cameras. Test the camera on the subject matter. Note that 4:2:2 can produce a satisfactory result in green screen (since the green channel has the highest resolution in these cameras), but one should not expect the ultimate in fine edge detail. (Consumer cameras typically record 4:1:1 and are not recommended for pro visual effects use.)

It bears repeating: Whatever the camera, any edge enhancement/sharpening should be turned off!

Filtration

In general, no color or diffusion filters other than color-temperature correction should be used on the camera when shooting greenscreen or bluescreen work. Compositing can be called "the struggle to hold edge detail"; obviously low-contrast, soft effects or diffusion filtering that affects the edge or allows screen illumination to leak into the foreground will have an adverse effect.

To ensure that the filter effect you desire will be duplicated in the composite, shoot a short burst of the subject with the chosen filter, making sure it is slated as *filter effect reference*.

Negative Scanning and Digital Conversion

The film frames, data recording, or video recording must be converted into frame-based digital files the software can use. It's important not to lose information at this step.

The three layers of the color negative are sensitive exclusively to the red, green, and blue portions of the color spectrum. When the negative is scanned, the RGB densities of each pixel in the image are translated into red, green, and blue numerical levels in a digital memory. The three color records of each frame are referred to as the red, green, and blue channels. They are usually recorded as Cineon or DPX frames, which are uncompressed formats.

Video and data must be similarly converted into frames. This step is sometimes called *digitization*, which is really a misnomer since the source is already digital. These frames are usually recorded in the DPX format.

Color Correction

Color correction at the scanning/conversion stage can be a major source of data loss. It should not be built in to image files intended for compositing. On the other hand, a few frames recorded with the desired color and filtration will be an invaluable reference during the composite step.

Software Functions

The software uses the difference between the backing color and the colors found in the foreground to accomplish four tasks:

1. Optimally, it will correct nonuniformity in the backing (the *screen correction* function, not available in all software packages).
2. It must create a *silhouette matte* (the alpha channel) of the foreground action (Figure 3.12, center frame).
3. It must create a *processed foreground* in which all traces of the backing color are suppressed (turned black or neutralized), while the foreground color is carried through unchanged (Figure 3.12, right frame).
4. Finally, it must bring all the elements together into a believable composite with the background (Figures 3.13 and 3.14). In the example shown, the greenscreen foreground was shot on an outdoor set, freely following the action with a Steadicam. Motion tracking information derived from the Steadicam foreground was applied to the panoramic combined background plate. (In the process of making the background, the Horseshoe Falls and the American Falls were moved one-half mile closer together.)

Figure 3.12 Original photography, silhouette (alpha) matte, and processed foreground from *Bruce Almighty* (2003). (Image courtesy © 2003 Universal Studios Licensing, LLLP. All rights reserved.)

Figure 3.13 Background seamed together from three VistaVision images. (Image courtesy of Bill Taylor, ASC)

Figure 3.14 Three frames from *Bruce Almighty* (2003) Steadicam shot. (Image courtesy of Bill Taylor, ASC. © 2003 Universal Studios Licensing, LLLP. All rights reserved.)

The Processed Foreground

The original image contains the green backing and the foreground subject. The green backing is automatically reduced to a black backing by a logic operation, and subtracting a proportion of the alpha (matte) signal in each channel. Green is limited so that it cannot exceed red or blue. As a result, all of the green color seen though transparent and translucent subjects likewise disappears.

If the foreground subject (actor) is close to the backing or standing on a green floor, the subject will have a green color cast due to reflected (bounce) light from the floor and from lens flare. (This reflected light from the screen is sometimes called *spill*, but it should not be confused with the spill light from the subject's lighting falling on the screen.) No attempt should be made to remove this color with filters on the lights or camera, or with color correction in transfer. All backing contamination is removed from the subject by the software's white, gray, and black balance controls.

Blue bounce is much harder to see on the set than green but is just as visible in the composite. There is no difference between green screens and blue screens of the same brightness as far as bounce is concerned. A dark blue or green will bounce less, but dark colors have too little color saturation to make a high-quality matte.

Once the backing has been reduced to black, and color contamination of the subject has been eliminated, the subject appears to have been photographed against a perfectly black backing. No evidence of the backing color remains. This is the processed foreground image.

The order in which the foreground is processed is important. Noise reduction on the foreground should happen when the processed foreground is made, before the alpha is created, whereas color correction should wait until the final composite.

Underwater Photography

In addition to underwater diving or swimming shots, underwater greenscreen photography creates a zero-g environment for spacesuited actors who have freedom of motion that is impossible to achieve on wire rigs.

The biggest challenge is keeping the water clear of sediment and particulates. Underwater diffusion causes the screen to flare into the foreground and vice versa; it's ruinous to the matte edges. High-capacity pumps, good water circulation, and a multistage filter are necessary to keep the water clear. It's also important that all personnel have clean feet when they enter the tank.

Composite Components' green material stretched on a frame works well under water in a swimming pool or a tank. Tip the screen back to catch light from above, with diffusion material floating on the water surface to kill caustic patterns on the screen. Build up the screen lighting level with green fluorescent units above the water. Underwater Kino Flo lamps are also available.

The high chlorine levels common in swimming pools bleach out the screen quickly; pull the screen out of the tank daily and rinse it off with tap water.

Working with the Cinematographer

The cinematographer is the visual effects creator's most important ally on the set. So much depends on the quality of the original photography! Befriend the Cinematographer early in the game, and keep him or her in the loop!

Invariably, the Cinematographer is eager to help achieve the best final result. Be sure he or she understands and believes that you can duplicate any final look required, if (for example) you need to shoot without diffusion on the lens. Be sure to shoot properly slated reference with the desired diffusion, filtration, and so forth, so that it can be matched in the composite.

Please refer to the ASC manual, which has a similar chapter on blue screens and green screens.

The Alpha Channel

The alpha or matte channel (the channel that carries transparency information) is a grayscale image in which the foreground image is a silhouette. The silhouette may be imagined as black against clear (and all the values in between) or, with its values inverted, clear against black.

The alpha channel represents the *difference* in color (hue, saturation, and brightness) between the backing color and the colors in the foreground subject. The matte's numerical level at any pixel is proportional to the visibility of the backing.

Compositing Software

Bluescreen and greenscreen compositing software is sometimes lumped into the collective category of *keyers*. Unfortunately, some early keyers such as Chroma Key were so crude that they harmed the reputation of the whole class by association. The present-day software described next has no relationship to those early keyers.

The software described in the following paragraphs is in wide use. All except IBK are available as plug-ins for most of the leading digital compositing packages, including After Effects, Nuke, Flame/Inferno, and so on. All contain filters to deal with less-than-ideal video like DV.

Each package has individual strong points; all are capable of first-class results with well-shot photography. Sometimes the best results come when two programs are used on a single shot. This list is by no means inclusive.

Keylight

At this writing, Keylight is the most used package, thanks to its bundling with After Effects Professional software. A straightforward user interface makes it very easy to use. Keylight has excellent edge transition controls and plenty of power to deal with off-color backings. The background scene may be used to influence the edges of the composite.

Keylight was developed originally at London's pioneering Computer Film Company by Wolfgang Lempp and Oliver James. It is marketed worldwide by The Foundry.

Ultimatte

Ultimatte and Ultimatte AdvantEdge are the tools of choice for difficult shots. AdvantEdge borrows from Ultimatte's Knockout concept by processing the edge transitions separately from the core of the foreground image, blending them seamlessly into the background without loss of detail.

The deep and rich user controls require an experienced operator to get the most from the software. The interface works as a black box within the compositing package, which can complicate workflow. One benefit of this architecture is that the interface is identical in the wide range of supported software packages.

The first-of-its-kind software was derived from the original Color Difference logic created by Petro Vlahos; Richard Patterson (then at Ultimatte) wrote the first digital version. The commercial digital implementation won multiple Academy SciTech Awards. Ultimatte HD and SD video hardware compositing devices are also available from the company.

Primatte

Primatte was originally developed at Imagica Japan by Kaz Mishima. The unique polyhedral color analysis allows fine-tuned color selections between foreground and background. The user interface is intuitive and uncomplicated while offering many options. The background scene may be used to influence the edges of the composite. It is bundled into Nuke.

The IBK (Image-Based Keyer)

The IBK was developed by Paul Lambert at Digital Domain. It is exclusively bundled with Nuke. It employs Ultimatte code carried over from earlier compositing software packages like Cineon and Rays, by agreement with Ultimatte. Like Ultimatte, it can deal with a wide variance in backing color by creating a synthetic clean plate. As in Keylight, the background scene may be used to influence the edges of the composite.

Updated contact information for these suppliers is listed in this book's companion website (www.VESHandbookofVFX.com).

With Thanks to Petro Vlahos

This document draws heavily on the Traveling Matte chapter that Petro Vlahos and the present author wrote for the last three editions of the ASC manual. Vlahos, a multiple Oscar winner, created the perfected Color Difference bluescreen film system in 1958 and in the following years led the creation of analog and digital hardware and software versions of Ultimatte, the first high-quality electronic compositing systems. At their core, all digital bluescreen and greenscreen compositing software systems employ variants of the original Vlahos algorithms.

ON-SET DATA ACQUISITION
Karen Goulekas

Ensuring that the proper visual effects data is gathered while shooting a film is one of the most important aspects of a VFX Supervisor's job. Decisions made about what data to get, and how to acquire it, will determine how efficiently the visual effects vendors will be able to create their final shot work in post-production.

A poorly planned visual effects plate shoot can result in wasting precious post-production time and money solving technical issues, rather than using the time on aesthetic and creative issues that will make the shot better. Examples of things that can make visual effects shot creation less than ideal include missing camera lens data, badly lit or nonexistent chroma screens, no (or too many) tracking markers, and rig removals that could have been better hidden in frame.

However, although it is the job of the visual effects team to gather this data, there are definitely circumstances when it is not feasible. For example, sometimes a plate shot on location that was not intended for visual effects work may very well become a visual effects shot in post as the edit comes together. And although it may not be an ideal plate, the hope is that, at the very least, the camera information can be found in the script supervisor's and/or camera assistant's notes—copies of which should always be obtained before the end of the shoot.

Also, due to the high cost of having an entire crew on location each day, it can quite often make more economic sense to choose the "fix it in post" option. The reality is that even if it's going to take "only an hour" to prepare a chroma screen behind the actors on location, that hour, multiplied by the cost of every crew member on set, can be a far more expensive option than paying extra for one roto artist to manually brute force the way through creating a matte to isolate the actors in the scene. Although this is not an ideal solution, it's the one that the producer will most likely choose, for the obvious financial reasons. However, although it is important for the VFX Supervisor to be flexible regarding the budget and time issues that are a part of every film shoot, they must consider not only the cost differences but also the potential quality differences, depending on the specifics of the shot. A poorly executed final shot won't be of any value to the film, regardless of how many dollars were saved.

Additionally, when a scene is taking place during sunrise or sunset (the magic hours), gathering the ideal visual effects elements, such as a clean plate or HDRI stills with all the actors and crew cleared from the set, will simply not take priority over filming all the required shots in similar lighting. Even something as quick as placing tracking markers cannot take priority over shooting the required action in the desired light. The visual effects team should be prepared to take advantage of any downtime during shooting to prepare and place tracking markers ahead of the shoot day so as to minimize slowing down the live-action shoot and missing the opportunity to gather important data on the day.

Camera Report

That being said, it is still important to plan for getting all the ideal data possible. The first and most basic piece of information is the visual effects camera report. Although the script supervisor and camera assists will be taking their own notes, they tend to only take down the basics, such as the slate number, lens, takes, camera roll, focus, and time of shot.

However, for the visual effects camera report, more data is good data! The on-set data wranglers should get as much info as possible, including the following:

- camera lens and serial number;
- camera roll;

- film stock (if using film cameras);
- filters;
- camera body;
- camera height;
- camera distance from subject;
- pan, tilt, and zoom info;
- time of day;
- weather;
- slate number;
- lighting info; and
- location.

Of course, not all of this data is required for every shot. However, if the data wranglers can get this information unobtrusively, then why not? It might be required to shoot an additional visual effects element for a particular plate later in post and, if so, it sure is nice to know the camera settings and where it was positioned relative to the actors and set.

However, it is important to note that a data wrangler should not gather information that is not mandatory to the creation of a shot if it slows down the camera crew or overall production in any way.

It's important to have a written description of both the camera's and actors' actions. For example, while the actors' action might be about the actors getting into a car and driving away, the camera action might be a crane shot starting on the actors as they get into the car and then craning up, panning, and tilting with the car as it drives away from the camera. The point is to be able to get a visual on what the entire shot is about based on these written descriptions.

Additionally, notes about the type of camera equipment used, such as dolly track, cranes, camera heads, etc., should also be documented. This is particularly important information if there will be additional plates for the shot, such as a miniature, and a need to re-create the motion control data to export to the camera crew shooting the models. It is also helpful to know how the camera equipment was set up to get the shot if there are any issues solving the camera track for the plate.

Another good practice is to list the 2D and 3D tasks and elements required for each plate shot, such as set extension, sky replacement, wire and marker removal, etc. This is a good way to gauge how many potential shots of each type, such as composite only, set extensions, or CG creature shots, there might be in the final shot list.

Many script supervisors will place a "V" for visual effects in front of the scene number on the slate to indicate when a shot will require visual effects work. It is also recommended to place a visual effects number on the slate of each plate shot that will require visual effects work. This is particularly helpful in editorial as a quick way for the editor and visual effects team to identify which shots in the cut will require visual effects work. Although most visual effects work needed is quite obvious, a visual effects numbering scheme is a sure way to remember wire and marker removals that are, otherwise, hard to spot on the editorial screens. It can also serve as a reminder about less obvious things discussed with the director while shooting, such as sky replacements, color corrections, speed ramps, etc.

For most visual effects projects, the anticipated body of work is generally broken down into specific sequences and shots during pre-production as a means of budgeting and bidding the work to award to visual effects vendors. One typical scenario is to use a two-letter code for each visual effects sequence in the script. For example, shots in a Brooklyn Bridge sequence would begin with "BB," followed by a four-digit number, such as BB0010, BB0020, etc.

Because multiple units are often shooting, one helpful practice is to assign a unique visual effects slate number for each camera setup that will involve visual effects work. Although any numbering scheme can work, one suggested methodology is to indicate the two-letter sequence code, such as the "BB" mentioned above, and then increment sequentially for each camera setup. It can also help to use a different numbering sequence for each unit—for example, starting at 1000 for main unit, 2000 for 2nd unit, 3000 for 3rd unit, etc. This is a quick way to know which unit shot each plate without having to look up the specific camera report. It is also handy for getting a quick count on how many visual effects plates have been shot overall.

The data wranglers simply start the visual effects camera setup as BB1000, BB2000, etc., depending on which unit they are covering, and then increment by one for each camera and setup that is shot for visual effects. If a particular shot is being covered by three cameras—for example, A, B, and C—each camera should get a unique visual effects number and associated camera report, such as BB1000, BB1001, BB1002.

When multiple cameras are being used as described above, it is also helpful to note on each camera report that it was part of a multicamera shot. For example, the camera report for A camera, named BB1000, should note that it was shot with BB1001 and BB1002.

Because camera slates can get quite full with all the information that needs to be documented about each take, there is often no room left to put the visual effects number. Or even if there is, if it is a tiny space, it defeats the purpose of having the number on the slate if it can't actually be read off the monitors in editorial during post. To address this, it is good practice to ask the camera assistants to write the visual effects slate number on the back of the camera slate—nice and big! When slating the cameras, they just have to flip the slate over for a moment to record the visual effects number.

Figure 3.15 is an example of a simple camera report filled out with sample data.

FILM NAME							
Camera data report							

Date	Time	Location	Weather	Slate #		VFX slate #	
07.24.09	10:15 am	Malibu-PCH Hwy	Sunny	88M (A)		BB1022	

Camera	Lens		Lens serial #	Aspect	Filter		Stock
Arri 235	17–80 mm Optimo T2.2		#1587760	1.33 (full ap)	ND3		5201

Stop	Focus	Cam height	Cam tilt	Shutter		Notes by	
T2.8 1/3	10' to 35'	12' to 43'	See takes	180		Joe	

Shot description

Jack gets into his car and drives away

Camera set up

Super techno crane 50'. Crane up and pan and tilt with car as it drives away.

VFX work required

Set extension, marker removal, sky replacement

Notes

Shot with BB1023. Tracking markers placed on road.

Take	Focal	FPS	Roll	Print	Comments
1	24–35 mm	24	A28		NG. False start
2	24–35 mm	24	A28	X	Good. Tilt ~15 up to 20 degrees down
3	24–40 mm	24	A29	X	Good. Tail slate. Tilt: ~15 up – 25 down

Figure 3.15 Camera report with sample data. (Image courtesy of Karen Goulekas.)

Tracking Markers

Tracking markers, in conjunction with the camera lens info, are the best way to ensure the ability to digitally re-create the practical camera motion that created the plate. While many programs are available that can calculate the camera motion with just the camera lens, it's still a best guess. However, with tracking markers in the scene, the tracking software can use a combination of the camera lens and triangulation of the tracking markers to calculate a more accurate match for what was actually shot.

When placing markers on a chroma screen, it is important to use a marker color that is well separated from the chroma screen color. A good rule of thumb for placing markers on a chroma screen is to place them 5 feet apart, which, in most cases, will ensure that markers show up in the shot. If a CU shot reveals too few markers, a data wrangler should always be ready to run in and place another marker or two to get the coverage needed. However, it is good practice to check with the crew members who will be doing the actual tracking as they might have additional requests or specifics to make their job easier.

Note that it is far better to add extra markers when/if needed, rather than place the markers too close together. On the other hand, too many markers means a lot more work for the compositing team, because it requires more paint-out work and/or multiple keys to accommodate the color of the markers versus the color of the chroma screen. Think twice about the work added to be done in post before plastering the screen with unnecessary markers.

It is also quite helpful to use different shapes for adjacent markers because camera tracking software can get confused when they are all the same. For example, if a particular "X" shape that is being tracked and calculated by the tracking software enters or exits frame during the course of the shot, the tracking software might jump to another "X" shape in the scene to track instead. This problem can be alleviated by using different shapes.

When dealing with placing markers on outdoor locations, any size and shape of markers can be used that will best address the terrain and tracking needs. For example, if the terrain to be tracked is relatively bare, use short markers placed on the ground in the areas where visual effects will be added. In Figure 3.16, tracking information was needed about the ground plane as digital vultures were going to be interacting with it.

Figure 3.16 Sample ground plane marker layout for the film *10,000 BC* (2008). (*10,000 BC* © Warner Bros. Entertainment Inc. All rights reserved.)

However, when faced with high foliage, taller markers are required. In this case, it is best to have stakes cut to a predetermined height so there is always a sense of approximately how high each marker is from the ground plane. Additionally, if Velcro is placed on all four sides of the stakes, the tracking markers can be quickly aligned toward the camera, rather than having to physically move the orientation of each stake for each shot.

When dealing with aerial plates, bigger markers are required. In one shot a grid of traffic cones was placed 15 feet apart from one another. The cones showed up perfectly in the aerial plates and it was very helpful to the visual effects artists to know the height of the cones, as well as their distance apart from one another as a guide to the scale of the location.

When dealing with dark sets or night shoots, LEDs placed around the set are the perfect solution. They show up clearly in the plates and are easy to paint out because they are so small. Also, the type of cloth being used for the chroma screens can determine the best materials to use to create the tracking markers. For example, grip tape works fine for Spandex chroma screens, whereas Velcro-backed markers work best on felt screens.

When visual effects elements will be added to actors, small dots placed on their face and body get the best results. Depending on what needs to be done in post, the number of markers can range from two or three to over a hundred placed in a grid across their face.

In general, the on-set visual effects team should always be armed with a variety of tracking markers, such as grip tape in various colors, LEDs, stakes and rods, precut X's, etc. However, along with the job of getting tracking markers into the scene quickly and without holding up the shoot also comes the responsibility of quickly getting those markers back out of the scene if the next camera setup does not require visual effects. No point in spending the visual effects budget on unnecessary paint-out work in post.

Props for the Actors

Quite often, actors have to perform and interact with "invisible" characters that will be added with visual effects during post-production. Not only can it be difficult for the actor to perform without being able to see and interact with his counterpart, but it can also be very difficult to add the digital character in the scene if the actor's eye line and body motion do not fit with the scale and proportions of the digital character. It also makes it very difficult for the camera crew to frame a shot without knowing how much space the digital character will take up in the final shot composition.

In a situation where the actor just needs to know the size and position of the digital character so he can get his eye line and body oriented correctly, a prop representing the size and position of the digital character may be sufficient.

For example, in Figure 3.17, a full-scale model of the in-progress digital tiger was printed out on fabric and stretched across a lightweight frame. This allowed both the camera operators and actors to rehearse a pass while the data wranglers walked the tiger stand in through the set.

Figure 3.17 Full-scale stand-in model used for camera and actor eye lines for the film *10,000 BC* (2008). (*10,000 BC* © Warner Bros. Entertainment Inc. All rights reserved.)

Then, when the scene was shot without the tiger stand-in, the actors and camera crew already knew what marks and eye lines they had to hit. It is also helpful to shoot a take of the rehearsal as a means of indicating how the shot was envisioned with the digital character during shooting.

If the digital creature is really large, a simple height stick indicating where the creature's eyes will be can be helpful. For example, in the case of the mammoths in *10,000 BC* (2008), they were 18 feet tall. To give the actors a correct eye line, an extendable rod was used and raised up to about 16 feet where the mammoth's eyes would be. This allowed the actor and camera crew to adjust for the framing and action needed when shooting the plate.

When dealing with lots of extras, make sure that they do not move through the areas on the set where the digital creatures will be added. Again, in the case of *10,000 BC* (2008) a technique was needed to indicate the total area on the set that the digital mammoths would require in the final shot as a means of preventing the extras from travelling through that area.

To do this, full size and lightweight mammoth shapes were built to indicate their size and position on set (Figure 3.18). And because space for four mammoths pulling up the stone blocks had to be accounted for, a base was built, representing their total required area, which served as a type of fence that kept the extras out during shooting.

Figure 3.18 Mock-up of elephants on set for the film *10,000 BC* (2008). (*10,000 BC* © Warner Bros. Entertainment Inc. All rights reserved.)

When actors need to physically interact with digital characters, one approach is to have the stunt team interact and fight with the actors using life-size props that represent the digital character. For example, the actors needed to fight and kill various 12-foot-tall Terror Birds in *10,000 BC* (2008). Because the actors needed to dodge the strikes of the birds, as well as strike at them with their swords, it made sense to have the stunt team perform as the Terror Birds. To do this, life-size Terror Bird heads were built and attached to rods so that the stunt team could raise the Terror Birds to the correct height and interact with the actors.

Any number of props and techniques can be used, but, unfortunately, most of them, as seen in the images above, do increase the amount of paint-out work needed in post. But that is better than shooting plates blind without any guidance as to where the characters will be and what they will be doing in the final shots.

Cyberscanning

For both props and actors that need to be created or enhanced with visual effects, cyberscanning offers the best solution to quickly gathering a 3D volume of their shape.

Because it can be difficult to have access to actors once principal photography has wrapped, most cyberscanning companies offer mobile services so they can come on location and cyberscan the actors during the shoot. Generally, when doing a full-body scan, it is good practice to have the actor wear a Lycra body suit, rather than the costume. This allows for the costume to be added digitally, as a separate model, so that cloth simulations can be added as needed.

The same holds true for hair. If the character will be relatively large on screen and it will be necessary to create digital hair and simulations, it is better to have the actor wear a skull cap for a clean scan of his head shape rather than have to remove all of his cyberscanned hair in post.

However, if the digital characters will be very small in frame and, therefore, not require any hair or cloth simulations, they can be cyberscanned in full costume. Using this technique, digital photos of the actor in costume can be directly projected right onto the cyberscanned model, thus avoiding the step of creating the costume and hair as separate models.

Digital Photos

For any props or actors that are cyberscanned, digital photos are also needed for use as texture maps and/or reference to create shaders.

When photographing props, it is best to take the pictures in neutral light for use as texture maps. However, taking pictures of the props in hard sunlight and shade is also a good means of seeing how the materials the props are made of react to different light situations.

For photos of digital crowds and extras that will be small on frame, about five photos of each extra in costume should suffice. It is best to photograph them against a white backdrop with no harsh lighting. It is also a good idea to put tape marks on the ground to quickly show the extras where they need to stand for their photos, which helps make things move a long a little faster.

When building a digital character that will be large in frame, many, many photos are needed! While the requirements of each digital character will be different, the number and detail of the range of photos should be relative to how close it will be to the camera in the final shot.

In general, it is a good idea to take photo references of all the props and sets during shooting in the event they need to be built as additional visual effects elements.

When there is a need to photograph large areas for a set extension or to create CG buildings, a good technique is to shoot the photos/textures as tiles. Very simply, the edges of each tile should overlap with the edges of its adjacent tiles to ensure there isn't anything missing in the scene because it accidentally didn't get photographed.

For example, if it is necessary to capture a city skyline for use in multiple shots, set the camera up on a tripod and pan and tilt to each section of the skyline, until overlapping tiles representing up to 360 degrees of the environment have been captured. Once these tiles are stitched together, they can be projected onto a dome to give a full 360-degree view of the world to use in the composites.

Lidar/Laser Scanning

Lidar/laser scanning of sets and locations is an incredibly useful tool to get a 3D volume of large areas for use in visual effects. Because lidar is based on line of sight in terms of what it can capture from where it's set up, the length of time to scan a set or location depends entirely on how crowded that area is.

For example, when scanning a natural location, such as a canyon, the scan can go very quickly because the lidar system can view and scan large areas at a time with few obstructions from any given location. However, when scanning buildings in a dense city, every building is obstructed to some degree by other buildings in the foreground and, therefore, the lidar system requires many more positions to set up and scan from.

To create the digital buildings in *The Day after Tomorrow* (2004), a lidar team scanned 12 blocks of buildings in New York City in high detail. This took 12 weeks to accomplish due to the many locations required to get full coverage. It also took a lot of time (and money) to get the approvals from the building owners to actually get inside and on top of various buildings from which to scan. During this time, a team of photographers took advantage of the various locations to take thousands of photos for use as textures for the scanned buildings. (Lidar scanning is discussed in more detail in the *Lidar Scanning and Acquisition* section later in this chapter.)

Lens Distortion Charts

Because camera lenses create varying degrees of lens distortion on the images they capture, shooting lens distortion charts is very helpful in dealing with this issue when creating visual effects.

Since no two camera lenses are the same, a large black-and-white grid should be shot for every lens that was used to shoot the film. So if the main and 2nd unit both used the same range of lenses, it is still necessary to shoot a unique grid for every lens in both kits. By doing so, the unique lens distortion created by each lens will be obvious based on how many the lines of the grid get bowed and distorted toward the edges of the frame.

For best results, the grid should have the same aspect ratio as the film or digital cameras that were used. For example, a grid that is 4 feet by 3 feet can be easily filmed to fill the frame of a full aperture film frame of 2048 × 1556 pixels as it shares a similar aspect ratio. When filming the grid, it should be placed against a flat surface, such as a wall, and the camera should be positioned along a dolly track until the grid fills the camera frame edge to edge.

Then in post, if a plate has a lot of camera distortion, use this data to create a version of the plate with the camera lens distortion removed for camera tracking and 3D element creation. This is done by matching the serial number of the lens used to shoot the plate with the corresponding grid that was shot with that same lens. Using the compositing software tool set, undistort the grid until the grid lines look completely straight and absent of any distortion or bowing.

Now when the CG elements are added into the composite, simply apply the inverse of the numbers used to undistort the plate to actually distort the CG elements by the amount needed to match them back into the original plate. Voilà!

A lens chart can be as simple as a series of grid lines or a checkerboard as seen in Figure 3.19.

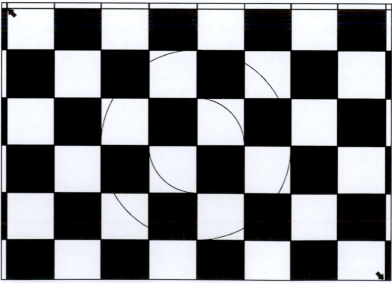

Please keep chart centered and leveled.

Figure 3.19 Lens distortion chart. (Image courtesy of Gradient Effects, LLC.)

HDRI and Chrome Balls

Matching to the practical outdoor and indoor lighting used to shoot the film is one of the more difficult tasks required for the visual effects teams to make their elements photoreal and fit them seamlessly into a shot.

One relatively quick method is to shoot a chrome ball on set for each camera setup. It is a quick way of seeing where the light sources are coming from and how the object reacts to light. It is also a good idea to paint half of the ball with a matte gray to see how dull surfaces react to the same light. When shooting the ball, the data wrangler can simply hold the chrome side of the ball up to the camera for a few seconds and then rotate the ball to reveal the matte gray side for a few seconds.

The advantage of using the chrome ball is that it can be done quickly for each setup without holding anyone up. It can be done any time but most often during the slating of the shot or at the very end as the last take. The disadvantage is that the chrome ball simply provides visual reference of where the lights were on set and how shiny and matte objects respond to that light.

Another technique, which provides a lot more information when re-creating a digital version of the position and intensity of the set or location lighting, is to use HDRI (high dynamic range imaging).

By photographing the same scene with a wide range of exposure settings and then combining those different exposures into one HDR image, an image is created that represents a very high dynamic range from the darkest shadows all the way up to the brightest lights.

Many visual effects houses have created their own proprietary software than can use these HDR images to calculate where the lights need to be placed in a scene and how bright they need to be. This technique has great advantages over the simple chrome ball because it greatly improves the ability to re-create photorealism and accurately light visual effects elements in a scene.

The disadvantage of taking HDR images on set, however, is that it can take a few minutes to set up and take all the bracketed photos needed and crew members should not be walking through the scene during this time.

If shooting on a set in which the lighting does not change, simply take the HDR photos during lunch hour without disrupting anyone. However, if HDR images are shot for an outdoor shoot with a constantly moving sun position, it can be quite difficult to get the set cleared after every camera setup.

So it is a good idea to still use the old-fashioned chrome ball during the slating of each scene as a backup, and grab those HDRs whenever there is a window of opportunity.

LIDAR SCANNING AND ACQUISITION
Alan Lasky

Modern visual effects production relies heavily on computer-generated imagery (CGI) for the creation of synthetic elements that will be combined with live-action photography. This blend of "real-world" cinematography and computer graphics necessitates a tight integration between the set and post-production. To facilitate communication between live-action production and digital post-production, a new discipline has evolved that has come to be known collectively as *on-set data acquisition*.

Digital visual effects are a relatively new addition to the craft of filmmaking and on-set data acquisition is still fundamentally an embryonic science. Capturing relevant data on set is often a delicate balance between the requirements of visual effects facilities and the practical realities of tight shooting schedules and limited budgets. Additionally, the rapid pace of technological change creates a "moving target" of data requirements that can become a source of frustration for all involved.

One of the most important aspects of on-set data acquisition is the capture of accurate 3D data from real-world sets and locations. Computer-generated characters, set extensions, and props all rely on precise data derived from the real world in order to create seamless visual effects. Many tools and techniques have been adapted from other industries to meet the demands of large-scale 3D capture in visual effects: photogrammetry, surveying, image-based modeling, and most critical for this section, lidar.

Lidar (*li*ght *d*etection *a*nd *r*anging) is a term that covers a broad range of technologies used in metrology, atmospheric research and military topographic mapping. However, for visual effects production the most important subset of lidar technology is that used in surveying and known collectively as 3D laser scanning. These tools and techniques are often referred to as *high-definition survey*. No matter what name is used, lidar represents one of the most powerful tools available for rapid, accurate 3D modeling of large-scale sets, locations, and props.

Lidar scanners work on a relatively simple principle. Because the speed of light is known, the scanner can measure the time light takes from a laser pulse emitter back to a receiver and record an *x*, *y*, and *z* coordinate in space for each reflected point. Through rapid scanning of these reflected samples, robust and descriptive 3D "point clouds" are created, providing extremely accurate coordinate information across millions of points. Using specialized software these point clouds can be stitched together and intelligently filtered to produce deliverables in a number of different formats. These formatted point clouds are then used as the basis for a number of visual effects techniques.

In practice, lidar scanning is not much different from conventional surveying. The scanner is connected to a host computer (usually a field laptop) where the collected laser range measurements (point clouds) are stored in a file. This collection of measured coordinates usually exists as a list of x, y, and z samples formatted as a standard spreadsheet table. Multiple scans are often necessary to fill in the 3D topology of an object from all angles and cover any occlusion that may occur from fixed point scans.

Some lidar scanners cover 360 degrees horizontally and, depending on the power of the laser, their range can be as long as 1000 meters (about 3280 feet). Quite large areas can be scanned, and by stitching together multiple point clouds there is no theoretical limit (exclusive of computer storage and processing) to the size of the area that can be captured. The trade-off in lidar scanning is always measurement range versus eye safety. As the range increases, so too must the power of the laser. Obviously the greater the laser power, the greater the threat to the human eye, so most lidar scanners (apart from those used in military applications) are limited to eye-safe power levels.

Several companies manufacture commercial, off-the-shelf lidar scanners for sale to the general public. Currently Leica, Geosystems, Trimble, Optech, and Riegl all make efficient, powerful, and portable systems useful for visual effects applications. While the costs have come down somewhat in recent years, lidar scanners represent a considerable investment. Large capital expenditure is necessary for the systems, support equipment, and personnel required to operate an efficient lidar capture team. Due to this high economic barrier to entry in the field, lidar scanning is usually subcontracted to professional service bureaus for visual effects production.

Lidar in Visual Effects

The integration of CGI and live-action photography is always a difficult problem, and lidar scanning provides significant advantages to the visual effects pipeline. Lidar can be used in a number of ways to assist the blending of computer-generated elements with live-action cinematography. In fact, use of lidar as early as pre-production can substantially affect the quality and efficiency of visual effects material. Lidar data links the art, camera, and visual effects departments through shared, highly accurate 3D data and visualizations. Lidar scanning has many roles in modern film production, from previsualization to visual effects.

Previsualization

Starting in pre-production, lidar can be used for the previsualization of complex scenes by sending a lidar crew out on a 3D location survey. Much as a location scout takes photographs, the lidar crew scans the location and delivers accurate 3D models to production. These models can be used to plan the logistics of a complex location shoot. Although it may seem extravagant to use lidar for this purpose, significant benefits can be gained from this process. Detailed 3D geometry representing a location can be used to plot camera angles with extreme accuracy. Camera moves can be designed with exact measurements of dolly track and crane clearance. Geographically referenced and aligned models can be used to track sun positions throughout the day to further facilitate production planning.

Art Department

Of course, precise 3D models of sets and locations provide unique benefits to the art department. Lidar scan data can be loaded into CAD software in order to enhance the set design process. A 3D scan gives precise data to construction crews in order to facilitate rapid fabrication of set pieces and props. Lidar scans of existing structures are sometimes called *as-built surveys*, and these surveys are equally useful to the construction crews and art departments. Certainly lidar data can be used anywhere accurate CAD drawings of existing real-world elements are needed in pre-production.

Set Extension

One of the more common applications of CGI in current filmed entertainment is the use of computer-generated elements to extend sets beyond the scope of what is physically built. These set extensions serve the same purpose as traditional matte paintings, and indeed they have been called 3D matte paintings in certain circumstances. However, the nature of 3D computer-generated imagery allows for much more freedom of camera movement on these set extension elements than was possible with traditional flat matte paintings.

Like all computer-generated elements, it is imperative that set extensions be precisely locked to the live-action photography in order to be convincing. To successfully blend a computer-generated set extension with a live-action set, some form of 3D model representing the physical set or location is necessary. Limited measurements can be taken on set, or blueprints from the art department can be acquired, but these are often imperfect solutions. What is needed is an as-built survey of the set or location to facilitate the creation of elements that register perfectly with their real-world counterparts. Lidar provides an effective method of gathering this on-set data for the creation of 3D set extensions. A point cloud version of the set provides all the measurement data essential for an accurate lock between the real world and the virtual world. A polygonal or surfaced version of the model can be used along with 3D camera projection techniques to further enhance the realism of the shot.

3D CG Characters

The use of 3D characters in live-action photography can greatly benefit from lidar scanning. If a 3D character is to convincingly inhabit a live-action scene, the visual effects artist must obtain an exact duplicate of the set or location where the action takes place. Lidar provides a quick and accurate method for deriving a 3D representation of these photographed areas. Lidar scan data can be used to lock 3D characters into a complex topology and to limit their action to the physical constraints of the photographed space. Models created from lidar data can also be used both to cast accurate shadows on 3D characters and to receive accurate shadows of 3D characters for projection on to real-world geometry.

Matchmoving

An important and time-consuming task for today's visual effects professionals is the art of matchmoving and camera tracking—literally matching the movement of the 3D virtual camera to that of its live-action counterpart. Although software exists to perform camera tracking, it is by no means an automated task. A great deal of manual input is required to successfully track a shot in 3D. Most current matchmoving software packages have the capability of incorporating measurement data into their mathematical camera solvers. Indeed, most matchmoving tools recommend the use of these "constrained points" to assist the algorithms in more accurately deriving a result.

Lidar scans are by definition measurement data. This measurement data can easily be incorporated into the matchmoving/camera-tracking pipeline. Sets and locations often contain many elements useful for feature tracking. Window corners, edges, architectural elements, and other features can be used as track points to better resolve 3D camera motion. Lidar can significantly enhance the use of these features by providing extremely accurate distance constraints between these tracked points. This measurement data is extremely valuable when tracking complex camera moves. Any point in the lidar scan can provide an accurate measurement reference; therefore, any tracked feature in the live-action photography can be referenced and measured in the scan data. Scanning sets and locations requiring matchmoving can save several weeks and thousands of dollars by eliminating guesswork and hand tracking.

Collision Geometry

One of the more interesting uses of lidar scan data is collision geometry for particle systems. A particle system is a computer graphics technique generally used to simulate natural phenomena such as fire, smoke, or rushing water. Particle systems are usually implemented in 3D space and can be programmed to appear subject to external physical forces such as gravity, wind, friction, and collision with other objects. Lidar data can be used as collision geometry to guide dynamic particle system simulations to the topology of real-world sets and locations. This is particularly useful for effects involving fire, water, and smoke where the particle systems must convincingly interact with live-action photography.

Lidar: Practical Realities

Like many new technologies, lidar scanning is not a panacea and must be used with caution. Anyone interested in utilizing lidar for visual effects should learn as much about the technology and process as possible before embarking on a large-scale scanning job—or hire a professional and ask a lot of questions. Planning and communication are essential when utilizing lidar in visual effects production. The live-action crew, especially the assistant director and camera department, must be aware of the capabilities and procedures of the lidar crew well in advance. Although the 1st AD is rarely happy about any on-set intrusion, a well-informed camera crew will often welcome lidar as an adjunct to their photography. Indeed lidar scans are often referred to as *3D plates* that will be used to enhance visual effects photography.

One of the main pitfalls of lidar scanning comes when hiring a 3D scanning service bureau that is not entertainment-industry savvy. Professional survey providers own most lidar scanning systems and the corporate cultures of these companies are often at odds with those of the entertainment industry. Fundamental misunderstandings over deliverables, on-set etiquette, schedules, and other factors are a constant cause of frustration when hiring outside scanning contractors.

Unfortunately, there are very few service providers dedicated solely to film production so it is inevitable that visual effects professionals will have to deal with nonindustry hires for scanning. Proper planning and communication with the service provider coupled with reasonable management of expectations will go a long way toward ensuring a smooth lidar scanning job. Do not assume the service provider knows anything about 3D, visual effects, matchmoving, or even where to find craft service on a film set. Economic constraints will often dictate a local hire so it is vital for the service provider to be thoroughly briefed by a member of the visual effects department on every aspect of the job. It will usually also be necessary for a visual effects department member to accompany a lidar crew on set in order to avoid friction.

Once the scanning is done another area that can cause problems is the management of deliverables. Lidar data is typically used by the survey industry, and their deliverable requirements are very different from those of a visual effects facility. Raw lidar scanning data is almost completely useless in a standard visual effects pipeline, so some form of processing and formatting will be required to create suitable deliverables. Again, communication is critical and a full test of the lidar pipeline is essential before production begins. Make sure the 3D deliverables are compatible with all facets of the production pipeline. Matchmovers may need a vastly different dataset than animators and all of those requirements should be worked out prior to production.

None of this is rocket science, however, and it usually only requires a meeting and some formal documentation to put everyone on the same page. After all of the issues of geometry, coordinate systems, and scheduling are worked out, lidar scanning can provide significant advantages for visual effects production.

ON-SET 3D SCANNING SYSTEMS
Nick Tesi

On-set scanning, in this section, refers primarily to the scanning of people; however, it could also refer to scanning animals, props, vehicles, and other items no larger than a car. This is different from lidar scanning, which is used to scan larger items such as buildings and environments.

On-Set Data Acquisition
How to Get the Most out of Your 3D Scanning Time on Set
An earlier decision has led to the need to do 3D scanning on set. To get the most out of the scanning crew the timing and scheduling of events should be well planned. Things to consider are:
1. Will the talent to be scanned all be available in a single trip of the scanning crew?
2. Will any facial expressions or facial performances need to be used with the scanned model?
3. Will other props and objects need to be scanned on site?
4. As a precaution, should other actors and objects be scanned now in the event those assets might be advantageous to have in digital form later?
5. Will the scanning charge be any more if the extra items are scanned but not processed?
6. Will a texture shoot be needed in addition to the scans or does the scanning company provide this service as well?

3D Scanning Systems

The two most popular scanning system services are structured light scanning and laser scanning.

1. *Structured light scanning:* Typically uses a projecting device to project a grid or light shapes on to the object or talent. To have a full 3D version of the subject, photographs of the subject need to be taken from all angles and applied appropriately.
2. *Laser-based systems:* Project a laser that follows the contours of the object or person. The output is typically a point cloud that then goes through a process of surfacing and then clean-up of that created surface.

Figure 3.20 Structured light-based system. (Image courtesy of Eyetronics.)

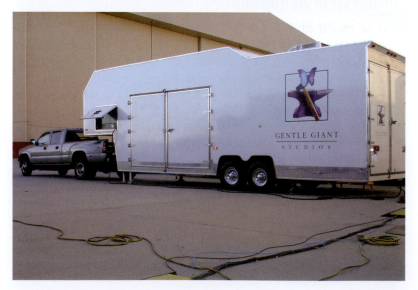

Figure 3.21 Laser-based system in a truck already set up on location as a portable studio. (Image courtesy of Gentle Giant Studios.)

Both systems will provide you with an acceptable final result, but selecting the correct system and company for your scanning needs is paramount.

To help determine the best system the project needs, look first to the project's visual effects facilities to see if they have a preference or, if there are several facilities involved, if there is a consensus of opinion. The next option would be to contact several vendors to determine prices, availability, and flexibility. This should happen in pre-production as early as possible.

After determining the system that will work best for the project references should be checked to ensure the selected team can achieve what is needed, how it is needed, and when it is needed. Communication is the key to success.

Key Questions to Ask

1. What does the scanning crew need on site to acquire the data? This will help with selection of a location that is suitable for scanning.
2. Will the area selected for the scanning allow for the most work accomplished in the least amount of time? Keep in mind that ADs, talent, and props may demand to have easy and close access to this area so as not to interfere with production filming.
3. How long does it take to scan the primary talent? Remember that the AD will need to schedule the talent for this process. Their involvement is integral to the success of the scans.
4. Is the scanning crew able to show samples of the scans to ensure the data has been captured correctly and in the detail required?
5. What is the data delivery schedule and is the scanning crew aware of it?
6. How much time is needed to set up, calibrate, and test the equipment? Based on the type of scanning choosen, this could take anywhere from one to several hours.

Prepping the Actors for Scanning

To prep the actors for scanning, start by determining what is needed from the actor in the scan. For example: Should the hair be covered up for the scan so that cyberhair may be added more easily later? Should the background characters be scanned with or without their hair showing? A foundation of makeup is also a good idea if the skin is slightly translucent. In most systems the body and head will be shot separately. With the actor in the seated position, expose the neck and upper chest as much as possible so the body can be matched later. The body is typically standing in a "T" pose or a modified "T" pose that will be used later as the neutral position. Check with the scanning operator to make sure that black or shiny pieces will not pose a problem.

Scanning Props or Cars

When it comes to scanning props or cars, always know in advance if you can spray or powder the items if need be. This is especially important for shiny, transparent, or translucent items and black or dark-colored objects. If a spray or powder is needed, have an idea of what material the scanning company will use and know if it can be removed without too much difficulty.

If scanning props or cars in addition to talent is required, plan on scanning them between talent scans if possible. Try to arrange to have a number of props available for the scanning crew to do while they are waiting on talent. Have the car and prep team on standby prepping the car so scanning can begin without delay. Typically this prep involves applying dulling spray, paper, or tape to the vehicle.

Review All That Has Been Scanned

When scanning is completed, but before releasing the scanning crew, it is important to compare the scanning list with what has been scanned. Here is a useful checklist:

1. Has the crew scanned everything required per the master list? If not, has another date been set for the second visit? Sometimes various actors are only needed on set at certain discrete points during principal photography, thus requiring a second visit by the scanning crew.
2. It is always wise to scan additional props, extras, and talent in case they are needed later. It may be very costly to find and bring in the talent for scanning in post-production. Additionally, the props and costumes may have been lost, destroyed, or not available in post. Try to think ahead and anticipate.
3. Check the samples of the scans while the scanning crew is still on site.
4. The scanning crew should send a shot sheet of all that has been scanned so that production is aware of all assets available and the costs involved. Make sure to ask for this list. Generally, they are available within a week after the scan session.

A shot sheet like the one shown in Figure 3.22 allows for the ability to select a blend shape or outfit. Most companies will have these models in storage should additional models or blend shapes be needed later. Shot sheets can also include props, cars, or anything else scanned.

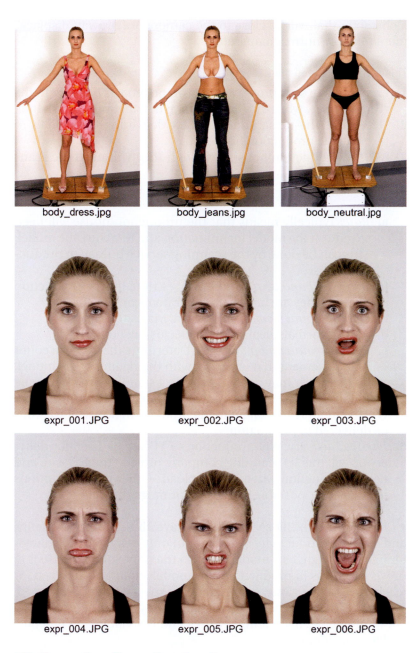

body_dress.jpg

body_jeans.jpg

body_neutral.jpg

expr_001.JPG

expr_002.JPG

expr_003.JPG

expr_004.JPG

expr_005.JPG

expr_006.JPG

Figure 3.22 Shot sheet with range of facial expressions and poses. (Model: Liisa Evastina. Image courtesy of Eyetronics.)

3D Scanning Post-Production

The scanning company will take all data back to their facility and make a copy for backup. They will then create a shot sheet of all that has been scanned for review and discuss the priorities. The shot sheet also helps eliminate the confusion of selecting the wrong model by the naming convention. The project lead will review the needs for detail in the scan— i.e., whether this is a character that will be close to the camera or far away, displacement maps or normal maps, etc.

Things to Help Speed the Delivery Cycle

1. Can orders to start processing any of the models be given to the scanning crew while they are on site? If not, the sooner the better.
2. Determine the turnaround time for delivering the models to the selected production house.
3. Ask the production house how soon they will need the scans for their shots.
4. The scanning crew will need guidance as to the delivery format for the scans:
   a. *Raw:* Typically means that the production house will need to remesh the model for animation and retexture the model. This can be done by the scanning service bureau or production house.
   b. *Remeshed and textured:* This saves time for the production house if they are busy with other items on the shot.
   c. *Type of digital format:* OBJ, Maya, Max, etc.
   d. *Maps:* Normal, displacement, occlusion, etc.
   e. *Polygon count and placement:* Determine the polygon count and placement that will work with the rigging of the model. Or the rigger may need to provide a sample wireframe to be followed by the scanning facility for delivery on the model.
5. Will the models go straight to the production house or will they be delivered to production?
6. *Physical delivery:* Will production's FTP site be used for delivery or will the 3D scanning company provide the FTP site and notify production when to download? Other delivery options include DVD, portable hard drive, or magnetic tape.

In conclusion, 3D scanning can save time, improve quality, and increase productivity overall. It not only delivers your character in its best light as a model but also the opportunity to use it in previs as well as in production. The model should be archived for use in the event a game, commercial, or special trailer is planned. The model may also be set up to make a physical model later as a gift or memento. 3D scanning works and is a viable and practical tool for consideration.

LIGHTING DATA
Charlie Clavadetscher

Gathering Lighting Data

To properly capture lighting data, and to ensure the person capturing the data can intelligently and quickly change his or her capture method when required, someone with CG lighting experience is required to perform the task. Without proper personnel assigned to the task, time and money spent during production are essentially thrown away, potentially slowing production and causing other problems with little benefit.

The key point when choosing a qualified lighting data capture crew member is to choose "someone with CG lighting experience." They must have actual, hands-on (recent) CG experience for the on-set job.

When selecting personnel for this task, try to avoid people who have only overseen CG lighting, "have a good idea about it," or other near misses for experience. There is no substitute for knowing what the artists need, knowing the technical details of CG lighting, and having seen a variety of stage lighting data in the past as CG reference.

Beware of False Savings!

Initially, it may seem like a bargain to hire a local or junior individual to perform the lighting reference data capture. The main production itself or other factors, such as local employment laws, may encourage or require you to do this. However, the initial saving will be obliterated when volumes of data, collected by inexperienced personnel, prove useless.

Goals

The main goals of lighting data capture are to acquire lighting information in a manner that has little to no impact on the on-set production process and to collect as much data as possible that will make the visual effects lighting process fast and accurate.

Generally speaking, this means gathering complete environmental references that can accurately measure light sources, their position, and intensity. This also includes other environmental information such as shadows and reflections and the color and characteristics of objects that reflect or otherwise influence the light. This information should provide a full range of lighting information from dark shadows up to and including bright light sources such as a 20K stage light (with filters if any were used), and even capturing the lighting characteristics of the sun.

Four primary methods of capturing lighting data are currently used, as discussed next.

A Lighting Diagram Combined with Photographs and/or Video

This is definitely the quick-and-dirty method for gathering lighting data. A sketch or diagram indicates the position of the camera, identifiable objects in the camera's field of view, and the locations and types of lights. These provide an overview of the scene's lighting. Additionally, one or more photographs, properly slated, can help make the diagram easier to understand and also fill in details that a sketch cannot show.

While better than nothing, this system is clearly the most primitive and, therefore, the least desirable.

Using a Scanner or Survey Equipment

Using a scanner or survey equipment can accurately locate the position of lights and lighting equipment in 3D. However, this method does not accomplish all of the basic goals of capturing the actual lighting environment as a whole. While this is also better than nothing and far more accurate and consistent compared to a sketch, it is not an up-to-date methodology and it does not record actual lighting values.

Using Colored and Reflective Spheres to Capture Lighting Information

While using spheres is an older, somewhat outdated method, it is greatly preferable to the two methods cited above.

The process generally uses a sphere painted standard 18% gray, which captures key light and shadow or fill lighting information in the visual form of a picture. A second picture of a reflective (mirror-like) sphere captures information that can assist in determining light placement and angles within the environment, as well as light source intensity. The reflective sphere may also be used to create a CG lighting sphere to light CG objects in the visual effects process.

Lighting reference spheres can vary in size, from as small as a few inches to 18 inches or more in diameter, usually dependent on the set and the distance from camera to sphere. While some productions have the resources and desire to purchase or custom build extremely clean and sturdy gray and reflective spheres, other productions may choose a more economical route and use lower cost spheres that contain varying degrees of imperfections.

Sources for lower cost and less precise spheres include manufactured plastic or chrome steel spheres that are widely available at garden supply stores and other similar outlets. These are oftentimes called *gazing globes* or *garden globes* or similar names. Chrome spheres like this are already mirror like and reflective, or they can be painted the appropriate color. Many of these already have threaded sockets installed to help secure them in a garden, which makes them ideal for visual effects. They can be mounted on a threaded post or pole and carried around without touching or smudging the surface. These predrilled and threaded mounts are generally stronger and preferable to drilling and mounting or gluing an attachment socket to an existing sphere.

Typically the lighting sphere capture process uses both types of spheres: a standard 18% gray sphere and one of reflective chrome. In some situations, a third all-white sphere may also be used to help evaluate the lighting.

Regardless of the source or type, the spheres are photographed by the production camera and/or by a visual effects reference still camera.

The spheres are usually placed in the location where the visual effects will occur, not necessarily where the actors are located. If the visual effects occur at the actors' location, then it may be easier for the film crew to have someone step in at the end of the last take, place the spheres, and roll the camera on the spheres at that position.

To make this process faster, some facilities have a sphere that is painted 18% gray on one half and chrome on the other half. This reduces the number of spheres needed and speeds the process. The gray side is shot, and the sphere is quickly rotated to photograph the chrome side, combining both types of surfaces in one object.

While it is convenient to have a single sphere with gray and chrome halves, it also limits which part of the sphere can be photographed to that exact half. Unfortunately, the surface may become dented, scratched, or develop other imperfections through travel, accident, and normal usage. In this case, a sphere that is half gray and half chrome can't be turned to use another area on the sphere as a clean side, which is an advantage when using all-gray and all-reflective spheres.

One or more backup spheres should be readily available in case serious problems occur with the main sphere. It also helps to have extra spheres in case a 2nd unit requires its own separate spheres during production. It is especially important to have backup spheres if the shooting will last for weeks or longer, and if a lot of travel is a possibility, all of which contribute to the chance that the spheres will develop physical problems, scratches, dents, broken sockets, and other imperfections.

The use of spheres has some potentially negative consequences:
- If the production film camera shoots the spheres far from the camera position, the spheres may be small in frame and thus difficult to analyze.
- Although it only takes a few minutes, time is money on set. Taking the time to slate and shoot a gray sphere and a chrome sphere will interrupt the normal flow of work on set and may be objectionable to the production process.

Alternatively, with proper setup and calibration, still cameras can be used in place of the production camera. This approach has a number of advantages:
- The film crew is not required to shoot the spheres and therefore bypasses all the production steps, such as editorial,

scanning, and film processing. Also, by using a digital camera, the images are kept in the realm of the visual effects production and team.

- The photographer shooting the spheres can bring the camera much closer to the sphere's location (as defined by expected location of the CG visual effects). Moving a visual effects still camera is much easier compared to moving the production's motion picture camera, and usually records an image with much more information compared to a sphere that is small in frame.

- Additionally, while the photographer can shoot the spheres from the camera's primary point of view, the photographer is also able to choose another direction to shoot the reference images—for instance, shooting the spheres from 90 degrees to each side of the production camera's point of view or from the complete opposite direction of the camera's point of view.

Shooting from the camera's point of view and then reversing 180 degrees to shoot toward the camera often provide a much more complete lighting reference than images shot from only one position. Specifically, the chrome sphere process now contains two sphere shots that mirror each other. This provides, at least in theory, a full reflective mapping of the entire lighting environment.

One problem remains, and that is the photographer and any helpers who might be assisting with the process will be picked up in the reflections of the chrome sphere. Additionally, some software utilizing the chrome sphere as a reflectance map may be more awkward to use and, thus, potentially less accurate. The gray paint and the chrome sphere are subject to dents and scratches and other physical imperfections over time, which can affect the quality of the reference images. Furthermore, all but the most expensive chrome spheres are not truly mirror like, and small imperfections over time can lead to lighting irregularities; plus multiple large spheres can be difficult to transport and keep clean and secure in production situations.

However, even with these potential problems, lighting spheres generally are greatly preferred to methods 1 and 2, a sketch and 3D-only measurements of light positions.

Using Direct Photography of the Entire Environment

Currently, one of the best choices for capturing lighting information is use direct photography of the environment rather than shooting a reflection of the environment off a chrome sphere. Typically, these direct photographs are used in a computer graphics 3D lighting process to create a virtual sphere or partial sphere of the entire environment. This direct photography process shows all lighting equipment, reflecting surfaces, and every other aspect of the environment that creates light and shadow in the real world as well as the CG world.

Direct photography may also be a better choice for unusual situations such as for specific reflections created on computer graphics reflective objects.

One of the immediate advantages of using a direct photography method, compared to other methods, is that it avoids seeing the recording camera and personnel in the image. Usually, these direct photography images are cleaner, including bypassing any dirt, dents, or other imperfections such as in the surface of a sphere. They are almost always more detailed and complete because the entire frame typically has usable image data instead of only a subsection of a photographed sphere.

Some specialized cameras are made specifically for this process, and they are able to shoot an entire environment in one single image through a type of image scanning or other process. Other similar specialized cameras are able to shoot HDRI (high dynamic range images) directly, capturing anywhere from 5 to 20 or more stops of information in a single image.

Using Conventional Still Cameras

Similar results can be obtained with less sophisticated equipment by using conventional still cameras and a 180-degree (fish-eye) lens to capture two opposing hemispheres of information. These two 180-degree half-sphere images fit together to create a complete photographic sphere of the lighting environment.

To successfully use this process with conventional cameras, it is best to perform tests to ensure the camera and lens work together to create a true 180-degree half-sphere. Some camera and lens combinations may crop the image, leading to an incomplete sphere and resulting in incomplete lighting data.

When using conventional still cameras, usually some determination is made as to the number of stops above and below normal exposure that are required to provide enough information about the lighting to perform CG visual effects lighting. Different facilities most likely have different objectives, procedures, and requirements for this approach. Some might require a great range of values, while others find that anything beyond certain limits to be irrelevant lighting information. For instance plus or minus 5 *f*-stops may be deemed adequate by some facilities, while others prefer a larger range.

Once the decision has been made for the required range of exposures, the camera is commonly set on a tripod and the range of photographs taken by shooting one direction. Then the camera is turned 180 degrees on the tripod and an identical range of images is shot in the reverse direction. The two sets of images, held steady by the tripod, form the basis for a complete, deep color space HDRI lighting sphere of the environment.

In some cases, facilities are able to calibrate the cameras and the process so that they can skip stops and still get a full range of lighting data with fewer pictures. For instance, when using high-bit-rate pictures, the amount of bracketing (additional exposures above or below normal exposure) can be established so that photographs are taken every two or even every three stops instead of every single stop, yet still give a full range of lighting data.

Skipping stops while shooting a range of images has several advantages. It is faster, and since time is paramount on set, cutting the process time in half by skipping stops can be the difference between being allowed to take the pictures or not.

The benefits to the visual effects process are a reduced number of photographs and, in turn, a reduced amount of data to catalog. In some cases a reduced number of photographs streamlines the lighting CG process itself.

Shooting Considerations

Make sure the lighting matches the production takes. The DP may make changes to the lighting up until the take or even between takes. Any prerecorded data will be less useful in these cases.

Depending on the production, it may be best to shoot the references at the start of the shot, if possible. Waiting until the shot is finished runs the risk the production may move too quickly, turn out the lights, take down a key rig, clutter the set with crew members, and so on. Any of these situations at the end of shooting would cripple or prevent gathering of the desired references.

If the individual capturing the lighting data can only get one-half of the sphere shot before being told to leave the area, that is still 50% done, and perhaps the other half can be accomplished 5 minutes later. It is better to have two half-spheres that don't match up exactly rather than have no data at all trying to wait for perfect conditions.

Gathering proper lighting data also usually requires the set or location to be clear of crew members, or at least as much as possible, so that lights and environmental information are unobstructed by people and equipment that will not be present during the actual photography. In other words, if something wasn't present during the production shot, it should not be present during the lighting data capture.

Always bear in mind that the individuals capturing the lighting data must be flexible and ready to move in at a moment's notice based on the rapid pace of stage operations yet also be attentive and sensitive to what is happening on stage so they know when to get out of the way—preferably before someone grabs them by the collar and yanks them out of the way.

Having the film crew wait for 3 or 4 minutes after every take while lighting reference is gathered will likely become intolerable for production. Therefore, every effort must be made to shorten this process—30 seconds or less is a good target; 15 seconds is better.

Speeding up the process can be accomplished via two different general approaches: streamlining the process itself and choosing other times to shoot the photographs.

Streamlining the Process

Any steps that can be taken to speed up or reduce the amount of time the process takes, such as shooting every three stops instead of every stop (described above), should be implemented whenever possible. Doubling equipment, such as running two cameras simultaneously, can cut the time in half if personnel are properly prepared and rehearsed for this situation.

Similarly, renting or purchasing specialized equipment that can speed up the process should be investigated and pursued whenever possible. The alternative is missing data or incurring the ill will of crew members and production.

Equipment purchases and rentals need to have speed and quality as the top considerations because the alternative may be no data at all.

For instance, if a laptop computer or other device can be programmed to run the camera faster than a human, it should be part of the process. Some cameras have internal programs that can automatically cover the range and options, like skipping stops. Be sure to test and fully evaluate these capabilities before arriving on stage.

Ensure that acquisition personnel know how to operate the cameras or similar devices correctly and can make changes or corrections on the spot as situations change. Also confirm that the equipment and results perform as expected. This should be a fully rehearsed and tested process before production and data collection begin.

Even with the fastest equipment, the key factor for successful capture may be the individual operating the process. He or she needs to be fast, knowledgeable, prepared to step in at the proper time, knows the priorities for making on-the-spot decisions, and is simultaneously able to stay out of the way of production.

Choosing Other Times to Shoot the Photographs

Another approach to increase speed and achieve successful capture is to be prepared to use any on-set delays, unexpected downtime, or other breaks in the shooting process to capture the required data and pictures.

In other words, don't wait for the end of the shot. Talk to the AD and DP early in the production so they are aware the reference images can be captured at other times to help the production. With this in mind, if an opportunity arises to shoot the images or collect data, be ready to jump in at a moment's notice. The production crew will appreciate your efforts to save their time and will likely be more cooperative if you show you are sensitive to their need to move fast and not interrupt the flow of production.

Examples of such opportunities may be when the actor's lighting double is standing in for camera rehearsal or when waiting for the actors to get ready. Other times might be during a video review of a take, or any other time you can find.

In some instances, if you talk to the AD and the gaffer they will be able to leave the lights on for a few minutes after lunch or wrap is called. But be careful this does not put the crew into an overtime situation that will cause problems later.

Remember the Goals

1. Acquire lighting information in a manner that will have little to no impact on the on-set production process.
2. Collect as much good data as possible that will make the visual effects lighting process fast and accurate.

CLEAN PLATES
Scott Squires

A clean plate[13] is footage that is identical to the actual shot, but without the actors and possibly other items (props, wires, rigs) in the shot that may need to be removed in the final shot. When an image of something needs to be removed from a shot, then it's necessary to replace that area with the "clean" background shot with the clean plate. This is the easiest and best solution for replacement.

Examples

Some examples of shots where this can be very useful include the following:

- Actor needs to appear as a see-through ghost or removal of part of the actor (such as missing legs).
- A prop or actor needs to teleport or disappear/appear during the shot.

---

[13] Plate: visual effects term for live-action footage to be used for later visual effects work. *FG plate* refers to foreground images, *BG plates* to background images, *BS plates* to bluescreen images, etc.

- Wires are being used to provide a safety line on the actor or stuntperson.
- A device or rig has to be in the scene during the actual shot (car ramp for car stunt, framework to hold wires for stunt-person, a reference needs to be in the scene such as a stand-in for a CG character).

Each of these examples would be shot normally with the actors and props in place for the actual shot and then shot again without the actors and objects to be removed. This actor-less version is the clean plate.

> The more accurate the clean plate matches the shot, the more useful it will be. This includes all aspects of the clean plate: position, exposure, focus, color, lighting, and activity in the background. Position implies not only *xyz* but also tilt, pan, and roll of the camera.

Figure 3.23 Original live-action plate, clean plate, final. (Image courtesy of Scott Squires.)

Shooting the Clean Plate

Shooting of clean plates should be discussed in pre-production with the Director, Director of Photography, and Assistant Director. This is to make sure production understands the need for the clean plates and provides the time during the shoot to film them.

If the visual effects shot is simple, once the takes for the shot are done and the director is happy with the shot, the clean plate is slated and photographed. The visual effects crew and script supervisor would note this take as the clean take. A better and safer method can be to shoot the clean plate first before the action takes.[14] Frequently there are changes between takes that will affect the usefulness of the clean plate. The camera angle, exposure, or focus may be changed by someone on the camera crew. Since the clean plate was shot first this ensures a clean plate always exists to match. Once a change is made a new clean plate should be

---

[14] Takes to be used with the actors or action.

reshot to match this new change. In some cases if there will be a change after every take, it may become necessary to shoot a clean plate for every take. The VFX Supervisor will have to determine the number of changes and balance that against the time issues on the set. If it's a small change, the time on set is limited, or the mood is frantic, it's best to deal with it in post. If it's deemed critical and unlikely to provide satisfactory results in post, then the supervisor will have to request a reshoot of the clean plate.

A simpler and faster alternative in some cases is to shoot the clean footage at the start or end of the actual take. The actors enter the scene after rolling off enough footage or they leave the shot once the take is done and the camera continues to roll. In this way no additional time is required for stopping, starting, and slating. Notes must be made that the clean footage is at the start or end of the take.

The clean plate should be shot to the same length (or longer) as the take whenever possible. If it's too short then it will be necessary to loop the footage back and forth, which could result in a noticeable change in grain, change in noise, or a repeat of any background activity.

The clean plate should be shot with the same focus setting as the actor. The requirement here is for the background between the actor and actor-less images to match exactly in appearance, not for the background to be sharp.

Locked-Off Camera

The simplest clean plate setup is shooting with a locked-off camera. The camera is ideally on a tripod that has the pan and tilt locked. This way the camera position will be identical for all takes, including the clean plate. If the camera is on a dolly, then everyone needs to step away from the dolly so it doesn't move. In some cases it may be necessary to have a 2-by-4-inch piece of wood available to brace under the camera head to make sure there's no shift.

It is critical to discuss the concept of a clean plate with the camera crew and dolly grip before shooting. Left on their own the camera team will tend to make adjustments that invalidate the clean plate. For a good clean plate the DP and the crew have to accept the camera settings and leave them for all the takes and the clean plate (or shoot additional clean plates as noted above).

Moving Camera

Getting a decent clean plate for a moving camera is much more difficult. A locked-off shot is much easier, faster, and cheaper.

For moving camera clean plates, the best solution from a visual effects requirement would be to use a motion control camera system, but this is unrealistic except where an absolute match is very critical. A motion control camera system can shoot multiple takes and the clean plate, exactly matching position and speed. But the extra time and effort on a live-action set is seldom allowed by production unless the supervisor deems it the only reasonable way of achieving the shots. (An example is a complex move with an actor performing as twins, special splits or dissolves between complex moving shots. In these cases the clean plate is actually being used as part or all of the background, not just to clean up an area of the image.)

The next best solution is to use a repeatable camera head. These are now readily available and should be requested for a project with a number of shots that might require repeatable motion. These are simple motion control heads but designed to be used for live action. The camera operator pans and tilts and the system is able to play back the same pan and tilt for other takes, including the clean plate. For a move that includes a dolly motion, the dolly grip will have to try to match the motion as closely as reasonable. Timing or distance marks can be placed on the dolly tracks as a guide.

For cases where the move is nonrepeatable, the idea is to make as close an approximation of the move as possible. These won't be great clean plates but a skilled compositor and paint person can work wonders, and certainly it's much better than having to create the clean images from scratch. In these cases the operator, dolly grip, and camera assistant all work in tandem to re-create the move. Sometimes it's best to do the clean plate a bit slower than the original plate. This can provide more material for the compositor to work with and less motion blur on the frames.

An alternative to a clean plate that mimics the original camera move is to shoot tiles of the area. In this case the camera is locked off and films an area for the duration of the shot. The camera is then panned and/or tilted a bit (overlapping previous tile by 15% to 20%) and another plate is shot. Repeat to cover the image range of the original camera movie. This tiled area can then be merged in software in post-production and a move can be re-created to match the original move or at least the images can be aligned. Note that due to the method of shooting any motion within the image will not continue past the tile edges.

Other Issues

Even if the camera motion matches exactly, a number of problems with the clean plate can arise that should be considered when shooting. Once again, it's almost always worth shooting a clean plate shot even if it's not ideal. The VFX Supervisor will have to make the determination balanced with on-set shooting time.

Some of these issues include the following:

- wind blowing the leaves or foliage in the background,
- rain, snow, dust, or fog (real or special effects),
- flickering or flashing lights,
- moving people and cars in the background,
- shadows on the ground moving, and
- time of day during which the lighting changes rapidly (such as end of the day), which might cause a different look and different shadowing.

If the length of the clean plate is long enough, then it may be possible to shift frames around to match flashing lights or to frame average to solve some of the basic issues. It's also possible in some cases to rotoscope and minimize specific areas that may be problems (i.e., blowing foliage).

Postprocess

In the composite stage the area to be removed (of the rig, wire, or actor) will require a matte. Usually this is done by rotoscoping. The matte areas are replaced by the clean plate in the composite.

Sometimes the area to be removed (such as the rig) is painted green or blue to make generating a matte easier but this usually isn't recommended. The problem is that if it's outside you will likely have blue sky or green grass, and for a dimensional object the shadows may make creating a matte more time consuming than rotoscoping. The other potential issue is color bounce from the reflection off the colored surface.

Alternates without Clean Plates

If a clean plate cannot be shot, then alternate shooting methods may be required. In the example of a partial or transparent actor, the actor could be shot on a greenscreen or bluescreen stage and the background could be shot without the actor (which would look just like the clean plate). Note that there is no real savings here. In fact two plates now have to be shot (at different locations) and then have to be lined up and composited in post-production. Matching exactly the lighting and angle on a stage to a background image is difficult; this is a common issue with blue- and greenscreen shots.

Wire removal can be done by advanced software tools but these work by blending from surrounding pixels of the original shot. This doesn't require a clean plate, but the larger the wire the less satisfactory this method is.

If no clean plate exists, in most cases the team of the compositor, roto artist, and painter will have to create one using whatever materials are available. This might mean cloning or painting areas from other parts of the frame or from different frames. If the wire or actor moved through the frame, then a frame earlier or later in the shot might show that area clear of the wire or actor. This is what would be used as the source. Essentially the matted out areas are patched by bits and pieces by hand so this becomes a time-consuming process that can still suffer from matching issues.

Other Uses for Clean Plates

Clean plates are shot somewhat frequently even on shots where removal of a foreground actor or items isn't planned. Post-production may require visual effects changes where a clean plate becomes very useful. The clean plate can also be used as part of the environment (including reflections) or environment lighting for the CG rendering.

- *Bluescreen:* Some blue- and greenscreen keying software can use a clean plate of the screen without the actor. This is used to compensate for any exposure variations in the original screen so a better matte can be created.
- *Difference mattes:* A difference matte is created by having the computer compare two images, in this case the foreground and background (clean plate). Any pixel the same color in both images would be made clear and any pixels that were different would be made opaque.

In theory, if an actor is shot against a background and then a clean plate is shot without the actor, the computer could extract the image of the actor since those pixels are different. The problem is that the film grain or video noise tends to lower the quality of the matte and any similarity to the background will make it difficult to create a matte with gradations. An example of this is in the Apple iChat software.

MONSTER STICKS
Scott Squires

Many visual effects shots involve adding CG characters, creatures, or objects in post-production. This can be a challenge for the camera operator and the actors when filming the original scene because they need to react to something that is not there. Without a reference of some sort, every actor is likely to be looking in a different spot and the camera operator could be cropping off the head of the CG character. To help with this, a stand-in or proxy is frequently used on the set to provide a reference for what will be added later in post-production.

For a tall (7- to 20-foot-tall) creature, a *monster stick* is often used. This is an adjustable pole (such as that used for painting) or an aluminum tube with drilled holes. A cross piece of wood or tubing is attached with a small disk at each end. These represent the eyes of the creature. The assembled device looks like a tall, narrow "T" with a disk on each side. The VFX Supervisor should have a list of the different heights and dimensions of the characters. The eye height is adjusted for the character and the particular pose required in the shot (standing, bending down speaking to the actor, etc.). A member from the visual effects crew holds the monster stick in place for everyone to reference. The Director and Director of Photography (DP) can check the location, and the camera operator can frame the shot accordingly. The actors and extras now know where to look for their eye line.[15] Film is usually shot of this reference so in post-production the director and visual effects team can reference the actual setup. In most cases the actors try to find something in the background (tree, cloud, etc.) in that same visual location to reference. Or they may remember the head tilt and eye angle. The monster stick is removed for the actual takes and the actor now acts toward where the monster stick was.

Figure 3.24 Monster profile (*center*). Monster stick with eyes (*right*) from *Dragonheart* (1996). (Image courtesy of Scott Squires.)

If the creature is moving, then the crew member holds the stick and walks with it using the path and speed as worked out by the Director and VFX Supervisor. For complex motions the

[15] Eye line: specific direction in which the actor looks. This is a point that is frequently off camera to represent another actor or object. Crew members need to avoid walking through this during the take since the actor is focused.

animation supervisor may aid in the timing and action. The pre-vis is likely to be checked as a reference. The height of the stick is adjusted to compensate for being held. Someone on the set may call out the time in seconds so the camera operator and actors can memorize the timing. This same timing is called out during the actual shooting so everyone knows where to look. It may be necessary to shoot with the stick being moved in the scene if it's particularly difficult to maintain eye lines and timings. In this case the crew member and stick are painted out using the clean plate in post-production.

A number of additional variations can be used to provide an on-set proxy for a character. For example, artwork or a rendering of the character can be printed out full size and mounted onto a sheet of foam core.[16] Printing is likely to be done at a specialty company onto multiple large sheets of paper. A handle of some sort would be attached to the back so this reference can be moved and held in place.

Just the profile or front view of the creature head can be cut out in plywood or foam core. A full-size print of the head could be glued on if desired. This would then be mounted onto a pole of some sort or include brackets for mounting. If it's on foam core then it could be mounted onto the monster stick to replace the eye reference.

If it's a large creature then a reference model or maquette[17] could be used in front of the camera (a posable model is even better if it exists). The distance to the desired location of the creature is measured. This distance is scaled by the scale size of the model. (Example: A 100-foot distance using a 1/50 model would make the scaled distance 2 feet.) Place the model at this scaled distance in front of the camera. Note that the model can be placed in front of the camera first to achieve the desired composition, and then the reverse calculation is done to determine where to place the actors. This will provide a guide at the camera and at the video monitor. Reference footage is shot of the model in place. The downside is that the actors won't be able to see the creature in front of them so someone at the video monitor will have to guide the actors about where to look. Shooting of the model in front of the camera may also require a split-diopter[18] to show the model and the background in focus.

---

[16] Foam core: white, strong, and lightweight sheets of poster-type material usually in 1/8- or 1/4-inch thicknesses.

[17] Maquette: sculpture of the creature or character for design purposes.

[18] Split-diopter: a diopter is an auxiliary lens that goes in front of the camera lens to allow for close-up photography. A split version is half lens and half plain glass so only half of the scene is focused for close-ups.

Figure 3.25 Monster profile (*top*). Posable model (*bottom*). Monster sticks with orange bands (*sides*). (Image courtesy of Scott Squires.)

All of the above techniques were used on the film *Dragonheart* (1996). An additional technique that may be of value is the use of an ultralight aircraft to represent a large flying creature. This was used for some of the flying scenes in *Dragonheart* (1996) where a large number of extras had to be watching the same location as the dragon flew over. At the end of *Dragonheart* (1996) a glowing spirit rises and moves over a crowd. The electrical department constructed a light box, and the special effects crew rigged it on wires to move. This supplied not only the reference for the crowd but also provided the practical light effects.

On the film *Van Helsing* (2004) an actor was fitted with a helmet that had a short post that held a flat foam core head shape. A printout of the Mr. Hyde artwork was glued to the foam core. This rig allowed two actors to work together. The main actor would use the foam core image of Mr. Hyde as an eye line while responding to the motion and dialog of the other actor. The reference actor was removed in post-production and replaced with a CG Mr. Hyde character.

For human-sized CG characters, actors are usually dressed in a representative costume. This was done for Silver Surfer in the film *Fantastic Four: Rise of the Silver Surfer* (2007) and for the droids in *Star Wars: The Phantom Menace* (1999) among others films.

For characters smaller than human size, a foam core cutout can be used or, as in the case of *Roger Rabbit* (1988), a rubber sculpture casting was used on the set. Stuffed toy animals can be used for small creature films, as they were in *Alvin and the Chipmunks* (2007).

When a creature is very close or small, then it may be useful to place ping-pong or tennis balls on rods. These would be placed at the eye position. This has the advantage of supplying not just the eye line for the actor but also something to motion track in post-production. The small size means the rendered CG creature will cover the reference and not require painting out of the rig.

For *The Mask* (1994) a real clock was hand moved on the set to represent the CG animation to be added later. This was not only a reference for the actor and director but also for the technical directors and digital lighting artists who could use the real clock as a lighting and material guide and for the animators to use the motion at least as a rough guide.

Shooting of reference materials is useful for the digital lighting artist to check the lighting and the material response on the actual set or location. This might be a square of fur, a piece of plastic, or a piece of cloth.

Tips

1. A C-stand[19] can be used to hold a reference or monster stick if it's not moving. A spud[20] may be taped to the back of a foam core cutout to allow mounting to a C-stand without damage. Heavier references (such as made out of plywood) may require a movable light stand.[21]
2. Cut holes in any large flat reference if it's to be used outside. The wind turns any large flat object into a kite that may be blown down.
3. For plywood references it may be good to have hinges to make it more compact when packed. A latch or lock mechanism would be needed to keep it from folding while in use.
4. Foam core can be easily damaged when moving it around from location to location in different weather conditions. Make two of any foam core references and handle them with care. A large box that can hold the reference is recommended.
5. By slotting the base of a full-size foam core cutout, a cross piece of foam core can be used to hold up the cutout when it's placed at 90 degrees in the slot.
6. A foam core cutout can be made of both the profile and straight-on views of the creature (head or full body). Each of these is slotted with one slot going halfway up and the other going halfway down. Once the two pieces are slid together

---

[19] C-stand: common three-legged adjustable stand used by the grip department to hold things such as lighting flags. Sand bags are placed on the legs to prevent it from falling over.
[20] Spud: short metal rod a few inches long mounted onto a flat plate in most cases. Used in conjunction with C-stands.
[21] Light stand: heavy-duty, three-legged stand used to hold motion picture lighting equipment.

at the slots, the cutout now represents both the side and the front view of the character. This provides a simple physical 3D representation of the character.

7. Remove the reference from actual shots when possible. When that is not practical, then keep an eye on any action behind the reference. Moving actors or other motion behind the reference will make painting out the rig even more difficult.

8. Try to keep the mounting system as small as possible since it will likely have to be painted out in some shots. Actors frequently give better performances when a reference is in the frame. This should be discussed with the director depending on the reference required and the specific actors involved. The budget should incorporate the rig removal in the shots.

9. Mark the monster stick for common heights (standing, bending over, etc.) to make it quick to change.

10. Mark the monster stick with alternating 1-foot bands of black and white or place bright tapelines every foot. This makes it quick to check the height on the set and in the filmed reference.

11. Record the monster stick or reference height information along with the other matchmove set data. If a surveyor's transit is used, then it's worth recording a point on the monster stick for reference.

12. The image of the reference can be outlined with a grease pencil on the on-set video monitor so it can be checked when shooting even if the reference has been removed. It's also possible for the video operator to do an overlay of the reference to check for problems with eye lines or placements. This can be useful when laying the running reference footage over the current shot to determine if there were timing issues.

13. Do not dress the crew member holding the reference in a blue or green outfit unless the shoot is against a colored screen. A colored suit is likely to have dark shadows and highlights that make it difficult to extract a matte so the reference will likely need to be painted or rotoed[22] anyway. The other problem is the colored material will likely cause colored bounce onto the actor or set in the scene that will require some work to remove in post. When possible the crew member and the reference should be dressed or colored to match the final creature (i.e., avoid a crew member dressed in white next to an actor if the final CG creature will be very dark).

14. The eye convergence of the actors will change with their focus. Normally this isn't a problem if the creature is large or more than 10 feet away. If the actor is supposed to be interacting

---

[22] Roto: short for *rotoscope;* process used to trace images by hand to create mattes.

with a creature 2 feet away but in real life the actor is focused on an object 30 feet away, then this can be a problem if both eyes of the actor are clearly visible. The actor may appear to be talking to something beyond the CG creature. Having a small reference in frame or having the actors memorize their exact eye angles will help.

15. Work out a consistent order of shooting references and be ready to do them as soon as the shot is set up.

ON-SET ANIMATION CAPTURE: WITNESS CAM
Joel Hynek

A witness camera setup generally refers to the use of one or more video, high-definition, or motion digital cameras on a live-action set for the purpose of capturing the motion of one or more of the actors while the production cameras are shooting. The preferred method is to use two to four cameras to capture true 3D information. After the shoot the action from the various camera perspectives is tracked and converged into one set of 3D motion data.

Capturing animation by tracking only the view from the primary production camera is, of course, possible but it is not as accurate, and an animation with conflicting information can result. For instance, because it's not possible to capture distance from only one point of view, the lower part of a body may resolve as being farther away than the upper part of the body when in fact it is the same distance.

It is appropriate to use one or more witness cameras when there is a need to capture more motion information than can be obtained from the production's primary or secondary taking cameras.

Generally witness cameras are used to gather 3D information. However, they can also be used as an aid to 2D tracking when the view of the subject from the taking camera is partially obscured or in and out of focus. In these cases a sharp unobstructed view of the subject from a nearby witness camera can provide the track (this assumes that either the taking camera is static or that it can be stabilized).

Wireless Nonvideo Motion Capture

Systems are available that can motion capture on set without video cameras but they require that the actor wear inertial motion sensors or optical motion sensors and usually wire tethers to return the information. This kind of on-set motion capture is beyond the scope of this section. Please refer to the discussion of motion capture in Chapter 4.

Factors Affecting Witness Cameras

Position and Setup

Witness cameras should be placed about 60 degrees apart. The height of the cameras is not critical but it is good to place at least one of the cameras at a different height (at least a foot) than the rest so as to get a greater range of view. Obviously, the most important thing is to place the cameras so that they get a good view of the subject. Placing cameras so they get an unobstructed view and do not interfere with other set equipment is often not easy.

Generally speaking, the witness cameras should be fitted with as tight a lens as possible to keep the action contained within the frame. However, panning with the action is also possible as long as the witness camera move can be tracked afterward.

It's important to align/register the cameras to each other. Some common objects on the set itself can be used for this as long as the dimensions of the common objects or features on the set are known. It will make tracking and converging the data later much easier.

Camera Synchronization and Phasing

Keeping the witness cameras in sync is a must in order to capture coherent data. This is best accomplished by using a common time code and common sticks. It is not necessary for the witness camera sticks to be the same as those of the production cameras but it is good if at least one of the witness cameras also captures the production sticks and slate for each take. This is so an "offset" can be captured, making the syncing of the witness camera information to the actual filmed plate easy.

Time Code

Time code can be driven from the production's time code generator or an independent time code generator employed by the witness camera team. This is accomplished with either a hard wire going to each camera or a remote device such as a "Lockit Synchronizer" that is jammed from the time code generator at the start of the day and which in turn genlocks each of the cameras so that they all have the exact same time code.

Keeping the cameras in phase is also a must if extreme precision is required. Letting the cameras run out of phase is not the end of the world but it does require the imagery or tracking data to be time shifted back into phase if higher accuracy is needed. If the nonprimary witness cameras are being used to just occasionally confirm a 3D position rather than locking every frame, then letting the cameras run out of phase and not time shifting back into phase will probably be acceptable.

Camera Resolution

The higher the better is the rule. Generally high-definition (HD) cameras are required. Production-quality cameras like the Viper or Red Camera are great as well as some prosumer-type HD cameras. Certainly a test should be performed to confirm camera quality, functionality, and result. In the case of the Red Camera or other complex cameras, it should be pointed out that they will require more training than a prosumer-type camera and cost more.

Actor Preparation

Putting markers on the actors wherever necessary is important. Markers on body joints work better than markers placed in the middle of a limb. Also, using Velcro with different colored patches is good. If the filmed image of the actor, either part or all, is to be used in the final composite, then it may be necessary to minimize the markers or choose a color that is close to flesh tone (if the markers are on flesh) so as to make it easy to remove in post. At some point it is good to take stills of the actor with a ruler or calibration structure to record the dimensional placement of the markers.

Crew Preparation

To keep the set running smoothly it is important to brief all concerned, especially the ADs, that there will be cameras and operators all around the set and that VFX will need to shoot their own sticks.

Generally, members of the visual effects crew operate the witness cameras. They need to be able to keep the action in frame, in focus, and properly exposed and to stop and start the camera. Sometimes the responsibility of running the witness cameras can be taken on by the assistant cameraman. This will reduce the size of the overall on-set crew and relieve the data acquisition team of the task. However, it is best to dedicate one person per camera. This also ensures that the camera doesn't get bumped during the process.

Dealing with the Data in Post-Production

The first step in post-production is to edit and line up all the takes from the witness cameras. An editing system like Final Cut Pro works very well because it has a feature that will automatically line up all the takes based on their time code. It also affords a four-way split screen so that up to four cameras can be viewed and confirmed at once.

The witness camera's images, once tracked, are then converged using a 3D package such as Maya. Either custom software or a plug-in to Maya are required to semiautomatically converge the tracking data into one coherent animating 3D rig.

Conclusion

Witness cameras are a great way to capture the 3D motion data of actors or moving objects while they are being filmed on a live-action set. It is like having a motion capture system on set except that the result of the capture cannot be viewed simultaneously in real time as on a motion capture stage. On-set discipline, adequate preparation, and time in post are required to successfully realize captured 3D motion data from witness cameras but the results can be totally satisfying.

REAL-TIME MATCHMOVING AND CAMERA-TRACKING DATA
Charlie Clavadetscher

Real-time camera tracking refers to a process in which the motion of the stage camera, and possibly other key objects involved with the recorded image, is invisibly followed or tracked through some technical process. This information is sent to a computer that has 3D data about the shooting location as well as computer graphics data for the intended effect for the shot.

The computer, or other technology, is able to combine these elements and generate a simplified video version of the intended final visual effect. This generated visual effect correctly follows along with the camera motions as the shot is photographed. This is roughly similar to the way some video games and cellular phones are able to take the user's motion and generate different imagery based on that motion. Although this comparison helps explain the concept, the comparison is limited because real-time visual effects for production require far greater precision, preparation, participants, and many other considerations and advanced technologies.

During production, the real-time visual effect (combined with the live-action camera image) may be viewed on video monitors, potentially through the camera eyepiece, and may also be viewed by stage personnel who trigger specific events such as a door opening, a window shattering, or other specialized action.

Seeing synchronized, generated effects at the time of photography may be of significant help to the camera operator, the director, the DP, and possibly to the actors, among others. Real-time visual effects may provide a better understanding of a scene and guide it to a more completely realized, fine-tuned, and approved version of the final visual effect shot instead of shooting a scene that is potentially blank and may otherwise be difficult to visualize.

At this time, such technology is still in the early stages and has not yet been developed for truly invisible use or use that does not conflict with other production priorities, such as lighting.

However, the benefits of seeing correctly scaled and tracked visual effects as the scene is photographed should be apparent.

To avoid confusion with virtual cameras, please note that the real-time visual effects described here only pertain to traditional stage situations, such as dressed sets, and traditional filmmaking locations, such as a forest, beach, street, etc. In these situations, a motion picture camera or equivalent works in the real-world environment, and real-time visual effects are combined with those real-world scenes. In contrast, virtual cameras, such as those found on motion capture stages, typically involve a very different physical situation. While some aspects of camera tracking may be similar, many of the conflicts and shooting considerations are very different.

Real-time camera tracking data and real-time visual effects have two main applications:

1. To provide a simplified but representative rendered composite scene that can be viewed by cast and crew members as the scene is shot (real time). Ideally, the camera is run as on any set; however, the camera operator and others are able to see the simplified version of the visual effects, such as sets and creatures, rendered on the fly and shown in sync with the live-action background.

2. To provide data and reference to be used later in the visual effects pipeline to speed up CG processes and to assist CG object and camera tracking.

Of the two uses, the first is by far the most attractive. The ability to preview visual effects on stage and in real time has enormous appeal to directors, actors, and crew. It may be very helpful in finding the most effective framing and blocking of the shot, particularly when important elements in the shot are imaginary. Being able to watch a camera rehearsal with a reasonable approximation of the effects in place helps everyone better understand the scene and react accordingly.

Real-time tracking records all physical camera motion and lens information: *xyz* motion, pan, tilt, roll, plus zoom and focus. With this data, the camera motion can be recreated in a CG environment which is then seen through monitors. While the final visual effects shot typically includes the original actors and any live set combined with finalized and realistic CG effects, real-time visual effects, for the foreseeable future, must be simpler and limited to the most important CG elements in the scene.

Some technical issues must be dealt with to get a precise and consistent match and provide acceptable and successful real-time visual effects:

• Noise in capture systems leads to random motion jitter. Large amounts of noise can make real-time visual effects swim or vibrate compared to the background. This type of problem can change the real-time visual effects from something attractive to something incomprehensible.

- Lens magnification can change with focus: for example, when focused close, a 50mm lens may become 54mm.
- Lens distortion can vary greatly across the frame.
- The roll axis of the camera system must be accurately located; bad roll data can invalidate all other motion.

Good tracking data is only the beginning. Having the correct path is at best only about one-third of the problem. Tracking the camera motion in relation to existing objects in places on the set is the other critical part of the process necessary to lock visual effects into the set. In a fully decorated set, it's often impractical to locate every object, but some key measurements will be invaluable to providing the foundation for this process. Fortunately, greenscreen and bluescreen sets are usually highly simplified and well suited to this process.

For example, imagine a large empty stage with a green screen. Assume the stage has a green sloping floor, stairs, platforms, and other green features on which the actors will walk, stand, or interact. With the dimensions and location of those features known plus known camera data, simplified visual effects can be related to the space and inserted into the camera's image as seen on a monitor or other device. Example technology for real-time tracking was used in the film, *A.I.* For specialized shots that used real-time visual effects, a multitude of special tracking markers were attached to the stage ceiling. A device on the production camera used these markers to track camera motions.

A.I. only used one process and this was a serious problem. The methods described next were not used on the film and are examples only. Other proposed real-time technical processes may use special markers on the camera itself, similar to the way a motion capture system operates. Both of these solutions, markers on the ceiling for *A.I.* and proposed markers on the camera alone, require additions to the production camera and changes in the stage that may have a direct impact on what is possible for lighting, stage design, and other considerations.

Other technical solutions and proposals involve using transmitters or sensors on the camera, with subsequently less equipment in the stage area. Such systems may use a technology similar to a GPS system or a technology that uses sensors on the camera to detect the camera's motion. Other proposals include ways to track the actual image coming from the camera video tap[23] and are therefore more passive in nature.

---

[23] Video tape: the video signal from the production camera that sends the camera's "through the lens view" to on-set video recording personnel and separate video monitors.

These are just examples of the types of technology that may be considered, though each may require additional equipment on stage or impose limitations on other aspects of the production process, such as lighting. Also, as productions change from indoor stage to outdoor locations, it may be necessary to use more than one system to lessen negative impact on production while still achieving the desired real-time visual effects.

Some practical considerations include the following:

- It's vitally important to have the production crew, and especially the camera crew, accept the technology which is used to track the camera and other parameters. Crews have a lot to deal with when performing normal photography, and there is plenty of equipment attached to the camera already, so any additional cables and technology must be minimal in order to be accepted and successful in a production environment.
- Motion tracking equipment should be low profile and low impact. Likewise, even if on-camera tracking equipment is lightweight, antennas or emitters sticking out in several directions can interfere with the crew's work. Likewise, LEDs, both visible and invisible to the naked eye, can create problems.
- It's also important to have equipment that can be quickly (as in "instantaneously") transferred from one camera to another, and once attached, won't come loose. It's ideal to have several sets of instruments already attached to any cameras and provide a means to electronically switch from one camera to another, rather than physically transfer connections from one to another. Any switch and initialization from one camera to the other must also be quick if not completely invisible.
- Visual effects personnel should be prepared for the possibility that multiple cameras may need to be tracked on certain shots, or a decision must be made if or when only one camera can have real-time visual effects.

Other on-set equipment may not be friendly to the tracking electronics, and it's critical that any real-time visual effects system likewise not interfere with existing production equipment and processes. The dense thicket of crew radio and video assist broadcasts, magnetic fields, RF interference from computers, stage grid work and building materials, hundreds of amps of lighting equipment, and even truck ignitions can pull down an untested system. It should go without saying: *Test any system extensively in the real world before using it for real work!*

The stakes and pressure can increase dramatically if the entire day or week of shooting is dependent on unfailing synchronization of computer graphics images with human-driven cameras for some critical or climactic scene or sequence. The systems are complex and the possibility of failure is high. Halting production for an hour to work out some technical glitch would likely be seen as a disaster.

Just a few examples of problems would be systems based on line of sight or ultrasonic or RF transmission, which suddenly becomes confused or unusable if blocked with flags, cast or crew, or other equipment. (This is why these systems require redundant information capture.)

Also, appropriate computer graphics models and computer graphics animated characters must be developed, approved, tested, and ready to go into existing real-time live-action scenes. This can require a substantial real-time visual effects crew before shooting begins as well as on set, and it may also demand flexibility and control over animated CG elements that may not match the camera or actor's expected timing. The amount of preparation and support crew may become much more demanding, and the magic of real-time visual effects may become cumbersome, unexpectedly expensive, and complicated compared to original expectations.

Also, keep in mind that real-time visual effects yield two possible recorded variations for every shot, and both may be required for immediate playback and archiving. These two recordings would be:

1. the normal video recording of the set without any real-time visual effects, which duplicates what is photographed by the production camera, and
2. the background with the real-time rendered visual effects as a separate recording.

This puts a heavier burden on stage video personnel to record and play back both versions of each take and likely later in production editorial. There are a number of situations where the director or others will want to review the take without the visual effects, for instance, to focus more on the actor's performance or anything else that might have been obscured or unclear by the insertion of the real-time visual effects. Similarly, on stage at the time of photography as well as later, people will want to view the recorded shot with the real-time visual effects.

For instance, during the editorial process, it may be advantageous to have either the clean plate or to choose the recording of the same take with simplified real-time visual effects. Normally editorial would be working from the images transferred from film or the original digital images. However since the on-set composites only exist in video form it would have to be integrated into the editorial process as needed. This possibility and other variations should be discussed with stage and production personnel before shooting begins, including editorial and other members of the production process who may be affected by having multiple video versions of the exact same take.

Certain technical difficulties and potential added complexity can arise when using real-time camera tracking and real-time visual effects. However, as technical problems are overcome and reliable, low-impact systems become commonplace, real-time visual effects and previewing could have an important positive effect on set and for the overall production process, and may even play a role in test screenings. Like storyboards and the camera video tap, it may become an important aid in understanding what will be seen in the final shot, and real-time tracking systems may become one more tool to expand options and give more freedom to the creative process and imagination.

TRIANGULATION AS A METHOD OF RECORDING CAMERA DATA
Stuart Robertson

Photorealistic visual effects require all elements within an image to share common image and lighting characteristics and, most importantly, a common perspective. Since the photographic perspective is entirely dependent on the spatial relationship between the camera and the subject being photographed, it is essential that this relationship be recorded and applied systematically to the photography or computer generation of each element that goes into the finished composite. When shooting the image that establishes the perspective for the shot (usually the background plate), the visual effects crew has the responsibility for recording the camera position data and then applying that data to the additional elements (greenscreen plates, miniatures, CG animation, etc.) to be combined in the final composite image.

Although much of this positional data can now be derived after the fact from software tracking and other computer applications, on some occasions this work is still most easily accomplished manually, for instance, when the appropriate computer application is not available. In particular, when multiple physical elements are to be laid out (green screen, miniature, etc.) the specifications for such a layout will have to be created, either manually as described in this section or specifically from software. Knowledge of the manual method is especially important if multiple elements will need to be shot during live action with no time to scan in the film, matchmove it on a computer, and send back all the data in a usable form. Therefore, it is worthwhile to review the traditional methods of manual camera data recording, and to offer a supplementary procedure that increases the accuracy of such data. This approach provides a simple method of re-creating the camera/subject relationship for additional photographic or CG element capture.

Camera/Subject Positional Information

This is the data that guarantees the matching of perspective for all elements in a shot. Positional data can be derived using a very simple tool kit, and should be recorded relative to the *visual effects nodal point* of the camera lens. The triangulation method discussed here provides an accurate and convenient approach for recording and applying this positional data.

Basics: The Tool Kit

The tools needed for manual camera data recording are simple ones, most of which have the great advantage of being powered by gravity: a universally available and unvarying reference for vertical measurement—regardless of scale. The tools shown in Figures 3.26 through 3.29 are the minimum necessary. Most of them are available at any local hardware store.

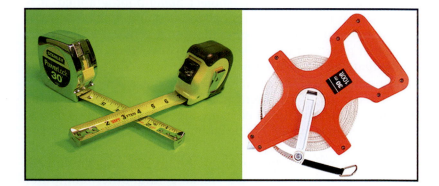

Figure 3.26 Measuring tapes (two are required, three are preferred). (All images in this section are courtesy of Stuart Robertson.)

Figure 3.27 Inclinometer (aka angle finder, angle dangle, etc.) A professional sighting inclinometer is shown at right.

Figure 3.28 Plumb bob and line (one required, two preferred).

Figure 3.29 Laser level (not essential, but very handy).

Basics: Nodal Point

Camera data should be recorded relative to the camera's visual effects nodal point[24], not from the film plane. Although current practice tends to favor data collection from the camera's film plane, measurement from the nodal point is more immediately accurate and will translate more accurately between differing lenses or image formats or between photographic and CG environments. It should be clearly noted in the data record whether the measurements are taken from the nodal point or from the film plane.

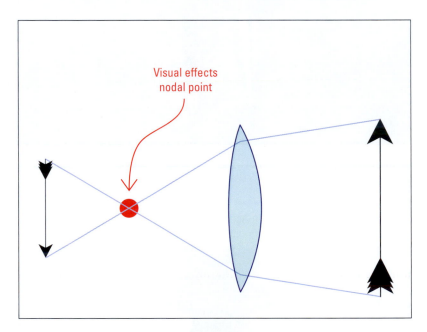

Figure 3.30 Visual effects nodal point.

The visual effects nodal point is considered to be the center of rotation and the perspective center for the image-forming function of a lens. Therefore, the position of the nodal point of any given lens will yield an equivalent perspective for any other camera lens, of whatever focal length, whose nodal point is placed in that same position.

And, because the infinitely small lens of a CG camera is by definition nodal to know the relative position of the nodal point of a

[24] Strictly speaking, the use of the term *nodal point* to describe the point within a lens around which the perspective rotates is contrary to the use of the term in geometric optics and lens design. In scientific optics, the nodal points (plural) of a lens are defined as "either of two points so located on the axis of a lens or optical system that any incident ray directed through one will produce a parallel emergent ray directed through the other" and in scientific usage the correct term for the point of rotation of a lens is *entrance pupil*. However, this section will continue to use the term *nodal point* as it is commonly and universally used by the visual effects community.

camera lens is to know the relative position at which to place a CG camera in a CG environment.

The degree of accuracy needed in determining the nodal point for data acquisition depends on the circumstances of each shot, varying inversely with the distance between the camera and the subject. For extreme close-ups (miniature or table-top work, for instance) the distance between the camera and the subject is very small and accuracy of all measurements is critical, so the nodal point needs to be determined very accurately, using techniques discussed elsewhere in this handbook.

At greater distances—6 to 8 feet or beyond—an approximation is usually sufficient (although this must always be a considered judgment based on the nature of the shot). A rule of thumb that has proven reasonably accurate takes advantage of the fact that *the entrance pupil of a complex lens can be found at the apparent depth of the image of the aperture stop as seen looking into the front element of the lens.* A visual estimate of the apparent depth of the aperture stop within the lens barrel will give a working location of the approximate visual effects nodal point, when an exact determination is unavailable or less than entirely necessary.

Tutorial: Camera/Subject Positional Information

The following tutorial demonstrates the procedure for recording and applying manual measurements of camera/subject relationships for a typical visual effects shot. In this typical case, the tutorial will deal with greenscreen characters walking along a path in an interior location but will also mention general considerations that would apply to other types of shots, such as the placement of a miniature building element within an exterior location. The tutorial will follow the desired shooting order for visual effects plates, first shooting the background plate and then shooting the elements (in this case, the greenscreen characters) that will fit into this background.

Figure 3.31 Background and greenscreen plates.

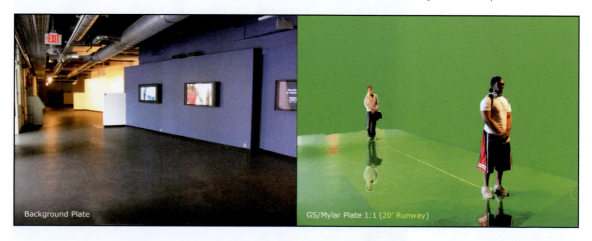

Step 1: Establish a Baseline

Once the camera has been placed to give the desired framing for the background plate, the visual effects crew will need to determine a *baseline* from which measurements will be taken. Determining an appropriate baseline requires careful judgment. A baseline must be long enough to provide accurate triangulation and must be chosen so that it will have a meaningful and measurable spatial relationship to common elements within both the background subject and the element plates that will be photographed to fit into it.

For instance, if one wanted to replace the front face of the building shown in Figure 3.32 with a pyrotechnic model, a sensible location for a baseline would be the lower front edge of the building face. This would be a common measurement for both the actual building and, if scaled, for the miniature.

For the tutorial example, the chosen baseline is derived from the path that the character will take as he walks through a hallway.

Figure 3.32 Baseline location on typical building.

A 20-foot tape measure is placed into the set to mark this baseline, and temporary tape markers are placed at either end of the measured baseline (these markers will be removed before shooting begins).

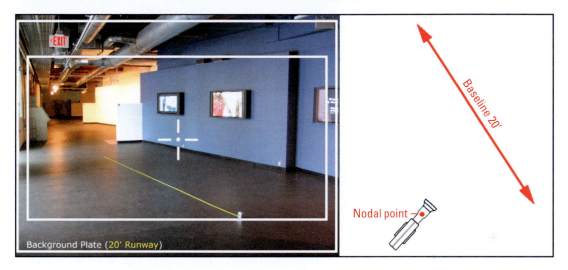

Step 2: Mark the Station Point

Drop a plumb line from directly underneath the nodal point of the lens to the floor below the camera, and place a square of tape to mark that spot. Designate this point (marking the camera's plan position on the set or location) as *station point (X)*.

Figure 3.33 Baseline established in background plate on set.

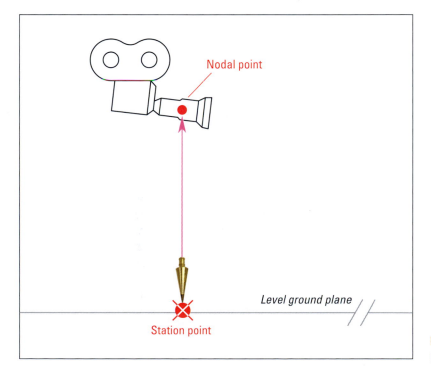

Figure 3.34 Station point— plumb line from nodal point.

Step 3: Create the Data Plan and Triangulate the Camera Position

Draw an overhead view floor plan of the setup, including the station point (*X*) and the baseline (this plan view does not need to be drawn to scale).

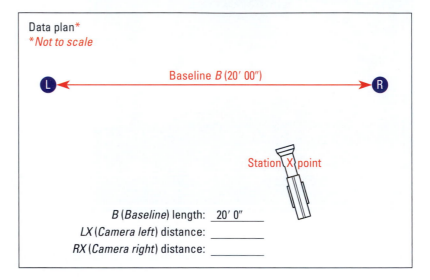

Figure 3.35 Data plan with baseline.

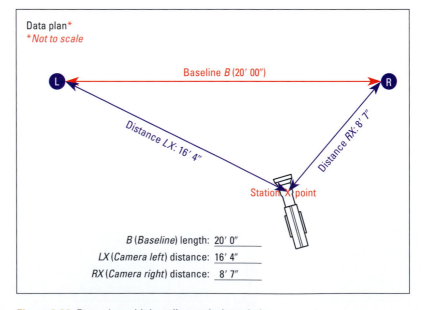

Figure 3.36 Data plan with baseline and triangulation.

Measure the length of a straight line from the left edge (*L*) of the baseline to the station point (*X*). Record this distance as distance *LX*. Record the distance from the right edge (*R*) of the baseline to station point (*X*) as distance *RX*.

Because of the rigid nature of a triangle, these measurements establish the only possible plan position that the camera could occupy relative to the baseline—and therefore relative to the subject.

Step 4: Record the Camera Height, Tilt, and Dutch Angle (If Any)

Using an inclinometer placed on an appropriate surface of the camera or camera mount, record the tilt and dutch (roll) angles of the camera. Assuming that the surface on which the camera rests is level with the height of the baseline, obtain the camera height by taking a direct measurement of the vertical distance from the camera's nodal point to the floor.

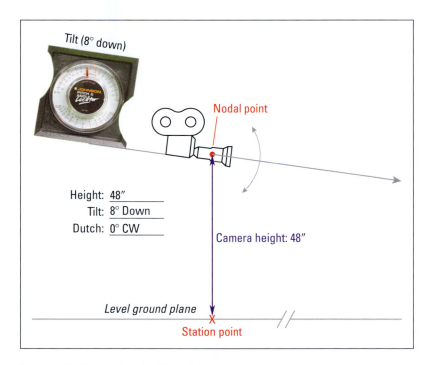

Figure 3.37 Camera height, tilt, and dutch.

If the baseline is *not* at floor level (in table-top photography, for example), one will need to offset the camera height to reflect the camera's height relative to the baseline instead of relative to the floor.

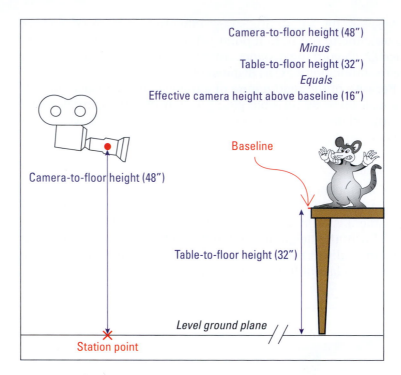

Figure 3.38 Camera height offset for baseline height.

Step 5: Determine and Record the Camera Pan Angle Relative to the Baseline

The measurements so far have recorded the camera's height, tilt, and Dutch angles, and the camera station point relative to the chosen baseline. This information is enough to re-create the position of the camera's nodal point and, therefore, the perspective of the shot (see following diagrams).

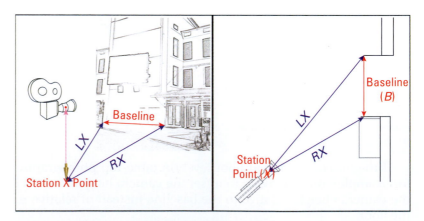

Figure 3.39 Station point established relative o baseline.

However, even the widest lens is sampling imagery from only a small portion of the panorama potentially visible from the position of the nodal point.

The data collected so far gives no information about the horizontal direction in which the camera is actually pointing. In fact, one could point the camera in the exact opposite direction from the original pan heading, and the data we've collected would still be valid. The only wrong thing would be the image.

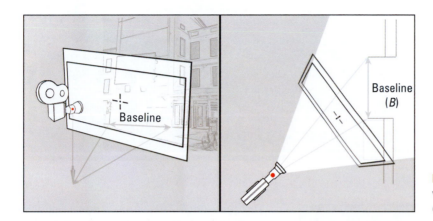

Figure 3.40 Camera field of view (one of an infinite number of views).

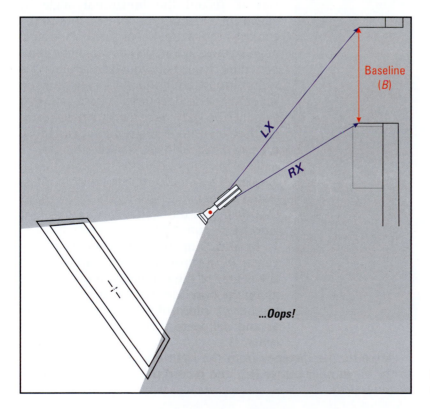

Figure 3.41 Right station point, wrong image ....

Figure 3.42 Camera crosshair establishes the center of field of view.

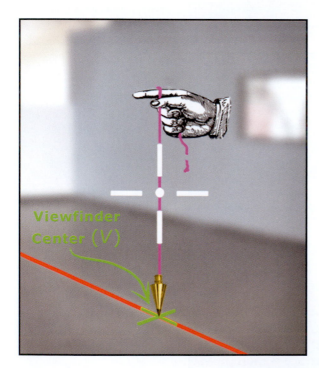

Figure 3.43 Plumb line to mark viewfinder center (*V*) on baseline.

To deal with this, one must have a way to record the horizontal angle by which the camera was pointed toward the subject—the azimuth or horizontal pan angle relative to the subject. Magnetic compass direction is notoriously unreliable due to local magnetic influences especially on set or in interior locations. A better strategy is to use the features of a professional camera itself as a survey instrument to establish the pan angle relative to the baseline.

Looking through the camera at the triangulated set, notice that a typical professional camera viewfinder has crosshairs that delineate the center of the image, as shown in Figure 3.42.

By dropping a plumb line from the center of the crosshairs one can establish the center of the camera frame as a point along the baseline. Mark this point with a temporary piece of tape or a chalk mark as and delineate this point as *viewfinder center* (*V*).

Measure the distance from the right end of the baseline (*R*) to the viewfinder center (*V*), and record this on the site plan as *distance* (*RV*).

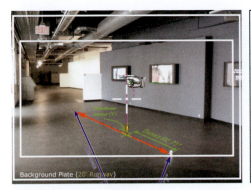
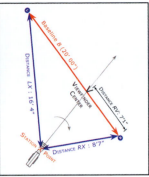

Figure 3.44 Record viewfinder center (*V*) on baseline.

To re-create this configuration on the greenscreen set, pan the camera so that the image center as shown by the viewer crosshairs will be directly above (*V*), thereby ensuring that the camera pan angle is correct. The camera data plan is now complete.

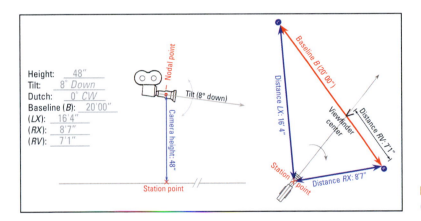

Figure 3.45 Data plan—completed.

Step 6: Apply the Positional Data to the Greenscreen Element

The first step upon beginning element photography is to reestablish the baseline—in this case, a 20-foot tape placed on the green floor. Viewfinder center (*V*) should be marked on the baseline at this stage.

Locate the camera station point by swinging two tape measures, set to the distances (*LX*) and (*RX*) and pivoted from the left and right edges of the baseline. The point at which the two tapes meet marks the station point (*X*).

Having established the station point, preset the camera to the heights and tilts previously recorded on the data plan. Placing the camera so that the nodal point is directly above station point *X* (the plumb line comes in handy here), pan the camera so that the center image crosshairs are directly above viewer center (*V*), and make adjustments as needed to reset the height and tilt to match the data plan.

Figure 3.46 Baseline reestablished on greenscreen stage.

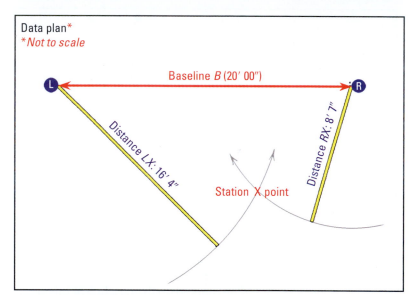

Figure 3.47 Station point located from baseline.

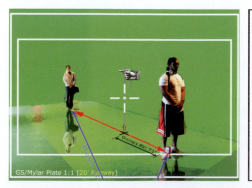
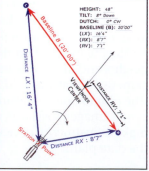

Figure 3.48 Data plan applied to greenscreen stage.

Proceed to shoot the greenscreen action, confident that the greenscreen elements will fit into the space of the background plate with little or no adjustment in post. (Don't forget to remove any temporary markers before shooting.)

GS/Mylar Plate 1:1 (20' Runway)
Background Plate (20' Runway)

Figure 3.49 Rough comp without adjustment.

Additional Notes 1: Scaling

Direct scaling of the data plan provides simple and accurate measurements for scaling of elements—in this case, for 2:1 scaling of the greenscreen characters (who will be positioned along a 10-foot baseline).

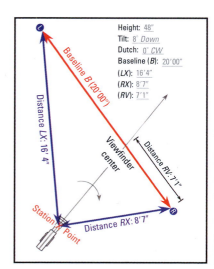

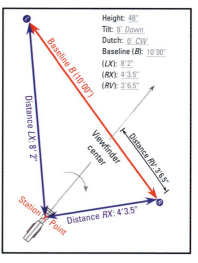

Figure 3.50 1:1 and 2:1 data plans.

Figure 3.51 2:1 greenscreen plate and rough comp.

Additional Notes 2: Uneven Ground Level

More often than not, the visual effects crew won't be lucky enough to be working from a level floor while shooting background plates—especially on outdoor locations. A more typical case might involve shooting with a low camera tilted upward, on ground that slopes unevenly downward away from the camera. Because the intention in this instance is to place a greenscreen character on the first stairway landing, a baseline has been established at that height—above the camera.

The problem is to determine exactly how far the camera is below this baseline—the negative camera height.

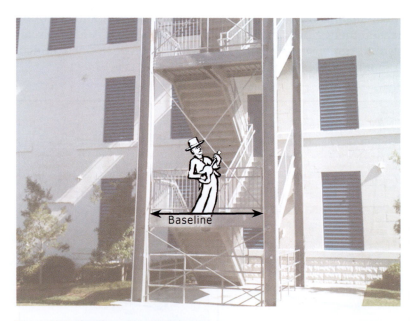

Figure 3.52 Baseline above the camera.

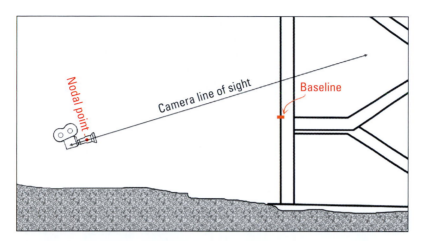

Figure 3.53 Side view—baseline above the camera.

This is a situation in which the laser level provides the simplest solution to the problem. Direct measurement from the visible line provided by the leveled laser gives the relative heights of both the camera's nodal point (Height *LLC*) and the baseline (Height *LLB*). Subtracting *LLC* from *LLB* gives the measurement of how far the camera is below the baseline—the measurement needed when setting the camera height below a greenscreen platform for the element photography.

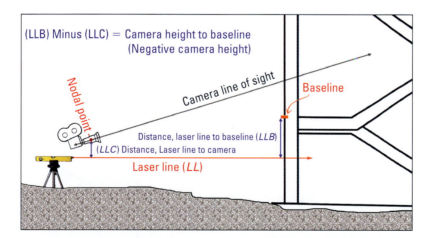

Figure 3.54 Heights measured from laser level line.

However, if the crew does not have access to a laser level, or if the distances and lighting conditions make it impossible to use one, one can obtain the information needed by using the camera itself as a surveying instrument.

The visual horizon is defined by the height of the observer, so the line of sight of a level camera is also a reference for the height of objects above and below the horizon and therefore the height of an object above or below the camera.

If one levels the camera and sight through it, one can obtain a visual horizontal reference shown by the viewfinder crosshairs. This of course would be done *after* completing the shot.

Camera Leveled to find Horizon/Camera Height   Camera Tilted Up for Shot

Figure 3.55 Camera leveled to determine camera height—view from camera viewfinder.

Direct measurement along the front edge of the subject, from the baseline to the spot on the subject on which the viewfinder center rests, gives the precise measurement of the distance by which the camera is below the baseline.

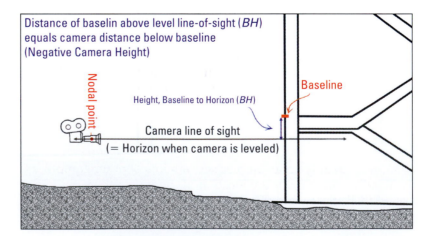

Distance of baselin above level line-of-sight (*BH*) equals camera distance below baseline (Negative Camera Height)

Nodal point

Baseline

Height, Baseline to Horizon (*BH*)

Camera line of sight
(= Horizon when camera is leveled)

Figure 3.56 C camera leveled to determine camera height—side view.

PHOTOGRAPHIC REFERENCE
Charles Clavadetscher

Oftentimes the individuals or teams capturing data will want to shoot photographs or video that visually document some aspect of the shooting situation, which may then be easier to understand later in the post-production process. These reference images provide a method to capture a very visual, active situation on set where written notes and diagrams won't or cannot convey clearly what can be seen in a few pictures.

This type of generalized reference photography is primarily helpful when specialized image and data gathering, such as for photogrammetry, textures, or lighting, fail to show some significant or unique factor. It can provide a better human-oriented angle of the set, or it may better emphasize specific components that other processes miss.

First, whenever possible, shoot a slate indicating that these images are for general or specific reference, and not for established areas, such as for lighting or matchmoving. Include the shot, sequence name, set name, and other relevant data (which should always be on a slate). When possible, make some note on the slate about the purpose of the reference shots. For instance, "flame rig and actor's position reference."

When shooting reference photographs, one way to highlight or direct the post-production artist's attention to a specific issue or detail is to shoot two nearly identical photographs in a row of the same scene or setup. The first picture is clean, showing the set without any special marker, while the second has a visual aid to direct the viewer's attention to a particular area in the image. Switching between the two images should make it clear what is being pointed out or noted.

For example, the first image may be the set and actor's position as an overview. The second image, shot with the same view, may have the photographer's finger pointing at the production film camera, which may be in a unique position, such as in a pit in the floor or under a table and therefore hard to see. The slate for these two photographs should say "camera location and actor's position reference."

Or the photographer's pointing finger may indicate the location of a special effects pipe that will emit water, but is otherwise hard to see and identify on a complex set with lots of other equipment. By literally pointing out the location of the pipe, others who were not on the set may find this reference image useful when trying to identify and work with the source of water in the production image.

Although it may seem somewhat crude, the technique of shooting one clean picture and a second picture with a pointing finger can be quickly accomplished by a lone photographer, and nothing fancy is required in terms of crew cooperation or the photographer's time or equipment, so the process has no impact on the production set itself, nor does it create obstructions. Plus, having only 2 photographs keeps the number of images low compared to having 5 or 10 images designed to highlight something from different vantage points and hoping the end viewer will figure out what's important.

The same technique can be used to help point out a person or object of special interest, a particular rig, unusual camera position, camera start and stop positions, a hidden camera, or a handheld camera that may be difficult to find in a single overview image. The almost limitless number of possibilities that can occur when shooting on a set, particularly for visual effects, can easily be pointed out using this simple technique.

As an alternative to the photographer's finger, someone else in the image may do the pointing, or a special marker could be placed as required. The problem with both a second person or a marker is that both require additional personnel or preparation. It may pose a problem for the production crew to have additional people or markers on the set, even temporarily. In contrast, a lone photographer can stand away from the set and use the pointing finger technique to passively and quickly record the item of interest and its location in relation to the rest of the set and then move on to more traditional data gathering.

When shooting references, keep in mind that on a busy set with many people and tasks, drawing the attention of a later viewer to one point of interest might be harder than expected. Whatever means is used to gain the attention of the post-production artist needs to significantly stand out and clearly indicate the exact detail of interest.

In some circumstances, a third photograph may be needed to act as a record of general changes or details. For instance, on a set that has wild walls, it may be hard for someone coming along later to understand the setup. In this case, a third photograph can help tie this together. The third photograph might be the set with and without the wild wall, taken from the exact same position, essentially showing a before and after situation. Or the third photograph may be of a set blueprint or diagram, and a finger points at exactly the same spot in the diagram as the finger in the second image. The common element of the pointing finger makes the purpose clear by guiding viewers to exactly what's important and ignoring what's not.

Don't forget to get feedback and do tests for this type of reference image. On the spur of the moment, it may seem like a good idea to shoot overview photographs of the sets. However, the artists themselves, looking at the images months later with no frame of reference, may only see a jumble of people and equipment, and the image is no help whatsoever. Worse, additional but useless images and data just add confusion to the other reference data and overall process.

Shooting Video as a Reference

Shooting video for reference sounds like a great idea for tying loose threads together, putting a helpful perspective on the production shot, or recording some minute detail in real time as the camera rolls. However, video reference can quickly transform into hours and hours of unusable and incomprehensible material.

This is not to say that video is without its use, but many factors need to be kept in mind in order to make video valuable:

1. First and foremost, get a slate shot for the video, preferably at the head. If this video pertains to a particular scene and/or sequence, make sure that is on the slate. Also it doesn't hurt to verbally read the slate as the video is slated since the video camera also captures audio, and it might make a hastily written slate easier to understand. Slates should always have the current date, time of day (to coordinate with other time-of-day information), and production shot number matching the production slate used to film/record the scene. Additionally, this slate should contain unique identifying information, such as the set name or location name. Because video is being shot for a particular purpose, it is always a good idea to put this on the slate as well as record that verbally.

2. The second priority is to use video precisely. This suggestion cannot be stressed enough. The most common reason video becomes useless is that by the end of the production there are hundreds of hours of video that someone must search through, log, copy, edit, organize, and/or perform other arduous and repetitive tasks on to make it usable. Plus, because the person organizing the video may not be the one who shot the video, the purpose and end usage may not be clear and may even be outright impossible to understand later. As a result, a lot of time spent shooting video has no benefit because it lies unused by the artists, misfiled, or thrown away because of the time-consuming, frustrating, and often impossible task of organizing or deciphering the video.

    Another issue is the willingness and ability of the artists to roll through the video themselves. In many cases, an alternate to video, such as photogrammetry, or other standard data gathering, would provide a more precise method of capturing the same information and would prove to be more useful and easier to access.

In this sense, shooting precisely is the key to successful video, or in other words, shoot just enough to get the job done and keep it organized

The idea of putting a video camera up in the rafters and having it run for the whole day sounds enticing—especially to people who never had to deal with the end results before. Now imagine 90 days of stage video that need to be sorted through. It could take 90 days just to watch it!

No wonder it gets tossed or deemed a waste of time compared to whatever benefit there might be. It would be cheaper to hire someone to operate the video camera on set, turning it on during the appropriate times and off as soon as its use is ended—all in order to reduce the overall mass of video to as little as possible. This reduces or prevents hiring someone later to sit and sort through video for days at some later date.

Another problem with video arises when it is intended to be in sync with production motion picture footage. One of the biggest problems in this scenario is the difference in standard video frame rate compared to film. Standard North American video is 29.97 fps and film is 24 fps. Even if video is somehow brought in sync with the film, there is a perceptible mismatch between the video image and the film and interlacing issues to consider. To correct this, if possible, use a video camera that shoots true 24fps, and test it under shooting conditions to make sure there is a solid, reliable system of sync throughout the production process, including editorial. The reference video and film images should be known, accessible, and usable to the post-production artist.

The other critical synchronization problem occurs when the visual effects artists get a small section of the photographed scene as the final cut, while the original video from stage contains the entire take from beginning to end. If the video needs to be synchronized correctly with the production footage, a solid and absolutely reliable system must be developed to get the video in sync with the much smaller cut shot.

Without this type of information, trying to synchronize a long video with a short take turns into an error-prone and expensive guessing game. While it may seem obvious on set as to which portion of the scene is connected to which motion, someone else who wasn't on set and is trying to figure this out later can face a frustrating, hopeless endeavor.

From all this, video may sound like a losing proposition. Yet, in some cases, and in support of some visual effects, it may be the ideal solution. For example, having video that is shot 90 degrees off the main production camera, or above it, may resolve some complex motion and timing issue that is otherwise open to guesswork or time-consuming tests and approval.

Those types of specific examples are covered in the earlier sections on witness cameras and matchmoving. However, other types of reference videos may be useful, such as walking through a set to explain some unusual setup, how a specialized rig was set up or used off camera, or how a wild wall moves in and out.

Using video for this type of reference is something that needs careful thought, preparation, and testing (when possible), before shooting, in order to get results that can be used as intended, and to make the effort worthwhile. It would be a mistake to have hours of video walking through sets. Make it concise; make sure it is both needed and useful and delivers significant information for later use. Given that visual effects data gathering has limited personnel, time, and equipment, choosing video for support reference, over or in combination with some other method, should be carefully considered and tested before production begins and before other methods are discarded in favor of video. In some situations, survey, scanning, or still images may be a better way to gather reference data or images. It bears repeating that shooting video which is never watched or can't be put in proper sync is not a good use of time and resources.

However, if captured correctly and in a way that is easy to manage, reference video may be just what is needed. But always be aware that video is unlike other data capture because it is a real-time process, generates many potential post-production processes and organization issues, and can overwhelm users and artists if it becomes confusing or cumbersome or doesn't seem to connect to the specific artist's process.

Overall, general photographic reference, either still image or video, provides a means to visually capture and organize production setups, data, and conditions that may fall outside the realm of other processes, such as lighting data capture. Recognizing this before production begins, discussing alternatives with acquisition personnel, and setting up procedures and guidelines can make this a flexible alternative to support the CG post-production process.

RULES, SETUP, AND TESTING
Charles Clavadetscher

As in many jobs, preparation is the key to success. Preparation helps prevent delays or interference with other tasks of the production/shooting process and helps all work proceed smoothly, working with the other departments to the completion of each shot.

As such, the job of acquiring visual effects data from stage or location begins well before the production starts shooting, beginning in pre-production, so that the first production shot is not a testing ground, which could waste time, cause confusion, or cause other problems on stage.

This is similar to nearly all other departments, which begin their work before the first shoot so they are fully prepared when shooting begins. For instance, the costume department goes through extensive fittings, visual tests, alterations, and fine adjustments of the actor's costumes, which are then ready and fitting properly when shooting begins.

In a similar vein, visual effects processes should be tested, rehearsed, and evaluated before the first day of shooting so that the data collection process proceeds as smoothly as possible, with the least impact or drag on production. The visual effects process should present a professional, nonconfused appearance to the rest of the production crew, which also ensures that the best results are obtained. Preparation for data collection helps avoid errors and conflicts on set, as well as errors in the collected data itself.

It is therefore a good practice to engage in a testing process in pre-production, in order to achieve successful and economic data collection for the visual effects process.

Before equipment is purchased or the cameras start rolling, the visual effects supervisor or on-set data wrangler(s) need to answer two basic questions:
• Who gets the collected data?
• How do they want it recorded and delivered?

Who gets the collected data breaks down into three separate people or entities:
1. The first person would be the VFX Coordinator/Editor/Supervisor or visual effects facility. Even if the person collecting the data has worked with a facility directly before, it's good to double check that previous data formats are still up-to-date and viable for the new production. Check to see if any improvements or changes can be made in how to record, capture, or deliver the data. If nothing else, new employees, or people in new positions, such as new supervisors or data handlers, may have different priorities compared to previous projects.
2. The second "who gets the data" question is answered by which department(s), and which techniques, of the visual effects process are the target for the data capture. Are the camera notes, such as focal length, intended only for matchmoving, or will they also be used for modeling, texture capture, stage/set extension, lighting reference, general photogrammetry, or other processes? Each user of the same data may require specific details

or an alteration to the data collection process that another user would not.

If the gathered data is for multiple visual effects processes, then clear priorities, as well as clear steps and expected results need to be defined and approved as early as possible. This must happen at the very least before production begins. Different processes have widely divergent data collection requirements, and it is common that one simply cannot reliably gather all of the data for all departments for any given shot. Setting established goals for the area(s) each person is covering depends on clear communication and priorities established during pre-production testing.

3. The third "who gets the collected data" question would be answered by identifying specific individuals at any facility who will receive the data, any intermediary individuals who might sort, collect, or process the data, and finally the end users, or at least a lead or supervisory member or representative of each area.

Understanding the three parts of "who gets the collected data" provides the foundation for the tests and connections necessary to ensure that the collected data is in the correct format and is usable. It also establishes the correct priority and expectations and ensures that communications have been opened between the different areas and specialists to discuss any special requirements, potential problems, or additional issues—all before production is started.

Do a Complete Test Shot!

Before arriving on set for the actual production photography, it is good practice and highly recommended for each member of the data collection process to perform multiple examples or test shots. The object of this exercise is to cover a variety of situations. Also, working on a group of shots helps uncover any problems arising from overlapping data on multiple shots, such as will occur during real production.

This may mean having test or example shots created in a nearby building or other location that represent reasonable approximations of the expected sets or locations.

To put this in perspective, consider the following scenario, wherein a very simple mistake in standardized practices created massive havoc and wasted time and energy in post-production. This is a mistake that could have been easy to avoid.

It is common practice in production to use both head and tail slates in shooting motion picture footage. For a head slate, the slate is held upright and reads correctly as the film is projected or viewed. A head slate indicates that the information on the slate applies to the shot that is following that slate. A tail slate is always turned upside down, indicating that the slate information applies to the shot before the slate's appearance. Additionally, a false start (without a slate) may be indicated by the camera operator holding his or her hand close in front of the lens.

The same rules apply to both still and video photography used in the visual effects data capture process.

In this example of the process gone wrong, during the rapid pace of production, the data gathering on set often used head slates, tail slates, and the hand in the frame techniques. Unfortunately, the individual accepting the raw, unsorted data was unaware of the standardized slating techniques listed above.

As a result, all the "hand" frames were deleted because it was assumed these were mistakes or irrelevant. Furthermore, the upside-down slates (indicating tail slates) were confusing and hard to read, so the slates were rotated to be easily read.

Problems started from the first day of using the collected photographs. Lighting reference images and their slates didn't match the plates. Modeling and photogrammetry pictures were mixed up or seemed nonexistent, even when submitted notes indicated the material had been shot. It took weeks to figure out the problem and even longer to correct it. One person in the chain had reorganized the data based on ignorance, costing time, money, and expedience.

This example also illustrates a simple rule of data handling, which is "never, ever manipulate the original data." If part of the process involves editing, reorganizing, or in any other way manipulating the original captured data, then first make a copy of the raw data and edit that, and leave the original version alone. A copy, even if it is much larger, disorganized, and potentially confusing, is left unaltered as insurance and a way to get back to a clean start.

Why Run Through Example or Test Shots?

Test shots help identify and avoid errors as in the preceding example. Test shots reveal the CG pipeline's weakest links so they can be corrected *before* problems occur with a real shot. The rule of test shots is that every aspect must be handled as if it were a real shot, by the same people, using the same process. It is an invitation for disaster to have one group handle or accept the test shot data and another group use the real production data. Real shots handled by different people may unwittingly use different processes, skip key procedures, or proceed with completely different understandings, expectations, and results compared to those who receive the real, final production data.

Running through a multiple-shot test process may reveal that the slates have both good and bad data. They may have the needed information, but be too small, poorly lit, cut off, or illegible (for instance, from bad handwriting). Or the slates may simply need rearranging for better understanding, sorting, and easier access by the final users.

Camera report forms may need to be simplified or expanded. It may turn out that the data collection equipment doesn't output the expected results or doesn't connect correctly with other data. For instance, "up" may be z in one system and y in another.

An example of an equipment setup problem would be a still camera that isn't set up for or capable of shooting the expected format. The camera may be recording single 24-bit JPEGs of the shot when the visual effects team expected 48-bit RAW images in a bracketed sequence. Or it may be that the camera and lens have unacceptable limitations or cropping compared to another preferred camera.

These sorts of problems may apply to other equipment as well, and the list of possible mismatches or missed expectations is quite lengthy. Running through multiple test scenarios will discover and correct these problems before production begins, and this testing procedure will fine-tune the equipment, the process, the people, and the expectations.

Complete testing also ensures that the data collection process will not suddenly change as production progresses. A change such as this could be complicated or confusing to stage personnel and the non–visual effects components of production, and it may be awkward or embarrassing, or changes to the data collection processes may even be impossible to accommodate in the middle of production once procedures have been established and planned.

Keep in mind that after running through one series of tests, it is prudent to run through them a second time to ensure that all the changes have been incorporated or accounted for correctly. That means doing more than one set of tests. At a minimum, two test shots or test sequences are needed to uncover and correct errors. Additional tests may find further problems or issues that need correction, resulting in yet another test sequence. The point is, do not go into production without knowing all of the expectations, techniques, and expected formats, and do not go into production without a system that has successfully produced a final set of test data that everyone agrees is good. If this can't be produced, there is a large chance errors will appear in the collected production data, and the cost will be many times greater than the cost for one additional test.

Comprehensive tests like these, including the review and correction process, can take well over a month. While some people may initially object to this process, skipping it is a guarantee that the data collected will be troublesome, likely very expensive, possibly unusable, impossible to fix during production, and may take weeks to correct, if it can be corrected at all.

This bears repeating: *Do not skip the testing process, which ensures that the data collection process is set up properly and will yield successful and economic data collection for the visual effects process.*

DIGITAL CINEMATOGRAPHY
Dave Stump ASC, Marty Ollstein, David Reisner

Shooting with a digital camera has advantages and disadvantages. This section introduces the issues that a VFX Supervisor should consider when planning to work with a digital camera.

Collaboration between the VFX Supervisor and the Director of Photography (DP) is always important in production. However, when the image is recorded on a digital camera, that collaboration becomes essential. The choice of camera, recording medium, image format, and workflow all affect the quality and nature of the work of the VFX Supervisor and the success of the visual effects that are produced. The possibilities and limitations that each decision entails should be fully understood before starting work in the digital realm.

The goal in choosing a camera is to provide the highest quality image capture that the production can afford. The VFX Supervisor is required to be both artist and engineer in researching the broad spectrum of eligible cameras, while staying fiscally responsible to the production.

Digital Definitions
- *Digital cinematography* refers to production shot with any digital camera on any digital medium.
- *High definition* refers to high-resolution digital cameras that have at least 1920 pixels horizontally or, for higher quality releases, 2048 or more pixels horizontally (which minimizes image resizing).
- *High definition*, *in television* and occasionally *in cinema*, refers to 1920×1080 cameras that record Rec. 709, subsampled, 8-bit color.[25]

---

[25] This type of HD camera pushes the low end of cinema color space and color resolution—a good deal below motion picture film. If using for cinema projects, one must do so with an understanding of the compromises that are being made and recognition that those choices have repercussions later in the workflow that will show in the final release.

- *Digital cinema* or *d-cinema* is the official Society of Motion Picture and Television Engineers (SMPTE) nomenclature for referring to feature motion pictures (and potentially other digital uses) distributed digitally and shown on digital projectors that meet SMPTE and DCI (Digital Cinema Initiatives[26]) specifications/requirements.

Dynamic Range

Dynamic range quantifies the recording latitude of a device or medium. In cinematography it is measured in *f*-stops. Modern color negative films have a dynamic range of 11 to 12 *f*-stops of latitude.[27]

In digital sensors, dynamic range is defined as the range of signals from the strongest to the weakest signal registered by the sensor. The dynamic range of the sensor is considered to be the difference between the photonic (electronic) noise in the system with no signal present, and the maximum signal the system can record without clipping or distorting the signal. This range, or latitude, of the sensor is measured in either units of decibels[28] (dB) or *f*-stops.

The signal-to-noise ratio (S/N) performance levels in digital cameras are stated in decibels to compare baseline noise to top signal power. To meaningfully understand the dynamic range of a photographic sensor, it is essential to define an acceptable level of noise at the lowest end of the scale. The level of noise selected will directly affect the image being recorded. The top end of the S/N equation is much easier to define. Even the novice can quickly learn to identify signal clip on a waveform monitor.

Noise is a factor in all digital cameras. Digital cameras record images in a very strict and methodical way. When presented with a quantity of light, they produce code values that describe an exact color and hue.

Noise is inherent in digital cameras and shows up as a bothersome dither or shifting in an otherwise stable and unchanging

---

[26] A consortium of major movie studios that have come together to set standards in the digital realm. D-cinema may be "2K" (nominally, 2048 × 1080) at 24 or 48 fps (which allows stereoscopic 3D at 24 fps per eye) or "4K" (nominally, 4096 × 2160) at 24 fps, with up to 16 channels of uncompressed audio. D-cinema content is compressed with JPEG-2000 at a maximum of 250 Mbps. D-cinema is intended to provide a quality comparable to 35mm film.

[27] In terms of the Ansel Adams Zone System, properly exposed film can record and reproduce highlights in zone 8, gray tones in zones 4, 5, and 6, and black details in zone 1, with room to print up or down by at least one *f*-stop.

[28] A decibel (dB) is a unit of measurement that expresses a ratio using logarithmic scales to give results related to human perception.

image.[29] This dither frequently attracts attention to itself and detracts from the storytelling. In certain lighting situations at the low end of the range, when the amount of light striking the image sensor varies minutely from frame to frame, the resultant change in tiny portions of the image can seem to flicker and change color. This results in a tendency to produce odd and unexpected image artifacts. These problems can be very difficult, if not impossible, to remedy in post-production.

Highlight Headroom

Highlight headroom is a complex concept. Put simply, it concerns the point at which the bright areas of the image are arbitrarily cut off and therefore not captured. Film negative handles overexposure extraordinarily well, but the highlight capture characteristics of digital recording have a tendency to lose overexposed highlight detail much sooner in its exposure cycle.

Digital cameras reach their saturation point decisively. When the light well of a photo site reaches saturation, it reaches that point with absolute certainty and is said to be at clip level. More light arriving at that sensor during that accumulation cycle is likely to spill out of that light well into adjacent light wells. This results in bloomed areas of overexposure that cannot be reduced in size or color corrected in post-production. Knowing the inherent differences in highlight and upper dynamic range issues between digital cameras is essential to success in digital cinematography and to all visual effects that utilize digital cinematography.

Sensitivity and ASA Ratings

The sensitivity of a digital camera's sensor to light is commonly stated as an ASA rating.[30] A digital camera with a higher ASA rating will usually perform better in low-light situations and contain less noise than one with a lower ASA rating.

Sensitivity and ASA rating are very important factors in any camera—film or digital. Film and sensors with lower sensitivity (lower ISO[31]/ASA speed) require more light and/or a longer exposure to achieve good color reproduction. Film or sensors with higher sensitivity (higher ISO/ASA speed) can shoot the same scene with less light or a shorter exposure, but that increased sensitivity usually comes at the cost of increased noise levels or film grain.

---

[29] Noise exists in film as well, but due to the nature of film grain, the noise is random, as opposed to the fixed pattern noise of digital. The random noise produced by film grain is more compatible to the human visual system and, when properly exposed and processed, does not call attention to itself.

[30] American Standards Association, renamed American National Standards Institute (ANSI).

[31] International Organization for Standardization.

Color Space

Color space describes the range or set of colors that can be represented by a given system, encoding, or piece of equipment. When talking about a color space, the standard starting reference point is usually the CIE XYZ color space, which was specifically designed to encompass all colors the average human can see. Color space is an area where film still holds a meaningful advantage over digital technology at the time of this writing.

Numerous factors must be understood when studying color space in digital cinema. For example, digital camera color space depends on the frequency response of the sensor(s) and on the characteristics of the path that light travels to reach those sensors—including elements used to split or filter the light. Additionally, digital color space is influenced by *which sensor data is recorded* by the camera, how it is modified in the process, and which camera mode and recording format are selected.

In both digital and film production, what the audience sees is ultimately dependent on the characteristics of the distribution medium. For a film release, there is a choice of print stock. For a digital release, it is the Digital Cinema Package (DCP). For the home, the DVD could be standard definition or Blu-ray (high definition). The display device used also affects the final perceived result, be it a 35mm or 70mm film projector, a 2K or 4K digital cinema projector, or a consumer video display.

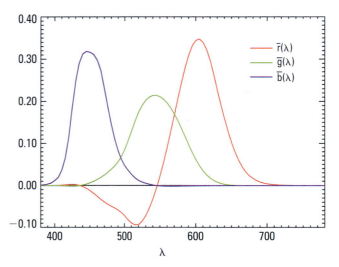

Figure 3.57 CIE 1931 RGB color matching functions. (From http://en.wikipedia.org/ wiki/File:CIE_1931_XYZ_Color_ Matching_Functions.svg. Reprinted with permission from Wikipedia.)

Color Space As It Relates to Cinematography

When colors are acquired by a digital camera or displayed on a monitor, they are usually defined in an RGB (red, green, and blue) color space. This is an additive process of making color, in which red, green, and blue light are added together to create color from darkness. The colors are defined by the amount of the red, green, and blue primaries that need to be emitted to produce a given color. Different display technologies produce different primary colors and thus display a different palette (sometimes referred to as *range* or *gamut*) of colors. While film intrinsically provides color references, digital cinematography uses display gamuts with standardized primary colors to allow the mapping from code values to specific colors.

When working in multiple media or with multiple technologies, it is sometimes necessary to convert the representation of a color from one color space to another. This color space conversion has the goal of making the colors of the transformed image in the new color space match as closely as possible the colors of the original image.

Cathode-ray tube (CRT) displays are driven by voltage signals for RGB. Full-bandwidth RGB signals require a relatively large capacity for storage and transmission. Reduced-bandwidth encodings such as YCbCr and Y'CbCr can do much of the same job using less capacity, but with some compromises and restrictions.

YCbCr and Y'CbCr (and their analog counterpart YPbPr) are practical ways of encoding RGB images as approximations of color with perceptual uniformity, but at much lower bandwidth for transmission. Y'CbCr is used to separate out a luma signal (Y') that can be stored with high resolution or transmitted at high bandwidth, and two chroma components (Cb and Cr) that can be bandwidth reduced, subsampled, and compressed for improved system efficiency. However, the use of this signal encoding system throughout the workflow can introduce substantial visible errors. Creating visual effects from subsampled images can be difficult and troublesome. For example, bluescreen or greenscreen mattes are more difficult to extract cleanly from chroma subsampled images.

The Calculus of Color Sampling

Current production digital cameras offer several different dynamic ranges for recording: 8 bit, 10-bit log, and 16 bit, to cite a few. Eight-bit-per-channel color can be simply described in this way: The sensor creates 2 to the eighth power values ($2^8 = 256$) for each of three color channels, that is, 256 shades of red, 256 shades of green, and 256 shades of blue. When the three color components are combined to define the entire color palette, $256 \times 256 \times 256$, the result is 16,777,216 colors, which is referred to as *8-bit color*. This color palette is an outgrowth of the display capability of phosphor CRT monitors, and it is intimately tied to the era of the genesis of television. CRTs are based on an old, inherently limited, and environmentally unfriendly technology that is now being replaced by LCDs, gas plasmas, LCOS, D-ILA, and DLP technology.

Some implementations of RGB use 16 bits per component for 48 bits total. Using the same color primaries, this results in the same range of color, but with a larger number of distinct colors (and smaller/finer steps between two adjacent colors). This is especially significant when working with wide-gamut color spaces where most of the more common colors are located relatively close together, or when a large number of digital transform algorithms are used consecutively, as is common in digital intermediate work.[32]

Color negative film is capable of rendering 12 to 13 bits per color component, or roughly 11½ stops of latitude. When scanned into the digital realm using today's standard production 10-bit log representation, each RGB color record is given between 886 and 1000 usable values out of the 1024 code values available in 10-bit encoding. When the three color records are combined, the overall resulting color space yields (loosely speaking) 1000 × 1000 × 1000 colors, meaning there are close to 1 billion colors from which to choose. Those colors are based on the color gamut that film can record, which is smaller than the color gamut that humans perceive (as documented in the CIE spec).

The Issues of Color Subsampling

What is 4:4:4? The term *4:4:4* has become HD slang for images and systems in which the three color records are sampled at equal maximum system frequencies. In the era of digital acquisition, 4:4:4 is a bit of a misnomer. Denoting an image as 4:4:4 traditionally refers to a standard-definition RGB (and occasionally YCbCr) video image in which all three color components have been sampled at 13.5 MHz. Because HD images are sampled at 74.25 MHz they should actually be said to be sampled at a 22:22:22 ratio. This indicates that none of the three color records has been subsampled at a lower rate to achieve system efficiency (and to save money).

Then, what is 4:2:2? Some smart engineers figured out that they could save money on storage and transmission if they reduced the signal through compression. The human visual system is much more sensitive to variations in brightness than in color, so a video system can be optimized by devoting more bandwidth to the brightness component (luma or Y'), than to the color components (color difference values Cb and Cr). A 4:2:2 Y'CbCr scheme requires only two-thirds of the bandwidth that 4:4:4 RGB requires, thus saving money in storage and transmission. Luma is sampled at full frequency, but the color

---

[32] Much attention is being paid to various 16-bit floating-point RGB formats as the eventual future of digital cinema color representation, and several research and development efforts are under way to implement 16-bit floating-point file formats for image acquisition, color correction, and display purposes. One of those efforts, the Academy of Motion Picture Arts and Sciences Image Interchange Framework (IIF) project, is an attempt to create an overall framework for motion picture color management that includes a 16-bit image file format that is intended to serve the industry all the way from acquisition through archive. IIF uses a constrained OpenEXR 16-bit floating-point container and a careful and extensive set of definitions to specify a highly capable and interoperable system.

components are sampled at half that frequency and then scaled back to full frequency using the brightness (Y′) channel as a multiplier for viewing.

The reduction in color bandwidth from 4:4:4 to 4:2:2 may only be perceived as a modest visual difference when viewed on a consumer CRT, but it can create significant problems for the visual effects compositor who is trying to create a convincing result from a greenscreen shot for theatrical release. The chroma subsampled images of 4:2:2 almost always result in matte lines and bad composites when viewed on larger screens. When creating visual effects for the big screen, then, you should shoot 4:4:4 or, technically, 22:22:22.

Subsampling Schemes

The 4:2:1, 4:1:1, 4:1:0, and 3:1:1 schemes are all subsampling schemes like 4:2:2, only worse. They are used in prosumer and HDV cameras. While any camera can produce the next Oscar for Best Cinematography, it is safer to ensure success with actual quality than to just hope for it with economy. A good rule of thumb is to capture the image with the best color you can afford, especially if visual effects work is involved.

The term *4:2:0* is used in many ways. All of them involve one form or another of subsampling of the chrominance channels in space (horizontal and vertical), and, in some cases, in time. The 4:2:0 subsampling scheme is used in MPEG-2 (the DVD format), DVCAM, HDV, and VC-1 (SMPTE 421M).

Another way to reduce or subsample the huge amount of image data generated by high-definition cameras is to use the mosaic pattern sensor layouts implemented in most single-sensor cameras. In 2/3-inch, three-chip cameras such as the Sony F900, each photosite on each of the three chips is sampled and assigned a code number that directly determines the color of the pixel. In single-sensor cameras, however, a mosaic pattern of filtered photosites is used to determine color. Each photosite is covered by a red, green, or blue filter in a pattern, and the samples of several adjacent photosites are combined to determine the color of each pixel.

One common pattern, used by the Arri D-21 and Red One, is the Bayer Pattern Mosaic Sensor Layout.[33] The Bayer pattern is a physical, sensor-level implementation of 4:2:0 subsampling. The manufacturers of some cameras that use 4K Bayer pattern sensors, such as the Red One, claim that they yield images with 4K resolution. However, that is extremely misleading. Bayer pattern single sensors (and any single-sensor camera) cannot sample color from co-sited photodetectors. A Bayer pattern sensor takes

---

[33] Bayer pattern: named after the inventor, Dr. Bryce E. Bayer of Eastman Kodak.

the output of four adjacent photosites to yield one RGB color pixel. This process yields an effective resolution that is one-half of the total number of photosites in the horizontal axis and one-half the total number of photosites in the vertical axis. Thus, a 4K Bayer pattern sensor can only yield 2K resolution. The fact that the camera system packages that effective 2K resolution into a 4K frame is irrelevant.

Resolution

Resolution is an area that is hotly debated in digital acquisition. HD cameras output a 1920 × 1080 pixel picture. In real-world terms, 1920 × 1080 pixels projected onto a 40-×-22½-foot movie screen would present pixels 1/4 inch square. It takes two horizontal pixels (one white and one black) to create one visible cycle, so the HD projection would yield 960 cycles of viewable information on such a screen. Viewing such an image at a distance of one and a half screen heights (33.75 feet) yields about 30.76 pixels per degree, and therefore approximately 15.36 cycles per degree of perceptible detail. The human eye is generally capable of detecting 40 to 60 (and in some cases up to 80) cycles per degree of detail. Images of 10 to 12 cycles per degree are almost universally perceived as blurry, whereas images of more than 20 cycles per degree are generally perceived to be sharp. This analysis demonstrates that the HD imaging system that operates at 15 to 16 cycles per degree is only minimally satisfactory for use in large-screen theatrical applications.

The widely used science of the modulation transfer function (MTF) considers that many factors enter into the effectiveness of any acquisition system. However, it can be roughly surmised that an image with 1920 pixels (960 cycles at 15.36 cycles per degree) is at least slightly inferior to the *de facto* digital cinema standard of 2048 × 1556 for Super 35 film (16.45 cycles per degree), which is inferior to 4K scanned negative at 4096 × 3112, which yields about 32.8 cycles per degree—a number more in accord with human vision.[34]

Keep in mind that once an image has been rendered at 1920 × 1080, that is the greatest resolution it can have. A camera original recorded at 1920 × 1080 is still 1920 × 1080 even when projected at 4K.[35] Likewise, once an image has been sampled into

---

[34] For a more in-depth discussion on the resolving powers and capabilities of the human vision system, Michael F. Deering's paper "A Photon-Accurate Model of the Human Eye" is recommended. It is a large (and intimidating) work, but once understood, yields many critical and valuable insights into the physiology and mechanics of how human beings see.

[35] It is important to note here that the original design spec for the 1920 × 1080 HD standard called for a viewing distance of four screen heights, yielding about 40 cycles per degree of resolution for the same pictures. But four screen heights is much farther than typical viewing distances currently found in either cinemas or homes.

8-bit color, it cannot acquire any additional color information or bits. Sampling and resampling errors are irreversible. *Data lost is data lost forever.* Color information lost in resampling cannot be recovered. Line resolution lost in resampling cannot be recovered.

Chip Size in Digital Cameras

The desire to work with a sensor the size of a 35mm film frame has become a strong force driving development in the area of sensor design, and many of the issues of digital cinema revolve around the basic differences between sensor technologies.

CCD vs. CMOS

CCD (charge-coupled device) and CMOS (complementary metal-oxide semiconductor) sensors both capture images by converting light into voltage, but they have different ways of converting the voltage into digital code values.

CCD imagers generally offer superior image performance and flexibility at the expense of system size and efficiency, whereas CMOS imagers offer better integration and smaller system size at the expense of image quality and flexibility.

Frame Rates

Loosely speaking, three frame rate standards are used with film cameras in motion picture and television production: 24 frames, 25 frames, and 30 frames per second.

The range of frame rates for acquisition with digital cameras is another issue. Many digital cameras are locked into a limited number of choices that correspond to the standard frame rates of broadcast television. Most digital cameras accommodate the frame rates of 23.98 fps (24/1.001), 24 fps, 29.97 fps (30/1.001), 30 fps, 50 fps, 59.98 fps (60/1.001), and 60 fps. Unlike film cameras, which may support a very wide range of frame rates, the current technology available for digital cameras is woefully lacking in its ability to acquire images at full resolution and full color bandwidth at more than 30 fps.

The term *60i* refers to 59.94 interlaced fields combined to create 29.97 frames, commonly known as 30 fps. This has been the standard video field/frame rate used for NTSC since its inception. The term *50i* refers to 50 interlaced fields combined to create 25 frames. This is the standard video field/frame rate used for European PAL and SECAM television.

The 24p (progressive) frame rate is a non-interlaced format and is now widely adopted for productions planning on migrating an HD video signal to film. The true 24-frame acquisition allows for direct, frame-for-frame, transfer to motion picture film. Additionally, cinematographers frequently turn to 24p for the cine look even if their productions are not going to be transferred to film, simply to acquire the look generated by the frame rate. The slower frame rate creates increased motion blur and flicker, both of which are associated with a film look. When transferred to NTSC television, the rate is effectively slowed to 23.976 fps, and when transferred to PAL or SECAM it is sped up to 25 fps. The 35mm movie cameras use a standard frame rate of 24 frames per second, though many digital cameras offer rates of 23.976 fps for NTSC television and 25 fps for PAL/SECAM.

The 25p format is a video format that records 25 progressive frames per second. This frame rate is derived from the original PAL television standard of 50i, which acquires 50 fields per second. Whereas 25p captures only half the motion resolution that normal 50i PAL registers, it yields a higher vertical resolution on moving subjects. It is also better suited to progressive-scan output, such as a transfer to film. Like 24p, 25p is often used to achieve a film look.

The term *30p* means 30-frame progressive, a non-interlaced format that records at 30 frames per second. This format evolved from 60i in much the same way that 25p evolved from the original 50i PAL standard. Progressive (non-interlaced) scanning mimics a film camera's frame-by-frame image capture and creates a cinematic-like appearance. Shooting at 30p offers video with no temporal interlace artifacts, resulting in greater clarity for moving subjects.

The 50p and 60p formats are new progressive formats used in high-end HDTV systems. While not technically yet part of the ATSC broadcast standard, they are quickly gaining popularity due to the superior image quality they offer.

Film Camera Aperture Sizes and HD Sensor Sizes

Digital camera sensors range from the size of a 35mm negative to a small fraction of that size. These sensors capture and reproduce images with varying degrees of success. Generally, the larger the sensor, the more faithfully it can reproduce the scene it records.

Lenses made for the 35mm format are not necessarily good for use on smaller format cameras, and lenses made for smaller format cameras are not necessarily good for use on larger format cameras. A lens made for a 35mm size sensor was designed and optimized to cover a much larger (and mono-planar) target surface area than that of a 2/3-inch sensor, and as a result, will almost always underperform when used with a smaller sensor. Still lenses made for full-frame 35mm film still photography will almost always underperform on cameras with smaller sensors.

Another issue is exclusive to three-chip digital cameras. The manufacturers of 2/3-inch three-chip cameras deliberately set the three color sensors at different flange depths from each other. Red light is notoriously hard to focus on mono-planar sensors, so the manufacturers of 2/3-inch three-chip cameras set the red sensor at a very different distance from the lens node than the green and blue sensors. Aware of this adjustment, the manufacturers of lenses dedicated to 2/3-inch three-chip cameras (such as the Zeiss Digi-Primes) expend great effort to focus red, green, and blue light at the particular distances set in the cameras, while bending each color of light to mitigate the resulting effects of chromatic aberration. Because of this, a lens made for a 2/3-inch three-chip camera would most likely exhibit very bad chromatic aberration if used on a larger mono-planar sensor.

Much has been discussed about the differences between the depth-of-field characteristics of 35mm mono-planar sensor cameras and 2/3-inch sensor cameras. In fact, their depth of field is subject to relatively simple mathematical formulas. The depth-of-field characteristics of 2/3-inch lenses can theoretically be matched to their 35mm equivalents by opening the f-stop as a scaled factor of the sensor size (that is, by a factor of 2.5), just as the focal length equivalent of a lens used with a 35mm sensor lens differs by a factor of 2.5 from the equivalent focal length of that lens used with a 2/3-inch sensor. The equivalent focal length and depth of field vary by the same factor. Accordingly, the focal length equivalent of a 50mm lens on a 35mm camera is a 20mm lens on a 2/3-inch camera. And the depth-of-field equivalent of a 35mm camera at f5.6 would be f2.4 on a 2/3-inch camera.

Table 3.1 Lens Focal Length Equivalency Chart

35mm Equivalent	2/3-Inch Equivalent	1/3-Inch Equivalent	Vertical Angle	Horizontal Angle
12.5mm	5mm	2.72mm	66.0°	87.0°
17.5mm	7mm	3.8mm	51.0°	69.6°
25mm	10mm	5.4mm	37.0°	52.0°
35mm	14mm	7.6mm	26.8°	38.4°
50mm	20mm	10.8mm	18.8°	27.0°
70mm	28mm	15.2mm	13.4°	19.4°
100mm	40mm	21.6mm	9.6°	13.8°
175mm	70mm	38.1mm	5.4°	7.8°

Red Channel Focus

The fact that the three sensors are set at different flange depths in cameras with 2/3-inch sensors makes a huge difference in perceived depth of field. No manufacturer of lenses for the 35mm format has ever succeeded in perfectly focusing all three color records on a mono-planar sensor, or for that matter, a film negative! Here's the biggest dirty little secret about film lenses: The red color record of every movie ever made on single-strip film was recorded out of focus!

What color is the human face? It is mostly red. So what is the most likely result of perfectly focusing red light on a 2/3-inch sensor? It will at least result in a very different-looking rendering of human facial features. Every pore, blemish, and nose hair will be in crisp focus. This is generally not desirable.

Being aware of this issue, there are many ways to deal with the variation in focus between the color channels produced by three-chip cameras. During post, some productions apply selective 1/2-, 1/3-, and 1/4-pixel Gaussian blurs to the red records with great success. Camera filters in front of the lens can also help. Keep in mind that the filter effects you might expect on 35mm (film or single-sensor) will be multiplied by a factor of 2.5 when used on 2/3-inch sensors.

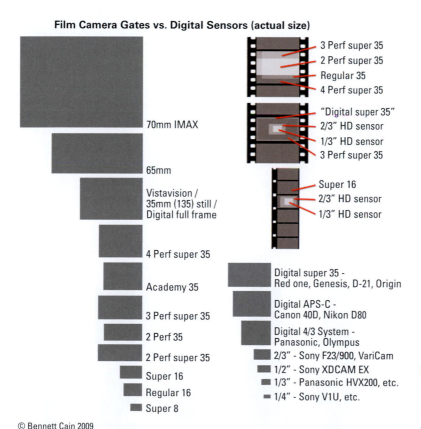

Film Camera Gates vs. Digital Sensors (actual size)

- 70mm IMAX
- 65mm
- Vistavision / 35mm (135) still / Digital full frame
- 4 Perf super 35
- Academy 35
- 3 Perf super 35
- 2 Perf 35
- 2 Perf super 35
- Super 16
- Regular 16
- Super 8

- 3 Perf super 35
- 2 Perf super 35
- Regular 35
- 4 Perf super 35

- "Digital super 35"
- 2/3" HD sensor
- 1/3" HD sensor
- 3 Perf super 35

- Super 16
- 2/3" HD sensor
- 1/3" HD sensor

- Digital super 35 - Red one, Genesis, D-21, Origin
- Digital APS-C - Canon 40D, Nikon D80
- Digital 4/3 System - Panasonic, Olympus
- 2/3" - Sony F23/900, VariCam
- 1/2" - Sony XDCAM EX
- 1/3" - Panasonic HVX200, etc.
- 1/4" - Sony V1U, etc.

© Bennett Cain 2009

Figure 3.58 Film camera apertures versus HD sensors. (Image courtesy of Bennett Cain, Negative Spaces, LLC. © 2010 www.negativespaces.com.)

Imager (Actual Size)	Lens Mount	ISO Base	Latitude	Frame Rates	Digital Sampling on Recording Media	Recording Format and Load Time	Bit Depth Recorded	Weight	Power Draw	Highlighted Positives	Average Rental Price
Phantom HD Gold — CMOS 36 Ø 25.5 × 25.5mm	PL PV Nikon Canon	250	10? Stops	5-1052 @ 1920×1080 4:4:4	2048 × 2048 Uncompressed RAW / 1920 × 1080 4:4:4	Uncompressed RAW 32G Internal RAM 8.9s@1000fps / 512G CineMags 2h12m @ 1000fps	14 Bit	12 lbs. / 14 lbs. w/ CineMag	80w	Compact Camera Size Uncompressed RAW CineStation Workflow Anamorphic Lenses 14 Bit RAW	$5000 w/2 CineMag (1TB) / $2500 Camera Only (16GB)
Weisscam HS-2 — CMOS 31.4 Ø 22.2 × 22.2mm	PL PV Nikon Canon	600	9 Stops	1-2000 @ 1920 × 1080 4:4:4	2048 × 1536 Uncompressed RAW / 1920 × 1080 4:4:4 or 4:2:2	Uncompressed RAW Internal RAM / DigiMag (2 TB) 1h31min @ 1000	12 Bit	13.2 lbs. / 29 lbs. w/ DigiMag	70w Camera / 85w DigiMag	Simultaneous HD-SDI & RAW Realtime RAW Playback Wireless Interface Anamorphic Lenses 35mm Depth of field	$3750 w/1 Digi-Mag (2 TB) / $3000 Camera Only (16GB)
Sony F35 — CCD 27.1 Ø 23.6 × 13.28mm	PL	640	12 Stops	1-50 4:4:4 / 1-50 4:2:2 (Docked) / 1-30 4:4:4 / 1-50 4:2:2 (Undocked)	1920 × 1080 4:4:4 or 4:2:2	HDCAM SR 50 Min / DPX s.two - OB-1	10 bit	29 lbs. w/SRW1 / 18 lbs. w/OB-1	106w w/SRW1 / 75w w/OB-1	Low Light Performance Easy HDCAM SR Workflow 4:4:4 Color Sampling	$3500 with SRW-1 & SRPC-1
Pana Genesis — CCD 27.1 Ø 23.6 × 13.28mm	Pana	500	12 Stops	1-50 4:4:4 / 1-50 4:2:2 (Docked) / 1-30 4:4:4 / 1-50 4:2:2 (Undocked)	1920 × 1080 4:4:4 or 4:2:2	HDCAM SR 50 Min / DPX Pana SSR	10 bit	29 lbs. w/SRW1 / 18 lbs. w/SSR	106w w/SRW1 / 75w w/OB-1	Low Light Performance Easy HDCAM SR Workflow 4:4:4 Color Sampling	$3500 with SRW-1 & SRPC-1
Sony F23 w/OB-1 — 2/3" 2/3" 2/3" CCD 11 Ø 8.8 × 6.6mm	B4	320	11 Stops	1-60 4:4:4 / 1-60 4:2:2 (Docked) / 1-30 4:4:4 / 1-60 4:2:2 (Undocked)	1920 × 1080 4:4:4 or 4:2:2	HDCAM SR 50 Min	10 bit	11 lbs. Camera Only / 29 lbs. w/SRW-1	106w w/SRW1 / 75w w/OB-1	Established Workflow 4:4:4 Color Sampling Wide Latitude	$3300 with SRW-1 & SRPC-1
Arri D-21 w/OB-1 — CMOS 29.6 Ø 23.7 × 17.8mm	PL	200	10 Stops	20-60p 4:2:2 / 20-30p 4:4:4 / 20-25p RAW	2880 × 2160 Uncompressed ARRIRAW / 1920 × 1080 4:4:4 or 4:2:2	ARRIRAW s.two - OB-1 30 min / HDCAM SR 50 min	12 Bit ARRIRAW s.two / 10 bit HDCAM SR	23 lbs. w/OB-1 / 16 lbs. Camera Only	60w Camera / 56w SRW-1	4:4:4 4:2:2 and/or RAW Optical Viewfinder Anamorphic lenses See outside frame lines	$3000 with SRW-1 & SRPC-1 or OB-1
Red One — CMOS 27.9 Ø 24.4 × 13.7mm	PL PV Nikon Canon	320* *next gen sensor advertised as ASA 800 (unconfirmed)	9 Stops	1-30p @4K / 1-60p @3K / 1-120p @2K	2K 3K 4K	Card (16GB) 9 mins / RAM (120GB) 60 min / Drive (320GB) 120 min	12 bit	9 lbs. Camera Only	65w	Cost vs. Performance Compact Size	$1100 with 16GB Cards RAM Drive

Camera	Imager (Actual Size)	Lens Mount	ISO Base	Latitude	Frame Rates	Digital Sampling on Recording Media	Recording Format & Load Time	Bit Depth Recorded	Weight	Power Draw	Highlighted Positives	Average Rental Price
SI-2K	CMOS 11 Ø 8.8 × 6.6mm (2/3")	PL	250	11 Stops	1-30p @ 2K & 1080p; 1-72p @ 720p	2K 1920 × 1080 4:4:4	2048 x 1152 CineForm RAW at 114Mbit/s; 1920 x 1080 CineForm RAW	12 bit	16 lbs. Standard; 1.2 lbs. Mini	60w	Configurable as a Standard or Mini Camera; Compact Small Size; Popular for 3D	$1200
Panasonic HPX-3000/3700	CCD 11 Ø 8.8 × 6.6mm	B4	500	12 Stops	3000: 24, 25p, 30p; 3700: 1-30p	1920 × 1080 4:2:2	5 - 32GB P2 Cards 200 min	10 bit	10.5 lbs.	43w	"HD D5" Quality; Cost vs. Performance; FCP 7.0 Supports Native AVC-I; 3700 Offers 4:4:4 Out	$1200 with two 16GB Cards
Sony HDW-F900	CCD 11 Ø 8.8 × 6.6mm	B4	320	F9 Stops 900R F900/3	24, 25 30p	1440 × 1080 3:1:1	HDCAM 50 Min	8 bit	12 lbs. F900R; 17.6 lbs. F900/3	34w F900R; 42w F900/3	Industry Workhorse; Proven Easy Workflow	$1100 F900R; $1000 F900/3
Panasonic HPX-2000/2700	CCD 11 Ø 8.8 × 6.6mm	B4	500	12 Stops	2000: 24, 25, 30p, 50p, 60p; 2700: 1-60p	1280 × 720 4:2:2	5 - 32GB P2 Cards 200 min	10 bit	10 lbs.	43w	HD D-5 quality @ Relatively low data & rental rates; Also Record 1080i	$575 w/five 16GB Cards
Sony PMW-EX3	CCD 8 Ø 6.4 × 4.8mm (1/2")	EX Mount	400	7 Stops	1-30p @1080p; 1-60p, 720p	1920 × 1080 4:2:0	2 - 32GB SxS Cards 200 min	8 Bit	4.2 lbs.	13w	Cost vs. Performance; Size; Flexibility to mount Professional 2/3" Lenses	$300 w/two 16GB Cards
Sony PMW-EX1	CCD 8 Ø 6.4 × 4.8mm (1/2")	FIXED	800	7 Stops	1-60p fps @ 720; 1-30p fps @ 1080	1920 × 1080 4:2:0	2 - 32GB SxS Cards 200 min	8 bit	6.2 lbs.	13w	Cost; 1/2" Imager; Full 1920 x 1080 imager and recording	$300 w/two 16GB cards
FILM	Full Aperture 31.1 Ø 24.9 × 18.1mm	PL, Pana, etc.	50 - 500	14 Stops	1 - 150p	1920x1080, 2K, 4K, 6K Uncompressed 4:4:4	3 Perforation 5m55s 400', 14m48s 1000'; 4 Perforation 4m26s 400', 11m 06s 1000'	16 bit (Linear); 10 bit (log)	25 lbs. 400' Load; 28 lbs. 1000' Load	55w	Established Workflow; Excessive Latitude; Proven Archival Value	$2000 w/two Mags
Thomson Viper	CCD 11 Ø 8.8 × 6.6mm (2/3")	B4	320	10 Stops	23.97, 24, 25, 29.97 30p 4:4:4; 23.97, 24, 25, 29.97, 30, 60i 4:2:2	1920 × 1080 4:4:4 or 4:2:2	HDCAM SR 50 Min; VENOM FLASHPACK 10 Min; DPX on all compatible Dual or Single Link DDR Systems	8 Bit; 10 bit HDCAM SR, DDR	7.5 lbs. Camera Only	40w	Cost vs. Performance; Compact Size Light Weight; Native Widescreen 2:35 Mode	$1000 Requires Separate Record System

Lenses

When prepping to shoot a production, begin by selecting the best lenses that the production can afford. Putting a poor lens on a good camera will make the camera look poor. Putting a high-quality lens on a lesser quality camera will make that camera look as good as it can. Rental houses offer various types of high-quality lenses that can be used on digital cameras, both with 2/3-inch and 35mm sensors.

Keep in mind that lenses designed for 2/3-inch sensors yield much greater depth of field than lenses designed for 35mm sensors. This is important to consider when selecting lenses.

The Viewing System

The monitoring of the camera image on set is immensely important when shooting digital. A camera system can *bake in*[36] the color space, the resolution, the bit depth, end even the noise level. However, in the event of a bad decision or a change of direction, a change may need to be made. And if the mistakes are baked in, they may not be able to be undone. There are several ways to prepare for such a situation:

1. Set up a Camera Control center with sophisticated color correction capability—the "lab-on-the-set" approach. This arrangement allows the Digital Imaging Technician (DIT) to carefully monitor many aspects of the digital recording and adjust levels as necessary. The role of the DIT in this work style is critical because the changes made have a direct effect on the recorded image (i.e., they are baked in) and in many instances cannot be reversed or modified at a later date.

2. Set up a Camera Control center with a Look Management System only. No color correction is baked in to the image being recorded on the set. The portable Look Management System allows the cinematographer to compare, adjust, and create looks on the set without risk.

3. Set up a Camera Control center where the image data is recorded in a raw format. The monitor is used exclusively for viewing.

The shooting work style is usually determined by the cinematographer, in conjunction with the director and the producer. Each style has its advantages.

Even without a viewing monitor on the set, the camera operator can always check the last few seconds of each take with the

---

[36] Bake in: take the various parameters and change the data to take those into account. This can eliminate some of the post-process work but also eliminates much of the flexibility later to make changes.

camera's record review function. The cinematographer and director can also use a portable HD monitor to observe and check details that concern them.

In the case of a live production, or one with a tight delivery schedule, on-set color correction can eliminate the need for a long and expensive post-production period. A disadvantage of this strategy, however, is that the visual choices made on the set get baked in. Highlight or shadow detail may be permanently lost due to choices made in exposure and contrast, and the color record may be biased in a direction that, upon later viewing, is seen as not serving the intent of the production, yet cannot be undone.

Viewing Environment

Human perception is very sensitive to ambient light. The color and intensity of the light surrounding a monitor or screen being used to evaluate an image will significantly affect any judgment made regarding the density, contrast, or color of that image.

SMPTE has published recommended practices to create a viewing environment for the evaluation of color television images (SMPTE RP-166). It specifies standards for monitor setup, screen size, viewing distance, the color and brightness of surrounding surfaces, and the color and intensity of ambient light. Most critical are the color and brightness of the area immediately surrounding and behind the monitor—what is seen in the viewer's field of view.

It may be difficult to meet all of these standards on a practical set. However, a shaded corner (created with flags), a gray piece of cloth draped behind the monitor, and a backlight setting the neutral reference source (approximately 6500°) may be adequate.

The Recording System

Media used to record digital images include magnetic tape, disk drives, and solid-state media. Digital cameras may record to magnetic tape, a disk drive, or flash memory in a wide range of configurations.

Several popular digital cameras (such as the Panavision Genesis) can have an on-board digital tape recorder. This gives the camera a similar configuration to a film camera. It can be handheld without the need for a tether cable connection to a remote recorder. Tapes must be changed, though less often than with film magazines.

By far, the most common digital tape recording format used today with cinema-level cameras is the Sony HDCAM-SR. SR recording offers two compression options: HQ (2.7:1) and SQ

(4.2:1). HQ records 4:4:4 10-bit; SQ records 4:2:2 10-bit. SR compression is considered by some to be visually lossless, but like many compression schemes, can sometimes present problems in compositing and greenscreen or bluescreen work. Testing is always recommended.

Other on-camera digital tape recording systems include HDCAM and DVCPRO-HD. HDCAM and DVCPRO-HD are suitable for high-definition television, but they are generally not suitable for digital cinema work.

Several popular digital cameras have solid-state digital recording systems. Flash memory cards or solid-state recording decks mount on the camera. Other devices record remotely with a cable connecting to the camera. Solid-state memory systems have several advantages: They are lighter, more rugged, and easy to back up or transfer to external storage.

Some digital cameras do not support any on-board recording system. These cameras must be tethered—connected to an external remote recording system. This remote system may range from a tape deck (HDCAM-SR deck with processor) to a breadbox (an S.two hard-drive system) to a computer disk array the size of a small refrigerator. External disk and solid-state systems require additional time and resources to back up data and transfer data to post, so as to free up space on the drive for future recordings. Some data recorder vendors (Codex, S.two) have devoted significant effort to addressing these issues. In the process, they have made it easier to record in data mode (which must be rendered) while still generating DPX files or other formats that can be used for immediate viewing.

Tethering a camera may sound inconvenient, and it does put restrictions on shooting, but it also brings some conveniences. The cable leads can often be quite long—300 feet or more when optical fiber is used. The tether provides a high-quality connection to the video village. The camera itself may be quite small and light and able to process high data rates, which allow for the high frame rates used for specialty purposes. The tether may also support two-way communication, motion control, and power.

Tape-based recording systems work in a streaming workflow. Cameras and sound recorders record to tape in real time. Signals play back from tape in real time. This is the closest digital equivalent to the analog arrangement where devices are connected by simple wires. Communication between devices by an HD-SDI connection is usually an indication that this approach being used.

File-based workflows treat data in a more computer-like way. Once data has been produced by a camera, typically recorded to disk or a solid-state device, it can be manipulated in a more versatile fashion. The random access retrieval capability of data saves time. Devices in a file-based workflow are connected with a computer networking protocol. There is a large installed base of streaming-workflow equipment. Although the industry is now in a transitional period, ultimately, all post-production will likely be done using file-based workflows.

Scene Files

Scene files allow camera users to move quickly from one saved look to another, without having to manually make multiple setting adjustments in the menu of the camera. These scene files feature preset menu settings that are suitable for sports, news, beauty, music videos, night scenes, and various creative looks.

They can be used to store and transport looks such as black-and-white, high contrast, low contrast, bleach bypass, as well as lens maps and tables for individually color-mapping zoom lenses and prime lens sets. Note that scene files vary widely in format from one brand of camera to another and are rarely interchangeable between makes and models of cameras.

Scene files have the serious disadvantage that when used, they destructively and permanently bake in the look being applied. They are not reversible in post-production, so use this method with caution, especially in visual effects work. Use of scene files is often unavoidable and necessary, such as when using an 8-bit camera system like the Sony F-900 and recording to its onboard HDCAM deck.

On-Set Look Management

Ideally, the full dynamic range of the original uncorrected scenes should be recorded during production. A look can be created or applied on set, either as an ASC CDL (color decision list) recipe or as a LUT (look-up table). The look would not be baked in, but instead attached to the original scenes as metadata and used throughout the workflow nondestructively to apply the cinematographer's look to the original camera images as displayed via a calibrated monitor or digital projector.

The basic (RGB primary color grading) look for a scene can be established on set and saved as a 3D LUT or as an ASC CDL (with compliant applications). It can then be used to maintain a consistent look for dailies, editorial, and preview screenings. With LUTs, this cinematographer's look reference can only provide a visual reference for final color correction in the DI. With the ASC CDL, this cinematographer's look reference can actually be used as a starting point for the final color correction.

LUT-based corrections are very powerful but hard to modify. A LUT-based workflow can often require applying several modifications to image data in series, which may introduce problematic amounts of noise. For maximum flexibility in final color grading, an ASC CDL-based on-set look should be used. In either case, the look should not be baked in to the original recorded image—until the final DI color correction sessions.

ASC Color Decision List (ASC CDL)

The ASC CDL is a cross-platform data exchange format for RGB primary color grading/color correction systems. It is a framework that allows the interchange of basic color corrections between color correction systems made by different manufacturers and different facilities. The ASC CDL defines functions and interchange formats for the basic primary correction operations of slope, offset, and power (similar to the standard lift, gain, and gamma, but consistent in all implementations) as well as saturation. It allows for the meaningful exchange of these values from one proprietary software or hardware platform to another.

FILMING LIVE-ACTION PLATES TO BE USED IN VFX
Bill Taylor, ASC

Large-format still rear projection came into its own in the 1930s alongside motion picture rear projection in the major studios. The extremely high-quality 8 × 10 images were shot on glass plate negatives with bellows-type view cameras. *Plate* became the generic term for any still or motion picture background photography.

Even though most composites are now created digitally in post, the background, or any live-action footage that will be used for visual effects, is still called the *plate*. For simplicity's sake, assume a simple two-element shot, containing a background (the original plate photography) and a foreground, which could be any added element, from an actor driving a car to gigantic fighting robots. Of course, the added element could actually appear to be behind the plate, as in a typical matte painting.

The requirements for plate photography vary from the simple to the complex. To produce a convincing composite, even a simple locked-off background has to match the eventual composited foreground in lighting, camera position, the angle of view of the lens, and the camera tilt. For some shots, clean plates are also required, that is, plates made without some specific element. (See the earlier section on clean plates.)

Camera Position (Station Point)

The camera height must match the height, or apparent height, of the foreground camera, unless a deliberate scaling effect is desired. Obviously, if the ground is not visible in the shot, some plausible place where the actor could be standing can be inferred, as on a mountain path where only the deep background is visible.

The distances to key elements in the foreground and background must match. If the camera cannot get far enough back to include the foreground, going to a mismatched wider lens may cause serious problems. Instead consider a pan or new composition that includes the desired elements.

Angle of View

If the entire background image will be used as the background to the composite scene, the horizontal angles must match. If the foreground and background are shot in different formats, equivalent lenses (matching degrees of view) must be used.

It is good practice to shoot the background plate one lens size wider than the foreground, allowing some movement within the frame. If the photographic quality is good, the slight blowup required will not be noticeable. The background image can be *much* wider than the foreground if multiple cameras are used. (See below.)

Lighting Considerations

Record the sun position and angle, as well as key/fill ratio and color temperature information (see the section on data capture). Regardless of the compositing technique, it's always preferable to shoot the background first. (For rear projection, the background obviously *must* be shot first.) The foreground will be lit to match the background, so the background lighting must be appropriate and congenial to the foreground.

For greenscreen compositing, it's possible to shoot foregrounds first (although not recommended), in the hope that the matching lighting condition can be found when the plate is shot. It's not always possible in practice if the weather doesn't cooperate, which can lead to great difficulties. [On Mike Nichols' *The Birdcage* (1996), the writer had a crew waiting fruitlessly for 10 days for sun in Florida to match high-contrast foregrounds already shot.] When there's no alternative, a study of maps of the eventual location will at least yield correct sun direction and elevation at the appropriate times of the day.

It's a challenging job to simulate single-source hard daylight on the stage. Fill light (supposedly sky light and bounce light from the environment) must be shadowless and the correct color balance to the key light. These issues are touched on earlier in this chapter in *Greenscreen and Bluescreen Photography*.

Camera Tilt

Tilt is probably the most important dimension to match, especially in scenes where the new foreground character must walk in depth (on the z axis) in the shot. The horizon (or vanishing point) in the foreground must match the horizon in the background. Even though overt perspective cues to the horizon may not be visible in a greenscreen foreground, it can become painfully obvious when there is a mismatch.

Background Quality

Because the background image must sometimes be scaled, heavily color corrected, and otherwise manipulated, the background should be of the highest possible quality to begin with. If the background is shot on film, use the finest grain, longest tonal-range film that's practical. Kodak Vision2 50D is perfect for day exteriors. If the foreground is 4-perf 35mm, consider 8-perf (VistaVision) for the background. Available 8-perf cameras such as the Beaucam are small and light, and though negative costs double for the plates, it's usually a minor increase in cost over the photography of an entire feature film.

If the show is digital, consider shooting the backgrounds on film, a more forgiving medium with (usually) a longer tonal range, especially for potentially harsh day exterior photography. If backgrounds are shot digitally, shoot and record full-bandwidth 4:4:4 uncompressed or with the minimum compression the camera system can deliver. Expose carefully to protect highlight details. Consider 3K or 4K photography for the backgrounds (essential if the rest of the film is 4K) as new high-resolution cameras come on line.

If shooting digitally, disable all sharpening or detail functions. Any needed sharpening can be added in the composite.

Moving Plates

Shooting from a moving camera adds new issues, since several reference points are no longer fixed. Because it's a typical problem, a car shot will serve as an example.

The first thing to establish is what the final composite is intended to simulate. Is the camera supposed to be mounted to the car, or is it supposed to be on a tow vehicle or a chase vehicle?

The second issue is mounting the camera or cameras so the correct point of view is accurately simulated. Mismatches can yield disconcerting or unintended hilarious results (such as giant cars looming in the background); in either case the illusion is destroyed.

Scouting the Camera Positions

With stand-ins in the key seats of the hero car, walk around the car with a finder and locate where the cameras should be to cover the scene. Find the appropriate focal length for each setup. Then measure each camera position and shoot still images from that position showing the actors and a slate.

Measure the camera height from the ground.

Locate the camera relative to the hero car: Once the height is known a triangulated measurement from two prominent points on the car to the lens will locate it with more than adequate precision. (Please refer to *Triangulation as a Method of Recording Camera Data* earlier in this chapter.) For more precision, measure to the iris diaphragm of the lens, which is usually at the nodal point, the place inside the lens where the principal rays cross. For example, the lens might be 8 feet 6 inches from the top left corner of the windshield and 9 feet 2 inches from the top right corner.

The vertical angle is easily measured with an inclinometer, but the horizontal angle is a bit trickier. It's very straightforward if the camera head has the pan calibrated in degrees: Zero the head on the centerline of the car and note the angle to the left or right of zero. If a calibrated pan is not available, find and note a feature on the car that falls somewhere on the vertical centerline of the viewer. Back that up with a visual estimate of the angle.

A Case Study

In a typical example, two actors have a long dialog scene in the front seat of the car. The storyboards show that the director wants to cover the scene in a two-shot looking back, two singles looking back, and angled side shots from both sides of the car. In an important distinction, the boards show that the two singles must be from cameras on separate parallel lines, rather than from a single vantage point matching the two-shot.

The distinction is important, because if the two singles were from the station point of the two-shot, it's likely that scaling and repositioning the background made for the two-shot would have sufficed for the singles if the background image were sufficiently high in quality. In any case, all three backgrounds must be in sync, since the editor will likely cut from the two-shot to the singles and back.

Any scheme that can reduce the number of trips down the road is worth considering. The time required to return to the start point can be significant, especially if there is a big entourage of picture cars to be repositioned. The rental costs of extra cameras is small compared the cost of extra days of shooting, risking mismatching weather, etc.

In the case in question, it was a straightforward job to rig three cameras on a camera car to cover all three rear-looking plates at once, in one trip down the road. On the head end of the setup, the hero car was lined up with stand-ins in the correct orientation to the road. A slate was shot on the film camera as well as still images from off-axis that showed the relative positions of the cameras and actors. Not only was there no doubt as to which scene those backgrounds belonged to, the actual lighting was recorded as a reference for the stage shoot.

Camera Cars

Camera cars have been designed for plate shooting that range from high-powered, high-speed electric carts to custom-built trucks like the Shotmaker. The most important feature on any camera car is a suspension that produces a smooth ride free of bumps and vibration. All camera cars feature fittings for camera mounts on all sides at any height from scraping the ground upward. Many of the trucks will accept booms for operated shots on the road. Booming shots are rarely useful for plates, but the booms allow quick repositioning of the camera, which is important when time is tight. Some booms allow mounting of multiple cameras, permitting (for example) tight and wider versions of the same backgrounds to be shot simultaneously.

Cameras are typically connected to monitors on the chassis or in the cab. These monitors are never big enough for critical playback inspection, so the footage shot should be checked on big screens before the shots are signed off and a retake becomes impossible.

Camera Car Safety Issues

Crew members have been killed or injured far too often on camera cars.

Camera crews and, particularly, crane operators riding on the chassis are potentially in danger. Crews riding in the cab are far safer than those riding outside.

Good safety practices are a must and cannot be overemphasized.

Just for starters: Every rider on a moving camera car must wear a crash helmet and be belted in. The moving car must have a protective buffer around it provided by police vehicles. If the job includes photographing stunt action by other vehicles, it should go without saying that it must be both safe and well rehearsed.

Purpose-Built Crane Cars

The Ultimate Arm (and similar equipment) is a remotely operated camera arm mounted to the top of a high-powered SUV. It can rotate 360 degrees around the vehicle and rise 12 feet or higher. Some arms can mount two lightweight cameras like the Arri 250 side by side.

Advantages of Crane Cars

Crane cars are much faster and more maneuverable than a vehicle like the Shotmaker.

Repositioning the camera between setups can be very fast, since there is no need to detach the camera, reattach it, reroute and reconnect cables, etc. Where a combination of plate work and location work must be shot, the crane can often substitute for a tripod for static shots. Particularly at freeway speeds, crane cars are much safer than cranes grip operated from the back of a truck.

Limitations of Crane Cars

Crane cars lack the flexibility of bigger vehicles like Shotmaker, don't have the variety of camera attachment points, and have limited space for crew members inside the vehicle. When operated at high road speeds, cameras on booms are vulnerable to wind buffeting. Matte boxes have a high wind load, so they should be kept small and, if possible, be replaced with a lens shade.

Monitors in crane cars tend to be even smaller than monitors in bigger vehicles, so it's even more essential to review work during the day on big screens to be certain that vibration, missed focus and equipment glitches have not ruined otherwise good takes.

Vibration and Camera Stabilization

A good camera vehicle will remove enough vibration by itself to produce useful footage on the highway with wider lenses (in 35mm film photography, 50mm lenses and wider). With longer lenses and on rougher roads, camera stabilization becomes important.

Note that the issue is not just stability of the filmed image. Unsteady film can be stabilized in post with common software. However, the sudden jarring motion produced by road roughness or wind buffeting can streak or blur the image, effectively destroying the frame. A software fix can interpolate a replacement frame from the frames on either side but this is not a sure thing if there are many frames to be fixed. It's much better to shoot an unblurred shot to begin with.

Gyroscopic stabilizers like the Libra head can produce stable shots with long lenses and big zooms under most circumstances. There's a wide choice of equipment in this category that is well worth testing.

Road Speed

High road speeds are sometimes unnecessary even if called for in the script. If all the foreground cars are under the control of production and background action permits, consider shooting at a slower road speed and undercranking. Wind loads increase geometrically with speed so even a modest road speed reduction can yield substantial dividends in vibrations and buffeting.

Road Speed Related to Camera Angle

When the camera is 90 degrees to the direction of travel, objects near the camera appear to whip past quickly and disproportionately to the actual road speed. Due to this effect it has been common practice to reduce road speed to 60% when shooting side plates, 80% when shooting at 45 degrees, and so on (60 mph becomes 36 mph at 90 degrees, and so forth). Obviously this is a problem when shooting front and side plates simultaneously unless the background action permits under- or overcranking of one of the cameras.

When the subject matter permits, consider overcranking the side-looking cameras. For example, if the forward-looking cameras shoot at 24 fps, shoot the side-looking footage at 40 fps. The footage can be sped back up in post if necessary.

The whole issue of modifying road speed to camera angle is somewhat subjective. As more and more traveling footage is shot on location with car-mounted cameras photographing the real actors from all angles, audiences have become more accustomed to the speed effect in the side angles. Some directors find the effect unobjectionable. If composited plates must cut in with real car-mount photography, they should be shot at the matching speed relationship to the real photography.

Of course, if the plate is shot with a panoramic multicamera rig like CircleVision, camera speed must be the same in all cameras.

Precautions

Lens flare must be carefully controlled (beware the vibrating sun shield), and constant vigilance maintained for dirt on the front filter surface. An air jet–type rain deflector can also deflect dust and smaller bugs.

Panoramic Rigs

When a sequence requires wide-ranging camera movement, or when it's uncertain what part of the background scene must be in frame at a given moment, a panoramic background can be created with a combination of several images. Usually the multiple images are filmed simultaneously with several cameras, but in some cases the background can be shot with a single camera at several successive angles.

On the first *Fast and Furious* (2001) film, all the night race car interiors were shot on a bluescreen stage. VFX Supervisor Mike Wassel suggested shooting the background plates with a modified CircleVision rig, which was built by Jim Dickson. (CircleVision normally shoots a full 360 degrees for special venue films with little overlap between panels. In the background plate mode, the lenses are one step wider than normal to allow a comfortable overlap for stitching the images together.)

To achieve the desired low vantage point and high road speed, the rig was mounted on a motorcycle with three of the usual nine cameras removed to allow for the motorcycle driver. Thad Beier and Hammerhead Productions took the resulting six strips of film, stabilized them, warped them, stitched them together, and projected the result onto a 240-degree digital cyclorama. (The same plate material was used as texture for a simple 3D model of the street.) The rig was flipped on the motorcycle to shoot the opposite side of the street. Only two trips down the street were necessary thanks to six cameras.

Variations on this idea involving wide lenses on 8-perf VistaVision cameras and 65mm cameras have been used on many other films for car and train backgrounds. Mark Weingartner has shot many HDRI panoramas, both still and motion picture, for *The Dark Knight* (2008) and several other films, in some cases creating full hemispherical coverage. Please refer to his section *Shooting Elements for Compositing* in this chapter.

Digital panoramic systems are under development. Dynamic range and bandwidth requirements for daylight, exterior, relatively uncontrolled photography stretch current digital systems to their limits. One obvious benefit is that the 30-minute reload for multicamera film systems is unnecessary.

On the Water

Gyro stabilization is vital on water to keep the horizon level. In *Bruce Almighty* (2003) an extended greenscreen sequence took place at Niagara Falls, supposedly on a tour boat. Panoramic plates were shot from a tugboat in the river below the falls with the Beaucam, a small, lightweight 8-perf camera, on the Libra head. The Libra kept the horizon level and ironed out the high level of vibration from the tug's engines, which had to work hard to hold the boat in place against the current.

Speedboats are even more of a challenge. The Perfect Horizon head from Motion Picture Marine is powerful enough to deal with heavy cameras and high rates of pitch and roll.

On the water it's critical to keep spray off the front filter surface. There are two basic approaches: electric rain deflectors in which a clear disk spins in front of the lens and throws off droplets by centrifugal force and an air squeegee system in which air nozzles blow the front filter surface dry. Camera equipment rental services often provide a choice of types.

The larger spinning deflectors drive the disk from the center while the lens sees through a radial off-center section of the disk. The disk must therefore be quite large to cover the front element of a big lens. The other approach is to drive the disk from the circumference, resulting in a much smaller and lighter package. A small air jet is needed to clear the tiny droplet that remains at the center of the spinning disk.

Don't use polarizers with spinning disk systems. The combination can produce flickering color shift.

Air squeegee systems position multiple nozzles around the front glass, usually on adjustable segmented tubes. These set-ups add less weight to the camera than spinners and occupy less space, but they use a lot of air, which must come from nitrogen bottles or a compressor.

Air to Air

The most versatile systems for aerial plates are the helicopter-mounted gyro-stabilized balls. A skilled pilot can "thread the needle" with the camera, making possible precision hook-ups and handoffs to other cameras, as in the main titles of *The Birdcage* (1996) and *The Fighting Temptations* (2003). In those two films, the shot began on a helicopter and was handed off invisibly to a camera crane and then to a Steadicam operator, who walked into the final set. The best known system of this type is Ron Goodman's pioneering Spacecam, which can be mounted to the nose or the side of several models of aircraft. Spacecam can shoot 4-perf and 8-perf 35mm film, as well as 5-perf and 15-perf (IMAX size) 65mm film, and can accommodate most digital cameras.

Spacecam can record very accurate GPS data synchronized to the camera, including aircraft speed, height, and direction as well as pan-tilt-zoom lens axis data. This data provides much of the information needed for motion tracking and matchmoving the plates, a real plus for visual effects use.

Small 35mm cameras and digital cameras can fly on purpose-built miniature radio-controlled helicopters. In the hands of skilled pilots, they can produce good results. They have the advantage that they can land and take off anywhere with little ground support. In practice there are some significant limitations. These small craft are easily blown off course by crosswinds and have a maximum height of 500 feet. They cannot be flown safely over people (think "upside-down, flying lawn mower") and in the past have had reliability problems in the field. There may be specific applications for which a test is justified.

To shoot high-speed fixed wing aircraft (and high air-speed photography in general), there's no substitute for a jet camera platform. One widely used system, the Nettman Vector Vision rig, is built into a Lear jet and can shoot digital, 35mm, 65mm 8-perf, and 65mm 15-perf from either top- or belly-mount lenses. The image is optically relayed to the camera inside the aircraft, so reloads can be done in the air. Although the optical path is complex, the resulting image is very high in quality.

Cable Systems

When the required plate camera POV is relatively near to the ground (below 200 feet), cable systems fill the gap between helicopters and camera cranes. Cable systems can operate safely over people and sensitive locations, with no prop downwash or dust.

Early cable systems flew a Steadicam operator point to point in a minimal cable car, similar to a ski lift. The operator could dismount from the car and continue the shot seamlessly on the ground. James Muro, ASC, operated the first shot of this type in *The Mighty Quinn* (1989).

Garrett Brown's original Skycam was the first multicable system that could fly the camera anywhere within the 3D space defined by the three or four computer-controlled winch stations. The prototype Skycam shot the plates for *The Boy Who Could Fly* (1986), but later found much more use in video sports photography than in film.

A highly refined system that has been through many evolutionary stages, Jim Rodnunsky's Cablecam, can fly film or digital cine cameras in very large 3D volumes (the size of a football stadium) or over great distances, all at very high speeds. Unlike earlier systems, Cablecam uses a central winch station running cables to high, lightweight stanchions, which can be erected nearly anywhere. Cablecam is the nearest thing to the proverbial "skyhook" with the ability to put a camera nearly anywhere with great precision. The only limitation is cable clearance, which can be overcome with clever set design. For example, set elements that conflict with the cables can be built to move out of the way at the appropriate moment, or they can be digital models tracked into the shot.

Spydercam is the overall trade name for a quartet of overhead cable systems. The system first became famous for traveling vertically at high speeds down the sides of buildings in *Spider-Man* (2001), but it can also travel long distances from point to point. Some Spydercam systems can now operate in 3D space. One Spydercam system (Talon) is motion-control repeatable, while another (Bullet) can fly 1 mile at 100 mph.

Both Spydercam and Cablecam can previsualize and program in Maya.

Believability

As with visual effects in general, the underlying secret to convincing plate photography is to ask, "How would this be photographed if it could really be photographed? Where would the camera really be, and how would it cover the action?" If the answer is simply impossible (the camera is hovering in space 2 feet from a surfer's face, for instance), proceed with caution! The result may never be believable, however well executed.

SHOOTING ELEMENTS FOR COMPOSITING
Mark H. Weingartner

The VFX Supervisor of the 21st century has access to the most complex 3D procedural solutions in order to generate smoke, clouds, flames, water, debris, and even crowds. Sometimes, however, the fastest, easiest, cheapest, and most rewarding way to get the elements is to have a special effects technician come to the nearest parking lot or stage, set up a camera, and just shoot!

What Is an Element?

In broad terms, an element is something or someone that is generally shot in such a way as to make it easy to separate from its background—grist for the compositor's mill—as distinguished from a plate, which is generally used as the background for a shot. Elements might be shot against black, white, gray, blue, green, red, or sky, depending on the material being photographed. Technically speaking, elements run the gamut from generic water dribbles and wafts of smoke all the way to multi-million-dollar movie stars acting in front of green screens or blue screens. Shooting elements can be complex—involving the lighting of giant green screens for high-speed photography or complicated motion control shots—or as simple as lining up a few coworkers in costume and shooting them with a prosumer video camera in order to populate a distant crowd scene.

The decision to shoot elements rather than to create them in a CG environment is situational. Since most visual effects facilities have abandoned their stages and camera equipment in order to make room for more workstations, the costs involved in putting together an element shoot can look daunting, but compared to the timeline involved in seeing successive versions of something being built in the CG world, an experienced visual effects camera crew with the support of a competent special effects team can experiment quickly and film many different versions of an effect in a short period of time.[37]

Generally, photography paid for by a studio is considered work for hire and rights to its use are retained by the studio. For this reason, it may be beneficial for the visual effects facility to arrange its own element shoots and to retain ownership of the material for future use on other projects.

Stock Footage

Some element needs can be filled with stock footage. Several agencies sell stock footage in various formats. Some of them even distribute specific collections of clouds, flames, or generic outdoor backgrounds. Finding appropriate footage involves wading through a lot of material and hoping that it is available in a usable format, but sometimes it works out. The explosion sequence of the big spaceship in *Event Horizon* (1997), a Paramount picture, actually incorporated a small piece of a space explosion from another Paramount film.

Types of Elements

In discussing element photography, it is useful to categorize the types of elements a couple of different ways. One can differentiate between full-sized elements and scaled elements, and one can also differentiate between shot-specific elements and more generic ones. These two sets of distinctions are not mutually exclusive—either miniature or full-sized elements can be destined for a specific shot. Likewise, one can shoot a library of generic elements as scale elements, full-size elements, or a combination of both.

---

[37] Unit Production Managers will often be inclined to get the Second Unit DP or one of the camera operators to go off and form a splinter unit to shoot elements, but real value is added when using an experienced VFX Director of Photography. A VFX DP thinks out of the box for a living with regard to frame rates, camera positions, and numerous other aspects of the job, and making use of that experience can often result in accomplishing the goal faster than a generalist's methodology of trial and error.

Generic versus Shot-Specific Elements

Resizing elements in the digital world is only a mouse-click away, but even with this ease of adjustment, there are benefits to shooting elements in a shot-specific way. In shooting an element for a specific shot, one has the advantage of being able to choose the appropriate lens and distance to match the perspective of the shot, the appropriate framing to make the shot work, and the appropriate lighting so as to integrate the element into the scene. Any camera position data from the original shot can be used to aid in line-up, but with elements such as water, pyro, flames, or atmospherics that are likely to break the edges of frame, it is best to overshoot (shoot a slightly wider shot), which will allow the compositor a bit of freedom in repositioning the element to best advantage without bits of the action disappearing off the edge of the frame. VFX Directors of Photography often use all of the area of full-frame 35mm or, when possible, VistaVision,[38] in order to allow for the most repositioning without sacrificing resolution when resizing or repositioning the image in post.

When it comes to shooting actors in front of blue screen, green screen, or sky, once the correct distance and angle have been worked out to ensure proper perspective, one frequent practice is to select a longer focal length lens in order to magnify the subject. As long as the subject does not break the edge of frame, this magnification yields better edge detail, which allows for easier, cleaner matte extraction.

Even though there are obvious advantages to shooting elements for specific shots, once the equipment and crew are assembled, one may realize a great return on investment by shooting a library of elements with variations in size, focal length, orientation, action, and lighting. These generic elements can be used as necessary in building many different shots, scheduled or added.

When shooting either generic or shot-specific elements such as flame, dust hits, atmosphere, etc., it makes sense to shoot some lighting, focal length, and angle variations—sometimes the correct setup ends up not looking nearly as good as some variation shot just in case.

Determining Element Needs

During the bidding and pre-production of a project, the numbers and types of elements needed for various shots are usually broken down and categorized.[39] During production it is common to

---

[38] VistaVision: a special format camera that shoots with horizontal running motion picture film to provide a large size image equivalent to a 35mm still camera.

[39] Elements shot for stereoscopic 3D production must be carefully shot with stereo camera rigs, because elements shot "single eye" will often be very difficult to integrate into a 3D shot.

keep a running list of new elements that are required. Additional elements may be added to the list after a review of the shots in the edited sequence or during the post-production work on those shots.

The first step is to review the list of desired elements with an SFX Supervisor and a VFX DP if at all possible. Their expertise can make things much easier and provide insights to alternate techniques. A skilled special effects person can do wonders with devices they have or with devices they can construct rapidly. Certainly elements that require anything potentially dangerous such as flames or explosions will require a special effects person with the appropriate license.

Cheating

The only hard and fast rule with regard to shooting elements is that they have to look right when they are incorporated into a shot. Since individual elements are shot one at a time, all sorts of tricks can be used when creating them. One can composite together elements shot in different scales, at different frame rates, with different camera orientations, and even with different formats of cameras. An element can be flipped and flopped, played backward, recolored, pushed out of focus, made partially transparent—in short, the VFX Supervisor has an arsenal that includes all of the different types of shooting tricks plus all of the various compositing tricks for creating the desired look.

Even as the bar is constantly being raised in creating realistic digital effects, numerous tricks of the trade of the old school creators of special photographic effects[40] are still valid. To paraphrase Duke Ellington, "If it looks good, it is good." Some types of atmospheric elements, such as smoke, steam, or fog, can be shot small and scaled up, often being shot overcranked in order to give the correct sense of scale. Water effects can be scaled up somewhat, though issues with surface tension limit the degree to which this works. Different materials can be used in clever ways; for *Star Wars: The Phantom Menace* (1999) large amounts of salt[41] were poured over a black background to create the illusion of waterfalls seen in a Naboo matte painting. For *Independence Day* (1996) a comprehensive library of steam, dust, glass, and debris elements was shot on a single day of thousand-frame-per-second photography. Those elements were massaged in countless ways and incorporated in many shots of destruction. To create the

[40] Before the rise of digital compositing and CG effects, most visual effects were referred to as *special photographic effects*.
[41] Care should be taken when filming any material that may produce dust or small particles. Use eye protection and breathing masks.

effect of a man whose skin was on fire in a zero-gravity environment for *Event Horizon* (1997) hundreds of individual bits of paraffin-soaked paper were attached to a specially constructed puppeted mannequin and burned in small groups to create small patches of flame that were not drawn together by convection. For the free-fall sequence in *Vanilla Sky* (2001), Tom Cruise was suspended upside-down and wind-blown with E-fans while the camera, turned sideways or upside-down at various times, hovered around him on a crane or whizzed past him on a 90-foot-long motion control track.

Miniature pyrotechnics that are supposed to be in space are often shot looking up (or at least upside-down) so that the arc-shaped paths of debris and convection-driven smoke propagation patterns don't give away the presence of gravity.

It is easier to cheat at some games than others, of course. As humans, we are highly attuned to the way other humans look, and when human elements are shot from the wrong angle, the wrong height, or the wrong distance, even the most nontechnical audience member will often sense that something is wrong with a shot. The cues that trigger this response usually have to do with a perspective mismatch—and the most common error in shooting actors on green screen is to shoot from too short a distance with too wide a lens, resulting in unnatural relative sizes of different parts of the subject. The best protection against this danger is to line up the shot with the same lens, distance, and angle as was used in the plate shot or as dictated by the action of the shot, but when this is not possible, a decent rule of thumb regarding perspective on a human that is allegedly being seen from a great distance is to get the camera at least 25 or 30 feet away.

Backgrounds

The choice of background against which to shoot is dependent on the type of element.

The object of the game is to end up with an image of the element with no background stuck to it so that the compositor can add the element to an existing plate. Ideally, the only criterion for choosing the background color would be to allow for the easiest and highest quality matte extraction, but in the real world, the costs involved in lighting blue screens or green screens (and the likelihood of damaging them) can weigh heavily in these decisions. Whenever possible, discuss the pros and cons of various backgrounds with both the VFX DP and the supervisor at the visual effects facility that will be responsible for the shots—different facilities have different preferences based on their particular experiences and the toolsets that they have created. A detailed explanation of bluescreen and greenscreen photography appears elsewhere in this book, but it is worth noting here that elements that contain transparent or translucent areas, motion-blurred edges, or highly reflective surfaces can create significant challenges when shot on blue screen or green screen unless all of the lighting and shooting parameters are very carefully controlled.

Black Backgrounds

One of the beauties of shooting against a black background is that in some circumstances, if the exposure on the background is low enough compared to the element being photographed, no matte extraction is needed at all. If a matte is needed, it can often be created as a luminance matte. Good candidates for shooting against black include flames, smoke, dust, debris, liquid splashes, and explosions.

Three types of black material are in common use:

- *Velvet:* The most luxurious (and expensive) option, velvet absorbs stray light wonderfully, but must be kept dry and unwrinkled. It is expensive to buy and hard to rent.
- *Velour:* Physically heavier than velvet, velour is the material of choice for theatrical drapes and masking and can be readily rented from theatrical supply companies. Like velvet, velour has a nap of fibers that extend out from the cloth and absorb light.
- *Duvetyne:* Sometimes referred to as Commando Cloth, duvetyne is much less expensive than velour or velvet but is not as light absorptive. This is the material most commonly used in making flags and solid frames or overheads used for controlling light on set. It is available for rent in various standard sizes and for purchase as raw goods by the roll.

Line-Up

If actors, objects, or atmospherics have to fit into a specific area of a shot, the camera should be positioned to match its position relative to the subject of the original shot.[42] This is a relatively simple prospect if the data from on set is accurate and available, but even without it, an experienced VFX Director of Photography should be able to match the angle and distance by analyzing the original shot. If the shot involves actor translational movement or any element interaction with the ground plane, it is vital that

---

[42] See *Triangulation as a Method of Recording Camera Data* earlier in this chapter for more information.

the line-up be accurate. Few things look worse than repositioning and tracking an element into a shot in order to solve a problem created by shooting that element incorrectly. Actors can be given tape marks and green or blue objects carefully placed in the set that correspond to the original scene. See the *Monster Sticks* section earlier in this chapter for more details about providing actors with interactive guides.

Traditionally line-up was accomplished by inserting a frame (or clip) of the original shot into a clip holder in the camera's viewing system, but in the modern world, this is facilitated by using a video switcher to combine video of the original shot with the output of the camera's video tap. Since film camera video taps show a larger image than what appears on the final framed shot, one must either use the video tap image recorded when the original shot was made or resize one of the images to match the other.[43] This calls for a video switcher that has the capability of magnifying or shrinking the image from one of its inputs[44] (or presizing the video to match using compositing software). The switcher should be capable of doing *DXs*[45] (semitransparent superimpositions) as well as rudimentary chroma keys. A number of tape- and hard drive–based video playback systems are used in the industry that are capable of doing all this, and hiring someone with all the right equipment is frequently easier than putting a system together for a single shoot.[46]

The most important rule for successful line-up work is this: *Perspective is determined by position, not focal length.*

Once the camera is positioned relative to the subject to create the right size image in the correct place in frame using the matching focal length, it is often desirable to change lenses to a longer lens that magnifies the subject more, preserving more detail for better matte extraction. In choosing to push in, be careful not to magnify the image so much as to allow any of the action to break the edge of frame—any action that is outside the field of view of the camera is gone for good, and any benefit gained from a magnified image is more than offset by the loss of usable action.

---

[43] Given a bit of lead time, the editorial department should be able to provide resized images to match the video tap, but they will need to see a sample of the tap image in order to do so.

[44] For standard-definition video taps and monitors, the standard switcher in the visual effects world for decades has been the Panasonic MX50. Long discontinued by Panasonic, they can still be found all over the world.

[45] DX is short for "double exposure."

[46] When working with HD cameras, be aware that if a downconverter and standard-definition video are used, the downconverter will delay the camera's signal by at least a frame, potentially causing temporal offsets.

If the camera move is complicated and/or creates significant perspective changes, the best way to shoot the elements might require the use of a motion control camera system, either driven by matchmove data from the original plate or from encoded or motion control data from the original plate shoot. See *Supervising Motion Control* in this chapter for specific information.

Figure 3.60 Author with motion control legs for flame, steam, and water reflection passes. (Photos courtesy of Mark H. Weingartner.)

Camera Format Considerations

A number of factors affect the camera and format choices. It is best to discuss these issues with the VFX DP as the shooting plan is developed:

- *Frame rate:* Does the shot need to be overcranked? To give miniature elements the proper sense of weight when interacting with atmospheric elements, wind, debris, flames, or explosions, it is necessary to overcrank the camera, but how fast? A starting point for choosing a frame rate is to multiply the base frame rate (generally 24 fps) by the square root of the scale of the miniature.[47] For example, if the miniature is 1:4 scale, the shooting frame rate would be $24 \times \sqrt{4} = 48$ fps. If the miniature were 1 inch = 1 foot (1:12 scale), the frame rate would be $24 \times \sqrt{12} \approx 83$ fps. It is important to test frame rates in order to find the right look for each situation. This formula does not take into account slowing down of action for aesthetic purposes but assumes that the intent is to show the action in real time on screen.

- *Shutter angle:* Does the shot require the use of a narrower shutter angle to reduce motion blur? The effect of narrowing the shutter angle is to shorten the exposure time. While this can benefit matte extraction, it can also lead to choppy-looking motion or strobing, depending on the subject's motion with respect to the frame. Be very careful when intermixing elements with different shutter rates from the original live action. When in doubt, test or shoot multiple versions.

- *Contrast ratios:* Film can handle a greater contrast range than any of the electronic cameras without clipping, but the trade-off is cost and processing and scanning time.

- *Resolution:* At one end of the scale—65mm and VistaVision film.[48] At the other end—MiniDV video. For elements that will be reduced considerably in the final composite, sometimes a standard-definition video camera is good enough. For projects as dissimilar as *Star Wars Episode I: The Phantom Menace* (1999) and *The Passion of the Christ* (2004) some of the deep background people were shot full frame with MiniDV video cameras and shrunk way down in the comp. These shrunk-down elements can be used directly or in more sophisticated ways. To fill the seats of the senate in *The Phantom Menace* (1990), the costumed actors were filmed by three MiniDV video cameras mounted at different heights and angles. The people were rotated and photographed from those different angles. A computer script was written to select the appropriate video clip to use for a given senate seat based on its angle to camera within a given shot.

---

[47] This rule of thumb can be found in an article on miniatures by L.B. Abbott, ASC, in the 1980 *ASC Manual* and has been repeated in numerous subsequent publications.
[48] The fireball elements for the title sequence of *The Dark Knight* (2008) were shot with a high-speed VistaVision camera in order to provide enough resolution for blow-up to IMAX for release.

Assorted Methods for Shooting Elements

Actors and Props

Actors are usually filmed against blue or green screen with attention to shot-specific angles, distances, and focal lengths for line-up. For *The Passion of the Christ* (2004), puppeteers in green-screen suits wielded canes and whips impacting green-wrapped sandbags in order to provide realistic interactive elements to composite onto the flagellation scenes of the film (which were shot with whip-less handles for obvious reasons.) *Van Helsing* (2004) used actresses dressed in blue against a blue screen to photograph their faces. They were suspended by wires and puppeted by people dressed in blue to match the action of the previs that had been created for an existing background shot. An infrared motion capture system was used to capture the actresses' movements, and that MoCap data was applied to the final animation so that the perspective of the photographic and CG elements matched.

Actors can be hung from wires, supported on pylons, rotated in rigs, or bounced around on motion bases to simulate horseback, monsterback, motorcycle, or other modes of travel.

Occasionally other backgrounds are appropriate. When a backing screen is not feasible, some exterior stunts have been shot against sky. For *Apocalypto* (2006), the descender-rig actor shots used in the waterfall jump-off scene were filmed by multiple cameras against an 18% gray-painted high-rise building wall.[49]

Explosions

Explosions are either shot against blue or green screens or against black, depending on the nature of the expected debris and the degree to which they are expected to be self-illuminated. One of the challenges in shooting scale model explosions is the need to shoot at very high frame rates, necessitating very high illumination levels for blue or green screens. Large explosions are frequently shot outside at night. An experienced special effects pyrotechnic technician will be able to offer up a number of different types of explosive effects by varying the proportions, placement, and deployment of different ingredients in the custom-made pyro charges. Safety is of prime importance—no shot is worth an injured crew member, and due diligence should be done with regard to protecting the camera, not only from fire and debris,

---

[49] The VFX Supervisor determined that given the uneven texture of the wall and the unavoidable proximity of the actors to the wall, it made more sense to rotoscope the actors off of the wall than to attempt to pull a key from a horrible blue or green screen.

but from water should it become necessary to extinguish a burning set. Some pyro recipes generate more smoke than others. This should be discussed with the SFX Supervisor. For some types of explosions, the meat of the action is over before the smoke has a chance to occlude what is being shot, but in other cases the smoke can create problems.

One of the benefits of shooting straight up for zero-gravity explosions is that convection drives the smoke up and away from camera. Shooting elements upside-down with the camera upside-down at least sends the smoke in an unexpected direction, and debris paths curve slightly upward instead of slightly downward in frame, which takes the curse off of the gravitational disadvantages of shooting on earth. Be sure to adjust framing to take into account the path of the debris. If necessary, shoot wider than needed—debris will break the edge of frame. Different materials create explosions with very different propagation speeds—the pyro technician and VFX DP will be able to advise with regard to suitable frame rates for different situations.

Flames

Flames are usually shot against black.[50] They are shot at normal speed if the flames are full size or at higher rates if the flames are to be scaled up or for aesthetic reasons. Some interesting effects can be achieved with different combinations of camera speed and shutter angle, but if one departs from normal practice, then testing or shooting multiple variations is vital. The special effects team is likely to have all manner of oddly named nozzles, flame bars, and flexible burners as well as different mixes of gas and various fuels and chemicals to create flames with different characteristics and colors. The flame can be further animated with fans. Safety is of prime importance. Aside from the dangers of fire, flame effects can throw off a tremendous amount of radiant heat—enough to damage things that are not remotely in contact with the flames themselves. Most decent blue screens and green screens are not fire retardant, and while much of the duvetyne used in the motion picture industry is treated with a fire retardant when new, once it has been wetted or washed, the retardant leaches out.

---

[50] Some shots call for flames filmed against green screen in order to allow for letting parts of the back plate bleed through the transparent parts of the flames. As always, consult with the visual effects facility that is working on the shot for their input. When in doubt, shoot it both ways—in front of black and in front of green. Blue screen is generally not a good choice for natural gas flames, which burn with a blue inner cone when sufficiently oxygenated.

Figure 3.61 High-speed VistaVision camera in flame-box being engulfed in flame. (Image courtesy of Mark H. Weingartner.)

Water Splashes, Swirls, and Streams

Water can be shot in an existing tank, but an impromptu shallow tank can be made by building a frame of 2 by 12 lumber on edge, forming a square or rectangular trough and lining it with black Visqueen or similar polyethylene plastic. In spite of the specular reflections from the surface of the plastic, resist the urge to submerge duvetyne in the tank, because the fire retardant will immediately start leaching out of the fabric, clouding the water in a nonuniform way. If the reflections are troublesome, consider using various woven fabrics designed for agricultural use that can be weighted down in the tank.

Water splashes usually look best when side and back lit, while ripples generally do best when large soft light sources are suspended over or behind the water. As a last recourse, adding a small amount of white tempera paint, milk, or soluble oil[51] to the water will reduce its transparency, but once that has been done, removing the adulterant requires draining and cleaning the tank. To create specific interactive splashes, use a black object of the appropriate shape and size and drop it in or pull it through

---

[51] Sold in industrial supply stores for use as lubricating oil for machining metal.

the water. If shooting a small-scale proxy of the true object, overcranking the camera will be necessary, but be aware that due to the surface tension inherent in the makeup of water, the effects can only scale so far. Once again, a quick test can be cheap insurance for getting lifelike elements. Air hoses and water hoses can be used to agitate the water, and all sorts of streams can be created with different types of nozzles and water pressures. Rainfall on water can be simulated with "rainbirds" from the special effects department. The special effects folk know how to generate everything from a mist to a torrent. Don't forget to bring a towel.

Underwater

Elements can be shot underwater to simulate weightlessness, slow motion, or just to create amazing swirly effects with hair and wardrobe. Water must be filtered in order to be clean enough to shoot through, and if people are working in the water without wetsuits (actors, for instance) the water should be heated. Some studios have shooting tanks with underwater windows that allow shooting without putting the camera in a housing and then in the water. A swimming pool with observation ports sometimes works just as well.

Lighting objects underwater carries with it its own challenges and dangers—make sure to use crew who are certified to work underwater and experienced with underwater lighting and the safe use of electricity around water. Any time crew is working underwater, expect the schedule to be slow—communication is difficult enough when people are face to face in air—underwater communication at its best is not so great.

Dust, Debris, and Breaking Glass

Interactive dust elements are frequently shot to add to the realism of large creatures or objects walking, falling, or otherwise impacting the ground. This can be done in a number of ways. Even if the "hero dust" in the final shot is going to be dark, the easiest way to film these elements is by using light-colored dust and black velvet mounted on a wooden backing. Dust is gently applied to the fabric and the light is flagged off of the velvet itself. The interactive dust hits can be created by dropping a black velvet-covered weight onto the velvet field or by shooting compressed air at it. As with any small dust or particle work, use air masks and eye protection.

Debris can be shot out of air mortars, dropped out of hoppers, or thrown by crew members in front of black, blue, or green screen. As with water effects, sidelight and backlight are often more effective in shooting debris than front light.

Breaking glass effects can be shot against black, of course, but sometimes work better against green screen or blue screen, especially when interactive reflections of various pieces of glass are to be incorporated into the composite. Different effects can be filmed looking up at glass (with the camera in a protective box, of course) looking down at glass, and looking across at glass as it is broken or shattered. The special effects team will have multiple ways of breaking different types of glass in order to create different types of effects. Glass effects will look very different depending on how they are lit. Large soft planar light sources create one type of look; very hard light creates a totally different sparkle. Be sure to order enough glass to allow some experimentation (and to allow for accidents).

Clouds

Clouds can of course be created by means of matte paintings or computer graphics. They can also be created in a liquid such as was done for *Close Encounters of the Third Kind* (1977) using a large clear tank (7 × 7 × 4 feet in this case) filled with saltwater on the bottom half and freshwater on the top half. White tempera paint was injected in the freshwater to create the illusion of cumulus clouds, which rested on the inversion layer of the saltwater. Other puffy clouds can be simulated by injecting soluble oil into clear water using various types of nozzles, and spreader bars can yield wonderful variations. *Independence Day* (1996) made good use of cloud tank elements for the atmospherics accompanying the arrival of the Destroyers.

Clouds can also be done using synthetic fiberfill mounted onto clear acrylic sheets as was done on *Buckaroo Banzai* (1984). Stratocumulus clouds can be built with cotton wool or fiberglass insulation.

Smoke and Fog

A number of different types of low-lying fog can be generated using dry ice fog machines alone or in concert with smoke generators and liquid nitrogen. Interesting effects can be obtained by sending dry ice fog over warm standing water, for instance. Different types of smoke machines are available, each with its strengths and weaknesses. Smoke and fog are generally shot against black. It is easy enough to recolor the element in post-production rather than trying to shoot dark smoke, but interesting effects can be created by burning acetylene and photographing the wispy, sooty smoke that it generates when burning. Consult the special effects team and the VFX DP for help making an informed decision.

Goo and Lava

Goo can be made using various food thickeners. There are various children's toy goo mixtures and simple things such as gum can be used for goo. Consider these examples of the use of goo in small amounts to help the finished shots: In *Van Helsing* (2004), a werewolf literally rips off his fur. Goo elements were shot to help with the final effect of the stretching, breaking flesh. Goo was also filmed by an animator working on *Dragonheart* (1996) using a DV video camera. This was manipulated and used to help show the saliva in the dragon's mouth. Lava can also be created as a separate photographic element, but will probably require some R&D before an agreed-on look is achieved.

Conclusion

Above and beyond elements containing actors, photographing elements of all sorts can be fast, easy, cost effective, and downright enjoyable. Sometimes the precise control made possible by developing CG elements procedurally is very important, but often the happy accidents that occur when special effects and visual effects get together to shoot elements can be truly wonderful, and the energy that this type of collaboration injects into the process can be quite beneficial.

HIGH-SPEED PHOTOGRAPHY AND FILMING ELEMENTS
Jim Matlosz

High-Speed Photography

High-speed photography, defined as a camera capturing moving images at a rate above 60 fps, in motion pictures was once relegated to miniatures and special effects. Today, however, with the advent of faster film stocks, bigger lights, and high-speed digital acquisition, high-speed photography is accessible to more filmmakers and artists and used by projects both great and small. In this section a number of topics are discussed to educate and inform those who have a need or use for high-speed photography, but also possess a basic understanding of cinematography and visual effects.

Cameras

The choice of cameras varies and many of these choices are covered in other sections of this book; however, two charts have been created to make your choice of high-speed cameras and deciphering a bit easier (Figures 3.62 and 3.63). The charts begin with film cameras, from the fastest 35mm on through the slowest of the 16mm. (Note: There are a number of high-speed, large-format IMAX 65mm 15-perf, 10-perf, and IWERKS 65mm 8-perf cameras in existence, but these cameras are seldom used anymore and have very limited application.) Then they list digital acquisition cameras from the fastest, highest resolution to the slowest, lowest resolution. Highlighted features include actual measured image size, pixel dimensions, capture medium, and weights of cameras.

CAMERA	FPS	RELATIVE FORMAT	MAX. IMAGE AREA	SHUTTER ANGLE
FILM				
35MM				
PHOTOSONICS 4C	125 - 2500	4 PERF ACAD ~ 35MM/S35 ~ (1.85)	24.892MM × 16.891MM	72 FIXED
PHOTOSONICS 4ER	6 - 360	4 PERF ACAD ~ 35MM/S35	24.892MM × 16.669MM	120 ADJ.
PHOTOSONICS 4ML	10 - 200	4 PERF ACAD ~ 35MM/S35	24.892MM × 18.669MM	144 ADJ.
WILCAM W7 VISTAVISION	2 - 199	VISTAVISION ~ 8 PERF ~ 35MM	36MM × 18.3MM	110 FIXED
WILCAM W9 VISTAVISION	2 - 99	VISTAVISION ~ 8 PERF ~ 35 MM	36MM × 18.3MM	175 FIXED
ARRI 435	1 - 150	3 & 4 PERF ACAD ~ 35MM/S35	24.892MM × 18.669MM	180 ADJ.
ARRI III	6 - 120	3 & 4 PERF ACAD ~ 35MM/S35	24.892MM × 18.669MM	180 ADJ.
PANASTAR	6 - 120	4 PERF ACAD ~ 35MM/S35	24.892MM × 18.669MM	180 ADJ.
MITCHELL	2 - 120	4 PERF ACAD ~ 35MM/S35	24.892MM × 18.669MM	180 ADJ.
16MM				
PHOTOSONICS ACTION MASTER	24 - 500	16MM	10.26MM × 7.49MM	160 ADJ.
PHOTOSONICS ACTION MASTER S-16 3000	10 - 360	S16MM	12.52MM × 7.41MM	144 ADJ.
PHOTOSONICS 1 VN SUPER16	24 - 168	S16MM	12.52MM × 7.41MM	120 ADJ.
ARRI 416+HS	1 - 150	S16MM	12.35MM × 7.5MM	180 ADJ.
DIGITAL	FPS / RESOLUTION	APPROX. FORMAT AT TOP SPEED	SENSOR DIM./MAX. RESOLUTION	
RAW/14 BIT				
PHANTOM HD (C-MOS)	2 - 1000 @ (1920 × 1080)	4 PERF ACAD ~ 35MM/S35	25.35MM × 25.5MM (2048 × 2048)	360 ADJ.
PHANTOM V10 (C-MOS)	2 - 978 @ (1920 × 1080)	4 PERF ACAD ~ 35MM/S35	27.6MM × 20.7MM (2400 × 1800)	360 ADJ.
PHANTOM V7.3 (C-MOS)	2 - 6600 @ (800 × 600)	3 PERF TV SAFE ~ 35MM	17.6MM × 13.2MM (800 × 600)	360 ADJ.
PHANTOM 65 (C-MOS)	2 - 150 @ (4096 × 2304) 16:9	5 PERF ~ 65MM	51.2MM × 28.0MM (4096 × 2440)	360 ADJ.
RAW/12 BIT				
WEISSCAM HS-2 (C-MOS)	20 - 2000 @ (1920 × 1080) (WINDOWED)	S16MM	22.18MM × 22.18MM (2016 × 2016)	360 ADJ.
PHOTRON SA2 (C-MOS)	2 - 2000 @ (1920 × 1080)	3 PERF ~ 35MM	20.48MM × 20.48MM (2048 × 2048)	360 ADJ.
*REDONE (C-MOS)	1 - 120 @ (2048 × 1152) (WINDOWED)	S16MM	24.4MM × 13.7MM (4096 × 2304)	360 ADJ.
*REDONE EPIC (C-MOS) *PROPOSED SPECS*	1 - 250 @ (2560 × 1350) (WINDOWED)	S16MM	30MM × 15MM (5120 × 2700)	360 ADJ.
ASA: DUE TO VARIATIONS IN REPORTED ISO/ASA RATINGS OF DIGITAL CAMERAS NO ISO/ASA RATINGS HAVE BEEN STATED.				
ASA NOTE: IT IS STILL BEST TO TEST AND MEASURE TO INSURE PROPER EXPOSURE INDEX RATINGS ON ALL DIGITAL CAMERAS.				
RAW: *RED CAMERAS CAPTURE TO REDCODE	A WAVELET BASED COMPRESSION FORMAT.			
WINDOWED: THE TECHNIQUE OF USING A SMALLER PORTION OR ZOOMING IN ON THE FULL SENSOR TO ACHIEVE DIFFERENT DESIRED EFFECTS.				

Figure 3.62 High-speed camera spec chart. (Image courtesy of Jim Matlosz.)

CAMERA	WEIGHT	APROX. DIMENSIONS	LENSE MOUNT
FILM			
35MM			
PHOTOSONICS 4C	125 LBS W/1000'	L18'' × W12'' × H12''	PENTAX, NIKON
PHOTOSONICS 4ER	125 LBS W/1000'	L18'' × W12'' × H12''	BNCR, NIKON, PL*, PV
PHOTOSONICS 4ML	28 LBS W/400'	L16'' × W6'' × H8''	BNCR, NIKON, PL*, PV
WILCAM W7 VISTAVISION	150 LBS W/1000'	L18'' × W15'' × H12''	PL
WILCAM W9 VISTAVISION	150 LBS W/1000'	L18'' × W15'' × H12''	PL
ARRI 435	32 LBS W/400'	L16'' × W10'' × H13''	PL, PV
ARRI III	23 LBS W/400'	L16'' × W 9'' × H12''	PL, PV
PANASTAR	50 LBS W/1000'	L20'' × W11'' × H24''	PL, PV
MITCHELL	50 LBS W/1000'	L12'' × W8'' × H8''	BNCR, NIKON, PL, PV
16MM			
PHOTOSONICS ACTION MASTER	20 LBS W/400'	L16'' × W6'' × H8''	PL, NIKON, C
PHOTOSONICS ACTION MASTER S-16 3000	20 LBS W/400'	L16'' × W6'' × H8''	PL, W/RESTRICTIONS
PHOTOSONICS 1 VN SUPER16	3.75 LBS W/200'	L14'' × W4'' × H5''	C-MOUNT
ARRI 416+HS	12.8 LBS (BODY ONLY)	L18'' × W6'' × H8''	PL, W/RESTRICTIONS
DIGITAL			
RAW/14 BIT			
PHANTOM HD (C-MOS)	13 LBS (BODY ONLY)	L12'' × W6'' × H8''	PL, PV, NIKON
PHANTOM V10 (C-MOS)	7 LBS (BODY ONLY)	L 9.5'' × W4'' × H4.5''	PL, NIKON, C MOUNT
PHANTOM V7.3 (C-MOS)	7 LBS (BODY ONLY)	L 9.5'' × W4'' × H4.5''	PL, NIKON
PHANTOM 65 (C-MOS)	13 LBS (BODY ONLY)	L12'' × W6'' × H8''	sPL, sPV, 645
RAW/12 BIT			
WEISSCAM HS-2 (C-MOS)	18 LBS (BODY ONLY)	L11.5'' × W7.5'' × H8''	PL, PV, NIKON, BNCR
PHOTRON SA2 (C-MOS)	15 LBS (BODY ONLY)	L10'' × W6'' × H6.5''	PL, PV, NIKON
*REDONE (C-MOS)	10 LBS (BODY ONLY)	L12'' × W5'' × H6.5''	PL, PV
*REDCINE EPIC (C-MOS) *PROPOSED SPECS*	6 LBS (BRAIN ONLY)	L 4'' × W4'' × H5.5''	SPL, *SPV
* ALL ABOVE WEIGHT AND SIZE SPECS ARE APPROXIMATED; WEIGHTS FOR FILM CAMERAS ARE DEPICTED WITH RELATIVE FILM LOADS.			

Figure 3.63 High-speed camera physical chart. (Image courtesy of Jim Matlosz.)

In Figures 3.62 and 3.63, the cameras listed are the most popular and those in current use as of this writing (early 2010). Photosonics, no doubt the leader in high-speed film acquisition, has the largest collection of cameras and formats available. These cameras are built and many of them are maintained around the world to this day by Photosonics Inc. itself. The reason for a detail such as this is that you must consider reliability when using high-speed photography. (For example, the Photosonics 4C will photograph up to 2500 fps, which means the film is traveling through the gate at roughly 102 mph—a thousand feet of film lasts a mere 8 seconds. With these types of speeds, a well-tuned machine is of utmost importance to not only capture the shot but also capture it well.) Photosonics also offers the fastest of all film cameras on the market to this day for motion picture use.

Other cameras that offer high speed options are: Wilcam, with its high speed Vista-Vision, 8-perf cameras; Arriflex, with the 435, peaking at an impressive and very stable 150 fps; and the legendary Arri III, a workhorse of the motion picture industry. In addition, Panavision offers the Panastar and there is the classic Mitchell camera, still in use nearly 100 years after it was first constructed. There were many makes of Mitchell cameras and all seem to look the same. The best way to determine if the Mitchell you are using is high speed is to determine whether it has a metal drive gear. Also a myth about the Mitchell camera is that it need be literally dripping with oil to run properly. Proper oiling is just that—proper: no more, no less. Too much camera oil can potentially leak onto the film and cause issues in processing and image quality. With 16mm high-speed film cameras, the choices are more limited. Once again Photosonics has the greatest number of offerings in both super and standard 16mm. Otherwise there is the Arri 416+HS, a camera that was introduced in 2008, which possesses all the latest bits of technology including speed ramps and integrated iris and remote capabilities.

Digital high-speed acquisition, still in its infancy, but no doubt moving as fast as all other types of digital cameras, has some very useful applications for both visual effects as well as practical effects. The largest manufacturer of high-speed digital cameras is Vision Research with its varied line of Phantom cameras; other cameras are the Weisscam HS-2, NAC, Photron, and the Red One. There are some pitfalls to be aware of with high-speed digital though. Almost all of these cameras can achieve higher frame rates by reducing image size and resolution. Often, however, this may require windowing in on the sensor (i.e., using a smaller portion of the sensor, acquiring less resolution; for example, reducing a 35mm frame to 16mm). This is a detail that is very important and something that may be overlooked or considered a nonissue.

If confronted with this issue, there is most likely a full-resolution camera available to achieve your high-speed goals. As always, proper research and application should be considered to achieve the highest quality results.

All of the above-mentioned cameras, both film and digital, do a fairly good job of capturing images, some better than others. For best results, testing is highly recommended. Do not rely on sales brochures, salespeople, conjecture, the Internet, fancy demo reels, or films you have seen in the theater to make a decision. Unless you were there working on the film with the camera and seeing it in post you may get yourself in trouble. With all of the intense post techniques used today, only an educated VFX Supervisor can make the proper decision.

Technicians

Along with just about any of these cameras, film or digital, comes a technician: a person dedicated to keeping the camera working, answering any and all questions, as well as proactively troubleshooting any issues that may occur, fixing them on site, and extending the education of the procedure beyond this writing. It cannot be stressed enough how valuable a good, well-trained, seasoned technician is. Many of these professionals have had years of experience with these cameras. They are kept up-to-date on the latest developments and are skilled in fixing most issues that may occur. These technicians also have a lifeline to manufacturers and other seasoned technicians that allows them to master and overcome many, if not all, potential issues. This is not to say that high-speed photography has issues, but one must consider, with film cameras, the speed at which the film is traveling, or with digital cameras, the speed at which it is capturing data and a superior high-resolution image. At times the cameras are teetering on the brink of discovery, every moment counts, and chances are when shooting high speed, the actual moment is fleeting.

Director of Photography

It is not a question of whether the DP is a master of high-speed photography, but more a question of does he or she have a good understanding of high-speed photography? Common mistakes in high-speed photography are underexposed elements and using the wrong lights. In fact, if you ask most technicians they will tell you the same. And while the VFX Supervisor may have no control over who the DP is, a few conversations and a bit of research prior to shoot day may help to alleviate many headaches and unwanted disagreements.

Lighting

When it comes to lighting for high-speed photography one must simply consider that for every time the speed doubles, one stop of light is lost (i.e., 120 to 240 fps is a one-stop loss), and with this loss comes the need for a greater amount of light. It's not uncommon to light a water droplet with a smattering of 20k lights. With this same thought comes the concern about lighting a larger area for proper exposure at the proper speed. When dealing with film cameras and light, one must first understand that many film high-speed cameras have limited shutter angles (see chart), which equates to less exposure and again the need for more light.

In addition to the concern about amount of light one must consider the type of light. While HMI lighting may offer a greater amount of light relative to tungsten, the electronic ballast needed to power the HMI light renders a flicker past 150 fps. Although this theory may be disputed, it has been proven time and again, to be true. That is not to say that HMI lighting cannot be used in flicker-free mode, but consider that even after testing, the light may flicker differently at different angles, relative to the camera. It may also flicker depending on the age of the ballast and duration of light use in a specific shot. The bottom line is that there is no surefire way to know flicker exists even through testing using HMI lights.

At the same time with digital cameras, one can see light flicker on a waveform monitor and troubleshooting can begin. Most qualified technicians can easily identify the flicker and inform the proper channels prior to shooting. As far as exposure goes, it is still a good idea to overexpose—get a solid healthy negative when shooting *film*. Digital on the other hand is much more critical; overexposure of any kind will lead to unwanted fringing and white levels that are deemed unusable. Underexposure in digital cinematography can lead to noisy black levels and render a muddy, unappealing, unusable image with both film and digital. Appropriate contrast levels should be maintained for both film and digital.

Application

As stated earlier high-speed photography was once limited to miniatures and simple visual effects, it eventually began to migrate into sports and be used for dramatic impact within movies and commercials. With the advent of digital high speed cameras, high-speed photography can now be used for the simplest of creative ventures. For the VFX Supervisor the question of which camera is right for the job is at hand. While there are arguments for both film and digital acquisition, it is still up to the educated professional to make that decision, a decision that is often based on application of effect, budget at hand, and complexity of elements to be shot. The choice of shooting speeds and needs will vary greatly and seem to be a bit more open due to digital post-production techniques; although slowing down an image in post to achieve a slower frame rate (i.e., shooting at 48 fps slowing to 96 fps) is possible, it is not recommended. However, shooting an element at a higher rate (i.e., shooting at 500 fps speeding up to 250 fps) and then speeding up in post has been very effective, so the new and simple rule for the most part is that if you are unsure, shoot it as fast as possible. Be forewarned that this philosophy does not mean that proper homework and planning are not needed; the more prepared and educated one is on proper speeds, the less reasoning and potentially future post work will be needed.

Elements

When considering elements, pieces of a visual effects puzzle shot in separate pieces, such as dirt, body parts, and debris, one must still consult proper frame rates per scale. These scale charts are tried and true and it is best to stick with these techniques. When shooting on film it is possible to shoot these elements with the most logical shooting technique, blue screen, green screen, black or white. As long as the screen and the elements are lit properly, the elements will be fine. Shooting on blue and green screen with digital high speed cameras is not as simple as shooting with film or even basic digital cameras. Testing exposures and processing the data as far as possible, through pipeline to finish, is highly recommended. These cameras, although great for elements, occasionally have issues with process screens. When it comes to water and fire, more thought must be used. Water only has one size, but variable speeds and proper depth of field will imply mass. Although one may be inclined to shoot a pool of water for the ocean at the highest frame rate possible, one must also consider depth of field. In many cases it is better to have more depth and less speed to convey size, and since depth of field (or f-stop) and frame rate work hand in hand relative to impact on exposure, choosing the proper speed for the proper scale should be observed. Elements should be shot as large as possible. Often overscale models of elements are created to avoid side affects like strobing and to increase the quality of the element themselves. Otherwise shooting the element in the proper framing should be observed. Things like lens distortion and travel of the element through the frame should also be observed.

As for fire, it is pretty much agreed that film will still render a better fire element than digital. It's a fact that film just has greater latitude and fire has a massive range of exposure from the brightest white to the darkest black. Popular opinion states that it is of the utmost importance to capture the greatest nuances of the fire to ensure the best look. When shooting fire, tests should be photographed, with a full range of exposures and frame rates, once again observing *f*-stops and speed to convey the right scale relative to your production.

Technique

There are certainly a few techniques and tips that should be observed to make your high-speed shoot go well. First and foremost, if you are shooting film, be very aware of start/stop times and how much film you will be using. When shooting with film and a camera technician or 1st AC, it is best to establish a streamlined verbal or visual cueing system of camera roll, camera speed, action, and cut. This will help to not only conserve film but also establish a safe, fluid, and productive shooting environment.

The same techniques should also be observed when shooting on a digital camera. However, the run and stop times on most digital high-speed cameras can be varied greatly. Techniques like *post-trigger* work more like a film camera, where you hit record and the camera records until it runs out of memory and stops. Another technique is *pre-trigger*, which means the camera will continuously record as much data as the buffer can handle and loop until the camera is cut. This second technique is generally more favorable, and it should be discussed with your technician to allow for maximum productivity.

Locking Down the Camera

Many film cameras have a tendency to vibrate, some more than others when running at selected high speeds. To ensure a solid and steady plate, the grip department, with the assistance of the camera technician, should lock down the camera and reduce this vibration. Of note, the Photosonics 4C, although an amazing camera, does have the largest amount of vibration as well as image weave due to the fact that it is not a pin-registered camera. Photosonics Inc. has made every effort to reduce these issues, often with great results. If, however, what you are shooting allows for camera movement, you will notice that much of the weave and vibration are considerably reduced upon viewing. Digital cameras have no vibration because basically they have no moving parts; however, it is still a good idea to lock this camera down when shooting critical plates to avoid any unnecessary human error.

Video Assist

All high-speed cameras have video assist. Film cameras all have standard-definition 30-fps video assist, and most are flicker free. High-speed digital cameras on the other hand offer a wide variety of real-time high-definition output; the HD video varies according to manufacturers and even your needs. It is highly recommended to take advantage of this HD signal; there is more advantage to capturing it than one could argue for not capturing it. Note, however, that this HD output is not always recommended for use as your hero footage. Although the image may appear to be very usable, on second inspection one may see anomalies generated by the camera performing a real-time conversion of a raw image.

Post

Post-production for film cameras is standard procedure; prep, process, and transfers require no special handling. Currently, digital cameras vary greatly depending on the manufacturer, current software, post facility, and what the final delivery format is. You should capture a RAW image whenever possible, first and foremost. Testing of the post technique you would like to establish should be performed. Capturing a standard Macbeth color chart and a focus chart is a good place to begin to establish color, focus, and resolution. Because all of these factors can vary greatly depending on the post technique, testing should be performed in a number of ways.

SUPERVISING MOTION CONTROL
Mark H. Weingartner

Motion control—these two words strike fear in the hearts of ADs and put scowls on the faces of UPMs,[52] bile on the tongues of DPs, and lines on the foreheads of directors.[53] It is considered by many to be the methodology of last recourse, and while developments in camera tracking software have reduced the need for motion control on live-action sets, judicious use of motion control can make difficult shots easy and impossible ones possible.

---

[52] UPM: Unit Production Manager.
[53] Painstakingly slow setup and programming time in the early days of motion control photography earned the technique a reputation for killing shoot schedules. It has somewhat outgrown this reputation, but the old attitudes persist.

What Is Motion Control?

A motion control camera rig is one that uses computer-controlled motors for accurate reproduction of camera movement with respect to time. Motion control rigs range from motorized pan/tilt heads to cranes with eight or more motorized axes of movement. A motion control programmer operates the rig with its highly specialized computer—choreographing camera moves that can then be edited in order to smooth out bumps, change timing, or adjust framing. In addition to moving the camera, the computer can be used to control lighting effects and movement of models or prop elements. Different types of rigs have different capabilities, strengths, and weaknesses—an understanding of how motion control can be used will inform equipment choices.

Four Basic Uses for Motion Control:

1. Precise choreography of camera movement
2. Repeat passes of a camera move
3. Scaling (temporal and/or spatial)
4. Import/export of camera move data

   The first three functions use pretty much the same hardware, while the last function can be accomplished either with traditional motion control equipment or with encoder sets, which can be attached to some live-action dollies, cranes, and associated grip equipment. In all of these cases, the choice of equipment is important. The supervisor must balance portability and speed of setup and execution against reach and the capability of the rig. A smaller lighter rig that is faster to set up is useless if it cannot get the camera where the director and DP want the camera to go. Similarly, choosing a large rig running on wide, heavy track sections for a simple shot that does not require that much reach only slows production down and reminds them how much they hate motion control. Some rigs are much noisier than others, whether due to their mechanical construction, motor and drive systems, or both. Knowing whether a shot is an MOS[54] shot or a sync sound shot will influence rig choice.

   While traditional motion control programming involves carefully setting key frames and using the software to fill in and modify the resultant camera move, many motion control vendors have developed multiple input devices that allow live-action crew members to control the rig directly while lining up and shooting the first pass of a shot. These input devices range from encoder wheels used to operate a pan/tilt head and follow focus controllers operated by the focus-puller, to encoded pan/tilt heads that

---

[54] MOS: no sync sound recording.

can be used as Waldos[55] to control the swing and lift axes of a motion control crane.

The decision to program using key frames versus learning a move controlled by live-action crew members using these input devices is situational. Often the programmer will program one or more axes (track or lift, for instance) for a move before the shot and then have the camera operator control pan and tilt while the 1st AC pulls focus to film the first pass. Sometimes a dolly grip will control the track axis of a rig in order to feather the move based on the action. Again, there are political as well as technical aspects to these choices: keeping a Director of Photography in his or her comfort zone by letting the shoot crew control the camera movement directly can be a useful goal in and of itself.

Figure 3.64 Grip operates motion control crane with Waldo. (Image courtesy of Mark H. Weingartner.)

Performance Choreography

Motion control can often make a difficult shot much easier to operate. Examples of this use of motion control include the classic "pull out from an ECU[56] of an eyeball to a wide shot" and its close cousin, the "push in from a wide shot to an ECU of an eyeball." Motion control has also been used for very precisely choreographed shots such as the slow reveals used in the popular Corona beer commercials. The capability of programming the combination of zooming, focusing, dollying, panning, and tilting

---

[55] Waldo: input device named after the Robert A. Heinlein short story *Waldo*.
[56] ECU: extreme close-up shot.

necessary to create these shots allows a degree of precision that human technicians cannot easily achieve. The ability to program the various axes separately and to edit the moves on the computer to smooth out problems allows the director and DP to fine-tune the shot until they are completely satisfied.

Sometimes a shot calls for a camera move that requires either a faster motion or more abrupt acceleration or deceleration than can be achieved with human-powered camera equipment. These shots can often be achieved with motion control rigs because of their powerful motorized axes.

Multiple-Pass Photography

Obvious examples of multiple-pass live-action motion control are *twin* shots where one actor plays two or more characters within a shot. Less obvious are *soft split* shots where actors and animals act in different passes, or actors run away in the first pass from a physical effect shot in the second pass. Another use of live-action motion control has been for shooting clean passes for rig removal—removing special effects tracks or other rigging for vehicle stunts, for instance.[57] Multiple-pass work also includes situations where motion control is used to duplicate a foreground greenscreen camera move when shooting the background plate, or conversely when playing back a move in order to shoot a greenscreen element to be composited into an existing shot.

Scaling

Motion control can be a powerful tool when either spatial or temporal scaling is required.

A simple example of temporal scaling would be a live-action shot with a time-lapse sky—clouds scudding across the sky and sun angles changing rapidly while the foreground action moves at normal speed. Accelerated actor motion would be another case of temporal scaling. These effects are accomplished by shooting different passes at different speeds. One of the big gotchas in temporal scaling occurs when one shoots a pass at normal speed and then attempts to play it back at a higher speed to create a slow motion effect. When playing a move back at a higher speed than recorded or programmed, the increased speed may exceed the physical limits of the rig itself, causing motors to stall or causing

---

[57] While the optical era of visual effects required great precision for this type of work, modern digital tools have relaxed some of those requirements—repeatable remote heads are often sufficiently accurate.

the rig to fail to repeat the move accurately. For this reason, it is advisable either to:

1. shoot the fastest pass first or
2. run a quick speed test before signing off on a hero pass if the hero pass is the slow pass.

While many people are familiar with the scaling done when combining live-action motion control shots with miniature motion control model work, a less familiar use of motion control involves shooting live-action shots of a normal-sized character interacting with a miniature or giant character. In these situations, a motion control move is scaled up or down and repeated with the other-sized character. The two elements are then composited in post.

When shots are scaled up or down, the rule of thumb is that angular camera movements and focal lengths remain the same, but linear movements scale proportionally. For example, if the big shot involved the camera tracking in from 10 feet to 5 feet and panning left 20 degrees, in a half-scale version of the shot, the camera would start 5 feet away and track in to 2 feet 6 inches away while panning left 20 degrees.

Now the tricky part: While the actual camera move scales according to this rule of thumb, the individual axes of the motion control rig do not necessarily scale that simply. Due to the geometry of the rig, the horizontal component of the arm's arc when it is going up or down is very different at different angles, so lowering the arm to get the second pass starting height correct, for instance, changes how that arm's move will scale.

The good news is that the software designers who have created the two most prevalent motion control packages have created tools within the software that allow the programmer to scale complex moves by taking all of this into account. This complexity, however, can lead to the same issues of exceeding the speed or acceleration limits of one or more axes of a rig. As with temporal scaling, it is important either to shoot the big shot first or to do a quick speed test after shooting the small shot before resetting for the next pass. Additionally, one runs the risk of creating a shot that the motion control rig will not be able to scale up due to its physical size. With these pitfalls in mind, it is prudent to spend the time in consultation with your programmer or motion control supplier *before* the job to ensure that you have the right rig on set when you start working.

Import and Export of Camera Move Data

In a world before optical flow tracking, motion control was one of the technologies of choice for matching bluescreen or greenscreen foregrounds to miniature or location background plates, and vice versa. The development of camera tracking software packages has greatly simplified and automated the painstaking task of extrapolating camera movement in a shot and applying it to the other elements for the composite. Situations still exist, however, where recording camera positional data against a frame-accurate time base or streaming camera positional data to drive a real or virtual camera's movement is advisable.

The equipment used for this in the live-action world can be divided into two types:

1. encoding devices that record angular or linear movement of the various axes of movement of a camera, whether it is moving on a pan/tilt head, dolly, jib, or crane, and
2. motorized motion control rigs that move the camera using a motion control program and programmer.

Data obtained by encoding live-action dollies, cranes, heads, etc., can be used to drive a motion control rig to shoot another element for the same shot. This data can also be applied to a virtual camera in a 3D program to generate the correct movement on CG elements or to drive a real-time visualization system such as EncodaCam.

Several suppliers of motion control equipment have created encoder kits that clamp on to existing cranes, dollies, and heads. There are also modified fluid heads and geared heads that have integral encoders. Some camera systems can output lens focal length and focus data as well, though these are not universally available. When using encoding data to drive a motion control rig, it is important to choose a rig that is capable of executing the move defined by the data with respect to both the physical operating envelope and the speed.

The Data

It is important to understand how the data will be used and to coordinate the formatting and transfer of the data from the motion control programmer to the visual effects house. When using a motion control rig, the programmer may choose to work in *virtual axes*, a mode in which the data recorded by the program is expressed as pan, tilt, roll, and *xyz* translations or, alternatively, by programming the various articulation axes directly, with the same results as with encoded rigs as described above.

If the data is not in virtual axes, it is vital for the facility to have all of the relevant dimensions of the rig on which the camera is moving so that they can model it in their 3D software. The actual move data is generally delivered as ASCII[58] files, which either provide a numerical value for each movement axis for each frame of

---

[58] ASCI file: pure, simple text file based on an American standard.

the move or, if in virtual axes, a linear numerical value for *xyz* and an angular numerical value for pan, tilt, and roll, as well as look-up table outputs for focus and zoom. The beauty of using ASCII text files is that they can be displayed, printed, and read by humans— and it is very easy to write a routine that looks at an ASCII text file and imports that data into a 3D CG program. If the data is going to be used to drive a motion control rig, it may be preferable to deliver the data as part of a *move* file—a proprietary file that can be read by another motion control computer. The motion control programmer will be able to advise which type of file will be of more use, but when in doubt, copy both, since these files are trivial in size.

A text file full of numerical angle and distance values is pretty much useless unless the user knows what they relate to. When sending encoder or motion control data to a facility or to a stage where the shot will be played back on another motion control rig, it is imperative that the end user of that data know how it relates to the set on which it was recorded. The data should be accompanied by data sheets showing the placement and orientation of the camera rig (whether motion control or encoded live-action equipment) relative to the set and to the actors, and describing the units, direction, and calibration of each of the move axes. Lenses should be noted by focal length and serial number. If the camera is not mounted nodally,[59] the nodal offsets should also be described and, if necessary, diagrammed.

Types of Motion Control Systems

Motion control rigs can be roughly split into live-action rigs and model/miniature/stop-motion rigs. The differentiation is primarily between rigs that can work at real-time speeds (i.e., working with production cameras that film at 24 fps) and rigs that are designed to move slowly while photographing at much slower frame rates, typically on the order of one or two frames per second. That said, there is no reason that one cannot shoot a scale model with a rig that is capable of live-action speeds.

Live-Action Rigs

Live-action motion control rigs are usually used to shoot multiple passes of a shot that is meant to look as though it has been shot as straightforward 1st unit photography, and to some degree, form follows function. Live-action rigs are designed to interface

---

[59] A camera is mounted nodally when the pan, tilt, and roll axes of the head pass through the rear nodal point of the lens. A nodal setup like this allows the camera to pan, tilt, and roll without creating any parallax shift between foreground and background elements.

with live-action cameras, lenses, and accessories, and their operating envelopes roughly emulate those of the heads, dollies, and jibs used in 1st unit photography.

Pan/Tilt Heads

The most basic of motion control rigs, a pan/tilt system consists of a motorized pan/tilt head, focus zoom and iris motors, a motion control computer with motor drivers, and a *bloop* light (which is held in frame at the beginning or end of the shot in order to put a one-frame flash or image—a bloop—on the film to aid in synchronizing passes). This type of system will typically include a set of encoder wheels that allows a camera operator to control the head in real time (as with any remote head) and a set of focus/zoom/iris controls that allows the camera assistant to adjust these settings on the fly when laying down the first pass.[60] Alternatively, the motion control programmer may program a camera move, controlling all of these parameters directly from the computer.

The pan/tilt head may be mounted anywhere, but it can only execute a true motion control shot if the device it is mounted on is completely static with respect to the scene being shot. Some motion control heads can accommodate a roll axis as well. This rig is capable of emulating a pan/tilt head on a tripod or other fixed mounting position and is ideal for simple twinning shots, morphs, and background changes where the shot is not all about camera movement. It is also a handy way to operate a camera remotely when a human operator might be in danger (e.g., car stunts) in the specific case where a second pass is beneficial for rig removal.[61]

Pan/Tilt Head on Track

The next step upward in complexity is the addition of a sled dolly on a track. Generally this is done by putting a tripod or fixed rig on a motion control sled dolly. The advantages of this type of rig are its portability and ease of setup. The disadvantage is that once the camera is tracking, the Director of Photography will often

---

[60] Traditionally, motion control stepper motors had to be mounted to control the focus, iris, and zoom lens rings, but in the past few years, several motion control equipment suppliers have begun using interface boxes that allow the use of Preston MDR wireless digital focus iris zoom motors and controllers. In a live-action situation, this can be quite beneficial because it allows the focus-puller to work with his or her usual tools, instead of having to become accustomed to a new piece of equipment.

[61] This sort of simple rig removal shot is rapidly becoming the realm of the *repeatable remote head*, which is a remotely operated head capable of recording and playing back moves. These heads are not truly motion control heads, lacking the accuracy of frame and phase synchronization, but they are often adequate to the task.

bemoan the inability to boom up or down during the shot, and the cost savings incurred by renting this simple rig can be somewhat offset by a Director or Director of Photography not getting exactly what he or she wanted.

Small Crane on Track

These rigs have jib arms of 4 to 6 feet in length and their movement capability tends to emulate a camera on a live-action dolly, but with some additional abilities. Though various designs appear to be quite different, conceptually, they can be described in terms of axes.

- *Track:* generally straight track, though some rigs can run on special curved track.
- *Swing:* the rotation of the entire mechanism above the track dolly.
- *Lift:* the raising and lowering axis of the jib arm.
- *Pan, tilt, focus, iris, and zoom:* as described earlier.

This is the most prevalent type of rig in live-action use—representing a good compromise between operating envelope and ease of setup and use. Not only can this rig achieve the full range of motion available on a live-action dolly on straight track, but with judicious use of the swing axis and careful placement of straight track, this rig can often emulate a dolly move that includes a combination of straight and curved track. Additionally, since the camera operator is operating the head remotely, it is possible to make shots that could not be done on a standard dolly or even a small jib arm with a manual head.

Figure 3.65 A very large motion control crane on its trailer-mounted track. (Image courtesy of Tom Barron.)

Big Cranes

There are a number of larger cranes that are still relatively easy to deploy on location. Built with the same axis configuration as small cranes on a track, these rigs sport jib arms of 8×12 feet and, in a few cases, as long as 24 feet. While the small cranes generally run on 24.5-inch gauge or 32-inch gauge track, most of the big cranes run on wider track and their larger size and wider track require a bit more time and effort to set up.

A couple of cranes on the market feature the best of both worlds: narrow, lightweight track and components coupled with a long arm. These recent designs take advantage of experience and modern materials and also take into account the fact that in the world of contemporary digital compositing, very small errors are not that hard to accommodate, compared to optical compositing, where steadying images was very difficult indeed.

Figure 3.66 VistaVision camera on a large motion control crane. (Image courtesy of Mark H. Weingartner.)

Purpose-Built Rigs

Every motion control equipment supplier has a pile of one-off rigs that were built for a particular shot or to solve a particular problem. If you have an oddball shot, it is worth asking your motion control supplier if he or she has a rig that can accommodate the shot. Most motion control suppliers are quick to rise to a new technical challenge.

Motors and Sound

The two types of motors commonly used in building motion control equipment are stepper motors and servo motors. From the VFX Supervisor's point of view, the main difference between them is that servo motors are virtually silent, while stepper motors emit a variety of harmonic sounds at different speeds. While the choice of motors is only one of the factors affecting the rig's impact on sound, it is a significant one.

Model/Miniature/Stop-Motion Rigs

While many miniature and stop-motion jobs have been shot with live-action motion control rigs, numerous rigs are still on the market that are fully capable of motion control accuracy but not at live-action speeds.

Figure 3.67 A large motion control rig designed to work at stop-motion and go-motion speeds. (Image courtesy of New Deal Studios.)

The resurgence of stop-motion animation features has resulted in the renovation and manufacture of smaller, lighter rigs that are only capable of stop-motion and go-motion speeds.[62] It is very unlikely that any rig that has not been built from the ground up to work at live-action speeds can be adapted to do so without performance compromises. When it comes to choosing a rig for shooting miniatures, models, or stop- or go-motion animation, it is best to discuss the specifics of the shots with your VFX Director of Photography, model shop supervisor, and motion control equipment vendor.

Motion Control Software

The two most prevalent motion control programs in current use are Kuper and Flair. Each has its proponents, and motion control programmers tend to specialize in using one or the other. Rigs from General Lift, Pacific Motion Control, Image G, and the companies that shoot miniatures in the United States are controlled primarily by Kuper software. Rigs that are built and supported by Mark Roberts Motion Control (a U.K. company) and their affiliates generally offer systems that use Flair software. For the most part, the ease and ability to accomplish a given shot will be determined by the physical rig and the skill of the programmer, not the choice of motion control software. On the other hand, if the data is being ported out real time to an on-set preview system, it is critical to determine that the specific preview system being used is compatible with the specific motion control software being used. As with all computer technologies, assurances over the phone are no substitute for actual tests.

Camera Types

Motion control can be used with a wide variety of camera types. Formerly used primarily with Mitchell cameras with stepper motors or Lynx Robotics motors, motion control rigs can be used with all manner of film, television, HD, and even digital still cameras.

Sync and Phase

What makes motion control "motion control" is the accurate correlation between each image frame and the matching camera position. To create this correlation, the motion control computer's time base either needs to be driven by the camera or needs to drive the camera. This requires the synchronization and phasing

---

[62] Go-motion photography is shot at very slow frame rates, but with the motion control rig moving continuously through the shot, rather than repositioning and stopping still for each frame. This allows for naturalistic motion blur when shooting miniatures.

of the camera to the motion control computer. When synchronized there is a one-to-one correlation between photographic frames and data frames, but when a camera has a 180-degree shutter, for instance, this frame-per-frame correlation can still have offsets of as much as half a frame. The camera and motion control computer are said to be *in phase* when the data frame correlates with the center of the open shutter period of the camera's cycle.

In practical terms, the importance of being in phase from pass to pass is greatest when there is fast movement in the motion control rig relative to the frame rate. Since a phasing error amounts to a timing error, the faster the movement, the greater the distance or angle offset per frame. The result of this offset is that multiple passes will not line up. The line-up error is not necessarily as simple as a global pixel offset. In the case of multiple objects in a scene at varying distances from the camera, the resultant camera path displacement caused by the timing offset can result in parallax variances from pass to pass between foreground and background objects.

With a little advance notice and fussing, pretty much any film camera that has an accessible shutter pulse signal can be made to work with a motion control rig at a variety of camera speeds. Standard-definition and HD cameras can be synced to a motion control computer using the camera's sync pulse (tri-level sync in the case of HD). When using HD cameras at speeds other than 23.98 or 29.97 fps, however, the likelihood of being able to obtain a once-per-frame pulse is much lower. For specific cameras and frame rates, it is imperative to research the possibilities with the motion control equipment supplier for the job. For obvious reasons, this is of particular importance when using motion control to create timescale effects, necessitating shooting the same shot at different frame rates.

Dealing with Production

The secret of a successful motion control shoot is good communication before the shoot. Part of the challenge is managing the expectations of the 1st Assistant Director and the Unit Production Manager. Many complaints about motion control arise from a lack of understanding on the part of the AD of what the shots entail and the AD's subsequent inability to plan the day appropriately. Find the time to talk through the on-set process with the AD. Let him or her know how much setup time the crew will need to get the rig on line and how much time you expect it to take in order to program the first pass. The AD also has to know what else has to happen before you can get to the second pass, whether that involves shifting scenery, flying in green screens, or moving the rig.

Talk with your set lighting crew and your grip crew. Make sure that the set lighting best boy knows how much power you will need and what, if any, special connectors you will need in order to power up. Motion control track is not difficult for grips to deal with, but the grips should be made aware of the necessity to support the track in such a way that there is no movement from pass to pass. When working with platforms, for instance, this often requires more legs, more plywood on top, or more bracing.

The Director of Photography needs to know how the shot will be programmed: whether the operator will be encoding the shot or whether the programmer will be building the move. Discuss the options with the DP before you finalize the equipment package—make sure the DP is happy with the process. Make sure to speak with the camera assistant and that there is a clear understanding of whose equipment will be controlling the lens and which camera body you will be working with. If necessary, have production bring a body to the motion control supplier's shop during prep. At least make sure that the body will be available to test for the sync pulse before the shot.

Conclusion

With a little research into the best ways of accomplishing the needed shots, and a little time spent communicating with production and the rest of the crew, it is possible to shoot motion control smoothly and efficiently. Every well-planned and well-executed motion control shoot helps makes for a smoother path for VFX Supervisors everywhere to use motion control when it serves the purpose of the project.

ACQUISITION OF MOTION/STILL PHOTOGRAPHIC TEXTURES FOR MAPPING ONTO CG
Mark H. Weingartner

Among the tools available for creating photorealistic panoramic backgrounds or photorealistic GC objects are elements that are created by photographing scenery, architecture, objects, and even people. While there are often considerations that suggest the use of procedurally generated textures, photographing real scenes or textures can provide a cost-effective and time-effective way to work.

Two general situations warrant the use of photographically acquired elements. One is the creation of naturalistic panoramic backgrounds onto which foreground elements are to be composited. This category includes not only static environments, but also moving background plates (for vehicles, for instance) that are built up from several overlapping images. The second application of photographic elements is in generating specific CG elements for which the skin might be more easily created using photographs than through CG synthesis—either modeling/painting or procedurally. These textures can be photographed with digital still cameras, film still cameras, motion picture film cameras of various formats, or digital cinema cameras. Additionally, many visual effects facilities have incorporated HDRI[63] fish-eye images into their automated lighting systems for CG elements.

Panoramic Backgrounds

When shooting the tiles that will be blended together to form a background, a number of factors inform the decision to shoot stills or motion pictures.

Resolution is a prime consideration. One must consider the resolution and intended viewing method of the final project, as well as the degree of magnification that might be called for in a given composite. Since the background is being assembled from photographic tiles, it is not necessarily the case that the resolution of the tiling camera need match the 1st unit camera, but one must be mindful of trade-offs. Insufficient resolution might result in backgrounds that need to be heavily processed to reduce grain or noise. Shooting much higher resolutions than needed can result in very large, unwieldy image files once the backgrounds have been assembled. In a bright day exterior scene where 1st unit photography can be expected to have a relatively deep depth of field, or when composites require focus thrown deep into the scene, more resolution is likely to be needed than if the tiles will form a deep background for a night scene that will be photographed with shallow depth of field. Resolution should be considered with respect to the field of view of a given tile, not just by looking at the resolution of the camera format that covers the same field of view.[64]

The anticipated dynamic range in a scene can strongly influence camera choice. Even as the dynamic range and bit depth of digital motion picture cameras and digital still cameras are improving, film stocks also continue to improve. Film can still

---

[63] High-dynamic-range imaging (HDRI) is a technique for capturing the extended tonal range in a scene by shooting multiple pictures at different exposures and combining them into a single image file that can express a greater dynamic range than can be captured with current imaging technology.

[64] It is advisable to shoot background tiles for an anamorphic show with VistaVision cameras, for instance, in order to allow for punching in to close-ups without having to shoot background plates for specific angles. The same resolution can be achieved with 4-perf cameras shooting longer focal length lenses, but more tiles will be needed to cover the same background area. Where camera size is an issue, a greater number of smaller tiles might make sense—a background made up of four VistaVision tiles will have the same resolution as an IMAX frame.

capture a greater dynamic range within a scene than digital cameras can at a given exposure setting. While the 1st unit Director of Photography can control exposure and contrast by changing the *f*-stop and adjusting lighting, backgrounds that encompass wide angles of view often have a great range of contrast—sunlit buildings with strongly shadowed streets, for instance. The desirability of shooting adjacent plates or tiles with the same exposure settings to facilitate stitching and blending suggests the use of film in high-contrast situations. If the 1st unit is shooting film, this approach has the collateral benefit of capturing the background material in the same color space as the foreground elements.

The advantages that film has in these respects are somewhat offset by handling costs and grain. Many projects choose to shoot their background tiles with digital still cameras, using bracketed exposures to compensate for the lesser dynamic range of CCD and CMOS sensors compared to modern film stocks. On the other hand, many backgrounds are assembled from tiles built from multiple film frames with grain averaging applied.

The choice of motion versus still capture is informed by several factors. If the backgrounds contain elements that show movement over time, such as wavy trees, rippling water, moving clouds, moving traffic, or flocks of birds, for instance, a strong argument can be made for shooting motion pictures. However, if the backgrounds are generally architectural or do not reveal movement, the lower costs, lower profile on location, and less voluminous data storage issues often suggest the use of digital stills.

Tiled Stills

In the past dozen years, the assembly of individual still photographs into a seamless image has gone from being a laborious manual process requiring sophisticated and expensive programs to something that can be done with free software available with many digital cameras. With either film or digital still cameras, a nodal head[65] is preferable when shooting environments containing objects at varying distances to the camera and including foreground objects, but if shooting distant backgrounds, perfectly acceptable results can be achieved with non-nodal camera heads. A certain amount of horizontal and vertical overlap is needed, generally on the order of 10% to 20% of the image. Prime lenses (non-zoom) should be used, both for optical quality and

---

[65] A nodal head is a pan/tilt head that is designed so that the pan and tilt axes can be lined up with the point inside the lens where the light rays forming the image cross. This allows the camera to be panned and tilted without revealing any parallax shift between foreground and background objects within the scene.

to ensure that image magnification and distortion are consistent from tile to tile. When photographing scenes that contain a wide tonal range, it is advisable to shoot multiple bracketed exposures for each camera position. These images can be combined to express an extended dynamic range in the scene. Different facilities have different specific requirements in order to feed their pipelines, so it is important to confer with the chosen facility before shooting whenever possible.

For remote applications and to solve certain other production issues, several automated nodal tiling systems are in use. These systems remove the difficulty of figuring out the appropriate overlap when shooting night scenes with few discrete visual reference points. The Tesselator system is a camera-agnostic system that calculates angles of view based on focal length, film-back size, and percentage overlap and drives a motorized head to shoot a user-definable matrix of tiles. Some visual effects facilities have built in-house solutions for automated tiling needs as well. Another approach to building a background from stills is the Panoscan system, which uses a motorized head to scan a panoramic scene and delivers a single large file integrated from the scan.

Motion Tiling and Synchronous Plates

If the needs of a project warrant the use of motion picture tiles, whether film or digital, there are two basic approaches: single-camera tiles or multiple-camera synchronous plates.

Figure 3.68 VistaVision camera on a nodal head atop a skyscraper.
(Photo courtesy of Mark H. Weingartner.)

A single-camera nodal tiling setup allows for all the tiles to be shot without any parallax[66] issues arising between foreground, midground, or background objects. This lack of parallax shift simplifies assembly of the background. In addition to shooting bursts at each position in the tile matrix, it is often advisable to shoot longer takes of tiles that are specifically framed to show traffic, crowds, or other moving elements. Even if the facility paints out the existing traffic and animates traffic across the tiles, these *traffic tiles* can serve as useful animation references.

Background plates for scenes that take place in moving vehicles or in front of movement-filled backgrounds are frequently shot with multiple motion picture cameras filming overlapping fields of view. Richard Yuricich, ASC, is generally credited with pioneering the technique of shooting a continuous panorama using a multiple-camera array with matched lenses in order to provide for tracking a moving foreground camera shot across a digitally stitched-up background. This method is now in common use, with overlapping plates shot digitally with 35mm cameras, VistaVision cameras, and even 65mm cameras.

(A)

(B)

Figure 3.69 (A) VistaVision cameras on a helicopter. (B) Rotovision cameras on a train. (Images courtesy of Mark H. Weingartner.)

While it is possible to set up two cameras to share a nodal point using a beamsplitter, whenever there are more than two cameras working, it is not possible to have them nodal to each other. The determination as to how many cameras and what focal length lenses to use involves weighing various factors—lens distortion, format resolution, lens vignetting, physical rig size, etc.— and coming up with the best compromise.

[66] Parallax shift is the apparent movement of objects relative to each other dependent on their distance to the camera when the camera pans or tilts.

If the background objects are all very far away, parallax becomes less of an issue and intercamera spacing becomes less critical. However, if dealing with foreground objects passing by slowly enough to be sharp, it is important to choose camera/lens/mounting combinations that create the least amount of temporal or spatial offset between an object's appearance at one edge of the frame of one camera and its appearance at the corresponding edge of the next camera over.[67]

To eliminate stuttering as objects cross from one frame to the next, the cameras should be synchronized and phased so that all the shutters are open at the same time and closed at the same time. If shooting electronically, cameras must be gen-locked. Because of the parallax shift caused by multiple cameras not shooting nodally, a bit of repair work can be expected in post. For this reason, if the Director and DP are willing and able to nail down specific angles for process work, there is some benefit to shooting *in-one* specific angle plates where possible or centering the tiled plates such that in-one plates can be extracted from single-camera shots.

Practical Considerations

Here are some rules of thumb that apply whether shooting with film or digitally and whether shooting still tiles or motion tiles:

- Maintain a consistent exposure. To fit tiles together, it is important that the exposure of each tile not need to be adjusted on ingest. Analyze the scene and set a fixed exposure that will work for the entire range of tiles to be shot. Do not vary the *f*-stop within a tile sequence, because this will alter depth of field and subtly change the bokeh[68] of highlights or out-of-focus objects.
- Use prime (fixed focal length lenses).[69]
- Use a deep enough *f*-stop to let the lens be the best it can and for the best depth of field possible, but avoid stopping down

---

[67] In the 1990s, Jim Dickson built a smaller, lighter, modular version of the CircleVision rig that aims up to nine cameras up into 45-degree mirrors. Portions of this rig have been used to shoot synchronous plates. It has the advantage of a relatively small nodal offset over the multiple cameras shooting a wide angle of view but does have some of the disadvantages associated with multiple mirrors on a moving rig.

[68] Bokeh: a photographic term referring to the appearance of point of light sources in an out-of-focus area of an image produced by a camera lens using a shallow depth of field. Different lens bokeh produce different aesthetic qualities in out-of-focus backgrounds, which are often used to reduce distractions and emphasize the primary subject.

[69] Some modern autofocus still lenses lack mechanical manual controls. With these lenses it is impossible to tape off the focus or aperture rings. When these cameras are powered up, they will hunt for a new position. With this in mind, it is important to come up with a routine that allows the photographer to reset these parameters if the camera is powered down during a tiling pass.

all the way, because lens performance can be degraded by diffraction.

- Most visual effects facilities will want lens distortion grids for any lenses used to shoot tiles. These grids will allow them to automate the removal of distortion of the individual tiles prior to assembly.

Stills for Textures and Lighting

The use of physical miniatures for set extensions and to photograph physical effects has been supplanted to a large degree by the use of models built in a CG environment, whether as wireframes or otherwise, and *skinned*[70] with the appropriate textures. Often the basis of this skin is a photograph or a series of photographs of a real object.

If called on to provide texture photos, either for direct use or as reference, it is important to find out exactly what the facility requires. Depending on the specifics of the job, the facility might want softly lit texture shots so that they can add their own drop shadows as needed, while other situations call for *baked-in*[71] shadows. In any case, it is important to use lenses that are of good quality, have decent contrast, and exhibit minimal spherical distortion across their fields. Backing up far enough from the subject to allow the use of relatively long focal length lenses ($\geq$50mm in full-frame 35mm still format at the widest) will help flatten the image and reduce the baked-in perspective.

Another evolution in 3D CG production is the automation (or semiautomation) of some of the lighting of 3D CG elements using fish-eye images shot on the live-action set. For years, common practice included shooting shots of chrome reflecting spheres along with 18% reflectance gray spheres in order to give CG artists lighting references, but gradually different visual effects facilities have built pipelines that incorporate fish-eye images, either of a reflecting sphere, or shot with a fish-eye lens, in their lighting systems. As with the software systems that assemble tiles into panoramic backgrounds, as the systems have become more automated, the specific shooting parameters have become more detailed and restrictive. Where these images were once visual references that allowed a 3D lighting artist to deduce what the light sources were on set that would have lit the CG element, they now drive the lighting programs directly.

---

[70] Skinning: process in which an image is overlaid onto a CG object; also known as *texture mapping*.
[71] The term *baked-in* is often used to denote a characteristic of an image that is integral to the image and cannot easily be modified in post-production.

The visual effects facility will generally specify how these fish-eye images are to be shot, both with regard to physical setup and with regard to exposure bracketing in order to best feed their pipeline. Several visual effects facilities and individuals have built their own proprietary hardware systems for recording the lighting impinging on a scene. The HDR-Cam Light Probe System developed by Hoyt Yeatman uses an array of multiple lenses whose images are integrated into a single HDR panorama. Others use motorized pan/tilt heads to map a scene with multiple exposures. Yet another clever approach to shooting panoramas for reference is a device that consists of a parabolic conical mirror into which a still camera is pointed. When photographed, the mirror records a 360-degree panorama.

Conclusion

With a variety of methods and uses for photographic textures, it is important to choose the most appropriate approach for a given situation. The gross distinctions between (1) film or digital acquisition, (2) motion or still capture, or (3) production use or reference use (e.g., HDRI lighting references) are further refined by the subtler choices of specific cameras and systems. Whenever possible, get a clear understanding of what the parameters are with regard to:

- visual effects facility pipeline requirements,
- contrast inherent in the material to be photographed,
- degree of resolution required for the specific use of the materials to be photographed, and
- color space matching issues.

Once format and exposure strategy have been decided on—have at it, and remember that in the digital world, data is not data until it is safely stored in two places.

STOP-MOTION
Pete Kozachik, ASC

Stop-motion is best known as a blend of animation and model photography, long the most versatile means to produce creature effects. Now it is chosen more for stylistic reasons, leaving computer graphics to produce footage that is required to be hyperrealistic.

At the heart of the process, a lone animator creates a performance by sequentially posing a flexible puppet and photographing each pose on a separate frame of film.

Without key-frame interpolation or Newtonian physics routines, stop-motion delivers a somewhat surreal take on real-world motion, further abstracted by the lack of motion blur.

For many decades, animating on film imposed a completely linear workflow; start at the beginning, and carry the shot to its end, only imagining how the work was progressing. The first opportunity to check one's performance was in dailies, when the shot was finished and baked in to the negative.

Evolution of Stop-Motion Photography

Recent advances in technology have made stop-motion a more user-friendly technique. But for most of its run, stop-motion was at a disadvantage with other forms of animation.

The classic means of estimating frame-by-frame continuity in stop-motion was a machinist's tool called a *surface gauge*. Basically a movable pointer on a heavy base, it was placed at a strategic point on the puppet such as the nose, before moving the puppet another increment. The gap between nose and pointer indicated how far the nose was moving between frames. Beyond that, the animator carried the entire shot in his head; the faster he could work, the better he could visualize the performance in progress.

Meanwhile, cartoon animation offered instant feedback; the animator could flip through his drawings to check motion and could shine a light through a sheaf of drawings to gauge increments of motion. Only when all was ready did the drawings go under a camera.

Beginning in the late 1980s, animators have been able to review stop-motion work in progress and service change notes midshot. Starting with surveillance video cameras and repurposed hardware frame stores, animators could scrub through their two most recent frames and a live frame. It was rudimentary and expensive but enough to gauge progress and verify that all those puppet arms and legs were moving in the right direction.

Soon after, hardware capture systems became available that could store hundreds of standard video resolution frames. Animators could review an entire shot in progress. And it was possible to cut back several frames and carry on in a different direction. The video camera image was not usable as production footage but was very helpful in gauging performance, while a film camera captured the end product.

Now such products are sold as PC or Mac applications, requiring only a video camera and a frame grabber card.

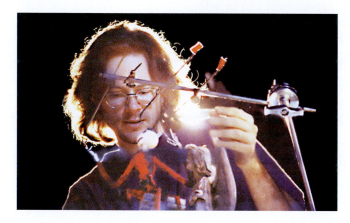

Figure 3.70 Anthony Scott animates Jack Skellington, using several surface gauges mounted on a grip stand. (Image courtesy of Jim Matlosz, Tim Burton's *THE NIGHTMARE BEFORE CHRISTMAS* © 1993 Touchstone Pictures. All rights reserved.)

As digital photography evolved, it became possible to capture images good enough for production footage. The first stop-motion feature to shoot without film cameras was *Corpse Bride* (2005), using instead a fleet of digital SLRs.[72] It was still necessary to feed the frame grabber animation aid from a live video camera placed at the dSLR eyepiece.

By the time the next stop-motion feature, *Coraline* (2009), was gearing up, it was possible to couple industrial machine vision cameras with a custom PC grabber application to handle both tasks, displaying animation in progress and capturing high-resolution production images.

As prosumer technology has evolved, the next such production will likely use the latest dSLR, now capable of live preview output, for the same purpose. This, coupled with evolving commercial frame grabber applications, will democratize stop-motion production, making high-end technology accessible to any budget.

The Time Required to Shoot in Stop-Motion

The actual shooting process takes time, but the supervisor can control some of it, not to mention the animator. Many factors affect production time; most notable are shot complexity, number of characters, accessibility to the puppet, and the work style of a given animator. Definitely include the animator and cameraman in prep to find ways of saving time.

There is a benchmark for high-end feature work. Average output from one animator on an average shot, working on *Corpse Bride* (2005), *Coraline* (2009), or *The Nightmare before Christmas* (1993), has been 2 or 3 seconds of screen time per day.

Figure 3.71 Buck Buckley sets up a challenging shot of multiple characters marching by torch light. (Image courtesy of Eric Swensen, Tim Burton's *THE NIGHTMARE BEFORE CHRISTMAS* © 1993 Touchstone Pictures. All rights reserved.)

[72] SLR: single-lens-reflex still camera.

Simpler visual effects work, or episodic TV character work, come in at 7 to 10 seconds a day. When the machine is humming, a stop-motion feature studio can put out a minute a week.

And once the shot is in the can, it is truly done. Lighting is done, camera work is done, and there will be no significant reworking of the performance. Good news for some and a scary scenario for others.

Sometimes a director will wish for a tweak on a finished shot, but usually she has infused her vision into the animator, and the first take has a strength and honesty about it.

Now that it is possible to stretch and squeeze time in selected parts of a shot, a director can massage a performance in post with a surprising degree of finesse. The animator's timing plays a major part in a performance, making retiming a powerful dramatic tool.

Preparation before Shooting

Preparation goes all the way back to shot design, character design, rigging, and building, before even entering the shooting stage.

Characters are designed with sketches and rough sculpts, followed by a fine sculpt. Since it is difficult to capture the exact look twice, it is a good idea to approve at the roughest acceptable stage and save the sculptor's mojo for the final master sculpt. This would be best done by applying clay over the armature, in a neutral spread-eagle pose, for best molding and casting.

An armature serves the same purpose as does rigging in CG animation. It is typically a framework of steel joints, machined to fit inside the puppet and hold any stance the animator imposes on it. A good armature can make a great difference in getting a subtle performance and can also save shoot time by making the animator's work easier. The armatures are usually designed to accommodate the range of motion called for in a breakdown of the character's planned performance.

Armature building is part art and part skilled machine work; some of the best armatures are made by animators with machining skills. They know just how the joints should behave when being moved. Each animator prefers a different amount of resistance, but they all like joints to move smoothly and hold their position the instant pressure is removed. That quality is best attained by lapping the joints, working them repeatedly until they are burnished smooth.

External rigging might also be used. More often these days, puppets have flying rigs and *helper* rigs, both used more for top-heavy puppet stability than for actual flying. Before rig removal became a catchphrase, puppet support came from finicky tungsten wires or just plain practical character design, usually including fat ankles.

Figure 3.72 Phil Dale uses support rigs to aid in animating Coraline and Cat. (Image courtesy of Pete Kozachik, *Coraline* © 2009 Laika, Inc. All rights reserved.)

Today, the animator usually does not make the puppet; a machinist makes the armature, a sculptor forms oil-base clay over it, and a mold maker casts it in foam latex, often lightly skinned with silicone. Then a painter paints it, a costumer clothes it, and yet another fabricator adds hair, scales, and so forth.

It is worth noting that these puppets wear out in use from constant handling. At the very least they need careful cleaning after a long shot. Inevitably the foam wears down, and the puppet is stripped down to the armature and recast. On a long project this must be accounted for.

Most puppet fabricators are freelancers, and there are a few one-stop shopping opportunities, entire companies that make animation puppets from scratch.

The same holds for stage crew; some, but not all, visual effects cameramen have shot stop-motion and are typically versed in the use of motion control. They have practical experience with shooting miniatures and can either match lighting from first unit plates or create dramatic lighting for a given scene or plot point.

Setting Up a Shooting Space for Stop-Motion

Stage sizes for most shows have centered around 20 by 25 feet, usually side by side with other setups, all separated by black duvetyne curtains. The biggest have been 40 by 60 feet, and the smallest have been 10 by 10. The higher the ceiling, the better, for cooling.

The setups use less electricity than live action, and a typical setup could work with 60 to 100 amps. This feed usually needs to be conditioned, held within a half-volt tolerance, so the shot doesn't flicker as line voltage varies throughout the day. Line regulators can be obtained in the form of a 60-amp variable transformer, constantly adjusted by a stepping motor and voltage sensor working in a closed loop. There are larger versions for permanent installation that can handle a whole studio.

Conditioning systems can save many hours on stage and in post; by presetting the line voltage down 5 or 10 volts, lamp life extends far beyond specifications. The difference in brightness and color is trivial, compared to dealing with a blown lamp during a shot.

Live-action-style overhead grids have disadvantages in a stop-motion studio, especially with multiple setups. While a camera crew relights one set, the grid may move over another set that is shooting. And grid heights are usually too high for table-top setups.

By populating the studio with simple floor-based individual grids, all that can be avoided, and the crew can still use the advantages of a grid. Given the scale of most setups, a grid can be no more than two parallel lengths of speed rail overhead, reachable by a 6-foot ladder.

Figure 3.73 Typical interior set, with a scaled down overhead grid holding most of the lighting. (Image courtesy of Galvin Collins, *Coraline* © 2009 Laika, Inc. All rights reserved.)

To date, most lighting for stop-motion has used small lights, scaled down to match puppet scale as much as possible. A typical setup relies mostly on 200W Mini-Moles and Arri 300W Fresnel units, with a few 650 and 1k units. A 2k is considered a big light in most cases, but some very large exterior sets have required 5k and 10k lights.

More recently, small banks of white LEDs have found their way onto stop-motion setups. They are good for hiding within a set, and run cool, which helps prevent the damaging of latex foam in proximity.

Practical lights, such as puppet scale table lamps and candles, tend to dictate how bright the movie lights can be. Practicals are usually made up from small but robust aircraft instrument panel lamps, typically 14 volt.

In planning for a workflow, one should have more setups than animators. While a camera unit works on lighting and motion control moves on one setup, the animator can be working on another setup. One of the primary goals for a production manager is to keep animators busy, and that means always having a set waiting for them once they finish their current shot.

Such redundancy should be used anywhere a production bottleneck could delay a shot. For example, there should always be an extra puppet waiting to fill in for a damaged one. Now that cameras and motion control rigs are easily obtained, there should also be a backup on them as well. As production ramps up, elements in short supply will reveal themselves, like it or not. An experienced production manager can identify them in advance.

Use of Motion Control in Stop-Motion

Motion control has allowed stop-motion to use camera moves like live action does. The rig need not be fast, pretty, or sophisticated. It should have somewhat higher resolution than typical live-action rigs, so it can smoothly advance from frame to frame. About one-half inch per motor turn is a good rule of thumb for tracks and booms. And pan/tilt/roll axes are good around 1-degree per motor turn.

Almost anything cobbled together will deliver a usable move, as long as its mechanical slop[73] is contained by bungee cords and counterweights. Plenty of motion control shots have been successfully filmed on rigs made with bicycle and car parts and hardware found in surplus stores.

---

[73] Slop: a degree of unwanted looseness in a mechanical system.

The best use of one's motion control budget is to obtain as many cheap, separate units as possible. Each will be tied up on a shot for several days, usually on simple moves, so simplicity and redundancy are the key requirements. That said, boom arms are preferred over tripod setups, because they help keep the animators' workspace clear.

Figure 3.74 Boom arm camera rig gives Eric Leighton easy access to animate. (Image courtesy of Pete Kozachik, *Coraline* © 2009 Laika, Inc. All rights reserved.)

Aside from camera cranes, motion control is useful in animating simple rigs such as color wheels, motorized dimmers, and moving props. Such mechanization helps to keep the animator's attention on character performance.

In the 1980s, ILM adapted motion control to animate creature effects, with 3 or 4 degrees of freedom on a puppet-sized rubber monster's head, limbs, and body. This change enabled animators to preanimate and edit the puppet's performance before committing it to film. Since it had the ability to create real motion blur, the process was named *go motion*.

Useful Caveats

Launching an animator is a serious commitment. Go through a checklist of shot-safety items before the animator begins. This can include securing camera and light stands, lens settings, camera and motion control cables, and props on the set. It is

Figure 3.75 Jan Maas uses a trap door to gain access to his puppets, while cameraman Peter Williams finishes camera checks. (Image courtesy of Pete Kozachik, *Coraline* © 2009 Laika, Inc. All rights reserved.)

common practice to hot-glue grip stands to the floor and check individual lightbulbs for signs of impending burnout. Pay special attention to making a clear path for the animator to move in and out of the set. Whether shooting film or digital, make sure the media won't run out midshot.

Camera supports and table-top sets shift over time, due to humidity and temperature variance. It only becomes a problem when shooting is interrupted for several hours, typically overnight. The effect on screen is a visible jump, usually slight, but not always. This problem is often fixable by carefully tweaking whatever shifted. Turnbuckles, jackscrews, and wedges are helpful. The frame grabber is used to compare last night's final frame with a live image, while making the adjustment. It is a good idea to build sets with some means of adjustment built in.

2D fixes in post sometimes help, but are often thwarted by motion parallax, which makes foreground objects shift more than in the background.

Prevention is the best approach, which saves valuable shoot time in the morning. Note that rigs made of unpainted thick-wall aluminum extrusions are especially good heat sinks, spreading temperature changes throughout, rather than bending from differential heating. And it is helpful to keep hot lights from hitting one side of a rig, regardless of the material.

Wood and composite materials are bones of contention regarding how best to prevent them from shifting. Humidity is the prime cause for wood shifting, so many consider sealing wooden structures.

In the age of flawless, photoreal computer graphics, the quest for perfection is a common hang-up in stop-motion. One can worry it to death, throwing a lot of resources at a minor problem. Or one can remember that such real-world anomalies are part of stop-motion's hand-made charm, perhaps the very reason for choosing the process.

Evolution of a Shot

On a mostly live-action film, the VFX Supervisor may be standing in for the director for visual effects animation. Working with animators and cameramen, he or she has to tailor direction to fit the individual, just as in CG animation. In the stop-motion feature model, a given shot begins in crude form, starting as a roughed-in response to an initial briefing.

Much like blocking a live-action shot, the performer (in this case, the animator) works directly with the cameraman/motion control operator. Based on the briefing, they make key position marks for the puppet to hit, and the motion control is keyframed to those marks. Several quick tests are shot to coordinate puppet location and camera move. When it is close enough, they shoot a *pop-through*, which is a run-through with minimal animation.

Typically, this is a first look at timing, with the puppet at least hitting key positions. It also informs detail work in lighting. Thus it is not the time for finesse, as many things may change when it is shown to the supervisor. It may be viewed on set, but more can be learned by cutting the pop-through into the reel.

Then the animator does a rough rehearsal, in response to comments on the pop-through. The amount of animation finesse is agreed on, so the supervisor gets what he needs, without the animator wasting time by overworking the shot. It should contain camera and lighting tweaks at this point as well; this could be the dress rehearsal, and such rehearsals have been known to end up in the movie. So if this is a possibility, everyone contributing should know in advance.

Depending on how that goes, and how the budget is holding up, the next event will be the final performance, the real deal. It may take several days to shoot, so broadband communication is crucial at this time to avoid a reshoot.

Thanks to digital photography, the supervisor can check in on how it's going, usually on set. If absolutely necessary, the shot in progress can be cut in. Once in awhile, segments of shots in progress go to visual effects so labor-intensive work such as roto can get started before the animator is done.

The traditional gut-wrenching moment as the projector is threaded up is a thing of the past; everyone involved has already seen the performance in progress, and camera/lighting issues have been seen as well, so the only surprise is how great it looks on the big screen.

Use of Stop-Motion in Visual Effects

Aside from creature effects, stop-motion was regularly used for supporting effects, such as enhancing motion-controlled miniatures where mechanization was not practical. Stop-motion has provided many stunt doubles over the years, such as the ubiquitous falling man, complete with flailing arms and legs.

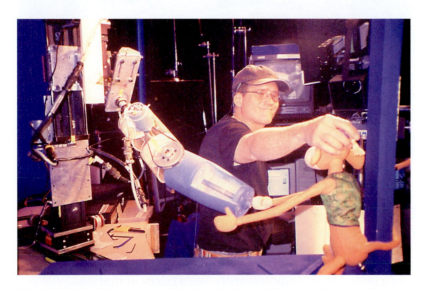

Figure 3.76 Tim Hittle animates a crazed simian grabbing a motion control arm, tracked to a live actor's arm movements in the background plate.
(Image courtesy of Pete Kozachik, *Monkeybone* © 2001 Twentieth Century Fox. All rights reserved.)

On rare occasions, the tone of a film fits the stop-motion look, and it is called on to deliver creature effects in a live-action setting. Modern filmmakers expect greater interaction between actors and puppets and more freedom for camera movement. This has become more possible for stop-motion effects thanks to advances in motion control and motion tracking, not to mention the powerful new capabilities in compositing. If a director wants the look, it can be done with confidence.

Figure 3.77 Brian Demoskoff animates Corpse Bride's wedding outfit, made with bendable wires sewed in. Animating cloth is a challenge in stop-motion as well as CG. Several shots used a CG wedding veil on the film. (Image courtesy of Pete Kozachik for Tim Burton's *Corpse Bride* (2005). TIM BURTON'S *CORPSE BRIDE* © Patalex II Productions Limited. Licensed By: Warner Bros. Entertainment Inc. All rights reserved.)

Good Moves to Make at the Beginning of a Project

VFX Producers and Supervisors new to stop-motion are wise to bring in an experienced adviser and go over script or boards. Get that person's take on how to maximize the use of stop-motion for the project's particular circumstances. He or she might have simple suggestions that could save a lot of money, on set or in post. Stop-motion isn't a minefield, but it can go smoother if someone on the team has already been there.

Similarly, supervisors can benefit by knowing why the director chose stop-motion as a technique; such an understanding will get the initial prep on the right track. The director may want enhancements such as motion blur added in post or may be seeking a period look, complete with sharp edges in motion.

Spend some time perusing this website: www.stopmotionanimation.com. It is hosted by an A-list stop-motion animator/animation supervisor and contains a comprehensive resource list.

WHAT ARE MINIATURES?
Matthew Gratzner

What Are Miniatures and Why Are They Used?

Miniature effects are one of the oldest visual effects techniques, dating back to the silent era. Miniatures, or models as they are sometimes referred to, are scaled replicas of the object they represent, designed and intricately detailed to photograph as a full-scale, real object. Miniatures have provided a practical solution to creating landscapes, cities, vehicles, and catastrophic events

Figure 3.78 A 1:24-scale period model of Grauman's Chinese Theater and Hollywood Boulevard. (Image courtesy of New Deal Studios for *THE AVIATOR* (2005). *THE AVIATOR* © IMF International Medin Unfo Film Gmbh & Co3 Produktions Kg. Licensed By: Warner Bros. Entertainment Inc. All rights reserved.)

through a technique that is not only physically practical but can be financially beneficial as well.

Though the explosion of digital effects has replaced the use of some miniature effects in today's filmmaking, the combination of digital and miniature effects has made it far more practical in cost and in post-production manipulation. With the advances in digital technology, particularly regarding tracking and compositing, miniatures have become more easily integrated into sequences, truly blurring the lines between the old and new techniques, giving audiences a hyperreality in visual effects.

The Advantages and Disadvantages of Miniature Effects

The advantage of employing a miniature effect is that a physical object is fabricated and photographed. Therefore the texture, highlights, shadows, and focal length are all within the photography and do not need to be created artificially as with digital effects. When dealing with destruction action, physically destroying a model will be affected by real physics and unpredictable random actions and imperfections that subconsciously fool the eye into believing it is real. Essentially, if the miniature is detailed correctly and photographs as a full-scale object, most of the battle of making it convincingly real has been won. The remaining challenge is integrating it into the scene.

Figure 3.79 A 1:6-scale 360-degree church interior miniature and effects from *End of Days*. (Image courtesy of New Deal Studios, © 1999 Universal Studios Licensing, LLLP. All rights reserved.)

Another advantage of miniature effects is cost. If a miniature is utilized in a number of shots, then the cost of the miniature's design and fabrication can be amortized over each shot, making it far more cost effective to use. Also when dealing with high-speed events, multiple cameras are used to capture the moment, in essence giving the filmmaker multiple angles or multiple shots in one take.

As dynamic as miniature effects can be to lend a sense of realism to a shot, the technique has one major disadvantage. Unlike the incessant versioning of digital shots, committal is the true deciding factor as to whether to use a miniature to achieve a shot. Even though most miniature effects are achieved in post, long after the first unit has wrapped, the decisions on what to fabricate, how to shoot it, and how it will be integrated into a scene need to be determined well ahead of time. The construction schedules on some miniatures can be as much as 4 months, so a well-executed plan is crucial to a miniature effect sequence's success.

In other words, once committed to a miniature, its scale, how its fabrication will be accomplished and how it is photographed, one is more or less committed to this technique. Certainly shots can and will be manipulated later, but the more a plan is adhered to, the greater success one will have using miniature effects.

Execution of Planning

Like any visual effects shot, a concise plan is the only key to success when dealing with sometimes hundreds of artists collaborating with the same goal. That plan should be in the form of storyboarding, followed by previs. In the storyboarding process, the director has the ability to very inexpensively commit his or her vision to paper. A VFX Supervisor should work with the director to determine how to achieve the shots and, at this point, depending on what's needed, miniature effects can be determined. Once storyboards are locked, a previs can be developed.

In designing the miniatures that match existing objects or feature-approved art department designs, the miniatures can be developed in a CAD-based software, such as Rhino. As digital technology becomes more prevalent in film, art departments are transitioning from the traditional techniques of drafting their plans on velum by hand to designing their sets, vehicles, and props in the computer. This process creates a 3D digital model that can be used to generate dimensionally accurate blueprints for the physical construction. These digital files can be converted to object files and then imported into Maya, thus becoming the assets to generate the previs. Then, the previs can be utilized to drive the motion control camera rigs, therefore shooting exactly what has been created in the virtual environment (more on this subject later). Once the miniatures have been photographed, any precomps[74] with the miniatures can be achieved using the previs as the guide, since the camera data should be the same.

The point is that from storyboarding to previs to miniature fabrication to shooting and finishing with post-production manipulation, creating a planning strategy that is a closed loop guarantees a consistent goal without the fear of deviation from the director's original vision.

Design and Integration within the Film

Far too often 1st unit pre-production schedules are shortened, not providing the proper design time art departments need for the 1st unit, let alone visual effects. It is imperative to keep the continuity throughout the film between 1st unit production and the visual effects unit. If a miniature is being used as a set extension, consult with the production designer to maintain a seamless blend between the 1st unit and miniature designs. Obtain every blueprint, concept sketch, and any paint samples used for the design and construction of the film's sets. If possible, go to the 1st unit photography and document the set with measurements and photographs. Photographs with a known scale object in each shot can help immensely since, even though an art department plan was generated, the final set construction could have changed or developed in a slightly different direction.

Photographic Continuity

One of the key reasons for a miniature effects shot standing out in a project is a difference in style in terms of how it was photographed. To keep the continuity of the film, meet with the director and DP and discuss their techniques for shooting the picture. If the film features an extensive amount of wildly moving cameras on cranes or cable rigs, then the miniature photography should mirror this look. In contrast, if a director favors more lock-offs and gentle camera moves, don't shoot the miniatures with dizzying shots that will not cut in to the live action.

Miniature Categories

For ease of explanation, the following two categories break down the types of miniature effects used: static models and action models. The term *static models* refers to any miniature used as a set

---

[74] Precomps: non-final composites that preview how elements will ultimately come together.

extension, a photographic element, or an in-camera background or foreground (i.e., forced perspective, hanging foreground miniature, or split scale). While there can be mechanized movement within the model, this category primarily refers to models that do not blow up or have any destruction effects designed into them. Static models tend to be models filmed with a single motion control camera rig or photographed as stills and used as textures to be applied to a computer-generated model. In this category the models also tend to be fabricated on a smaller scale since there is no reliance on any nonscalable elements (i.e., water, fire, smoke) to manipulate their actions.

The term *action models* refers to a miniature designed to be destroyed, that is, blown up via explosives or air mortars, crushed, or in general used for scaled physical effects and stunts. In this category the scales will be much larger and the photography is usually achieved with multiple high-speed cameras.

Scale Determinations

A miniature scale is the ratio of size compared to the full-sized object. As written, a 1:12 scale miniature is 12 times smaller than the actual object. In 1:12 scale, a person who is 6 feet tall is 6 inches because 6 feet 0 inches divided by 12 = 6 inches. In 1:12 scale, 1 foot equals 1 inch; 1:24 scale is 24 times smaller than the actual object. In 1:24 scale, a person who is 6 feet tall is 3 inches because 6 feet 0 inches divided by 24 = 3 inches. In 1:24 scale, 1 foot equals 0.5 inch.

When determining a scale it is always best to choose even numbers that break down the larger units of measurements into manageable increments; this makes the calculations easier. It also helps if the scale of the model is used within the field of architecture, therefore utilizing a three-sided architectural scale ruler for smaller measurements. Arbitrarily making up sizes for miniature scales (i.e., 1:13.5 scale) makes it more difficult for the fabrication and photography personnel.

Another consideration for determining a scale is choosing a scale that is commonly found in the hobby industry. This affords the use of prefabricated objects, from the simple vacuum-formed brick-patterned sheet to military vehicles and aircraft to beautifully detailed furniture. Common hobbyist scales are as follows:
- Dollhouse: 1:12
- Model train: G-gauge, 1:24; O-gauge, 1:48; HO-gauge, 1:87
- Militaria: 1:35

The determining factor for the scale at which to design a miniature effect is based primarily on sheer practicality. The driving factor in the fabrication of static models is how small it can

Figure 3.80 A 1:24-scale house and yard model with intricate garbage details for Matthew Gratzner's short film *Huntin'* (2009). (Image courtesy of New Deal Studios.)

be made without compromising detail and depth of field. Most importantly, can the lens physically fit within the area that needs to be photographed? The number one factor that gives away a model shot is poor depth of field, that is, are the foreground, mid-ground, and background holding focus? In the early days of film, if objects within the shot or the camera required movement, prior to the advent of motion-controlled cameras that could shoot with longer exposures and faster film stocks and lenses, miniatures tended to feel "modelly." It was not that the models were poorly made or detailed, it was just that the equipment to capture the image on film was not as advanced. So with today's equipment, models can be constructed in much smaller scales and photographed at slower camera speeds. (Motion control photography is covered in more depth in the section titled *Photography of Miniature Effects: Motion Control* later in this chapter.)

As for scale considerations for action miniatures, build them as physically large as possible to fit within the selected stage or location and within the allotted budget. The larger the scale, the better smoke, fire, and water look in an effects shot. Depending on the shot requirements, these could be physically real or digitally created elements layered in the compositing stage. There are trade-offs among interactivity, scale, and control when determining the use of practical versus CG. Sometimes it's far easier to utilize a controlled destruction of miniatures with prescribed breaks and rehearsed mechanical actuation than dealing with the difficulty of dynamic CG simulations.

Figure 3.81 A 1:5-scale stylized city of Venice and canals for *The League of Extraordinary Gentlemen* (2003) from New Deal Studios. (Image courtesy of *The League of Extraordinary Gentlemen* © 2003 Twentieth Century Fox. All rights reserved.)

These physical elements cannot be scaled very easily, so through the use of a larger miniature and high-speed photography, the shot becomes more convincing. Just remember scaling is exponential. If the sequence requires an airplane hangar that is surrounded by a tarmac section to blow up, consider the entire size of both hangar and surrounding terrain. While it makes sense to build the hangar in 1:6 scale, meaning the miniature will be 12×16 feet, if the surrounding area is included, now the whole table-top including the hangar becomes 40×80 feet and may not fit within the stage/location parameters or, more importantly, may exceed the allotted budget. In this case, the scale chosen would need to be smaller and photographed at a higher frame rate. (High-speed photography is covered in more depth in *Photography of Miniature Effects: High-Speed Photography* in this chapter.)

As an example for the 2004 film *The Aviator*, a section of a Beverly Hills neighborhood was fabricated for a miniature plane crash sequence. Because of the high-speed nature of the shot, 1:4 scale was determined as the size that would provide a large enough miniature for the destruction action but would also be small enough to ship the models on trucks to the location where they were to be photographed. Each of the three neighborhood houses fabricated in 1:4 scale was approximately 20 feet long by 8 feet wide. These dimensions scaled up to full size would make each house 80 feet long by 32 feet wide. The layout with all of the houses, foliage, and dressing measured approximately 160 feet long by 60 feet wide. This may seem colossal in size, but relative to the actual size of the matched location, it was quite manageable. The layout's size allowed access and the control needed to crash a 1:4 scale aircraft in the complex scene without compromising the space for camera rigs, lighting, or crew.

Figure 3.82 A 1:4-scale model of the Howard Hughes XF-11 plane crashing into a Beverly Hills neighborhood. (Image courtesy of New Deal Studios for *The Aviator* (2005).

With today's advancements in digital technology, anything imagined can be created for a film. But are the images convincingly real? Though miniature effects may not be cutting edge in the current state of technology, that doesn't mean that the technique should be cast aside as outdated and unusable. By combining old and new technology, these visual effects disciplines can give today's audience images that won't appear to look dated in 2 years. Remember, a miniature effect will look as real 10 years from now as the day it was photographed. Taking a photographic image and combining it with digital animation and compositing gives the filmmaker an arsenal of visual effects tools that keeps sequences and shots looking new but also stands up to the test of time.

FORCED PERSPECTIVE MINIATURES[75]
Dan Curry, ASC Associate Member

In-Camera Compositing of Miniatures with Full-Scale Live-Action Actors

Hanging or *foreground* miniatures have been a valuable method of creating production value since the earliest days of filmmaking. In-camera compositing makes the use of miniatures an attractive alternative when post-production compositing may

---

[75] Reprinted from the *American Cinematographer Manual*, 9th Edition with permission from the American Society of Cinematographers.

not be possible. These techniques may be of special interest to any filmmakers working with extremely small budgets.

With the exception of 3D, photographed images are two dimensional. The camera, and the audience, cannot tell how far or near an object may actually be as there is no stereoscopic depth perception. The only clues are linear perspective, aerial perspective (caused by natural atmospheric density), and focus. Filmmakers can take advantage of this by placing a miniature within the frame to create the illusion that it is part of the full-scale world being photographed. There are many ingenious ways to incorporate live actors into foreground miniatures using platforms, ladders, and devices to cast shadows. Once the basic principles of photographing miniatures are understood, filmmakers can expand on them to suit their specific needs.

Some Advantages of Hanging Miniatures

- In-camera compositing eliminates compositing costs.
- One miniature can be photographed from many different angles and therefore used for different shots.
- Good miniature builders may be as easy to find as matte painters.
- When shot in daylight, light on the miniature will naturally match the light in the scene.
- Nodal pan/tilts can be utilized to achieve camera moves.
- When carefully aligned, people can be positioned inside or on the miniature.

Important Considerations When Photographing Hanging Miniatures

- Scout and shoot reference photos of the location in advance and prepare the miniature for specific location requirements.
- Establish adequate depth of field.
- Plan proper setup for accurate perspective and miniature stability.
- Make sure that light angles and cast shadows work with the illusion. A backlit structure that would naturally cast a shadow on the ground in front of it (which it cannot do unless the ground is built into the miniature set piece) will shatter the illusion of reality without a properly cast shadow. Key light should be forward of the miniature. When scouting locations note time of day for the best light angle.
- If actors are to appear inside or on the miniature, provisions must be made to cast shadows on them where needed to complete the illusion.
- Short focal length lenses offer the greatest depth of field.

- Aerial perspective (natural atmospheric density) can be simulated with diffusion sprayed onto a foreground glass in appropriate areas. Clear varnishes and dulling spray work well. In interior situations, judicious use of smoke can be an effective way to scale air density.

It is impossible to predict every situation that may arise, but the following examples may provide useful guidelines:

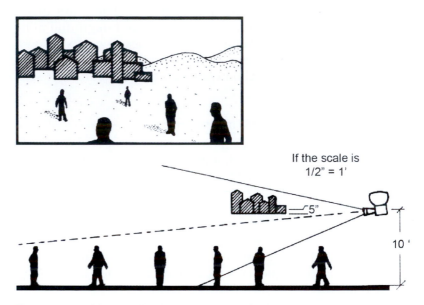

Figure 3.83 In this example actors approach a distant city or structure. (Image courtesy of Dan Curry and the American Society of Cinematographers.)

- If the actual height of the lens is 10 feet, the ground level on the miniature must be set below the lens an equal distance in scale. If the scale of the miniature is 1/2 inch = 1 foot, then the ground level on the miniature should be 5 inches below the lens.
- Depth of field must be determined (use any depth-of-field chart such as the one found in the ASC Manual) to carry focus to include the miniature and the appropriate area of the full scale environment. If the nearest point on the model is 4 feet from the camera with an 18mm lens (on a 35mm camera) an *f*-stop of 5.6 with focus set at 6 1/2 feet will carry focus from 3 feet 6 inches to infinity.
- Note that shadows can be a problem. It is generally wise to have the sun or key light behind the camera so that the shadow cast by the miniature falls away from camera where the viewer would not expect to see it on the ground, otherwise

provision must be made to cast an appropriate shadow on the full scale environment.

- Foreground miniature ceilings can be useful on sound stages where lighting grids must be used to illuminate the set and there is no room for a practical ceiling.

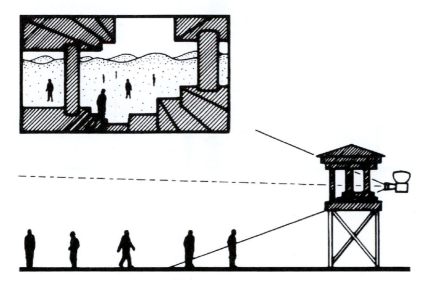

Figure 3.84 Using a miniature as a foreground cutting piece.
(Image courtesy of Dan Curry and the American Society of Cinematographers.)

Figure 3.85 Three-point perspective from a tall structure. (Image courtesy of Dan Curry and the American Society of Cinematographers.)

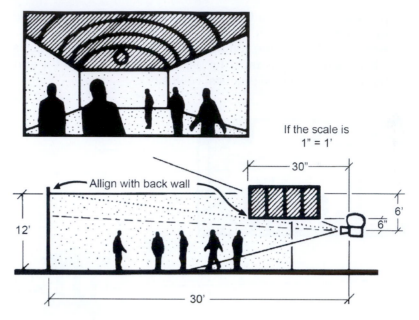

Figure 3.86 Using a hanging miniature as a ceiling extension. (Image courtesy of Dan Curry and the American Society of Cinematographers.)

Nodal Pans and Tilts

Pans and tilts are possible if the camera is mounted so that the pivot point is set at the nodal point of the lens. A simple way to confirm that the camera is properly mounted at the nodal point is to set two objects (C-stands, stakes, etc.) directly in line with one another in front of the camera. Try a test pan. If the foreground object appears to move in the opposite direction of the pan against the background reference object, then the camera is mounted in front of the nodal point; slide it back on the head until the two objects remain in alignment when the camera pans.

Forced Perspective

Situations may arise where forced perspective or constantly changing scales may provide the best solution to production needs. If this is the case, close coordination between director, director of photography, VFX Supervisor, production designer, and a highly skilled model maker is required, as there is no room for error if the illusion is to be successful.

Mixed Scales

To gain a greater illusion of distance, elements within a miniature scene can be built working from larger scale in the foreground to smaller scale the farther away objects are intended to appear.

THE FABRICATION OF MINIATURE EFFECTS
Brian Gernand

Methodologies and materials selected for miniatures are entirely based on the requirements of the specific shot or series of shots to be accomplished. For instance, the types of materials used to create a model that is going to be used in an action sequence (where miniatures blow up, burn, crash, or crumble) are going to be very different from a scene where miniatures will be photographed for a nonaction beauty or establishing shot.

Scale and Purpose Requirements of a Miniature

The first step is to identify the requirements for the miniature; that is, to define the action and uses for the model through script, previsualization, and discussions with creative leads. Next comes the conceptual phase, in which the scale and construction techniques are determined based on shot requirements. If the model is a static model to be photographed from a distance, the scale can be much smaller; a 1:48 scale or 1:96 scale could work. This allows for slightly less detail to be added to the miniature or miniature environment. It is also important to take into consideration stage space, ceiling heights, etc., when determining the best scale to use in a miniature scene. If the model is going to be photographed as a static model and the camera is going to be very close, the scale must be larger and the miniature will require more detail to give it a realistic look.

Frequently miniatures are selected as the visual effects technique when the model must perform action. This includes pyro models depicting vehicles or architectural models that need to

Figure 3.87 VFX DP Pat Sweeney surveys a large-scale miniature in preparation for pyro destruction for *Terminator Salvation* (2009). (Image courtesy of Kerner FX and The Halcyon Company. All rights reserved.)

blow up. Or the miniature may be a landscape that will experience a natural disaster such as a landslide or earthquake. It might also be some large architectural structure that collapses on camera. In all of these cases, the material requirements and the choices of materials are very different from a typical static miniature construction because the model needs to break apart or crumble in the proper scale and have the desired action, look, and feel of a realistic event.

When models/miniatures are destroyed—crashed, blown up, crumbled, and broken apart in dramatic ways—they need to interact with their environment. Air, water, fire, and smoke are key elements that help sell realism in a miniature. Typically this action type of miniature is constructed at a much larger scale than a static model in order for the event to be believable. Common scales for action miniatures are 1:3, 1:4, and 1:6. Sometimes a smaller scale can be used; however, that increases the risk of destroying the reality by having an event where the fire, smoke, or debris is out of scale.

Figure 3.88 For *Terminator Salvation*'s (2009) climactic finale, this large-scale miniature was constructed using laser cut acrylic and glass. (Image courtesy of Lucasfilm Ltd. and The Halcyon Company. All rights reserved.)

Most of the reason for the expanded scale of these miniatures is that it is very difficult to control the scale of natural elements like fire, smoke, debris, and water. For instance, a drop of water is a drop of water and it is nearly impossible to change the scale of that element. If a miniature must interact with water, then it must be built at a large enough scale so the difference between the water and the miniature is not noticeably in conflict.

The choice of materials to construct a miniature is critical and depends on the scale chosen. The designer/artist must imagine how this model is going to act in its environment and choose materials carefully to give the miniature the desired look. For instance, if a building is going to be blowing up, constructing this model using conventional materials like plywood would not give the event a realistic look. In the design phase determining what the real object is made from is paramount; for example, if it is a building, is it concrete or wood? If it is an airplane, then most likely it is made from metal, but not always—and the type of metal and construction play a part as well. The ingenuity of the model crew comes into play at this point because designing and choosing the correct materials and constructing a large miniature will require a lot of creativity and vision to accomplish this task in order pull off shots that have a 100% believable look and scale.

Construction Materials

Frequently, the type of material used in model making is acrylic, which can be laser cut in a variety of thicknesses. Wood is another standard building material. Depending on the way the model is to be used, different types of wood in various thicknesses are selected in combination to obtain structural integrity—or carefully constructed with lack of integrity to achieve a weak point or breaking point in a model where it must come apart. Typical wood materials are plywood and particle board. However, there are no definite rules to what materials are used and sometimes materials as simple as cardboard can be used. All types of metals are often used and can be manipulated in many different ways. A favorite is brass etching, which will provide tremendous detail from a very thin brass sheet, and often helps with the detail of a fine scale model. Laser cutting is also an option to achieve a variety of different looks; however, a fairly powerful laser is required for this technique if metal is selected. The look of concrete can be done by using faux finishes in the paint stages of a miniature project. However, if the concrete must crumble, then often tinted plasters are used, enabling the model to crumble appropriately.

The material choices relate directly to how a model must specifically perform. A performing model can be anything from a crashing airplane, a burning building, or a miniature that will blow up. In all of these cases, the material choice is critical. For instance, in the case of the burning building, a nonpoisonous flammable material should be the obvious choice. For the crashing vehicle, oftentimes lead sheeting is used to give the event the realism of crushing metal.

Figure 3.89 Fire, smoke, and pyro interact with brick and wood building structure leading to dramatic collapse in *Backdraft* (1991). (Image courtesy of Lucasfilm Ltd. and Universal Studios Licensing, LLLP. All rights reserved.)

When pyrotechnics are involved and a miniature is being blown up, it is important to use materials that will react properly and have the appropriate scale. Some commonly used materials like glass, acrylic, or various thicknesses of ultrathin aluminum are often prescored so the materials break in a pre-designated area. The balance of materials is tricky. If the balance is too light, it will vaporize in the pyrotechnic event; if too strong, the model may not come apart properly or a scaled look will not be achieved. All of this must be balanced and depends on the size of the pyrotechnic event and the scale of the model.

Figure 3.90 Kerner model crew sculpted the Geonosian Arena out of high-density foam. (*Star Wars: Episode II—Attack of the Clones*™ & © 2002 Lucasfilm Ltd. All rights reserved. Used under authorization.)

Many models will have sculptural aspects (or multiple sculptural aspects) to accomplish the desired look of the miniature. In these cases, a sculpture can be created from clay or foam. The type of clay chosen depends on the detail level of the sculpture and ranges from very hard oil-based clay to super soft water-based clay. Foam is another favorite material for miniature builders and is also available in a variety of densities, which usually must be sealed.

The sculpture is then molded, oftentimes out of silicone or a hard-cased fiberglass. It is then cast by using a variety of resins or stone, depending on the look, size, and application of the model part or sculpture. If a miniature has a large quantity of repeating elements, then molding and casting can be a very efficient solution to creating the volume required to accomplish a highly detailed look or dense environment.

Vacuum forming is another tool in the production of miniatures. Vacuum forming is the process of pulling a heated sheet of plastic over a pattern and applying vacuum, thus forming the heated plastic to the shape of the created pattern. The pattern is usually made of wood, metal, various densities of polyurethane, or whatever material is appropriate to achieve the proper look from the pattern as long as the material is hard and will not collapse under the extreme vacuum pressure that will be applied. This technique is typically used to create multiples of any given shape when the requirements for the shape allow or require it to be hollow. This technique is very useful when a shape must be clear and cannot be flat, like the windshield of a car or airplane, or when weight is a factor or if sheets of a very specific texture are required.

The molding process is used to add small details, re-create beautiful sculptures, and mold large shapes like an airplane fuselage, wings, or even the whole airplane. In this case high-detail patterns are created, again using the appropriate materials. In the case of a large airplane construction, high-density urethane foam is a good choice for its ability to be shaped and sealed upon completion. These parts are then given to the mold maker, who will create a mold. The mold is then used to create a casting of the original part. In the case of a large airplane, this casting is usually done out of fiberglass or carbon fiber if weight and strength are a factor. These parts are then cleaned up and assembled.

At this point details are added and electronics are installed. If needed, this is the point where a high-strength metal armature to support the miniature and provide a mounting point is integrated. This mounting point enables the miniature to be mounted on whatever rig has been designed for it, from motion control to pneumatic special effect rigs, to motivate it to move at any speed required.

Mechanical devices are also frequently incorporated in the model build process. Typically, these mechanical devices are designed in CAD and then created in a machine shop, usually out of a variety of metals. They are typically designed to be a functioning mechanism. Oftentimes these functioning mechanisms are motivated through the use of pneumatics, hydraulics, or a servocontroller. A good example of functioning mechanics would be functioning landing gear for an airplane or possibly a vehicle that is required to transform in the middle of a shot.

Electronics are used in almost every miniature project whether they are used simply to add a few miniature streetlights, light dozens of architectural structures, power the rotor blades of a miniature helicopter, or assist in the transformation of a vehicle. For miniatures that require mechanical movement, this is achieved by using servos or compact electric motors. These servos and motors must contain the ability to be controlled so speed can be adjusted. This will enable any mechanical movement to move faster or slower depending on the camera's frame rate or the desired look of the mechanical movement. For instance, if a miniature is being photographed using motion control, servos able to read electronic pulses are used so the motor moves extremely slowly in conjunction with a very slow frame rate, or in the case of photographing a miniature helicopter where the frame rate is overcranked, a high rpm motor would be used to enable the rotor blades to rotate much faster, achieving the proper scale rpm for the rotor blades.

Figure 3.91 Kerner model crew puts finishing touches using miniature lights to enhance ambient lighting within model. (*Star Wars: Episode II—Attack of the Clones*™ & © 2002 Lucasfilm Ltd. All rights reserved. Used under authorization.)

Miniature lights are frequently used to help the Director of Photography sneak some lighting into an area impossible to get to by conventional stage lights. Usually the type of lighting selected is dependent on how the model is to be photographed. For instance, when shooting at a higher frame rate, the miniature lights typically must be very bright and often need to be run at levels beyond their standard rating in order to achieve the proper light levels. This will cause the life of the bulb to be severely shortened, so these lights should be run at higher levels only when the camera is rolling or during exposure wedges. It is also important to design miniatures so the lights can easily be replaced on set in the event of a burnout. In most cases when miniature lights are used the DP will need to do exposure wedges to determine light levels and color temperature. In some cases a separate light pass will be required when the proper exposure for the miniature lights is different from the proper exposure for the beauty photography pass. Using miniature lighting and other types of electronics, including mechanical movement, provides depth, richness, and realism that help bring scale miniatures to life.

Figure 3.92 Kerner crew applying paint to enhance the aging process on this architectural structure for *A.I. Artificial Intelligence* (2001). (Image courtesy of Lucasfilm Ltd. All rights reserved. *A.I. ARTIFICIAL INTELLIGENCE:* © Warner Bros., a division of Time Warner Entertainment Company, L.P. and DreamWorks LLC. All rights reserved.)

The Paint Process

Along with all of the other processes required to get a miniature ready for shooting is the paint process. The paint process is an extremely important step in creating realistic scale miniatures. With regard to the sheen of the base coat, the specularity must be balanced. Too much shine and the kicks of light are going to give away the scale. Too dull, and a lifeless miniature may result. If reference photos are available they usually stand as an invaluable guide toward realistic representation.

Aging is the key to realism with miniatures. Almost every miniature, model or environment, will require the use of some age-enhancing techniques. A subtle layer of dirt or aging usually helps a model feel planted in its environment. For miniatures that require heavier aging or are representing a dirtier environment, it is important to keep in mind the scale of everything that is being applied. The drips must be in scale and have the right weight and feel for a naturalistic environment. For a vehicle model, all of the appropriate places on the vehicle should have some dirt and wear, as well as things like exhaust output. If there's damage, the paint job may require tiny little bits of metal showing through. All of these types of treatments add up to make the miniature look real and totally believable.

The same is applicable for landscapes. All of the materials chosen to create a natural landscape environment must be carefully selected and based on the scale of the miniature. The larger the scale, the easier it will be to use natural materials. When working in smaller scales, great care must be taken when choosing materials. For instance, at a 1:96 scale natural sand cannot be used to represent sand; the grains of sand will be too big and give away the miniature, so a much finer material like ground walnut shells should be utilized to represent sand.

Previsualization and Miniatures

When building any type of model, previsualization is a handy tool. If previsualization is available, then the object can be brought in from Maya to AutoCAD and broken down into individual planes, allowing a model maker to choose laser cutting as a starting point for the general geometry of the model. This can work for both architectural or vehicular models and for any other compound three-dimensional shapes. As an example, when using AutoCAD and a laser cutter, a 3D object can be built by creating notched bulkheads strung together by stringers and ultimately clad in the material of choice, enabling the model maker to create a 3D object out of laser-cut 2D shapes.

The Basic Standard Tools

Not all miniature construction requires the use of high-tech equipment and tools such as a laser cutter. Much of the construction can be done in a traditional model shop, as long as the shop is equipped with a standard tool set like table saws, band saws, radial arm saws, router tables, sanders, and nail guns. Using just these standard tools, a skilled craftsman will be able to create many different types of miniatures and miniature environments.

THE INCORPORATION OF MECHANICAL, PRACTICAL, AND PYROTECHNIC EFFECTS WITH MINIATURES
Ian Hunter

Many miniature shots rely on the integration of mechanical, pyrotechnic, and practical effects for their success. These effects can take many forms such as flying, traveling along a road or track, collapsing, or exploding. Miniatures used like this differ from statically shot miniatures in that they perform an action and could be called *action miniatures*. The action that the miniature performs can be as important to the shot as the miniature itself, and therefore thought should be given to incorporating the mechanical or pyrotechnic effects into the miniature.

The miniature maker and the special effects technician should work together concurrently when building a miniature for an action effects shot. For instance, if a model of a truck or train is to travel down a road or track, then the method used to move the model down the track should be designed at the same time as the model itself. Provisions should be made in the model to accept a reinforced frame and mounting plate to allow the special effects crew to attach whatever motorizing system will be used to pull the model, such as a cable. Models that are to be flown should have a frame with mounting tabs for flying wires. The model maker and special effects technician should also work out the estimated weight and size of the model beforehand so that the effects technician can accurately size the flying trapeze, carrying wire, pull cables, etc.

Too often a model will be built without the input of the special effects department and the resulting miniature is either too heavy for the effects rig or too weakly constructed to survive the stresses put on it. Conversely, special effects rigging built without consideration of the miniature can often be oversized and not fit the miniature or be made too lightly and not have the strength to lift or pull the miniature. Since it is always easier to run a motorized system at less than full speed versus making a motor pull more than its rated load, it is advisable to design a drive system with greater pulling capacity than the projected miniature's weight.

Figure 3.93 A 1:5-scale F35 fighter plane crash sequence for *Live Free or Die Hard* from New Deal Studios. (Image courtesy of *Live Free or Die Hard* © 2007 Twentieth Century Fox. All rights reserved.)

The effects rig should be built and tested with a matching sized and weighted stand-in or *mule* of the miniature so that speeds and actions can be practiced and refined before risking the detailed camera-ready miniature. Only after thorough testing should the picture miniature be mounted onto the effects system. This usually means that the miniature becomes dressing to cover the effects rigging. By rehearsing an effect before getting to the stage, the special effects crew is more likely to have a successful take in front of the camera, where shooting delays due to untested and unreliable special effects can become expensive quickly.

Water Effects

Miniatures that will be used with water effects such as water tanks or ships should obviously be made of waterproof materials or sealed with waterproof coatings. Also, water can exert a great deal of force on a miniature and its special effects rigging, so models used in water should be very strong. For sinking effects a way to evacuate air and flood in water should be built into the model. Don't make a sinking model out of a material that is naturally buoyant, because even more powerful winches or pull-down rigging will be needed to overcome the model's tendency to float. Pick points should be attached to the miniature's frame to allow the mounting of line or cables to hoist the miniature back up after a take is completed.

Figure 3.94 A 1:4-scale ice waterfall action sequence for *The Chronicles of Narnia: The Lion, The Witch and The Wardrobe* (2005). (Image courtesy of New Deal Studios © 2005 Disney Enterprises, Inc. and Walden Media, LLC. All rights reserved.)

Fire, Explosives, and Collapsing

Miniatures that will be used with fire or explosives have their own special considerations. If a model is going to sustain a long fire or burn, then fire-retardant materials or coatings should be used on the miniature to allow it a fighting chance of surviving more than one take. On the other hand, if the intent is to have the flames consume the miniature, then the model should be constructed out of flammable materials. Pyro sources such as copper flame bars can be built into the model during its construction. Materials that could give off noxious fumes should be avoided for a model exposed to flame.

For models used in collapsing or exploding shots, the material used to make the model and its framing should be weakened so that minimal amounts of explosive will be needed to destroy the miniature. Balsa wood is a good example of a relatively weak yet safe material from which to build breakaway miniatures. Often safer air cannons and pneumatic pull cables can be used to supplement the actual explosives, further keeping the pyro materials to a minimum. Weak knees, weighted pull cables, etc., that can be triggered from a timing box should be used to motivate the action and direction a model will take in an effects shot. The primary use of pyrotechnics should be to provide a spectacular filmable flame coming from the miniature, with some form of mechanical effect actually being used to bring down the model.

Figure 3.95 A 1:8-scale collapsing federal building for *The X-Files: Fight the Future* from New Deal Studios. (Image courtesy of *The X-Files: Fight The Future* © 1998 Twentieth Century Fox. All rights reserved.)

Shooting Locations and Conditions

The shooting location and conditions the miniature will be shot in need to be examined. If installation of a miniature at a location involves mounting of the frame to the building's foundation with bolts or screws, then permission to alter and later repair the site needs to be asked and given. Room to carry the miniature and special effects crew and their equipment should also be allowed for. Space will always fill up with every department's gear, so designating the proper space for the miniature and the location of the cameras at the proper distance should be established from the beginning. Remember, miniatures are like actors and sets in that they are the items that are photographed. Everything else is there to support achieving the shot through the use of the miniature.

Often measurements can be made of the potential location and a simplified digital model can be made along with digital models of the miniatures, cameras, cranes, etc., in volume to verify that everything will fit. Don't forget the third dimension, height, such that one only scales the floor and finds that the stage is not tall enough to get the required camera angle. If a miniature cannot be built adjacent to its shooting location and must be transported there, then the model department will need to know the maximum size any component of the miniature can be built to in order to transport it to location by truck. While the term *miniature* suggests a small, table-top item, action miniatures used in film are often 1:4, 1:3, or even 1:2 the size of the real objects and sets and can in reality be quite large.

When using miniatures for an action sequence, it is important to clearly define the effect that the miniature will perform and to build it and its integral practical effects with the common goal of accomplishing the action asked of it. The VFX Supervisor, model makers, effects technicians, and pyrotechnicians should work together to define and achieve this common goal.

PHOTOGRAPHY OF MINIATURE EFFECTS: MOTION CONTROL
Matthew Gratzner

What Is Motion Control and What Are Its Benefits to Miniature Photography?

Shooting a miniature with motion control equipment (*moco* for short) involves the use of a computer-controlled camera system. Motion control is a technology in which all axes of the camera and rig are controlled by a series of stepper or servo motors driven via computer using preprogrammed commands. This allows the camera moves to be precisely repeatable, which in turn allows for any number of identical camera passes.

The motion control process allows individual elements to be photographed with an identical, registered camera move. The separately photographed elements can then be composited, with each element locked together in the same camera move, without misalignment or sliding. Typical passes include a beauty light pass, practical light pass, rim light pass, fill light pass, focus pass, smoke pass, and matte pass. Each pass is photographed featuring only certain lighting or conditions that are set. Since these passes are exposed on the film separately, they can be dialed up or down within the composite. A smoke pass is a photographic pass in which the model is shot in a water-based atomized "smoke" that gives the model a level of atmosphere. This pass, when composited with a beauty light pass, can give the sense of atmospheric distance and depth in a shot.

Figure 3.96 A 1:4-scale replication of a hallway at the Louvre Museum into which computer-generated characters were composited. (Image courtesy of New Deal Studios for *Looney Tunes Back in Action* (2003). *LOONEY TUNES BACK IN ACTION* © Lonely Film Productions GmbH & Co. KG Licensed By: Warner Bros. Entertainment Inc. All rights reserved.)

The concept of shooting individual elements was used as early as 1914, but the camera and dolly movement was achieved not with a computer, but manually, with the aid of reference marks and precise timing. The recording and playback of camera moves has developed from the analog technology of vinyl records in the 1940s, to magnetic tape in the early 1970s, to digital technology in the mid-1970s, developed for the film *Star Wars* (1977) by John Dykstra and his team. Some of these early digital systems used strictly electronics, which were later replaced with computer-based systems.

Other pioneers in the use of motion control photography, particularly in motion graphics–prominent television commercials, were Robert Abel and Con Pedersen of Robert Abel & Associates. These motion control systems were adapted from systems that Con Pedersen, Douglas Trumbull, and his team developed for *2001: A Space Odyssey* (1968). Commercials featuring elaborate motion graphics sequences benefited greatly from the ability to shoot separate elements with the use of these motion control systems capable of repeatable camera moves.

Today motion control camera systems are computer driven, but physical camera moves can be created in a computer-generated previsualization or previs, using a virtual camera. This method, if properly planned, has the advantage of allowing the shot to be designed before the miniatures are fabricated and working out any photography issues well before the stage is rented and the camera equipment is ordered.

But the main advantage in shooting miniatures using motion control is the ability to control exposure and increase the depth of field. Depth of field is the one make-or-break factor in shooting miniatures. Motion-controlled photography enables the shutter to be opened and closed at a preprogrammed rate, synced to the camera move. This, combined with a stopped-down aperture, can, depending on how long each frame is exposed, provide an almost infinite depth of field—thereby emulating the exposure and associated depth of field that would be associated when filming a full-size real event.

Figure 3.97 A 1:6-scale bomb bay and bomb launcher from *Broken Arrow* from New Deal Studios. (Image courtesy of *Broken Arrow* © 1996 Twentieth Century Fox. All rights reserved.)

Another great feature with motion control photography is the ability to photograph fly-through shots that when played back, travel at an extremely high rate. Because the shutter speed and exposure are synced to the camera movement, a miniature can be photographed at a very slow speed, say 2 fps, with the programmed move negotiating the lens in and around tight spaces. This slower speed allows the system to be free of the physical speed limits of the equipment. When this footage is played back at 24 fps, the camera move is 12 times faster than as photographed, giving the illusion that the camera is racing through the scene. Shooting at slower frame rates also enables the DP to use less light since the exposures are much longer. Each pass can be shot at a different speed and exposure depending on the needs of the shot.

The disadvantage to shooting at slower frame rates is that the model makers, grips, and technicians need to be extremely careful during the photography not to bump the miniature or have any component within the miniature move or be affected by wind. This movement, when played back, will be exaggerated and could possibly ruin the shot because it is being photographed at a very slow rate. It is also very important not to displace or adjust the model between photographic passes; this action will cause misalignment of the objects being photographed and result in errors that will have to be fixed at the subsequent compositing stage in post.

Execution and Technique Using Previs

When planning a visual effects shot using miniatures, it is always best, if possible, to have the previs approved and locked before commencing any fabrication or production. The previs can be used to determine miniature scale, live-action components, digital characters and elements, and most importantly, the feasibility of a camera move. When prevising a motion control camera move, it is advisable to create the camera and rig as a 3D model within the previs. The model should accurately represent all of the dimensions of both the camera and rig and especially all of the pivot and movement points that enable pan, tilt, roll, dolly, etc. The virtual camera should be linked to the 3D model of the camera and rig, with all of the camera's movements slaved to the CG rig itself. Also, setting the previs in a computer-modeled stage or location space will help in the practical design of a shot. This simple step can help alleviate camera clearance issues. Far too often a beautifully designed camera move is created in a previs only to find out that the camera move starts with the camera traveling through the ground plane of the miniature set and concluding in a dramatic move exiting through the quite immovable wall of a skyscraper miniature. (Previs is discussed in depth in Chapter 2.)

Photography

One of the dynamic aspects of motion control photography is the ability to shoot full-scale, live-action elements and then rescale the camera move to a corresponding scale that represents a miniature set that could be integrated into the shot in post. Essentially, one is creating the exact camera move that was created for full-scale photography but scaled for a miniature set. With both live-action and miniature elements photographed with the same camera move, the two components should assemble in the compositing stage relatively seamlessly.

If motion control is not an option during principal photography, then motion control data can be derived from digitally tracking the principal photography in post. This post-tracked data can be generated with the use of 3D tracking software programs such as Boujou, Syntheyes, or Maya Live or as a 2D track with Nuke, Moca, or Shake. But again, data acquisition of the 1st unit photography is crucial to the success of creating an accurate digital track of the camera move in post. While tracking software can estimate a focal length of a lens and distance to a subject, the more accurate the information from the 1st unit utilized in the post-tracking, the easier it is to line up the elements in the composite.

When photographing any miniature or element to be combined with a live-action image, if possible, always use the same focal length of lens with which the live action was shot. If the live action was shot with a 21mm lens, shoot the model with a 21mm lens. The same goes for camera angle. If the live-action camera had a 15-degree tilt-up, the miniature shot should have the same 15-degree tilt-up. *Lenses and angles are not to be scaled in miniature photography.* In contrast, camera distance from the subject and speed *do* need to be scaled. (See the discussion of scale determinations in the *What Are Miniatures?* section for how to scale an object.) As for film stock, again, if possible, use the same stock that was used in the 1st unit photography. This is one of the necessities for comprehensive data acquisition during live-action production photography.

Because models photographed with motion control tend to be of a smaller scale, lens configuration is the first task at hand in production. If the set features a large number of shots tightly framed in and around the miniature, a periscope lens[76] will probably be needed. The advantage of using a periscope lens is

---

[76] A periscope lens is a lens mounted to a tube that extends out from the camera (typically 20 inches or so) and can photograph objects at a 90-degree angle to the body of the camera. This extended tube is engineered with a series of mirrors and lenses that reflect the image back to the film plane. It is also known as a *snorkel*. In some cases a small mirror at 45 degrees will be enough to allow the camera to scrape over the surface of a model.

the ability to get the lens into a small area without having to deal with the mass of the camera body or camera head colliding with the surrounding miniature. This configuration of lens is ideal for shooting fly-throughs of elaborate table-top models that need to travel though a confined space. This lens can also be configured into a *straight shooter* or *probe* lens by removing the 90-degree bend and mounting the lens directly to the tube. For *keyhole* shots where the camera needs to pass through a relatively small opening this lens can be ideal. The disadvantage of a periscope lens is that because the photographed image is being reflected by mirrors and lenses over a distance in a tube, a loss of a couple of stops can be expected. This needs to be considered when lighting and for length of exposure. Also with some periscope lenses, because the mirror is used to reflect the image back to the film plane, the filmed image might need to be flopped in post.

Motion control photography can take advantage of the pre-planning of a shot developed though previs or with the use of tracking software by tracking an existing shot, thus expanding the scene by photographing miniatures with a matched move. Motion control gives the filmmaker the freedom to use extremely small-scale miniatures shot in various lighting conditions and environments. Essentially, motion control photography bridges the gap between practical photography and the digital world, allowing the filmmaker to craft scenes seamlessly with the regimented nature of production but with the control and flexibility of post.

Figure 3.98 A 1:4-scale XF-11 complete with contra-rotating propellers and puppet of Leonardo DiCaprio as Howard Hughes. (Image courtesy of New Deal Studios for *The Aviator* (2005). *THE AVIATOR* © IMF International Medin Unfo Film Gmbh & Co3 Produktions Kg. Licensed By: Warner Bros. Entertainment Inc. All rights reserved.)

PHOTOGRAPHY OF MINIATURE EFFECTS: HIGH-SPEED PHOTOGRAPHY
Ian Hunter

Oftentimes a film will require an effect to be photographed, but doing the effect full size can become costly and logistically difficult. An alternative is to carry out the effect using a miniature shot at high speed. High speed denotes any frame rate at which a camera will run that is greater than the base speed of the camera for the venue being used. For this section 35mm film rates of 24 fps are considered standard. But if one is shooting for a television commercial, then that medium's base frame rate should be used (29.97 fps, which can be rounded up to 30 fps for miniature photography). The primary reason for shooting miniatures at higher frame rates is to slow the miniature's action down when the film is projected back at its normal frame rate. A miniature is proportionally smaller than its full-size brother—but because gravity is a constant, the action of the miniature at a normal frame rate gives away its apparent size. Therefore, to cinematically increase the apparent screen time it takes for the motion of the miniature and any debris the action might create, the miniature is filmed at a proportionally higher frame rate. The film is then projected back at its normal rate and the slower action is revealed.

Figure 3.99 Collapsing 1:5-scale Warner Bros. water tower. (Image courtesy of New Deal Studios for *Looney Tunes Back in Action* (2003). *LOONEY TUNES BACK IN ACTION* © Lonely Film Productions GmbH & Co. KG Licensed By: Warner Bros. Entertainment Inc. All rights reserved.)

Following is the formula to determine the proper frame rate to the scale being used:

$$(\sqrt{m}) \times (r) = f$$

$$m = \text{Miniature's scale}$$
$$r = \text{Base frame rate}$$
$$f = \textit{New frame rate}$$

1:4 scale at 24 fps = $(\sqrt{4}) \times (24) = (2) \times (24) = 48$ fps

High-speed frame rates for miniature effects will vary depending mainly on scale. The basic formula for estimating a frame rate to account for adjusting the apparent speed of objects affected by gravity (things falling) is to take the square root of the miniature's scale (m) and multiply it by the base frame rate (r). An example would be a 1:4 scale model truck falling off a cliff. The square root of the scale factor 4 is 2. Multiply by the base frame rate for film (24) = $2 \times 24 = 48$ frames per second. As expected, the smaller the scale, the greater the frame rate: 1:5 scale square root = $2.23 \times 24 = 53.66$ fps, 1:8 scale square root = $2.82 \times 24 = 67.88$ fps, and so forth. In practice, the frame rate can be rounded up to the nearest even number.

Following is the formula to determine the proper actual speed of a scale object at a scaled frame rate:

$$(rs/m) = (b)$$
$$(b) \times (r) = (as)$$

36 mph $\times$ 1:6 scale car = 8.8 feet per second
8.8 feet per second $\times$ 2.5 normal frame rate = 22 feet per second

When estimating the traveling speed of an object, such as a car or train in miniature, divide the real sized object's speed (rs) by the model's scale factor (m) to get the base speed (b). Then multiply that base speed (b) by the increase in frame rate factor (r) to get the actual speed (as) of the object while filming. For instance, a 1:6 scale car traveling a simulated 36 mph should travel 8.8 feet per second at 24 fps, but should be photographed at 60 fps or 2.5 times normal speed, meaning 8.8 feet per second (real-time scale distance) $\times$ 2.5 (frame rate factor over normal) = 22 feet per second real time. It is surprising how often that "22 feet per second" travel rate for miniatures will come up regardless of scale and frame rate.

Shooting high speed requires a camera that can record the event at the proper frame rate. Older Fries Mitchell 35mm cameras can get up to 120 fps and have the advantage of pin-registered camera movement for a stable image. While a stable image was vital during the optical/photochemical period of film compositing, stabilizing software can now be used to take out unwanted movement. The Arri 435, which is capable of 150 fps, is another commonly used high-speed camera. For ultrahigh speeds, in the 200- to 360-fps plus range, Photosonics cameras can be used. Newer digital cameras also have the ability to shoot high speed but with the downside of the image being created at less than maximum resolution depending on the frame rate (the higher the frame rate, the less resolution per frame).

Depth of Field

A major consideration to make while shooting miniatures is that in order to create sufficient depth of field and keep the majority of the miniature in focus, the camera needs to be stopped down. Therefore, the lighting on a high-speed miniature set will need to be increased due to the shorter exposure times. The higher the frame rate and the smaller the stop, the greater the amount of light needed. Typically each time the frame rate goes up by a factor of 1 (two times base frame rate, three times base frame rate, etc.), the amount of light needs to go up a stop from the normal exposure. Adding tremendous amounts of light to compensate for frame rate and stop can put a great amount of heat onto a model and its setting, which over anything but a short period of time can cause damage through melting or warping of the miniature. The shooting lights should only be brought up to full power just before rolling the camera and turned off when the take is completed to avoid damaging the miniature.

Figure 3.100 Freeze-frame diorama of a battle built in 1:11 scale for the *Halo 3 "Believe"* campaign. (Image courtesy of New Deal Studios.)

Pyrotechnics

The square of the scale times base frame rate equation should only be considered a starting point to determine shooting speed (but it's a good one). Pyrotechnics can have a major influence on frame rate. Pyrotechnic explosions in miniature happen over a much shorter time than their full-size counterparts. Shot at the base high-speed frame rate for gravity may make the explosion appear to happen too quickly, so the frame rate can be increased to compensate or the pyro can be timed with an electronic timing box so that the apparent explosion can be sustained using multiple explosions overlapping to appear continuous. If the explosion cannot be stretched out, then the main components of a miniature that will be falling may need to be accelerated faster than gravity to pull the miniature down at a speed that balances out the higher frame rate set by the pyro. This could be considered the application of "forced gravity." Pneumatic pistons attached to cables can be used to pull down the model. Another method is to attach the model to cables that are in turn attached to weights on a trip release. The dropped weights are run through pulleys with a mechanical advantage (2:1 or more). The dropped weights pull the cable that the model is attached to faster than gravity would and force the miniature down at a rate faster than gravity.

Smoke, Fire, and Water

Often a high-speed miniature shot will require some physical element to interact with the miniature. The most typical elements are smoke, fire, and water, with smoke generally being the easiest to make look scale, followed by fire and then water. Fire flickers at a rate that when reduced to a scale makes it appear that the size of flame flicker is not fast enough and the size of the flames edges are overscale. This makes flames look too big on a model. Flames that are used in a sustained burn need to be executed in a bigger scale. Flames that are being pushed around by explosions or the movement of the model can be done in a smaller scale if needed. Building and shooting the model in as large a scale as possible will help this problem.

As the scale of the miniature decreases, a way to increase the flicker rate of the flame must be added. Blowing on the flames with locally placed compressed air jets or using a high-airflow fan or air mover blown against the flame will help break up the flame to make it look more scale. The main point is to agitate the flames using some external method to increase the flame's flicker rate. Too fast a camera speed can have the reverse effect and make the flames move too slow, which makes the shot cry out "effects"! So while shooting flames, frame rate tests should be done to determine the proper shooting speed. Fire creates smoke, so unless the smoke is desired within the shot, the lighting should be flagged to avoid lighting up the smoke. An off-camera fan can be directed at the smoke and away from the camera to help dissipate the smoke.

Water is even harder to deal with when shooting in miniature. The main issue is that the surface tension of water makes the droplets appear out of scale and therefore as large a scale miniature as possible should be used. Standing or flowing water shot as an element should be built in as large a scale as possible also. Water being agitated through wind, rocking, or an explosion can mean a slightly smaller scale. If the water element will fill a large part of the frame, then a scale no less than 1:4 should be used (if not larger.)

Blowing water with compressed air, shooting water out of a high-speed washer nozzle, and hitting the water on the edges with an external fan helps break up the droplet size and therefore increase the apparent scale size. Shooting water at pressure through a fire hose with a fine-mesh grating will help break up the water droplet size. Large bodies of water that are agitated also can create foaming within the water, which has a telltale white look to its edges. To help add this subtle look to a miniature, add diatomaceous earth or 2% white milk to the water, which will increase its translucency. Food coloring can also be added to the water to increase apparent depth. Using agitation and foaming agents will allow the use of scales slightly smaller than 1:4 scale.

Smoke and other elements such as dust and debris can be integrated within the shot or shot separately and composited into a shot. Elements such as these can be shot at high speed and added to otherwise static matte paintings to impart some life to the shot. Smoke is usually shot against black screen to make pulling the element easier for the compositor. However, some elements such as dirt or dust have color and are better shot against blue or green screen.

Smoke can often be shot at a smaller scale if being added to a shot as long as the frame rate is sufficient to slow the smoke's motion. Smoke should be shot inside if possible where the air current can be controlled, because even a light breeze will break up a smoke plume. A light amount of fanned air can be directed over the top of a smoke plume to break up or redirect the smoke for the shot. Black smoke can be problematic, because it is illegal in most places for environmental reasons. Consider shooting white smoke and reversing the lighting direction and then process the smoke as a negative to get the dark smoke. Talcum powder, Fuller's earth, and decomposed granite can be shot out of air cannons or blown with air jets against black to create swirling dust effects or impact hits.

At times it is appropriate to shoot an effect using a high-speed miniature. This method utilizes real objects reacting to real physics. It can convey mass and scale at a smaller size. This allows complicated action effects to be performed in a controlled situation for reduced costs.

THE USE OF MINIATURES IN THE DIGITAL WORLD
Ian Hunter

Though the ease and availability of digital animation and compositing have enabled filmmakers to create credible renderings of impossible effects constrained only by the limits of the imagination, there are still times when, due to the nature of the desired effect, a traditional effects technique like the use of miniatures is still the best way to achieve impossible shots that look convincingly real. Even though great advances in computer-generated renderings are occurring on an almost regular basis, they still require a great commitment of time, talent, and expense to create a fully digitally rendered object or environment with an end result that often lacks substance or some ineffable quality that makes it seem less than real. Sometimes, for this reason alone, a practical model or miniature provides an easier path to tricking the brain into believing that something is really there—because subconsciously, the brain knows it really *is* there.

Figure 3.101 The 1:3-scale "tumbler" Batmobile and 1:3 scale Lower Wacker Drive for *The Dark Knight* (2008). (Image courtesy of New Deal Studios. *THE DARK KNIGHT* © Warner Bros. Entertainment Inc. All rights reserved.)

The archetypal situation that would suggest the use of miniatures would be a shot or sequence where real-world physics can be relied on to achieve the effect more convincingly and with less effort than computer-generated physics simulators. Quoting Terry Gilliam, "The behavior of real physical interactions is much more unpredictable than computer-generated action, and we seem to empathize with it subconsciously."[77] Simply put, if an effect requires interactive destruction through collapse, explosion, implosion, fire, flood, or other calamity and is too expensive or impractical

---

[77] Terry Gilliam, "Salman Rushdie Talks with Terry Gilliam," *The Believer*, March 2003.

to achieve full scale, then miniatures are the obvious next best solution. By necessity such miniatures are usually larger in scale than miniatures or models that are not going to be destroyed or interact with destruction. Most destructive miniature effects will fall somewhere between 1:8 scale to 1:2 scale but larger is almost always better. Many factors determine the ideal scale for an effect including distance to lens, size of effect, material being affected, and cost.

There are other times where the emotional impact of a cinematic moment relies on absolute acceptance of the reality of an image on screen that must be delivered as a visual effect—for whatever reason. The technology certainly exists to deliver impressive simulations of real-world geology, architecture, and natural phenomena, but again, it is sometimes more cost effective and easy for the viewer to accept the visual truth if the thing is built, lit, and photographed using the same real-world techniques as the film into which the effect is going. When speaking about a large-scale digital visual effect Gilliam went on to say, "It's very impressive, but it doesn't resonate. I think somehow, subconsciously we can see it even if we can't see it."[78] And that reflects a common belief among practitioners. The surface textures of miniature buildings, vehicles, landscapes, and even alien planets and spaceships have a certain magic about their physical reality that would need to be painstakingly added when fully realized in the computer. And these types of miniatures—the towering cliff, the bombed-out city, the snow-covered town, or the perfect lighthouse at dawn—can often be achieved in a very small scale without sacrificing verisimilitude.

Figure 3.102 A 1:48-scale church and snow-covered landscape, shot against a blue Los Angeles sky from New Deal Studios. (*DECK THE HALLS* © 2006 Twentieth Century Fox Film Corporation and Regency Entertainment (USA), Inc. in the U.S. only. © 2006 Twentieth Century Fox Film Corporation and Monarchy Enterprises, S.a.r.l. in all other territories. All rights reserved.)

[78] Gilliam, "Salman Rushdie Talks."

Scales from 1:12 down to 1:48 are common and can result in the most startling and emotionally powerful visual effects.

Often the call to build and shoot miniatures comes from the digital artists themselves. They, more than anyone, know how critical credible imagery is to creating a believable visual effect. As digital technology has evolved, much more can be done using much less. A puff of dust against a blue screen photographed practically can help create a convincing hoofprint from a digital Centaur. A miniature frozen waterfall, even in a very small scale, looks real compared to a fully digital version because humans have an ingrained ability to recognize the subtle infinite cues that distinguish between when something is actually there and when it's made up of pixels.

As digital compositing has become so advanced, it is a fairly easy task to integrate miniatures into live-action photography. High-resolution still photographs can be taken of miniatures and used to texture computer-generated 3D objects to give digital shapes and forms some of the richness and physicality of miniatures. Even when digital artists are generating the majority of elements in a scene, select real-world objects and/or subjects photographed in a real-world setting can generate live-action elements that can then be composited with the digital elements to create a more convincing image.

Another advantage of using miniatures in visual effects is revealed by the use of 2D and 3D programs such as AutoCAD and Rhino. These applications allow the resulting digital object to be used not only to generate construction drawings, but also as a digital model that can be transferred into digital applications such as Maya for CG production. With today's shortened production schedules, this sharing of assets is increasingly valuable. Thus, in a shot where a fighter plane crashes, it can be a miniature, but in the shots where it is chasing another fighter plane, it can be a CG model. Texture reference from the miniature can be used to enhance the look of the digital model so it appears to be an exact match of the miniature. This has immense value in terms of time, money, and look.

Miniatures do not lend themselves to last minute changes or reversioning the way digital effects might. To commit to the use of a miniature, certain decisions about design need to be locked up ahead of time. Using previsualization to aid in this task allows miniature sequences to be conceived, manipulated, fully explored, and designed before a single piece of wood, foam, or metal is cut or shaped.

The best visual effects use a combination of all available techniques. One recent real-world example, *The Good Shepherd* (2006), involved a flyover of a burned-out 1940s Berlin neighborhood lining up to a shot of extras in a street setting. Drawings and photographs of the set along with reference images of the real postwar Berlin were used to design the destroyed setting. Built in Rhino, the 3D model buildings were transferred into Maya and used to animate the flyover. The resulting previs animation was used as a guide to determine which sections would be full size, which would be miniature, and which would be matte paintings. To construct the models, laser-cut details and wax-printed patterns were combined with handmade parts. To ensure that the head end of the shot (the miniature) lined up with the tail end of the shot (a camera crane over the set), the moving miniature photography needed to match up with the moving live-action plate. The shot was scanned and tracked with a 3D program and a camera move was derived from the live-action shot. This move was then used to drive a motion control camera that photographed the miniature. Scaling the move to film the model with the same move allowed the combination of miniature and live-action settings to integrate into a single sweeping dramatic shot, perfectly matching the director's vision.

The decision to use miniatures is sometimes a matter of taste and cost. If a director decides at the last minute that a cliff needs to be not 50 feet but 100 feet tall, the digital model can more easily accommodate the requested change. But if molds, castings, sculptured foam, and surface detail need to be doubled in size after the physical construction of a miniature has already begun, the cost and time required to accommodate the requested change may be catastrophic. But if there is a shot where a historical character has a life-altering small plane crash, it might be important that the crash seemed real. The use of a miniature may be appropriate here. On the other hand, if there is a shot where giant robots crush vehicles as they fight each other in the streets, the use of digital models or a hybrid of both might be more appropriate.

Finally, it's important to remember that the richness of detail provided by miniatures is somewhat diminished if the intended viewing platform is smaller than a theater screen. The bigger a miniature effect is projected, the better it looks. Depending on the nature of the visual effect in question, miniatures can often be the most reliable, affordable, spectacular technique.

SPECIAL EFFECTS FOR MINIATURES
Clark James

Shrinking Reality

Scripts often call for sets, props, and characters to be destroyed in some spectacular manner that serves the excitement level of the story. Events such as downing a building, exploding a planet, flooding a town, sinking an ocean liner, triggering an avalanche, and so many other imaginative events can often be created in miniature for less expense and more photographic control than if it were accomplished on a full-scale set or with digital effects. Creating these effects full scale on location can be prohibitively large or expensive, extremely unsafe, or not permitted at a particular location. Alternatively, creating these moments digitally can be a time-consuming and expensive challenge that yields less directorial control and unconvincing physics.

Creating the special effects in miniature reduces the size of the event and makes it more manageable and cost efficient. Simply slowing down the playback speed (overcranking[79] while shooting) can take advantage of the true physics associated with the event, making it appear larger in scale. Part of the secret is to find that magic ratio between the full-scale and miniature-scale shooting speeds. Camera shoot speeds and scaling are not exactly proportional. In other words, shooting a 1:4 scale set and event doesn't necessarily mean it needs to be shot at 96 fps (24 fps × 4) to look real. There is a middle ground that provides a more realistic appearance. Finding that middle ground is a matter of testing, experience, and style. (Please consult the other sections on miniatures in this chapter for more details and formulas on this subject.)

This section examines the choices for miniature special effects, the scales and construction methods, and the camera settings used in popular movies and sequences, providing examples of what's been accomplished in the past in order to offer some guidance on how to develop new effects for films to come. Meanwhile, remember that there are always new methods to be developed, and new materials that can be included in future miniature special effects. A creative shortcut can be worth tens to hundreds of thousands of dollars to a project. Be inventive and remain open to new possibilities.

And a final and important reminder: Although the scale is smaller, miniature effects can be just as dangerous as full-scale effects. Do not become complacent just because it's smaller. The technologies often use the same high-energy devices: hydraulics, bungee rigs, explosives, high-velocity wind, rushing water, falling objects, etc.

Safety First

Maintaining safety must be a priority. Use only trained professionals to operate dangerous and specialized effects.

---

[79] Overcranking: shooting at a higher frame rate than normal to achieve a slow motion effect (above 24 fps for film).

As with full-size effects, foster an atmosphere of vigilance toward safe practices and always watch for ways to improve that safety. One can never know how many injuries, or lives, will be spared by this thoroughness, but it's much better than knowing for sure how many were not. Slow down; think.

Scale Considerations

Determining scale can be a process unto itself. Many factors play into the choice. One-third to 1:20 scale or so is a favored range when realistic action and close visual detail are needed. Downward toward 1:200 scale or even smaller is acceptable for static background elements where close-up detail isn't as important.

Determining the best scale for a miniature that will optimize the look requires some familiarity with the limitations of various elements to be miniaturized such as water and fire. Many factors figure into the decision of scaling: camera distance, lighting, shot lengths, visual effects, etc.

Some miniatures work well at 1:200 scale. Some require the detail found in 1:4 scale models or larger. Still others might be optimized somewhere in between. There are no hard-set rules, but various processes have been used to help choose the optimal scale. One of them is to build and test shoot a mock-up of the planned miniature effect, even if it's shot on video. Testing leads to knowledge, improvement, and greater reliability of the event. Don't be shy about conducting tests. It can help prevent headaches and delays down the road.

Scales can also be combined. It works fine to have a 1:4 scale foreground object in front of a much smaller scale background— a spaceship flying over a town, for example. They can also be connected and blended together. A forest can be 1:3 scale in the foreground and gradually taper into 1:12 scale or smaller in the background. To aid the illusion of depth, the background surface should ramp slightly upward to raise the apparent horizon line, making it appear farther away. This is known as *forced perspective*. Cut-outs are a great way to camera test these kinds of layouts. Likewise multiple scales can be digitally composited together. If a camera move is included, it might need to be accomplished with motion control; then camera moves for each scale must be proportional to one another to create the proper parallax effect.

Camera

The camera itself has requirements that will help determine the scale that is appropriate to the effect. Here are some questions that will help determine the scale:

• Will the camera fit in the set?
• Can it move as needed?

- How will the set be lit?
- Can the focal depth be increased and appropriate lighting be incorporated to accomplish this focal stretch?
- Can the camera move scale down in proportion to the miniature's scale?
- Are the shots motion control?
- What film speed is needed?
- What lens angle is preferred?
- What will the shutter angle be?
- Is a previs available?

One of the first issues to determine is the camera lens's depth of field. This is a major key that reveals scale to most viewers. When shooting an actual cityscape, the camera's focus is typically set to infinity. Everything is so far away from the camera that everything is in focus. When shooting a miniature, however, everything is much closer, requiring setting focus to specific distances. Unfortunately, this reduces the depth of field, making the near-background much softer than the sharply focused foreground. Because of this, the depth of field must be forced to expand. This is accomplished by setting the camera's aperture as small as possible.[80] This will significantly reduce the amount of light entering the lens, but increase the depth of field. Shooting in a bright environment using bright lighting, using faster film, and/or increasing the exposure time of each frame can counter this loss of light. Using a wide-angle lens also helps increase the apparent depth of field and helps to avoid the problem of reducing the amount of light entering the lens.

Figure 3.103 Focal study comparing a sharp image of a Legoland ride to a variation showing less depth of field. (Images courtesy of Clark James.)

[80] Very small apertures may result in diffraction and softer images. Best to test.

The image on the left of Figure 3.107 was shot at a full-size amusement park, with people standing behind the white wall on the left. The image on the right is the same image doctored with a gradient blur to reduce the apparent depth of field. Notice how the blur creates the illusion of a miniature set. When shooting miniatures to appear full scale, keep the entire frame sharp unless style dictates otherwise.

Water

Physical realities often limit the degree of scaling down that is possible with some effects. If moving water is involved, for instance, the size will probably be limited to a minimum of 1:4 scale. This is because water doesn't scale down well. The surface tension of water creates splashes and droplets of familiar sizes that reveal its scale.

Most importantly, the water surfaces must be broken up by some means. Whether it is accomplished with turbulence, surface froth, and/or debris, large smooth surface areas must be broken up because not doing so will reveal the scale. Splashes that look glassy also reveal the scale.

Figure 3.104 Possibly the largest miniature ever built, a portion of this set featured a bridge that was swept away by turbulent flood waters as victims made their escape. (Image courtesy of *Dante's Peak* © 1997 Universal Studios Licensing, LLLP. All rights reserved.)

In the film *Dante's Peak* (1997), Digital Domain built the river bridge portion of the set at 1:4 scale. The background hills with trees tapered down to 1:12 scale. That limited the shooting angles but compressed the set and reduced expenses. The 1:4 scale water surface in the bridge sequence was broken up using water pumps, turbulence pipes, air injectors, debris, and a giant dump tank (about 700,000 gallons) to cause a flood wave; quite a spectacular feat of engineering.

A quick note here: Chemicals known as *surfactants* can reduce the surface tension of water (reduce the normal droplet size), thus reducing the visible physics involved. These include certain detergents, solvents, and photographic chemicals such as Photo-Flo. Using them can reduce the surface tension and droplet size about 30%. Be very careful, however, when using and disposing of such chemicals, because they are considered hazardous waste and must be disposed of accordingly.

Even without chemical additives, large amounts of water used in special effects are typically considered hazardous waste. Be very aware of this issue. There are companies that will send out trucks to suck up all of the liquids and dispose of them properly. And by all means, *do not pour these liquids down the street sewers.* They usually lead straight to natural rivers, lakes, or oceans without any processing or purification.

Rain

Rain is an element that is hardly ever created in a miniature set, thanks again to physics and the very perceptive brains of the audience. The size of raindrops can be reduced using spray heads, but they are then much lighter, fall slower, and are easily disturbed by the slightest breeze. A full-size raindrop makes a familiar looking splash when it hits a puddle; miniature droplets give no splash when they hit a puddle. What a miniature needs to look real are small drops that fall fast. That's a bit of a challenge.

Miniature rain has its best hopes of usage in high-velocity situations such as a storm sequence where the smaller raindrops can be swirling through turbulent wind streams created by fans and blended with puffs of smoke to simulate the mist. Miniature rain also works well as small raindrops swooshing over and past a miniature aircraft using high-velocity wind machines. Even splashes look nice as they impact surfaces when combined with high-velocity wind. The fast wind counters the surface tension of the droplets and speeds up the physics. Of course, the scale needs to be kept as large as possible, perhaps no smaller than 1:6 scale. As always, thorough planning and testing will reveal the sweetest drop sizes, angles, and speeds to achieve the best look.

Full-size rain can work as foreground elements for miniatures. A curtain of rain properly placed can blend in well with a miniature shot. Also remember that rain, like smoke, is most visible when backlit and can be invisible when only frontlit. Just don't let the splashes of the drops be visible unless the foreground perspective is being shifted to full scale.

Misty rain can also be useful in the background of a miniature set and can help fog out the deeper background. Mist sprayers can reduce the drop size and place the rain behind a set. When back-lit, this mist becomes a blanket of light; when frontlit, it's almost invisible. The key is finding the best balance in light direction. Be careful not to reveal any dripping from surfaces on which the mist collects, because the droplets would appear too large for the miniature.

When rain is used in conjunction with a miniature, it's usually added in post, whether it's a filmed element or created wholly on the computer. Filmed elements typically involve plumbing together a rain rig and shooting it against a black or green background. The droplet splashes can also be used. It can then be composited onto the miniature shot with its physics appearing properly in scale. Digital rain can also work really well. The methods ultimately used to create rain on a miniature are a matter of taste and comfort level.

Fire

Fire is very dangerous in the hectic environment of a film set, miniature or not. Think about how intense and distracted everyone is prior to rolling cameras. Think about how to safely fit fire into this mayhem. Recognize the many risks that are involved. Plan sufficient safety measures and use them religiously. Always have sufficient fire suppression equipment on hand—charged water hoses, H_2O fire extinguishers, CO_2 fire extinguishers, wet burlap, sand—anything that will efficiently extinguish the flames. Designate someone with expertise to be the fire supervisor. Assign additional security to monitor the flames if it helps. Determine emergency exit routes. Conduct a safety briefing with the entire crew prior to lighting any flames to communicate the risk level, shoot procedure, emergency procedures, and warnings.

Most importantly, obtain a permit from the local fire jurisdiction. This cannot be emphasized strongly enough. Contact the local fire authority and tell them what is being planned no matter how small. Be completely up-front and cooperative with them. They may require the presence of a fire safety officer on set and enforce stringent safety constraints, but it's worth it. Cooperate with them and they'll cooperate with the production. Safety is in everyone's best interest.

Fire in miniature presents similar challenges as water. The fire can shrink, but its visible physics can't. Miniatures incorporating fire, therefore, are usually limited to a minimum of 1:2 to 1:4 scale. Again, there are ways to push the visible physics such as adding additional flammables to give the fire more details, adding air turbulence to break up the fire, and overcranking the camera.

Figure 3.105 A 1:3 scale miniature rooftop on fire, built by New Deal Studios for the film *Watchmen*. (Image courtesy New Deal Studios and Paramount Pictures for *Watchmen* (2009). *WATCHMEN* © Warner Bros. Entertainment Inc., Paramount Pictures Corporation, and Legendary Pictures. All rights reserved.)

New Deal Studios constructed a 1:3 scale miniature for the film *Watchmen* that featured a rooftop fire along with a collapsing water tower. The fire was fueled by propane fed through plumbing that snaked through the model. Its many flames could be precisely controlled individually. Of course, the building is designed and constructed to be highly fire resistant where necessary using drywall and plaster-type materials. The cameras shot the action at 48 fps.

When working with fire, to help push the scale, the flames need to be smaller and more turbulent. Dark turbulent smoke blended in can also aid the look. However, sometimes a cleaner shot is preferred to which smoke can be added later. When the flames require more visual detail, propane is sometimes substituted with MAPP gas (a mixture of methylacetylene and propadiene). Handled similar to propane, MAPP gas burns with more color variations, produces a black smoke[81], and burns hotter than pure propane.

Turbulence can be introduced by adding a velocity-amplifying nozzle or some light wind sources (more and smaller wind sources work better than one giant breeze). Experimentation will be needed to determine the best source and direction to achieve the desired look. There are also liquid formulas that can produce an excellent miniature flame, but these sacrifice the ability to turn the flame on and off at will. These are all important considerations when planning such an event.

---

[81] Production of large amounts of smoke, especially black smoke, is highly regulated or outright illegal in many counties. Check with the local fire department and air quality management prior to engaging in such activities.

Figure 3.106 The command module of Apollo 13 makes its reentry into Earth's atmosphere. (Image courtesy of *Apollo 13* © 1995 Universal Studios Licensing, LLLP. All rights reserved.)

For the reentry sequence in the film *Apollo 13* (1995), fire physics was also scaled down to simulate traveling at 12,000 miles per hour. To accomplish this, a 1:4 scale capsule shape was made out of sheet steel. No details; just a bottomless cone. Several replaceable heat shields were shaped out of fiberglass and attached, and plumbing was fitted inside to feed propane through hundreds of small holes in the "heat shield." This was positioned upright, high on a black stage with a heat-dissipating baffle hanging above it. An E-fan[82] was positioned below the model and aimed straight up. The camera ran at 2 seconds per frame to achieve lots of motion blur, and the flames were brought up very slowly over a 16-minute shot.

By the end of each take, the "heat shield" had burned out all of its resin (the smell of which could be detected on that stage and in adjoining offices for almost a year after). New "heat shields" were repeatedly installed and more takes were shot. Another 1:4 scale heat shield was painted with fluorescent paint streaks and shot without fire under UV lighting as a glowing shield element for compositing. Also, a detailed 1:4 scale capsule model was painted with fluorescent paint applied mostly to leading edges and surfaces that the heat would make glow. After the shots were completed and layered, some additional digital elements were added along with a background for a very realistic rendition of reentry. Again, research, creativity, and testing led to a beautiful solution.

Smoke

Essentially, two categories of smoke are used in miniature photography:
• general haze and atmosphere, intended to enhance scale and image depth, and
• practical miniature smoke effects.

---

[82] E-fan: Abbreviation for "effects fan". Manufactured by the Mole Richardson Company in Hollywood, it is commonly used because of its portability, ease of control, and powerful airflow.

Atmospheric smoke is used to increase the apparent depth of an image or set. A series of mountains or hills in the distance appears grayer and softer the farther away it is from the viewer. This is because of the moisture and dust suspended in the air between the viewer and the hillsides. The smoke simulates this effect on a miniature scale. Smoke needs light from the proper direction relative to the camera to be seen. When it's frontlit, it is transparent; but when it's backlit, it glows brightly and obscures the objects behind it. Therefore, if the smoke is too light, perhaps just add some backlight to thicken it up.

This type of atmosphere is also used during motion control photography. In the film *The Fifth Element* (1997), the flying car chase sequence in a futuristic Manhattan was shot on a motion control stage dressed with about 25 miniature skyscrapers, built to 1:24 scale, each about 30 feet tall. A custom smoke system was installed on the stage that could maintain an exact smoke level for long periods of time. The smoke was shot in three camera passes: (1) light smoke, (2) medium smoke, and (3) heavy smoke.

In compositing, the light smoke was used for the buildings just past the foreground. The medium smoke was used for the buildings behind those. The heavy smoke was used for the buildings farthest away. Digital set extensions completed the background and sky. This layered smoke level process also helped push the physics of the smoke, causing a greater difference of visibility between the foreground and background buildings, making the distances appear even greater.

In contrast to a smooth haze effect, specific puffs or clouds of smoke as an element don't scale down well, such as from a miniature house chimney: 1:2 to 1:3 scale is typically the limit. It is a common practice to shoot a full-scale smoke element on black and then digitally composite it into the image or just generate it completely on the computer. Unless there is a lot of turbulent velocity behind it, like from "rocket engines" or a "storm environment," specific smoke plumes are almost useless in smaller miniatures.

When associated with the force of an explosion, smoke can be imparted with enough turbulence to pull the scale down and can work quite nicely. Another method creates smoke plumes by blasting quantities of dust (Fuller's earth or FX Dust) with air cannons or air blasters. Fuller's earth is a finely ground calcium-based diatomaceous earth mineral. Health implications are associated with this dust due to the grinding process, which leaves some silica residue in the mix. FX Dirt is the same thing but without the health risk of Fuller's. It does, however, cost about 10 times as much as basic Fuller's earth. Use either or both of them, but pay close attention to air ventilation, visibility, breathing protection, and general safety with whatever is chosen.

Explosives and Fire

A fire safety officer (FSO) from the local jurisdiction might be required for any shoot involving pyrotechnics. Keep him or her in the loop on all plans and changes. Check into potential permit requirements long before any pyrotechnic activity begins.

Explosions

Due to the extreme dangers involved, explosives must be handled only by qualified pyrotechnicians, typically holding valid state and federal licenses and working under the guidelines of a temporary permit provided by the local fire jurisdiction. Safety rules and procedures must be followed. Especially since the tragedy of 9/11, the explosives industry is heavily regulated. Always approach pyrotechnics with respect for protocol and safety.

Explosions, when properly designed, can work in the range of 1:4 to 1:12 scale. The chemicals used, such as naphthalene and MAPP, generate fireballs full of contrasting intricate details. This hides the true scale and looks beautiful on screen. As in the 1:8 scale explosion shown in Figure 3.111, which was created for *The X-Files* (1998), smoke, secondary explosions, air cannons, and carefully rigged breakaway elements can accompany such fireballs.

Figure 3.107 This 1:8 scale miniature explosion was engineered by Ian O'Connor for the *The X-Files: Fight the Future* (1998) from New Deal Studios. (Image courtesy of *The X-Files: Fight the Future* © 1998 Twentieth Century Fox. All rights reserved.)

These processes use the same technologies as full-scale effects. One difference, however, is that they are triggered using a firing box that uses microtimers that can be precisely sequenced to 1000th of a second. This is necessary for cameras shooting at 96 to 120 frames or more per second. During the take, all of the events happen really fast but then look much bigger during slower playback.

Breakaways

The same methods used in most full-scale effects are used in miniature effects:

- electronic
- mechanical
- steel cable pull-rigs
- air cannons
- prescoring and weakening of materials
- pneumatics
- motion control

Miniature breakaways are approached in much the same way as full-scale breakaways. The only difference other than that of size is the choice of materials. Full-scale materials scale down fine in appearance, but their physics don't. Wood structures snap with a visible grain and look strange in miniature breakaways. Steel beams look like mush when a real building collapses but are too rigid when scaled down. Therefore, other materials need to be substituted when displaying their physics in miniature. Preshattered and reassembled balsa wood can replicate the wooden structures in miniature. Sheet lead and annealed aluminum make good substitutes for steel framing and sheet metal. Sometimes pyrotechnics are used to cut cables or embellish impacts. It is important to suppress any visible flash from these charges, because that can not only look out of place but can reveal true scale as well.

Following is a partial list of full-scale materials and common miniature-scale counterparts used in breakaways.

Full-Scale Materials	Miniature-Scale Materials
Steel Bars and Beams	Annealed Aluminum, Formed Sheet Lead, Solder
Sheet Metal	Aluminum, Sheet Lead, Foil
Wood and Lumber	Balsa Wood, Rigid Foam
Snow	Sodium Bicarbonate, Gypsum
Ice	Resin, Wax, Hot Glue, Super Glue, Acrylic
Glass	Plexiglas, Candy (Breakaway) Glass, Cellophane, Glitter
Cement	Snow Plaster, Urethane Carving Foams
Flowing Fabric	Silk, Flexible Fabrics
Brick and Mortar	Plaster, Snow Plaster, Urethane Carving Foam
Practical Lighting	Grains of Wheat/Rice Bulbs, Microfluorescent Bulbs, L.E.D.s
Assorted Fasteners	Super Glue, Hot Glue, Tape, Baling Wire

... And Remember Safety

Most of all, as the creative plan of the miniature effects evolves and comes together, remember to keep safety as the highest priority. Be willing to wait for any safety issues. *Don't forget:* It is better *not* to know how many lives or injuries were spared due to this diligence than it is to know for sure how many were not. Be safe.

4

PERFORMANCE AND MOTION CAPTURE

WHAT IS MOTION CAPTURE?
John Root

Motion capture is the process of encoding motion from the real world into the digital medium in three dimensions. More simply, motion capture is a technique for measuring things. Used cleverly, it can be used to measure the motions of the human body. Once recorded, that motion can be used to drive a digital character or breathe life into inanimate objects. *Performance Capture* is a term that usually refers to a subcategory of Motion Capture where an actor's face and body performance are recorded simultaneously.

Motion capture has become a widely used technique in visual effects for its ability to deliver high-fidelity character animation in a time frame not practically achieved through other methods. While many technologies fall under the umbrella of motion capture, including piezoelectric, magnetic, inertial, radio-frequency, resistance, and a wide range of computer vision techniques, the most prevalent is a form of computer vision called *passive optical, discrete point capture,* or just *optical* for short.

The term *passive optical* refers to the white spheres that are being captured by high-speed digital cameras. These balls, called *markers*, are passive in that they do not emit light or any other information. *Discrete point capture* refers to the fact that the system is returning three-axis, positional information for each marker on each captured frame. The practical upshot being that a motion capture system can record the position in space of the markers on the motion capture stage.

This chapter delivers a broad spectrum of information regarding motion capture technology, techniques, and process.

The number of different technologies available to capture motion makes it almost impossible to meaningfully cover all of them in a single chapter. This chapter, therefore, focuses primarily on the most

The VES Handbook of Visual Effects. DOI: 10.1016/B978-0-240-81242-7.00004-1

prevalent form of motion capture, optical. Where possible it will cover alternate and variant technologies.

OTHER TYPES OF MOTION CAPTURE
John Root, Demian Gordon

Motion capture is simply a tool for measuring real-world motion and encoding it into a digital medium. Therefore, a very patient man with a ruler could be said to be a form of motion capture. Optical motion capture may not be appropriate for all productions. This section serves to inform readers about alternate technologies that might be worth exploring given their unique project needs.

Resistance-Based Technologies

- *Potentiometer:* Analog potentiometers measure conductivity and convert it to a digital signal. By using a variety of potentiometers, it's possible to create a wearable exoskeleton that can record its own movement.
  Examples:
  Gypsy-6 from Animazoo
  Cyberglove from Immersion
- *Light:* Light is shone down fiber-optic cables, and the amount of light that hits the far end and comes back to the emitter is measured and converted into data that relates to how bent the cable is.
  Examples:
  Shape Tape from Measureand
  5DT Data Glove from 5DT
- *Piezoelectric:* Piezoelectric motion capture systems work by measuring the electrical charge given off by a piece of piezoelectric material. The more the piezoelectric strip is bent, the more electricity it gives off.

Electromechanical-Based Technologies

- *Gyroscopic:* Gyroscopic motion capture systems use an array of gyroscopes to detect movement. Usually multiple gyroscopes are used per rigid object being tracked, to determine orientation.
  Examples:
  Playstation 3 6DOF controller from Sony
  IGS-190 from Animazoo
- *Accelerometer:* Accelerometers measure motion relative to a known starting position or velocity. An accelerometer can be as simple as a spring, fulcrum, and counterweight. To increase

fidelity, accuracy, and repeatability, an accelerometer is often augmented with additional technology. For instance, by reading the conductivity of the spring as it expands and contracts, more information can be gleaned from the mechanism.
Examples:
Wiimote from Nintendo
iPhone from Apple

- *Magnetic:* A magnetic field is generated from an emitter. Sensors are then introduced into the field that cause magnetic disturbances. The position and orientation of the disturbance can be measured. By placing sensors all over an object and placing the object inside the magnetic field, the movement of the object can then be tracked over time.
Example:
Flock of Birds from Ascension

Computer Vision

- *Dense stereo:* Cameras are arranged in stereo pairs, which is to say they are placed about the same distance apart as the human eyes are from one another. The overlapping views from the cameras are analyzed and each matching pixel in the resulting camera images can be reconstructed into a 3D point cloud.
Examples:
Di3D from Dimensional Imaging
Contour from Mova
- *Structured light:* A structured pattern of light is projected onto an object. Several cameras record images of the structured light pattern as it is deformed on the surface on which it is projected. The details that make up the structured pattern are triangulated by comparing the various images that were recorded. This data is then reconstructed into 3D geometry.
Example:
MaMoCa from MaMoCa
- *Light stage:* The subject being measured is placed into a light-controlled environment where the timing and direction of light, as it strikes the object being captured, can be measured. The light stage then emits light from the top, bottom, left, right, front, and back of the object. The resulting images are analyzed to determine the normal amount of displacement at each pixel. This information is used to create a normal map that can be used as a displacement map to increase the resolution of the basic 3D shape that was generated by the structured light scan.
Example:
ICT from Aguru Images

Time-of-Flight Technologies

- *Light:* The time that it takes light to be sent out and return to an emitter is measured and turned into a distance calculation that can be triangulated. A single time-of-flight measurement system generates 3D depth and 2D shape measurements. Multiple emitters are required to generate 3D shape and depth.
  Example:
  Swiss Ranger from Mesa Imaging
- *Sound:* Ultrasonic emitters and detectors are utilized. The emitters send out an ultrasonic chirp that is detected by the detectors. The amount of time it takes for the chirp from an emitter to reach the detector array can be measured. The amount of time it takes for the sound to reach each detector can be equated to the distance away from the emitter that each detector is.
  Example:
  IS-900 virtual camera from Intersense

IS MOTION CAPTURE RIGHT FOR A PROJECT?
John Root, Scott Gagain

Motion capture is still a relatively new tool in the world of entertainment and already it has opened up a treasure trove of creative capabilities. During the past 15 years or so, motion capture has risen to become ubiquitous as a de facto content creation tool for the visual effects community. So is motion capture right for a project? To figure that out, it's important to first recognize the role that motion capture can play in a production.

The most common use for motion capture is to capture human motion and apply it to a digital double. In this manner, high-fidelity character animation can be delivered at a price point and in a time frame not practically achievable by other methods. Using motion capture, virtual actors or fantastic characters can be convincingly integrated into live-action backplates or into digital environments where they previously did not exist such as in The *Curious Case of Benjamin Button* (2008). Actors can be made to play non-human characters such as Andy Serkis playing the starring role in *King Kong* (2005). The scope to which this technique can be extrapolated and executed is near limitless, such as in the marauding waves of Orcs in *Lord of the Rings: The Return of the King* (2003). Entire films can be made with motion capture such as Disney's 2009 *A Christmas Carol*. Motion capture can even be used to replace actors who are no longer available or even alive!

However and perhaps most importantly, even though a production may benefit from motion capture, that does not mean it is ideally suited to accommodate it. The following points should be considered:

- What are the basic production requirements?
- What is the proper entry point?
- Which technology best suits the production needs?
- Does the production have the right resources available to meet expectations?

What Are the Basic Production Requirements?

Most successful projects go through a substantial amount of preplanning before the actual production wheels can get moving. This is true for all types of media whether it be commercials, feature films, music videos, television shows, or video games. Once the storyline has been accepted, it may be storyboarded or previsualized, at which point decisions must be made as to how the vision will be realized. If something can't be done in the live-action arena, a number of options are available to help bring an effect to life. This is typically where the "Is motion capture right for the project?" question comes into play. The biggest factor to weigh is whether the desired animation outcome is a lifelike look or something more stylized. Motion capture or hybrid MoCap keyframed approaches are ideal for scenarios where more lifelike performances are desired.

What Is the Proper Entry Point?

Once the decision to use motion capture has been made, additional questions need to be addressed: What type of budget is available? Should a system be purchased, or should the motion capture be done by a third-party service provider? Perhaps a stock motion library is appropriate? Finding the right entry point is important. The size of the project, what the company is looking to accomplish, and the company's future MoCap needs are all deciding factors.

What Are the Budgetary Constraints?

If price is not an issue, the company may look into building out a facility and purchasing its own system. If the company doesn't have extremely deep pockets and a long-term production forecast, it may be better to outsource the project to one of the many MoCap service providers. A range of cost-effective options is available that can help provide a good starting point in the world of motion capture.

Should a System Be Purchased?

Motion capture equipment, especially optical, is expensive. Not only are there significant up-front costs, but motion capture equipment needs a stage area and people to run it. Properly managed, however, it's worth its weight in gold. A top of the line system will last 6 or 8 years or more before it becomes obsolete. If the company plans on using motion capture heavily during the next 6 to 8 years, purchasing a system will definitely pay off.

Some hardware vendors will entertain leasing a system, but this is not common.

Should the Work Be Outsourced?

A number of companies offer motion capture services. The benefit to outsourcing is of course to skip all of the up-front costs associated with purchasing a system. If the project is in need of some motion capture, but a long-term investment does not make sense, outsourcing is probably the best choice. MoCap service providers can typically provide anything from raw data capture, which can be processed in house, to complete ready-to-render animation.

Should a Stock Motion Library Be Used?

Many animation libraries are available. These are collections of animated motions pertaining to a specific genre or character type. Motion libraries are typically used for crowd simulations or ambient background characters.

Stock motion libraries suffer from nonexclusivity and are often incomplete for the needs of a professional production.

Which Technology Best Suits the Production Needs?

The technology to choose should be based on what needs to be captured. Optical systems such as Vicon and Motion Analysis are the most widely used in the industry because of their accuracy and flexibility. Optical systems have become a trusted resource for visual effects professionals around the globe during the past decade. They have been battle tested for years and have proven to withstand just about any production scenario. If the production requires extreme attention to detail; multiple character interactions; highly accurate data; high-impact stunts; on-set, real-time, full-performance (face, body, and fingers), dialogue-driven sequences, etc., then the best possible option would be to use a passive optical system either in house or with a third-party vendor.

However, if the project is dependent on real-time performance or being streamed live for network television; has heavily occluded animation (i.e., shot inside a car or under bed sheets, etc.); is capturing facial animation only; or involves animated cloth, it may be better to use an alternative MoCap solution from a vendor like PhaseSpace, Moven, Animazoo, Mova Contour, Image Metrics, Measurand, or Dimensional Imaging.

Are the Resources Available?

Whether data is outsourced or captured internally, a fair amount of post-processing is likely required. Processing motion capture data can run the gamut of skill sets. Some parts of the pipeline are fairly objective, while others are highly subjective. The types of talent required will range from highly specialized animators to trackers and solvers.[1] Do not take these people for granted. Ensure that the company has secured the services of skilled artisans. Do not underestimate the ability of someone skilled in working with motion capture—they can, will, and have made the difference between quality data and a useless mess.

PREPARING FOR MOTION CAPTURE
John Root, Demian Gordon

Stage time can be very expensive. Actors, directors, cameramen, grips, props, and all of the expense that comes with a typical production add up really fast. However trackers, solvers, riggers, animators, and all of the expense of the post-shoot team aren't exactly cheap either. Because the post-shoot team is trying to re-create what happened on stage, they are at the mercy of what happened on the stage. This section explores how to minimize stage time while still providing the post-shoot team with quality data.

Understanding the technology, showing up prepared, and working with skilled motion capture professionals are all essential to quality motion capture.

What Can Be Captured

Motion capture is ideal for real-world timing of objects, people, and things moving in a 3D space. Weight, timing, balance, velocity, and acceleration are just some of the things that can

---

[1] Trackers and solvers: motion capture specialists who process data off the stage and turn it into useful animation.

be acquired with motion capture. With motion capture it is possible to record human and animal performances. Body, face, fingers, articulated puppets, and to some extent cloth can all be captured. It is even possible with some technologies to record the shape and texture of the object along with the articulated motions.

What Cannot Be Captured

Each technology has its limitations. Optical motion capture, for example, is vision based and therefore requires line of sight to prevent marker occlusion. It requires controlled lighting conditions, including reflections and refractions. Additionally, passive optical systems are marker based and are therefore limited to capturing things to which a marker can be affixed. This makes eyes difficult to capture. Further, an object's motion needs to be able to be expressed as a point or several points in space. This makes water and cloth difficult to capture.

There are, however, lots of different capture technologies, each with different limitations. To date, no one technology can do it all without significant limitations. It is common in motion capture to combine technologies into a larger, more complete package. For instance, you could capture face and body separately or employ several types of capture devices: one for body, one for face, and possibly another for hands or eyes. Using various scanning or photogrammetry[2] techniques to acquire a mesh that is later driven by motion capture is also common. Knowing the limitations of the technology is the key to success.

Motion Capture People

Motion capture is not a turnkey solution. Talented people are needed to run the hardware and to process the data. At each step in the motion capture pipeline, a different skill set comes in to play. Any production gearing up for a motion capture shoot should be sure to include hardware technicians, trackers, solvers, and animators skilled in working with motion capture data.

Hardware Technicians

Running the stage and operating the motion capture equipment is mostly an objective process. A hardware tech should be comfortable in a stage environment, have a cool demeanor and be an absolute ace when it comes to troubleshooting hardware issues. If the hardware goes down in the middle of a shoot, a lot of money

---

[2] Photogrammetry: process in which information is derived from a 2D image.

will be wasted as the production sits idle. Hardware techs are responsible for ensuring that the capture technology is running like a well-oiled machine.

Motion capture hardware techs are also responsible for setting up the system. This benefits greatly from a strong knowledge of computer vision, camera technology, networking, general computer technology, and some light programming and scripting.

Trackers and Solvers

Once the data is captured, it needs to be processed. Processing optical data is usually broken into two steps, tracking and solving. Tracking is the process by which data from the stage is made usable for solving. A tracker is typically a person with strong technical skills and a keen eye for animation. Technical or junior animators with a strong ability to learn new things can make good trackers.

Solvers are the people who turn tracked data from the stage into actual character animation. A solver is typically an animator with a strong technical background. Riggers or Character Setup Technical Directors (TDs) with a keen eye for animation can also make good solvers.

MoCap Animators

Once data has been solved, it becomes character animation on a rig. At this point it is typical to want to modify the performance, which requires an animator. Finding an animator who can work with motion capture is important. It is also important to be clear when hiring animators that they will be working with motion capture because some animators prefer not to work with motion capture.

Service Providers

When a long-term investment in motion capture is not an option, it is typical to use a motion capture service provider. A service provider is a company or individual with which motion capture can be outsourced. Most providers offer services ranging from a complete solution to isolated tasks depending on need. Isolated tasks might include consultation, capture, tracking, solving, and integration. A complete solution would mean the delivery of animation to spec in a ready-to-render state. Some service providers are better than others. You are encouraged to shop around and ask lots of questions. Get lots of quotes and request sample data. Don't be afraid to ask for a test capture session.

Most large VFX houses will offer some level of motion capture capability. Additional studios include, but are not limited to:

Accel Animation Studios
Thiruvananthapuram, India
www.accelanimation.com

Black Powder Media
Los Angeles, CA, USA
www.blackpowdermedia.com

Centroid 3D
Buckinghamshire, UK
www.centroid3d.com

Deakin Motion Lab
Melbourne, Australia
www.deakin.edu.au/motionlab

Elektrashock
Venice, CA, USA
www.elektrashock.com

House of Moves
Los Angeles, CA, USA
www.moves.com

Just Cause
Los Angeles, CA, USA
www.for-the-cause.com

Mobility Art Studios
Hyderabad, India
www.mobilityart.com

MocapLab
Paris, France
www.mocaplab.com

Motion Analysis Studios
Hollywood, CA, USA
www.mastudios.com

Motus Digital
Dallas, TX, USA
www.motusdigital.com

Perspective Studios
New York / Santa Monica, USA
www.perspectivestudios.com

Red Eye Studio
Hoffman Estates, IL, USA
www.redeye-studio.com

Xtrackrz
Culver City, CA, USA
www.xtrackrz.com

Animation Vertigo
San Diego, CA, USA
 www.animationvertigo.com

CaptiveMotion LLC
Tempe, AZ, USA
www.captivemotion.com

Critical Moves USA
Detroit, USA
www.criticalmovesusa.com

EA Motion Capture Studios
Vancouver, Canada
www.mocap.ea.com

Giant Studios
Atlanta / Los Angeles, USA
www.giantstudios.com

Imagination Studios
Sweden
www.imaginationstudios.com

Metricminds
Frankfurt, Germany
www.metricminds.com

MoCap Latte
Washington, D.C., USA
www.mocaplatte.com

Motek Entertainment
Amsterdam, Netherlands
www.motekentertainment.com

Motion Werx / Animazoo USA
Emeryville, CA, USA
www.motionwerx.com

Parallax 360
Southfield, MI, USA
www.parallax360.com

Rainmaker Entertainment Inc.
Vancouver, BC, Canada
www.rainmaker.com

Sony Computer Entertainment of America
San Diego, CA, USA

Rigging for Motion Capture

Character rigging can mean many things, but for the purpose of this chapter it means the adding of controls to a digital character such that a mesh is made to be easily animated. To drive a digital character with motion capture, it will need to be rigged first. The rig is typically a simple hierarchical collection of forward kinematic pivots represented as joints or bones on which the captured data is solved. Rigging and solving are closely intertwined. Each must take the other into consideration for optimal results.

Motion capture rigs should be lightweight and straightforward. More complicated deformation and animation rigs are typically kept separate for compatibility and flexibility and then driven by the motion capture rig via constraints or remapping of the data. Compatibility is important when it is common in motion capture to involve many different software packages, each with its own limitations.

If real-time previsualization will be used during the motion capture shoot, the rigs must be sorted out beforehand. Otherwise, the rigging process can happen after and, in fact, be informed by the captured data.

Joint Placement

Creating a digital skeleton that closely matches the proportions of the actor is important to generating quality animation. However, a human skeleton is not rigid. Its pivots are speculative and often involve compound motions. Further, short of an X-ray the joint positions of the capture subject cannot easily be known because they are covered by muscle, skin, and the motion capture suit. For these reasons the *range of motion* is used. A range of motion, commonly referred to as a ROM, is a motion capture exercise whereby an actor is asked to move each of his or her limbs to their extremes such that the motion capture software can learn the physical limits of each limb. Some software uses the ROM to generate a skeleton automatically. If no such software is available, a skeleton is typically generated manually by visually analyzing the ROM.

Degrees of Freedom

Degrees of freedom (DOFs) are the prescribed axis by which a joint is allowed to move. Motion capture is commonly solved to six basic degrees of freedom: translation in x, y, and z and rotation in x, y, and z. It is typically not desirable to allow a joint complete freedom on all axes. For instance, knees and elbows are often solved as hinge joints. Different solving methods work better with different degrees of freedom.

Mesh Deformations

While it is best to keep complex deformations separate from the motion capture rig, it is usually desirable to have a visual representation of the character beyond the skeleton. The mesh the skeleton is driving should be segmented, parented, or a simple smooth bound skin. This is because the various motion capture software packages do not support more complicated deformation techniques.

Shotlist

A shotlist is a document that is prepared before the motion capture shoot. The purpose of the shotlist is to predetermine everything that is going to be captured for the sake of minimizing stage time into a focused shoot. A good shotlist will list those performances in an order that plays into the technology and the stage requirements. A great shotlist will be flexible and expandable because quite often most of the information contained within a shotlist is actually filled in on stage. It is typically the job of the script supervisor, assistant director, or director to extract a shotlist from the script. Shotlists generally contain file names, brief descriptions, and important technical information.

Technology Considerations

For the most part, motion capture is liberating to the shooting process. Camera, lighting, and exacting specifics can be figured out post-shoot. There are, however, a few things to consider.

Time

There is commonly an upper limit to the length of a take when dealing with motion capture. Find out what this length is and be sure to take it into account when breaking out a shotlist.

Wardrobe

If actors are expected to be getting in and out of stunt gear or similar such wardrobe changes, it would be a good idea to group those takes together because the marker positions on the actor will likely change as the wardrobe changes.

Set

Tearing down and building up a set on the motion capture stage can be time consuming, complicated, and in some cases dangerous. If possible, shoot everything in that set before moving on.

Scene, Setup, Pass, Take

The filename is generally concatenated from the relevant information. In a feature film environment, this might follow the *scene, setup, pass, take* nomenclature, where each bit is separated by an underscore or dash. It is ideal to pad the individual parts such that they sort properly in a list.

002_B01_001

In this example, scene 2 is ready to be recorded using stage setup B01 (Bravo 1). This will be take 1. It might not have been known at the time the shotlist is created that a setup B was even required. However, because of the concatenation this filename is flexible and expandable.

Tiles

When breaking a script into a shotlist it is important to consider the limitations of the technology. The size of the volume[3] will be limited, as well the number of actors and perhaps even the types of motion. For these reasons scenes may need to be broken up into multiple tiles. A tile is an action that is intended to be composited with other actions. For instance, technology may limit a shoot to 10 actors in the volume. Therefore, shooting a large-scale battle scene might seem impossible. In this case several tiles are invoked where the actors are playing different characters in each tile. Then, in post, all of these tiles are composited together in 3D to create the desired masses. In another example, an actor might have to run a distance that is farther than the capture volume permits. In this case, tiles are invoked, and the resulting animations are stitched together in post such that the actor is playing the same character only in a different time and space.

Actors

When casting for motion capture talent, it is helpful to cast for individuals who have excellent body control and a highly developed sense of physical awareness. The technology can be very demanding. Cast actors who will be comfortable in very tight suits surrounded by technology. And above all, look for actors who can remove their mind from the motion capture set and bring it to the story world because the motion capture set is limited in its props and set decoration.

Ideally, actors should be of the same size and shape of the character they will be playing. Following these simple rules will reduce time in post and save money. However, unlike traditional

---

[3] Volume: term that describe the motion capture stage. However, unlike "stage," it implies a 3D space.

filmmaking, this is not required. The magic of motion capture is that it is possible for actors to play characters of completely different proportions to their own, at different ages, and in different times, scales, and states.

In traditional optical motion capture, some types of actors are more difficult to capture than others. Overweight actors, for instance, can be difficult to record as the markers tend to jiggle on the soft tissue rather than measure the bones and joints directly. Also, very small people can be difficult because they can present challenges to marker placement.

Briefing the Actor

It's sometimes challenging to prepare actors for the experience of motion capture. The technology involved can be overbearing to them or it may take them a little while to acclimate to the difference between normal filmmaking and motion capture. Primarily they need to be made aware of the technology and processes surrounding them. Explain what things are, how they work, and what they do. Explain the limitations of the technology. For instance, explain that the markers should not move; explain that the cameras are extremely delicate and should not be touched; explain that a proper T pose[4] is important and to respect the boundaries of the capture volume. Typically it is the job of the assistant director to brief the actors on such things but this might also fall on to the motion capture supervisor or stage lead.

Often, several technical actions must be captured that are not related to the performance but are required for the technology. These actions, such as the ROM or FACS,[5] should be explained ahead of time such that they are rehearsed and taken seriously. Let the actors know that a proper ROM and FACS session is essential to good data on the back end.

Animals

It goes without saying that an animal's natural habitat is not that of the sterile, high-tech motion capture studio. They hate having things glued to them, they hate wearing tight suits, and they are not very good at performing rigidly perfect moves such as the T pose of a FACS session. For these reasons and countless others, animals make poor motion capture subjects. That said, they can be captured like anything else. Their articulate joints can be measured with strategically placed markers just like those of the human.

---

[4] T pose: an action performed by the actor. It simply consists of standing with one's feet straight down from one's hips and arms out to the side, palms facing down. This pose is easy for the motion capture software to identify and label.

[5] FACS: short for Facial Action Coding System, which is a method by which almost all possible facial motion can be encoded.

Markers on Animals

A human can be instructed to not touch the markers. They can be made aware that the markers are meticulously placed and should not be moved. Animals don't listen so well in this regard. For this reason, it is best to have a motion capture suit custom made for them with the markers sewn into the suit such that they cannot be easily removed … or eaten. This suit should be tight, such that the suit itself doesn't move and the markers stay true to the joints they are measuring. Of course, the suit should not be so tight that it disturbs the animal.

If custom making a tight suit is not an option, affixing the marker directly to the animal is the next best option. This is best done with a medical-grade, hypoallergenic adhesive. If applicable, and possible, shave the animal's fur/hair such that the marker can be glued directly to the skin. If shaving the animal is not an option, fur/hair can be matted down with soluble glue and the marker then glued to the matted fur.

Animals are animals, and as such cannot be counted on to respect the technology. It goes without saying that the less obtrusive a technology, the better for animal capture. Nothing can be farther from an animal's happy place than a motion capture studio. When shooting with animals, the set should be locked down and distractions minimized.

Suits

A motion capture suit is a tight-fitting suit to which markers are attached. They can be made from any material, but a black material with a stretchy, loop Velcro property is common. A suit should be as tight as the actor can stand it. This will keep the markers true to the joints they are measuring. However, a suit should not be so tight that it restricts the actor's movements. Suits are typically black to reduce light reflection and prevent camera blowouts. A black suit is not necessarily required, nor is it ideal. A shiny black material can reflect light just as unfortunately as a white surface. A material that diffuses light serves the same technical requirements and is much easier to see in reference video. A video image of a bunch of actors in pitch-black suits can be difficult to discern. A good suit is worth the money because the resulting data is more usable.

Suit Slide

Even the best fitting suits are going to slide across the outside of the actor as they contort. Because the markers are affixed to the suit and not drilled into the actor's bones directly, suit slide can make it difficult to accurately solve for joint rotations. A well-made suit will minimize the slide, but not eliminate it. When fitting an actor for a motion capture suit, it is ideal to have him or her perform a variety of motions and stretches to get an idea of where the suit is falling short. Different swatches of material can be sewn in to minimize the sliding affect. Commonly, high-quality suits have an altogether different material around the bendy parts such as the elbows, shoulders, and groin.

Marker Placement

Optical markers are placed to measure translations. Given that, markers should be placed such that when the thing they are measuring moves, the marker moves with it. Markers are primarily placed for the benefit of solving, but also need to consider tracking. Additionally, they should be placed such that they don't endanger or hinder the performer. Markers should be placed with respect to safety and comfort over the course of the performance. The quantity of markers that can be used is limited as is the size, so it's important to maximize these factors.

Figure 4.1 A medium-resolution, 57-marker body placement. (Image courtesy of John Root.)

Stay Rigid

Markers should be mounted rigidly to the objects they are measuring. When measuring the motions of the human body, markers should be mounted on or near bone such that they pick up the least possible muscle bulge or skin slide. When placing markers on humans, it's important to get a good sense of the actor and suit he or she is wearing. Place markers with consideration of all the possible ways in which the actor might move and the suit might deform.

Distance

A marker defines a point in space. Any three points in space will define a triangle. A triangle defines a plane, and from a plane an orientation can be derived. Even the best marker data, however, contains errors. This error can manifest as jitter, spikes, or slip. Because of this error, the wider and larger the triangle that is created by the markers, the better the resulting rotation will be. This is because a sharp, narrow triangle will have one poorly defined axis. Any marker error on this axis will manifest as gross error in the resulting rotation. For this reason, always place markers as far from the joints they are measuring as possible and also as far from each other as possible.

Redundancy

Redundancy helps in re-creating missing or occluded markers. Through rigid body math missing markers can be gap filled during times of occlusion by placing them at their last known offset to still present markers. For this to work properly four markers per rigid segment is ideal. While gap filling with three markers or less is possible, it usually involves some kinematic or statistical knowledge of upstream and downstream hierarchical connections. Because rigidity can be speculative, the more markers placed on a rigid object, the better the gap fill will be.

Marker Placement on Faces

Not only is the human face incredibly detailed in its motion and subtleties, but the human eye is very adept at sensing its slightest movement. Capturing these motions with optical discrete point capture is difficult. This is because packing enough markers onto the face to capture every little motion presents problems for the technology, the performance, and the process. While there is no clear winning strategy, there are two common marker placement methods.

Muscle-Based Marker Placement Method

All faces are different, but under all that skin and fat, a common muscle structure can be found. One common face marker placement strategy is to lay out markers that measure the contractions of the underlying face muscles. By placing markers along the length of these muscles, the amount any given muscle is engaged can be approximated by measuring the markers' relative distance to one another or a common point. Some muscles always flex along with other muscles and can be skipped entirely because they can be inferred from other muscles. Having captured the amount a muscle or collection of muscles is capable of flexing is only a small part of a much larger problem. Building a rig capable of using the captured muscle information is then required. Additionally, muscle bulge, fat, skin, and physics must then be modeled and rigged to build a final, photoreal face.

Advantages
- Provides a universal marker set across all actors.

Disadvantages
- Muscles can be hard to locate and capture on some actors.
- Requires complex tools to infer muscle information from point data.
- Requires complex rigs to make use of muscle information.

Peak Motion Based Marker Placement Method

Not quite as objective as a muscle-based approach would be to find independent peak motions. This means motions not easily inferred from other motions, motions whose lines of action differ from those around them. If, for instance, an actor raised an eyebrow and five folds appeared on his forehead, each fold would get some number of markers along its length. A different actor might only have three folds and therefore receive only three rows of markers. Peak motions are quite often perpendicular to the muscle motion or the result of a muscle's motion. This is because as a muscle contracts it bulges the skin. Marker data collected in this manner is immediately usable in a direct drive or wrap deform fashion.

Advantages
- Data is more easily usable.
- Measures physics, gravity, etc.

Disadvantages
- Every actor has a different marker set.
- Time required to locate peak motions can be significant.

Hybrid Approach

A hybrid approach would be to be measure both the muscles and the peak motions. Together, information can be known that is not easily derived from either. In this method markers are placed at both the points required to measure the muscles and any motions that are caused by the muscle, gravity, or external physics. A hybrid approach that measures everything often requires more markers than can be practically captured with traditional optical markers.

Advantages

• Data for all common types of solving is acquired.

Disadvantages

• Requires a lot of markers!

Marker Masks

In large-scale productions where many actors are captured across many days, it is common to create a markering template mask. This template is a clear plastic mask made from the actor's face. Once the actor's face has been markered for the first time, the mask goes on and is marked so as to project the markers from the face to the mask. Then these marks are drilled and holes created. Each subsequent capture day, the mask template goes on and the marker locations are projected back down. In this manner the markers' locations do not need to be reidentified every capture day. This ensures consistency and affords efficiency.

HARDWARE
John Root, Andrew Smith

An optical motion capture system is image based and as such its primary component is digital cameras. The motion capture camera is designed for a very specific purpose: to capture a narrow spectrum of high-intensity light at very fast speeds. This

Figure 4.2 A high-level overview of the motion capture hardware pipeline. (Image courtesy of John Root.)

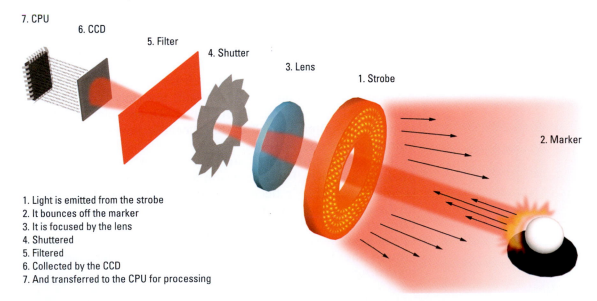

7. CPU
6. CCD
5. Filter
4. Shutter
3. Lens
1. Strobe
2. Marker

1. Light is emitted from the strobe
2. It bounces off the marker
3. It is focused by the lens
4. Shuttered
5. Filtered
6. Collected by the CCD
7. And transferred to the CPU for processing

light is emitted from the strobe, reflected back by the marker, and focused by the lens through the filter onto the image sensor. Then the captured image is sent by the charge-coupled device (CCD) to the CPU where it is processed, compressed, and finally offloaded to the data collection station for reconstruction. This is done typically between 60 and 240 times per second.

The entire motion capture process hinges on collecting quality 2D images. Bad 2D images will generate bad 3D reconstructions, so when considering hardware, collecting quality 2D images should be a primary concern. This section is intended to give a better understanding of the camera and its various elements and how to leverage them to give the best 2D data for a given application. Primarily the information contained in this section refers to Vicon and Motion Analysis hardware, but much of this information is also applicable to other systems as well, such as Phase Space and Standard Deviation.

The Strobe

Sometimes called ring lights, the strobes are the typically red, infrared, or near-infrared light-emitting diodes (LEDs) that are mounted on the front of the camera. The term *strobe* comes from the fact that the LEDs are flashing in unison with the camera taking pictures. This is, in most cases, happening faster than the human eye can perceive and thus they appear to be always on when in fact they are strobing. The strobes send light out that is reflected back by the marker and captured by the CCD image sensor. Picking the right strobe for the camera and lenses is important because they come in multiple varieties and can make a significant difference in volume setup.

Field of View

Field of view (FOV) is the angular extent of a scene that is illuminated by the strobe. FOV is determined by the type of LED and the orientation at which the LED is mounted on the board. Assuming all LEDs are facing forward, the only factor to consider is the FOV of the LED itself. If the LEDs are splayed outward to gain FOV, intensity will be lost because fewer LEDs will be pointed in any one direction.

The amount of light a strobe can emit will vary in both intensity and FOV. For this reason a proper lens/strobe pairing is important. This is because precious light would be wasted in the case where the strobe's FOV exceeded that of the lens. Concurrently, if the FOV of the strobe were narrower than that of the lens, the resulting image would appear to be poorly lit around the edges. This artifact is sometimes referred to as *vignetting*.

Strobe Intensity

The intensity of a strobe refers to its brightness level. A strobe's intensity is defined by the power and focus of the LEDs contained within it. The filtered strobe light has to travel to the marker and reflect with enough intensity to register on the camera sensor. Since light intensity follows the inverse square law (two times the distance equals 1/4 the light) these strobes need to be extremely bright. The intensity required for capture depends primarily on the size and distance of the fiducials (markers). Smaller volumes (capture area) generally do not require as much light as larger volumes. Strobes typically allow for brightness control and as such the brightest strobes permitted should be used.

Markers

A marker is a capture fiducial, meaning that it is a point within a captured image that can be easily identified and tracked. Sometimes referred to as *jewels* or *ping-pong balls*, markers should technically not be called sensors because there is no sensing going on in the optical marker—all of the action is at the observer.

Off-the-shelf solutions use one of three styles: passive, passive retroreflectors, and active. Though there are different styles of markers, the main goal of each is to provide something easy to identify and consistently track in the camera image. Markers are usually circular or spherical, which provides an easy-to-find center from all angles. The following types of markers all accomplish these goals by slightly different methods, and each has its niche, as dictated by application and the economics of scale.

Passive Markers

A passive marker is a fiducial that offers little to no optical advantage. Passive markers are commonly used to aid in matchmoving or live-action film shoots. In recent years passive marker motion capture has been made popular for its ability to digitally record animation simultaneously with live-action footage. A passive marker is typically of high contrast compared to its surroundings. Examples of passive markers are ink dots on an actor's face or cross-hairs on their clothing. As such, passive markers are most difficult to track and are rarely used in conventional motion capture.

Retroreflective Markers

When people think motion capture, this is the type of marker that most likely comes to mind. Typically these markers are small rubber spheres wrapped in Scotchlite tape. The nature of a retroreflective surface is that it reflects light straight back at the source with a minimal degree of scattering. This creates tiny hot spots of light in the collected images that can be easily distinguished from background information. In this manner, markers are easily separated from the rest of the image and therefore more easily tracked.

Typical sizes include 10 to 18mm spherical markers for the body and 2 to 5mm spherical or hemispherical markers for the face. A marker's size is primarily determined by the distance and resolution of the camera but is also affected by strobe intensity, *f*-stop, and the subtlety of the performance being captured. Prices range around $6 per marker, and given that a single actor may wear 60 or more just for body capture, markers are not a trivial cost that shouldn't be overlooked. The life span of a given marker depends on what it is used for, but they can lose effectiveness over time by mishandling (particularly if you just ate some greasy pizza), scuffing, rips in the tape, and general capture. Expect to replace markers fairly frequently if stunts or if lots of action are involved.

Active Markers

The less common active marker is a tiny solid-state LED that emits the same spectrum of light the cameras are looking for. Active markers require power so are typically tethered to a battery worn by the actor. Because active markers do not bounce light, they are brighter and more clearly visible to the cameras. Active markers, however, typically emit light in a particular direction and, hence, are most visible from the direction they are facing. Light from an active marker can be diffused to cover a wider FOV but in doing so becomes less bright and can lose some of its advantages. This cone of effectiveness can induce noise in the data as cameras come in and out of view. Some hardware can detect the frequency at which active markers are strobing and automatically identify the marker's label. This advantage makes active markers ideal for real time but with the disadvantage of an upper marker limit. It is possible, albeit impractical, to mix retroreflective and active markers in the same capture volume.

Lenses

A camera's lens is its window into the capture volume. Motion capture requires an intricate understanding of exactly how any given lens gathers light from the volume and focuses it onto the camera's image sensor. This understanding is known as *calibration* and is required so that any given 2D pixel can be traced back out into 3D space. Calibration is so delicate that a mathematically perfect lens is required for mathematically perfect data. However, such lenses do not exist. A good motion capture lens will be a lens with near-perfect radial symmetry, no filter coating in the spectrum in which the capture occurs, high speed, and as close to diffraction limited as possible. Hardware providers generally recommend and resell a variety of lenses for various volume configurations.

Focal Length

The focal length is the distance from the lens to the image sensor when the lens is focused on an object at infinity. That is, it is the number used to define the FOV of a camera's lens. Because the size of the image's sensor will be fixed and the parameters of the lens may vary, focal length does not directly correlate with FOV. Generally speaking, however, a wide-angle lens will have a smaller focal length number, whereas a narrow-angle lens or long lens will have a high focal length value. Focal lengths typical for a motion capture volume range from 12.5 to 45mm or anywhere in between. However, focal lengths can go as low as 2mm in special cases such as head-mounted cameras.

Generally speaking, and assuming a list of fixed parameters, long lenses are used to capture things very far away, while wide lenses are used to capture things very close. However, distance can be traded for accuracy. A long lens focused on a close object would be more accurate, but have a smaller capture volume than if the same object were being captured by a wide lens. Inversely, a wide lens focused on a far object would be less accurate but have a very large capture volume. Given these trade-offs, balancing distance and focal length against marker size and accuracy is a delicate process.

One additional thing to consider when talking about focal length is camera handoff. Camera handoff occurs when a marker is well inside the capture volume, but leaves the view of a camera. While this marker is still being seen by other cameras, the resulting position of the marker will suffer from its number of contributing cameras having changed. For this reason, simply throwing more cameras with long lenses at a volume does not necessarily make it better.

F-Stop

The *f*-stop of a lens is focal length divided by the aperture diameter. In practical terms it defines the amount of light that is let in through the lens. This is done by adjusting the aperture, which is a mechanical iris. Closing this iris, referred to as *stopping it down*, reduces the amount of light captured, while opening this iris allows more light in to be captured.

It is ideal, in the world of motion capture, to be taking pictures that are a frozen instant in time. This means using very fast shutter speeds. Faster shutter speeds capture less light. For this reason it is common to open up the *f*-stop to let more light in. This, however, has the negative by-product of decreasing the depth of field, meaning objects are out of focus. Balancing *f*-stop with strobe intensity and shutter speed is a delicate process.

Depth of Field

While not a property of the lens, depth of field (DOF) is closely related to the lens settings. While a lens can only truly be focused on one point in space, the DOF refers to the acceptable distance from that point where an object is still considered to be in focus. Naturally, a deep DOF to increase the range where markers are in focus is preferred. To obtain this, it is typical to stop the aperture down, thereby letting less light in. However, decreasing the amount of light let in to the camera makes for a darker image of the marker. Ideally, markers should be in focus to a camera at the farthest extent of the capture volume while also being fully lit. Finding this sweet spot is a balance between *f*-stop, strobe intensity, and shutter speed.

Prime versus Zoom

A prime lens is a lens whose focal length is fixed, while a zoom lens is a lens with an adjustable focal length. While the flexibility of a zoom lens is attractive, they should be avoided because they contain many complex elements that decrease the amount of light and increase the amount of difficult-to-calibrate image artifacts. It is possible to find high-quality zoom lenses without such aberrations, but they come at an extremely high price.

Which Lenses Are Ideal?

Which lenses to use is going to depend primarily on the number of cameras present, their resolution, and the size and scope of the markers they are trying to capture. Here are some typical system configurations:

- 20 × 20 × 10 ft, 16 cameras, 16mm focal length, 15mm marker minimum, 2 actors;
- 10 × 10 × 7 ft, 32 cameras, 24mm focal length, 5mm marker minimum, 1 actor;
- 30 × 30 × 7 ft, 32 cameras, 16mm focal length, 15mm marker minimum, 4 actors; and
- 20 × 20 × 7 ft, 64 cameras, 24mm focal length, 5mm marker minimum, 2 actors.

Filter

The purpose of the filter is to eliminate all light except that emitted from the strobe. Sometimes a filter is mounted in front of the lens, sometimes behind it. Given the retroreflective nature of the markers and the position of the strobes, the resulting filtered image should contain only bright white spots of light reflected by the markers.

Charge-Coupled Device

Light emitted from the strobe and reflected back from the marker will land on and be captured by photoelectric image sensors and transferred by the CCD to camera memory for processing. The speed and resolution of a CCD will vary based on the camera model, but it is typically in the neighborhood of 4 megapixels at 120 fps. While quality data can be collected at 1 megapixel, some cameras offer resolutions as high as 16 megapixels. The CCD is arguably the most important piece of the motion capture camera when recognizing that higher resolutions and faster frame rates have the biggest impact on data quality. In addition to the primary factors of resolution and frame rate, the shutter, gray scale, and sensitivity must be considered.

Resolution

The resolution of the camera is determined by the number of photoelectric sensors contained within the image sensor. All things being equal, resolution will have the biggest impact on data quality. This is because the circle fitter will have more pixels to work with when attempting to fit a centroid[6] to any "blob" of pixels returned by the CCD. More information on circle fitting is given in the reconstruction section under *Software*.

A higher resolution CCD would allow a wider angle lens or finer precision with the same lens. Higher resolutions can capture smaller markers or farther distances. Higher resolution could also equate to fewer cameras. The benefits to a higher resolution are so vast that it is the single biggest factor to consider when purchasing a camera.

Frame Rate

Frame rate is the number of images captured per second. Maximum frame rate is determined by how many times per second the CCD can read from the image sensor and offload data to memory for processing by the CPU. Beyond the obvious benefits of being able to capture high-velocity actions such as the swing of a golf club, frame rate will also improve data quality. More temporal samples of a marker's position in space will average down to a more accurate position when filtered. More on filtering can be found in the tracking section under *Software*.

---

[6] A centroid is the geometric center of a blob of pixels that are determined to be circular.

Shutter

The image sensor is read by the CCD at the specified frame rate. Without first *blanking* the sensor, residual light information would be left on the sensor and would manifest itself as a motion trail in the image the next time the CCD went to read. By exposing the sensor to dark it will more quickly "forget" what it saw. This is not literally the case in many cameras. Some cameras use an electronic shutter, which blasts the image sensor with a jolt of electricity to blank the information off the sensors. A sensor outfitted with an electronic shutter is always exposed to light. In the case of an electronic shutter, the image sensor is blanked just before the CCD goes to read.

The amount of time a shutter is open before the sensor is read will affect the brightness of the image. Shutter speed is another factor to consider when trying to get a good solid image of the markers.

Gray Scale

Images taken by the camera are likely either black-and-white or gray scale. White represents the presence of the desired color spectrum, black the absence of color, and grays being the values anywhere between white and black. Black-and-white cameras take images whose pixels are either black or white, whereas grayscale cameras take images whose pixels can be one of up to 256 values between black-and-white. Some less common CCDs are capable of more than 256 shades of gray scale while others are capable of less. A CCD capable of delivering gray scale is ideal because it will unquestionably yield better data over just black or white.

A black-and-white camera has a threshold value. This value determines what brightness a pixel needs to be before it will be captured by the CCD. If a pixel is determined to be bright enough, it will leave a white pixel on the image. If it is not bright enough, no pixel will be created and the image will remain black. Black-and-white cameras are binary in this regard. One possible advantage to black-and-white over gray scale is that it's faster to transfer and process than gray scale.

A grayscale camera, on the other hand, is capable of capturing pixels whose brightness ranges from nearly black to pure white as long as they are in the spectral range being sampled. Having this information allows the system to more accurately detect edges of markers during circle fitting, resulting in a more accurate centroid.

Sensitivity

There are two kinds of sensitivity. The first is determined by how large the photoelectric sensors are. At equal resolutions a CCD with larger sensors would result in a larger chip, onto which the lens would focus a larger image. The result is that more light will be absorbed by each individual sensor. The second kind of sensitivity is how many different shades of any given color that sensor can register. The image sensor is usually tuned to be more sensitive to a particular wavelength of light, typically red, near infrared, or infrared. By ignoring some colors, the sensor can focus its spectral resolution in the narrow band of light being captured.

Onboard Processor

Most motion capture hardware providers now offer cameras with onboard image-processing capabilities. This means that the images captured can be analyzed and processed before being sent back to the data collection station. The processing power contained within a camera will vary depending on manufacturer and model. Typical image-processing tasks include feature detection, feature identification, and compression.

Feature Detection

The process of analyzing an image in an effort to find some sort of pattern is called *feature detection*. Features vary based on the particular type of motion capture being deployed. However, in the case of passive optical, discrete point capture the algorithm will be looking for blobs of pixels it determines to be circular. If a blob of pixels is determined to be circular, it is probably the captured image of a marker. When a circle is detected the algorithm can discard those pixels and just retain the centroid information. By only sending a coordinate plus a radius that describes the found circle, the amount of data sent back from the camera can be dramatically reduced, affording much faster frame rates.

Feature Identification

Once a feature has been found, it may be desirable to temporally correlate its existence with similar features found on other frames. This is accomplished by first assigning an arbitrary identification to all of the markers found on a given frame. If a newly found marker on a subsequent frame is similar to a previously found marker, it is assumed to be the same marker and given the same identification. Feature identification is a key component to real-time motion capture.

Compression

Bus speed, network bandwidth, and disk access are limited, so to further enable high frame rates, motion capture cameras typically deploy image compression. Most pixel information is discarded in favor of the centroids; therefore, the majority of the pixels in the images collected are black. The only nonblack pixels would be those to which a centroid could not be fit. These leftover pixels are run-length encoded and sent back for a more complex circle fitting. Run-length encoding expresses the image as long runs of data. For instance, scanning an image from left to right, top to bottom, many thousands of black pixels would be found before encountering a white or gray pixel. Run-length encoding is a type of lossless compression.

Inputs/Outputs

A motion capture camera will have several connections in the back, for both incoming and outgoing purposes. Incoming connections will include power, networking, and sync, while outgoing information will include network and video. In some cameras these are combined into a single cable. In motion capture systems containing hundreds of cameras, cabling can be a complex practical issue as the sheer number of cables becomes difficult to wrangle.

Setup

Cameras should be mounted in a secure fashion and preferably to the foundation of the building in which the studio is housed. A sturdy box truss in a temperature-controlled room is ideal. Motion capture cameras are delicately calibrated instruments so that the slightest nudge or shift in its position can throw the resulting data out of alignment.

Balance

A motion capture volume can be configured in a nearly infinite number of ways. With all of the variables at play, configuring a volume is more of an art than a science. There are a few guidelines, however:
- It is ideal to see at least 5 pixels of resolution for a marker in a captured image.
- Marker images should have a nice full, white center with a crisp gray outline.
- Position cameras and choose lenses such that no marker is smaller than 5 pixels when inside the volume.
- A good maximum marker size for body capture is 16mm. Any larger and they start to impede the actor. Use the smallest marker that still allows for 5 pixels of resolution.
- A good marker size for face capture is 5mm. Any larger and they start to collide with each other on the face and impede the actor. Smaller markers can be captured with very specific camera configurations.
- More resolution is generally better, but that does not mean that more cameras are better.

SOFTWARE

John Root, Demian Gordon

Motion capture software can be broadly divided into two categories, acquisition and post-processing. Acquisition software is typically supplied by the hardware provider for the purpose of setting up and running the system. Post-processing software, which might also be provided by the hardware vendor but can involve off-the-shelf tools, is meant to turn the acquired raw data into usable animation for the project. Some software is capable of both acquisition and post-processing activities. This section describes each of the algorithms at play by translating the complex math into plain English.

Acquisition

Acquisition is the process of triggering the cameras to take pictures. In order for the acquired images to be meaningful, the system must be synchronized and delicately calibrated. Synchronization, or sync, is important to all forms of motion capture. Sync is the process by which all of the optical cameras are made to capture in unison. Taking synchronized pictures of an object from multiple angles and then comparing those captured images against one another is the basis of all optical and most computer vision-based motion capture technologies.

Calibration

Calibration is the process by which the intrinsic and extrinsic parameters of a camera are made known. Properly calibrated cameras are essential for quality data during reconstruction. Camera extrinsic values are the values that define the camera's position and orientation in space. Camera intrinsic values are values required to map any given pixel of the 2D image out into 3D space. Because it is not possible to know one without knowing the other, calibrating intrinsic and extrinsic values often involves a third parameter, a calibration object. A calibration object is an object whose exact dimensions are known. By placing the calibration object in the capture volume and photographing it from multiple angles, it is possible to reverse engineer the camera parameters by assuming that what is seen is the same as what is known. This is done by performing a bundle adjustment. A bundle adjustment is a mathematical process by which a best fit of the unknown parameters is found through reverse projection and optimization of the known parameters. It is ideal to use a calibration object that defines every point in the field of view of the camera including the depth axis. For this reason, a wand calibration is typical.

Calibration should be performed regularly. It is common practice to calibrate the capture system at the beginning of each capture day and at the end. Additional calibrations should be performed if any of the camera's intrinsic or extrinsic values might have changed, for example, if a camera is bumped or moved. Most capture systems allow arbitrary assignment of calibration files to capture files. This allows users to back apply an end-of-day calibration to some earlier capture data to account for degradation in data quality due to, for example, a slip in calibration.

Camera Extrinsic Parameters

The extrinsic parameters of a camera are the x,y,z position and x,y,z orientation of the camera in space, relative to the zero point and world scale of the capture volume. The camera extrinsic parameters can be static or dynamic. In the case of a dynamic extrinsic parameter (where the cameras are moving), calibration is recomputed per frame by either re-projecting reconstructions from static cameras back to dynamic cameras or assuming a known calibration object in the scene to be "true."

Camera Intrinsic Parameters

The intrinsic parameters of a camera are the values needed to re-project any 2D pixel out into 3D space. These values typically include a lens distortion model, focal length, and principle point, but can contain additional parameters. If it is known exactly how a camera bends light and captures it onto its image sensor, the system can reverse project any pixel back out into 3D space and assume the point to exist somewhere along that ray.

Dynamic Calibration

Dynamic calibration is the process of capturing a moving object of known measurements, most commonly a wand. Wands come in many shapes and sizes. Typically, a calibration wand is a rigid stick with some number of markers attached to it. The exact distance of each of these markers to one another is measured and known to a high degree of accuracy. By photographing these markers from many angles, and assuming the known measurements to be true in all images, a 3D representation of the capture volume can be built and the camera intrinsic and extrinsic parameters can be calculated.

When performing a wand calibration, the wand is waved about the volume so as to completely cover each camera's field of view, including the depth axis. It is also ideal, at any captured instant, for the wand to be seen in at least three cameras. Not doing so will result in poorly calibrated areas of the capture volume. These captured images of the wand are then digested by

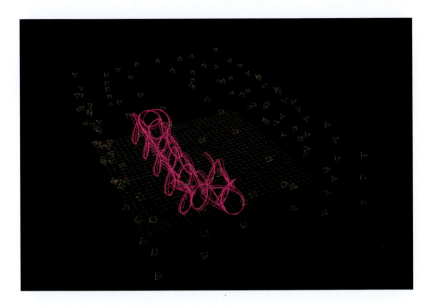

Figure 4.3 ImageMovers Digital main capture volume during a wand calibration. (Image courtesy of ImageMovers Digital.)

the software and an accurate model of the camera's intrinsic and extrinsic parameters is established.

Static Calibration

While the most common form of calibration is wand calibration, some systems use static calibration. Static calibration does the same thing as a wand calibration except in a single instant. Static calibrations are performed by placing a single known object in the capture volume and capturing it from all cameras simultaneously and in a single instant. The advantage of this is that the calibration is less subject to error induced by the person performing the wand wave. The disadvantage of an object calibration is that the capture volume is limited to the size and shape of the calibration object.

Checkerboard Calibration

Some less common machine vision-based systems use a checkerboard calibration. A checkerboard calibration is similar to a wand or object calibration in that an image of a known checkerboard is put before the camera and photographed from multiple angles.

Post-Processing

Once data is acquired it must be processed in order to be made usable. With optical data this usually involves reconstruction, labeling, cleaning, and solving. Each of these steps generates data that is usable in the next step.

Some systems can acquire and process data simultaneously, thereby giving the user data in real time. Real-time data often involves shortcuts or approximations that result in lesser quality data than data derived from more complex post-processing techniques. Depending on the production requirements, real-time quality data may be sufficient.

Reconstruction

The term *reconstruction* as it applies to optical motion capture is the process of creating 3D data from 2D images. The software first finds all of the places in each camera's 2D image where it detects a marker. During the marker detection phase, often referred to as *circle fitting*, the software is typically looking for a round blob of pixels to which it will fit a circle. Because blobs of pixels are not perfect circles the 2D position of the resulting circle's centroid is somewhat inaccurate. Once all the circles are found across all cameras, the process of turning these centroids into 3D trajectories can begin.

Once the cameras are calibrated, the system knows how light is bent and captured on the image sensor. By reversing this path the system can shoot (calculate) an imaginary ray back out into the volume somewhere along which the marker is known to exist. By shooting many of these imaginary rays from all cameras and then looking for intersections among them, the system can begin to reconstruct 3D data in the form of discrete marker positions.

While a point can be reconstructed with a mere two intersections, more intersections are better. This is because each of these rays is somewhat inaccurate and more rays will amortize the error down to yield more accurate information. Additionally, a ray's contribution to a marker reconstruction will be intermittent as it is occluded or leaves the camera's view frustum. So while a marker's position is derived from the average of its contributing rays, the number of rays contributing to this average is constantly changing, thereby inducing spikes in the trajectory.

Once marker positions are reconstructed they need to be temporally correlated such that the software can determine that a given trajectory is the same marker through time. This process, called *trajectory fitting*, is usually the final step of reconstruction or the first step of labeling depending on the company view of the pipeline. Trajectory fitting most commonly utilizes 3D velocity predictions but can also involve more complex 2D information from the cameras.

Labeling

Labeling is the step after reconstruction where the yielded marker trajectories are assigned names. Marker trajectories will be some number of frames long depending on the quality of the trajectory fit and the accuracy of the reconstruction. The process of assigning labels is actually correlating fragmented animation curves rather than naming individual marker points. Having labeled data is essential for the solver to know what any given trajectory is measuring. Unlabeled data, often called *raw* or *uncorrelated*, is not useful because it exists sporadically in time, blipping in and out of existence.

By incorporating some biomechanical information into the labeling process, the software can make an informed guess as to where a marker should exist. For instance, it could be said that markers on the head are always a given distance away from one another or that a marker on the wrist can be found within some rigid distance of markers on the elbow. With these sorts of rules at play, should a marker on the head or wrist disappear it's possible to look for an unlabeled marker in a prescribed location. In this manner the more markers that can be identified, the easier it is to identify the entire set.

Gap Filling

Sometimes no marker was reconstructed. This is usually because it was occluded (no camera could see it). When this happens, the same biomechanical rules involved in labeling can be used to create a marker at the location the missing marker is thought to be. This process is called *gap filling*. Gap filling usually involves rigid body reconstruction but can also involve more complex biomechanical assumptions. An example of such an assumption might be informing a missing marker's location by assuming the knee to be a hinge. In this case, there might be information about a thigh and a foot, which could be used with this assumption to reconstruct a missing marker at the knee.

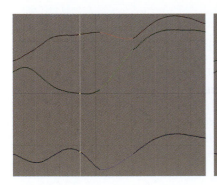 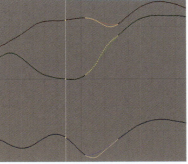

Figure 4.4 The image on the left is a marker trajectory that contains a gap. In the image on the right, the gap was filled using a rigid body transform. (Image courtesy of ImageMovers Digital.)

Rigid Bodies

A rigid body is a transform derived from three or more markers thought to be rigid with one another. Imagine that any three points in space would define a triangle and that from a triangle

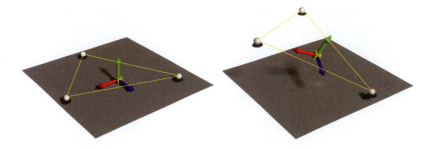

Figure 4.5 Any three nonlinear points in space define a triangle. From a triangle, a rotation and translation can be extracted. (Image courtesy of John Root.)

it is possible to extract a rotation. That rotation, plus the average position of the markers would give a rigid body transform.

Cleaning

Optical data is unfortunately noisy. This is primarily due to inaccurate calibration, poor circle fitting, and occlusion. Whatever the cause, these errors manifest as trajectory spikes and high-frequency jitter that must be removed. This process is often referred to as *cleaning*. If the data is not cleaned, the spikes and noise will come through in the resulting animation.

Cleaning typically involves some amount of identification and removal of large data spikes, followed by application of a light filter, where the filter is a mathematical algorithm in which the animation is smoothed to remove noise. Many types of filters are available, but all should be used with caution because they can be destructive to the animation. Overfiltered data can look mushy and lack the subtlety and nuance that makes motion capture so realistic. Most filters benefit from high frame rates. This is because the more data they have to average or analyze, the more accurately they can distinguish between noise and performance.

Solving Motion Capture

Solving is the process of turning processed data into usable animation. Most commonly this involves manually fitting a skeleton into marker data, defining a relationship between the markers and the skeleton, and then having the solver attempt to hold that relationship over the course of the animation. Because the physical relationship between a marker and a joint can vary due to a variety of factors including joint type, suit slide, muscle bulge, and skin stretch, holding the corresponding digital relationship can be a tricky process.

Rigid Body Solvers

A rigid body solver takes groups of three or more markers that are assumed to be rigid to one another and extracts a 6 degree-of-freedom transform. Extracted transforms, in the form of joints, can

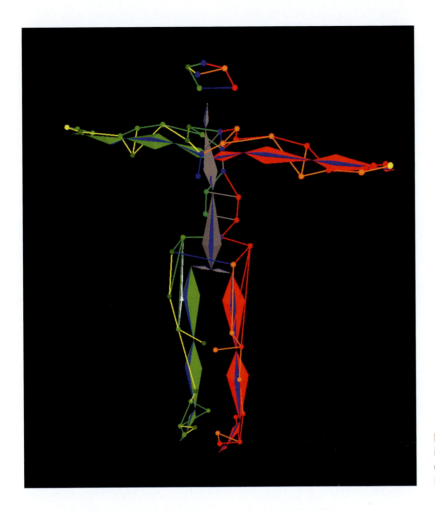

Figure 4.6 A skeleton fit into its markers using Vicon's Blade. (Image courtesy of ImageMovers Digital.)

be parented relatively to one another such that they describe a skeleton. Although a skeleton derived from rigid bodies might visually look correct, it typically contains transforms on undesirable axes that need to be rectified in a second step often involving constraints. Motionbuilder's Actor solver is an example of a rigid body solver.

Constraint-Based Solvers

A constraint solver is very similar to and often used in conjunction with a rigid body solver. With a constraint solver, the markers themselves are used to directly drive the skeleton's rigging controls, which in turn drive the skeleton. Using a motion capture marker as an IK[7] handle would be an example of a

---

[7] IK is short for Inverse Kinematics. It most commonly refers to the solving of a chain of joints to reach a known destination. (Example: Moving the hand on a 3D model moves the rest of the arm and elbow correctly.)

constraint-based solving method. Motionbuilder's Actor solver is an example of a constraint-based solver.

Global Optimization Solvers

A global optimization solver attempts to find a best fit for a skeleton into its marker data. The best fit is considered to be the solution with the least amount of error. Error can be described in a number of ways, but is most commonly described as variations in distance. Distance is the user-defined initial offset between a marker and a joint in the target skeleton. In this case a global optimization would attempt to animate the skeleton such that all of the distances between markers and joints are offset the same throughout time as they were in the initial user fitting. Vicon's Blade, Motion Analysis's Calcium, and the Peel Solver are all examples of globally optimized solvers.

Physics Solvers

A physics solver uses the marker data to actuate the skeleton in a number of ways. Once a marker is assigned to a bone, the bone might be asked to take on the velocity of that marker or to gravitate toward the marker. Endorphin is an example of a physics-based solver.

Behavioral Solvers

A behavioral solver reinterprets the marker data into a common language spoken by the rig. To accomplish this, data is analyzed and statistically strong patterns are extracted—be it FACS[8] values, phonemes, emotions, intentions, or some other meaningful animation data. A behavioral solver has the advantage of being able to solve and retarget simultaneously. Behavioral solvers are typically used for the face or other nonrigid deformable surfaces where joints are inappropriate. The ImageMetrics solver is an example of a behavior solver.

FACIAL CAPTURE
John Root, Nick Apostoloff, Oleg Alexander

Facial motion capture is the younger and less developed sibling of body motion capture. Where body motion capture aims to capture and reconstruct the joint angles of an articulated skeleton, facial motion capture measures the subtler deformation of facial tissue. Perceptual motion plays a more important role in facial motion capture because it is the actor's emotion

---

[8] Discussed in more detail in the *Facial Capture* section.

as well as facial articulation that is required rather than well-defined skeletal motion. The importance of perceptual motion makes facial motion capture in some ways harder and in other ways easier than body motion capture. Small facial motions such as the slight squinting of the eyes when somebody smiles to a trembling upper lip offer immediate insight into the character's emotions and are hence crucial to capture accurately. Alternatively, because the character's face is often very different from the actor's, the global deformation, though still important, can be represented less accurately. This leads to different requirements and techniques for capturing and solving facial motion as opposed to body motion, where perhaps the desire is to represent a skeletal motion as accurately as possible. Capture techniques can estimate a dense reconstruction of the actor's face or compute the location of a sparse set of markers, as discussed first in this section. In both cases, complex solving techniques must be employed to translate this geometry into character animation and this is the focus of the later part of this section.

Capture Techniques

Methods for facial motion capture can be broadly divided into two categories: marker based and markerless. Marker-based methods use markers applied to the actor's face so that a capture system can measure their motion. These markers may be in the form of optical retroreflective markers, makeup markers, or noise pattern makeup. Markerless methods simply use the actor's facial structure as tracking features.

Marker-Based Motion Capture

By adding markers to the face, a performance can be easily and accurately captured because the markers offer a clearly delineated fiducial that can be tracked and differentiated in multiple views. A unique surface texture like this is crucial in any system where 3D geometry is created from images of an object. Given the position of a fiducial in two or more cameras, its 3D location can be computed using techniques of multiple-view geometry such as triangulation (Hartley & Zisserman, 2000). The downside of a marker-based approach is that the markers themselves can hinder a performance and impose limitations on the actors, capture volume, and the production itself.

Optical Markers

Optical retroreflective markers commonly used in combination with filtered lens cameras create easily detected features in each camera. In a similar fashion to optical body motion

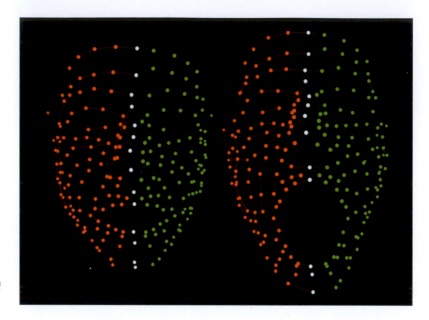

Figure 4.7 Marker-based facial capture. (Image courtesy of ImageMovers Digital.)

capture systems, the 3D accuracy is directly correlated to the number of cameras used and the size of the volume they cover. Facial motion capture is slightly more susceptible to inaccuracies because smaller markers must be used on the face than the body. To counter the inaccuracies introduced by smaller markers more cameras must be used in a smaller volume (i.e., closer to the face), which inherently restricts the performance that can be made.

A significant advantage of these systems is that the software used to compute the marker positions is automatic and only requires supervision by a human operator. With enough cameras in a small enough volume, very accurate results can be achieved. However, in the past these volumes have been too restrictive. Large volumes that allow simultaneous body and facial capture have usually produced poor facial data. Conversely, small volumes produce good 3D but require the facial performance to be conducted separately from the body performance.

From a robustness standpoint, a disadvantage of optical systems is that the markers look the same in each camera; therefore, it is difficult to find the same marker across multiple cameras. Remember that an object must be seen in two or more cameras to reconstruct its 3D location. In general, the more cameras that see a marker, the more accurate the 3D data will be. For this reason, calibration of the cameras in these systems is as essential as a high camera count. The calibration is important because if the positions of the cameras are known (as well as their internal calibration), it is possible to restrict where a 2D point in one camera might appear in another camera (see epipolar geometry[9] in Chapter 8 of Hartley & Zisserman, 2000).

A high camera count is important for two reasons. First, there is always error in the location of a 2D point in an image (e.g., image quantization, motion blur, inaccurate marker segmentation, etc.). Though these 2D errors produce errors in the 3D location, this error can be reduced by seeing the marker in many cameras. Second, as in body motion capture, occlusion is a problem in facial motion capture. Occlusion errors manifest themselves as pops in the data, sometimes because a marker is suddenly seen by fewer cameras or because the system has mislabeled the marker across the cameras. As mentioned previously, and repeated here because it is important for reducing these inaccuracies, the number of cameras required is related to the size of the capture volume—the larger the volume, the more cameras required.

Another disadvantage of optical marker systems is the markers themselves. First, they are expensive. Second, they are difficult to apply to the skin and often fall off. Furthermore, the data captured is limited to locations where markers are present. If, after capture, it is decided that more markers around the eyes are required, it would be necessary to recapture the performance with more markers.[10] For this reason, careful planning of marker locations and count is extremely important. Typically, regions of the face that deform considerably require more markers. It is also important to consider both the actor and the character when it comes to marker placement. For example, if the character does not have a nose, then there is no point having markers on the nose of the actor. If the actor has deep wrinkles around the mouth, then it would be wise to avoid placing markers on those wrinkles as they will be occluded when the wrinkles engage.

Makeup Markers

Some of the shortcomings of an optical marker solution can be overcome by using makeup markers, usually in the form of solid circles drawn on the face. Makeup markers are generally more comfortable for actors, and they do not fall off and do not hinder the performance. Makeup markers can be tracked

---

[9] The epipolar geometry of two cameras defines the possible locations of a point seen in one camera in the other camera. For an ideal pinhole camera, a point seen in one camera exists along a line in another camera.

[10] The chances of this happening can be mitigated somewhat by capturing a reference session of each actor with a higher marker count. A statistical model can then be used to predict the position of the extra markers from the markers captured during the shoot. This is often referred to as gap filling.

and reconstructed just like optical retroreflective markers. However, unlike retroreflective markers, makeup markers typically require the capture of standard noninterlaced video footage. Unfortunately this can equate to lower frame rates and lower resolution because the storage of the image data can be prohibitively expensive. However, the switch to video opens up new hardware options including head-mounted cameras, and the captured video also provides an excellent animator and editorial reference. Most important, a head-mounted solution frees the actor from the restrictions of a small performance volume.

Makeup markers are most commonly used in conjunction with head-mounted cameras and these systems must be kept lightweight. The reduction in weight is usually at the expense of high-end features including on-board feature detection, high frame rates, and image compression. Some design specifications that may be important in these portable capture systems include the following:

- *How many cameras to use:* With special statistical models it is possible to reconstruct 3D given only one camera, but in general two or more are required.
- *Frame rate for capture:* Higher frame rates (48+ fps) make marker tracking easier and allow temporal filtering to be used to smooth the data, at the cost of having to store more images.
- *Compression of captured images:* From the perspective of marker detection, uncompressed images are the best, but this is not always practical given the storage requirements.
- *Use of color versus monochrome cameras:* Color can add additional texture that can be useful for marker tracking and labeling (i.e., different colored markers) but requires more data be stored.

In both the case of optical markers and makeup markers, the daily shooting schedule has to factor in the application of the markers, which can take considerable time depending on the number of markers used.

Noise Pattern Capture

An all-together different capture method employed by some in the industry to create high-resolution facial geometry is noise pattern capture. In this method, some form of noise pattern is applied to the face to create many unique features that can be tracked across multiple cameras. The noise pattern may be in the form of makeup applied in random patterns over the face or through structured light projected onto the face. Even the skin itself can be used as the noise pattern as long as the skin has enough high-contrast texture.

Some Motion Capture studios employ normal makeup while others, such as Mova Contour, use phosphorescent makeup and synchronize their cameras and lights such that every second frame is captured in the dark and the cameras see only the phosphorescent makeup. This is incredibly useful because it removes noise artifacts generated by the background in the scene and only the geometry of the face is captured. Noise pattern techniques can produce geometry with 100k+ vertices and pore level detail.

A major problem with noise pattern techniques is temporal coherence. For rigging purposes, each frame of mesh data usually has the exact same topology. While noise pattern techniques can usually produce excellent high-resolution meshes, the meshes tend to drift over time in such a way as to make them difficult to use for motion capture purposes. In addition to this, these techniques usually require complicated hardware setups that have a small operating volume. The lighting often had to be very bright, or consist of many flash units, which can be uncomfortable for the actors. Sometimes the actors may also have to remain still over a number of seconds during the capture process.

Markerless Motion Capture

The advantage of marker-based techniques lies in the method in which the markers are captured. The markers form unique signatures in the image data that can be easily detected. In the case of markerless capture, these signatures are no longer available and similar information must be derived from features inherent to the actor's face, and more advanced techniques must be employed for their capture.

Active Appearance Models

One prominent method in the vision community for markerless facial motion capture is active appearance models, or AAMs (Cootes, Edwards, & Taylor, 1998; Matthews & Baker, 2004). An AAM is a statistical technique that learns the appearance of salient facial features and builds a deformation model of those features so that tracking can proceed automatically. Typical features that are tracked include the eyebrows, corners of the lips, and the nose.

Once the AAM has been trained, it can then automatically capture the locations of these facial features in 2D or 3D from one or more cameras. A crucial point here is that these models must be trained. This training requires the salient facial features in many images of the actor to be hand labeled, which is a time-consuming process. These methods are often limited to only working with the person they have been trained with and are sensitive to rotations of the person's head. Another disadvantage of these techniques is that there aren't many salient features on a person's face. The eyes, eyebrows, mouth, and nostrils can all be captured, but the deformations of the cheeks and brow and the subtler motion that occurs away from fiducials are often lost (i.e., squinting).

Pictorial Structure Models

In a similar fashion to the AAM work of Matthews and Baker (2004), the pictorial structure model (PSM) work of Felzenszwalb and Huttenlocher (2003) learns a statistical model of the appearance of features and their relative motion. Like AAMs, this requires hand-labeled training data, but this is encapsulated in a robust estimation framework that computes the optimal solution given the image data. What this means is that the PSM can compute the feature locations for each frame of data with no prior knowledge of where they were in the previous frame. The AAM needs an initialization process to get started and may drift away from the correct solution over time.

Dense Stereo Reconstructions

Like the noise pattern techniques discussed previously, there are other methods that focus on computing temporally coherent dense reconstructions from two or more cameras (Furukawa & Ponce, 2009). These techniques work well with even-lit images from many high-resolution (10+ megapixel), low-compression cameras, to create the coarse geometry of the face, but they don't typically capture the high-frequency pore-level details, are computationally expensive, and can produce temporally noisy results. In addition, it isn't clear how advantageous it is to have dense reconstructions for rigging purposes, if the character is significantly different from the actor.

Stabilization

Captured facial performance data will be in the form of marker positions relative to the world coordinate system (WCS) of the scene. This means the data contains not only motion caused by facial deformations but also the motion of the actor's head. In many cases, for solving, the captured data must be relative to a stationary head; that is, the head motion must be removed from the marker data. This results in any given point actually describing a motion of the face. For instance, given a marker placed on the forehead whose motion is relative to world zero, its motion might describe the raising of an eyebrow or a nod of the head. Alone and in the WCS, it cannot be known. If the marker's motion is known to be relative to the head or skull, the marker can be said to be describing the skin of the forehead sliding over the skull. The process of removing the head motion from the marker data is referred to as *stabilization*. Stabilization is not unique to facial motion. The technique can be applied to any hierarchical motion. It is, however, common for facial motion to require stabilization because the subtleties of facial deformation cannot be easily seen or measured unless they are separated from the head motion.

One common method for stabilization is to find three or more rigid points on the subject's head. From these points a rigid body can be derived under which the entire data set is expressed relative to. However, the human head doesn't have any rigid surfaces that can be practically measured. Even the most rigid-like points will slide as the face deforms and will cause errors to be embedded into the facial motion.

More complicated methods of stabilization include complex statistical models based on manually stabilized datasets, complicated physical devices attached to the head for reference, or machine learning techniques that automatically separate the facial motion from head motion (Torresani, Hertzmann, & Bregler, 2008).

The Face Model

In recent years it has become popular to capture the face model or models with one form of motion capture and then drive those models with a different form of motion capture. However, to date, many of the capture technologies that yield high-resolution polygonal meshes suitable for facial rigging do not correlate the resulting surfaces temporally. This means that while each captured mesh may appear as a highly detailed representation of the capture subject, each frame is in fact a completely different mesh that only appears similar. This dissimilarity makes working with the resulting meshes very difficult. For this reason it is common to require resurfacing of the resulting meshes to a universal topology. Whether meshes are captured or individually modeled, in an ideal world all of the meshes in the data set would contain a universal topology.

Universal Topology

Universal topology refers to a static number of vertices and edges with prescribed locations that describe any given shape in a dataset. For example, vertex number 256 might describe the tip of the nose and will be located at the tip of the nose in any given facial expression or point in time. For this reason any given facial pose can be described as a vertex position delta to a base pose (commonly a neutral pose). In this way a facial dataset with universal topology enforced across all frames makes easily available the process of facial rigging with blend shapes.

When choosing a universal topology for a mesh, all permutations of the mesh need to be considered. What poses can the character achieve and what is the desired look of those poses? If, for instance, a character is expected to have fine wrinkles when it smiles, sufficient resolution in the mesh will need to be present even in poses where it is not required. Further, the edge direction of the mesh should follow the flow lines of the character's wrinkles and possible actions. Edge directions that contradict the flow of a character's face can result in a poor quality result or the need to subdivide the mesh to the point of impracticality.

Facial Rigging

Facial rigging is the process by which a face model becomes animatable. Often it is the face rig that is driven with motion capture and not the mesh directly. It is for this reason that the face rig is a critical component of the facial motion capture pipeline. If the rig cannot drive the mesh to achieve what the director requires, there is little the animator can do to improve the performance.

Because captured marker data from the face can be sparse, it usually falls on the rig to make up the missing information. Rigs will commonly engage a number of sophisticated techniques to fill in uncaptured details such as fine wrinkles or deep skin folds. The rig should be well understood before stepping foot in a capture volume. Both rigging and capture stand to benefit from finding the right balance between what should be captured and what can be algorithmically re-created.

The facial rig consists of three primary components: the deformers, the user interface, and the model.

Facial Deformers

A deformer is a method by which the model is made to move. Several different types of deformers are used, each with its own advantages and disadvantages. For this reason, it is common for face rigs to contain multiple types of deformers. Some types of motion capture data are better at driving certain kinds of deformers than others. Rarely does captured data directly drive the deformers. Instead, captured data is typically interpreted into a common language spoken by both the data and the rig.

Blend Shapes

A blend shape deformer, sometimes referred to as a *morph target*, is a subset of vertices that have moved from their neutral position. A blend shape gets its name from the notion that it can be blended on or off with a multiplier value from 0 to 1. For example, a blink shape can make a character's eyes go from neutral (0) to sleepy (0.5) to fully closed (1). In this manner, many shapes can be created so as to give the face rig a complete range of facial motion.

Note, however, that blend shapes are prone to crashing. This is a peculiar artifact that manifests when certain combinations of blend shapes don't work well together and the resulting mesh is "off-model," or not character achievable. To counter this effect, corrective shapes are often added that automatically trigger when bad combinations are encountered. For this reason a high-end facial rig built from blend shapes might easily contain hundreds of blend shapes.

Joints

The same joints used in body rigging are often used in face rigging. While typically associated with articulated rotations, a joint is really just a method by which collections of points can be made to move through a single motion's influence. This influence can be made to drop off over a distance such that when the joint is moved, its effect on the mesh is soft and natural.

Setting up a rig with joints is fairly straightforward and results can be obtained quickly. However, rigs made with joints are typically unconstrained and prone to generating off-model shapes.

Wrap Deformers

A wrap deformer is most commonly a low-resolution model that deforms a high-resolution model. In facial rigging, this allows a much more manageable number of points to control a much higher, unmanageable number of points. One method is to create a wrap deformer from motion capture data and use it to control a high-resolution model. In this manner a hundred or so points captured on an actor's face can be made to control a high-resolution version of that same actor's face.

Other Deformers

There are many other different types of deformers, including clusters, lattices, wires, and muscles. New deformers come out of the research labs every day. Some are better for facial rigging than others. As new types of deformers come online, the facial rigging landscape changes as does the facial motion capture pipeline.

Face User Interface

In regard to rigging, the user interface is a set of controls exposed to the user allowing the face to be animated in an intuitive way. With a cleverly designed user interface, it is possible to control many deformers with a single slider, dial, or control. A face rig might have 30 blend shapes, 20 bones, and a heap of special case scripts and algorithms required to simply make a face smile. Engaging all of these elements in the manner required to achieve a smile could be set to a single slider labeled "smile." However, setting these controls with motion capture data can be a tricky process.

Solving for the Face

Captured marker data manifests as a cloud of translating points that sparsely and speculatively describe the actor's face. The face rig is a collection of complex deformers that when engaged in very specific ways will yield the desired character mesh. These two things are inherently very different and bringing them together to generate convincing animation is a problem to which other problems step aside and nod with respect.

Direct Drive

A relatively straightforward approach to driving the rig is one called *direct drive*. In a direct-drive approach, marker data is directly connected to the deformers. This means that the translations of a captured marker are directly applied to a joint, wrap deformer, or similar such deformer such as to animate that deformer exactly as the captured marker is animating. A direct-drive approach is a reasonable method for 1:1 scenarios where the capture subject and target model are the same. However, the marker data is sparse, so information will be missing and fine details lost. To re-create this missing information, additional blend shapes can be added to the rig and triggered to appear when the marker data hits prescribed poses.

One downside to the direct-drive approach is that there are inherent subtle inaccuracies in all forms of captured data. Applying these inaccuracies directly to the face where the most delicate of motions can be perceived as wrong is a risky endeavor.

A second downside to the direct-drive approach is that it offers little to no path to success for characters that are not 1:1 to the actors who play them. This is because direct drive, by its nature, is a literal interpretation of the data on the rig.

Behavioral Model

Another and very much more difficult approach to applying captured marker data to a rig is that of a behavioral model. A behavioral model is a Rosetta stone of sorts that sits between the data and the rig and serves to transcode the data into a format meaningful to the rig. Behavioral algorithms range from simple expressions to complex statistical models.

By translating data into a different format it can be qualified in ways not possible in a more literal direct-drive method. For this reason, resulting animation can be made to stay "on model," or legal. For instance, in a behavioral model based on muscles, an algorithm might measure the relative distances of a set of markers on an actor's forehead and infer percentages to which the underlying frontalis muscle is engaged. In doing so a behavioral model can be used to filter out jitter or illegal motions that are unlikely or impossible based on a statistical model of the frontalis. Once the motions of the markers are transcoded into muscle space percentages, any rig with controls capable of achieving a similar pose can be made to work with the resulting animation data, thus affording retargeting.

In a behavioral model information is typically lost. It is not only possible, but likely that the recorded performance will contain actions not present in the behavioral model. In the muscle space example, the effects of gravity, friction, or velocity would be lost whereas those elements are retained in a direct-drive method.

There are many different behavioral approaches to converting translations into facial animation. Some of the more common are muscle based and eigenfaces, but the most prevalent is FACS.

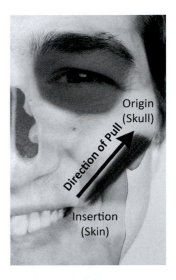

Figure 4.8 Markers placed along the zygomaticus major can measure the amount to which the muscle is flexed. This information can be used in post to drive a rig. (Image courtesy of Oleg Alexander.)

Facial Action Coding System

The Facial Action Coding System (FACS) was designed by Dr. Paul Ekman to give psychologists a common language when discussing facial expressions. The FACS process can encode all possible face motions into a set of 32 poses called *action units* (AUs). This means that, barring external influences, every possible facial expression can be broken down into some combination of these 32 poses. While Ekman accurately described 32 action units, he did not do so with computer animation in mind. It is therefore common to split some of the shapes into left and right. Additionally combination, in-between, and corrective poses are typical to counter artifacts from blend shapes and linear interpolations.

FACS is not limited to human faces. It can fully describe the movement of all kinds of faces, from cartoony to hyperreal. FACS action units and their meaning are so powerful they are studied by criminal psychologists, behavioral scientists, actors, animators, and riggers for their ability to describe human emotion in a quantifiable manner.

Before capturing an actor's performance, it would be typical to perform a *FACS session*. A FACS session is a survey of the actor's facial range of motion. In a FACS session an actor would perform some or all of the FACS poses in as isolated a manner as possible. This means that when performing any given FACS pose, that portion of the actor's face would ideally be the only thing that moves. Performing a FACS session in this way allows for the pose to be more easily identified against a neutral pose.

Depending on the needs of the character and the production, the pre-capture survey may vary. In addition to neutral, full-open, and full-compressed, some commonly captured poses to inform rigging and animation are shown in Figures 4.9, 4.10, and 4.11.

Figure 4.9 FACS reference images. (Images courtesy of Oleg Alexander.)

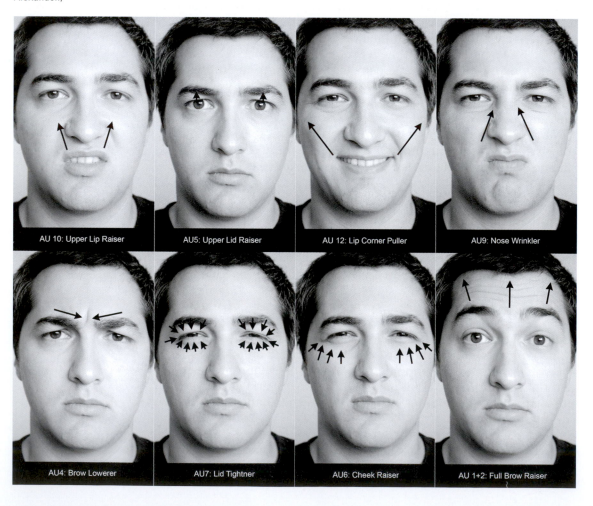

AU 10: Upper Lip Raiser   AU5: Upper Lid Raiser   AU 12: Lip Corner Puller   AU9: Nose Wrinkler

AU4: Brow Lowerer   AU7: Lid Tightner   AU6: Cheek Raiser   AU 1+2: Full Brow Raiser

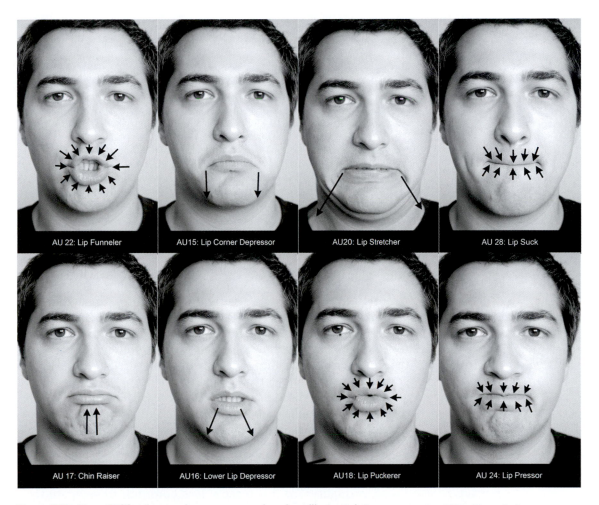

Figure 4.10 More FACS reference images—eyes closed not illustrated. (Images courtesy of Oleg Alexander.)

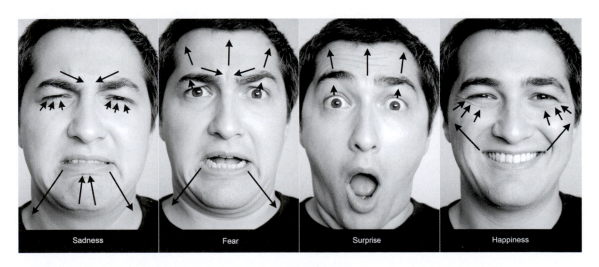

Figure 4.11 Emotional expressions. (Images courtesy of Oleg Alexander.)

References

Cootes, T. F., Edwards, G. J., & Taylor, C. J. (1998). Active Appearance Models. European Conference on Computer Vision (pp. 484–498). Freiburg: Springer.

Felzenszwalb, P. F., & Huttenlocher, D. P. (2003). Pictorial Structures for Object Recognition. International Journal of Computer Vision, 55–79.

Furukawa, Y., & Ponce, J. (2009). Dense 3D Motion Capture for Human Faces. International conference on computer vision and pattern recognition.

Hartley, R., & Zisserman, A. (2000). Multiple View Geometry in computer vision. Cambridge: Cambridge University Press.

Matthews, I., & Baker, S. (2004). Active Appearance Models Revisited. International Journal of Computer Vision, 135–164.

Torresani, L., Hertzmann, A., & Bregler, C. (2008). Nonrigid Structure-from-Motion: Estimating Shape and Motion with Hierarchical Priors. IEEE Transactions on Pattern Analysis and Machine Intelligence, 878–892.

REAL-TIME MOTION CAPTURE
John Root

Real-time motion capture refers to the capture, processing, and visualization of motion capture in a time frame that is, or appears to be, instant. Real-time MoCap is most commonly used as a tool to help actors get accustomed to their characters. Standing before a screen or monitor and being able to see yourself as a completely different person, creature, or thing is invaluable as an actor. Real-time MoCap can also be used for such things as director's previsualization, camera layout, to animate live performances, or to immerse the person being motion captured into a virtual reality environment. However, because processing motion capture data is time-consuming and requires skilled technicians, real-time MoCap often involves strict limitations and compromises in quality. For this reason, it is common to separate real-time data from actual performance capture data.

Limitations

Real-time motion capture is an emerging field. It gets better every year. To date, however, significant compromises must be made to achieve real time. While some hardware providers are able to achieve remarkable real-time data, passive optical-based motion capture is inherently bad at real time.

Line of Sight

Optical motion capture is computer vision based and therefore the cameras must have an unobstructed view of the markers. In post, it is common for the tracking team to sort out glitches induced by cameras losing line of sight or markers having been occluded. Because real-time MoCap forgoes this post-processing, it is common to reduce the number of actors, limit the props, and govern the performance to maximize marker visibility. It would be a very hard, for instance, to generate real-time data for 13 actors rolling around on the floor.

Markers

Trying to make sense of the markers on the stage in real time is a daunting task. Beyond simply using fewer markers, inducing asymmetry into the marker placement will make them easier to identify. When the labeler is measuring the distance between markers, it is less likely to get confused and swap markers when the markers are placed asymmetrically. An asymmetrical marker placement, however, may be less than ideal for solving.

Solving

Some methods of solving are very processor intensive. As such they might not yet be possible in real time. Solving methods that are currently possible in real time often involve approximations and limitations that will yield a resulting solve that does not look as good as an offline solve. Given this, plus the compromises induced by marker placement modifications and performance alterations, what comes through in the real-time previsualization might not be indicative of the final quality of the animation.

Visualization

Real-time rendering technology is catching up with offline rendering technology at a radical pace. Some of the games on the shelves these days look nearly as good as the movies in the theatres. Using real-time game rendering technology to previs a film is becoming a common practice but one that requires significant investment. Off-the-shelf solutions including Autodesk's Motion Builder offer a complete turnkey package to visualizing motion capture in real time. Expect that real-time-rendered characters and environments will come with compromises to visual quality, most notably in lighting and lookdev (look development).

Alternate Technologies

If real time is a requirement, passive optical technology might not be the best choice. Passive optical is known for its quality, not for its real-time ability. Some optical systems such as Giant and Motion Analysis are quite good at real time considering the limitations inherent in the technology. At the expense of quality, alternate technologies can deliver more reliable real time.

Active Optical

Active optical is similar to passive optical except that the markers are actually brightly lit LEDs. In an active marker system, the LEDs can be made to flash in a pattern that is recognizable by the cameras, thereby automatically identifying each marker for what it is measuring. In this manner the complex post-production process of labeling can be made obsolete and qualified data made available for the solver instantly.

Active optical systems suffer from significant limitations. They are limited to the number of markers they can track and limited also in that those markers are tethered to a battery pack. While the battery pack is small, light, and can be worn on the actor, this limitation makes capturing props and set decoration difficult.

Mechanical

Mechanical motion capture refers to motion capture that involves the technology itself being worn on the actor. With mechanical capture, a sensor of some sort is directly measuring a joint, limb, or object. Its information is transferred via a wireless or tethered connection and applied directly to a digital character. Often with mechanical capture, several technologies are combined into a more complete package. Potentiometers or bend resistors might be used to measure joint rotations while accelerometers could be used to measure limb velocity. While neither measuring technique is entirely accurate, when combined, they can produce very convincing animation.

Mechanical capture technology also enjoys several other benefits. Depending on the technology, a mechanical solution can be deployed under a costume or in a lighting environment not suitable for optical capture. Mechanical solutions often enjoy a significant range advantage over optical and do not suffer from occlusion.

The downside to mechanical solutions is that they commonly have little or no information about the global position of the capture subject. This means that while they can generate convincing joint rotations, the position of the character within the capture volume can be prone to error. By adding more technology, this limitation can be overcome. Other limitations of mechanical capture are mostly practical. The suits can be cumbersome and the sensors delicate.

5

STEREOSCOPIC 3D

HOW 3D WORKS
Lenny Lipton

Cinema, since its inception in 1895, has been three dimensional: three dimensional in the sense that there have been depth cues that can be appreciated by a person with only one eye. Movies have been based on a one-eye view of the world as captured by a one-lensed camera. But the medium has depth cues that produce a 3D picture. And filmmakers have learned how to control the 3D effect by means of lens focal length, lighting, additions of fog or mist to the background, a moving camera, and other techniques. But the stereoscopic cinema works only for people with two normally functioning eyes.

It is important to recognize that the cinema has always been three dimensional because the new 3D cinema is not a revolution—rather it is part of an evolutionary process. The technology now exists for practical stereoscopic cinema and in this article an effort will be made to review several things creative people need to know in order to control the appearance of the stereoscopic image.

Accommodation and Convergence

It is important to know something about how the eyes work. When one looks at an object, the optical axes of the left and right eyes are crossed on that object. The eyes rotate inward and outward (vergence) to make this happen. This inward and outward rotation of the eyes allows the principal object in the visual field to be seen singly on the central part of the fovea, but objects at other distances will be more or less seen as doubled. Try an experiment by holding a finger in front of the face. When attention is paid to the finger, with introspection, the

The VES Handbook of Visual Effects. DOI: 10.1016/B978-0-240-81242-7.00005-3

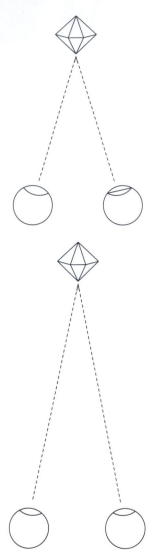

Figure 5.1 The eyes converge. The eyes rotate so that their lens axes cross on the object of interest. That object, and a locus of points in space, called the *horopter*, and a region in space in front of and behind the horopter, called *Panum's fusional area*, are not seen to be doubled. Everything else in the visual field is seen doubled and produces retinal disparity. (Image courtesy of Lenny Lipton.)

background points appear to be doubled. If attention is paid to the background points, the finger will appear to be doubled. It is this doubling of the images that produces retinal disparity, which in turn creates the depth sense of *stereopsis* (solid seeing), that is, the basis for the stereoscopic cinema.

In addition to the eyes verging on the object, they also focus. The lenses of the eyes are stretched by muscles (accommodation) that pull on them to change their shape so that they can focus. Accommodation and vergence (or convergence) are interlocked by habit but they have separate neurological pathways and separate muscle systems.

The change of the focus and the vergence of the eyes are not important depth cues. Far more important is retinal disparity; and it is this retinal disparity that produces the depth sense of stereopsis. The stereoscopic cinema reproduces retinal disparity when one looks at a stereoscopic movie with 3D glasses. Without them, two images will be seen. The horizontal difference between those two projected images is called *parallax*. It is the parallax that produces the disparity, and it is the disparity that produces stereopsis.

When looking at a 3D movie, the eyes are accommodated at the plane of the screen, but they verge (or converge) at different points depending on the value of the parallax at that point. This phenomenon is called the breakdown of accommodation and convergence (A/C), and it is often cited as a cause for visual fatigue. But when looking at well-prepared motion pictures projected on a large screen, from the usual seating distances, this "breakdown" is of little significance in terms of viewer comfort. Unless sitting in the closest rows, the breakdown of accommodation and convergence for well-shot stereoscopic images does not cause eyestrain, and this is emphasized because it is so frequently cited as a problem. If there are humongous values of parallax (consistently measured in feet) there is a problem. But well-shot stereoscopic movies in which parallax values are measured in inches will not produce discomfort.

This is not true for small screens from close distances. When looking at small screens, such as desktop monitors or television sets, A/C breakdown is a consideration, and the cure is to restrict parallax values to much less than those used for the big screen. This chapter, however, concerns itself with the cinema as projected on big screens.

Interaxial Separation

Compared to planar photography, stereoscopic photography has two additional creative controls: (1) setting the distance between the camera heads or lenses (which controls the strength of the stereoscopic effect); and (2) controlling that which appears in the plane of the screen.

The term *interaxial separation* refers to the distance between camera heads' lens axes. These can be real camera heads, like those in a stereoscopic camera rig, or they can be virtual camera heads in a computer space. Here is an important nomenclature distinction: The distance between the eyes is called the *interpupillary* (or *interocular*) *separation*. (It is given as being between about 2 and 3 inches for adults.) Most on-set stereoscopic photography can usually be better accomplished at some interaxial separation less than the interpupillary. The choice of interaxial

Figure 5.2 Four kinds of screen parallax. (A) Zero parallax. (B) Infinity parallax. (C) Crossed parallax. (D) Divergent parallax. (Image courtesy of Lenny Lipton.)

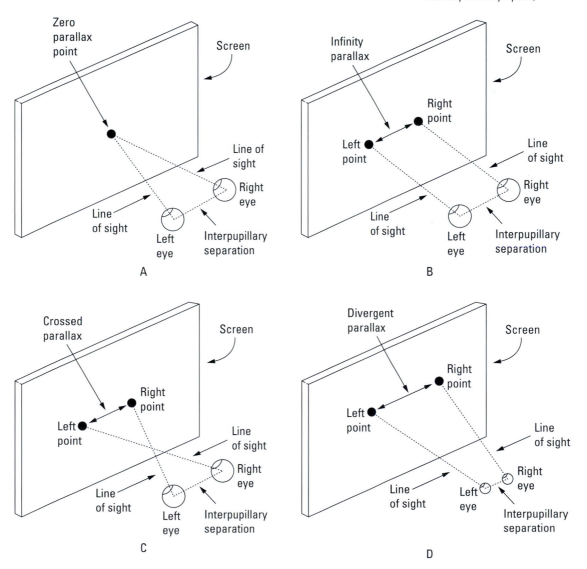

separation is to a large extent an artistic decision based on certain constraints. Typically, for shots on a sound stage with the usual kinds of distances of actors from the camera and the usual choice of focal lengths, good cinematography requires an interaxial separation that is less than the interpupillary. If this advice is not followed, parallax values for background points may become so large that they will invite A/C breakdown, and in addition the image can look elongated.

Toe-in versus Horizontal Image Translation

The other means of control in stereoscopic composition is setting that which will appear in the plane of the screen, that is, at zero parallax. That which is perceived to be within the screen has positive parallax, and that which appears to be in the audience space has what is called negative parallax. The screen location, at zero parallax, can be thought of as a boundary between screen and theater space. Camera rotation or "toe-in" is not the best way to achieve the zero parallax setting because it creates asymmetrical trapezoidal distortion (which can be fixed in post), but most of the twin camera stereo rigs use toe-in.

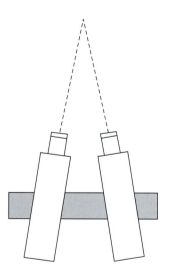

Figure 5.3 Camera head toe-in. Most stereo rigs use toe-in (also called *convergence*), or the rotation of the heads to cross the lens axes on the object of interest (that which is to appear at the physical plane of the screen). (Image courtesy of Lenny Lipton.)

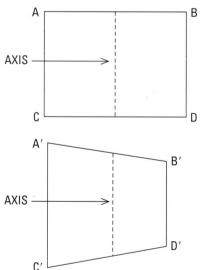

Figure 5.4 Trapezoidal distortion. Toe-in produces vertical parallax for image points away from the center of the screen. Points A, B, C, and D, compared to points A', B', C', and D', are either higher or lower than their corresponding points. (Image courtesy of Lenny Lipton.)

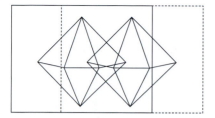

Figure 5.5 Horizontal image translation. A better way to place the object of interest at the physical plane of the screen is to horizontally shift the left and right images with respect to each other so the points of interest overlap. This can be accomplished during photography with a properly designed camera or in post. (Image courtesy of Lenny Lipton.)

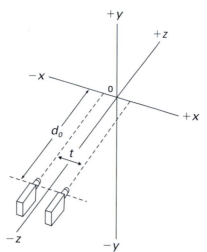

Figure 5.6 Recipe for a properly designed stereo camera. Distance to the object of interest O is d_o. The camera lens axes are parallel and induce no trapezoid distortion; t is the distance between lens axes. (Image courtesy of Lenny Lipton.)

A geometrically superior way to achieve the zero parallax condition is through horizontal image translation, which is easy to achieve in a computer-generated universe. By horizontally shifting the left and right image sensors (or lenses) so that upon projection the corresponding points overlap, the geometric distortion that toe-in produces is avoided. Moreover the aforementioned trapezoidal distortion is asymmetrical, producing vertical parallax, especially when using wide-angle lenses or objects close to the camera, and are more easily seen at the edges of the screen. Vertical parallax image points are hard to fuse and can cause discomfort. Vertical parallax is hard to look at because the eyes have to verge in the vertical, which they ought not to do when looking at a 3D movie. However, there is no point in remaining a dogmatic purist in this matter since most of the 3D camera rigs in use do use toe-in and the distortion can be fixed in digital post.

Parallax or Depth Budget

Two related concepts are discussed next: depth range and parallax budget. The depth range concept applies to the visual world during cinematography. There is a certain range of distances in the shot (this is an idea that sounds a lot like depth of field) that should not be exceeded, because parallax values may become too large for easy fusing (seeing the image as a single rather than double image).

Parallax on the screen is a function of image magnification, so using long focal length lenses will produce bigger parallax values. Another factor that is important is the distance that objects are from the zero parallax plane. The farther things are from the plane, the greater the parallax values. If a certain range of parallax values is exceeded, the image can be difficult to look at. This is especially true for background points. If the background parallax points exceed the interpupillary separation by very much, the viewer may experience discomfort. The screen size matters too; the larger the screen, the greater the parallax because the greater the image magnification.

Parallax budget refers to projection. Recall that screen parallax is what creates retinal disparity and thus binocular stereopsis. But too much parallax can lead to viewer discomfort, both for theater space and screen space parallax points. The proportionality here shows that screen parallax, *P*, is directly proportional to the product of screen magnification (the ratio of the image sensor width to the projection screen width), the focal length of the lens(es) *f*, and the interaxial distance, *t*, but inversely proportional to the distance to the zero parallax point. This is the simplified version of the depth range equation:

$$P \propto Mft/\mathbf{D°o}$$

Prior to the digital cinema, stereoscopic photography was much more difficult. One of the wonderful things about the digital stereoscopic cinema is that one can see a stereo image during the shoot or, when creating computer-generated (CG) images, can properly adjust the photography so that it is both easy to look at and beautiful. Images can be viewed using one of the many types of off-the-shelf stereo monitors that are available. There is also a lot of information to be gained by viewing the left and right images superimposed and viewed on a planar monitor—the parallax values can be checked. Many people on location screen what they are shooting by projecting images on a theater-size screen when available—it is admittedly difficult to visualize how a stereoscopic image will play on a theater-size screen unless viewed on a theater-size screen.

Positive and Negative Parallax

As noted, images that appear in screen space have positive parallax and images that are in theater space have negative parallax. So there are two kinds of parallax and a boundary condition (the plane of the screen). As a rule of thumb, there are maybe 3 inches of positive (in screen) parallax with which to work. Longer distances may produce discomfort by means of a condition called *divergence*, in which the eyes (which normally would have their lenses' axes parallel when looking at distant objects) now have their lenses' axes splayed outward or diverged in order to fuse background points.

An important concept with regard to parallax is not its absolute measure in terms of inches (or pixels); instead, it should be thought of in terms of angular parallax—because angular parallax directly relates to retinal disparity. If it is known where somebody is sitting in a theater, how big the screen is, and the angular parallax values, retinal disparity can be determined. And retinal disparity is the key to how much the eyes have to verge in order to fuse image points. People can more easily fuse image points when they are sitting in the middle or the back of a big theater than when they are in the closest rows. The people in the close seats need to be considered, but people who sit in the front rows are seeking a special experience and experience may, when all is said and done, guide the audience to their favorite seats. A rough rule of thumb to use when judging projected stereoscopic images is that the less doubled or blurred they look without the glasses, the more comfortable to view they will be with the glasses. Of course, if this idea is taken too far the result is nothing but a planar movie.

Hard and fast limits or formulas are not as much help as one would suppose when it comes to predicting image comfort or image beauty. Stereoscopic composition remains an art. Hard and fast rules may do more harm than good by overtly restricting creative decisions. There is also a temporal issue. Strictures with regard to stereoscopic composition may become obsolete as viewers gain experience. What is a difficult image today may pass without notice in a few years. That is because most people have relatively little experience viewing stereoscopic movies. A collaboration is going on between filmmaker and audience. One can look at the present stereoscopic cinema as a great big learning experience, but the situation is not much different from that which occurred during the introduction of sound, color, or widescreen and scope.[1]

Floating Windows

Modern stereographers have developed the concept of floating windows. This is going to be a convoluted train of logic, so stay the course. The concept of parallax budget was discussed earlier.

---

[1] For those who seek a mathematical basis for understanding the perceptual geometry of stereoscopic display space, download a free PDF version of the book *Foundations of the Stereoscopic Cinema* at www.lennylipton.com.

Although it is one of several depth cues, the more parallax there is, the deeper (rounder) the image. The cliché "less is more" applies to parallax. The lower the values of parallax required to produce a deep-looking image, the easier the picture is to look at—and the more flexibility there is when playing the image on screens of different sizes. That is because the values of parallax are a function of linear screen magnification. So images that are prepared for one size screen have a better chance of looking good on bigger theatrical screens if parallax is chosen judiciously. (Stereoscopic images created for big screens work fine on smaller screens, but stereoscopic images that are composed for very small screens are often difficult to look at when projected on big screens.)

Floating windows are designed to increase the parallax budget. Here is how it works: People are aware of the rectangular surround when looking at a stereoscopic screen. Most Western art, that is, drawing, painting, photography, and cinematography, is informed by the rectangle. It is the rectangle that determines the composition. IMAX projection gets away from that and here the confines of the rectangle are obviated because the viewer is so close and the screen is so large it is hard to see the surround, or the hard mask that surrounds the edges of the screen. IMAX 3D movies can have large values of parallax because there is no conflict with the screen surround—the vertical edges especially—of the screen.

For the vast majority of theatrical projection situations, unlike the so-called immersive IMAX experience, people looking at a stereoscopic image have the feeling that they are looking through a window. If the stereoscopic image is a theater-space image emerging into the audience, but is cut off, especially by the vertical edges of the surround, there is a *conflict of cues*. If the image appears to be in front of the surround but is cut off by the surround, the stereoscopic cue is conflicted with a planar cue. The planar cue is called *interposition*, and it says that if something is cut off by a window, then it must be behind the window; but if the stereoscopic parallax information says it's in front of the window, then there is a conflict of cues and for most people the perceptual experience is one of confusion. Floating windows cue the problem. They materially extend the parallax budget, allowing for deeper images.

The paradox in stereoscopic cinematography is that, while there are only a few inches of positive parallax to stereo-optical infinity in screen space within which to work, there are a few times (three or four times) in which that value of parallax will work within theater space. Floating windows save the day by eliminating the conflict and allowing more action to play with negative parallax. Black bands at the edges of the frame are added to create a new projected screen surround having off-screen parallax values. In this way objects that might have conflicted cues at the surround are no longer hard to view. The floating or virtual windows can be added in post. In effect this approach redefines the plane of the screen. In a way the floating window (sometimes called the *virtual window*) becomes the new plane of the screen. The effect of adding a virtual or floating window is identical to that which could be achieved by adding a physical black frame or aperture placed in space between the audience and the screen. In effect, the use of floating windows achieves the same thing and is identical to viewing the screen through such an aperture. Now the image plays behind the aperture and objects that might have produced a cue conflict play at or behind the new virtual surround.

The technique of floating windows harmonizes with the esthetic of the current stereoscopic cinema. In reaction to prior practice, modern stereographers, for the most part, use a modulated approach to depth effects and off-screen effects judiciously. Floating windows, by expanding the usable parallax budget into the audience space, tend to reduce off-screen effects. But when needed the windows can be withdrawn or adjusted to allow for off-screened effects. In many shows floating windows are changed from shot to shot, or the values of the effect are different from one side of the screen to the other, or on occasion, the

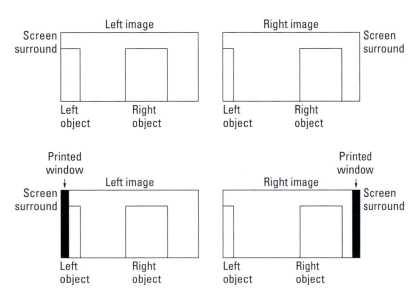

Figure 5.7 Floating or virtual windows. Top stereo pair is without floating windows, the bottom with. The rectangle labeled "right object" is not occluded by the vertical edges of the surround, whereas the left rectangle, which has off-screen negative parallax, is occluded by the left edge of the surround. A conflict of cues is avoided by adding the black bands to produce a new vertical surround with negative parallax to match that of the occluded object. If viewers can free-view stereo they can see the problem and the cure. (Image courtesy of Lenny Lipton.)

windows tilt, and they can be moved during a shot. Floating windows work if the audience doesn't notice them.

Fix It in Post

While the phrase "fix it in post" sounds like an old cliché, for stereo 3D it is a daily routine. For more than half a century cinematographers baked in the look on film they were trying to achieve with the camera. With the advent of the digital intermediate (DI) step or shooting with digital, the trend is now to capture raw or neutral data so that corrections and the look of the film to be determined can be created in post. Specifically this takes place in color timing, and the equivalent for 3D, stereo timing, is emerging.

Two major products have been released in the past 2 years, one from Quantel, the Pablo, and one from Avid. The Pablo allows camera errors to be fixed and it also allows the zero parallax setting to be adjusted, most probably as a step after the film is cut. The Avid off-line editor treats stereo the way it treats color. Films are cut before they are color timed but Avid lets the editor see color—albeit untimed. The same thing is true for stereo. The editor will see the untimed stereo effect, probably on a TI DLP RPTV using shuttering eyewear. The Avid uses the *above and below* (also called the *over and under*) *format* to organize the left and right images.

Arguments have arisen about whether raw or neutral digital data should be used for controlling zero parallax in post. When cutting shots together, there is the ability to figure out how the shot should play with respect to the others. Visualizing how a stereo image looks is difficult to do at the time of photography and visualizing how one shot will work with adjacent shots in post is even more daunting. For one thing the monocular cues play a large part in how deep the image will look and it is hard to visualize how they weight the stereo cue.

It would also be a good thing to be able to control, for live action, the interaxial (and, hence, the strength of the stereo depth effect) in post as well as the zero parallax setting. While the technology to do this could be developed, as of early 2010 there was no product on the market that does the job of allowing the depth strength of a shot to be dialed in.

STEREOSCOPIC DESIGN
Sean Phillips

"If people were meant to see 3D movies they would have been born with two eyes."

—**Apocryphal quote attributed to Sam Goldwyn**

The Emerging Grammar of 3D

Digital projection has, for the first time, made flawless mass 3D presentations possible, and digital imaging tools now give filmmakers sufficient control over the stereo image. The future promises complete control and pixel-perfect stereo accuracy. At this very moment, a grammar for the creative use of 3D in motion pictures is being invented. Each new 3D film is a step forward and a lesson. For 3D to be a meaningful part of the grammar of film, however, it has to contribute to a film's ability to tell a visual story that engages the emotions of an audience.

Creative Use of Depth

Analogies to Color and Visual Design

An audience doesn't consciously think about color or space when watching a story told on the screen. Instead, the response to it is immediate and emotional. Conversely, a typical story involves conscious attention by the viewer and is told through actors—human, animal, or virtual—that engage the audience with empathy and stir their emotions through conflict. The visual elements of a film usually overlie this drama. Used well, the visual design of a film can give it a style and, more importantly, a unique emotional feeling that augments the underlying story. Today 3D is a novelty and any form of it looks interesting to audiences, which sells tickets. The same was true when Technicolor first came out, but the industry was quick to put it into service to enhance a film's visual design. Stereo design will follow a similar pathway but, because it is so new technologically, it doesn't have as much history as color did in other media like painting and photography. The important creative question to answer is "What does 3D add to a film?"

Stereo adds a new level to a film's visual design. In its purest form 3D gives the viewer a palpable connection to the images of a film. An actor looks real and alive. It is intimate, sensual, tactile, and immersive. In its raw form 3D is not subtle and it is not ambiguous, but with good design both of these qualities can be introduced as needed and used with great precision. Like the saturation of a color image, a stereo image can be very dimensional or have the stereo cues completely removed by the taking cameras. The stereo effect can also be exaggerated or twisted to defy reality. The control obtained over real and virtual stereo cinematography is such that there are very few aesthetics of a 2D film that cannot be part of a 3D film as well.

A 3D movie expands a filmmaker's working space in front of and behind the screen. In addition to screen right and screen left, there is now a stereo window, dividing stereo space into theater space and screen space.

The Stereo Window

The stereo window was born out of the need to make a stereo image work within a photographic composition. When an object in a 3D movie appears closer to the viewer than the physical space of the theater screen, there is an inherent visual conflict when that object breaks the edge of frame. This problem can happen on the left or right sides of the screen, but it is not so much of an issue on the top or bottom of the screen. The reason for this is simple: The left and right eyes are separated horizontally, so the left and right sides of the screen are where stereo cues are perceived. The top and bottom of the screen are, by contrast, stereoscopically ambiguous.

To solve this problem, the stereo window was created, which is a construct that stereographers use to minimize depth conflicts at the left and right frame edges. The interocular[2] is adjusted so that nothing in the background has a divergent offset on the typical movie screen of more than 2.5 inches as measured on the screen. This keeps the viewer's eyes from diverging or going "walleyed" when watching the film. Since screen sizes vary from 20 to 40 feet or more, a safe divergent offset value used for widely released 3D films is 1% of the screen width. That means that the positive stereo parallax seen behind the screen plane shouldn't exceed 1% of the screen width. That would be 20 pixels on a 2k image. There are times when this rule can be exceeded, especially when using soft backgrounds, but care must be taken. (Please refer to the *Stereoscopic Window* section later in this chapter for a detailed in-depth discussion of the stereo window.)

Theater Space

Things that appear in front of the stereo window are said to be, not surprisingly, in *theater space* or *off-screen*. The stereo offsets in front of the screen are called *negative parallax*, because the distances are getting closer to the viewer. For shots of actors it is usually acceptable to break the bottom of the screen in theater space but not the top. It is good practice to keep the actor's head from breaking the top of the frame and to keep people and objects in theater space from breaking the left or right side of the frame—unless it happens very quickly. Actors can make quick entrances and exits in theater space, but slow entrances and exits are best avoided. Those are the major *don'ts* of theater space.

---

[2] Interocular: distance between the lenses of the left and right eye cameras. Also called the *interaxial*. In a mirror rig this distance can be typically varied from 0 to 4 inches.

Theater space is an area where the most immersive and palpable forms of 3D can be created, and it is vastly underutilized because of the time and effort required to properly design its use. A traditional dialogue scene with reverses and even over-the-shoulder shots can be played in theater space with the right design—but this requires all departments to work together with a common vision. Playing a scene like this at, or behind, the screen plane is easier, safer for editorial, and in many cases appropriate, but in as many cases it is not using the 3D medium to its fullest.

Screen Space

Screen space is all the remaining stereo space the audience can see behind the screen, or stereo window. This space is often referred to as having *positive parallax*. Objects in this space can move with no restriction on traditional framing. Actors can enter and exit any time they want as long as they are at, or behind, the point of convergence. Cinematographers may frame traditionally in screen space, and even very high contrast lighting is unlikely to cause ghosting issues.

Less is More

The stereoscopic depth effect is very powerful, but it is very important to use it in moderation. If a scene is played at reduced interoculars, the next scene, if played at wider interoculars, will appear much richer in depth. This is simple contrast, just like light and dark and complementary colors, and it can be just as effective.

Practical Storytelling in 3D: Two Extremes

One director wanted to shoot his 3D film the same way as he would shoot a 2D film, but this approach does not make very good use of the 3D medium's capabilities. A blanket direction to the 3D team was "Just give it as much depth as possible." This kind of director is going to produce a very unsatisfying 3D project, thus mitigating the very reason for doing it in 3D in the first place.

At the other extreme, a different director used a camera that had only convergence control. The lenses were fixed at 63mm (2.5 inches) apart. Not being able to reduce the interocular is a severe constraint in 3D, but the director was eager to stage and design the film to work best for 3D. Tests were shot where the stereo was pushed far beyond its limits. This was very important because it allowed the director to see what worked and didn't work in 3D. By seeing those boundaries a common frame of reference was created, allowing the 3D team to design the film's 3D to its creative limits. Shots of actors on green screen were layered in order to build up depth of field and work within the stereo budget. Every shot was staged with 3D in mind, and in the end the film was far more effective in stereo than the first film discussed because of its design—despite a much smaller budget and the serious working constraint of a fixed interocular.

The stereo design should be discussed between the director, DP, and stereographer in pre-production because it will become the 3D road map for the film. Which scenes are played heavily in theater space, at the screen plane, or in screen space? Where are unique or complex 3D effects needed? This dialogue also facilitates choosing the best 3D capture systems for the particular film.

Previsualization

Three-dimensional photography can be previsualized in CG with extreme accuracy. This accuracy can be used to predetermine at what interocular and convergence settings a visual effects–laden scene will be shot. Stereoscopic previsualizations are most helpful when doing greenscreen work with actors who will interact with CG characters. When actors are photographed on green screen, the interocular distance is baked in to the scene. So if there is only a vague idea of what's to happen in the CG portion of the scene, there is good chance that the interocular chosen on set could prove to be wrong. By previsualizing the CG characters' motion in stereo space, the best interocular setting can be predetermined for the live action greenscreen photography. One important aspect to previsualization in 3D is that the virtual world should use real-world units (feet, inches, meters, etc.) to define that world. This makes everything previsualized completely accessible to the stereography, camera, and art departments in meaningful units, hence enabling successful execution of principal photography. When virtual units are arbitrary, simple errors that can be expensive or impossible to fix later are difficult to spot.

Avoiding Painful 3D

The 3D process can actually cause physical pain if used incorrectly. Because of this there are a lot of noncreative issues that have to be respected before 3D can be used aesthetically.

Painful 3D is caused by an unacceptable difference between the left and right eye images. In a properly aligned 3D image pair, a slight left-right shift in the perspective of the stereo images should only be visible if toggling between them on a workstation or digital intermediate suite. This horizontal shift varies with an object's distance from camera, but is usually not more than 4% of the image width and often much less.

Vertical misalignment, where one image is set higher or lower in the frame compared to the other eye, is a very disturbing thing to see in 3D. However, this usually can be eliminated in post by shifting the images up and down in relation to each other until they appear aligned.

Color hue, color saturation, image sharpness, contrast, brightness, and image geometry should all be consistent between the image pairs. If not, they need to be carefully balanced in post. Stereo errors in photography can have catastrophic results. For example, shooting with too wide an interocular can bake in a stereo offset that is unwatchable in the theater. It might have looked acceptable on a little 3D screen, but a big theater screen changes everything.

Additionally, improper stereo synchronization of any of the camera functions—frame rates, shutters, focus, iris, and zoom controls—can also doom a shot. And keep in mind that these are just the basics. With all of these potential issues, it is not surprising that stereo cinematography has been a slow, laborious process where most of the effort is directed at avoiding humiliation rather than furthering the creative use of 3D. Digital capture and the digital intermediate process are now typically used on most projects to ensure that the image streams are well aligned and presentable.

The Aesthetic of Scale

In a traditional film the perception of the scale of an object is defined by 2D cues such as texture, aerial perspective, depth of field, and proximity to and occlusion by other objects. In its raw form 3D wants to assign scale to everything. It becomes very specific and unambiguous. On a small screen, or in combination with a wide interocular, it will create the effect of apparent miniaturization. This effect is usually unwanted on people—unless the film is about miniature people.

One of the great charms of going to the movies has been the way the screen makes characters look larger than life—not smaller. This is a design aesthetic that is desired in 3D movies as well. Audiences are very comfortable watching 3D movies when actors appear, in the back row, normal in scale or larger. Audiences feel uncomfortable when people look miniaturized in 3D movies. The acceptance of larger than life appearances of actors in the cinema has made apparent gigantism in 3D movies something that audiences do not perceive. An actor can have an apparent scale of 22 feet in a 3D cinema and it doesn't look unnatural unless there is a relative error in scale. For example, if a 12-foot actor is standing next to a car whose apparent scale is normal, he will look like a giant relative to the car. The process of creating a stereo window generally tends to increase the apparent scale of the subject because it narrows the interocular to reduce divergence and it pushes the subject away from the camera to put him at or behind the stereo window. It is an open question whether audiences will get very picky about scale as their stereo sophistication grows. However, it is a safe bet that people will still want to see actors who appear larger than life.

Lens Choices

In general, you should shoot with wider lenses in 3D. A wide lens expands space in a way that is pleasing to the eye—especially for architectural interiors. Wider lenses also have more depth of field, which is especially helpful for foreground objects. When moving in for close-ups on actors, it is better to get physically closer and use a wider lens. For example, if an 85mm lens would ordinarily be used for a close single, a 50mm lens would probably work better in 3D. Longer lenses compress space in ways that are more subtle and flattering for close-ups in 2D than 3D. Long telephoto lenses compress space even more, and the effect in 3D is like looking through a pair of binoculars at a series of flat cutouts with exaggerated expanses of space in between them. That might be the right look for some films, but not most. This "cardboard cutout" effect can be compensated for to a degree with wider interoculars and staging that carefully places objects in space—within very strict limits.

Fish-eye lenses have a unique look and can work surprisingly well in 3D, but only for an occasional shot as the vertical alignment drifts at the edges of frame. Many minutes of looking at fish-eye shots will create eyestrain. A side benefit is that because fish-eye lens designs are compact and have an ultra-wide field of view, they can be used in very tight spaces and the fish-eye distortion can be corrected in post. When the distortion is removed, they behave like an ultrawide spherical lens in 3D. Ultra-wide lenses, and especially fish-eye lenses with 180 degree fields of view, translate left-right stereo parallax at the center into z-axis shifts toward the edges of the frame, minimizing the 3D effect.

A good rule of thumb is that 3D needs a lot of depth of field, and that rule is true most of the time—but not all of the time. In many instances a narrow depth of field is highly effective and can be used to make the depth effect ambiguous when creatively desired. Another rule is that if there is something that needs to be looked at in a shot that something should be in focus. They eye always goes to the person or object that is in focus.

Cutting for 3D

The stereo space of a film needs to flow through the edit just like the motions of actors, angles of cameras, and progress of the story. Being able to preview the edit in 3D in the edit bay is essential. It is also imperative to review the full edit on a theatrical-sized screen with the filmmakers sitting at the range of seats that resemble a normal cinema. A 3D edit isn't done until it can play to all of the seats in the house.

It has often been said that 3D films have to be paced more slowly because of the time it takes to accommodate 3D images. It is certainly true that big 3D in-theater effects need to be given sufficient time to read to the audience and then withdrawn before cutting to the next shot. In general, however, a 3D film can work at just about any pace if it has been properly designed. The challenge is creating a flowing continuity of space for the eye to follow. If the stereo depth flows across the edits, it is possible to cut a scene very quickly.

Over the course of a scene, the intercutting of 3D shots creates a spatial relationship between characters. If the space between characters is too great, it will appear unnatural, as will jumps in the space of characters. Most of these issues are solved in photography by keeping the intercut action close to the stereo window. Oftentimes the director will want to move beyond this convention and play action more in theater space, but the scene must be carefully designed and essentially edited in advance if it is to be successful.

When the space of two shots is very different and those shots are juxtaposed, a stereo jump cut is created. The classic example is cutting from a wide scenic vista to a single of an actor well out into theater space. A cut happens instantaneously, but the viewer's eyes take time to accommodate a stereo image that is on a different plane in space. Eyes are relaxed and nearly parallel when they look at objects far away in space, easily fusing two almost identical images into about the same place on each eye's retina. The amount of eye cross tells the brain how close things are—the closer things are, the more the eyes have to cross. Cutting from deep space to close space instantly makes the eyes try to cross and takes the audience out of the story. Conversely, it is far easier to cut from something close in space to something far away as the eyes are actually relaxing across the cut.

Floating Windows

The stereo window does not always have to stay at the theater's screen plane, and that is where floating windows come into play. Imagine if the black masking around the frame had a stereo offset all its own. The floating window itself could then be placed deeper in space than the real screen or, more commonly, closer. Floating windows are part of the domain of editorial because they are almost always used in post to fit a stereo image whose depth budget has exceeded the normal screen plane. It is also a powerful tool for converting films shot in other formats with large depth budgets like IMAX 3D for presentation in RealD theaters. For a more in-depth discussion of these topics, please refer to the previous section, *How 3D Works*.

Designing for Multiple Release Formats

The technology of 3D is constantly evolving, and it needs to. At present, most 3D camera systems look like science projects. As high-resolution motion picture cameras move toward lower and lower price points, and as integrated electronics become available, the stereo camera systems will become much more "set friendly." Presentation technology is also evolving quickly. 3D screen sizes are currently limited by projector brightness, but new generations of projectors, and multiple projector tiling based on automated machine vision, are already entering the special venue field and will soon be scalable to a mass audience. Because of constant change one can never be sure where a 3D film will show or under what conditions. A 3D feature film will appear in RealD and Dolby theaters, possibly in IMAX 3D, or on the Internet. And the truth is that 3D cannot be shot in a way that works perfectly for all formats. All that can be done is to shoot and design a film for its primary market. If it is a feature, shoot it for a RealD-sized screen. If it goes to IMAX, it will need to be reconverged to fit into that format.

Immersion-Based versus Convergence-Based Stereo

Traditionally 3D in motion pictures has been called *convergence based*, meaning it uses convergence to place the scene within a stereo window, as discussed so far. There is another way of designing 3D films that emerges from a construct known as the *orthostereo condition*. To create this condition, one shoots with a lens that has the same angular field of view that the viewer's eyes have to the theater screen. The two cameras are also the same distance apart as the viewer's eyes (about 63mm or 2.5 inches) and the cameras are completely parallel, meaning that their convergence is set to infinity, as are the projectors. What this condition creates is an exact, one-to-one re-creation of reality in the stereo space of the theater.

The problem with using orthostereo has always been that anything in the image closer than the screen that is cut off by the edge of the frame collapses in depth. This is why the convergence-based stereo window was devised in the first place. But there is a way to get around this problem.

3D IMAX and Giant Screen Venues

Something very interesting happens on a movie screen when the audience sits within two-thirds of a screen width away from it: The image becomes completely immersive. In other words, the audience no longer thinks about the edges of the frame, there is no "stereo window," and the image space can be designed to float anywhere between the eyes and infinity. This is the essence of immersion-based 3D. It demands a huge shift in thinking away from traditional frame-based filmmaking, where convergence has always been used to make 3D fit the traditional 2D compositional window. However, when viewing from two-thirds of a screen width away from a typical movie screen, the image is so magnified that its quality is extremely poor. What has made immersion-based 3D possible is the higher resolution (about 8k) of film formats like IMAX and the giant screens on which they are displayed.[3]

A convergence-based projection system, whether it is one or two projectors, always strives to align a grid pattern from each eye into a single identical grid pattern on the screen when viewed without 3D glasses. In an immersive system, like IMAX 3D, the grid image from the left and right projected images are offset exactly 63mm, or 2.5 inches, on the screen—the average distance between human eyes. Although 63mm, or 2.5 inches, may not seem like a lot, especially on an 80-foot-wide IMAX 3D screen, that separation is essential because it makes objects appearing at near infinity to the camera appear at near infinity to the viewers in the theater.

An IMAX 3D film is shot in a very different way from a traditional, convergence-based film. Because there is no stereo window, almost everything is staged in theater space. This is a huge break, not just from traditional 3D but also from traditional frame-based filmmaking. Scenes need to be essentially pre-edited when they are shot because a continuity of space needs to be maintained independent of a stereo window.

There is no question that the future of theatrical motion pictures is written on bigger screens. As large HD screens fill homes, the public cinema has to offer something bigger, better, and more immersive. Already theater chains are adding 4k digital screens and larger digital screens are filled as soon as brighter projectors are available. The push for larger theatrical screens is inevitable and will make the possibility of mass distribution of immersive 3D a reality.

---

[3] This is not referring to the recently deployed IMAX digital system, which is essentially oversampled HD with a screen size slightly larger than that of a RealD system.

VIRTUAL 3D PHOTOGRAPHY
Rob Engle

Virtual 3D Photography Defined

The current renaissance in stereoscopic filmmaking can be closely attributed to the use of digital techniques both for production and exhibition. While digital techniques have revolutionized the acquisition of moving pictures in the physical world, no technology has more profoundly impacted stereoscopic content creation than computer graphics. The use of 3D digital techniques to build a stereoscopic image pair is called *virtual 3D photography*. CG features are the best example of virtual 3D photography with numerous examples driving the state of the art in 3D filmmaking. These same techniques have been shown to create high-quality 2D-to-3D conversions. This is in contrast to many of the 2D compositing (image-based) techniques that are used for 2D-to-3D conversion of material in which a virtual world, representing a physical world, is never built. By creating a virtual stereoscopic camera and placing it into a scene, one is able to simulate the effect of actually photographing the scene in stereo, producing the highest quality images while gaining a tremendous degree of flexibility in creating the final stereo pair.

Pros and Cons of Virtual 3D Photography

One of the chief advantages of using both image-based digital techniques and virtual 3D photography is the ability to create so-called "perfect" 3D. While the human visual system is very flexible to a wide variety of differences between the images seen by the left and right eye, any differences other than horizontal parallax can lead to fatigue when extreme enough or viewed for an extended period of time. By not being bound by the limitations of physical optical systems, it is relatively straightforward to create stereo pairs with only horizontal parallax. Additionally, by its very nature the post-production process allows the stereographer the flexibility to review the results of his work in the context of the film's cut, tuning individual shots and cuts to provide the highest quality 3D effect. In many cases this tuning might involve matching the depth of the primary subject matter from shot to shot to minimize the impact on the viewers' having to adjust their eyes' vergence. In other cases the stereographer may be making creative choices about the overall depth of a shot or to what extent the subject matter should extend in or out of theater space.

Another benefit of using a virtual camera to render a stereo image is that it is possible to create 3D compositions with very deep focus. In the physical world, assuming the viewer has good vision, everything will be in sharp focus. This means the technique of using a narrow depth of field, which has been commonly practiced in planar cinema, runs counter to creating a truly deep 3D experience. The virtual camera with its idealized "pinhole" properties allows the stereographer complete control over depth of field. While many cinematographers would use a narrow depth of field to direct the viewer's gaze, the 3D cinema is a different medium and benefits from different techniques. If you are trying to create a truly immersive 3D experience, it is generally better to use lighting, movement, and deliberate 3D staging to direct the viewer rather than to rely on a narrow depth of field.

The single biggest disadvantage of virtual 3D photography is that all objects must be modeled and exist in proper scale and location in the virtual world. Objects that do not adhere to this requirement will require special handling and, in the worst case, may need to be converted from 2D to 3D and then integrated into renders of the virtual world.

Multiple Camera Rigs

A technique that is somewhat unique to virtual 3D photography and has been applied on numerous CG features is that of photographing a virtual scene using multiple stereoscopic camera pairs. By isolating individual objects or characters in a scene and tuning the stereo parameters on a per-object basis, you can achieve a higher degree of control over the use of the parallax budget for a shot.

Oftentimes, many of the same effects of multiple-camera rigs can be achieved by judicious selection of lens focal length and object distances. However, the multiple-camera rig technique enables a significantly greater degree of flexibility and allows one to compress and expand the 3D effect in ways that are very difficult to achieve by any other means. For example, with normal stereoscopic photography, a foreground object will have more internal dimension (roundness) than objects that are farther from the camera. In the case of an over-the-shoulder shot, it may be desirable to compress the roundness of the foreground and minimize the distance to the primary subject while enhancing the roundness of the subject.

If a scene has multiple characters, it can be helpful to subtly compress the space between the characters while giving them more roundness to minimize the cardboard effect. Selectively applying roundness to individual objects can also be used to heighten the emotional impact of the film. In Robert Zemeckis' performance capture epic, *Beowulf* (2007), individual characters were often isolated and given extra roundness when they were in a position of power while their roundness was minimized when

Figure 5.8 In this shot the apparent roundness of the main character as well as the other characters was manipulated using the multiple-camera rig technique for *Beowulf* (2007). (Image courtesy of Paramount Pictures. BEOWULF © Shangri-La Entertainment, LLC and Paramount Pictures Corporation. Licensed By: Warner Bros. Entertainment Inc. All Rights Reserved.)

they were in relatively weaker positions. In addition to using this technique as a creative tool, it is also possible to use multiple-camera rigs to correct technical problems such as incorrect eye lines or unusual character scaling that would normally require sending a shot back to animation.

Note that the multiple-camera rig technique will often not work when applied to separate objects whose interface is visible in the shot. For example, it would be difficult to apply two separate stereo settings for a character and the surface on which it is standing because it is important that the character still appear to be on the surface. If the character is standing still or one is using a results-driven camera rig, it may be easier to make this example work, but, in general, these kinds of shots don't benefit from this technique anyway. Additionally, while this technique can be used for live-action photography with the use of greenscreen matting to isolate elements, it is somewhat impractical to implement on a large scale.

Figure 5.9 In this example from *Open Season* (2006) the animator used forced perspective to get the right-hand character to feel smaller (placing her farther away from the camera). A multiple-camera rig was used to correct the characters' eye lines without changing their scale. (Image © 2006 Sony Pictures Animation Inc. All rights reserved.)

Creating a finished multiple-camera-rig shot involves rendering each group of objects through their associated camera pairs and compositing the renders, taking into account the depth sorting order. Because it is very easy to create unnatural depth effects and interfere with the viewer's sense of scale using this technique, it is very important to visualize the final result as early as possible. In many production environments custom viewing software is required in the layout and animation package to allow for live preview of multiple-camera-rig shots since most animation packages do not have native support for this feature.

The 3D Camera Rig

When implementing the virtual 3D camera rig, three primary strategies are used most commonly.

When mixing virtual photography and practical photography, it is very important for the two virtual cameras to match the plate photography as accurately as possible. Since physical cameras rarely are perfectly aligned with matching focal lengths, the matchmoved cameras cannot simply be driven by an interaxial spacing and convergence value. They must be allowed to freely translate and rotate in all dimensions relative to each other. As a consequence, this style of rig imposes the fewest constraints on the left and right cameras, but also gives the stereographer the least intuitive controls.

The "direct" style of rig constrains left and right cameras to each other such that only horizontal offsets can be obtained and are driven by the interaxial spacing and convergence parameters. This rig is probably the simplest to implement and offers the stereographer a set of controls with the closest parallels to real-world stereoscopic cameras.

Layered on top of the direct rig, it is also possible to implement a "results-driven" rig that allows the stereographer to adjust controls such as on-screen parallax, an object's perceived distance from the viewer, and object roundness. This type of rig would normally have locators or measuring planes that can be placed in the scene at a near and far location along with specifications for the desired apparent distances or expected parallax values. A results-driven rig that allows control based on the viewer's perceived distances will need to make assumptions about the distance from the screen at which the viewer is sitting as well as the size of the screen.

Implementing Convergence

When building a physical stereoscopic camera it is common practice to implement convergence by rotating the individual cameras (typically only one camera actually rotates) toward each other. On long focal lengths or when the amount of rotation is small, this technique works quite well. In other circumstances, however, it is possible to create a fair amount of vertical keystoning as a result of this rotation. Since the keystone effect is different on each side of the image (the left eye will be taller on the left

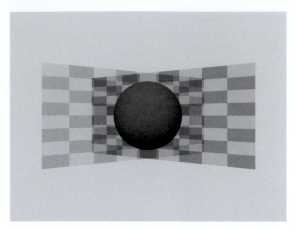 

Figure 5.10 On the left a stereo pair has been converged using toe-in of the cameras. On the right the stereo pair has been converged using horizontal image translation.

side than on the right), this technique can cause vertical parallax, making the images difficult to fuse when viewed as a stereo pair.

In contrast, the virtual stereoscopic camera is typically built such that, rather than rotating the left and right eye cameras, the film planes of each camera are shifted horizontally. By simply shifting the individual eyes, no keystoning occurs and a near "perfect" stereo pair is produced. This is a direct result of keeping the individual eye film planes parallel to each other.

If desired, it is possible to simulate this technique using practical photography. On the stop-motion animated film *Coraline* (2009), the filmmakers used a single camera on a motion control base that would move the camera left and right, keeping the film backs parallel. By using a large imaging array (wider than the film's release format), it was possible to converge the cameras as a digital post move. Additionally, it is possible to build a stereo camera with a tilt-shift lens or film back or to embed a wide imaging chip in the camera.

Whatever technique is ultimately used to implement convergence in the virtual camera rig, it is important for the entire camera model (including convergence) to match the physical camera rig in the event of integrating CG elements with real-world photographed plates. This requirement may limit one's options on a mixed live-action/CG production.

Manipulating the Screen Surround

Floating Windows

When the composition of a shot is such that objects in the foreground intersect the left and right edges of the screen, a phenomenon known as the *paradoxical window effect* comes into play. Objects that appear in depth to be closer than the edge of the frame they intersect create confusion for the viewer. Suppose a close object intersects the right side of the frame. In this situation, without some form of correction, the viewer is able to see more of the object in the right eye than in the left. This experience runs counter to the normal experience of looking through a window in which the left eye would be able to see more than the right. A very simple solution to this problem was employed by Raymond and Nigel Spottiswoode in the early 1950s. They moved the edge of the frame closer to the viewer by imprinting a black band on the side of the frame in the appropriate eye. The black band effectively hides the portion of the image that wouldn't be visible if looking through a window.

While use of this technique allows one to avoid the visual paradox created by the edges of the frame, it also can be quite useful as a creative tool and to subtly convey the context of a shot as well. By moving the window closer to the audience than would be needed simply to correct the screen window paradox, one could convey, for example, a given shot as a character's point of view or make a flat, far-away shot feel deeper. This floating window technique is especially useful for smaller screen presentations in which the screen edges are a distinct part of viewing the film.

It is especially important when using this technique to make sure the theater does not allow the sides of the image to overlap the theatrical masking. If the theater introduces its own masking to the image, the effect of the floating window will be lost. It is now common practice for films using a floating window to include a "guard band" of black on either side of the frame and to include a reference framing chart to aid the projectionist in properly framing the film.

Figure 5.11 An example framing chart from the film *G-Force* (2009). (Image courtesy © 2009 Disney Enterprises, Inc. All rights reserved.)

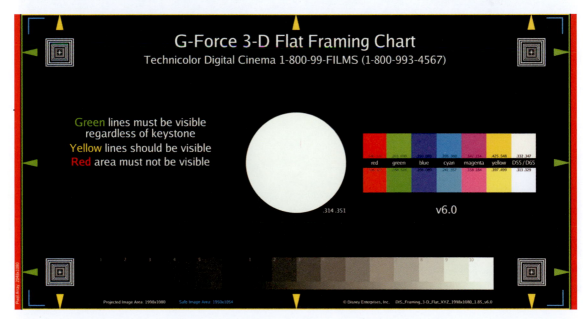

Breaking the Mask

The very purpose of the floating window technique is to ensure that objects which cross the edge of the frame do not appear to conflict with the frame itself. Another technique, rather than forcing the objects which cross the edge to appear behind the frame, is to matte them such that they appear to be in front of the masking. A black border can be introduced on any side of the image with select foreground parts of the composition allowed to extend over the border. The resulting effect reinforces the audience's sense that these objects extend into theater space. On *G-Force* (2009) this technique was employed heavily to allow objects to appear to be farther into theater space than they really were. By masking objects to appear in theater space but limiting their negative parallax to near screen level, the film was made more dynamic without sacrificing audience visual comfort. One of the dangers of this technique (common to many theater-space effects) is that it can distract the audience from the narrative flow of the film if used at the wrong time. Limiting the use of the effect to action scenes often works best, and subtler uses, such as placing spark and debris elements over the mask, will keep the audience involved in the film.

Note that neither of the above two techniques for treating the screen surround are truly limited to use in films created with virtual 3D photography. It is relatively straightforward to implement

Figure 5.12 Breaking the mask as illustrated in *G-Force* (2009). Note that the shards of glass fall both in front of and behind the black masking helping to fix the depth of the mask itself. (Image courtesy © 2009 Disney Enterprises, Inc. All rights reserved.)

a floating window in any digital release, and post-production tools for their creation continue to be refined. The breaking-the-mask technique is probably easiest to implement when all of the elements are easily isolated (as in a CG film) but wouldn't be out of the question in films created using other methods. (For a more complete discussion of stereo windows, see the *Stereoscopic Window* section later in this chapter.)

Special Cases for Virtual 3D Photography

One of the primary rules that cannot be broken when creating virtual stereoscopic photography is that you cannot "cheat" 3D. Artists who are well versed with creation of planar CG features and live-action visual effects films are used to a variety of 2D shortcuts to achieve convincing and high-quality imagery. Many of these shortcuts do not lend themselves well to 3D filmmaking. For example, it is important that renders use proper holdouts and proper shadow casting objects. In 2D filmmaking, it is common practice for simple effects elements (e.g., smoke or sparks) to be rendered without any object holdouts and then composited into the scene. When translated to 3D, however, without proper holdouts, these effects elements will now intersect objects because the depth of the element may be behind something but not held out by the object.

Another common practice is to use compositing techniques (rotoscoped shapes or drop shadows) to enhance a shadow or color correct an element. If the 2D shape being used to correct the effect is not properly mapped onto the surface being manipulated, the shape may appear to float in 3D space.

Reflections and transparency are another special case because they must be rerendered in order to get a convincing effect. If one were to use a 2D technique (offsets or image warping) on an element with obvious reflections or transparency, the effects would appear to stick to the object surface rather than having the expected look. For a fully CG film, it is usually sufficient to simply rerender objects that are highly reflective or transparent. In the case of a 2D-to-3D conversion (whether using 2D techniques or virtual 3D photography), it is important to isolate the surface of the reflective object from the image in the reflection.

Last, note that one of the biggest "cheats" in filmmaking is the use of matte paintings to create entire backgrounds (and sometimes foregrounds) in 2D rather than having to actually model them. Any time a 2D matte painting is used (unless it is in the extreme distance), some 2D-to-3D conversion work is likely to be needed to integrate it into the rest of the scene.

2D TO 3D CONVERSION
Matt DeJohn, Anthony Shafer

The recent resurgence of stereoscopic 3D (stereo) motion pictures means that the visual effects artist of today can be called on to create a new level of visuals, an area of expertise that was previously handled in obscurity. The intimacy with which the audience participates in a stereoscopic picture is an important aspect of the experience and, therefore, for projects not shot in 3D, the conversion. The stereographer[4] must understand the director's overall intent with the film, as well as the contextual composition of each shot, because this information will alter the amount of depth and style used in the conversion process.

The 2D-to-3D conversion process generates alternate perspectives from a 2D image. When these images are appropriately displayed, the viewer fuses[5] the two images into one to create a stereoscopic effect. A 2D-to-3D conversion can be done with any type of footage, including live-action footage, or animation. Live-action 2D-to-3D conversion is uniquely different from live-action stereo camera capture in that the entire stereoscopic effect is created in post-production. This allows live-action production to capture footage with typical equipment in a typical time frame. A positive aspect of the post-production conversion is that the depth can be significantly altered to match the edit, the director's developing artistic desires, or any other reason. The concession for these positive aspects is longer post-production time. Performing conversion simultaneously with other post-production processes can mitigate this, but some additional post-production time should be allowed for.

Depth Creation Preparation

Before creating a stereoscopic pair from a monocular image, the image must be analyzed to identify depth cues to help determine the shape and depth of the original image. The human visual system derives *perceived depth* using both physiological and psychological cues. Retinal image size, linear perspective, texture gradient, overlapping, motion parallax, aerial perspective, shading, and shadows can all be used to help determine the depth of an image and the shape of an object. Individually, each cue provides an indication to the original depth and shape of an object. Identifying as many cues as possible will provide a more accurate representation of the original image depth.

[4] Stereographer: person who has the responsibility for making sure all shots of a project are properly composed in terms of stereoscopic depth.
[5] Fusing: act of perceiving two images' perspectives as one.

Visual Analysis of 2D Depth Cues

A 2D depth cue is the visual perception of depth without an alternate perspective. In the 2D-to-3D conversion world they are referred to as *implicit depth cues*, as they already exist in the original 2D image. Some of the most important implicit depth cues are occlusion,[6] relative size, height in visual field, motion perspective, aerial perspective, and depth of field (see Figure 5.13).

Occlusion Relative size Height in visual field Motion perspective   Aerial perspective

2 Km/h for 20 sec.

2 Km/h for 20 sec.

Figure 5.13 Implicit 2D depth cues. (Image courtesy of Matthew DeJohn.)

Occlusion indicates general object ordering implied by overlapping objects. Relative size indicates depth based from the size relationship of objects in the scene. Height in the visual field indicates depth because humans see the world from an elevated perspective in relation to the ground. Given this fact, the bases of distant objects appear higher in one's visual field than nearer objects. (The example in Figure 5.13 specifically shows this relationship with no consideration to the relative size difference that would be present.) Motion perspective indicates depth based on the distance an object travels in one's visual field during its own movement or the movement of one's point of view, such as during a crane, dolly, or trucking shot. Aerial perspective indicates depth through a loss of detail and contrast present in distant objects. This is caused by the amount of atmosphere between the viewer and the subject; therefore, in space there would be no aerial perspective depth cue.

One needs to understand these implicit depth cues in order to accurately analyze an image for conversion. The artist's explicit choices of convergence and binocular disparity must be consistent with, or at least not conflict with, the implicit depth cues. For example, if two men, who in reality are the same height, appear to be different sizes in a 2D image, there needs to be sufficient separation in Z-space[7] to justify their size difference in the image. Also, the degree of these implicit depth cues helps indicate the amount of volume and separation necessary to properly convert the image. Take the example of the two men again: The greater the apparent size difference between them on the 2D image, the more separation is needed to support that implicit depth cue.

---

[6] Occlusion: state in which objects or portions of objects are not visible because they are blocked by other objects or portions of objects.

[7] Z-space: way of stating where an object is in relation to the camera on one axis—close to near.

It is important to note that the more depth that is built into the scene, the more accurate the artist's analysis of the scene must be because the viewer is more likely to see any disparities between explicit and implicit depth cues. In a sense, the more depth that's created in a scene, the more definitive the explicit depth choices are.

Main Artistic Stages of 2D-to-3D Conversion

Most successful 2D-to-3D conversion techniques requires three broad artistic phases: element isolation, occluded surface reconstruction, and depth generation. Although some approaches can yield results without these artistic phases, they are not adequate for most shots.

Element Isolation

The goal of element isolation is to define the elements in the image that had substantial physical separation between them in order to offer flexibility when creating the 3D effect. A pen on a desk would not need to be isolated; however, the desk would need to be isolated from the ground. Even if portions of elements connect, such as the desk and the floor, it is often advantageous to isolate them separately. This allows for independent shaping, positioning, and perspective control. It is important to note that this specific approach is more applicable to the pixel displacement workflow (discussed later).

Another way to determine which elements to isolate is by analyzing which elements are not visually connected (see Figure 5.14). This approach is specifically applicable to the re-projection workflow. Consider a medium shot of an actor in a room; even though the audience knows the actor must be standing on the floor, there is not a visible connection with the floor since the framing is on the torso and not revealing the connection. Therefore, the actor can be isolated from the background because he does not exhibit connection to room, specifically the floor, within the frame. Element separation allows more flexibility when creating a realistic 3D effect.

Element isolation reveals the necessity for another artistic phase, occluded surface reconstruction. When foreground elements

Figure 5.14 *Left:* Subject visually connected to floor. *Right:* Subject not visually connected to floor. (Image courtesy of Anthony Shafer.)

Connective tissue   No connective tissue

are isolated, that area also indicates the occluded surface that may be revealed by 2D-to-3D conversion. The occluded surface lacks appropriate image data and so may require image reconstruction.

All standard visual effects methods for isolating elements apply to 2D-to-3D conversion. Those methods include rotoscope, manual paint, procedural paint, and procedural keys.

Isolating elements for a 2D-to-3D conversion process can be quite challenging. Artists are required to isolate an element with the same degree of accuracy as would be expected if the shot was properly captured on a green screen. If this level of accuracy is not met, the audience immediately sees the errors. Poor matte creation in 2D-to-3D conversion can actually make a shot look like a bad greenscreen shot even if it never was. Particularly challenging elements to isolate are out-of-focus objects, objects with motion blur, hair, and highly other intricate objects such as trees.

Occluded Surface Reconstruction

A 2D-to-3D conversion creates at least one alternate perspective. This new alternate view commonly reveals new surfaces that were not visible in the original perspective. These revealed surfaces must be filled with accurate image information to complete the 3D effect. This occluded surface reconstruction (OSR) can be achieved by a variety of visual effects methods such as clean plate reconstruction, re-projection, automatic temporal filling, or frame-by-frame paintwork.

The goal when performing any OSR is to maintain consistent textures, motion, grain, color, and luminance between perspectives in order to avoid fusion errors. While that's easy enough to understand, OSR is generally the least forgiving process. To illustrate this, consider a medium shot of a character shot in front of an ocean. When the additional perspective is created, more ocean is revealed. When reconstructing that surface, the texture of the waves needs to be maintained. This is challenging enough on a single frame, but this texture needs to move in a way consistent with the rest of the ocean. This type of moving texture is difficult to re-create because the human brain is so attuned to how the ripple should progress into the occluded space. Also, in this example, the ever changing color and luminance must be maintained accurately.

Many paint tools (procedural, nonprocedural, and autopaint) can be used for OSR. Autopaint tools generally fall into two categories, temporal-filling[8] and pattern matching.[9] It is best to

---

[8] Temporal filling: process by which missing image data is replaced from frames elsewhere in a shot where that image area is revealed.

[9] Pattern matching: process by which missing image data is synthesized by continuing patterns that are found elsewhere in the image into the missing area.

attempt to get as far as possible with a temporal-filling algorithm and then move to a pattern-matching algorithm.

Results with automated tools can vary greatly and so manual paint tools (procedural and nonprocedural) are almost always necessary. It is advisable to do as much as possible in a procedural fashion, because paint and/or depth revisions are inevitable. The full range of paint, rig-removal, and matchmoving techniques will need to be used at one point or another during OSR. However, there are a few specific things to keep in mind when painting in stereo. For instance, cloning from a source directly next to the target can cause the viewer to fuse a portion of the background at an unintended position in Z-space. Given this common mistake and others, it is imperative to regularly view one's work in stereo. In general, all source material should be cloned from the new perspective only. Cloning from the original perspective will potentially neutralize shaping.

Grain management is essential in the OSR process. First and foremost, grain must be consistent in nature between layers regardless of the Z-depth position. Some paint techniques, like matchmoving a single clean plate to fill occluded surfaces, can result in static grain, so grain must be generated to effectively blend this area with areas that have dynamic grain.

A seemingly viable approach would be to de-grain the footage on the front end and then add grain to each perspective after all depth and paintwork is complete. Unfortunately this approach fails because the grain will actually play at screen level like a curtain of grain. In areas of low contrast, the viewer will fuse the grain at screen level and this will likely conflict with the depth of that low-contrast element. Different grain in either eye is not a viable option either. This approach can lead to a discomforting left eye and right eye discrepancy. Grain should map to the surface of the objects in the scene. This will prevent the sheet-of-grain phenomenon and avoid stereo discrepancies.

Depth Generation

The broad artistic depth-generation phase of the process creates one or more additional perspectives, thereby creating a 3D effect. The primary goal when generating depth should be to create a comfortable viewing experience. Even with the inherent benefits of conversion, like perfectly aligned perspectives and perfectly matched exposure, it is possible to cause the viewer discomfort.

Viewers' interpupillary distance (IPD) needs to be taken into account. Adults have an average IPD of 6.5 cm (2.5 inches) and children ages 6 to 11 have an average IPD of 5.1 cm (2 inches). Along with this knowledge, target screen size should also be considered. If the positive parallax of the image is more than the target audience's IPD, the viewers' eyes may diverge or go walleyed. This can cause discomfort, like headaches, especially in children and is likely to take the viewer out of the story because of eyestrain. Since the stereographer will not have control over the final screen widths, with the exception of an IMAX venue, positive parallax values must be averaged. Many digital feature animation studios use a starting positive parallax value of 17 to 20 pixels of separation to represent infinity—based on a 2048 resolution image. Often the final released parallax limit is 11 pixels. These decisions are usually driven by the current average digital 3D screen size. A free application called the Depth Machine can be used to analyze parallax and its implications in terms of perceived depth and screen size. This tool can be found at http://thedimensionalists.com.

Depth continuity is another important factor in creating a comfortable viewing experience. It is essential to be sensitive to how depth transitions from shot to shot in terms of where the focal element is placed in Z-space and what the range of depth is. Range of depth refers to the negative and positive parallax extremes of a shot. In effect, the negative and positive parallax limits built into a shot define the overall depth of the world, commonly known as a *pixel parallax budget*. If those limits are changed dramatically from one shot to the next, the viewer's visual system will attempt to accommodate, or reorient itself, to the new visual world, thus potentially missing the film's intention or performance and may cause eye fatigue. These considerations are not meant to imply that the focal element's placement in Z-space or that overall depth must be exactly the same from shot to shot. Rather, these decisions should be made consciously in order to provide a comfortable experience that allows the viewer to experience the story.

Continuity of depth is used in 3D feature animation and 3D performance capture to control the volume of the characters throughout the film based on their importance or emotional performance. Depth grading is commonly used to enhance the character performance or the audiences' participation in the scene. On *Meet the Robinsons* (2007), the viewing distance to a character equated to the emotional distance of the character, creating an emotional void for the viewer. Likewise, emotionally involved performances were graded closer to the viewer, encroaching on the viewer's personal space as a way to increase the emotional intensity. Another technique is changing the volume of a character to draw the viewer's eye. Generally the character volume should be consistent throughout a scene. However, on *A Christmas Carol* (2009), character volume was occasionally used to determine character importance in the scene. In test screenings, it was revealed that rounder characters were perceived as more important than flatter characters.

A 2D-to-3D conversion has a level of dimensional flexibility challenged only by 3D feature animation and 3D performance capture. This flexibility provides great artistic opportunities. Generally, it is advisable to reinforce the director's intent. As an example of this, consider two shots, A and B. Shot A is a long-lens shot toward a woman running from a monster that pursues her from behind. Shot B is a medium-lens shot following the woman from behind as she runs down an open trail, with no chance of escape. It is reasonable to infer that the director used a long lens in shot A to "compress," in a 2D manner, the depth between the woman and the monster. It is also reasonable to infer that shot B was shot with a short lens to make any avenue of escape appear far away. The director's intent in shot A can be reinforced by creating minimal separation between the woman and the monster, and hence increasing the sense that she will be caught. In shot B the depth of the road can be extended far out into positive parallax, to make her salvation seem impossible to reach.

Another way to capitalize on the flexibility of conversion is to tailor the depth to the edit. If a scene is made of long shots, a viewer has more time to take in the depth. If a scene is made of short cuts, the viewer may have a hard time taking in a shot with a lot of depth. So, for short cuts, it may be advantageous to have a modest depth budget so the viewer can more easily see what is happening. The same theory can be applied to camera motion as well.

When choreographing position and volume, it is important to consider the scale these depth choices imply. Think of a wide shot of a 100-foot giant projected where his image is 10 feet tall on the screen. In a 2D environment the viewer is used to seeing this scenario and relies on the implicit 2D depth cues to infer size and distance. Once explicit depth choices are made, it is important to be sensitive to the scale that is implied with the depth choices. Consider a scene where the skyline plays at 2.5 inches positive parallax and the giant plays at the screen level; the giant will likely be perceived as "miniaturized." The position in Z-space of the giant is definitive and so is his perceived size. Because he is placed at the screen plane and his projected image is only 10 feet tall, he will be perceived as 10 feet tall. If he were placed at about 2.2 inches of positive parallax he would appear to be the correct size. Because the giant's height on screen is only 10 feet he needs to be positioned beyond the screen, at a point where the 100-foot giant would occupy 10 feet of the viewer's visual field (Figure 5.15). Generally, issues of accurate scale pertain, to a larger degree, to shots captured with lenses that approximate the human eye (50mm on 35mm film).

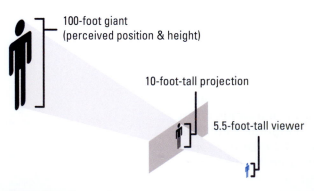

100-foot giant
(perceived position & height)

10-foot-tall projection

5.5-foot-tall viewer

Figure 5.15 Perception of scale. (Image courtesy of Matthew DeJohn.)

Miniaturization tends to be an issue with objects that are larger in reality than they are when projected on the screen. The opposite phenomenon is present with objects that are smaller in reality than they are when projected on the screen, such as a 10-foot-tall projection of a normal person's face. However, the scale issue present when this person's face is positioned at the screen level does not seem to be as offensive to viewers.

Another consideration when dealing with the scale position in Z-space is the way it can be used to tell the story. If a director wants to make a person feel more powerful during a dialogue scene made up of neutrally framed medium shots, the director can place the dominant character farther in screen. This will create the sense that this person is larger and perhaps more powerful.

Some other items to consider when generating depth: Is the content a still or a motion clip? A still will require much more detail because it has to be compelling when viewed for long periods, and motion depth cues cannot be leveraged to help sell the 3D effect. A motion clip can more heavily rely on motion depth cues and can have detail commensurate with the length of the clip. The longer the clip, the more detail necessary to sell the effect. What is the effect on occluded surface reconstruction? The amount of depth greatly affects how long occluded surface reconstruction will take. The greater the depth, the more image data that needs to be reconstructed.

Major 2D-to-3D Conversion Workflows

There are as many approaches to extruding an image as there are software packages. The two major approaches to 2D-to-3D conversion are *re-projection mapping* and *pixel displacement*. Both of these approaches share the three major artistic phases described earlier: element isolation, occluded surface reconstruction, and depth generation. These two main approaches are distinguished by their depth creation paradigms. Re-projection mapping creates a stereoscopic effect within a virtual 3D environment by projecting images onto geometry from one perspective and rendering from the alternate perspective. Pixel displacement creates a stereoscopic effect by horizontally displacing pixels from a mono image to create one or more alternate perspectives. In both workflows, by using a single perspective as the master view, the alternate view can be synthetically generated and art directed. The choice of methods is determined by software and skill sets. The fundamental result is a pair of image streams that, when presented to the audience, create the sensation of stereoscopic depth.

Special Cases

Reflections, transparencies, motion blur, and deep focus all need special consideration when organizing the depth generation of the image. The approach is rarely easy or straightforward when planning depth extraction of these elements.

Transparencies

Images with transparent surfaces encode two levels of depth, the pixel displacement representing the spatial position of the transparent surface and the pixel displacement of the surfaces behind the transparent surface, both of which are described on a single surface. The complexity of the depth generation depends on the complexity of the surface on the transparent object. If it has intricate details care should be taken to retain the surface integrity. However, the occasion may arise when surfaces may need complete reconstruction. A two-step approach could include a surface reconstruction of both respective surfaces, followed by a traditional visual effects comp to combine the surfaces as originally shot.

Motion blur and deep focus should be handled as a subset of transparent surfaces, where similar depth generation may be applied in the blur boundary overlap between foreground and background surfaces.

Reflections

Mirrored reflections can present an additional challenge, especially if the reflective surface is a narrative or focal point of a shot. Although not initially apparent in a 2D image, a mirrored surface does represent additional depth in the scene and if not taken into account could introduce IPD disparity. Allowances should be made if mirrored surfaces exist while calculating the overall stereo pixel parallax budget. Additionally, all of the depth-generation techniques can be used to shape a reflection or transparency; labor and production costs should be considered because diminishing returns are a potential consequence.

Re-Projection Mapping Method Workflow

The benefit of this approach is that it provides flexibility to manipulate the scene and is a familiar concept for artists to grasp. Organizing elements by volume is essential in this workflow. One method for organizing elements is identifying objects that visibly touch. This is commonly called *connective tissue* (see Figure 5.14). Objects with connective tissue are tied into the same volumetric space as surrounding objects and cannot be individually graded for depth. Generally the connective tissue is obvious, such as a character embracing another character; obviously both characters are occupying like space and are of similar volume. Any object that interacts with any other object, within the frame, should be considered "touching." Easily overlooked but equally important are atmospheric effects such as snow, rain, fog, and particulates.

The following represent the basic steps in this process workflow:

1. *Matchmove the camera to the plate:* The success of the re-projection workflow relies on a proper camera matchmove. Accurate real-world position, rotation, and focal length will allow for properly scaled set geometry and camera interaxial values, which help the stereographer define the depth. If this method is approached like a traditional visual effects shot, it will make the remaining steps less burdensome.

2. *Isolate the objects in the plate:* A number of industry techniques are used to isolate elements from a plate, the most common of which are rotoscoping, luminance or difference mattes, or a combination of any or all. Use the connective tissue guideline to decide which elements are rotoscoped. It is easy to overthink rotoscoping of articulated mattes. But keep in mind that sometimes loose and rough mattes will suffice; thorough testing should be done prior to investing in articulates. Try to keep objects on similar parallax planes in the same roto spline or at least grouped together. Beware of objects that recede into the distance—they may need additional rotoscoping of overlapping depth, depending on the negative parallax amount.

3. *Model low-resolution approximate set and environment geometry:* The brain is quite forgiving when presented with a stereo pair, so accurate geometry isn't always necessary for most depth generation. Simple geometric shapes augmenting depth cues already present will produce a rich and interesting stereoscopic image.

4. *Model and rig low-resolution character geometry:* Character models can be as rough or as detailed as the scene demands. A small library of generic bipeds is recommended as a base, and higher resolution models can be created when more topological detail is required. Most characters will need simple forward/reverse IK rigs, but keep it simple for the animation team.

5. *Match-animate the characters and geometries:* Animate characters to the best possible space approximation. Accurate placement of the character in the environment with respect to the camera lens is critical for proper depth generation. Be aware that spatial tricks will be quickly spotted in the stereoscopic

medium. It is recommended that the animation team be accurate in the placement of props and characters.

6. *Re-project the plate through the left camera:* Digital feature animation and most major visual effects houses consider the *left* camera perspective to be the original plate as shot. By projecting the plate through the left camera and onto the set and character geometries, a virtual set is created that can be rendered by a right camera perspective, thus creating a convincing stereoscopic synthesis of the 2D plate. Additionally, by using an off-axis stereo rig for the *right* camera, the post-production workload is simplified. It is highly recommended that toe-in camera rigs be avoided for depth generation because they eliminate the flexibility for simple parallax pixel shifting that is afforded by an off-axis pair.

7. *Occlusion surface reconstruction:*

   a. The right eye render will reveal interposition occlusions that are now visible because the right perspective now reveals surfaces that were previously behind foreground objects. To sustain realistic stereo, this missing information must be "painted" back into the plate where the object was moved to create the effect (previously discussed as OSR). A number of paint packages or simple pixel filling algorithms can be used to accomplish this feat, but be forewarned that complex and nonrepeating texture structure such as human faces as well as unique patterns will be difficult, if not impossible, to synthesize via these methods. Laborious frame-by-frame paintwork may be called on to complete a reconstruction effort.

   b. Organizing one's paint will help identify problem areas and alleviate frame management issues. Begin work at the background and work forward, layering each isolated element. Each element will be re-projected onto the geometry and re-rendered as a right eye perspective. Proper organization of layers will help guide a clean composite. Ensure that any object between the camera and the isolated element is painted from the element's surface; otherwise a "doubling" effect will be experienced when viewed in stereo.

   c. If there are multiple objects that interweave or overlap and contain a large distance between them, occlusion reconstruction becomes exponentially more difficult and may require a smaller parallax pixel budget. Proper depth planning at an early stage will result in an easier and possibly less expensive extrusion.

   d. Each reconstructed layer should be stored in a fashion that is easy to access by a compositing package. Some complex depth extrusions can generate half a dozen or more layers per eye, so rigid naming conventions are recommended.

8. *Rendering the right eye perspective:*
   a. Render each piece of geometry with its respective clean texture mapped using an off-axis or parallel right eye camera into a new image. This new image should be considered the "stereo pass" for each subsequent isolated element.
   b. In a compositing package, read each stereo pass, associated roto, and/or procedural alpha mattes. Cut the stereo pass image with the alpha matte and composite background-to-foreground for each respective element for each eye.
   c. The resulting composite should be run for left and right eyes. The left image should closely resemble the original plate; the right should produce a synthetic view that is pixel-parallax-shifted for each level of depth.

Pixel Displacement or Pixel Shifting

Pixel displacement is the other major approach to 2D-to-3D conversion. This process works by displacing a 2D images pixels in order to simulate an alternate perspective, hence creating a 3D effect when viewed by the audience. Through whole-pixel and subpixel moves, distinct separation between elements and fully featured shaping can be achieved. Basic pixel shifting, and even some rudimentary shaping, can be achieved in a 2D composite.

For more accurate shaping, mesh warp tools or depth mattes generated by a variety of methods (match-animation, extraction from a color channel, paint) can be used. This approach can be very flexible if every object has its own depth matte. As with the other major 2D-to-3D conversion approach, this process requires extensive element isolation and OSR. This approach is often attempted with off-the-shelf software, which can be complicated because many applications do not support sufficient stereoscopic display methods and are not able to efficiently handle layer ordering issues that arise during conversion.

Dimensionalization, used by In-Three,[10] is a process that employs the pixel displacement concept. This patented process makes use of custom software that allows an artist to quickly match-animate a scene to drive pixel-shifting algorithms. Similar to the re-projection workflow, an artist creates a 3D geometry, but unlike the re-projection workflow, the 3D effect is generated without the use of virtual cameras. This approach allows depth to be controlled very quickly and granularly.

---

[10] In-Three Inc., 4580 E. Thousand Oaks Blvd., Westlake Village, CA 91362. www.in-three.com.

Minor 2D-to-3D Conversion Workflows

Other 2D-to-3D conversion workflows, including automatic conversion, temporal offset, and dynamic temporal offset, are used less frequently because they are limited in applicability and/or quality.

Automatic Conversion

For the purposes of this chapter, automated conversion refers to a process that extracts depth through an algorithm with little to no user input. Optical flow technologies can be used to automatically convert a shot. Camera motion or, less commonly, subject motion, in any direction will yield different perspectives of the scene. Similar to how humans can perceive depth through motion parallax, optical flow technologies, detect motion parallax. Motion vectors, created by optical flow technologies, can be converted to depth maps, which can be used to drive pixel displacement. The amount of displacement will correspond to the intensity of the motion of that pixel, creating an alternate perspective. This approach is very useful for highly complex objects that are static as the camera moves through space.

The benefit of this approach is that it has the potential to yield highly accurate results with little work from the artist. The downside is that the objects within a shot often have their own independent motion, which can make the motion vector unusable. Also, this approach still requires OSR.

Temporal Offset

Temporal offset is another approach that can yield highly accurate results very quickly. In this process a copy of the original 2D image sequence is offset in time and then assigned as the other perspective. This approach only works with a trucking shot[11] of static objects. The advantage of this technique over an automated process is that there are no algorithmic inaccuracies and usually no paint is required. Pans while trucking complicate the approach, but are still possible to accommodate. The cons of this process are that the subject must be static, and there is limited control over the depth of the scene. Depth choice is limited to offsetting the images in 1/24th-of-a-second increments.

---

[11] Trucking shot: camera movement that is perpendicular to the direction of the camera lens.

Dynamic Temporal Offset

Dynamic temporal offset capitalizes on the benefits of the temporal displacement process while allowing for some dynamic objects in the frame. For example, consider a trucking shot of a house with kids playing on the lawn. Without the children this shot would be perfect for temporal displacement. So, if the children are painted out, the shot can be temporally offset to create a stereo pair. Then the children, who could be converted via a major 2D-to-3D conversion method, would be composited into the stereo pair.

Is "Real" Always Right?

In 2D-to-3D conversion, and 3D in general, "real"[12] is often not right. Everything about the theater environment is not real. A human face can be projected 10 feet tall, one's view of the world changes in 1/24th-of-a-second intervals and the eyes always focus on the screen while converging somewhere else in space. Recognizing that 3D film is only an artistic representation of the real world provides the freedom to find the best way to represent it.

While compressing depth for a quickly edited scene may not be a real representation of parallax, it likely is the most comfortable way to present that scene in 3D. While the example of the woman running from the monster does not realistically portray the distance from her to the monster, those views help the viewer better experience the danger she is in. The realization that "real" is not necessarily "right" is why CG 3D employs multiple virtual camera rigs. So in 2D-to-3D conversion it is not necessary to feel constrained by real geometry or other measures of "real." The goal should be to find what is comfortable, what feels right, and what is most effective to present and tell the story.

3D STEREOSCOPIC VISUAL EFFECTS
Christopher Townsend

The world of visual effects presents an ever-changing landscape. From simple wire removal, to the seamless integration of a digital character in a live-action set, to the compositing of an actor into a complex computer-generated organic environment, every sequence can be a challenge. Creating visual effects for a stereo film increases all of those challenges dramatically. Two versions

---

[12] *Real* means that the relative relationships between an object's position, perspective, and volume are mathematically accurate and consistent with the results that are achieved if the scene was captured with a stereoscopic camera rig.

of every shot have to be created that not only work as individual images in their own right, but also have to coexist as a single version—a single stereo pair—so that every nuance and subtlety created for one eye has to be exactly duplicated in the correct manner to be seen with the other.

During the past 50 years or so, visual effects professionals have developed a big bag of tricks; they have come to rely on certain techniques and assumptions that have allowed them to wow an audience or trick the audience into believing they are seeing something that they are not. Is that crop duster really flying over Cary Grant in *North by Northwest* (1959)? Is that dinosaur really tossing that Jeep around like a toy in *Jurassic Park* (1993)? Is Johnny Depp really out at sea in a maelstrom in *Pirates of the Caribbean* (2007)?

These mono films, as spectacular as they are, lack one entire real-world part of the experience: the second eye. As a consequence, any visible depth cueing doesn't have to deal with that aspect of reality. If something needs to be pushed farther away, the standard things to do are to make it smaller, reduce its contrast, and put it behind something else, all of which help define its spatial place in the cinematic world. That is in mono. In a stereo presentation, the object's literal place, as defined by how the left and right images compare, describes exactly where that object lies relative to everything else. This means that not only do those same subjective mono tricks need to be employed, but they also need to work alongside the far more objective science of stereography. If it is wrong, then a tree in the far background is suddenly not so far away. Maybe its scale doesn't work with its relative spatial placement, implying that the tree must be miniature and creating a scale anomaly; or maybe it is occluded by the person apparently walking in front of it but spatially walking behind, creating a stereo contradiction.

Making a stereo feature film requires using everything already known about visual effects, along with the science of stereography. Currently, there is a renaissance in stereo filmmaking, so consequently some obvious stereo moments with things jumping off the screen are what an audience expects. However, as this part of the industry matures, stereo films will have to do less of that and simply rely on the added dimension to naturally make it a far more immersive experience than a normal mono presentation.

In creating a full-length dramatic feature, rather than a short-format piece, filmmakers have to be incredibly sensitive to an audience's comfort. For many stereo presentations in the past, eyestrain, headaches, and fatigue have been a very real problem. In a 10-minute stereo ride film, making a viewer perform eye gymnastics is probably acceptable; however, for something long form, particularly one that has a narrative, things will be too painful and viewers will just get up and leave.

Prepping for the Third Dimension

As natural binocular viewers, humans are incredibly sensitive to stereo anomalies. One of the fundamental rules going into a stereo project is that the stereo space can't be cheated, which means, in terms of production design, that sets can't be created that rely on forced perspective or use painted backdrops: One eye will tell the audience member that something is far away (for example, a cityscape behind the actors is clearly in the distance, because the buildings are small and there's a lot of atmospheric haze in the air), but with both eyes they will realize that it is actually only a few feet behind the actors and all on one flat plane (because stereo vision reveals its placement in space).

That working methodology translates directly to everything in visual effects. The virtual sets have to be similarly created; if the environment is supposed to be huge, it has to be created with 3D geometry. When a shot is being planned, it has to be designed so that it uses the depth effectively: rather than putting a wall parallel to the camera, placing it at an angle will lead the eye deeper into the image; when an object smashes into something, having the debris fly off the screen into the audience will take advantage of the stereo fun factor; rather than having a vast open space, placing things in the foreground and midground will help describe the volume better.

Even though 3D films have been around since the 1920s, stereo filmmaking today is in many ways in its infancy; high-definition cameras and projectors have transformed this aspect of filmmaking, where quality and consistency are now paramount. In many ways there are no defined standards yet, so there is not necessarily a right way to do things or a particular way to solve problems. A stereo pair of images should differ from each other only as a horizontal offset, often called the *convergence* or *image separation* (this describes where an object is in space), and as a perspective view, which is dependent on the distance between the lenses, often called the *interocular* or *interaxial distance* (this describes the stereo volume). However, photographed stereo imagery is likely to have various technical issues. Lenses, however well matched optically, will always have some discrepancies, particularly with their optical centers. Technical adjustments may be needed if the left and right eyes are differently scaled; not vertically aligned; if one is more rotated or skewed; or if any exposure, color, or specular value of one is different from that of the other. Any keystoning may need to be removed to rectify the images. Keystoning occurs when a pair of cameras is toed in, resulting in mismatched trapezoidal images caused by the film planes not being parallel to the view.

Shooting the Third Dimension

There are generally two different types of stereo camera rigs: a side-by-side rig and a beamsplitter. The side-by-side rig is the larger of the two units, with both lenses set parallel to each other and the cameras mounted on a symmetrical motorized rig. Changes in interocular distance result from altering the physical distance between both cameras (the minimum interocular distance is dependent on the lens diameters); changes in convergence result from rotating both cameras. The beamsplitter's right camera is on a horizontal motorized plate, allowing for rotation (for convergence) and translation (for interocular) and shot through a 45-degree one-way mirror. The left camera is on a vertical fixed plate, pointing down, and shoots the reflection from the mirror.

Though initially it may seem like a side-by-side rig is a far simpler and more robust solution than a beamsplitter, the physical limitations of the cameras and lenses limit how close the lenses can get to each other. If large lenses are used, then it is likely that the interocular is greater than the human stereo viewing interocular (the eyes are only about 2.5 inches apart), so this will immediately cause everything to look smaller. On long-lens shots or big vistas, a larger interocular is often desirable, because it increases the stereo effect. On close-ups or shots using a wide-angle lens, however, often an interocular between 0.5 and 1.5 inches is preferable and more comfortable.

The advantage of the beamsplitter rig is that the interocular can go down to 0 inches. However, along with the inherent geometric differences in the two lenses, the mirror introduces another layer of problems: The left image may be slightly softer and flopped, and there may be color and exposure differences, and more geometric warping will be introduced.

Geometric differences between the left and right images need to be corrected on a take-by-take basis, and when possible should be done during shooting. At the start of every shot, a chart should be placed several feet in front of the rig, perpendicular to it. Convergence should be set on the chart and then the angle of the mirror should be adjusted. The tension on each corner of the mirror may need to be tweaked, and the individual cameras may need to be repositioned. The aim is to line the images up, when viewed as a 50/50 mix. Depending on the tilt angle of the rig, gravity may cause different parts of the rig to sag, thus causing unwanted geometric differences between the lenses. This means that an average setting has to be found for a shot with a big move (particularly a tilt) because, depending on the rig's position, the geometric differences will change.

Image sharpening can be handled as a post-production process where necessary. Because most people are right-eye dominant, and with two images giving essentially very similar information to the brain, some slight softness in the left eye is possibly acceptable. When using the beamsplitter, the left image should be flopped when it is recorded. However, sometimes due to technical issues, this may not always happen, so it has to be flopped later by the visual effects facility. Along with handling all of this, color and exposure have to be closely monitored and corrected as much as possible during shooting.

The stereo shooting process is complex to say the least, with a lot of time needed to prep and test in pre-production, and then during principal photography, to monitor the quality of the stereo space. A huge effort has to go into making the rigs and lenses as robust and accurate as possible during the pre-production period. The camera crews have to do major recalibrations of the stereo system prior to the start of shooting and tweak the setup throughout the day.

Images can be recorded onto tape, hard drive, or portable memory card. A good argument can still be made for using a tape-based system, because this uses the most familiar current workflow, and testing has shown that there is negligible, if any, quality difference between, for example, Sony HDCAM SR tape and a hard-disk solution. Creating a whole new workflow with extreme data management issues may be required for a hard-disk solution, though this will become less of an issue as the industry becomes more familiar with a digital start-to-finish process.

Visual Effects in the Third Dimension

For shooting visual effects shots, a lot of tracking markers and cubes should probably be used to assist in the camera tracking process. Even with metadata (general lens information including focal length, *f*-stop, convergence, and interocular), which can be supplied with every shot to a visual effects facility, tracking can easily become a nightmare. Having a large quantity of markers and cubes to paint out will be painful for the paint/roto/comp crews, but the shots will fail if they can't be tracked. Seeing tracking mistakes in stereo is doubly bad!

The no-cheating rule, when it comes to dealing with stereo space, follows into post-production. Layout, environment design, and compositing all have to follow the rules. This means that if something is supposed to be 100 feet away, physically (in the virtual world) it has to be placed that same distance away, with the correct corresponding CG environment to support it. Matte paintings have to exist in 3D space, projected onto CG geometry rather than just being painted on a flat plane or a cyclorama.

Some visual effects techniques, such as adding extreme camera shake, need to be reevaluated in a stereo film, because it is very hard to resolve a fast-moving image that is too different frame to frame. This is the same reason why fast-paced editing can be less comfortable to watch and less effective in stereo. Lens flares also pose an interesting dilemma. They are often added for creative reasons in mono films, but suddenly in stereo they need to be more carefully created, in an artificial way, to work volumetrically, but not necessarily photographically.

Perception of the volume of a space is obviously affected by not only the mono cues, but by the stereo ones too. It is often challenging to determine how the geometry, the camera move, the lenses used, the interocular, the convergence point, and the lighting or the compositing is influencing the scale of an environment relative to the actors in it. More often than not, it is a combination of some of these things. So, if an environment looks flat, what should be changed? If it looks miniature, or multiplaned rather than volumetric, what should be altered? All of these questions have to be asked, and many iterations created, in order to determine the solutions based on perception of stereo, while viewing the results on a big screen.

Flares and lens artifacts often appear only in one eye and sometimes need to be painted out or replicated so that both eyes match. The right eye may look correct, as may the left, but together, while reviewing on a stereo screen, the issues will become apparent. It is often down to a personal judgment call as to whether these need to be fixed; some people's stereo perception is far more acute than others'.

Photographed Elements

Stereo photographed elements need to be accurately occluded in stereo space; cheating doesn't work. For example, trying to combine photographed dust or splash elements with CG creatures can be extremely challenging. If incorrectly done, in stereo it will be totally apparent that part of an element, which should be behind a creature, is actually composited in front. Generally, elements (dust, splashes, smoke, etc.) need to be photographed in a shot-specific way, using a totally accurate animated mandrel (a solid form that replicates the volume of the CG creature that will be added later) as a holdout object. Often this is not practical. Broad volumetric elements (rain, etc.) need to be very carefully placed in stereo space in order not to intersect another object. A mono photographed element projected onto a plane often does not work. If an element would be volumetric, it generally should be volumetric (dust, smoke, fog, etc.), so in most cases it is easier to work exclusively in CG rather than try to incorporate photographed elements.

Accuracy and Attention to Detail

Subpixel accuracy is required for correctly placing elements in stereo space, whether it is to ensure a correct eye line (for interaction between an actor and a CG creature, for example) or contact between CG elements and photographed ones (feet contact on a CG ground plane, splashes on a CG ocean, etc.). Artists are required to work with a much higher attention to detail, so they need higher quality screening systems (projected stereo HD) in order to see, understand, and solve the stereo issues. Artists also need to appreciate these new higher technical standards and embrace this new aspect of visual effects.

Artistic Skill Level

The overall skill level of artists being able to understand and analyze stereo problems is currently quite low, because most people have little experience working with dual-stream imagery. As artists work more on stereo projects, these skill levels will increase and the work will evolve to the same standards as those for mono features. Technically it is far harder to work in stereo, because everything has to be carefully considered and calculated, rather than allowing the artist to rely on past visual effects experiences.

If an image looks wrong it could be for any number of reasons: Any individual element within the shot could be swapped, left and right; it could be offset in some other way rather than just horizontally; it could be in the wrong stereo space, conflicting with something else in the shot; the left and right eyes could be at different exposures or different hues; or any of the usual visual effects gotchas could apply (exposure, matte lines, blur value, etc.). More than likely, a combination of some of these will be the problem. Soft-edged elements (steam, smoke, etc.) are particularly difficult to analyze. Currently, too much effort and too many resources are required just to make a shot work correctly in stereo space, leaving less time to finesse the actual visual effects within a shot.

Data Management

With twice the number of images for every shot, data management becomes dramatically harder, both for production and for the visual effects facilities. Editorial notes need to be accurate, are often far more complex than their mono equivalent, and need to be followed absolutely at initial shot setup. Attempting to correct any errors created early in the process, once a shot is in progress, can be extremely challenging. Photographed plates, bluescreen elements, mattes, all individual render passes, pre-comps—everything is doubled. Accidentally swapping the left and right eye of an individual element or creating the left and right eye out of sync will cause headaches, both from a data management point of view and literally, if not caught, from the viewer's perspective. All of this points to the need to create a robust input/output workflow that is accurate, efficient, and capable of handling large amounts of data.

Not only do the technical aspects of correcting the stereo need to be addressed, but also the creative challenges. Stereo perception is so heavily based on screen size that stereo-specific creative calls can only be made on a screen that accurately replicates the intended theatrical one. This means that visual effects facilities should have a projection screening room, accessible by artists, in which they should be frequently reviewing their work. The VFX Supervisor also needs a screening room to review stereo dailies and to present shots to the Director. Depending on the editorial workflow, the only place to see shots on a large screen in cut context is possibly at the digital intermediate (DI) stage. From an editorial perspective, depending on cutting workflows it may be necessary to make convergence changes as the cut is viewed in stereo on a large screen, within a stereo-capable DI suite.

Conclusion

So, is it worth it? Absolutely. Making a stereo movie is definitely more complex and challenging than making a mono one, and creating visual effects for such a movie follows this truth. But when it works, and the audience reaction is witnessed, it is soon realized that the cinematic experience is much more immersive when in stereo. Whether it is as viewers reaching out toward the screen to "catch" that object floating out toward the audience or ducking when a creature flies over their head, or just sitting, enthralled at being within the world showing up on the screen, it is soon realized that this represents the future of filmmaking. As big and as important a step as the one from silent films to talkies or from black-and-white to color, the transition from mono to stereo represents another huge leap forward toward a more realistic representation of the world, where stories and visuals work in harmony to take the viewers on the ride of their lives. As more films are made in stereo, so too do we, in the visual effects community, have to go along for that ride.

3D STEREO DIGITAL INTERMEDIATE WORKFLOW
Jeff Olm, Brian Gaffney

This section features post-production processes and challenges leading up to the 3D stereo digital intermediate (DI) stage. The items discussed include 3D dailies workflows, the editorial and viewing options available, and the post-production challenges that need to be addressed to help complete the entire end-to-end workflow for 3D stereoscopic post and DI.

An essential part of any digital workflow process is organizing the material and data. It is very important to set up the proper structure before the post-production process starts to make sure the clients' creative expectations are realized for this exciting visualization technique.

The 3D stereo colorist is an essential part of the creative process because the overall look will help support the story and complement the 3D images with shadow, depth, and overall color. The colorist and the DI team are responsible for the final technical quality of the image and will use the DI tools to refine the look and feel of the stereo images. Various software tools are used to correct for imperfections in the stereo image pairs as detailed in the following paragraphs. The 3D stereo colorists' toolbox will include image pre-processing tools and additional post-production techniques used for convergence fixes, ghosting, grain, and noise reduction.

Stereoscopic 3D Process Milestones

The project must be broken down into a series of milestones. These include the final edit or locked cut, reel conform, technical color correction, creative color correction, preview screenings, and final deliverables. It is essential to work hand-in-hand with the I/O, data management, off-line, and creative editorial teams to make sure that a proper conform can be accomplished and verified. A variety of camera systems and data acquisition formats are available that allow for good organization of the stereo images.

Film is still a viable image capture option for 3D; however, due to the cost of post-production for 3D stereography, digital acquisition is more widely used in production. These have been outlined in previous sections; however, Figures 5.16 and 5.17 will

Camera	Resolution	Video/data	File format
Sony F900, F950, HDC-1500 F23, F35	1920 × 1080	HD video output	n/a
Red	4096 × 2304	Data output	R3D
SI-2K	2048 × 1152	Data output	CineForm

Figure 5.16 Commonly used cameras for 3D capture. (Image courtesy of Technicolor Creative Services.)

Type	Recorder description
Solid state	Includes flash packs, compact flash, SSR-1, OB-1, etc. Capture camera output as data. Lightweight and lowest power requirement. Usually mounted on camera. Dailies may be played out to HD tape or a data archive may be created. Capacity varies per unit from 4–43 minutes.
CODEX	Can record single stream (one eye) or dual stream (two eyes) to multiple disk packs (removable drive array). External device requiring cables running from camera. Video or data inputs. Offers redundant recording if desired. Can output capture data as DPX, DNxHD. MXF, Quick Time, AVI, BMP, JPG, and WAV. Data must be archived or played to HD videotape.
S. Two (OB-1 covered in solid state)	Records uncompressed DPX files to drive array. External device requiring cables running from camera. Video or data inputs. Data must be archived or played to HD videotape.
HD CAM SRW-1	Can record single stream (one eye) to a single tape as compressed 4:4:4 on dual stream (two eyes) to a single tape as compressed 4:2:2. Major advantages are the ease of working with a commonly adopted tape format and no need to archive data after each day's shoot. External device requiring cables running from camera.

Figure 5.17 Common 3D capture media. (Image courtesy of Technicolor Creative Services.)

help you review the most commonly used cameras for 3D stereo acquisition and the recording systems used for 3D image capture.

Understanding what the production needs are to properly visualize a story will typically define the camera choice. Understanding what the expectations are for editorial, visual effects, and overall budget constraints will also help define what workflow choices exist to provide an efficient post-production process. These are some of the first milestones to set when planning any post-production workflow in 2D, let alone in 3D stereoscopic production.

Like all 2D productions, the direction and cinematography are assisted by the use of production dailies, a well-understood and mature process for broadcast and feature film. Although not new (in fact, it was developed by Sir Charles Wheatstone in 1840), 3D stereo image acquisition is still not a standard, and the use of digital 3D stereo dailies is not a mature process. Hence, many different techniques have been deployed to address the viewing experience and to support the editorial experience and still provide a process by which the media is cost effectively produced.

Viewing 3D Dailies

Dailies are used for many reasons and depending on the role in production the requirements may be different. An executive who views dailies may be more interested in how the main talent looks and is responding to the Director, but for the Director of Photography, it is more about the lighting and focus of the 3D images.

Affordable dailies are usually standard definition DVDs sent to set. DVDs are currently not 3D, so another process is required to support the DP, the Director, the Producers, and the Editor. Viewing 3D Blu-ray media or even 3D QuickTime files requires a 3D display.

The current 3D viewing environments range from traditional anaglyph viewing on any monitor to custom projection environments and polarized LCD displays.

The choices for 3D viewing can be summarized as follows:

- anaglyph,
- active glasses and passive glasses,
- dual stacked projectors,
- single projector,
- circular polarization,
- linear polarization, and
- triple flash/120Hz LCD displays.

Linear and Circular Polarization

The above examples of 3D viewing choices review linear and circular polarization. The effect of polarization is that it separates the images and allows for the brain to be fooled and to visualize the Z-depth between the interaxial offset of the left eye and right eye sources.

Linear polarization polarizes each eye by 90 degrees. The light is then projected with two projectors, and the screen used maintains the polarization state. The process has minimal crosstalk between the eyes (image leaking from one eye to the other eye). Linear polarization is not tolerant of head tilt, and ghosting can increase if the polarizer's are not exactly 90 degrees apart.

Circular polarization uses left- and right-hand polarization to separate the images. The eyewear also employs circular polarization of the lenses.

This process can be used with dual stacked projectors or with one using circular polarization switching such as the RealD system and their patented Z-screen, which is a silver screen that maintains the polarization state. This technique is much more tolerant of head tilt, which makes for a more comfortable viewing experience.

Active Glasses versus Passive Glasses

A single projector with active glasses can make use of a matte white screen, the most common installation in theaters. When the switching cycle of the glasses and the time when the shutter is closed are factored in, the lens efficiency of the glasses yields about an overall 17% efficiency rating (including the screen gain).

If a second projector is added, the efficiency (or brightness) will increase. Replacing the matte white screen with a silver screen has a gain component of approximately 2.4× this value.

On the other hand, a single-projector setup with passive glasses deals with other issues that affect the efficiency rating. There is absorption from the active modulator inside the projector. The left eye and right eye are only on half of the time, reducing light output. There is blanking in the left eye and right eye between frames due to modulator switching. There is absorption at the glasses and then gain from the silver screen.

Projection Screens for 3D Stereoscopic Viewing

The United States has more than 30,000 theater screens and about 5,000 are 3D enabled at this point. The number of 3D stereo projection theaters is growing more slowly than expected due to general financing issues in the marketplace more than anything to do with the technology. However, the number of 3D theater screens is expected to grow with each subsequent release, with this growth typically happening around "tent pole" features such as that exhibited by James Cameron's *Avatar* (2009).

Developments in film projection for 3D projection have resurfaced with new lens assemblies from Technicolor that support "over/under" imaging. Using film projection for playback has been around since the 1940s, but the subsequent development of digital film recorder technology allows for the proper registration of two stereo images, positioned one on top of the other inside a single academy film frame. This has improved the stability, image brightness, and quality. Warner Brothers Studios released *Final Destination 4* (2009) in 3D using both digital projection with a RealD system as well as film projection with the Technicolor system. The advantage is that the system does not require a silver screen and this will certainly help increase the adoption of 3D theater screens in the marketplace.

In summary, the screen for 3D projection can be simplified such that if use of a matte white existing screen is desired, active glasses must be used. If using a RealD system with circular polarization, a silver screen must be installed. These screens have suffered from damage (the silver can flake off if rolled or scratched) and can exhibit light distribution issues such as hot spots. The improved brightness provided by the reflective silver screen, however, is the reason it is being deployed despite the cost and other issues.

LCD Displays for Viewing Dailies in Boardrooms and for Editorial Support

Due to the cost of 3D projection systems plus scheduling access to a theater to view 3D dailies, portable LCD displays of 24 to 46 inches and now even 100 inches in size are now being offered. These displays are nowhere as big as theater projection screens and limit the total viewing experience for color correction;

however, they offer the on-set, editorial, and executive board-room clients an affordable and high-quality way to view dailies.

These displays are primarily based on passive glasses technology. The Hyundai 46-inch display using the DDD[13] circular polarizing filter attached to the inside of the panel allows for the use of passive glasses and is the right size to fit into an editing bay or small conference room for viewing dailies.

The limitations are calibration to the DI theater and light leakage around the edges of the filter installed on the inside of the LCD glass panel. The monitors are HD capable and are usually 720p with resizing hardware to scale the image to 1920 × 1080. The refresh rate on these monitors is usually 60 or 120 Hz.

The Hyundai 46-inch monitor has been used by the studios, production and post-production facilities, and even at museums for 3D exhibits. A common use for a 3D LCD monitor of this size would be during editorial and visual effects visualization. Being able to view the 3D during the editorial process is key, especially when pacing the cuts of the story.

High-speed motion and quick cuts distract the viewer from the immersive experience they are having within the 3D space. Jarring the viewer out of this pace of motion loses the 3D immersive feeling and the images can revert to 2D in the brain. Therefore, the viewers "feel" pressure or fatigue on their eyes. Being able to view in 3D while still at the editing console can really assist an editor and director to modify the pace and flow of the storytelling process in 3D.

3D Editorial Processes

The 3D editorial process is twofold. First one must consider the acquisition camera and recording device, which may, in turn, define the editing system used and/or the workflow designed.

The editing systems discussed here are limited to the two systems actually used for 90% of all broadcast and feature productions: Avid's Adrenaline and Apple's Final Cut Pro (FCP).

Both of the systems are 2D editing systems and as of early 2010 had very little direct 3D viewing and editorial support. Avid uses a plug-in called MetaFuse that supports the tracking of left eye and right eye video timelines but does not allow for 3D viewing without a render pass. These are the early development days of the digital 3D stereoscopic tools for post-production; in the near future this market area will certainly have upgraded or reinvented itself.

---

[13] A commercial company that developed and patented a 3D polarizing film technology for LCD panels and has licensed this technology to several monitor manufacturers.

Final Cut Pro with support of the CineForm codec can allow for two timelines to be locked and played together through one single stream over HD SDI and with a quality that surpasses HDCAM SR in SQ mode. This output can then feed a RealD projection system or come out as HS SDI and feed a Hyundai display (via HDMI).

The CineForm toolset, within the Final Cut Pro editing system, supports image modification tools for offsetting the left eye and right eye with horizontal and vertical parallax to address issues from production. The issues arise during production when camera rigs are not properly aligned. When one camera is not properly converged with the other or the rig has been shifted and one eye is offset from the other, the parallax is observable and the editor can correct for some of these problems using these tools.

Human eyes are separated by approximately 66mm (approximately 2.5 inches) from center to center. This is known as the *interocular distance* between the eyes. In camera, this term is known as *interaxial*.[14] The essence of 3D stereoscopic production is separating the objects for left and right views and adding depth with lighting. The process is fundamentally based on replicating this ocular offset, called *interaxial offset*, which creates different views for each eye. If the two cameras are not properly aligned, parallax issues can arise that affect post-processing during editorial, visual effects, and the final DI.

Figure 5.18 Example of horizontal parallax. (Image courtesy of Matt Cowan, RealD.)

Horizontal parallax indicates a different distance between the viewer and objects between each eye. This type of parallax is normal (as the eyes are horizontally positioned). See Figure 5.18.

Vertical parallax is unnatural in the real world and can cause headaches and the feeling that the eyes are being concentrated on a small area of interest (like when crossing one's eyes). Real-world parallax is always in the direction of separation of the two eyes and is normally horizontal. See Figure 5.19.

With proper on-set monitoring, these gross examples

Figure 5.19 Example of vertical parallax. (Image courtesy of Matt Cowan, RealD.)

[14] Interaxial: term for offset between cameras on a stereo camera rig.

should be caught and resolved before they get to post-production; however, due to the challenges of 3D stereoscopic production and the time pressures, shots are sometimes affected and therefore tools are needed in post to resolve these issues.

Beyond the CineForm tools in their development kit for the codec they released for Final Cut Pro and other specialized plugins, a minimal toolset is available for editorial that allows for 3D stereo images to be easily fixed and rendered and addressed in a database for replication in visual effects and during the final conform and DI. As post-production shares these issues with software manufacturers, tools will become more readily available to address these issues in a more direct, straightforward, and easy way.

As described in the next section of this chapter, one of the 3D "eyes" will usually be chosen to be the "hero" eye or mono master. This is due to the fact that not all systems can display and play back two streams of SD or HD content from one timeline. Also, due to the fact that less than 10% of the screens today are 3D enabled, to secure a distribution deal, a studio will dictate that the product must be released in multiple formats (2D, DVD, Blu-ray, and 3D).

The editorial process typically cuts with one eye and then will have a post partner render and create the stereo version for the partner to preview and review the cut before it is locked to get a sense of the 3D stereoscopic feeling of the story.

The edit decision list (EDL) exported must be frame accurate and any ALE (Avid Log Exchange) file must reflect this so that when creating deliverables for dailies, encoding, and DVD creation, the elements can be married in stereo without any latency effects (one eye out of sync with the other eye).

3D Stereoscopic Conforming

The most important milestone for the digital intermediate team is the stereo conform process. It is essential for the stereo conform to be tested and reviewed by the editorial team to make sure that the process is perfect. A series of initial conforming tests should be completed before and as the reels are assembled. The digital intermediate process normally breaks down the project deliverables by reels. After each reel is conformed, the 2D color correction can begin or continue if an on-set solution was utilized. Although the final deliverable is 3D, the product is always released as a 2D deliverable to accommodate the broader audience. The majority of the color correction work is done in the 2D creative grade. This allows post to use the resources available in the digital intermediate software systems to treat and grade the images. The corrections are then applied to the other eye and viewed in 3D to measure and test the results.

Overall Stereo Workflow and Conforming Process Options

The traditional DI assembly method is much like any final conform. An EDL is used as a reference to the image selects, and the finished audio files in the AIFF format from the editorial off line as the starting point for the conform. It is very advantageous to have access to both left and right images at all times during the grading process. But not all DI systems can maintain good operational performance levels in stereo mode. If good stereo asset management tools, solid stereo tools, and an experienced team are on hand, the conform and shot update process should be a relatively straightforward process.

When to Start the Post-Production Process

Involving post-production during the early pre-production planning stages of a 3D stereo project can be a beneficial first step in helping guide the production direction of the show. Depending on the post-production demands of the project, the feedback from post-production may in fact guide some of the production processes if clearly understood early. The post-production process can take place in parallel and be used as part of the daily review and off-line deliverables process.

The DI theater may also be utilized by production to assist in the review and development of visual effects shots throughout the post-production process. It is essential to budget adequate time to allow for the large amount of data that is generated by stereo cameras and visual effects facilities. It is also very important to allow the visual effects and data teams' additional time to deal with the idiosyncrasies of managing a stereo pair of images on a large production.

Many studios have chosen to bring some of these processes in house and have integrated them alongside their CGI workflow. This is more common among the larger 3D animation companies who can build a direct pipeline and control the process. The facilities may even purchase their own software DI systems. This allows them to maintain creative control of their assets and maintain control of their schedule by not being at the mercy of their DI facility and their other clients.

Other traditional post-production facilities have added new equipment and additional capability to allow for stereo post-production to take place. Stereo post-production is a rapidly evolving segment of the market that will have a large amount of growth in the next 5 years.

Testing with the post-production partner or in-house facility should ideally begin before production to establish proper pipelines and establish proper review techniques for 3D dailies. Constant evaluation of 3D stereo images through dailies reviews and visual effects reviews on a variety of displays is required. This includes reviews on a variety of displays: large theater screens, stereo delivery systems, and smaller home video displays.

Selecting Left or Right Eye for the Mono Master

For a live-action 3D film, the right eye is sometimes chosen as the primary eye or "hero" eye. Depending on the camera rig chosen for a particular scene, the left eye may be reflected from the beamsplitter. The images reflected off the beamsplitter may have lifted blacks, flaring, or slight color distortion depending on the quality of glass used. This is a big consideration for choosing a proper stereo rig but typically more of a reality for the dailies and final colorist to address. The "hero" eye or the mono master should be derived from the best image available.

Two types of workflows are currently available for live-action stereo projects: data-centric and tape-based workflows. Note that the camera choice may define the workflow due to the fact that the camera itself may be file based, for example, the Red One camera. However, depending on budget, editorial preference, and the planned conforming and DI process, a workflow can be established on either tape or maintained as files in a data-centric workflow.

Any 3D stereo workflow should utilize metadata and timecode to keep the left and right eyes in sync with each other. It is very important for proper timecode procedures to be followed throughout the entire process to ensure that the left and right eyes maintain their sync relationship at all times. A frame offset on a matte used for a composite on a 2D project may not be noticed during motion, but a simple frame offset between the left and right eye will not be tolerated in 3D stereoscopic images. The offset between the two eyes will be immediately "felt" when viewing the images.

The source tapes can be ingested (imported) utilizing the EDL from the off-line system to do a batch capture on the conforming system. A set number of handle frames is normally established to allow for slight changes during the post-production process.

The ingest path for the left and the right eyes must be exactly identical. A difference in the procedure, hardware, or color path used during the ingest process may produce unacceptable stereo results. This would manifest itself by creating differences in the left and right eyes that will cause viewer fatigue.

The stereo camera image capture process inherently has left and right eye differences because of physics and imperfections in camera optics. Use of the beamsplitter to achieve specific interaxial offsets for image capture within 10 feet of the subject for close-ups may soften the focus and may sometimes introduce differences in the luminance levels between the two cameras, which causes viewing issues. It may be desirable to remove these left and right eye differences in a pre-processing step after the initial conform. The Foundry's Ocula software has some tools available for left eye/right eye autocolor matching.

This is also something that an assistant colorist could do before the stereo creative grade using the digital intermediate software by using tools to compare the two images to minimize the difference in color balance between the eyes.

The final conform should be viewed in stereo to check for editorial inaccuracies and to make sure the stereo was ingested properly. Once the stereo ingest is complete, the workflow takes on similar characteristics to the data-based workflow.

Data Workflow

A stereo data workflow should use timecode procedures that are identical to the tape-based workflow procedures. Careful data management processes should be followed to properly identify left and right eyes and maintain image continuity. Normal data workflow procedures should be followed with use of RAID storage systems and storage area networks (SANs) with proper tape backups throughout the entire process.

Standard 2D color correction techniques can be used throughout the grading process. This includes primary and secondary grading, hue and value qualifiers, static or animated geometry, and image tracking techniques.

The mono creative grade should be done on a DCI-compliant[15] projector at 14 foot-lamberts in a completely calibrated environment according to SMPTE[16] specs. Stereo creative grading can be done on a RealD projection system calibrated between 3.5 and 5 foot-lamberts as specified by RealD for their projectors in the field.

Mastering light-level options are currently being debated by many organizations. The new RealD XL Z-screen achieves increased light efficiency and is able to achieve more than 12 foot-lamberts. This will be something to keep an eye on as RealD deploys the XL light doubling technology.

The ideal grading environment would have mono and stereo projection systems available and use a white screen for mono grading and the silver screen for the 3D grading. This system should be able to transition from the 2D grading environment to the 3D grading environment in less than 1 minute. This will allow a user to quickly check the stereo settings in the stereo grade to make sure that the shots look as expected.

A 3D projection system may also require ghost reduction, commonly referred to as *ghost busting*. Stereo ghosting is caused by

---

[15] DCI: Digital Cinematography Initiative for Digital Projection.
[16] SMPTE: Society of Motion Picture and Television Engineers; a forum that sets standards for transmission, projection, recording, storage, and archiving of images.

inefficiency in the projection system and the viewing glasses. If the projector and the glasses were 100% efficient, there would be no need for ghost reduction.

The 3D films also require a stereo blending pass to minimize ghosting effects in the animation. This provides the ability to set the stereo convergence of the shots to minimize viewer fatigue and allow for good stereo continuity. In addition to the stereo blending pass, other techniques may be used such as floating windows. Floating windows are used to move the object in front of the screen plane or behind the screen image plane to set the depth of the scene for the viewing audience. Blending and stereo windows will normally animate from shot to shot to allow for proper stereo viewing continuity.

In addition, convergence changes can be made to the images by means of pixel shifting the images on the x-axis in the digital intermediate software. This along with stereo blending will allow the colorist and the stereographer to set the depth and post-production to achieve the optimum experience for the viewer.

The use of stereo disparity and depth maps such as those generated in the Ocula plug-in will allow an artist to use a stereo shifter that creates new pixels and new stereo convergence settings for live-action photography. This is evolving technology and is not always artifact free.

CG-animated films can use stereo disparity maps that are easily generated with the CG process to help in the convergence of images. This allows for greater manipulation, more precise rotoscoping and increased working speed during the post-production stereo manipulation process.

2D versus 3D Grading

It is best if the stereo rotoscoping process could be done utilizing software intelligence or use of the stereo disparity map. This technology is currently evolving and is only used in shot-based compositing systems such as the Foundry's NUKE software.

As these technologies mature, the use of more rotoscoping shapes and greater freedom in the stereo color correction process will become more commonplace. Currently, intricate rotoscoping must be manually offset and tracked as the image moves through 3D space.

CGI animation stereo projects have the added benefit of rendering out character, background, and visual effects element mattes, which allows for greater freedom than does a live-action stereo project.

It is essential for the digital intermediate system to allow the use of mattes. In the future, systems will allow for unlimited use of mattes, which will greatly reduce the amount of manual stereo rotoscoping offsetting.

Stereoscopic color grading is normally done in addition to the mono creative grade. Warmer hues appear closer in 3D space. Cooler colors such as light green and blue appear farther away since the brain perceives these as normal background colors. The director of photography will normally use a color palette that complements the 3D stereo environment. On an animated feature, the production designer will normally choose the color palette and develop a color script[17] for the entire animated feature. This is complemented by a stereo script that is normally set up by the stereographer for future use.

3D Stereo RealD Mastering Considerations

Stereo projects use the same approach to reel-by-reel workflow. Depending on the delivery schedule, there may be a request to move directly to the stereo reel immediately after delivery of a mono reel. The RealD grading environment should ideally be the same system and room as the mono grade. A silver screen will be put into place, and the RealD Z-screen will be used to create the 3D effect when viewed with the passive glasses.

The addition of the Z-screen polarizer and passive glasses reduces the amount of light that reaches the viewer's eyes. The RealD stereo deliverable must compensate for these additional devices needed to create the stereo effect for the viewer. As of early 2010, a RealD deliverable was mastered at 3.5 to 4.5 foot-lamberts as measured through the passive glasses. For the near future this will remain the current configuration. The colorist may use a LUT (lookup table) or the primary color tools to match the look of the mono DCM (digital cinema master) without glasses to the stereo image through the RealD system with glasses.

Geometry and Correction of Undesirable Binocular Disparity

Use of tools to fix and optimize the stereo defects and stereo effects, such as Foundry's Ocula software, stereo disparity maps, and interaxial pixel shifting, are geometry issues that need to be addressed and fixed in post if not realized during production.

Each DI system will have its own way to manage the transition from stereo to mono. Current 3D stereo DI technology does not use stereo disparity maps, as used in the Ocular software for stereo compositing. For certain situations an outboard tool external to the DI system may be needed for stereo reconciliation.

Frame shifting uses x-axis frame adjustment controls that need to be able to be viewed in stereo. This is used to adjust the

---

[17] Colors used for scene-to-scene and character design to match image depth requirements per script.

stereo from shot to shot for live-action stereo productions. The Quantel Pablo DI and compositing system's additional new tools from 3D Stereoscopic Production Company, 3Ality, can provide a "green = good, red = bad" stereo quality control report and tuning system. Stereo blending is more common in animation where virtual stereo cameras allow shot-to-shot adjustments to blend stereo depth transitions.

As with any new and emerging technologies, there are many ways to approach their use and apply these tools to an applicable project. It will depend on the project, team, talent, and gear to create a proper stereo workflow.

3D Stereo Deliverables

Each deliverable has its own characteristics and needs proper compensation for the delivery system. The mono deliverables include film, digital cinema master, and mono home video. The stereo deliverables include stereo IMAX and a RealD stereo master with ghost reduction and a Dolby stereo digital cinema master.

3D Stereo Home Video Deliverables

The 3D stereo home video market is developing rapidly with a variety of systems contending for home delivery. Traditional cyan/red anaglyph and magenta/green anaglyph are existing forms of stereo home video. The deliverables for these media should be optimized for the delivery system and judged on a variety of displays with the associated glasses to ensure their enjoyment by the largest number of viewing audience members.

Current home video active glasses technology includes checkerboard, left/right split, or stereo interlaced images. These technologies use active glasses with an infrared emitter to synchronize the glasses. New technologies will continue to emerge for the home video market.

The SMPTE is also actively trying to set a standard for delivery, display, and formatting of 3D stereo video. Once set, this will open the floodgates for manufacturing to proceed with product development and shipment. In the spring of 2010, more product offerings in the consumer electronics space emerged.

References

1. Wikipedia: Source of Definitions and Anaglyph Images
2. RealD 3D specs and Roadmap: www.reald.com/Content/Cinema-Products .aspx
    - IMAX 3D Film and 3D Digital PDF
    - Home 3D Technologies and recent SMPTE standards PDF
    - Images courtesy of RealD provided by Matt Cowan, Chief Scientific Officer at RealD, from an IBC presentation, dated 11/15/07, "Stereoscopic 3D: How It Works"

3D Stereoscopic links and short descriptions, spec sheets of available stereo DI systems

- Quantel Pablo www.quantel.com/list.php?a=Products&as=Stereo3D
- da Vinci Resolve www.davsys.com/davinciproducts.html
- Autodesk Lustre www.autodesk.com
- Assimilate Scratch www.assimilateinc.com
- Iridas Speedgrade www.speedgrade.com
- Digital Vision NuCoda www.digitalvision.se/products/index.htm
- RealD www.reald.com
- Technicolor Creative Services www.technicolor.com

STEREOSCOPIC WINDOW
Bruce Block, Phil McNally

This section is extracted from a forthcoming book by Bruce Block and Phil McNally about the overall planning and production of 3D films.

The dynamic stereoscopic window is an important new visual tool available to the filmmaker using 3D. This article describes the window and how it is controlled and suggests a variety of ways in which it can be used for directorial purposes.

The Stereoscopic Window

In a traditional 2D movie, the screen is surrounded by black fabric creating a flat, stationary frame or window.

Figure 5.20 A 2D movie screen. (All images courtesy of Bruce Block.)

The screen and the window share the same flat surface. The movie is viewed within this window.

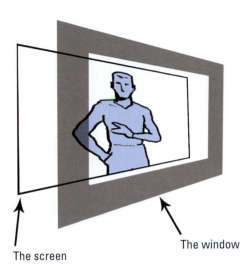

The screen

The window

Figure 5.21 A dynamic stereoscopic window.

In 3D this window is called the *dynamic stereoscopic window*. This window is not black fabric, but an optical mask that is part of the projected image. The dynamic stereoscopic window is movable so it doesn't have to share the same flat surface as the screen as does the 2D window. The dynamic stereoscopic window can be moved forward, pushed back, twisted, or separated into pieces and each piece set in a different depth position in relation to the objects in the 3D picture.

World space

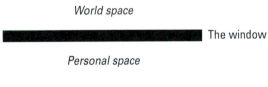 The window

Personal space

Figure 5.22 The area in front of the window is called *Personal Space* and the area behind the window is called *World Space*.

The dynamic stereoscopic window is a threshold between two separate visual spaces.

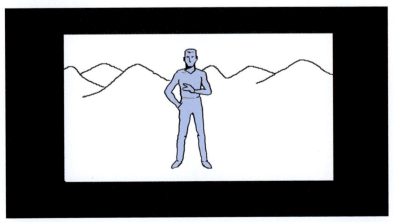

Figure 5.23 Traditionally in 3D, objects appear *behind* the window in the World Space.

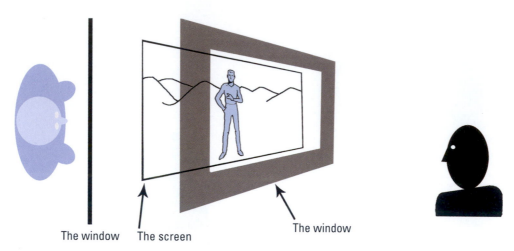

The window   The screen   The window

Figure 5.25 This overhead view illustrates how the window appears in front of objects. The 3D picture exists in the World Space *behind* the window.

Figure 5.24 The window acts as a frame in front of the scene.

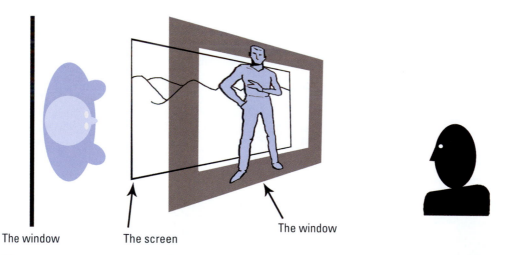

The window   The screen   The window

Figure 5.27 This overhead view shows how the window is behind the object. The object exists *in front of* the window in the Personal Space.

Figure 5.26 Objects can also appear in the Personal Space *in front of* the window.

Placement of the Window in Relation to the 3D Scene

The window location is one factor that determines where the audience experiences the 3D space.

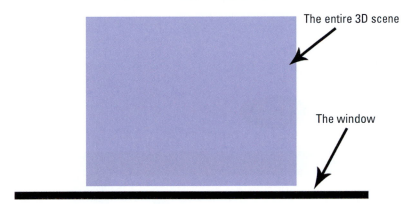

The entire 3D scene

The window

Figure 5.28 In this overhead diagram looking down on the audience, the entire 3D scene (indicated by the blue square) exists behind the window in the World Space.

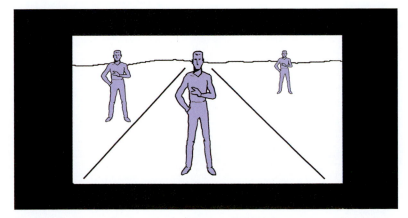

Figure 5.29 The audience sees the 3D scene behind the stereoscopic window like a theater proscenium.

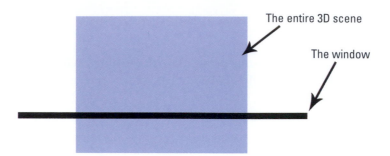

The entire 3D scene

The window

Figure 5.30 The window location has now been shifted away from the viewer so that about one-third of the 3D scene extends into the Personal Space.

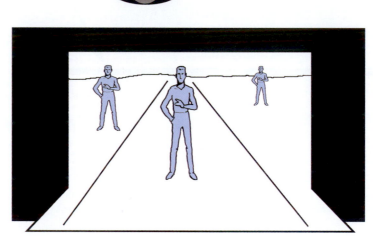

Figure 5.31 The front of the scene extends through the window.

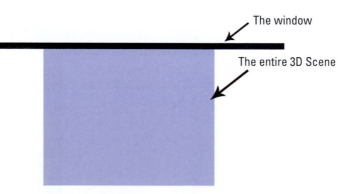

The window

The entire 3D Scene

Figure 5.32 In this third example, the window has been moved even farther back.

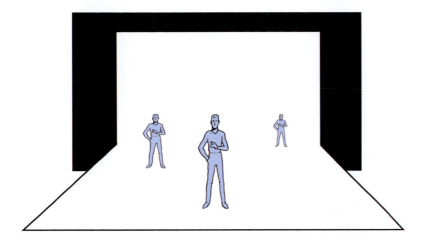

Figure 5.33 The 3D scene now exists entirely in front of the window in the Personal Space.

Window Violations

Window violations can occur when an object appears *in front of* the window. There are two types of violations: horizontal and vertical. Horizontal window violations are visually minor. A horizontal violation occurs when an object in front of the window is cut off or cropped by the horizontal upper and lower borders of the stereoscopic window.

Figure 5.34 This is a horizontal window violation.

In the example shown in Figure 5.34, a tightly framed actor appears in the Personal Space in front of the window. This creates a horizontal window violation because the window is behind the actor, yet it crops the actor on the top and bottom. The violation: How can a background window crop a foreground object?

An overhead view (Figure 5.35) illustrates how the audience's vision system may accommodate for the horizontal window violation by bending the window in front of the object. The audience's vision system assumes that the window has curved outward in front of the foreground object to crop it. Only about 50% of a 3D audience can visually bend the window.

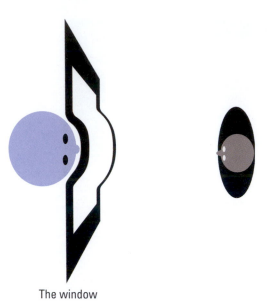

Figure 5.35 Overhead view. The window wraps around the image.

The window

Vertical window violations are more problematic because of the way human stereoscopic vision works. A stereoscopic window violation occurs when the vertical sides of a background window crop a foreground object.

Figure 5.36 A vertical violation occurs when an image is cropped by the window behind it.

When an object in the Personal Space (in front of the window) is cropped by a vertical window edge behind it, a violation occurs. The basic violation is the same: How can a background window crop a foreground object?

Figure 5.37 To solve the vertical window violation, all or part of the window must be moved in front of the object.

Figure 5.38 The window violation is corrected.

Window violations can be corrected during a shot or from shot to shot. The manipulation of the window during a shot can go unnoticed by the audience if it is motivated by camera movement or object movement within the frame. Placement of window parts can also be altered from shot to shot without the audience being aware of the manipulation.

Window Placement Logic

Directorially, window placement should be linked to the geography of the scene. What is far away should be placed behind the window. What is closer can be brought in front of the window.

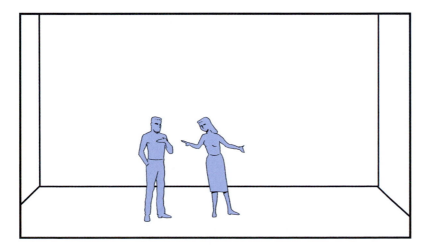

Figure 5.39 The actors appear in the mid-background. To create a visually normal space, the window should be placed in front of this scene.

Figure 5.40 The actors are now closer to the camera. The window could be placed just in front of the actors or the window could be moved behind the actors, placing them in the Personal Space (creating a minor horizontal window violation).

Figure 5.41 This is a close-up. The window position is now optional. The window could be placed in front of the actor, keeping her in the World Space, or moved behind the actor, placing her in the Personal Space.

The concept of window position may seem obvious, but it becomes an important visual cue allowing the audience to understand the geography of the space, the physical relationship of the objects in the space, and the position of the camera. Duplicating the way people perceive space in the real world is important in keeping the audience acclimated and involved in a 3D movie.

There are times in a story where deliberately confusing the audience about the 3D space can be useful. By placing the window at inappropriate distances, visual intensity can be created that makes the audience excited, confused, or even anxious. Sequences can become more chaotic, intense, or unreal by placing the window in unnatural positions. The danger here is creating a 3D sequence that disrupts the known space so completely that the sequence becomes impossible to follow.

The position of the window can create visual intensity, but other characteristics can be assigned to the window placement, too. Any story, emotional or dramatic value can be attached to the World Space or the Personal Space.

Interestingly, any of the meanings assigned to the Personal or World Space lists can be reversed. The Personal and World Spaces can be given almost any definition needed for the story. The concept is to assign a meaning to the World or Personal Spaces and then use that choice to tell the story visually.

As more of the depth appears in front of the window, the audience becomes "part of the action" because it is taking place in the Personal Space. Occupying the Personal Space usually creates more visual intensity because it breaks with traditional movie-viewing experiences.

Personal space	World space
Peace	War
Emotional	Unemotional
Aggressive	Passive
Antagonistic	Friendly
Intimate	Public
Quiet	Loud
Exposition	Conflict
Calm	Turmoil

Figure 5.42 Possible meanings of window placement.

How to Create a Stereoscopic Window

Figure 5.43 shows a stereoscopic image pair. Each image is seen by only one eye. This image pair does not have a stereoscopic window, so the only window the audience will see is the traditional black fabric masking that surrounds the actual projection screen.

In Figure 5.44 optical masking embedded in the stereoscopic images has been added. Additional masking on the right edge of the right eye image and the left edge of the left eye image will place the stereoscopic window *in front of* the screen.

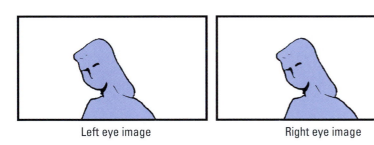

Left eye image   Right eye image

Figure 5.43 Stereoscopic image pair.

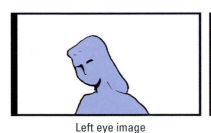

Left eye image   Right eye image

Figure 5.44 Optical masking embedded in the stereoscopic images.

Increasing the width of the optical masking will bring the stereoscopic window closer to the viewer.

Changing the position of the optical masking embedded in the stereoscopic images changes the location of the stereoscopic window. Using an optical mask on the left edge of the right eye image and the right edge of the left eye image will place the stereoscopic window *behind* the screen. As the width of the optical mask increases, the window will appear to move farther from the viewer.

A variety of combinations are possible using the embedded optical mask so that different sides of the stereoscopic window can exist in front of or behind the screen surface. Generally, a viewer is completely unaware of any optical masking changes during a movie because the edges of the movie screen are already bordered with black fabric. The additional optical mask blends into the existing black fabric border.

PRODUCING MOVIES IN THREE DIMENSIONS
Charlotte Huggins

A producer's role in the filmmaking process is to create the best possible conditions for getting movies made. From the initial spark of an idea through to the moment of the movie's release, producers are there to guide, facilitate, promote, defend, and support all aspects of a production. As the principal partner of the director and responsible to the studio and/or financiers, producers simultaneously supervise and serve all production departments during development, physical and post-production, and marketing and distribution. It is a big job. It is a great job. In 3D the job is even bigger and better. There are many differences between producing in 3D versus 2D and this section explores them and an even larger question: *Why make a 3D movie in the first place?*

The process of producing in three dimensions comes (naturally) in three parts: development, production, and the experience.

Development—Getting the Greenlight

Physical production of a 3D movie is similar in many aspects to that of a 2D project—putting together and managing the not-so-simple combination of a great script, a great director, great cast, and a great on-set and editorial team. For 3D, the inclusion of a few key 3D experts, appropriate planning, and suitable technology for the 3D process, which are detailed below, are needed for the *capture* (aka *filming* or *principal photography*) phase of production.

But before any movie is made, it must be written, packaged with a director and/or talent, and financed and often must have also secured distribution. This is a time-consuming, competitive, often relentlessly frustrating process. For a 3D project in development, unusual questions arise: How is 3D sold when it is so inconvenient and often technically complicated to show to people, and even more difficult to verbalize to those with little or no experience with it? How can a meaningful schedule and budget be created for 3D when the production tools and methods are new and ever changing? How is the revenue potential of 3D accurately estimated when the number of theaters at the time of the film's release is unknown and distributors have so little precedent from which to run the numbers? These questions, often quite simple or nonexistent in a 2D world, can be huge obstacles in getting a 3D project off the ground.

The production of a good 3D pitch is one of the single biggest obstacles to overcome when selling 3D to studio and creative executives, investors, distributors, theater owners, and audiences. Especially since pictures sell pictures. So, 3D development has certain rules. Rule number one:

Take the potential studio, distributor, talent, director, or financier to see 3D movies!

As obvious as this seems, it often proves more complicated than expected. As industry professionals, such people are used to being able to judge movies by watching them in a theater convenient in proximity or schedule or on DVD in the comfort of their homes. Often the seemingly simple act of screening a 3D movie or test clip proves difficult technically and organizationally because of the paucity of 3D screening rooms and complexity of preparing the material for projection in 3D. No one, not even a 3D film expert with many movies under his or her belt, can make an informed decision about what works and doesn't work in 3D without seeing it in a 3D theater.

To create a substantive production plan and budget, a producer must know all options. There are a variety of technologies, production and post-production people and pipelines, and release platforms in 3D. They all need to be known and understood before a plan can be created that will pass vetting. Rule number two:

Get informed about 3D. Learn everything possible about it technically, creatively, and financially.

All 3D suppliers and most 3D production and editorial people are used to answering questions about the process and demands of 3D. Find them, talk to them, ask the questions, look at the options, hire the experts, go to seminars, and, if possible, test the equipment and rigs that seem right for the production. The more that is known before production, the better and easier life will be on set and in post, and ultimately the better the 3D will be.

As for 3D financials such as future screen counts and box office in 3D, happily more and more 3D movies are being released, creating more and more statistics from which to base projections. The box office numbers for 3D movies are now available on a variety of websites. However, while the number of 3D screens in the RealD, XpanD, Dolby, IMAX, and other networks is growing, it continues to be difficult to get reliable forecasts of the number of future 3D screens either in the United States or worldwide. Quite a few websites and blogs discuss 3D screen and box office growth, but perhaps the most reliable sources of information about the number of screens and their growth pattern are from the British publication *Screen Digest* or recent articles in both *Daily Variety* and *Hollywood Reporter*. Rule number three:

Track down the most trustworthy statistics possible, because the estimation of the number of 3D screens and per-screen averages is critical to estimating potential box office, which is also critical to knowing what the budget will support.

Some important figures: In 2003, *Spy Kids 3D: Game Over* gave the visual effects industry the first modern sense of what 3D could mean to the box office bottom line. It was released only in 3D and earned almost $200 million in worldwide gross box office revenues. It was clear from audience response that they loved this anaglyphic (red/blue glasses, discussed in another section) 3D movie experience. The next year, *The Polar Express* (2004), originally intended only for 2D, was converted to a spectacular version for IMAX 3D release and earned 25% of its gross on 2% of its screens—the 3D screens. Analysts were quick to point out that revenues from the 3D version of the film not only justified the cost of conversion, but that presenting the film in a showcase platform increased awareness of the property and the 2D bottom line in the process.

Chicken Little in November 2005 earned 10% of its gross on 2% of its screens, the digital 3D screens. *Meet the Robinsons* (2007) again pushed box office numbers up, with 3D screens outgrossing the 2D release nearly 3-to-1 on a per-screen average. And the 3D hits just kept coming. The rerelease of Tim Burton's *The Nightmare Before Christmas* in 3D has earned this original 1993 2D film another $75 million with its 2006 and 2007 digital 3D release. *Beowulf* (2007) also earned approximately three times as much in 3D as in 2D; *Hannah Montana* (2009), a 3D-only release, broke all records with a whopping $65 million on 687 digital 3D screens in 3 weeks; *Journey to the Center of the Earth* (2008) earned over $250 million in a 2D/3D release with

66% of its domestic revenue coming from 30% of the screens (the 3D screens) and 47% of foreign revenues from only 15% of screens—again in 3D. The numbers speak to the excitement and audience approval of 3D experiences.

What do all of these numbers mean to producers of 3D feature film content? James Cameron pointed out in his keynote address at the Digital Cinema Summit in 2006 that the higher per-screen averages for 3D over 2D show that audiences are willing to seek out the premium experience of 3D and pay for it with an extra $2 to $5 per ticket up-charge. According to Cameron, "The costs associated with 3D will be paid for by the upside." This type of financial information and thinking can be strategic in getting a 3D movie greenlit.

Production—What to Look Out For

Once you are lucky (and persistent) enough to launch a 3D movie, new and different issues arise: new personnel, new equipment, new budget line items, new on-set rules, new visual effects challenges, and a new post-production pipeline. Furthermore, from concept to editorial, every step in the making of a 3D feature film must be infused with the goal of creating a thrilling yet comfortable 3D experience. This is true whether the intent is to release only in 3D (as only a handful of films in history have done) or in a more traditional 2D/3D release. Either way, the filmmakers have the responsibility of satisfying the same storytelling needs of a 2D movie, but for the 3D release the shots and sequences must be balanced with framing and pacing successful for 3D.

From pre- through post-production, a number of details and issues surrounding the use of 3D should be considered. Here is a partial list:

Pre-Production

- If the director, director of photography, or production designer isn't already familiar with the format, head to a 3D theater and watch as many 3D movies as possible together. The goal is to have all of these members of the team experience the technical and creative possibilities of 3D.
- Consider creating 3D previs for complicated sequences or all segments of the movie that are visual effects driven.
- For animated features, much can be learned from seeing initial animation tests in 3D projected on a theatrical-sized screen.
- Story/script sequences/shots should take into consideration 3D issues such as subject, pacing, framing, depth, on- and off-screen effects/opportunities, and art direction.

- Have all camera crew trained on 3D rigs as necessary.
- Budget must provide for additional crew, 3D rigs and additional cameras, stock (film or tape) or drive storage space, additional 3D screenings, and important post-production support. For these items, the increase above the 2D budget is approximately 20% of the below-the-line costs depending on the size and complexity (mostly visual effects) of the production.

Production

- Have on-set stereoscopic expertise and support.
- Have 3D rigs and support for particular set/location requirements.
- Install room to screen dailies in 3D on set or location.
- Have editorial staff necessary to conform 3D dailies for screening and on-set visual effects support.
- Have on-set VFX Supervisor with 3D experience or training to ensure the creation of proper 3D plates.
- For animated features, have frequent 3D test and sequence reviews with film and studio creatives on a full-sized theatrical screen.

Post-Production

- Provide the 3D conform for editorial assessment throughout post.
- Have in-house 3D screening capability, preferably on a screen large enough to judge 3D as it will be seen in a commercial theater.
- Visual effects facilities need 3D expertise or support and 3D screening capability—preferably on a full-size theatrical screen. If multiple visual effects facilities are used, they must all be calibrated equally to match the specs of the screen on which the director is viewing shots so that everyone is seeing the same thing.
- The editorial department must have stereoscopic expertise and support. If possible it is preferable to have an assistant editor dedicated to 3D issues.
- DI and final visual effects sign-off must be in 3D (and 2D if applicable).

Details of physical production notwithstanding, the two most important production considerations needed to create a great 3D motion picture are summed up in rules four and five:

See the footage in 3D often during filming and throughout post.

Have the best 3D creative and technical people possible in key positions on the production team.

The Experience—Why Make a 3D Movie in the First Place?

There are positive financial considerations in the distribution of a 3D movie, but the number one reason to produce in 3D what might otherwise have been a 2D film is the experience. Eric Brevig, director of *Journey to the Center of the Earth* (2008), once noted that as a filmmaking tool, 3D allowed him to engage audiences on a more subconscious, visceral level. According to Brevig, "People are able to experience the excitement and adventure of the story as if they are physically alongside the characters in the film."

Successful 3D can be expansive and breathtaking or quiet and intimate. Some of the best 3D experiences take viewers to a place they would never otherwise get to go or put them up-close-and-personal with intriguing people: front row at a sold-out concert, miles into outer space or deep under the ocean, within reach of someone who is loved or feared, in the middle of a fully rendered game where the viewers are players, or on a journey to an imaginary world.

It was once believed that less successful 3D concepts would be stories that took place in environments people see every day in real live 3D. It was commonly thought that an all-live-action story that took place primarily in an office, home, or school, for instance, seemed neither tight enough to create an intimate sense of space nor expansive enough to give a feel of wonder or awe. In general, it is now understood that such movies can be captured routinely in three dimensions, as the tools have become universally available, and the option of 3D seems always to be desirable as a distribution option. In fact, some feel a small comedy or intimate drama might actually be funnier or more poignant in 3D than 2D, drawing the viewer even closer to the events and on-screen personalities.

To get a feel for how different the experience of 3D is versus 2D, go see the same movie in the two different exhibition dimensions—preferably first in 2D and then in 3D, which is possible for many films currently in release. Go to theaters with as many people, preferably non-film-industry people, as possible for the full experience. In 3D, the sensation of "being there" is undeniable, and in a theater with an audience, you will see people enjoy and react to the events of the movie, believing that what's on the flat screen really exists in three dimensions. *That experience is what the joy of telling a story in 3D is all about.*

All producers are required to sell their movie projects in order to get a greenlight. Producers of 3D movies are required also to sell and often help develop the technology to make the movie and present it to audiences. By the late 2000s, with a substantial quantity and quality of 3D movies in the production and distribution pipeline and the number of digital 3D theaters over the 1000 mark, the technical expertise and financial models have given 3D a chance for long-term, broad acceptance.

Just as with the introduction and ultimate acceptance of sound as an integral part of the movie going experience in the late 1920s and color in the 1940s, digital 3D brings a few critical elements to the growth of the movie business: 3D gives filmmakers a new palette with which to create motion pictures and enhances the immersive nature of the theatrical experience, both of which justify an increase in ticket price and get people back into movie theaters for the "next dimension in cinema."

6

POST-PRODUCTION/IMAGE MANIPULATION

RESOLUTION AND IMAGE FORMAT CONSIDERATIONS
Scott Squires

Formats

Capture Format

The capture format for a film is decided in pre-production by the Director and Director of Photography (DP) along with the Production Designer and the VFX Supervisor. Creative choices along with camera size, post workflow, and costs are all a factor when determining the particular format.

Typically the choices are a 35mm film camera or digital camera (HD resolution or higher). With 35mm film there is the choice of a 1:85 ratio[1] (traditional aspect ratio) or 2:35/2:40 ratio (anamorphic or widescreen). The ratios are achieved either by using an anamorphic lens that squeezes the image or by using a Super 35 format[2] to record as a flat image that will be extracted. If the final film is to be shown in IMAX format,[3] then this will need to be considered as well since IMAX requires higher resolution for the best results.

There are a number of variations when it comes to digital capture formats. The selection of the codec[4] used will have a large impact on the quality of the image as well as the storage requirements for the initial capture.

---

[1] 1:85 and 2:35 are ratios of width to the height of the image.
[2] Super 35 takes advantage of the full 35mm image area, including what would have been the optical soundtrack.
[3] IMAX is a 70mm film running horizontally through the projector to provide a very large image projected onto a very large screen.
[4] Codec refers to the specific type of compression used on images.

The VES Handbook of Visual Effects. DOI: 10.1016/B978-0-240-81242-7.00006-5

Film needs to be scanned before doing digital visual effects, but currently film supplies a higher resolution and greater dynamic range than digital formats. Digital formats don't require scanning and therefore might provide a cost and time savings when importing the footage for visual effects work.

Film stock choices will be important for the style of the film and the visual effects work. Green and blue screens require film stock consideration to ensure the color response and resolution is sufficient to pull keys. This is especially true in digital formats where some codecs produce full color and others produce reduced color response and compression artifacts (which is a potential problem for blue or green screens). Full-color digital is usually referred to as 4:4:4, but some codecs provide image data that is sampled at lower color resolution (such as 4:2:2), which results in matte edges that are very blocky and obvious. See *Digital Cinematography* and *Greenscreen and Bluescreen Photography* in Chapter 3 for more information.

Whatever capture source is chosen will set the specifics for graining and degraining in post and subtle but important issues such as the shape and look of lens flares, out-of-focus highlights, and image edge characteristics so the finished visual effects shots match the live-action shots.

File Formats

Each company determines what image formats they will use internally. A scanning company may supply DPX[5] images but the visual effects company may import these and work internally with EXR[6] or other formats. Footage from digital cameras is imported and then resaved in the internal format of choice. Intermediate file formats are chosen to maintain the highest level of quality throughout the pipeline. This avoids any artifacts or other problems when combining images, processing them, and resaving them through a few generations.

File format issues also come into play when determining what to supply editorial. These could be specific QuickTimes or other formats depending on the editorial workflow setup. This should be sorted out in pre-production so the visual effects pipeline includes being able to export in the correct format, including color and gamma space.

Film delivery formats for exporting the final shots are another file format that needs to be chosen. In the past, film-outs[7] from digital files to film were required for film-based projects. Now

---

[5] DPX: Digital Picture Exchange format based on the original Cineon format. ANSI/SMPTE (268M-2003).

[6] EXR: image format; also known as OpenEXR since it's an open standard. It is a flexible and high-quality raster image format.

[7] Film-out: the actual recording of the digital image data onto motion picture film.

most film projects use a digital intermediate (DI) process. All live-action shots are scanned and imported for DI to be color corrected. In this case the finished visual effects digital files are submitted to the DI company in their requested format.

Target Format

Most films are delivered for both film and digital projection distribution. This is typically handled by the DI company and film labs. In some cases a film will be released in IMAX as well. This will require a special film-out process.

Transport

All of these digital files need to be moved from one location to another—both within a visual effects company and between the visual effects company and other vendors on the project. Files are typically distributed locally within the company using Ethernet. When going to or from another company, the images may be transferred by secure high-speed data connections or they may be transferred to large hard drives and physically shipped. In some cases storage tapes can be shipped if they are compatible. HD input and final output can be done using HD tape transfers although hard drives and Internet connections are probably more common.

Resolution

Most film production has been done at 2k (2048 pixels wide). As more 4k (4096 pixels wide) digital projectors become available, there has been a push to use 4k throughout the entire process. While this does technically increase the quality of the image, some issues still need to be addressed. To support a given resolution, every step in the process has to maintain that same resolution or higher. If the initial source is HD resolution, then working in 4k would require an initial resize and the up-ressed (resized larger) results would not provide as much of an increase in quality as a 4k film scan source would. As with digital still cameras, diminishing returns are seen as the pixel count goes up.

Scanning is frequently done at a higher resolution to allow better quality images even if they will be scaled down. Resolution of 4k will allow the full detail typical of a typical 35mm film shot to be captured and maintained through the production pipeline. This allows the digital images to be the best they can be from 35mm film; in addition, the images will be less likely to require rescanning for future formats.

However, a number of issues should be reviewed before settling on the resolution. A resolution of 4k means that the image will be twice as many pixels wide and twice as many vertically. This is four times the amount of data required of a 2k image. Although not every process is directly linked to the size, most visual effects steps are. When visual effects companies went from 8-bit per channel to 16-bit floating point, the size of the image data doubled. This increase in pixel resolution will require four times as much data.

A 4k image will take four times as much storage space on disk so a given hard drive will now hold only a one-quarter of the frames it could hold for 2k projects. It will also take longer to load and save images. This increases the time the visual effects artists may have to wait on their workstations. Some software may be less responsive since the image is occupying much more memory, and live playback will be an issue since only one-quarter of the frames can be loaded. Also, 4k requires more pixels to paint if one needs to work in full detail. Transferring images to other machines on the network or off site will also take four times as long. Archiving of material will require more time and storage as well.

A typical monitor does not support the full 4k, so users will need to resize images to 2k or less to see the entire image and then zoom in to see the full resolution. Projection equipment at the visual effects company will need to support 4k if pixels are to be checked on the big screen. Any hardware or software that doesn't support 4k efficiently will have to be upgraded or replaced. In some steps, 2k proxies can be used just as video resolution proxies are sometimes used in normal production. This can be done for testing, initial setups, and processes where the image is a guide such as rotoscoping.

How noticeable will the results be? If the results are split screened or toggled on a correctly configured large-screen projection, then they may be obvious. But when projected without a direct comparison, it's not likely the audience at the local theater will notice. For a number of years after digital visual effects came into being, visual effects were done on very large films at slightly less than 2k with 8-bit log color depth. These shots were intercut directly with film. Not too many people complained to the theater owners. Some theatrically released films were shot in the DV format (Standard Definition Digital Video; typically for consumer video cameras). These were used for specific purposes but in most cases audiences will ignore the technical issues and focus on the story once the film is under way. (Assuming it's a good story being well told.)

Today Blu-ray DVD movies are available. They are a higher resolution and use a better codec than regular DVDs, but many people are finding the upres (resizing) of their old DVDs to be pretty good. When DVDs came out there was a very large quality difference and ease of use compared to VHS tapes. People purchased

DVD players but the leap from DVD to Blu-ray is not as apparent to the average person so there has been slow acceptance of this new format. Note that high-quality resizing software and hardware also allows 2k film to be resized to 4k probably with better results than expected. This can be done at the very end of the pipeline.

The quality comparisons assume a locked-off camera using the highest resolution of the film. If a film is shot with a very shaky handheld camera with frenetic action and an overblown exposure look, the results may not show a noticeable difference.

Summary

A resolution of 4k will likely be used for visual effects–heavy films and eventually for standard films. At the time of this writing (early 2010), it may or may not make sense for a specific project.

Visual effects companies will need to review their pipelines and ideally run a few simulated shots through to make sure everything handles 4k and to actually check the time and data sizes being used. From this they can better budget 4k film projects since these will cost more and take some additional time.

For the filmmakers and studios that wish to have 4k resolution, they will need to determine whether it is worth the extra cost. With tighter budgets and tighter schedules, it may not make the most sense. Would the extra budget be put to better use on more shots or other aspects of the production? It is unlikely that 4k itself will sell more tickets to a movie, so ultimately it's a creative call versus the budget.

As new resolutions and formats (such as stereoscopic) are introduced, these will have to be evaluated by the producers and the visual effects companies to see what the impact will be and to weigh the results.

IMAGE COMPRESSION/FILE FORMATS FOR POST-PRODUCTION

Florian Kainz, Piotr Stanczyk

This section focuses on how digital images are stored. It discusses the basics of still image compression and gives an overview of some of the most commonly used image file formats. An extended version of this section, which covers some of the technical details, can be found at the *Handbook*'s website (www.VESHandbookofVFX.com).

Visual effects production deals primarily with moving images, but unlike the moving images in a television studio, the majority of images in a movie visual effects production pipeline are stored as sequences of individual still frames, not as video data streams.

Since their beginning, video and television have been real-time technologies. Video images are recorded, processed, and displayed at rates of 25 or 30 frames per second (fps). Video equipment, from cameras to mixers to tape recorders, is built to keep up with this frame rate. The design of the equipment revolves around processing streams of analog or digital data with precise timing.

Digital visual effects production usually deals with images that have higher resolution than video signals. Film negatives are scanned, stored digitally, processed, and combined with computer-generated elements. The results are then recorded back onto film. Scanning and recording equipment is generally not fast enough to work in real time at 24 fps. Compositing and 3D computer graphics rendering take place on general-purpose computers and can take anywhere from a few minutes to several hours per frame. In such a non-real-time environment, storing moving images as sequences of still frames, with one file per frame, tends to be more useful than packing all frames into one very large file. One file per frame allows quick access to individual frames for viewing and editing, and it allows frames to be generated out of order, for example, when 3D rendering and compositing are distributed across a large computer network.

Computers have recently become fast enough to allow some parts of the visual effects production pipeline to work in real time. It is now possible to preview high-resolution moving images directly on a computer monitor, without first recording the scenes on film. Even with the one-file-per-frame model, some file formats can be read fast enough for real-time playback. Digital motion picture cameras are gradually replacing film cameras. Some digital cameras have adopted the one-file-per-frame model and can output, for example, DPX image files.

Though widely used in distribution, digital rights management (DRM) technologies are not typically deployed in the context of digital visual effects production. The very nature of the production process requires the freedom to access and modify individual pixels, often via one-off, throwaway programs written for a specific scene. To be effective, DRM techniques would have to prevent this kind of direct pixel access.

Image Encoding

For the purposes of this chapter, a digital image is defined as an array of pixels where each pixel contains a set of values. In the case of color images, a pixel has three values that convey the amount of red, green, and blue that, when mixed together, form the final color.

A computer stores the values in a pixel as binary numbers. A binary integer or whole number with n bits can represent any value between 0 and $2^n - 1$. For example, an 8-bit integer can represent values between 0 and 255, and a 16-bit integer can represent values between 0 and 65,535. Integer pixel value 0 represents black, or no light; the largest value (255 or 65,535) represents white, or the maximum amount of light a display can produce. Using more bits per value provides more possible light levels between black and white to use. This increases the ability to represent smooth color gradients accurately at the expense of higher memory usage.

It is increasingly common to represent pixels with floating point numbers instead of integers. This means that the set of possible pixel values includes fractions, for example, 0.18, 0.5, etc. Usually the values 0.0 and 1.0 correspond to black and white, respectively, but the range of floating point numbers does not end at 1.0. Pixel values above 1.0 are available to represent objects that are brighter than white, such as fire and specular highlights.

Noncolor Information

Digital images can contain useful information that is not related to color. The most common noncolor attribute is opacity, often referred to as *alpha*. Other examples include the distance of objects from the camera, motion vectors or labels assigned to objects in the image. Some image file formats support arbitrary sets of image channels. Alpha, motion vectors, and other auxiliary data can be stored in dedicated channels. With file formats that support only color channels, auxiliary data are often stored in the red, green, and blue channels of a separate file.

Still Image Compression

A high-resolution digital image represents a significant amount of data. Saving tens or hundreds of thousands of images in files can require huge amounts of storage space on disks or tapes. Reading and writing image files requires high data transfer rates between computers and disk or tape drives.

Compressing the image files, or making the files smaller without significantly altering the images they contain, reduces both the amount of space required to store the images and the data transfer rates that are needed to read or write the images. The reduction in the cost of storage media as well as the cost of hardware involved in moving images from one location to another makes image compression highly desirable.

A large number of image compression methods have been developed over time. Compression methods are classified as either *lossless* or *lossy*. Lossless compression methods reduce the size of image files without changing the images at all. With a lossless method, the compression and subsequent decompression of an image result in a file that is identical to the original, down to the last bit. This has the advantage that a file can be uncompressed and recompressed any number of times without degrading the quality of the image. Conversely, since every bit in the file is preserved, lossless methods tend to have fairly low compression rates. Photographic images can rarely be compressed by more than a factor of 2 or 3. Some images cannot be compressed at all.

Lossy compression methods alter the image stored in a file in order to achieve higher compression rates than lossless methods. Lossy compression exploits the fact that certain details of an image are not visually important. By discarding unimportant details, lossy methods can achieve much higher compression rates, often shrinking image files by a factor of 10 to 20 while maintaining high image quality.

Some lossy compression schemes suffer from generational loss. If a file is repeatedly uncompressed and recompressed, image quality degrades progressively. The resulting image exhibits more and more artifacts such as blurring, colors of neighboring pixels bleeding into each other, light and dark speckles, or a "blocky" appearance. For visual effects, lossy compression has another potential disadvantage: Compression methods are designed to discard only visually unimportant details, but certain image-processing algorithms, for example, matte extraction, may reveal nuances and compression artifacts that would otherwise not be visible.

Certain compression methods are called *visually lossless*. This term refers to compressing an image with a lossy method, but with enough fidelity so that uncompressing the file produces an image that cannot be distinguished from the original under normal viewing conditions. For example, visually lossless compression of an image that is part of a movie means that the original and the compressed image are indistinguishable when displayed on a theater screen, even though close-up inspection on a computer monitor may reveal subtle differences.

Lossless Compression

How is it possible to compress an image without discarding any data? For example, in an image consisting of 4,000 by 2,000 pixels, where each pixel contains three 16-bit numbers (for the red, green, and blue components), there are $4,000 \times 2,000 \times 3 \times 16$ or 384,000,000 bits, or 48,000,000 bytes of data. How is it possible to pack this information into one-half or even one-tenth the number of bits?

Run-Length Encoding

Run-length encoding is one of the simplest ways to compress an image. Before storing an image in a file, it is scanned row by row, and groups of adjacent pixels that have the same value are sought out. When such a group is found, it can be compressed by storing the number of pixels in the group, followed by their common value.

Run-length encoding has the advantage of being very fast. Images that contain large, uniformly colored areas, such as text on a flat background, tend to be compressed to a fraction of their original size. However, run-length encoding does not work well for photographic images or for photoreal computer graphics because those images tend to have few areas where every pixel has exactly the same value. Even in uniform areas film grain, electronic sensor noise, and noise produced by stochastic 3D rendering algorithms break up runs of equal value and lead to poor performance of run-length encoding.

Variable-Length Bit Sequences

Assume one wants to compress an image with 8-bit pixel values, and it is known that on average 4 out of 5 pixels contain the value 0. Instead of storing 8 bits for every pixel, the image can be compressed by making the number of bits stored in the file depend on the value of the pixel. If the pixel contains the value 0, then a single 0 bit is stored in the file; if the pixel contains any other value, then a 1 bit is stored followed by the pixel's 8-bit value. For example, a row of 8 pixels may contain these 8-bit values:

$$0 \ 127 \ 0 \ 0 \ 10 \ 0 \ 0$$

Writing these numbers in binary format produces the following 64-bit sequence:

00000000 01111111 00000000 00000000 00001010 00000000
00000000 00000000

Now every group of 8 zeros is replaced with a single 0, and each of the other 8-bit groups is prefixed with a 1. This shrinks the pixels down to 24 bits, or less than half of the original 64 bits:

$$0 \ 101111111 \ 0 \ 0 \ 100001010 \ 0 \ 0 \ 0$$

The technique shown in the previous example can be generalized. If certain pixel values occur more frequently than others, then the high-frequency values should be represented with fewer bits than values that occur less often. Carefully choosing the number of bits for each possible value, according to how often it occurs in the image, produces an effective compression scheme.

Huffman coding is one specific and popular way to construct a variable-length code that reduces the total number of bits in the output file. A brief description of how Huffman coding works can be found in the extended version of this section on the *Handbook*'s website (www.VESHandbookofVFX.com); further material can also be found in Huffman (1952).

Transforming the Pixel Distribution

Encoding images with a variable number of bits per pixel works best if a small number of pixel values occur much more often in an image than others. In the example above, 80% of the pixels are 0. Encoding zeros with a single bit and all other values as groups of 9 bits reduces images by a factor of 3 on average. If 90% of the pixels were zeros, images would be compressed by a factor of nearly 5. Unfortunately, the pixel values in correctly exposed real-world images have a much more uniform distribution. Most images have no small set of values that occur much more frequently than others.[8]

Even though most images have a fairly uniform distribution of pixel values, the pixels are not random. The value of most pixels can be predicted with some accuracy from the values of the pixel's neighbors. For example, if a pixel's left and top neighbors are already known, then the average of these two neighbors' values is probably a pretty good guess for the value of the pixel in question. The prediction error, that is, the difference between the pixel's true value and the prediction, tends to be small. Even though large errors do occur, they are rare. This makes it possible to transform the pixels in such a way that the distribution of values becomes less uniform, with numbers close to zero occurring much more frequently than other values: Predict each pixel value from values that are already known, and replace the pixel's actual value with the prediction error. Because of its nonuniform distribution of values, this transformed image can be compressed more than the original image. The transformation is reversible, allowing the original image to be recovered exactly.

Other Lossless Compression Methods

A large number of lossless compression methods have been developed in order to fit images into as few bits as possible. Most of those methods consist of two stages. An initial transformation stage converts the image into a representation where the distribution of values is highly nonuniform, with some values occurring much more frequently than others. This is followed by

---

[8] In fact, if the lowest or highest possible value occurs a lot in a photographic image, then that image is generally underexposed or overexposed. Many digital cameras can display a histogram of the pixel values in captured images; a fairly flat histogram without tall spikes at the left or right end is a sign that the image has been exposed correctly.

an encoding stage that takes advantage of the nonuniform value distribution.

Predicting pixel values as described above is one example of the transformation stage. Another commonly used method, the discrete wavelet transform, is more complex but tends to make the subsequent encoding stage more effective. Huffman coding is often employed in the encoding stage. One popular alternative, arithmetic coding, tends to achieve higher compression rates but is considerably slower. LZ77 and LZW are other common and efficient encoding methods.

Irrespective of how elaborate their techniques are, lossless methods rarely achieve more than a three-to-one compression ratio on real-world images. Lossless compression must exactly preserve every image detail, even noise. However, noise and fine details of natural objects, such as the exact placement of grass blades in a meadow, or the shapes and locations of pebbles on a beach, are largely random and therefore not compressible.

Lossy Compression

Image compression rates can be improved dramatically if the compression algorithm is allowed to alter the image. The compressed image file becomes very small, but uncompressing the file can only recover an approximation of the original image. As mentioned earlier, such a compression method is referred to as *lossy*.

Lossy compression may initially sound like a bad idea. If an image is stored in a file and later read back, the original image is desired, not something that looks "kind of like" the original. Once data have been discarded by lossy compression, they can never be recovered, and the image has been permanently degraded. However, the human visual system is not an exact measuring instrument. Images contain a lot of detail that simply cannot be seen under normal viewing conditions, and to a human observer two images can often look the same even though their pixels contain different data.

The following subsections show how one can exploit two limitations of human vision: Spatial resolution of color perception is significantly lower than the resolution of brightness perception, and high-contrast edges mask low-contrast features close to those edges.

Luminance and Chroma

Human vision is considerably less sensitive to the spatial position and sharpness of the border between regions with different colors than to the position and sharpness of transitions between light and dark regions. If two adjacent regions in an image differ in brightness, then a sharp boundary between those regions is easy to distinguish from a slightly more gradual transition. Conversely, if two adjacent regions in an image differ only in color, but not in brightness, then the difference between a sharp and a more gradual transition is rather difficult to see.

This makes a simple but effective form of lossy data compression possible: If an image can be split into a pure brightness or "luminance" image and a pure color or "chroma" image, then the chroma image can be stored with less detail than the luminance image. For example, the chroma image can be resized to a fraction of its original width and height. Of course, this smaller chroma image occupies less storage space than a full-resolution version.

If the chroma image is subsequently scaled back to its original resolution and combined with the luminance image, a result is obtained that looks nearly identical to the original.

The top-left image in Figure 6.1 shows an example RGB image. The image is disassembled into a luminance-only or grayscale image and a chroma image without any brightness information. Next, the chroma image is reduced to half its original width and height. The result can be seen in the bottom images in Figure 6.1.

Scaling the chroma image back to its original size and combining it with the luminance produces the top-right image in Figure 6.1. Even though resizing the chroma image has discarded three-quarters of the color information, the reconstructed image is visually indistinguishable from the original. The difference between the original and the reconstructed image becomes visible only when one is subtracted from the other, as shown

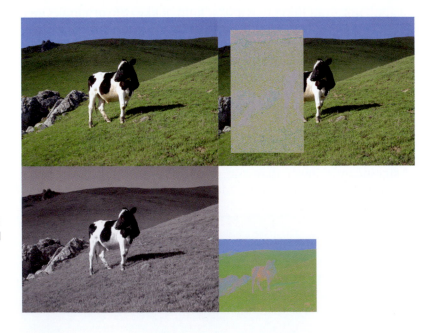

Figure 6.1 *Top left:* A low-resolution RGB image used for illustrating the use of chroma subsampling in compressing images. *Top right:* Reconstructed RGB image, and the difference between original and reconstructed pixels. *Bottom left:* Luminance of the original image. *Bottom right:* Half-resolution chroma Image. (Image courtesy of Florian Kainz.)

in the inset rectangle. The contrast of the inset image has been enhanced to make the differences more visible.

The specifics of converting a red-green-blue or RGB image into luminance and chroma components differ among image file formats. Usually the luminance of an RGB pixel is simply a weighted sum of the pixel's R, G, and B components. Chroma has two components, one that indicates if the pixel is more red or more green and one that indicates if the pixel is more yellow or more blue. The chroma values contain no luminance information. If two pixels have the same hue and saturation, they have the same chroma values, even if one pixel is brighter than the other (Poynton, 2003, and ITU-R BT.709-3).

Converting an image from RGB to the luminance-chroma format does not directly reduce its size. Both the original and the luminance-chroma image contain three values per pixel. However, since the chroma components contain no luminance information, they can be resized to half their original width and height without noticeably affecting the look of the image. An image consisting of the full-resolution luminance combined with the resized chroma components occupies only half as much space as the original RGB pixels.

Variations of luminance-chroma encoding are a part of practically all image file formats that employ lossy image compression, as well as a part of most digital and analog video formats.

Contrast Masking

If an image contains a boundary between two regions that differ drastically in brightness, then the high contrast between those regions hides low-contrast image features on either side of the boundary. For example, the left image in Figure 6.2 contains two grainy regions that are relatively easy to see against the uniformly gray background and two horizontal lines, one of which is clearly darker than the other.

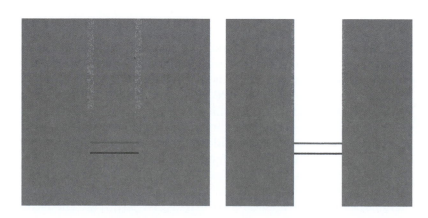

Figure 6.2 Synthetic test image illustrating the contrast masking exploit in image compression. Note how introducing a much brighter area effectively masks any of the underlying noise and minimizes the differences in the brightness of the two horizontal lines. (Image courtesy of Florian Kainz.)

If the image is overlaid with a white stripe, as shown in the right image in Figure 6.2, then the grainy regions are much harder to distinguish, and it is difficult to tell whether the two horizontal lines have the same brightness or not.

The high-contrast edge between the white stripe and the background hides or masks the presence or absence of nearby low-contrast details. The masking effect is fairly strong in this simple synthetic image, but it is even more effective in photographs and in photoreal computer graphics where object textures, film grain, and digital noise help obscure low-contrast details.

Contrast masking can be exploited for lossy image compression. For example, the image can be split into small 4 × 4-pixel blocks. In each block only the value of the brightest pixel must be stored with high precision; the values of the remaining pixels can be stored with less precision, which requires fewer bits. One such method, with a fixed (and fairly low) compression rate, is described in the extended version of this section (see the *Handbook*'s website at www.VESHandbookofVFX.com).

Careful observation of the limitations of human vision has led to the discovery of several lossy compression methods that can achieve high compression rates while maintaining excellent image quality, for example, JPEG and JPEG 2000. A technical description of those methods is outside the scope of this section.

File Formats

This subsection presents a listing of image file formats that are typically found in post-production workflows. Due to the complexity of some of the image file formats, not all software packages will implement or support all of the features that are present in the specification of any given format. The listings that follow present information that is typical to most implementations. Where possible, references to the complete definition or specification of the format are given.

Camera RAW File Formats and DNG

RAW image files contain minimally processed data from a digital camera's sensor. This makes it possible to delay a number of processing decisions, such as setting the white point, noise removal, or color rendering, until full-color images are needed as input to a post-production pipeline.

Unfortunately, even though most RAW files are variations of TIFF there is no common standard in the way data are stored in a file across camera manufacturers and even across different camera models from the same manufacturer. This may limit the long-term viability of data stored in such formats. Common filename extensions include RAW, CR2, CRW, TIF, NEF. The DNG format, also an extension of TIFF, was conceived by Adobe as a way of unifying the various proprietary formats. Adobe has submitted the specification to ISO for possible standardization.

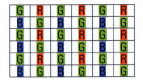

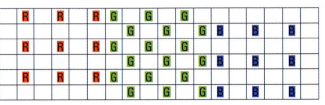

The image sensors in most modern electronic cameras do not record full RGB data for every pixel. Cameras typically use sensors that are equipped with color filter arrays. Each pixel in such a sensor is covered with a red, green, or blue color filter. The filters are arranged in a regular pattern, as per the top example in Figure 6.3.

Figure 6.3 *Top:* Arrangement of pixels in a typical image sensor with a red-green-blue color filter array. *Bottom:* The interleaved image is separated into three channels; the missing pixels in each channel must be interpolated. (Image courtesy of Piotr Stanczyk.)

To reconstruct a full-color picture from an image that has been recorded by such a color filter array sensor, the image is first split into a red, a green, and a blue channel as in the lower diagram in Figure 6.3.

Some of the pixels in each channel contain no data. Before combining the red, green, and blue channels into an RGB image, values for the empty pixels in each channel must be interpolated from neighboring pixels that do contain data. This is a non-trivial step and various implementations result in markedly different results.

Owner: Adobe
Extension: DNG
Reference: www.adobe.com/products/dng

Cineon and DPX

DPX is the de facto standard for storing and exchanging digital representations of motion picture film negatives. DPX is defined by an SMPTE standard (ANSI/SMPTE 268M-2003). The format is derived from the image file format originally developed by Kodak for use in its Cineon Digital Film System. The data itself contains a measure of the density of the exposed negative film.

Unfortunately, the standard does not define the exact relationship between light in a depicted scene, code values in the file, and the intended reproduction in a theater. As a result, the exchange of images between production houses requires additional information to avoid ambiguity. Exchange is done largely on an ad hoc basis.

Most frequently, the image data contains three channels representing the red, green, and blue components, each using 10 bits per sample. The DPX standard allows for other data representations including floating point pixels, but this is rarely supported. One of the more useful recent additions to film scanning technology has been the detection of dust particles via an infrared pass. The scanned infrared data can be stored in the alpha channel of a DPX file.

The Cineon and DPX file formats do not provide any mechanisms for data compression so that the size of the image is only dependent on the spatial resolution.

Owner: SMPTE (ANSI/SMPTE 268M-2003)
Extension: CIN, DPX
Reference: www.cineon.com/ff_draft.php; http://store.smpte.org

JPEG Image File Format

JPEG is an ubiquitous image file format that is encountered in many workflows. It is the file format of choice when distributing photographic images on the Internet. JPEG compression was developed in the late 1980s. A detailed and accessible description can be found in the book *JPEG Still Image Data Compression Standard*, by Pennebaker and Mitchell (1993).

JPEG is especially useful in representing images of natural and realistic scenes. DCT compression is very effective at reducing the size of these types of images while maintaining high image fidelity. However, it is not ideal at representing artificial scenes that contain sharp changes in neighboring pixels, say, vector lines or rendered text.

JPEG compression allows the user to trade image quality for compression. Excellent image quality is achieved at compression rates on the order of 15:1. Image quality degrades progressively if file sizes are reduced further, but images remain recognizable even at compression rates on the order of 100:1. Typical JPEG implementations suffer from generational losses and the limitations of 8-bit encoding. Consequently, visual effects production pipelines where images may go through a high number of load-edit-save cycles do not typically employ this format. It is, however, well suited to and used for previewing purposes. It is also used as a starting point for texture painting.

In 2000, JPEG 2000, a successor to the original JPEG compression, was published (ISO/IEC 10918-1:1994). JPEG 2000 achieves higher image quality than the original JPEG at comparable compression rates, and it largely avoids blocky artifacts in highly compressed images. The Digital Cinema Package (DCP), used to distribute digital motion pictures to theaters, employs JPEG 2000 compression, and some digital cameras output JPEG 2000-compressed video, but JPEG 2000 is not commonly used to store intermediate or final images during visual effects production.

Color management for JPEG images via ICC profiles is well established and supported by application software.

Owner: Joint Photographic Experts Group, ISO (ISO/IEC 10918-1:1994 and 15444-4:2004)
Extension: JPG, JPEG
Reference: www.w3.org/Graphics/JPEG/itu-t81.pdf

OpenEXR

OpenEXR is a format developed by Industrial Light & Magic for use in visual effects production. The software surrounding the reading and writing of OpenEXR files is an open-source project allowing contributions from various sources. OpenEXR is in use in numerous post-production facilities. Its main attractions include 16-bit floating point pixels, lossy and lossless compression, an arbitrary number of channels, support for stereo, and an extensible metadata framework.

Currently, there is no accepted color management standard for OpenEXR, but OpenEXR is tracking the Image Interchange Framework that is being developed by the Academy of Motion Picture Arts and Sciences.

It is important to note that lossy OpenEXR compression rates are not as high as what is possible with JPEG and especially JPEG 2000.

Owner: Open Source
Extension: EXR, SXR (stereo, multi-view)
Reference: www.openexr.com

Photoshop Project Files

Maintained and owned by Adobe for use with the Photoshop software, this format not only represents the image data but the entire state of a Photoshop project including image layers, filters, and other Photoshop specifics. There is also extensive support for working color spaces and color management via ICC profiles.

Initially, the format only supported 8-bit image data, but recent versions have added support for 16-bit integer and 32-bit floating point representations.

Owner: Adobe
Extension: PSD
Reference: www.adobe.com/products/photoshop

Radiance Picture File—HDR

Radiance picture files were developed as an output format for the Radiance ray-tracer, a physically accurate 3D rendering system. Radiance pictures have an extremely large dynamic range and pixel values have an accuracy of about 1%. Radiance pictures contain three channels and each pixel is represented as 4 bytes, resulting in relatively small files sizes. The files can be either uncompressed or run-length encoded.

In digital visual effects, Radiance picture files are most often used when dealing with lighting maps for virtual environments.

Owner: Radiance
Extension: HDR, PIC
Reference: http://radsite.lbl.gov/radiance/refer/filefmts.pdf

Tagged Image File Format (TIFF)

This is a highly flexible image format with a staggering number of variations from binary FAX transmissions to multispectral scientific imaging. The format's variability can sometimes lead to incompatibilities between file writers and readers, although most implementations do support RGB with an optional alpha channel.

The format is well established and has wide-ranging software support. It is utilized in scientific and medical applications, still photography, printing, and motion picture production. Like JPEG, it has a proven implementation of color management via ICC profiles.

Owner: Adobe
Extension: TIF, TIFF
Reference: http://partners.adobe.com/public/developer/tiff/index.html

References

DPX standard, ANSI/SMPTE 268M-2003 (originally was version 1 268M-1994).

Huffman, D. A. A method for the construction of minimum-redundancy codes. In: *Proceedings of the I.R.E.* (September 1952) (pp. 1098–1102).

ISO/IEC 10918-1:1994. Digital compression and coding of continuous-tone still images: requirements and guidelines.

ISO/IEC 15444-4: 2004. *JPEG 2000 image coding system: core coding system.*

ITU-R BT.709-3. Parameter values for the HDTV standards for Production and International Programme Exchange.

OpenEXR image format, http://www.openexr.org

Pennebaker, W. B., & Mitchell, J. L. (1993). *JPEG still image data compression standard.* New York: Springer-Verlag, LLC.

Poynton, C. A. (2003). *Digital video and HDTV: algorithms and interfaces.* San Francisco, CA: Morgan Kaufmann Publishers.

Young, T. (1802). On the theory of light and colors. *Philosophical Transactions of the Royal Society of London, 92.*

4K+ SYSTEMS THEORY BASICS FOR MOTION PICTURE IMAGING

Dr. Hans Kiening

Five years ago digital cameras and cell phones were the biggest thing in consumer electronics, but the most popular phrase today seems to be "HD." One would think that the "H" in HD stands for "hype." Although professionals have a clear definition of HD (1920 × 1080 pixels, at least 24 full frames per second, preferably 4:4:4 color resolution), at electronics stores, the "HD-Ready" sticker on hardware offers considerably less performance (1280 × 1024 pixels, 4:2:1, strong compression, etc.).

On display are large monitors showing images that are usually interpolated from standard definition images (720 × 576 pixels or less). The catchphrase "HD for the living room" means (on a different quality level)—comparable to the discussion of 2k versus 4k in professional post-production—expectations, and sometimes just basic information, could not be more contradictory. Yet an increasing number of major film projects are already being successfully completed in 4k. So, it's high time for a technically based appraisal of what is really meant by 2k and 4k. This section strives to make a start.

Part 1: Resolution and Sharpness

To determine resolution, a raster is normally used, employing increasingly fine bars and gaps. A common example in real images would be a picket fence displayed to perspective. In the image of the fence, shown in Figure 6.4, it is evident that the gaps between the boards become increasingly difficult to discriminate as the distance becomes greater. This effect is the basic problem of every optical image. In the foreground of the image, where the boards and gaps haven't yet been squeezed together by the perspective, a large difference in brightness is recognized. The more the boards and gaps are squeezed together in the distance, the less difference is seen in the brightness.

Figure 6.4 Real-world example for a resolution test pattern. (All images courtesy of Dr. Hans Kiening.)

To better understand this effect, the brightness values are shown along the yellow arrow into an *x/y* diagram (Figure 6.5). The brightness difference seen in the *y*-axis is called *contrast*. The curve itself functions like a harmonic oscillation; because the brightness does not change over time but spatially from left to right, the *x*-axis is called *spatial frequency*.

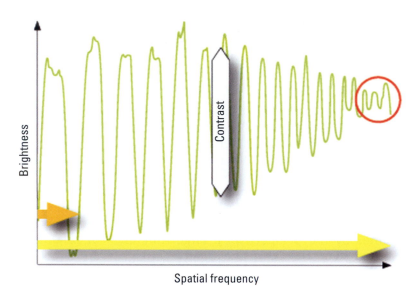

Figure 6.5 Brightness along the picket fence in Figure 6.4.

The distance can be measured from board to board (orange arrow) on an exposed image such as a 35mm. It describes exactly one period in the brightness diagram (Figure 6.5). If such a period in the film image continues, for example, over 0.1mm, then there is a spatial frequency of 10 line pairs/mm (10 lp/mm, 10 cycles/mm, or 10 periods/mm). Visually expressed, a line pair always consists of a bar and a "gap." It can be clearly seen in Figure 6.4 that the finer the reproduced structure, the more the contrast will be smeared on that point in the image. The limit of the resolution has been reached when one can no longer clearly differentiate between the structures. This means the resolution limit (red circle indicated in Figure 6.5) lies at the spatial frequency where there is just enough contrast left to clearly differentiate between board and gap.

Constructing the Test

Using picket fences as an example (Figure 6.4), the resolution can be described only in one direction. Internationally and scientifically, a system of standardized test images and line pair rasters to determine and analyze resolution has been agreed on. Horizontal and vertical rasters are thereby distributed over the image surface.

To carry out such a test with a film camera, the setup displayed in Figure 6.6 was used. The transparent test pattern was exposed with 25 fps and developed. Figure 6.8 shows the view through a microscope at the image center (orange border in Figure 6.7).

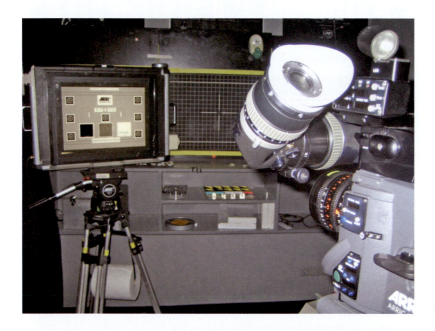

Figure 6.6 Setup for resolution.

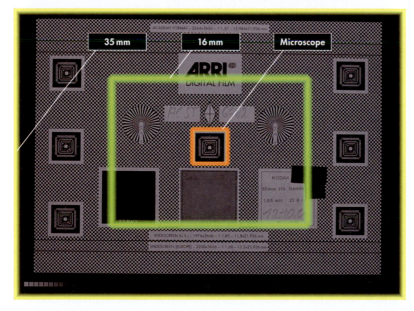

Figure 6.7 Framing.

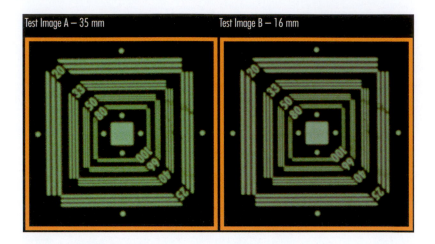

Figure 6.8 View through the microscope at the negative (center).

Resolution Limit 35mm

Camera: ARRICAM ST
Film: Eastman EXR 50D Color Negative Film 5245 EI 50
Lens: HS 85mm F2.8
Distance: 1.65 m

It is apparent that the finest spatial frequency that can still be differentiated lies between 80 and 100 lp/mm. For these calculations, a limit of 80 lp/mm can be assumed. The smallest discernible difference was determined by the following:

$$1mm/80\ 1p = 0.012mm/1p$$

Lines and gaps are equally wide, ergo:

$$0.012mm/2 = 0.006mm\ \text{for the smallest detail}$$

Resolution Limit 16mm

Camera: 416
Film: Eastman EXR 50D Color Negative Film 5245 EI 50
Lens: HS 85mm F2.8
Distance: 1.65 m

If a 35mm camera is substituted for a 16mm camera with all other parameters remaining the same (distance, lens), an image will result that is only half the size of the 35mm test image but resolves exactly the same details in the negative.

Results

This test is admittedly an ideal case, but the ideal is the goal when testing the limits of image storage in film. In the test, the smallest resolvable detail is 0.006mm large on the film, whether 35mm or 16mm. Thus, across the full film width there are

24.576mm/0.006 = 4096 details or points for 35mm film and 12.35mm/0.006 = 2048 points for 16mm film. Because this happens in the analog world, these are referred to as points rather than pixels. These statements depend on the following: (1) looking at the center of the image; (2) the film sensitivity is not over 250 ASA; (3) exposure and development are correct; (4) focus is correct; (5) lens and film don't move against one another during exposure; and; (6) speed <50 fps.

Digital

The same preconditions would also exist for digital cameras (if there were a true 4k resolution camera on the market today); only the negative processing would be omitted. Thus in principle, this test is also suitable for evaluating digital cameras. In that case, however, the test rasters should flow not only horizontally and vertically, but also diagonally and, ideally, circularly. The pixel alignment on the digital camera sensor (Bayer pattern) is rectangular in rows and columns. This allows good reproduction of details, which lie in the exact same direction, but not of diagonal structures, or other details that deviate from the vertical or horizontal. This plays no role in film, because the sensor elements—film grain—are distributed randomly and react equally good or bad in all directions.

Sharpness

Are resolution and sharpness the same? By looking at the images shown in Figure 6.9, one can quickly determine which image is sharper. Although the image on the left comprises twice as many pixels, the image on the right, whose contrast at coarse details is increased with a filter, looks at first glance to be distinctly sharper.

The resolution limit describes how much information makes up each image, but not how a person evaluates this information. Fine details such as the picket fence in the distance are irrelevant

Figure 6.9 Resolution = sharpness?

to a person's perception of sharpness—a statement that can be easily misunderstood. The human eye, in fact, is able to resolve extremely fine details. This ability is also valid for objects at a greater distance. The decisive physiological point, however, is that fine details do not contribute to the subjective perception of sharpness. Therefore, it's important to clearly separate the two terms, resolution and sharpness.

The coarse, contour-defining details of an image are most important in determining the perception of sharpness. The sharpness of an image is evaluated when the coarse details are shown in high contrast. A plausible reason can be found in the evolution theory: "A monkey who jumped around in the tops of trees, but who had no conception of distance and strength of a branch, was a dead monkey, and for this reason couldn't have been one of our ancestors," said the paleontologist and zoologist George Gaylord Simpson (2008). It wasn't the small, fine branches that were important to survival, but rather the branch that was strong enough to support the monkey.

Modulation Transfer Function

The term *modulation transfer function* (MTF) describes the relationship between resolution and sharpness and is the basis for a scientific confirmation of the phenomenon described earlier. The modulation component in MTF means approximately the same as contrast. Evaluate the contrast (modulation) not only where the resolution reaches its limit, but over as many spatial frequencies as possible and connect these points with a curve, to arrive at the so-called MTF (Figure 6.10).

In Figure 6.10, the *x*-axis illustrates the already established spatial frequency expressed in line pairs per millimeter on the *y*-axis, instead of the brightness seen in modulation. A modulation of 1 (or 100%) is the ratio of the brightness of a completely white image to the brightness of a completely black image. The higher the spatial frequency (i.e., the finer the structures in the image), the lower the transferred modulation. The curve seen here shows the MTF of the film image seen in Figure 6.8 (35mm). The film's resolution limit of 80 lp/mm (detail size 0.006mm) has a modulation of approximately 20%.

In the 1970s, Erich Heynacher from Zeiss provided the decisive proof that humans attach more value to coarse, contour-defining details than to fine details when evaluating an image. He found that the area below the MTF curve corresponds to the impression of sharpness perceived by the human eye (the so-called Heynacher integral) (Heynacher, 1963). Expressed simply, the larger the area, the higher the perception of sharpness. It is easy to see that the coarse spatial frequencies make up the largest area of the MTF. The farther right into the image's finer details, the smaller the area of the MTF. Looking at the camera example in Figure 6.9, it is obvious that the red MTF curve shown in Figure 6.11 frames a larger area than the blue MTF curve, even if it shows twice the resolution.

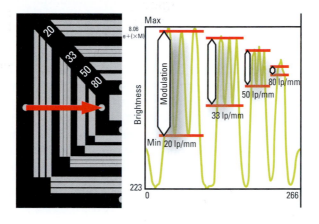

$$\text{Modulation} = \frac{[I_{Max} - I_{Min}]}{[I_{Max} + I_{Min}]}$$

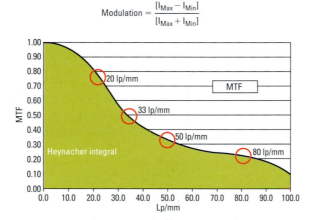

Figure 6.10 Modulation transfer function and the Heynacher integral.

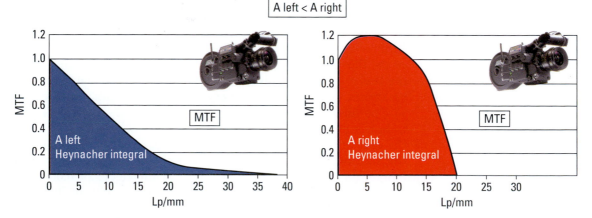

Figure 6.11 MTF and Heynacher integral for Figure 6.10.

For Experts

An explanation of the difference between sine-shaped (MTF) and rectangular (CTF) brightness distribution in such test patterns will not be offered here. However, all relevant MTF curves have been measured according to ISO standards for the fast Fourier transform (FFT of slanted edges).

Part 1 Summary

Sharpness does not depend only on resolution. The modulation at lower spatial frequencies is essential. In other words, contrast in coarse details is significantly more important for the impression of sharpness than contrast at the resolution limit. The resolution that delivers sufficient modulation (20%) in 16mm and 35mm film is reached at a detail size of 0.006mm, which corresponds to a spatial frequency of 80 lp/mm (not the resolution limit <10%).

Part 2: Into the Digital Realm

How large is the storage capacity of the film negative? How many pixels does one need to transfer this spatial information as completely as possible into the digital realm, and what are the prerequisites for a 4k chain of production? These are some of the questions addressed in this section.

The analyses here are deliberately limited to the criteria of resolution, sharpness, and local information content. These, of course, are not the only parameters that determine image quality, but the notion of 4k is usually associated with them.

Film as a Carrier of Information

Film material always possesses the same performance data: the smallest reproducible detail (20% modulation) on a camera film negative (up to EI 200) is about 0.006mm, as determined by the analysis done earlier in this section. This can also be considered the size of film's pixels, a concept that is well known from electronic image processing. It does not matter if the film is 16mm, 35mm, or 65mm—the crystalline structure of the emulsion is independent of the film format. Also, the transmission capability of the imaging lens is generally high enough to transfer this spatial frequency (0.006mm = 80 lp/mm) almost equally well for all film formats.

The film format becomes relevant, however, when it comes to how many small details are to be stored on its surface—that is the question of the total available storage capacity. In Table 6.1, the number of pixels is indicated for the image's width and height. Based on the smallest reproducible detail of 0.006mm, Table 6.1 gives an overview of the storage capacity of different film formats.

Table 6.1 Number of Film Pixels per Height and Width

Format	Width × Height (SMPTE/ISO Camera Gate)	Pixels
Super 16mm	12.35mm × 7.42mm	2058 × 1237 pixels
Super 35mm	24.92mm × 18.67mm	4153 × 3112 pixels
65mm	52.48mm × 23.01mm	8746 × 3835 pixels

Scanning

These analog image pixels must now be transferred to the digital realm. Using a Super 35mm image as an example, the situation is as follows:

The maximum information depth is achieved with a line grid of 80 lp/mm. The largest spatial frequency in the film image is therefore 1/0.012mm (line 0.006mm + gap 0.006mm). According to the scanning theorem of Nyquist and Shannon, the digital grid then has to be at least twice as fine, that is, 0.012mm/2 = 0.006mm. Converted to the width of the Super 35mm negative, this adds up to 24.92mm/0.006mm = 4153 pixels for digitization.

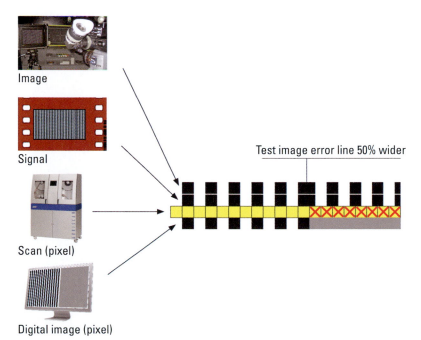

Image

Signal

Test image error line 50% wider

Scan (pixel)

Digital image (pixel)

Figure 6.12 Principle of aliasing.

Aliasing

Stick with the line grid as a test image and assume a small error has crept in. One of the lines is 50% wider than all of the others. While the film negative reproduces the test grid unperturbedly and thereby true to the original, the regular digital grid delivers a uniform gray area, starting at the faulty line—simply because the pixels, which are marked with an "x," consist of half a black line and half a white gap, so the digital grid perceives a simple mix—which is gray.

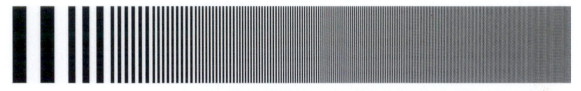

Figure 6.13 Frequency sweep.

So if the sample to be transferred consists of spatial frequencies that become increasingly higher—as in Figure 6.13—the digital image suddenly shows lines and gaps in the wrong intervals and sizes. This is a physical effect whose manifestations are also known as acoustics in the printing industry. There, the terms *beating waves* and *moiré* are in use. In digitization technology, the umbrella term for this is *aliasing*. Aliasing appears whenever there are regular structures in the images that are of similar size and aligned in the same way as the scanning grid. Its different manifestations are shown in Figure 6.14. The advantage of the film pixels, the grains, is that they are statistically distributed and not aligned to a regular grid and they are different from frame to frame.

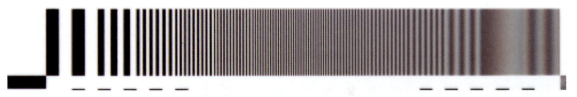

Figure 6.14 Aliasing.

Figure 6.14 shows an area of incipient destructive interference and an area of pseudo-modulation. This describes the contrast for details, which lie beyond the threshold frequency and which, in the digital image, are indicated in the wrong place (out of phase) and have the wrong size. This phenomenon does not only apply to test grids—even the jackets of

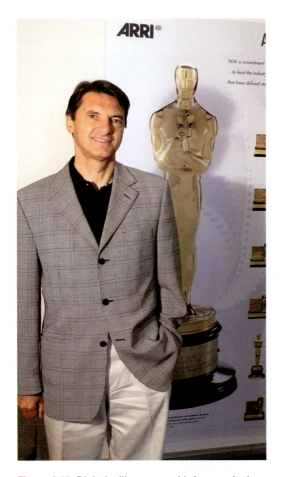

Figure 6.15 Digital still camera with 2 megapixels.

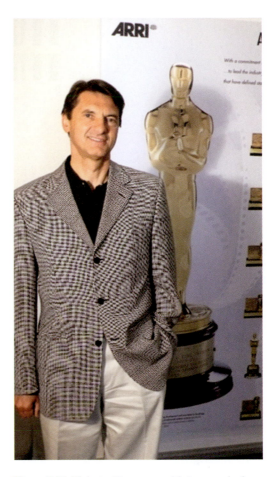

Figure 6.16 Digital still camera with 1 megapixel.

Academy Award winners may fall victim to aliasing (Figures 6.15 and 6.16). *Note:* You can see from these figures that aliasing is a nasty artifact for still pictures. It becomes significantly worse for motion picture because it changes dynamically from frame to frame.

Impact on the MTF

It is very obvious that the aliasing effect also has an impact on the MTF. Pseudo-modulation manifests itself as a renewed rise (hump) in the modulation beyond the scanning limit Pseudo, because the resulting spatial frequencies (lines and gaps) have nothing to do with reality: Instead of becoming finer, as they do in the scene, they actually become wider again in the output image (Figures 6.17 and 6.18).

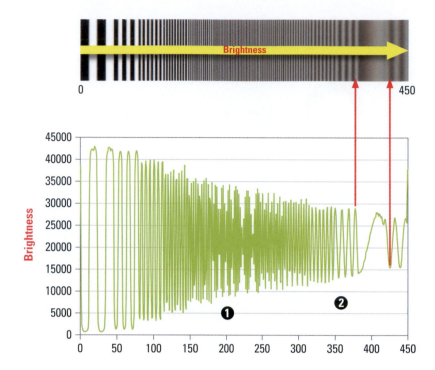

Figure 6.17 Luminance along the frequency sweep.

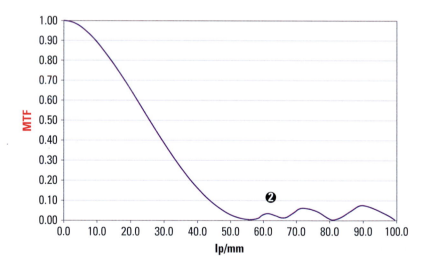

Figure 6.18 Resulting MTF.

Avoiding Alias

The only method for avoiding aliasing is to physically prevent high spatial frequencies from reaching the scanning raster; that is, by defocusing or through a so-called optical low pass, which in principle does the same in a more controlled fashion.

Unfortunately, this not only suppresses high spatial frequencies; it also affects the contrast of coarse detail, which is important for sharpness perception.

Another alternative is to use a higher scanning rate with more pixels, but this also has its disadvantages. Because the area of a sensor cannot become unlimitedly large, the single sensor elements have to become smaller to increase the resolution. However, the smaller the area of a sensor element becomes, the less sensitive it will be. Accordingly, the acquired signal must be amplified again, which leads to higher noise and again to limited picture quality. The best solution often lies somewhere in between. A combination of a 3k sensor area (large pixels, little noise) and the use of mechanical microscanning to increase resolution (doubling it to 6k) is the best solution to the problem.

Table 6.2 Required Scanning Pixels

Format	Width	Pixels	Scanning Resolution/ Digital Acquisition	Final Image Size
Super 16mm	12.35mm	2058 pixels	3k	2k
Super 35mm	24.92mm	4153 pixels	6k	4k

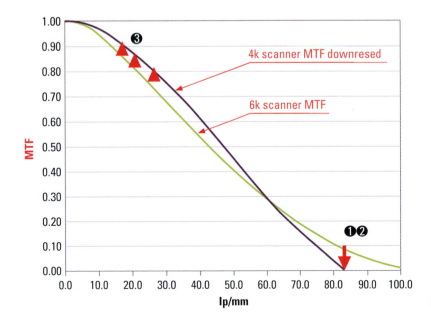

Figure 6.19 Scanner MTF.

The currently common maximum resolution in post-production is 4k. The gained 6k data is calculated down with the help of a filter. In the process, the MTF is changed; thus:

(1) The response at half of the 4k scanning frequency itself is zero.

(2) Spatial frequencies beyond the scanning frequency are suppressed.

(3) The modulation at low spatial frequencies is increased.

Whereas measures (1) and (2) help to avoid aliasing artifacts in an image, measure (3) serves to increase the surface ratio under the MTF. As discussed earlier, this improves the visual impression of sharpness. To transfer the maximum information found in the film negative into the digital realm without aliasing and with as little noise as possible, it is necessary to scan the width of the Super 35mm negative at 6k. This conclusion can be scaled to all other formats.

The Theory of MTF Cascading

What losses actually occur over the course of the digital, analog, or hybrid post-production chain?

The MTF values of the individual chain elements can be multiplied to give the system MTF. With the help of two or more MTF curves one can quickly compare—above all—without any subjectively influenced evaluation. Also, once the MTF of the individual links of the production chain is determined, the expected result can be easily computed at every location within the chain, through simple multiplication of the MTF curves.

Figure 6.20 Theory of MTF cascading.

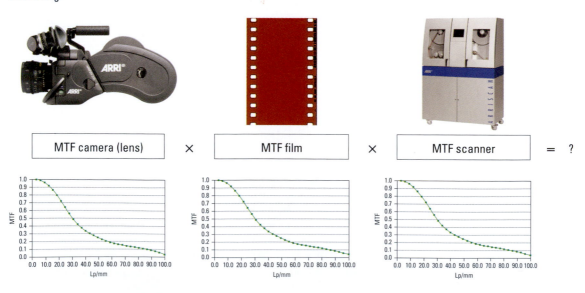

MTF camera (lens) × MTF film × MTF scanner = ?

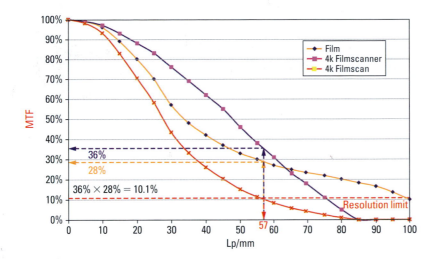

Figure 6.21 Resulting MTF in a 4k scan.

MTF Camera (Lens) × MTF Film × MTF Scanner = ?

An absolutely permissible method for a first estimate is the use of manufacturers' MTF data for multiplication. However, it must be remarked that there usually are very optimistic numbers behind this data and calculating them in this way shows the best-case scenario. Actual measured values are used for the calculations here. Instead of using the MTF of the raw stock and multiplying it by the MTF of the camera lens, the resulting MTF of the exposed image is directly measured and multiplied by the MTF of a 4k scanner.

What Does the Result Show?

The MTF of a 35mm negative scanned with 4k contains only little more than 56 lp/mm (the equivalent of 3k with the image width of Super 35mm) usable modulation. The resolution limit is defined by the spatial frequency, which is still transferred with 10% modulation. This result computes from the multiplication of the modulation of the scanner and of the film material for 57 lp/mm:

MTF_4k_scanner (57 1p/mm) × MTF_exposed_film (57 1p/mm) = MTF_in_4k_scan (57 1p/mm) 36% × 28% = 10.08%

The same goes for a digital camera with a 4k chip. There, a low-pass filter (actually a deliberate defocusing) must take care of pushing down modulation at half of the sampling frequency (80 lp/mm) to 0, because otherwise aliasing artifacts would occur.

Ultimately, neither a 4k scan nor a (three-chip) 4k camera sensor can really transfer resolution up to 4k.

This is a not an easily digestible paradigm. It basically means that 4k data only contains 4k information if it was created pixel

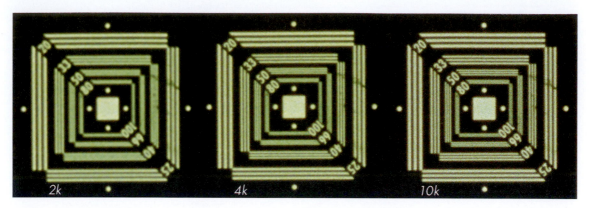

Figure 6.22 From left, 2k, 4k, and 10k scans of the same 35mm camera negative.

by pixel on a computer—without creating an optical image beforehand. However, this cannot be the solution, because then in the future there would be animated movies only—a scenario in which actors and their affairs could only be created on the computer. This would be a tragic loss and not just for supermarket tabloid newspapers!

Part 2 Summary

In the foreseeable future, 4k projectors will be available, but their full quality will come into its own only when the input data provides this resolution without loss. At the moment, a correctly exposed and 6k/4k scanned 35mm film negative is the only practically existing acquisition medium for moving pictures that comes close to this requirement. By viewing from a different angle one could say that the 4k projection technology will make it possible to see the quality of 35mm negatives without incurring losses through analog processing laboratory technology. The limiting factor in the digital intermediate (DI) workflow is not the (ideal exposed) 35mm film but the 4k digitization. As you can see in Figure 6.22, a gain in sharpness is still possible when switching to higher resolutions. Now imagine how much more image quality could be achieved with 65mm (factor 2.6 more information than 35mm)!

These statements are all based on the status quo in the film technology—for an outlook on the potential of tomorrow's film characteristics read Tadaaki Tani's article (Tani, 2007). The bottom line is that 35mm film stores enough information reserves for digitization with 4k+.

Part 3: Does 4k Look Better Than 2k?

The two most frequently asked questions regarding this subject are "How much quality is lost in the analog and the DI chain?" and "Is 2k resolution high enough for the digital intermediate workflow?"

The Analog Process

"An analog copy is always worse than the original." This is an often-repeated assertion. But it is true only to a certain extent in the classic post-production process; there are in fact quality-determining parameters that, if controlled carefully enough, can ensure that the level of quality is maintained: When photometric requirements are upheld throughout the chain of image capture, creating the intermediates and printing, the desired brightness and color information can be preserved for all intents and purposes.

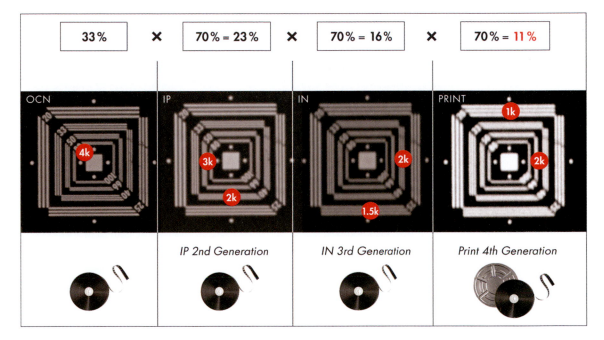

Clear loss of quality, however, indeed occurs where structures, that is, spatial image information, are transferred. In other words, resolution and sharpness are reduced. This occurs as a result of the rules of multiplication. Table 6.3 shows how 50 lp/mm with a

Figure 6.23 10k scans (green), photochemical lab from camera negative to print.

Table 6.3 MTF Losses in Photochemical Lab

MTF at 50 lp/mm	
Exposed Film Image Kodak 5205 (camera + film)	33%
Kodak 5242 Intermediate (copy to IR)	70%
Kodak 5242 Intermediate (copy to IN)	70%
Kodak Print Film 2393	70%

$$33\% \times 70\% = 23\% \times 70\% = 16\% \times 70\% = 11\%$$

native 33% modulation in the original is transferred throughout the process.

This, however, is an idealized formula, because it assumes that the modulation of the film material and the contact printing show no loss of quality. This is not the case in reality, which can be seen in the differences between the horizontal and vertical resolutions.

Is 2k Enough for the DI Workflow?

Although the word *digital* suggests a digital reproduction with zero loss of quality, the DI process is bound by the same rules that apply to the analog process because analog components (i.e., optical path of scanner and recorder) are incorporated. To make this clearer, again perform the simple multiplication of the MTF resolution

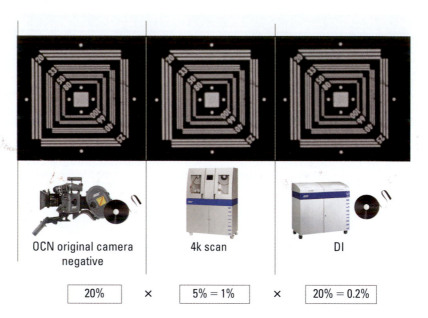

OCN original camera negative   4k scan   DI

$$20\% \quad \times \quad 5\% = 1\% \quad \times \quad 20\% = 0.2\%$$

Figure 6.24 DI workflow.

Table 6.4 DI MTF Losses in 4k DI Workflow

MTF at 80 lp/mm	
Exposed Film Image 5205 (ARRICAM, VP, OCN)	20%
Film Scanner MTF at 4k (ARRISCAN)*	5%
Recorded Internegative Fuji RDI (Film + ARRILASER)	20%

$$20\% \times 5\% = 1\% \times 20\% = 0.2\%$$

Per definition to avoid alias.

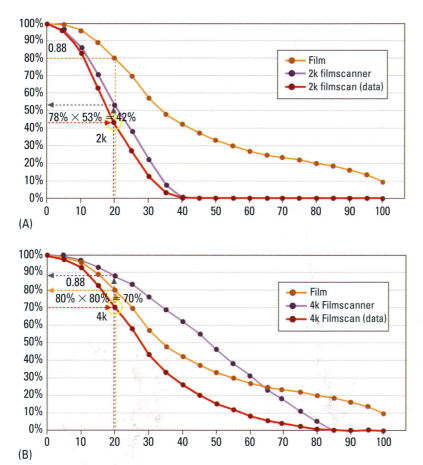

Figure 6.25 (A) 2k scan. (B) 4k scan.

limit in 4k (= 80 lp/mm). The MTF data illustrate the best filming and DI components that can be currently achieved.

As the multiplication proves, inherent to the 4k DI chain, modulation cannot occur at 80 lp/mm, even though the digitally exposed internegative shows considerably more image information than can be preserved throughout the traditional analog chain. An *internegative*, or intermediate negative, is a film stock used to duplicate an original camera negative. Conventionally it is generated with film printers alternatively exposed from the digitized data on a film recorder. Then it is called a *digital intermediate*.

Why, then, is a 4k digital process still a good idea, even though it cannot reproduce full 4k image information? The answer is simple, according to the Heynacher integral (the area beneath the MTF curve): The perception of sharpness depends on the modulation of coarse local frequencies. When these are transferred with a higher modulation, the image is perceived as sharp. Figure 6.26 shows the results of a 2k and 4k scan.

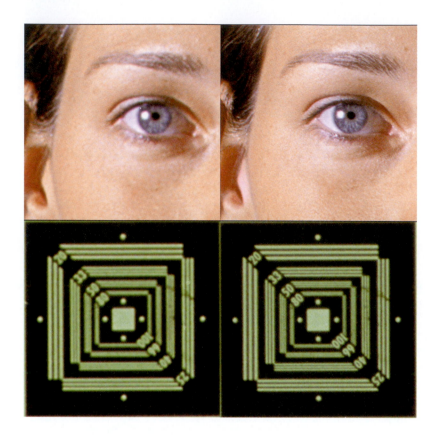

Figure 6.26 Cutout of a 2k (*left*) and a 4k (*right*) digital internegative.

Because a 4k scanner offers not only more resolution but also more modulation in lower local frequencies, the resulting 4k images will be perceived as being sharper. When this data is recorded out in 4k on Fuji RDI, for example, it produces the results shown in Figure 6.24.

Part 3 Summary

A 4k workflow is advantageous for DI and film archiving. The MTF characteristics seen in 4k scanning will transfer coarse detail (which determines the perception of sharpness) with much more contrast than 2k scanning. It is thereby irrelevant whether or not the resolution limit of the source material is resolved. It is very important for the available frequency spectrum to be transferred with as little loss as possible.

Part 4: Visual Perception Limitations for Large Screens

The section discusses the most important step in the production chain—the human eye. Again, the focus is resolution, sharpness, and alias. More specifically, the focus is now on general perception at the limits of human visual systems, when viewing large images on the screen. This limitation shows how much effort one should put into digitization of detail.

A very common rumor still circulates that alleges that one could simply forget about all the effort of 4k, because nobody can see it on the screen anyway. The next sections take a closer look to see if this is really true!

Basic Parameters

Three simple concepts can be used to describe what is important for a natural and sharp image, listed here in a descending order of importance:

(1) Image information is not compromised with alias artifacts.
(2) Low spatial frequencies show high modulation.
(3) High spatial frequencies are still visible.

This implicitly means that an alias-affected image is much more annoying than one with pure resolution.

Further, it would be completely wrong to conclude that one could generate a naturally sharp image by using low resolution and just push it with a filter. Alias-free images and high sharpness can be reached only if oversampling and the right filters for downscaling to the final format have been used.

Resolution of the Human Eye

The fovea of the human eye (the part of the retina that is responsible for sharp central vision) includes about 140,000 sensor cells per square millimeter. This means that if two objects are projected with a separation distance of more than 4 m on the fovea, a human with normal visual acuity (20/20) can resolve them. On the object side, this corresponds to 0.2mm in a distance of 1 m (or 1 minute of arc).

In practice, of course, this depends on whether the viewer is concentrating only on the center of the viewing field, whether the object is moving very slowly or not at all, and whether the object has good contrast to the background.

(A)

(B)

Figure 6.27 (A) 3mm (to be viewed at a 10-m distance). (B) 2mm.

As discussed previously, the actual resolution limit will not be used for further discussion but rather the detail size that can be clearly seen. Allowing for some amount of tolerance, this would be around 0.3mm at a 1-m distance (= 1.03 minutes of arc). In a certain range, one can assume a linear relation between distance and the detail size:

$$0.3\text{mm in } 1-\text{m distance} \approx 3\text{mm in } 10-\text{m distance}$$

This hypothesis can be easily proved. Pin the test pattern displayed in Figures 6.27A and B on a well-lit wall and walk away 10 m. You should be able to clearly differentiate between the lines and gaps in Figure 6.27A (3mm); in Figure 6.27B (2mm), however, the difference is barely seen. Of course, this requires an ideal visual acuity of 20/20. Nevertheless, if you can't resolve the pattern in Figure 6.27A, you might consider paying a visit to an ophthalmologist!

Large-Screen Projection

This experiment can be transferred for the conditions in a theater. Figure 6.28 shows the outline of a cinema with approximately 400 seats and a screen width of 12 m. The center row of the audience is at 10 m. An observer in this row would look at the screen with a viewing angle of 60 degrees. Assuming that the projection

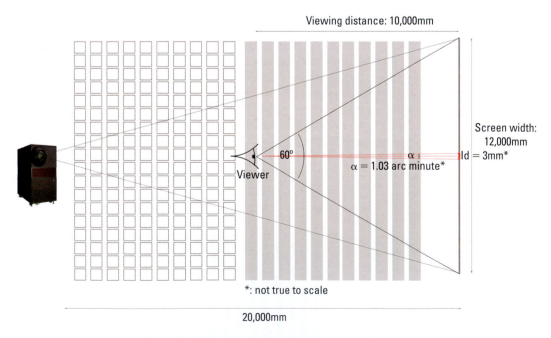

Figure 6.28 Resolution limit in the theater.

in this theater is digital, the observer could easily differentiate 12,000mm/3mm = 4000 pixels.

The resolution limit is not reached below a distance of 14 m. In other words, under these conditions more than 50% of the audience would see image detail up to the highest spatial frequency of the projector.

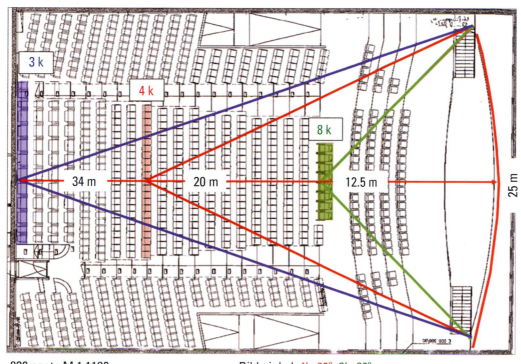

830 seats M 1:1190   Bildwinkel: 4k: 60°; 8k: 90°

Figure 6.29 Resolution limit for large screens.

Large theaters generally have screens with widths of 25 m or more. Figure 6.29 shows the number of pixels per image width that would be needed if the resolution limit of the eye were the critical parameter for dimensioning a digital projection.

Part 4 Summary

It can be concluded that the rumor is simply not true! A large portion of the audience would be able to see the 4k resolution of the projector. At the same time, the higher resolution inevitably raises the modulation of lower spatial frequencies, which in turn benefits everyone in the theater.

Conclusion

The discussions in this section have shown that a scientific approach is necessary to get a clear view of the real problem instead of merely counting megapixels. This section has addressed only the static image quality factors: sharpness and resolution. As mentioned at the start of this section, there are many more parameters to consider; therefore, an article about the transfer of photometry (sensitivity, contrast, characteristic curve) from scene to screen is being written.

References

Heynacher, E. (1963). Objective image quality criteria based on transformation theory with a subjective scale, Oberkochen, Germany. *Zeiss-Mitteilungen, 3*(1).

Simpson, G. <http://de.wikipedia.org/wiki/George_Gaylord_Simpson>. Accessed January 2008.

Tani, T. (2007). AgX photography: present and future. *Journal of Imaging Science and Technology, 51*(2), 110–116.

FILM SCANNING AND RECORDING
Charles Finance

Scanning

Scanning is the process by which the analog image that is visible on film (that is, what one considers as a traditional image composed of continuous tones of gray and infinitely varying colors) is converted into a digital file of zeros and ones. Every filmed element must first be scanned and converted to a digital format before it can be worked on in a computer.[9]

The fundamental function of every scanner is to produce a faithful digital replica of the filmed image. In doing so, scanners must deal with and reproduce the negative's resolution, dynamic range, density, and color. In scanning, the analog film image is converted to a digital file and stored in one of several formats. Common formats in use today are Cineon (developed by Kodak), DPX (Digital Picture Exchange), and TIFF (Tagged Image File Format). These formats are favored because they preserve the original raw image data of the film.

When scanning with raw image data formatting, as much of the original data as possible is captured and stored by the scanning device. By extension one can easily recognize that the scanning device's limitations will have a severe impact on the information that is captured. Therefore it is essential to have at least a passing understanding of scanning and the options available. And it is

---

[9] Scanning is needed only when starting with film, an *analog* process. There is no need for scanning when a project originates in digital form.

equally essential that tests be performed before one commits an entire project to a specific scanning company.

A scanner is comprised of several key elements: a film transport system, a light source, a digital sensor, electronics that convert the image to zeros and ones, a user interface (usually a computer workstation), and a storage device. That storage device—normally an array of hard drives—is not necessarily part of the scanning system but is nonetheless still important.

During scanning, film is moved past the scanner's light source and digital sensor, or light detector. Current scanners take two different approaches to how film is transported during scanning. In some models the film moves past the scanning aperture in a continuous path (continuous-scan). These types of scanners are descendants of earlier telecine technology that evolved primarily in television. The other type of scanner uses an intermittent pull-down in which the film is pulled down one frame at a time and is momentarily locked in place by register pins in the aperture as the image is scanned. These scanners are descendants of film technology.

Scans must have maximum image stability. The best scanning systems achieve image stability by pin-registering the film as it is scanned, similar to pin-registered cameras. Other scanning systems attempt to stabilize the image through utilization of optical registering. This is a system in which the sprockets of the film are measured optically and the image is digitally registered frame by frame to match the previous frame's sprockets. In spite of repeated attempts by manufacturers to produce truly stable images, these types of systems are not satisfactory for visual effects work because they cannot, at present, provide the reliably stable images necessary for critical effects shots. By paying close attention to the stability of the image at the scanning stage, one can hopefully begin the visual effects work without performing further stabilization of the image.[10]

Engineers have developed several methods for converting an analog image into streams of digital data. The details of that process are beyond the scope of this book. In each method, the scanner looks at almost 2.5 million points on a standard Academy 35mm frame, detects the color and luminance value of the light at each point, and converts that into a packet of digital data. This is accomplished by using a line array, frame array, or spot sampler type of digital sensor or chip.

Resolution

Of great importance to the visual effects practitioner is *resolution*. Scanning can be done at various resolutions, but as of this writing 2k is the most common. In a 2k scan the digital sensor reads

---

[10] Note that "tracking" of a plate is not the same as stabilizing the image.

the color and density of approximately 2000 points horizontally across the width of a full 35mm frame, and approximately 1500 points vertically.[11] This resolution has been found to be satisfactory for standard film projection in movie theaters.

Resolution of 4k is rapidly becoming more common in 35mm film work as the technology continues to improve. This represents not just a doubling, but effectively a *quadrupling* of the resolution over 2k. Scanning in 4k and then downsizing the resolution to 2k before the visual effects work is begun has also become an increasingly standard practice. Many VFX Supervisors and scanning scientists agree that "A superior scan requires a superior resolution source, generally twice that of the working resolution. For example, if a true 2k image is desired, then the scan has to be derived from a 4k scan and scaled down to the 2k image. This technique produces a superior scan more suitable for digital work."[12] It takes a fairly educated eye to tell the difference, but many leaders in the industry feel that even average viewers may be subliminally sensitive to the difference between 2k and 4k resolution.

Higher levels of resolutions of scanning are possible, and 65mm, IMAX, and other special-venue film formats usually employ 6k, 8k, and even higher resolutions. It is important to recognize that *resolution* is a term that is often misunderstood. For example, 4k on a 35mm frame is effectively a higher resolution than 4k on an IMAX frame. For a better understanding of the term and its ramifications, please see the preceding section on resolution and perceived sharpness of an image.

Storage

The scanning of film results in digital data. That data must be stored as it is scanned and then archived for later use. Usually, the scans are stored on large active hard drives on site and then backed up and also transferred to another storage medium that the client uses. Until recently this would have been onto several commonly used digital tape formats: DLT, DTF, Metrum, or Exabyte. The choice differed according to the tape drives that were being used by different digital facilities and their clients. However, like so much else in the industry, advancing technology has made these forms of digital storage obsolete. Today, data from digital scans are stored on portable or external hard drives or flash memory. From there, the data can be distributed to their end users, including visual effects facilities, on physical media or via secured Internet connections.

---

[11] The exact measurements are 2028 × 1556 pixels for a full-aperture (Super 35) frame.

[12] E-film website: www.efilm.com.

Estimating the Cost of Scanning

On most visual effects–heavy shows, a VFX Producer will have prepared a digital shot breakdown that lists the number of layers (meaning filmed elements) that need to be scanned. Since scanning costs are charged by the frame, it is essential to know how many layers are needed in each shot and the length in frames of each layer. Obviously, there is no way to know the exact number until the shot is filmed, edited, and sometimes temp or rough-comped together. To get around this dilemma in pre-production, VFX Producers use an industry-wide rule of thumb that assumes that a shot runs 5 seconds, or 120 frames (based on 24 fps). Experienced VFX Producers and Supervisors may also budget for an extra scan layer for each shot as a contingency because of the frequent changes that occur on set.

To the customary 120-frame length of a shot a *handle* is added, which is generally a minimum of 8 frames at the head and tail of each element or plate, for a total of 16 frames (though handles may be longer or shorter). As with all services, scanning costs vary and are negotiable. At the time of this writing, scanning services ranged from $0.45 to $0.55 per frame, and they may well continue to drift lower as the technology improves and competition from image capture by digital cameras becomes more common.

To gain an appreciation of how rapidly these costs can escalate, assume that there are 200 live-action plates to be scanned running an average of 5 seconds each, plus 16 frames of handle, for a total of 136 frames per layer. At $0.50 per frame, the scanning costs come to $13,600.

Be aware that most scanning facilities will charge a setup fee. These basically pay for a line-up person to take the negative supplied by production and prepare it for scanning. There is a certain amount of labor involved, and it is a delicate task since the line-up person must handle the original negative. As a general rule, the negative of several shots should be grouped together and sent to the scanning facility in batches. The number of setups, therefore, will be a fraction of the number of scan layers.

Recording

Recording—putting the digital image back on film—is currently the final step in the process of creating a visual effects shot.[13] This is where the digital file that represents each frame of an effects shot is converted from the digital into the analog (film) medium.

---

[13] However, it is increasingly more common to hand the digital files over to the digital intermediate (DI) facility where they are inserted into the DI version of the project, timed, and then output to film as the final step of the DI process. This topic is covered in the *Digital Intermediate* section later in this chapter.

In other words, it goes from a computer (which "thinks" in zeros and ones) back out to film (which is an actual image that is projected). Normally, the digital files are output to a new negative, which is then cut into the negative of the completed show.

Images are recorded out for a number of applications:
- delivery of visual effects shots,
- digital intermediates,
- HD-acquired productions,
- digital trailers,
- tape-to-film transfer,
- archive to film,
- digital film restoration, and
- long-form 65mm productions.

Approaches to Recording Out

Two technologically distinct approaches are used for recording digital files to film. In one method, the final images are photographed off a high-quality cathode-ray tube (CRT) not unlike the picture tube in a TV set but far superior in resolution. In the other, a laser beam is used to expose the film. Both methods result in a new negative that is cut into the completed show's negative.

Film-Out Requirements

A good film-out must meet the highest standards of the following critical qualities:
- *Resolution:* A measure of the sharpness of an image or of the fineness with which a device (such as a video display, printer, or scanner) can produce or record such an image, usually expressed as the total number or density of pixels in the image (e.g., a resolution of 1200 dots per inch).[14]
- *Dynamic range:* Visually speaking, the film, charge-coupled device (CCD), or sensor's ability to hold the brightest point to the darkest point. This ability, or range, is usually expressed as a curve. The distance between the highest and the lowest points *and* how smooth that curve is connecting the two visually demonstrates the dynamic range of the film or device.
- *Color fidelity:* The successful interoperability of color data, from image creation or capture to output across multiple media such as film, broadcast, DVD, etc., such that the color reproduction quality remains consistent throughout.

Both recording technologies—CRT and laser based—have their advocates. Of the two methods, laser-based recording is now widely recognized as yielding better results for 35mm theatrical projects. However, it should be noted that recording

---

[14] *Merriam-Webster's Dictionary.*

from CRT is still used extensively for large-format films, such as IMAX, because a CRT tube offers a larger target from which to record.

It is good practice to test film-out technologies across several different facilities, using the same negative before choosing a facility to execute the work. The differences among facilities can be significant.

Estimating the Cost of Recording

As with scanning, recording is charged by the frame. On average, record-out costs tend to be slightly higher than scanning, but can also be negotiated to $0.65 to $0.75 or less, especially if a high volume of work can be guaranteed to a facility.

To continue with the previous example, assume that the number of visual effects shots that actually ends up in a movie is 100, each averaging 5 seconds for a total of 12,000 frames to be recorded out to film. To estimate record-out costs under this scenario, one would apply the formula of number of shots (100 in the example) × 120 (the number of assumed frames) × cost per frame. At a median price of $0.70/frame, recording costs would come to $8,400.

Whereas scanning is usually acceptable on the first try, that is not the case with recording or filming out. Visual effects shots typically have to be recorded two or three times before they are deemed acceptable (and that's not counting the tests a facility may record for its own purposes). In large part this is because digital artists view their images on monitors, and no matter how good a monitor is it is extremely difficult—even for a discerning eye—to see tiny flaws that are readily visible when the shot is projected on a theater screen. What is more, a shot may not "cut in" well with the surrounding shots in terms of its color, density, contrast, graininess, and other qualities. So the first record-out may serve more as an opportunity to tweak the shot than as the final accepted version of the shot. Using these common practices, by the time the 100 shots are approved, thousands of additional dollars will have been added to recording costs. And that does not include additional items such as color or resolution tests, rescans, and lab costs.

Ideally one would record out only the exact number of frames of each shot as it appears in the cut. However, in actual practice it has become relatively common for a visual effects facility to be asked to output shots up to 3 feet longer than they are in the cut to give directors and editors the ability to change the cut up to the time of making the digital intermediate.

Most facilities that perform this service will also have a setup charge. As with scanning, finished effects shots are sent to the recording facility in batches whenever possible. But because final composites can sometimes dribble out of a visual effects facility one at a time, it is difficult to guess at a consistent average for the number of shots per batch. Three is probably as good a number as any.

Recorders also should be pin registered. Output is commonly recorded to Eastman 5242 or Fuji intermediate stock. It is best to have the facility do the record-out at the stock's full dynamic range. Virtually all recorders run at much lower than real-time speed, capable of recording only a few frames per second. Only one system, whose use is confined mainly to Europe for limited film releases, is capable of recording out at real-time speed.

COLOR MANAGEMENT
Joseph Goldstone

Any visual effects professional whose personal contribution is judged on color should read the three guidelines below; anyone building a workflow from scratch or integrating existing workflows should read (or at least skim) this entire section.

The Three Guidelines

1. Make critical color decisions in the screening room, not in an artist's cubicle.
2. At the desktop, use an open-source or commercial color management system if possible, but don't expect too much.
3. Understand and document the color image encodings produced by a production's digital motion picture (DMP) cameras, renderers, and film scanners, and the encodings consumed by displays, film recorders, and digital projectors that deliver production output to clients.

Digital Color Image Encodings and Digital Cameras

Visual effects work now includes a bewildering variety of image representations: 10-bit log scanner output, 8-bit *display-ready* images *baked* for sRGB monitors, Adobe RGB-encoded *wide-gamut* reference plates from still cameras, and now *raw* (sometimes inappropriately termed *log*) data from digital motion picture cameras. The best way to compare two image encodings (*encoding* encompasses not just the image bits but their meaning and expected viewing environment as well) is to map them onto the same standard conceptual framework.

Compared here are two color image encodings usually available from high-end digital single lens reflex (DSLR) still cameras: a well-defined display-ready Adobe RGB image encoding and a less-well-defined *camera raw* image encoding. This situation closely parallels the traditional HD and raw image encodings employed by digital cameras from Panavision, ARRI, Thomson, Red, and other manufacturers. The terminology in Figure 6.30 will be explained as these two image encodings are discussed.

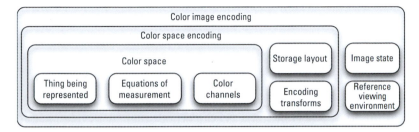

Figure 6.30 Conceptual color image encoding hierarchy. (Image courtesy of Joseph Goldstone.)

At the lowest level—and in the diagram's innermost boxes—Adobe RGB's color space is defined[15] to represent colors as they would be measured by some physical device.[16] Measured colors, with the measurement results expressed in terms of what are termed the *CIE X, Y,* and *Z* primaries (described in detail shortly), can be converted to corresponding amounts of Adobe RGB's R, G, and B primaries by multiplying X, Y, and Z against a 3 × 3 matrix given in the Adobe RGB specification. The RGB values are represented as normalized numbers (i.e., between 0.0 and 1.0).

Adobe RGB's color space encoding specification provides for two methods of digitally encoding RGB color space values for storage: as unsigned 8-bit integers and as unsigned 16-bit integers. The normalized values are put through a simple power function with exponent 2.19921875, the output of which is scaled to either 0.0 to 255.0 for the unsigned 8-bit integer encoding, or 0.0 to 65535.0 for the unsigned 16-bit integer encoding, and finally the interpolated value is rounded to the nearest whole number and stored in the 8- or 16-bit field.

Finally, Adobe RGB's color image encoding specifies that the image colors as a whole are those of an image ready for display. Several terms are used to express this idea: Such an image

---

[15] See http://www.adobe.com/digitalimag/pdfs/AdobeRGB1998.pdf.
[16] Physical device measurement is not the only basis for color systems; some spaces are defined in perceptual terms and thus include color processing done by the brain. All of the color spaces listed in this section are measurable; that is, they represent color stimuli, not perceptions of color stimuli.

is said to be *output-referred* or—in an unfortunate collision with an existing visual effects term—such an image is said to be *color rendered. Color rendering* in the language of color science and color management means the transformation of an image to account for differences in viewing environment. A digital still camera producing JPEG files (typically encoded in either the Adobe RGB color space or sRGB[17]) will color render the captured image to account for the difference between, for example, the image subject standing in bright sunlight on a desert mesa, and the image reproduction in a typical office on a monitor whose peak white luminance is hundreds of times less powerful than desert sunlight. Such color rendering is usually performed prior to the quantization and rounding specified by the color space encoding.

Adobe RGB says nothing about how the color rendering was performed; the specification is concerned solely with displayable imagery, and any details of how the displayable image came to be are irrelevant. The details of display, on the other hand, are very relevant: The colors are intended to be viewed on a display with a peak white luminance of 160 cd/m² (roughly 47 foot-lamberts), whose contrast ratio is roughly 290:1, with the white's chromaticity being that of D65 (roughly the color of overcast daylight), and with the area immediately around the image being a gray of identical chromaticity but with 20% of the luminance of displayed white.

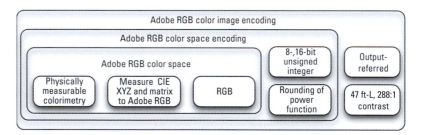

Figure 6.31 Color image encoding hierarchy for Adobe RGB. (Image courtesy of Joseph Goldstone.)

Turning to camera raw formats for digital still and motion picture cameras, Figure 6.32 shows those color image encodings are quite different from that of Adobe RGB.

Like Adobe RGB, the camera raw colors represent physically measurable colors. Unlike Adobe RGB, there is no mandated breakdown into particular image channels; some raw formats used by single-sensor cameras, for example, provide for two green channels if the camera sensor contains twice the number

---

[17] sRGB: a color space designed to support the use of desktop displays.

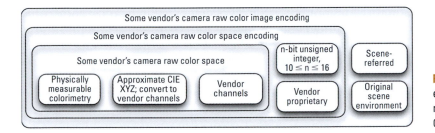

Figure 6.32 Color image encoding hierarchy for camera raw. (Image courtesy of Joseph Goldstone.)

of green-filtered pixels as it does red-filtered and blue-filtered ones.

The encoded colors leaving the camera are similarly unconstrained, but typically the encoding provides for three or four channels and the bit depth (not necessarily the same for all channels) ranges between 10 and 16 bits.

With all of this uncertainty it is reasonable to ask why anyone would want camera raw encodings. The answer is that the image data are not color rendered; in color management terms, they are *scene referred*. If the vendor provides some post-processing tool that converts the image data to a more standard RGB encoding without losing the raw nature of the image data (that is, without color rendering it for some display device), then this scene-referred data may play very well with CGI renderers and compositors. For digital still cameras, Adobe's DNG Converter and Dave Coffin's open-source dcraw program can be used to perform this type of extraction. For digital motion picture cameras, there are no such well-publicized, freely available tools at the time of this writing (early 2010), although the input device transforms of the Academy of Motion Picture Arts and Sciences' Image Interchange Framework (discussed elsewhere in this chapter) will provide this ability when available.

With raw encodings, color rendering will need to be done downstream before the completed shot is shown in a theater. Color rendering is more easily done by the visual effects team, however, than it can be undone if the camera manufacturer has baked in color rendering in a non-raw format.

The color image encoding for camera raw implicitly has as its viewing environment the original scene itself.

CIE XYZ Colorimetry and CIE Chromaticity Coordinates

In introducing Adobe RGB, it was mentioned that Adobe RGB's definitions of red, green, and blue are provided by mathematical derivation from CIE XYZ values—but what are CIE XYZ values? The psychophysics and mathematics by which colors are specified was worked out in the early 20th century and standardized by the

Commission Internationale d'Éclairage (CIE); the most commonly used device-independent metric for colorimetric specification is known as the CIE 1931 Standard Observer, which describes colors in terms of their relative proportions of three primaries: X, Y, and Z (often pronounced "big X," "big Y," and "big Z" or "cap X," "cap Y," and "cap Z"). These proportions are called a color's *tristimulus values*. Any color thus described can be used to derive a second CIE quantity, known as that color's *chromaticity*, a measure that expresses the aspects of color disregarding luminance. The usual way to express chromaticity is in terms of chromaticity coordinates x and y (pronounced "little x" and "little y"). The equations relating x and y and X, Y, and Z are shown in Figure 6.33.

x, y chromaticity coordinates are derived from *X, Y, Z* colorimetry:

$$x = \frac{X}{X+Y+Z}, \; y = \frac{Y}{X+Y+Z}$$

For chromaticity coordinates *x, y* recovery of *X, Y, Z* colorimetry is possible if *Y* is known:

$$X = Y\frac{x}{y}, \; Z = Y\frac{1-(x+y)}{y}$$

Figure 6.33 Equations relating x, y and X, Y, and Z. (Image courtesy of Joseph Goldstone.)

Commonly Encountered Primaries and White Points

A projection of the chromaticity coordinates of a color space's primaries onto a 2D plane is often (and misleadingly) used to compare a color space's coverage of the set of all possible colors. Figure 6.34 gives chromaticity coordinates for primaries and white points of color space data metrics used in visual effects practice. Figure 6.35 shows the primaries projected onto a chromaticity diagram. For a better way to compare color spaces, see Figure 6.36.

6D-5 Primaries and white points

Name	red x	red y	green x	green y	blue x	blue y	white x	white y
BT.709	0.6400	0.3300	0.3000	0.6000	0.1500	0.0600	0.3127	0.3290
sRGB	0.6400	0.3300	0.3000	0.6000	0.1500	0.0600	0.3127	0.3290
AdobeRGB	0.6400	0.3300	0.2100	0.7100	0.1500	0.0600	0.3127	0.3290
ACES	0.73470	0.26530	0.00000	1.00000	0.00010	−0.07700	0.32168	0.33767
DCI-P3	0.6800	0.3200	0.2650	0.6900	0.1500	0.0600	0.314	0.351

Figure 6.34 Primaries and white points of various encodings. (Image courtesy of Joseph Goldstone.)

Camera Color Analysis Gamuts

The portion of the color space where a camera's output (or other capture system's output; scanned film will be described later in this section) distinguishes color variation is sometimes termed its *color analysis gamut.* For DMP cameras the color analysis gamut is limited by both what the camera sensors can differentiate and by the set of colors the camera output encoding can represent.

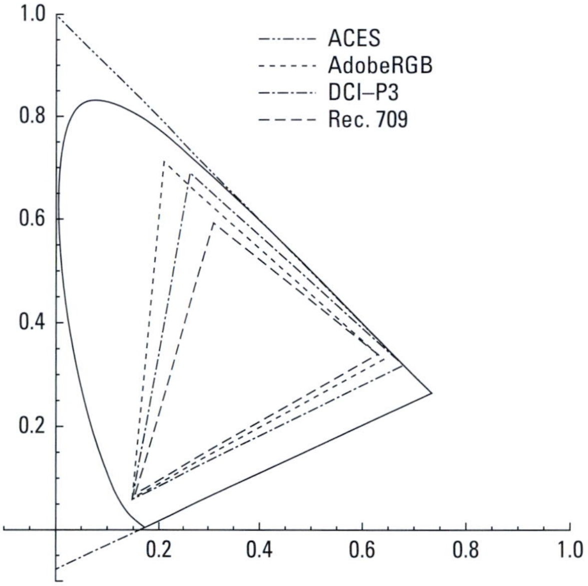

RGB Triangles on the Chromaticity Diagram

If a camera were to output CIE XYZ signals, those signals could represent any captured color (since CIE XYZ by definition represents all colors). No commercially available DMP camera outputs XYZ signals, however; usually the color space output encoding is some form of RGB (as RGB, or internally processed to YCbCr). Placing the three BT.709 RGB primaries on a chromaticity diagram (within a vaguely horseshoe-shaped boundary representing the spectral locus) makes it clear that many commonly used encoding primaries cannot be combined in positive proportion to represent the full range of colors. (Emergent schemes for wide-gamut color encodings allow RGB weights below zero and above unity but these schemes aren't yet well standardized, nor therefore widely deployed.)

Figure 6.35 Primaries and the set of chromaticities perceived by humans. (Image courtesy of Joseph Goldstone.)

Display Reproduction Gamuts

The counterpart to the camera color analysis gamut is the display reproduction gamut, the set of all colors that a display can reproduce. In an effort to satisfy the needs of the graphic arts industries, desktop monitor manufacturers have expanded the reproduction gamuts of their high-end products considerably in the past few years; today's best monitors can match all or nearly all of the colors in the reproduction gamut of exhibition-venue commercial digital projection (although high-end projectors in darkened theaters still have a bigger gamut near black because of substantially higher contrast than desktop displays).

This expansion has had the benefit of allowing visual effects artists to see colors at the desktop that previously might have been clipped to the boundary of a smaller (typically sRGB) reproduction gamut volume. On the flip side it means that whereas previously an sRGB-compliant display might have properly reproduced the colors of the encoded image, a wide-gamut display supplied with sRGB-encoded imagery will—in the absence of color management—misinterpret the encoded image. The most common sign of this is when certain memory colors (green grass, for example) are reproduced with extreme oversaturation.

Figure 6.36 compares[18] the reproduction gamut of a laptop monitor with that of a monitor reproducing most of the colors produced by a commercial theatrical venue digital projector. The point is not to denigrate laptop capabilities; it is that reproduction gamut comparisons should be made volumetrically.

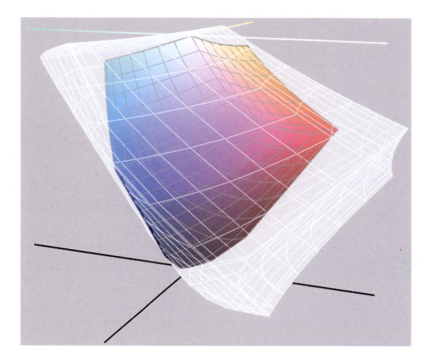

Figure 6.36 Comparison of monitor reproduction gamuts. (Image courtesy of Joseph Goldstone.)

Transcoding versus Color Rerendering

The complexity of transforming color image data optimized for one display into image data optimized for another display will depend, obviously, on the degree of difference between the two. If the displays' black levels, white luminance, and viewing conditions are identical, and if the displays' relationships between signal level and output (a display's gamma) are similarly so, but the primary chromaticities are different, for example, then the encoded colors can be transcoded by linearizing[19] the first display's encoded RGB values, converting them to CIE XYZ values, converting those CIE

---

[18] Note that the comparison adds a new dimension (luminance) and is thus volumetric. Gamut comparisons based on chromaticity diagrams alone (in CIE x, y space, or related planar spaces) are extremely misleading and benefit only marketers and vendors, not artists.

[19] *Linear* here means radiometrically linear: Double the luminance reflected or emitted by an object, and the code value representing that luminance doubles as well. This is how users of CGI renderers understand the term *linear*; it is *not* how video engineers understand the term—they believe *linear* implies a power function.

XYZ values to the corresponding RGB values for the second display, and reimposing the encoding nonlinearity.[20]

If the contrast or white levels or viewing conditions are grossly dissimilar, then the best solution is probably color rerendering: Any color rendering implicitly or explicitly done for the first display is undone, and the non-color-rendered CIE XYZ values are color rendered for the second display.

Gamut Clipping, Gamut Warnings, and Gamut Mapping

CG artists frequently use monitors that cannot accurately display image data created by large-gamut capture systems. How this can happen with film will be described shortly, but the particular gamut of film isn't required to exemplify the problem.

Consider once more a camera producing images encoded in Adobe RGB, which has a more saturated green primary than many other encodings. If that camera captures an image of an extremely green object—one with many different shades of a green so intense they are almost at the limit of what Adobe RGB can represent—and those images are displayed on a DCI-P3-compliant projector, and if the green shades are legal Adobe RGB values falling outside the DCI-P3 gamut, the intense greens may "block up" as the projector reaches its limits in reproducing those shades.

Such gamut clipping is almost always objectionable. The alternatives are to provide some warning when it occurs (for more subtle instances of the problem) or to systematically transform the encoded image data by nonlinearly compressing it into the reproduction gamut in some visually acceptable fashion. Gamut mapping strategies can be quite complex and are outside the scope of this chapter.[21]

Color Management at the Desktop

With the above as background, the responsibilities of any color management system are thus to:

- Interpret image data according to the image's associated color image encoding.
- Provide a path to and from some common color space in which the correctly interpreted captured image data can be combined (a "working space").
- Display those original or combined image data as an accurate reproduction of what the final consumer (e.g., moviegoer) will see.

---

[20] See "Appendix H: Color-Primary Conversions," in Edward J. Giorgianni and Thomas E. Madden, *Digital Color Management: Encoding Solutions* (2nd ed.) (John Wiley and Sons, 2008).
[21] *Color Gamut Mapping* (Jan Morovic, Wiley, 2008) provides a comprehensive treatment of gamut mapping strategies.

The description of the relationship between capture device code values and some reference colorimetric space is held by what is variously called an *input profile*, or an *input device transform,* or some similar nomenclature.

The space in which image data is combined is often based on some form of CIE colorimetry, either CIE XYZ, or a derived space such as CIE LAB (which has the advantage of being more perceptually uniform than CIE XYZ: In the 3D CIE LAB color space, a distance of one unit between any two represented colors means that they are just barely perceptible as different).

The relationship between the encoded image data accepted by digital display devices and the CIE colorimetry that those devices then produce is described by an output profile (or in some systems, an output device transform). Typically this is an analytical or empirical mapping between RGB code values and the resultant displayed CIE XYZ colorimetry; also typically, what is needed is the inverse of this mapping.

If one color renders the colorimetry of the captured, synthesized, or composited scene, the result is CIE XYZ, or some RGB values that can be related to CIE XYZ by a simple 3×3 matrix. What needs to be sent to the display device, however, are device code values, so the output device profile must be inverted to get an analytic or empirical mapping from the color-rendered, displayable colorimetry to the device code values that will produce that colorimetry. Note that any color management system doing this will have to deal with the case where the output of the color-rendering algorithm is outside the reproduction gamut of the chosen device; how this is handled tends to be specific to the particular color management system.

The ICC Color Management Architecture

As a first illustration of such systems, consider the color management architecture proposed by the International Color Consortium (ICC). This is the color management system underlying most Adobe products; in addition to proprietary implementations by Adobe, Kodak, Apple, Microsoft, Canon, Sun, etc., there are at least three open-source[22] ICC implementations as well.

In the ICC architecture, an input profile defines the mapping of input code values from a capture device into the Profile Connection Space (PCS). The ICC PCS was originally created to meet the needs of the graphic arts industry, but has been used with some success in DMP work. ICC PCS values represent col-

[22] As can be found by searching for "color management" on http://www.sourceforge.net.

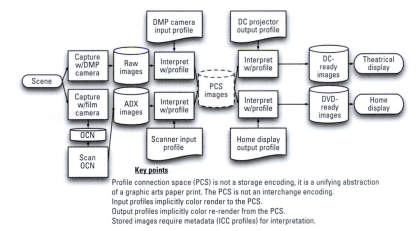

Key points

Profile connection space (PCS) is not a storage encoding, it is a unifying abstraction of a graphic arts paper print. The PCS is not an interchange encoding.
Input profiles implicitly color render to the PCS.
Output profiles implicitly color re-render from the PCS.
Stored images require metadata (ICC profiles) for interpretation.

Figure 6.37 Color management using the ICC architecture. (Image courtesy of Joseph Goldstone.)

ors ready for printing on a graphic arts press and thus are already color rendered. In Figure 6.37, ICC input profiles map captured image data code values from a digital still camera (DSC) and a digital motion picture camera (DMP) into the PCS. An ICC output profile maps PCS values into digital projector code values, appropriately rerendering the PCS colorimetry for the darker cinema-viewing environment. Additionally, an ICC display profile may be used in conjunction with the digital projector output profile to preview the appearance of the cinema projection on a desktop monitor (within the reproduction gamut limits of that desktop monitor).[23]

Almost every commercial desktop display calibration system is capable of creating an ICC display profile once the device has been calibrated and characterized. Some vendors offer hardware and software to calibrate digital cameras. As for hardware and software to calibrate film-based capture and projection systems (to jump ahead slightly), there are no prominent vendors offering such products based on the ICC system; specific characterizations are done in house or by consultants. That said, recent Adobe products include ICC profiles for some common original camera negative (OCN) and print stocks.

Note that in the ICC system, image data are stored using a wide variety of color encodings: The color management depends critically on metadata in the form of ICC profiles and there is no emphasis on—in fact, there is active discouragement against—storing image data in the PCS.

[23] For more detail on the use of ICC profiles, see Phil Green (ed.), *Color Management: Understanding and Using ICC Profiles* (New York: Wiley, 2010); also see the ICC website's white papers, available at www.color.org.

The AMPAS Image Interchange Framework

A second open-source[24] color management system is the Academy of Motion Picture Arts and Sciences (AMPAS) Image Interchange Framework (IIF). At the time of this writing (early 2010), the IIF is unfinished but under active development and testing. In the IIF, the emphasis is on conversion of image data to a common colorimetric format. The barest bones of the IIF architecture are shown in Figure 6.38.

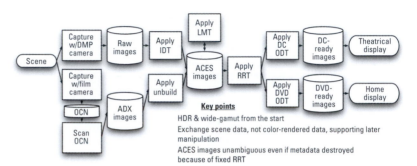

Figure 6.38 Color management using IIF. (Image courtesy of Joseph Goldstone.)

Input transforms process the image data code values produced by digital cameras and convert those data into Academy Color Encoding Specification (ACES) RGB relative exposure values. Color image data converted from various devices are brought together as ACES values, much as (roughly speaking) the ICC brings together data from various devices as PCS values.

The ICC architecture depends on metadata, in the form of ICC profiles. Transformed images identified as being encoded as per the ACES document are unambiguous without further metadata. Figure 6.39 maps the encoding given in the ACES document into the conceptual hierarchy of Figure 6.30.

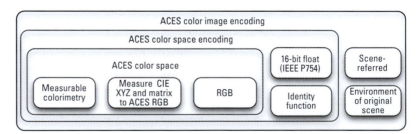

Figure 6.39 The ACES color image encoding. (Image courtesy of Joseph Goldstone.)

The color rendering performed on ACES data is always the same: a reference rendering transform (RRT) takes the ACES RGB relative exposure values representing the scene and transforms them into colorimetry suitable for display in a darkened theater

[24] See http://www.stcatp.org.

by some idealized display device. The output of the RRT is then mapped through a device-specific output device transform (ODT) designed to approximate best the appearance of the ideal darkened theater image on some particular class of display and in some viewing environment, whether a digital projector, a desktop HDR display, or a Rec. 709 broadcast monitor.

Commercial Color Management Packages

As of early 2010, there were two commercial color management systems with substantial market penetration in the DMP industry: the Truelight system from FilmLight Limited and the cineSpace system from Cine-tal (originally developed by Rising Sun Research). Both are well engineered, widely used, and provide comprehensive documentation to supplement the information in this section,[25] both in the particulars of those systems and on color management for motion picture work. Neither uses the ICC or the IIF in their architecture or implementation.

Intersection with On-Set Practices

As discussed at the beginning of this section, the advantage of acquiring DMP image data in raw mode is that creative decisions are not irrevocably baked into the encoded image data. The disadvantage is that capture-time review of raw data requires some form of on-set color rendering for display. This is typically done by special-purpose hardware that interprets the video stream, applies color rendering for a high-quality on-set display, saves the transform, and passes that transform on as metadata to post-production.

The color rendering is normally accomplished by a 3D lookup table (LUT) built by a manufacturer, by a digital imaging technician (DIT)—possibly at a rental company—or by a DP. The look of this transform may be portably encoded in the color decision list (CDL) whose format is defined by the American Society of Cinematographers (ASC); some parts are not yet standardized and call for careful documentation and cooperative testing between the production and post-production facilities. Without such cooperation and in the absence of a full standard for the description of the desired look, a raw workflow may produce images that may be firmly locked to scene radiometry but which are aesthetically adrift, disassociated from the DP's intent.

---

[25] Both provide downloadable white papers describing not just their products, but their take on the industry problems they are attempting to address. In evaluating the utility of commercial or open-source color management, *all* of this documentation—proprietary and open-source alike—should be considered required reading.

Some Desktop Color Management Caveats

Always buy displays after doing side-by-side comparisons that keep the considerations here in mind. Never buy monitors based solely on a vendor's datasheet.

Ideally (from a color engineer's viewpoint, not a producer's viewpoint) every artist would have his or her own screening room, and the issues about to be listed would not apply. Given that color-critical judgments will inevitably be made at the desktop, however, visual effects staff should be aware[26] of the following five factors that influence the artist's perception of a displayed color, and two factors that influence the displayed color itself:

- Glare from incidental light sources (a skylight, a neighboring cubicle's desk lamp, etc.) reflecting off a display's surface will lower color contrast and saturation. If the unwanted light is chromatic, the color's hue will also be affected.
- Viewing-angle dependencies (especially with LCD displays) can cause observers clustered near a monitor to each see a different color. The classic publicity shot of the heads of an artist and VFX Supervisor bent over a monitor virtually guarantees they are seeing different colors on the display surface.
- A display's correlated color temperature (CCT) is not an accurate predictor of its neutral chromaticity.[27] Use hardware and software that can calibrate a monitor's neutrals to match a particular pair of CIE x, y chromaticity coordinates, since many perceived colors can share the same CCT.
- Inappropriate color cues, such as a to-do note on a monitor bezel or even a white memo taped to a nearby wall,[28] will cause observers to misjudge the chromaticity corresponding to neutral colors. Movie audiences "white balance" to the content based on their memory of objects they "know" are white: snow, a white coffee cup, and the white letters on a road sign. Artists should adapt to neutrals in the subject material, as theatergoers do.
- A light surround inflates perceived image luminance contrast. If a shot's colors are chosen or adjusted with the image surrounded by a lighter background, that image might look low

---

[26] Mark Fairchild, *Color Appearance Models* (New York: Wiley, 2005) covers this topic in depth; see also the previously mentioned *Digital Color Management: Encoding Solutions* by Giorgianni and Madden.

[27] Wikipedia's "Correlated Color Temperature" article has a particularly good section showing many different chromaticity coordinates mapping to the same CCT.

[28] Inappropriate color cues can also result when on-screen elements that the artist traditionally regards as neutral (such as gray-colored system or application menus) have their displayed color changed by color management systems that rewrite low-level 1D lookup tables in the graphics card. Such low-level manipulations unfortunately affect all on-screen elements, not just the image data being color-managed.

contrast in theatrical presentation. Craft-store black velvet or even stage duvetyne are better approximations to theatrical projection than a light aluminum bezel.

- The absolute luminance levels of colors affect the perception of their colorfulness. If a desktop monitor's peak white luminance (measured with a colorimeter or even a spot meter) is several times that of the luminance of projected white in a theater, the projected image will appear less vivid than its preview at the desktop.[29]
- The angular subtense of a color stimulus influences its appearance, as most people have learned when repainting their kitchen with colors chosen from small paint chips in a store rack. In the theater, always make color judgments from the same seat, and try to emulate this in the cubicle.

Two other things should also be kept in mind:

- Monitor color reproduction gamuts merely approximate digital and film projection reproduction gamuts. Use desktop image review software that can flag regions where the color on the desktop display is known to be an inaccurate preview of the color of the final projected image.
- That said, remember that a desktop display's inability to preview a color that a digital projector might produce (or a film projector might project) is not a liability as long as none of the production's content uses that color. The colors of a documentary on strip-mining for coal will probably not suffer if a desktop display cannot match the deepest indigo or most brilliant red of digital projection.

Bringing Color Management to Film Workflows

Today there are many more film theaters than there are digital theaters, and film projection will have a long tail-out. The dyes present in processed film register scene colors by modulating the way in which the film transmits light of various wavelengths. Any data metric for film-captured images, then, must have as its foundation some wavelength-dependent function; in the parlance of color science and international standards work, these wavelength-dependent functions are known as the *spectral condition defining density*.

Spectral Conditions Underlying Densitometric Data Metrics

For the motion picture industry, five spectral conditions are relevant. Two of them are used for process control: ISO Status M density's underlying spectral condition helps in keeping negative development steady (or can be used forensically when

---

[29] This also accounts for a mismatch in vividness when a monitor is brought into a screening room for a misguided side-by-side comparison.

development goes awry) and ISO Status A density's underlying spectral condition serves the same function for print development. When a production assistant calls out lab variances at dailies, he or she is basing that assessment on Status A density. Process control densities are less than optimal for predicting projected color. For that purpose, three spectral conditions are used to determine printing densities, which numerically encode the way the print will register the colors encoded on the negative:

1. Cineon printing density's (CPD's) spectral condition,
2. the spectral condition of SMPTE RP-180,[30] and
3. Academy printing density's (APD's) spectral condition.

Graphs of two of the three spectral conditions are shown superimposed in Figure 6.40, with the older RP-180 spectral condition indicated in thin lines and the newer APD in thick lines.

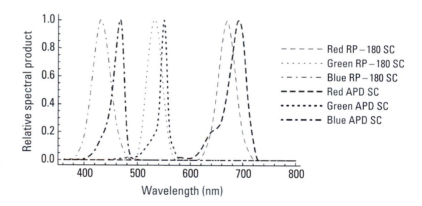

Figure 6.40 Spectral conditions defining density. (Image courtesy of Joseph Goldstone.)

The spectral condition for Kodak's original Cineon printing density (circa 1993) was proprietary and never made public; the consequence was considerable scanner vendor-to-scanner vendor and facility-to-facility inconsistency in producing "Cineon" scans of the same negative; scanner vendors reverse-engineered the Cineon spectral condition independently.

Densitometric Color Spaces and Data Metrics

Not only are CPD and the printing density associated with SMPTE RP-180 showing their age in terms of applicability to contemporary print stock, but also the ranges of their associated color space encodings are now unable to cope with the extended

---

[30] This spectral condition is sometimes mistakenly termed *DPX density* because it was intended to define a densitometric data metric to be used with SMPTE 268M, "File Format for Digital Moving-Picture Exchange (DPX)."

density range registered on contemporary original camera negative (OCN) stocks such as Kodak 5219. Cineon and DPX both encode printing density into three 10-bit fields with the minimal pixel-value change indicating a 0.002 increment of printing density over average OCN base density. Cineon encoded the OCN average base density at code value 95, to avoid clipping pixels whose individual densities scanned at below the OCN average base density. When code value provision for this headroom is included, the larger contemporary OCN density ranges shown in Figure 6.41 cannot be encoded in a 10-bit field with single-bit changes indicating a 0.002 printing density increment.

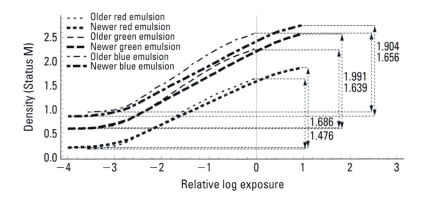

Figure 6.41 Encoding ranges and contemporary OCN densities. (Image courtesy of Joseph Goldstone.)

Users of Cineon or DPX color image encodings whose image content uses the full range of newer emulsions must either clip highlight values or use a nonstandard and nonportable printing density increment to squeeze the densities into the storage layout of the encoding. Although there appears to have been provision to indicate a nonstandard density increment in Cineon or DPX headers, no Cineon or DPX I/O libraries known at the time of this writing pay attention to the relevant header fields, and therefore production must carefully make each internal and farmed-out user of the image aware of the nonstandard encoding.

Academy Density Exchange Encoding (ADX) in its recommended ADX_{16} form will provide 16-bit rather than 10-bit fields, supporting a density range of nearly 8.192 over base,[31] and thus avoid this problem entirely. ADX-compliant scanners were estimated to become commercially available as soon as mid-2010.

---

[31] ADX also offers finer granularity in encoding densities (a single-bit change represents an increment of 0.000125 in density) and per-channel scaling factors to maximize encoding efficiency while preserving the property that equal encoded values imply neutral colors.

Characteristics of Film Scanners as Image Capture Devices

Whereas the relationship between scene colorimetry and digital camera sensor linear output values can be reasonably approximated by a 3×3 matrix transform (much as is the case with additive displays), the relationship between scene colorimetry and scanner transmission sensor output values is much more complicated. The sensitivity of the multiple layers of film is complicated by crosstalk that can vary with the intensity of the exposing light, and by films that are designed to deviate from literal capture of scene colorimetry in favor of more pleasing colorimetry (exaggerating the green of grass, for example, or the blue of captured sky). Moreover, any crosstalk in film sensitivities is compounded by possible crosstalk at the scanner sensor level.

Film Unbuilding and Film Building

Analytic models of the relationship between scene color and captured density are considerably more complex than their digital counterparts. Most such models are proprietary, although Kodak and FujiFilm have cooperated with the AMPAS IIF effort in creating a transformation from APD densitometry to ACES colorimetry (that is, ACES RGB relative exposure values). In the IIF architecture, using this transform is termed *unbuilding*[32] the film; inverting the transform (*building* the film) produces APD values from ACES RGB relative exposure values.

The Film Reproduction Gamut

Film's continued use as a delivery medium is not just habit, nor is it purely a matter of the cost of converting theaters for digital projection. For those who originate their project on film, or who digitally capture or synthesize images using an encoding that supports a wide gamut, film provides certain colors that are not produced by any current commercially available digital projection system. Glacier ice, for example, contains a wealth of dark cyan detail that typically is clipped by digital projection, and certain deep pure yellows can be produced with film but not with current digital projection technology. That said, no film print can ever hit the deep red of a freshly painted fire engine, but digital projection systems can easily achieve the needed luminance and chromaticities.

---

[32] Note that IIF *building* and *unbuilding* transforms produce and consume colorimetry that includes the unique per-stock characteristics of the film. If a DP chooses an OCN stock for its warm highlights, that warmth will be in the ACES RGB relative exposure values resulting from the unbuild.

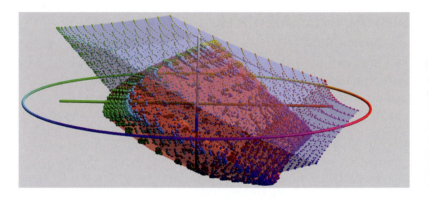

Figure 6.42 This color plate shows the relationship between the reproduction gamut of commercial-grade digital projection (sharp-edged color solid) and that of projected film (rounded edges).
(Image courtesy of Joseph Goldstone.)

Film at the Desktop

The difficulty of modeling the nonlinear relationship between densitometrically encoded image data (that is, printing density values) and reproduced colorimetry is such that the traditional video card's three independent 1D LUTs cannot provide the processing required for a credible prediction of projected film. Instead, 3D LUTs can be created to express the interdependencies between the color channels, usually by spectral measurement of filmed-out color cubes, each frame of the film-out being a full-frame patch of color. The resultant transmission spectra are combined with a spectral measurement of a film projector's open-gate light bounced off a theater screen to predict the projected colorimetry of a film-out. Such characterization is available from most providers of color management software or through independent consultants.

Figure 6.43 Spectral transmission measurement of a filmed-out color cube. (Note film loaded into right-hand unit.)
(Image courtesy of Joseph Goldstone.)

DIGITAL INTERMEDIATE
Christopher Townsend

The digital intermediary is a part of the post process that is gathering more importance and relevance within the filmmaker's toolbox. This phase of post-production is also known as *color grading, timing, finishing,* or more commonly, the *DI.* It has become a stage that can alter the entire look of a project. By enhancing, among other things, the color, saturation, and contrast palette, filmmakers can add drama and nuance, hence changing the mood of a piece. Knowing that most films go through a DI stage adds one more layer about which visual effects professionals need to be aware. Now, the image that leaves the visual effects facility and is "finaled" by the director is not necessarily the same image that appears in the final film in the theater. The line between what was traditionally done by a visual effects company and what can be done at the DI stage is getting more blurred all the time.

The DI stage can be an incredibly powerful finishing tool, allowing filmmakers to tweak a shot, often separating the image into different areas or layers, using power windows, rotoscoping, or mattes provided by a visual effects company.

Power windows are traditionally simple geometric shapes that are used as mattes or stencils, through which an image is enhanced in certain areas. For example, a circular power window may be used to brighten just the area of an actor's face, or a rectangular one can be used to darken a sky.

Rotoscoping is basically a more complex (and more accurate and more versatile) version of power windows. The operator creates a spline around the area that needs to be enhanced, keyframing it if necessary.

Mattes from a visual effects company, for certain areas or objects, may be requested by the DI team to be used to protect or adjust specific areas of the shot. Creating mattes can add expense and additional workload for a visual effects company but can be very useful. The fear that all of those meticulously constructed composites can quickly be torn apart if mattes are not used judiciously is well founded, so such work should be carefully supervised.

What does this mean to the visual effects community? It means that images need to be protected; that is, they should have as much dynamic range as possible so that they can be pushed and pulled around without breaking. Sometimes a director, colorist, or cinematographer goes into a DI suite early in the process and creatively pregrades a sequence. If so, that information can be used while creating the visual effects. Depending on how different the intended look is from the original source photography, various approaches may be applicable.

Film is an analog process, with each piece of negative reacting slightly differently to light, to the chemical processing baths, to the

scanning process, etc. As a consequence, there will always be undesirable discrepancies between shots, whether they be exposure or
color related. As more and more productions are shot on HD, some
of these variables are removed. Technically pregrading the plates,
matching shot to shot, so that the same CG lighting rigs and basic
composite color calls can be used, is often a good idea. Note that
this sort of pregrade isn't a creative one; it's sometimes known as
normalizing or *neutralizing* and is merely a unifying pass, rather
than one that indicates the final look. This pregrade could be done
as the shots are scanned or by a visual effects company. Generally,
if the visual effects work seamlessly in the pregraded plates, with
matching black levels, etc., then whatever is done to the final image
should take everything in the same direction.

However, subtle nuances in the visual effects may be lost if the
image is taken too far away from the original working color space.
If the DI team, based on a creative pregrading session, knows
exactly where it will take the final images, then working directly
on these new color-corrected plates may be a good idea. Again,
these color-corrected plates may be provided by the DI suite or
scanning facility or created by a visual effects company, based on
specified reference timing or match clips. These clips, which are
individual frames, represent the intent for the entire sequence.
In this case, a visual effects company would deliver its work integrated into plates with the final look.

A display LUT can be created to emulate the final desired look.
This doesn't affect the actual data within the image, but is an
adjustment layer that is applied and shows what the final color
correction will look like. Working on the original plates (or neutralized pregraded plates) may offer the best and most protected
workflow. Artists and clients should both review the shots using
the display LUT. However, the artists should also check that their
work still looks integrated in the non-LUT version, because this is
what will be delivered back to the DI suite.

If an extreme color correction is going to be desired, a more
complex approach is often necessary: a combination of all of the
above. First, the colorist technically pregrades the plates to *neutralize* them shot to shot. Then, based on the intended final look,
the colorist *creatively* grades the plates. Depending on how far
away that is from the original photography, a percentage of that
look (maybe 10, 20, or 50%) should be used to color correct the
shots, which now become the plates with which the visual effects
company will work, and the color space in which the completed
shots are sent to the DI. However, a supplementary LUT needs to
be created to emulate the final look and should be used by artists
and clients to review the shots. Again, the artists should also check
that their work still looks integrated in the non-LUT version.

So, how does one choose the best approach? As is often the
case in visual effects, there is not necessarily a correct answer. If

the final look is not far off from the original photography, then working directly on the technically pregraded plates is the best solution. If the director and his team know exactly where they want the images to end up, then working on creatively pregraded plates makes sense. If there is any doubt that the final look is undetermined, then a combination is preferred.

As stereographic filmmaking becomes more popular, it is worth noting the differences and complexities that this adds. Often left and right images have different colors and exposures, so this needs to be addressed. Frequently, there are geometric differences between the eyes, and again, using scaling and image warping tools, these can be corrected in the DI. In stereo, a matte has to be offset for each individual eye. However, its shape also needs to be adjusted, because the shape of the object will be different, due to perspective shifts between one eye and the other.

Many DI suites offer toolsets that are the equal of some basic compositing systems. This means simple compositing (keying, tracking, stabilizing, keyframe animating, and layering as well as the expected color controls) can be done within the suite. Huge advantages are realized by working on the final shots in a known calibrated environment on a large screen. Having the director (and other members of the creative team) work directly with the artist (usually the colorist in this case) removes any feedback loops and potentially saves a huge amount of time. The problem, however, is that it usually costs a huge amount of money to use time in the DI suite, so this is often not a good use of resources, but it illustrates the potential power of such a tool. Whatever approach is chosen, discussing it with the key members of the DI team early in the process is vital; confirming the specific technical requirements and testing that pipeline to check the results are also highly recommended. After all, the digital intermediary is something that should be embraced as an integral part of the visual effects pipeline.

VFX EDITORIAL
Greg Hyman, David Tanaka

This section is not intended to be an absolute description of a VFX Editor's job. Each visual effects movie represents its own set of challenges and each studio, or visual effects facility, has its own unique pipeline. The purpose of this section is to give a brief history and overview of the many standard responsibilities and procedures a VFX Editor typically faces on a modern visual effects movie.

This section describes the responsibilities and procedures inherent to visual effects editing. It also provides key background information on how the role has evolved through the years, as well as a better understanding of how editorial information is organized and disseminated clearly and accurately in the modern age.

Much of what VFX Editors do is process oriented and deals with numbers—numbers such as shot lengths, handle lengths,[33] cut lengths, key numbers,[34] timecode,[35] scene numbers, take numbers, lab roll numbers, and on and on. Then they translate those numbers into other numbers so that producers, VFX Supervisors, scanners, animators, lighting technical directors, and compositors can understand and work with them. Finally, they disseminate these numbers to companies hired to create the visual effects: scanning, visual effects, post-production, and digital intermediate facilities. And when the numbers change (and they will often), VFX Editors start the process all over again.

On large shows multiple VFX Editors may be tracking this information: one in the cutting room and one in each of the visual effects facilities, for example. Regardless of where VFX Editors work, their jobs are basically the same: They track and exchange the same set of numbers. The numbers they track are vital to the creation of visual effects shots because they define what elements are to be used in a shot, the order in which these elements are to be composited, how long the shot is, and how the shot has changed over time. They also give VFX Producers the information necessary to budget the creation of the shot(s). If these editorial numbers are wrong or incorrectly interpreted, they can cost the visual effects facility and the production valuable time and money.

Given the complexity of the job, the VFX Editor is often one of the longest serving crew members on a movie.

Editing within a Shot: The Art of Pre-Compositing

Before dividing the visual effects editing process into various procedures, it is important to first explain what *visual effects editing* is exactly and how it began.

VFX Editors actually do edit, just not in the traditional sense. They edit shots, not sequences. A traditional editor, called a *picture editor*, cuts together scenes by editing together different

[33] Handles are extra frames scanned at the beginning and end of a shot that don't appear in the cut. They give the picture editor additional frames to work with when finessing the cut after visual effects shots begin arriving from the visual effects facility.

[34] Key numbers (also called Keykode by Kodak): latent numbers printed onto the edge of film negatives that are used to identify and distinguish between individual frames for 35mm, 70mm, and 16mm film. The numbers progress in terms of feet (as in distance). KU 22 7711 1842 is an example of a key number. Like fingerprints no two key numbers are ever the same.

[35] Timecode: used to identify and distinguish between frames on videotape. It progresses in terms of time: hours, minutes, seconds, and frames (01:41:10:05, for example). Unlike the key numbers, timecode is never unique and can be duplicated across multiple tapes. Because of this, the tape names must be unique in every case.

camera angles, called *shots,* to tell a story. For example, a scene may begin with a close-up of a general's face looking through a telescope followed by a wide shot of a group of soldiers marching toward him on a battlefield and finally ending with a medium shot of the general riding away on his horse. By contrast, a VFX Editor edits within an individual shot by compositing together different elements and assembling them one on top of the other. Pacing and composition within a shot need to be experimented with and locked down before they can blend seamlessly into the larger context of an edited sequence. This process is called *pre-compositing.*

To illustrate pre-compositing, let's say the wide shot of the battlefield sequence described before is a visual effects shot containing multiple elements requiring compositing: a BG (background)[36] plate of the battlefield, several small groups of soldiers marching on different areas of the field (that when composited together give the impression that hundreds of people were filmed marching at the same time), and pyrotechnic (pyro) elements of shells exploding in the distance. The VFX Editor works with the VFX Supervisor, the Director, and the picture editor to decide which takes of the BG plate, soldier, and pyro elements work best in the shot and on what frames the different pyro elements should enter the shot. The selected elements are layered on top of each other in a digital editing program starting with the BG plate, then the shells, and concluding with the soldiers. To make the shot work, some, or all, of the elements may require a combination of cropping, keying, keyframe animation, resizing, repositioning (repoing), scaling, or retiming.

In essence, the VFX Editor's job is to help determine what elements are needed for a shot and how they are to interact with each other. The information describing how elements interact with each other in a shot, as referenced in a precomposite (precomp), is called *line-up information.* Once the Director approves precomps, the line-up information must be delivered to the visual effects facility.

To help facilitate precomping, the VFX Editor should carefully track and organize elements as they are shot so they can be easily located when needed. This is especially important when the Director or VFX Supervisor needs to quickly see alternate takes for a given element. Knowing where all of the elements are ahead of time speeds up the process greatly.

Multiple tools are available to the VFX Editor: nonlinear editing software such as Avid's Media Composer, Apple's Final Cut Pro, and Adobe's After Effects. All or some of these tools may be used on a show. So the more platform-neutral an editor is, the better.

---

[36] Background (BG) plate: the farthest background element in a visual effects shot on which all other elements, like bluescreen elements, are layered. BG plates can be anything from a single wall to a desert vista.

How It Came to Be

In the beginning (circa 1910s), visual effects editing was accomplished in-camera. The Director, actors, and cinematographer would film an action and then literally backwind (rewind) the footage in the movie camera to expose another piece of action over the first. The Director and crew would have to roughly estimate when the second piece of action should start in relation to the first before the camera began rolling again for a second pass. As time went on, this practice of in-camera double exposure soon established itself as an accepted form of trick photography from which more elaborate techniques and hardware would be built. The process was originally crude and imprecise, but it did acknowledge that pacing within a visual effects shot was important to its overall impact.

From the mid 1930s on, visual effects editing was accomplished using the optical printer. The optical printer allowed for individual elements to be composited together photochemically, using a precise projector-to-camera photography setup. The results were exposed onto a new piece of film stock, which then had to be processed at a laboratory in order to be seen. Because visual effects no longer had to be done in-camera, actions intended for a visual effects shot could now be filmed separately to be combined later via optical printing. The VFX Editor could examine the projected pieces of film individually on a viewing device, such as a moviola,[37] to get a feel for each element's timing. The elements could then be placed side by side on a light table to determine exactly how each piece of action should line up, frame for frame, in relation to one another.

Once a *locked-sync* between elements was determined, the VFX Editor ran test composites on the optical printer, or literally overlaid one piece of film over another on a moviola (a process called *bi-packing*), while keeping track of how the elements lined up. The routine was time consuming and contained errors that could not be detected until the film was processed overnight and screened the next day, but it was still a huge leap forward from the early days of in-camera compositing.

The digital revolution of the 1990s, with computer graphic animation and digital compositing, not only opened the floodgates on visual effects in general, but also changed the way visual effects editing would be performed from that point forward. Just as most traditional hand-drawn and stop-motion animation would be replaced with computer graphic animation, visual effects editing would no longer be hand tooled using moviolas,

---

[37] Moviola: a mechanical viewing device that allows film editors to project film on a small screen, also allowing for convenient stopping, reversing, vari-speeding, editing, and playback of film.

light tables, and optical printers. Instead of actual footage to hold up to a light source, photographed imagery could now be digitized into a nonlinear file format to be used with a computer.

As a result, precomposites could now be rendered electronically in minutes as opposed to overnight. Nonlinear editing software allowed the VFX Editor, VFX Supervisor, and Director the ability to closely collaborate in formulating the pacing of a visual effects shot and determine what elements would be required in a fraction of the time it took using the optical printer.

Note also that at this time visual effects editing did not come without its own set of unexpected challenges. For example, Avid's Media Composer was originally introduced via commercial television as opposed to feature filmmaking. As such, feature picture editors and VFX Editors both had to adapt to the new digital technology. Hence, the VFX Editor was given the challenge of performing multiple checks simply to keep the flow of visual effects editorial information running as smoothly as possible throughout the production pipeline; from visual effects facility to client cutting room (and vice versa), from one visual effects department to another, and from one format to another.

Today, visual effects editors are at a point in which the responsibility of tracking numbers equals or even supersedes the editing process itself. Modern technology allows for the making of visual effects shots to be shared across all visual effects disciplines in order to yield the best results possible for the project at hand. Out of production necessity, the role of the VFX Editor has evolved. The VFX Editor is still responsible for adapting to new techniques and collaborating with all key contributors in order to decipher the most precise visual effects shot count information.

Modern Day Tracking and Disseminating of Information

The Cutting Room's VFX Editor

As mentioned before, dissemination of information is one of the most important tasks of a VFX Editor. Gathering this information begins when a sequence is far enough along in the editing process, as determined by the Director, VFX Supervisor, or in some cases, the Producers and or the studio, to be turned over[38] to a visual effects facility so that artists may begin working on the shot(s). While the type of work for some shots may be obvious,

---

[38] Turnover: an official handing off of visual effects work from a film's editorial department to the visual effects facility. The work usually consists of individual visual effects shots from a specific sequence.

other shots may not be so obvious. Therefore, the VFX Editor must carefully look through the sequence, examining all shots for any potential work, and then check with the VFX Supervisor or picture editors to notify them of what was found that they may not have been aware of.

Before an artist can begin working on a shot, the required elements must be scanned (if they were filmed as opposed to digitally captured) and delivered to the visual effects facility. Some shots may only have a BG plate, while others may have many elements. In addition to the elements visible in the shot, there may also be reference spheres,[39] clean plates,[40] and various other references that need to be scanned. These may be selected by either the production's VFX Editor or the visual effects facility's VFX Editor. The two editors should discuss who should select the pertinent reference elements before the first turnover. Regardless of which editor selects these elements, it is the VFX Editor in the cutting room who will request the scans from the scanning facility.

The scanning facility usually requires key numbers, lab roll numbers, and possibly timecode numbers, which can be exported from the VFX Editor's editing system into a database, such as FileMaker Pro. How the scanning facility wants the information delivered and in what format can vary. Therefore, the VFX Editor should establish a procedure with the facility ahead of time. The naming convention of scanned files is crucial. As mentioned before, some shots may have multiple elements; therefore, the VFX Editor must distinguish between the different BG, BS (bluescreen) elements, and reference scans to ensure that it is clear to the visual effects facility what each scanned element is for. A typical filename is as follows:

BF010.bg1.1-125.cin

where

BF010 = the shot name[41] (i.e., BF = Battle Field and 010 = the tenth shot in the sequence),

bg1 = the element (i.e., background plate #1),

---

[39] Reference spheres: globes, about the size of a human head, that come in chrome and neutral gray. When filmed on the set, they visually record the placement of lights within a scene. CG artists later use the sphere reference as a guide for placing CG lights within the shot to help make CG and live-action objects appear to be from the same environment.
[40] Clean plate: a captured element containing the same camera composition and movement as the recorded main action footage, but does not include any actors or props. It is used to digitally erase unwanted rigging and to correct mishaps inherent in the selected action footage during the visual effects compositing stage.
[41] Sequence names and abbreviations are usually determined in pre-production by producers in the budgeting process. However, the shot numbers are officially assigned by the Director and Producer prior to the sequence being turned over to the visual effects facility.

1-125 = the frame range (i.e., 125 frames, starting on frame 1 and ending on frame 125), and

cin = the format extension (i.e., the element was scanned in Cineon format).

Some visual effects facilities and cutting rooms require specific naming conventions. Therefore, how elements are named should be discussed with the facility's VFX Editor prior to scanning. Some sequences may also have shots going to different visual effects facilities. It is the responsibility of the VFX Editor to ensure that the scanning facility knows exactly where to send the scans.

In addition, not all shots within a sequence are ready to be turned over at the same time. When this happens, the situation is referred to as a *partial turnover*. The VFX Editor must keep track of which shots have been turned over versus which shots are still being edited or undergoing the bidding process.

Once scanning is complete, it is time to deliver all relevant information to the VFX Editor at the visual effects facility. This

Figure 6.44 Sample count sheet. (Image courtesy of Tom Barrett and Greg Hyman.)

COMP SHEET		**THE BATTLEFIELD**			

EFX #	Vers #					☐ **COMPLETE SHOT**	
BF040	-	**1**	Date	**May-17-03**	**Company**	**VFX HOUSE**	☐ **PARTIAL SHOT** PAGE 1 OF 1

Comp Fr #	Slate W307-3(A) Element BG Plate File Name **BF040.BG1.1-80.CIN** Scan Frame #/ Key Number	Slate XB307-1(B) Element Blue Screen Plate 3 File Name **BF040.BS3.62-102.CIN** Scan Frame #/ Key Number	Slate Element File Name Scan Frame #/ Key Number	Description
x 001	x 001 EH 05 2133 4552 + 3	x 062 KL 54 1234 4002 + 1		1st Frame of Comp
x 009	x 009 EH 05 2133 4552 + 11	x 070 KL 54 1234 4002 + 9		1st Frame of Cut
x 041		x 102 KL 54 1234 4004 + 9		Last frame of Blue Screen plate
x 072	x 072 EH 05 2133 4556 + 10			Last Frame of Cut
x 080	x 080 EH 05 2133 4557 + 2			Last Frame of Comp

Notes	Notes	Notes

☐ **SEE ATTACHED SHEET FOR CROSSOVER INFORMATION**

Cut Length	4 + 0	or	64	fr
Total Length	5 + 0	or	80	fr

Handle/Hds	8 fr	Tails	8 fr
Counts include hds & tls handles			

information comes in two forms: count sheets and media consolidation. A count sheet is a document that contains all relevant information about a visual effects shot including the total length, handle lengths, key number range scanned, scene and take information, camera report, and lab roll number. It is usually generated from the VFX Editor's database.

Some shots will be built entirely in the computer (called *virtual shots* or *all-CG shots*) and, therefore, won't have any elements or plates to be scanned. In those cases, the only information on the count sheet might be the length of the shot and any specific notes from the Director or VFX Supervisor. In cases where it may not be clear what needs to be done with a shot, it is essential to highlight that information on the count sheet. Count sheets may be delivered either as part of a database file, as printed documents, or both. The VFX Editor should check with the visual effects facility on what they prefer.

The second requirement for a visual effects facility is an exact copy of the sequence being turned over. This is achieved with a "consolidation" from the picture editor's editing system that copies all media files associated with the sequence, including picture, sound, and visual effects renders. With these files, the visual effects facility can look at the cut exactly as it is seen by the picture editor. This allows the facility's visual effects editor access to all metadata (numbers) found on the count sheets that is needed when requesting scans from the cutting room. The consolidation also allows the visual effects facility's VFX Editor to deconstruct the precomps created by the cutting room's VFX Editor, thereby, in turn, allowing him or her to pass the line-up information to the artists. If the visual effects facility is small and does not have a VFX Editor or an editing system, then a consolidation is not useful. In those cases, the precomp line-up information must be included in the count sheets.

The Visual Effects Facility's VFX Editor

Once a sequence has been turned over, the job of the facility's VFX Editor really begins. After receiving the count sheets and consolidation from the client, the VFX Editor must distribute all pertinent information about the shots to the show's producers and artists. This usually begins by entering shot information from the count sheets into the facility's database system. (How much information a production needs is company specific.)

If the visual effects shots have not already been titled by the production's VFX Editor, the facility's VFX Editor will need to do that so crew members know what shots in the sequence correspond to which count sheets. QuickTime files of the sequences are usually put online so the artists working on the show may reference them. If the show is heavy with animation requiring lip sync, audio files for each shot will also need to be created and put online for animators to reference for lip sync.

Once scans start arriving from the scanning facility, the VFX Editor must import each element into the editing system and check it against the cut to ensure that the correct number of frames was scanned and delivered. If a problem is discovered with any of the scans, the production's VFX Editor should be notified so that the problem can be corrected as soon as possible.

Line-up information from the precomps may be the most complicated to pass on to the visual effects crew. This is because the metadata found in the timeline contains numbers that mean nothing to most other crew members: timecode, key numbers, and scene and take numbers. It is the job of the VFX Editor to translate this information into numbers that the visual effects artists and production personnel can use. The best way to do this is to re-create the precomp using the scanned files brought into the project. Basically, layer the elements as they appear in the cut, and reapply all of the effects from the precomp to the scanned elements. Once done, it becomes much easier to tell the artists where each element appears in the shot and when it enters and exits the frame, because the scanned elements are a common point of reference for all involved (i.e., they contain the same set of numbers). This is done in terms of frames, not time. For example, let's return to the battlefield shot described earlier: Frame 7 of a pyro element explodes on frame 25 of the shot. The line-up note for this element may look like this:

BF010.fg1.1-52.cin

Element frames 7–52 sync up with comp frames 25–70.

(Please scale down to 70% and repo screen right to match reference movie.)

Matters can get complicated when elements need retiming using curve ramps, so using precise language in the instructions is essential. Talking with artists directly about how they prefer to have instructions worded will also help avoid miscommunication. How line-up information is made available to the artists differs with each visual effects facility. It is best to have a database track this information, or at least a spreadsheet that the artist can view easily.

Once all of the information has been distributed to the appropriate people on a show, work on the shots can begin. As different departments (i.e., animation or compositing) run takes,[42] the VFX Editor imports them (from digital files) into their editing system so they may be cut into the appropriate sequence(s) and, if need be, exported as an updated QuickTime file for review. This is the

---

[42] Run takes: in-progress versions of a shot, designated by specific numerical take numbers, that serve as a record of the shot's progress at a particular point in its production history.

dailies process for the VFX Editor and allows artists and supervisors to see their work in context with the rest of the sequence. It is important to make sure that all of the shots received are the correct length and that specific line-up info has been followed correctly. If something is wrong, the artist needs to be informed as soon as possible.

Sometimes the facility's VFX Editor needs to precomp shots as well. A visual effects facility is often responsible for shooting elements on a stage (miniature elements like ships or planes, debris and smoke), which need to be incorporated into a shot. The VFX Editor will go through the same process as the production's VFX Editor in determining, with the VFX Supervisor, which takes should be used and how they will interact with the other elements in the shot. For scanning, the VFX Editor may have a counterpart in the production's cutting room order the scans, or the VFX Editor may communicate with the scanning facility directly. As always, all appropriate line-up information must be communicated with the artists.

When preparing scan requests the VFX Editor must make sure that all key numbers are being tracked correctly in the editing program in case a nonstandard film format was used to shoot the elements. For example, the standard film format used today

Figure 6.45 4-perf 35mm versus 8-perf 35mm film formats. (Image courtesy of David Tanaka.)

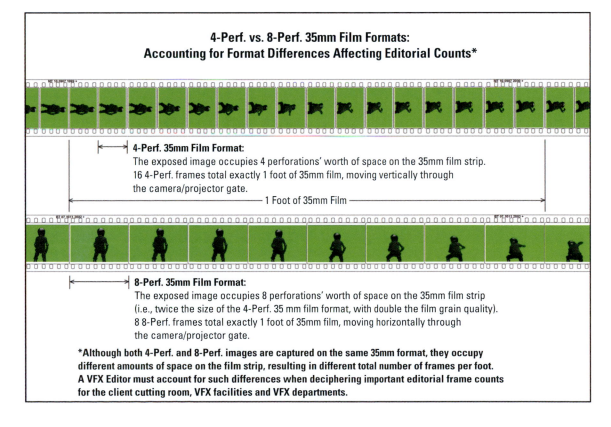

4-Perf. vs. 8-Perf. 35mm Film Formats: Accounting for Format Differences Affecting Editorial Counts*

4-Perf. 35mm Film Format:
The exposed image occupies 4 perforations' worth of space on the 35mm film strip.
16 4-Perf. frames total exactly 1 foot of 35mm film, moving vertically through the camera/projector gate.
— 1 Foot of 35mm Film —

8-Perf. 35mm Film Format:
The exposed image occupies 8 perforations' worth of space on the 35mm film strip (i.e., twice the size of the 4-Perf. 35 mm film format, with double the film grain quality).
8 8-Perf. frames total exactly 1 foot of 35mm film, moving horizontally through the camera/projector gate.

*Although both 4-Perf. and 8-Perf. images are captured on the same 35mm format, they occupy different amounts of space on the film strip, resulting in different total number of frames per foot. A VFX Editor must account for such differences when deciphering important editorial frame counts for the client cutting room, VFX facilities and VFX departments.

is referred to as *4-perf 35mm*. This means that there are four perforations per frame of film (16 frames per foot) that run vertically (top to bottom) through a projector. However, some films shoot VistaVision, which is 35mm film but with eight perforations per frame (8 frames per foot) that run horizontally (left to right) through a projector. As a result, if the VFX Editor orders a scan from an 8-perf element using 4-perf key numbers, the scan will be wrong.

Periodically, shots need to be sent to the cutting room for the production's VFX Editor to cut into the movie for the Director to review and give feedback. These files are usually delivered as QuickTime movies. It is the VFX Supervisor's responsibility to determine what files should be delivered, and it is the facility's VFX Editor who must keep track of what versions, or takes, of shots are sent and when. If there is a problem with a shot, such as an incorrect length, that information must be communicated to the production's VFX Editor.

While working with film is becoming rarer because of the dominance of digital editing and compositing, it is still necessary. Some directors prefer to view visual effects shots in a theater on film rather than from HD tape. This is because film is the medium on which most people will watch a movie theatrically, making some directors feel that it is the best context in which to evaluate the quality of the work. Therefore, instead of sending down digital files, the VFX Editor may send film rolls that need to be prepared for projection. As such, it is important for all VFX Editors (whether working in the production's cutting room or visual effects facility) to understand how to use a traditional flatbed,[43] rewinds, and a sync block.[44]

As the Shot Changes

Even though a sequence may be far enough along in the editing process for delivery to a visual effects facility, the cut is by no means locked.[45] The Director and VFX Editor continue cutting the film even as visual effects shots are being worked on and delivered. Because the cut is always fluid, many shots will change in some way, requiring updated information be sent to the visual effects facility. Sometimes a change can be as simple as a shot

[43] Flatbed: a picture and sound playback machine on which multiple film and audio tracks are loaded separately and arranged flatly on a motorized table-like surface, allowing film editors easy access to hand-edit all materials.

[44] Sync block: a device used to measure film in total number of frames. Film is loaded onto a cylinder that is calibrated at 1 foot per rotation. An attached counter reads and updates the total amount of footage that winds through.

[45] A locked cut means that the Director has determined that no more editing is needed; the edit is 100% complete.

being shortened by several frames at the head or tail. Other times a shot may be extended or new elements added, requiring new scans. Shots could also be omitted and new ones added. In all of these cases, new count sheets, called *change notes* (paperwork describing the changes), and new consolidated media need to be sent to the visual effects facility. It is essentially the same process as a turnover only more focused on the changes.

Depending on the Director's editing style, changes may come weekly or even daily. As a result the VFX Editor must stay on top of cut changes and ensure that the visual effects facilities are updated with the latest information. While picture editors try to inform the VFX Editor of any changes, they are often too busy editing the film to keep track of everything. Therefore, the only way to know for sure what has been changed in a sequence is for the production's VFX Editor to go through the updated sequence, shot by shot, and compare it against the previous cut. As a double check, the facility's VFX Editor should do the same when an updated cut is received just to make sure that no changes have inadvertently slipped through the cracks.

It is not only the production's VFX Editor who has to communicate changes. Oftentimes the visual effects facility is also making changes that need to be communicated back to the cutting room. If a sequence requires a lot of animation or has many all-CG shots, the VFX Supervisor may suggest length changes to better accommodate the wishes of the director. For example, a 50-frame shot was turned over to the visual effects facility with an animatic[46] of a CG character reacting to something off screen. But once the actual animated character is added to the shot the animation supervisor realizes that 50 frames are not enough time for the reaction the Director requested. In this case the shot would have to be extended to accommodate the action. In cases like these, the facility's VFX Editor must inform the production's VFX Editor of the change needed and why. The production's VFX Editor then must inform the Director and/or the picture editor to get approval.

Wrapping It Up

As the show approaches completion, much of the production's VFX Editor's job is dealing with final renders (called *finals*[47]) from the visual effects facility. This can be made more challenging if the director is still making cut changes. On large shows

---

[46] Animatic: a series of illustrated or animated images run together, in sequence, in order for filmmakers to previsualize a scene ahead of time. They are usually created in the early preplanning stages of visual effects development.

[47] Final: a shot that no longer needs any work as determined by the Director. It is 100% done.

the facility's VFX Editor may send dozens of shots to the cutting room every day in order to finish the show on time. The VFX Editor in the cutting room cuts these shots into the movie so the Director and the picture editor can evaluate them in context. However, the Director will not be finaling shots in this context because the files are compressed and lack detail. Instead, the Director will look at the shots in a theater, projected from film or an HD format.

Oftentimes the Director sends the shots back to the visual effects facility for additional fixes or changes. It is usually the VFX Coordinators, at both the visual effects facility and the cutting room, who track which shots are finaled and which still require work. But the facility's VFX Editor still needs to keep track of everything sent to the cutting room and when.

All during this process the production's VFX Editor is communicating with the digital intermediate (DI) facility to ensure that they have accurate edit decision lists (EDLs) and corresponding film negative from which to conform the movie. As the cut changes, or new shots are delivered, new EDLs may be required.

The frantic and harried nature of the show's final weeks can lead to mistakes and confusion. Both VFX Editors, with help from the VFX Producer(s), VFX Coordinator(s), and VFX Supervisor(s), need to make sure the DI facility is working with the correct finals to avoid problems during the conform process. Shot lengths are especially important to check during the final weeks of a show. If a short shot is sent to the DI facility, an uncomfortable and costly delay may result.

Conclusion

Over the years a VFX Editor's job, like many other jobs in the visual effects film industry, has changed, evolving from handling film on flatbeds to punching pixels on a computer. Yet through all the changes, the core responsibility of disseminating vital editorial information regarding visual effects shots to all necessary parties has remained the same.

Not long ago a movie with 200 shots was considered large. Now a large movie exceeds 1000 shots, which in turn translates into a great many precomposites, scans, count sheets, consolidations, and change notes. In other words, a lot of numbers! It is the commitment to keeping these numbers accurate and understood by all involved that has remained a constant to the VFX Editor's contribution to the art of visual effects. As visual effects movies continue to grow in size, the role of the VFX Editor will continue to grow with it and become all the more essential to the filmmaking process.

COMMUNICATION WITH ARTISTS
Eric Durst

Starting

Visual effects in motion pictures are often the combined work of hundreds of people. The responsibility of the VFX Supervisor is to guide and lead the communication between all of these artists, focusing on a single goal: the visual effects blending seamlessly into the final film.

Because visual effects is a subjective art form, combining aesthetics with large doses of science and mathematics, there is no exact formula. There are, however, certain principles that one can look to for guidance in order to succeed in this process. Regardless of the number of artists involved, whether it is one individual or a massive team, these methods of navigation are similar.

People trying to describe how they want visual effects to look often use words and phrases like "magical," "ethereal," and "something that we've never seen before." But in truth, these words and phrases do not represent how things look; they represent how one feels once one has seen them. When guiding artists, it is essential to define the difference between what it takes to manufacture the image and the feeling the image emotionally projects.

A visual effect, regardless of how fanciful or "otherworldly" it may appear, is always made up of specific, definable, and tangible elements from the real world. Color, light, and movement are what the film displays and this is the palette the artist has to work with. So the building blocks are specific descriptions that show the range of colors, the properties of light and how it reacts within the image, and the way these elements move through the frame.

How the viewer responds to this color, light, and movement is an emotional response to the shot and this is independent from the building blocks used to construct the images. This response is what gives the shot meaning and understanding, and the impact these elements produce drives one's decisions and judgments about what does and does not work.

For every shot and sequence that has visual effects, one must have answers to three basic questions: What? Why? and How? These answers give a context for the visual effects and a supervisor uses this to guide all the artists working on the project

> *What?:* What is the effect is being created? What does it look like? What are the attributes that make it up, and what are all the specific details about the visuals that are being constructed? What are the emotional beats of the shot? What is the feeling that one has when one sees it?

Why?: Why do these visual effects exist? Why is it important in the story? Is it a transition, punctuation, or a seamless shot that goes by without calling any attention to itself?

How?: How can it be achieved? This involves all of the technical and logistical aspects of visual effects pre-production, production, and post-production. This includes how to design the shots and sequences, the principal and visual effects photography, and any elements and source materials that are needed. This also includes all camera equipment, software, workstations, personnel, pipelines, and finances that are required to produce the visual effects shots.

Based on the complexity of the visual effect shots, answers to these questions range from very simple decisions to something short of a Ph.D. thesis.

Working with Teams

Communicating with a team over a period of time can be a little like the Telephone Game, where a message is passed around a circle of people—one by one—only to get a distorted version of the original message at the end. It is important when translating information through a group of people to make sure it is done in a way that is clear and understandable, so the message remains intact. However, communication is often much harder than duplicating a sentence correctly because visual effects must carry both dramatic impact along with visual perfection.

Consider this example: A statement, "THERE'S A FIRE IN THE BACKYARD!!!!," is passed around a circle of people, delivered with a sense of passion and urgency. This travels around the group and the last person is told, "There's a fire in the backyard," delivered in a complete monotone. This is mechanically accurate, but because the delivery is flat and nonemotional, it is not a completely acceptable interpretation of the original statement. In visual effects terms, the shot is technically perfect, but does not work because it lacks the intended impact.

The game is played again, but this time the message at the end of the circle is "THE BACK OF THE HOUSE IS ABLAZE! WE MUST GET OUT IMMEDIATELY!," delivered with the original sense of passion and urgency. Even though the words are different, the message is more thoroughly understood. In visual effects terms, the shot may not look exactly like the original design, but it feels right so it is successful.

The point is that it is essential to communicate both the visual and emotional parts to get a result that truly works. The supervisor needs to understand how to read between-the-lines and have great insight into what is needed and expected from the shots they are delivering.

Reference and Perspective

To give the clearest possible direction to the artists constructing the shots, many resources need to be brought to the table:

1. Gather and review specific images and reference material that visually describe the shot(s).
2. Gather and review specific motion reference material that describes the kinetic feel of the shot(s).
3. Review all production artwork, pre-production templates, and animatics.
4. Make sure the artists understand the context of their shot(s) by reviewing edited sequences, especially showing the shots surrounding the ones they are working on.
5. Review the expectations of each shot and the degree of detail that is required.
6. Describe the properties of the objects in the frame as being:
   - Transparent, translucent, or opaque.
   - How visible—do they stand out or do they recede?
   - How does light interact—do they emit, absorb, or reflect light?
   - What materials are they similar to (plastic, metal, glass, crystal, gas, etc.)?
7. Describe the emotional feeling of the shot in terms of volume. Use phrases that express the visual effect's impact outside of technical or artistic language that everyone understands.
   - How hot or cold is this shot?
   - Does the visual effect whisper, speak normally, shout, or scream?
   - How bright or dark is it, going from total blackness (0) to the sun (10)?
8. Describe the intent of the visual effects in the sequence.
   - Are the visual effects used to punctuate a sequence?
   - Are the visual effects a transition?
   - Are the visual effects introducing a new idea or concept?
9. Separate technical and artistic considerations to gain an understanding from each perspective.
   - Describe the shot from the artistic viewpoint (without any technical considerations).
   - Become the disciplined technician and figure out how to accomplish what the artist needs for the shot to work.
   - Become the problem solver and create the best result knowing all sides.
10. See the work with fresh eyes, as if one were a member of the audience.
    - View shots from how they look and feel, not from how much money or effort was required to create them.
11. Understand all of the visual firepower that can be utilized:
    - Software—what software tools are available?

- Machine power—what hardware resources are needed to complete the shot(s)?
- Team—what individual artists are ideal for each shot/sequence?
- Experience—how much artist experience is needed for each shot?
- Time—what is the time needed and allocated for each shot?
- Finances—what are the financial resources for the project?

Shot Production

Filmmaking is evolutionary, and changes and adjustments often occur throughout the post-production process that alter the original plan. The artists follow the lead of the VFX Supervisor, so during this phase it is essential to maintain a clear perspective at all times to keep everyone focused in the right direction.

The VFX Supervisor heads the shot review process, where each shot is analyzed and critiqued on an incremental basis as it progresses to its final state. During this process, his or her thoughts are communicated, as well as those of the director and others, in the clearest manner possible. This is most often accomplished with a phone/video conference call or a face-to-face meeting with the artists.

These reviews also include written, audio, or visual notes to further specify and clarify particular points, ensuring that everyone is in full understanding with each other. A dated record of all comments for each shot should be maintained throughout the production. Because shots can take weeks or months to produce, this history of information can be enormously helpful to everyone in the production pipeline.

Communicating with Artists in Other Departments

Visual effects often join with other departments to help expand their work into the digital realm. Communication of the VFX Supervisor with the artists in these departments is important, so there is a direct connection between the visual effects and live-action areas.

Digital Sets, Environments, and Extensions

When new environments are needed, whether they are sets or locations, visual effects are often used to create them digitally. In live-action production this is the domain of the Production Designer, so good communication between the art department and visual effects is essential to bring the physical and digital worlds together successfully.

Figure 6.46 Visual notes from the film *Knowing* (2009) with review comments. (Image courtesy of Buf and Summit Entertainment, LLC.)

Digital Actors

Actors and stunt actors are often enhanced or created digitally through the visual effects process, whether with full figures or partial figures (face replacement, etc.). The use of digital techniques is frequently underestimated during live-action photography. The VFX Supervisor should make sure that all needed resources are available, so if digital replacements are required later in the post-production process, the visual effects team is prepared. To ensure this, make certain that extensive photographic reference of the actors, their costumes, and any relevant performance material has been collected. Reference of extras for crowd enhancement is also extremely useful. Communication and coordination with the assistant directors, stunt coordinators, costume designers, and actors are essential for this to go smoothly.

Digital Cinematography

Visual effects shots that require digital lighting and camera moves are extensions of the roles of the Director of Photography and camera operator. Maintaining consistency and visual style in digital shots is enhanced greatly by communication with the DP and camera department. Understanding the look and feel of the original live-action photography goes a long way toward helping the visual effects blend in with the live-action footage.

Digital Sequences

Visual effects is often called on to perform the role of a digital 2nd unit. This is parallel to the work performed by a live-action 2nd unit. By having the ability to generate total environments as well as digital actors, visual effects often creates complete sequences for the film, along with digital shots that cut within the live action. These shots also extend the special effects department's role by expanding, or digitally manipulating and enhancing practical effects.

Completion

The visual effects in a film represent the efforts of many artists and technicians who have worked together to create images that form a unified vision. This is a challenging task. To succeed requires great communication skills, the ability to motivate and guide a wide variety of personalities, and a high degree of patience and persistence between all parties. The end result, the reward of seeing the final visual effects shots cut into the completed film, is a spectacular thrill that continues to inspire visual effects artists worldwide.

THE HISTORY OF COMPOSITING

Jon Alexander

The History of Optical Technique

In the 1920s simple optical printers were made to duplicate exposed movie film. They consisted of a camera with raw film stock and a projector with previously exposed film that needed to be duplicated. Using machine tool technology, a camera, projector, and lamp house were placed on a lathe bed with mounting platforms that allowed for precision alignment. The camera was focused on the movement of the projector that held the exposed film.

In the 1930s at RKO Studios, Linwood Dunn used traveling mattes to create some of the earliest motion picture special effects. Examples of those effects were basic wipes used as transitions from one scene to another. Using a second projector on the printer to hold traveling mattes, he could expose part of the raw stock film frame, roll it back to a starting frame, and then put the inverse of the matte in the second projector and expose the raw stock a second time without double exposing the originally exposed portion of the film. Although the black-and-white matte film was not totally opaque, it held back enough light that the raw stock would not get any exposure.

In 1940 Larry Butler expanded on this basic premise of holding out one part of a film frame from exposure with a second opaque piece of film. He won an Academy Award for inventing the blue-screen technique to make traveling mattes of moving objects photochemically. This technique would pretty much be the only way to efficiently composite moving objects into film scenes for the next 50 years. It was not until the early 1990s that it made economic sense to move away from film compositing to digital compositing on computers.

Traveling Matte Technique and the Digital Age

In the simplest film composite, one photographed object is cut out so as not to double expose the film and is put over a different background. To cut out an object on film, the object needs to be photographed in such a way that it can be separated from its original background. To do this, the foreground action phase is photographed against a plain backing of which there are various types and colors and methods of illumination. The goal is to create a duplicate negative with a composite of the foreground object over another piece of film of the background. This requires a traveling matte that is a silhouette hold-out that can change from frame to frame with the action of the foreground object. Then the foreground object can be put over the new background without double exposing that area.

Figures 6.47, 6.48, and 6.49 show images used in making a composite. This is not a very good composite. The foreground character does not integrate well with the background. The mat is a bit dense and the beauty lighting of the model does not match the background. One doesn't have to be an expert to recognize a

(A)

(B)

Figure 6.47 (A) Background. (B) Blue screen. (Image courtesy of Jon Alexander.)

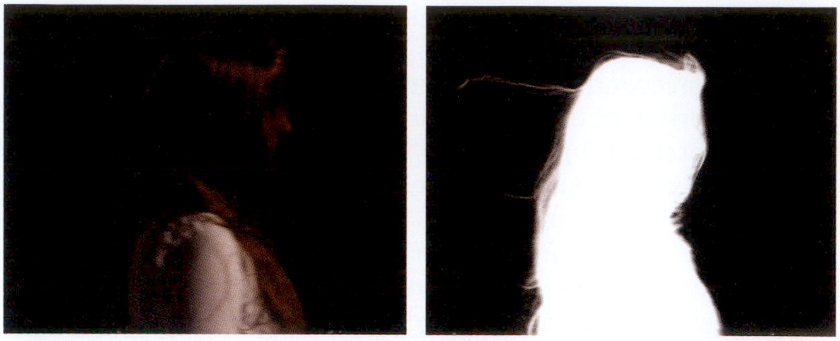

Figure 6.48 (A) Extraction. (B) Matte. (Image courtesy of Jon Alexander.)

(A) (B)

Figure 6.49 Composite. (Image courtesy of Jon Alexander.)

bad composite. A perfect composite is one that gives no clue to its separate origins.

The basic technique for shooting images with the objective of making traveling mattes from the negative for computer graphics compositing is the same as it was for making mattes for film compositing. The nature of computer graphics, however, is such that there is much more latitude in what is acceptable exposure of the original negative.

Making precise mattes with film requires a very specific and narrow range of the color spectrum. If one looks at a perfect blue screen through a corresponding red glass, no color will be seen. The eye (or the camera) just sees black. If that blue does not exist anywhere else in front of the camera, then the rest of the film will get some bit of exposure from which a matte can be made.

It is pretty easy to test for the perfect blue photochemically. A series of exposure wedges reading the processed negative with a densitometer is run. Kodak published AIMs[48] for their films. Kodak's AIMs were suggested values read from the densitometer that, depending on the film stock, would give the maximum separation of the blue screen in order to make hold-out mattes. Through trial and error one can come up with the best negative film exposure AIMs to get the cleanest most precise mattes for the filters. The ideal negative AIMs for digital compositing are still the same as they were with film. The closer to the AIMs, the easier it is to get a perfect matte result. Deviations to a certain extent will make pulling the matte more difficult, but not necessarily impossible as it was in film compositing. Optical compositing techniques might be able to get a reasonable matte even if one-half stop off on film. But values beyond that just can't get a clean edge. However, the complex algorithms of digital compositing allow for much more latitude.

Once the mattes are extracted, the second and perhaps more important step is replacing the color of the matte screen. Better blending is possible in computer graphics compositing than optical compositing because of the ability to replace the color regionally and to choose the hue of the replacement color. With good mattes and replacement color, making the actual composite is a simple final step.

The advent of computer graphics compositing has also made it possible to use colors other than blue for the matte screen. In older types of films the emulsion layer that was sensitive to blue light always had the biggest grain because silver halide reacts the least to those wavelengths. The larger film grain allowed for a balanced response to the emulsion layers that were sensitive to red and green light. Skin tones also have little blue in them, so if a blue replacement is performed to get rid of the screen those tones will be affected to a lesser extent than a green replacement will. In addition, the blue replacement will have less apparent film grain. Since it is easier now to isolate edges in digital compositing there is more latitude in choosing a background screen color. However, the color replacement of the edge still needs to be dealt with.

Historical Notes on Blue Screen

A short review of some of the requirements for shooting with optical compositing in mind should be of value since these are basically using the same techniques as digital compositing.

---

[48] *AIM* refers to a value measured in the Laboratory Aim Density (LAD) printing control method. By exposing a LAD patch, the value of the exposure of that piece of film can be determined. Kodak publishes suggested density tolerances for each type of film in the duplicating and print system.

This will also give an opportunity to comment on requirements that used to be mandatory and are now just suggested. Most of the current confusion in shooting stems from misunderstandings about what is possible today versus what was possible yesterday.

The original traveling-matte system was based on consistency, quality control, and the limits of the optical-photochemical process and dictated by the limitations of three little square pieces of glass in the filter set of the optical printer. These red, green, and blue filters were used to make the bluescreen extractions, mattes, and separations from the original negatives. The resulting elements were used to make the composites.

The biggest problem with the optical-photochemical compositing process was that one fit for the whole matte was necessary. There was really no practical way to make different fits for different parts of the object being matted (although this is something that is done on nearly every digital extraction shot today). Because the matte needed to fit as one, that meant that the colored screen had to have a very consistent exposure over the width of the screen. In addition to the requirement of being evenly lit, a very narrow range of exposure was allowable on the original negative for successfully pulling a matte. Variations in the exposure would mean variations in the density of the mattes and thus dark or light fringing in the composite.

Not only was a good original negative needed, but there also had to be incredible care taken while making the elements, so that all wedge picks[49] would match into the final composite. Both wedge and element obviously have to go through chemical development, often several days apart. If the processing were not in control during developing, the elements would have to be made again from the start. Black-and-white film processing has greater tolerance to mixing and temperature variations than color film in general. The tricky part was the close tolerances needed to develop the various gammas of the black-and-white elements. Lack of control in developing could come from any number of reasons. The chemical mixing needs to be extremely consistent. Care needs to be taken not to use the chemicals too long before refreshing. Controlled bath temperature can be tough if the room temperature fluctuates too much. The mattes could not be easily tweaked with additional rotoscoped elements like they can today.

In the years before compositing on computers, most composites were done on optical printers. The exception at ILM would be shots done completely in camera in the matte painting department. In the optical department at ILM, the vast majority of the

---

[49] Wedge: a series of test frames varying the exposure slightly of a single frame.

original elements for the composites were made on the Anderson Printer in a VistaVision format.[50]

The majority of the final composites were delivered as normal 4-perf 35mm images. Working in the larger VistaVision format helped to compensate for the natural loss of quality in film as it is duplicated. Manipulation of the images was completely photochemical and optical as opposed to mathematical as it is in the computer graphic world. (The math of course is based on the same physical laws of light that dictated the optical printing process.)

The goal in optical compositing was for one matte to work overall to isolate the object in front of the blue screen. This way the optical camera operator could make one fit of the mattes. This matte fit was a visual adjustment and its repetition over a series of takes was based on the skill of the operator to exactly repeat the same placement with the same elements. If the element was damaged it would have to be remade and a different fit would be necessary. This refitting each time the comp is done no longer happens. In computer graphics, once the matte is blended successfully, a compositing script exists that will exactly repeat the line-up. That precise refitting on the optical printer was up to the camera operator.

The other aspect of compositing an element shot in front of a blue screen is replacing the blue of the screen. Ultramarine blue is a natural pigment historically used to give the richest blues to paintings. Because it can eliminate the yellow of white light, it is ideally suited for bluescreen work. The pigment choice has been refined somewhat over the years depending on the medium with which it is to be used. More common terms today are *chroma* or *digital blue*. Ultramarine blue was a good choice for pre-Vision films. A considerable amount of light could be thrown on an actor or model without washing out the rich blue hue.

In optical compositing replacing the blue was accomplished by rephotographing the image through a red filter, which would, in a perfect world, make all the blue disappear into black and thus not be carried to the new duplicate negative. Assuming the elements were made successfully, the composite was then in the hands of the optical camera operator. The composite would have to run at least several times. Each time the operator had to line up the camera and elements exactly the same way, and then hope the lab processing was consistent. Each composite was created on film and projected because there was no other way to preview the composite. Today, composites are previewed on computers or servers.

---

[50] The 8-perf format with the image sideways on 35mm film versus 4 perfs vertical as in traditional movie film.

Ideally, a compositor would like to have a bluescreen negative with as much information in it as possible for the sake of pulling a matte with as many details as available. Using the color-difference matting technique means the optical printer compositor will be pulling the mattes from a protection interpositive[51] of the original negative. Blue light is the hardest part of the visible spectrum to capture on film and as such the blue record[52] silver halide crystals[53] are proportionally bigger than those found in the green or red records. The blue resolving power of the film is never as good as the green or red records. Thus, there will not be as much detail in the blue record as in the red or green. In any color-difference matting system, the underlying premise is that the color of the screen that is being used is thrown out. With the exception of rich blues or violet little is lost. Furthermore, little is lost chromatically by throwing out the blue channel and a greater detail of the red and green channels is retained.

The perfect blue color for the screen lies at the center of the blue region of the film spectrum. (The blue region runs between 400 and 500 millimicrons, green 500 to 600, and red 600 to 700.) The peak transmission of a blue screen lies at 450 millimicrons. For practical purposes this color is referred to as ultramarine blue. Because ultraviolet light has a shorter wavelength than visible light, which contaminates the blue record, the photographed matte image will be slightly smaller than the color action image. Thus an enlarging compensation must be made in the printing steps unless corrected lenses are used on the camera to offset image reduction. This aberration often shows up in older lenses whose coatings have deteriorated. But, unlike in the old optical compositing days, this chromatic aberration is easy to fix in computer graphics compositing. A histogram of an image with ultramarine blue shows almost no red or green. In the mathematical world of computer graphics, it is thus easy to isolate and eliminate this color. If there are no transparent objects in the scene or a great amount of motion blur, the threshold of recognition of the color-difference matte can be raised to reproduce medium blues and violets while still maintaining a major discrimination against the blue backing. This means pure blue is not necessary to pull a satisfactory matte digitally. That latitude is very narrow when extracting blue photochemically.

Green screen works the same way as far as color-difference matting (with the obvious subtraction of green rather than blue). The

---

[51] Interpositive: a positive film copy of a negative. It is used to protect a negative from overuse. From this interpositive, a duplicate negative could be made, if necessary.
[52] Blue record: the layer of the film that captures blue light.
[53] An enlargement of a piece of film shows thousands of little sand like particles. They are commonly referred to as *film grain*. What is being seen are the silver halide crystals.

problem with green screen, especially with anything other than fine-grained film, is that by subtracting the green record an incredible amount of detail around the edges is lost. There is also the problem that the green record lays physically below the blue layer and the yellow filter layer. Because of this it is very common to see halation in the optical composite from a greenscreen extraction.

A densitometer can measure how far off the blue/greenscreen AIM[54] on the negative is. Following are the neg AIMs with the less than sign (<) indicating that the goal is to get that AIM below the number following it. For example, at ILM's optical department the bluescreen AIM was "Red 20, Green less than 100, and Blue 235." The AIMs can vary per film stock and with the red, green, and blue filters used to pull the separations. These ILM values have been adapted from Kodak's suggestions. They worked with ILM's particular filters and processing techniques. They would be a good place to start but should certainly be adapted to give the best results for specific red, green, and blue filters, as well as the lab where the film will be processed. Following the AIMs is a little chart that shows how far off in stops the blue or green screen would be based on the densitometer readings.

Bluescreen Neg AIM 20 <100 235
Greenscreen Neg AIM 20 180 <145

Green screen/blue screen
20 120 85 –3 stops 20 40 175
40 140 105 –2 stops 20 60 195
60 160 125 –1 stop 20 80 215
80 180 <145 AIM 20 <100 235
100 200 165 +1 stop 40 120 255
120 220 185 +2 stops 60 140 275

The old rule of thumb for shooting in front of a self-illuminated blue screen[55] was that the subject should be shot about 25 feet in front of it to prevent, or at least reduce to a minimum, the blue spill that occurs if the subject is closer. Self-illuminated blue screens are wonderful for the compositor because they tend to be the most even across the field. Of course, this implies availability and by the nature of how they are built, the field of view can be fairly limited. The blue spill is not nearly the problem today that it was

---

[54] The "AIM" refers to a value measured in the Laboratory Aim Density (LAD) printing control method. By exposing a LAD patch there is a way to determine the value of the exposure of that piece of film. Kodak publishes suggested density tolerances for each type of film in the duplicating and print system.

[55] A self-illuminated blue screen is one that would have a series of lights behind the translucent blue screen that would illuminate evenly. They are very easy to use because in general an "on" switch turns on all of the lights sitting in a fixed position. But due to their design they are not very flexible or portable.

in the photochemical compositing world because now a large inner matte can be used to isolate just the edge of the object for the mattes. The color difference of the blue spill to the screen color tends to be severe enough to allow a successful edge blend matte between the spill area and the edge.

In motion control work where there is the luxury of repeating the action, it is always helpful to the compositor to use strong yellow light on the models during the matte pass in order to reduce the amount of blue spill. Since this pass is only shot to make the matte and not to color or shade the model, a strong yellow light will not hurt anything.

It has become more popular to shoot with a frontlit screen (blue or green) during the past few years. As far as compositing goes, there is no advantage to this other than the reduction of potential blue spill. The most important thing about the frontlit screens is that they be consistent side to side. If they are not, problems could occur. For example, assume a screen is uneven; that is, it has seams or is fluttering in the wind. Depending on the object being matted, some allowances are possible. If it is impossible (or not economical) to have a flat consistent screen, then a bit of common sense should rule. For objects with no solid shape (smoke or dust, for example), a screen with a wavy blue would be better than one with seams because it is nearly impossible to separate the seam without leaving some remnant. Conversely, a seam behind a model is easier to deal with because the roto work can be done the same way connection points are matted on bluescreen models. If the perfect chroma AIM can't be met, then it is better for the screen to be lighter if the foreground object is darker; conversely, the screen should be darker if the foreground object is light. These suggestions applied in the past when the shots were going to be optically composited as well as today. Unlike digital compositing, it was certain that straying too far from the ideal exposure would make it impossible to successfully create a good, clean photochemical separation of the blue screen.

Another large change from days past is the ability of rotoscoping to fix matte problems fairly interactively. In the past it could take days, if not longer, from the time mattes were ordered to when they were drawn and processed. Nowadays if the mattes have problems, it is easy to go back and tweak the specific sections that have problems rather than having to start all over again. Medium to close-up full-body articulation is still very labor intensive, but many other types of roto help are relatively cheap compared to the cost of the time a crew may take on the set or on location. Today, there are a number of good edge-detection algorithms, and short of that there are different ways to extract elements digitally that just were not possible photochemically. Keep in mind that the farther off the target the AIMs are, the less relevance there is to even set up a screen. A lot of money could be wasted lighting a screen that doesn't ever get used.

Probably the biggest improvement in compositing in computer graphics over the old optical compositing is in matte color replacement. In optical compositing the technique was to attempt to turn the blue screen to black so there would be no exposure added to the final comp due to the blue of the screen. The problem with this approach is that light naturally wraps itself around any edge it encounters. The edges on any image contain contamination of the edge foreground object by whatever color is directly behind it. Obviously as the object travels in front of lighter or darker objects, the light wrap changes. Also all blue cannot be completely eliminated from the foreground objects or their colors won't look correct. The midtones especially will look processed and have too much contrast.

In optical compositing, an attempt was made to solve the foreground blue replacement problem by using a color-difference matte. The color-difference matte is produced by bi-packing a black-and-white green color separation[56] positive with the original negative. This matte registers as density only in those areas of the scene where the blue content is less than the green content. This matte, together with the green positive, represents a faithful duplication of the blue color content within the scene (except of course where the blue content does not exceed that of green). All colors except blue and violet will therefore reproduce in normal values. Desaturated blues (like blue jeans) reproduce acceptably. The blue backing reproduces as black and makes possible normal reproduction of transparent objects in the scene such as smoke, glass, etc., without fringing. But that system is based on the necessity of tying the composite to a single blue replacement.

Due to the interactive nature of matte manipulation within CGI composite scripts, different areas can be tweaked with different screen color replacements. Generally the screen color is only digitally replaced with a dark or a light value run through a luminance mat. In theory, the whole edge could be queried, detecting the color of all regions and replacing the screen color appropriately. It is this ability to manipulate the screen color replacement that allows computer graphics to accept less than perfectly chromatic screen colors. Matte lines do still exist because the extractions are not perfect. But now the screen color is replaced with more appropriate colors behind the objects, so what used to appear as matte lines now appears as nearly correct color edge wrap.

---

[56] Optically speaking, a color separation positive is one of three black-and-white pieces of film that will be exposed to recreate the red, green, and blue layers on the original piece of film.

Film versus Digital

One historical advantage of film over digital images is tonal range, in particular detail at the low end. As file size transfer becomes less of an issue with better technology, this difference is disappearing. For the longest time nothing has looked better than a new print in a large format projected to SMPTE[57] standards. And nothing has been more disappointing than viewing that same film print after it has been run several hundred times.

Optical compositing obviously was all about manipulating a collection of original negatives. The first step was always to make an interpositive to work from, so the original (read "irreplaceable") was touched as little as possible. Over the years Kodak, in a nod to the marketing advantage of being involved in the Hollywood film industry, developed and changed film emulsions to suit the needs of visual effects. No one has pressed the limits of film manipulation like the visual effects industry. The old standard film emulsions had huge blue grain compared to the modern Kodak Vision films. And certainly the bottom line for shooting is that no matter how much performance is desired of a piece of film, it is still a photochemical reaction that has absolute limits in science.

In optical compositing the bluescreen negative is re-created using fine-grain black-and-white films. Red, green, and blue records were made and recombined on a new piece of color negative. Mattes were also made on black-and-white acetate or Estar-based film.[58] It was a laborious process that required a very precise choreography by the printer operator. Something as simple as a change in the order of placement of color correction filters from one take to another could make the composite unusable.

For years the standards were Panchromatic Separation Film 5235 and SO202 (Estar base). These are no longer being produced by Kodak (2238 is the replacement). The first color negative Vision films greatly reduced grain if properly exposed. They did help, but reacted just like any other film if under- or overexposed. Kodak's 5277 film[59] in particular exhibited very ugly blues if underexposed. The blues were so bad that the blue channel needed to be reprocessed with a mix of the green in order to get any sort

[57] SMPTE: Society of Motion Picture and Television Engineers. It was founded in 1916 and works to establish industry-wide technical standards for every aspect of the motion picture industry.

[58] Estar: a polyester film base that is much more rugged than acetate film base. It is thinner and much stronger than acetate. It can damage the moving parts of a camera or projector if it jams, whereas acetate films will just tear. Its durability allows its use for compositing many takes of a scene.

[59] Kodak films have four-digit labels with different stocks for specific purposes (e.g., shooting outdoor live action, under tungsten, or in the optical printer or film laboratory processes).

of definition. It also got very milky in the blacks when underexposed. The S0214 film was developed to get rid of halation,[60] especially when using green screens (but it is not yet in wide use). The 5245 film got contrasty outside but could look great with the use of some scrims. The 5274 film was punchier but tended to be a bit contrasty, whereas 5293 film was pretty predictable for a midspeed film. The 5298 film probably shouldn't have been used for visual effects, unless the visual goal is that 16mm look (i.e., very grainy).

Optically speaking, some of these adverse film characteristics were impossible to overcome since the frame needed to be dealt with as one image. Area mattes could be made but the process of hand drawing and photographing them could take days, so it was not economically feasible. Artists were quite particular in optical compositing about the AIMs and requirements for how things were shot because there truly were physical limits as to what could be fixed. These requirements would translate back to greater expense on the set because of care needed in shooting. That is probably the ultimate reason for the death of optical compositing because even though it is not necessarily any quicker, digital compositing doesn't have the photochemical restrictions. And one poor digital compositor laboring away to fix a less-than-ideal blue screen is far less expensive than holding up a complete first unit while the backing gets perfectly lit.

Optical Underexposure Generalizations

- More apparent grain,
- less saturated colors,
- smoky blacks,
- lower contrast, and
- less sharpness.

Optical Overexposure Generalizations

- Less apparent grain,
- more saturated colors,
- richer (blacker) blacks, and
- increased contrast.

Vision films replaced the old standard emulsions of the 1980s and 1990s. Currently Kodak has pushed out Vision 3 emulsions. Sadly, in some respects, the end of shooting on film is in the not too distant future. But just as digital compositing is a vastly superior technique to optical compositing, one would hope HD

---

[60] Halation: the spreading of light beyond where one would like the film to be exposed. Most films have an anti-halation backing to keep the light from the exposure from bouncing around in the camera and adding additional unwanted exposure.

cameras will eventually have the same latitude as film, with manageable file sizes.

As romantic as it may appear to have been compositing on film, the physical restrictions were a huge detriment to the artistry of making a movie. A printer breakdown in midshot or a mistake at the photo lab could mean hours or days wasted and no quick way to recover. Because of deadline restrictions that meant a limited number of effects shots per movie. A huge show in the 1980s might have had 300 to 400 shots, nothing like the several thousand of today's big shows.

COMPOSITING OF LIVE-ACTION ELEMENTS
Marshall Krasser

Modern Digital Compositing

With the release of *Star Wars* in 1977, the magical world of compositing was introduced to the masses on a scale not seen before. In fact, most of the digital artists practicing the trade today were influenced and inspired by this movie. A great deal of the current bluescreen/greenscreen (BS/GS) methodology and technology stemmed from the groundbreaking optical processes that were developed and refined in the 1970s. As just discussed, the photochemical process remained the leading form of screen compositing for feature films until the early 1990s, when more affordable desktop computers became available. The software engineers utilized the knowledge of the photochemical process and developed methods that would allow the same type of work to be done digitally. This opened the door to unlimited possibilities and development.

Prior to this adoption by the film industry, a great deal of groundwork had been developed in the commercial production facilities and broadcast video networks. A simple example was the real-time keying of the local weather forecaster over the weather map. Since film required more resolution than video, it took the development of high-resolution, pin-registered scanning equipment to finally allow the migration from film stock to pixels.

Regardless of the medium, the processes that are in use today are very similar, but the final techniques vary depending on the specifications of the final image (i.e., Film, PAL, NTSC, HD, IMAX, etc.).

Capturing the Image to Composite

Chapter 3 of this book focuses on how to properly acquire/shoot an image for visual effects work. The section titled *Bluescreen and Greenscreen Technology* specifically delves into great detail on BS/

GS methodologies and technologies. Therefore, the topic is only touched upon here in a general way.

Thanks to computer and digital technology, many problems with badly lit or shot elements can be corrected. However, a properly shot element will save time and resources that translate into costs and quality. Having the proper color screen, evenly exposed with a subject the correct distance away from the screen, can only help deliver a better composite—on time and budget.

Emerging Capture Technology Issues

Be aware that most, if not all, video cameras utilize an edge enhancement feature to artificially sharpen the image. This sharpening adds edge ringing artifacts that will result in very undesirable results when keying. Make sure this feature can be disabled on any HD system that is being used. If there is a sharpness issue with the image, it can be corrected in the composite later. Other cameras, such as DVCAM, have very low sampling in chrominance and tend to heavily compress the video data. This adds even more artifacts (noise) to the image that cannot be corrected and makes screen extraction difficult, if not impossible. (Please refer to the section *Digital Cinematography* in Chapter 3 for more detailed information.)

Emerging Approaches

A new emerging technique, which adds to the BS/GS set of tools, is the *retroreflective* curtain approach. This uses a retroreflective curtain in the background and a ring of bright LEDs mounted around the camera lens, which mitigates the need for any additional lights to illuminate the background. The advantage is that an extremely small amount of power is used and the LEDs require little or no rigging. This new approach stems from the invention of blue LEDs in the 1990s, which also allow for green LEDs. This process is still being developed but shows excellent potential for small-scale productions and has already been used on a few major projects.

Another emerging technology is color keying that uses a part of the light spectrum that is invisible to the human eye. Called *Thermo-Key*, it uses infrared as the key color. It isolates the living subject from the background and allows the artist to create a matte of the subject without the need for a screen. This is still in an early stage of development but could hold vast potential in specific situations.

As the capture side of the technology continues to advance, so will the compositing side of technology. But regardless of where the state of the art is at present, one thing remains constant: the need to create a believable composite that is of high quality and is on time and on budget.

After the Shoot

After the files are scanned and loaded online, a first pass at primary color correction to achieve a consistent and standard color basis for compositing is highly recommended.

One approach is to load all of the screen shots into a color correction application that allows images to be viewed sequentially in a thumbnail proof sheet mode. By conforming and setting a base color for the screens, a set of default extraction values can be set for the sequence, which can save time. However, the final subject color conform will need to be handled later in the final composites.

Another approach is to conform all of the subjects in the first pass and let the screens fall as they may. This allows the timer to set the primary color of the subject(s) and removes the need for individual artists to attempt color conforming on their own.

Extractions and the Magic Bullet

The general consensus is that there is no magic bullet when it comes to extractions. All of the techniques and tools available today have strengths and weaknesses. Ultimately, a combination of several techniques is usually most successful. Granted, at times quick and easy extractions can be made on perfectly lit and stationary subjects. However, those are the exception to the norm when budgets and time constraints are factored in. Ultimatte and Primatte are two well-known and powerful extraction tools and, when used alone or combined, can provide excellent results. The Image Based Keyer (IBK) is another tool that is quickly gaining popularity.

One widely used method for keying BS/GS photography involves pulling three primary keys:

1. *Inner key:* for the inside of the subject, which involves getting a solid interior matte that does not bleed out to the edge. This is a core matte in essence and should be solid enough to kill any small internal errors in the extraction. A good trick to eliminate any stray holes: Max filter the matte +11 and then Min filter it by −11 (values are an example only).

2. *Outer key:* for the exterior of the image that removes the exterior of the subject and does not bleed into the subject. This is a looser version of the next key below, the edge key, and is there to provide a good edge base on which to build.

3. *Edge key:* consists of a finer detailed key for the edge material, including hair or clothing fibers. These mattes might be built from a combination of luminance mattes isolated from the individual RGB channels.

These keys should then be used in combination to preserve fine edge detail while maintaining a pure clean and clear core matte.

Other Factors

There has been a recent trend to shoot "dirty," which is the introduction of elements such as rain, smoke, and dust into screen shoots. This can result in an interaction that cannot be achieved in a sterile screen shot and is increasingly becoming the norm. Shallow focus is another area that can cause special handling of the extractions. These and other factors can force an artist into isolating different areas in a frame (with a garbage matte) and pulling a separate extraction that is later combined into an extraction composite matte.

In the case of smoke being shot in the background plate, the ideal situation is to have the smoke contained spatially behind where the subject needs to be composited. Later in post, additional smoke can be added in front of the screened element. But this cannot always be controlled, so in situations where there is foreground smoke, this smoke should be isolated if possible. Difference matting can work if there is a locked-off camera and action and a clean, smoke-free frame.

Difference matting can only really work in limited situations but is a good first approach. Other options include simply placing the element over the background and then layering additional or "matching" smoke to blend it into the scene. This will cause some modification to the existing look of the plate but is necessary. There have been situations, in extreme conditions, where the entire background scene has been digitally re-created and then the smoke was reintroduced in the composite using CGI or practically shot elements.

Motion Blur

Motion blur can be difficult in any composite. For the best looking composite, one needs to retain as much of this motion blur as possible to avoid strobing. As with most screen extractions, first extract a good core matte and mix it with a softer edge matte extraction. This method will allow the edges to be processed and treated differently and will provide the most flexibility in the end. It is this control and flexibility that discourages some artists from using tools that prebake the "composite" inside of the plug-in. For many reasons, the safest route is to never "composite" in the plug-in.

If motion blur is still an issue, evaluate all of the channels separately to see if the motion blur can be isolated with a luminance extraction. Once it has been isolated and restricted to the desired areas, create a color card that best represents the original color of the subject(s) edges. Composite the color card into the matte, place this result over the background, and composite the keyed subject over this. In special cases, and if the action allows, the element that is being keyed can be translated to fill the motion blur matte. This will give a more accurate and complex color than what may be achieved with a single color card. This trick can work and save the artist from having to resort to the final option of manually re-creating motion blur by painting on the final composite. This method can also be used to capture extremely fine edge detail that the keyer cannot isolate.

Incorrect Exposure

If a subject or the blue or green screen is improperly exposed, there will more than likely be some noise or chatter occurring along the extraction edges. The solution in the past was to expose the screen one stop under the foreground subject to get the greatest saturation and minimize screen spill. Currently, there has been a trend to expose the screen at the same exposure as the foreground subject. This will help eliminate grain issues unless the subject is being lit for nighttime or a darkened environment. Ideally it is better to shoot these dark scenes a stop or two brighter than the target and later reduce the exposure in the composite. The key to this working is having good communication with the Director of Photography prior to the shoot. (Please refer to *Digital Cinematography* in Chapter 3 for more information on this topic.)

Spill Suppression

With the exception of a black screen, all screens will have a certain amount of color pollution (spill bounce) affecting the subject. Even if the distance from subject to screen is set correctly, some amount will always be there. Most software packages have spill suppression options built in, and these are fairly effective in eliminating the spill. Do *not* suppress too much of the target color when utilizing this option. This overuse of suppression is one of the big giveaways when it comes to being able to visually detect screen composites. If the plate has been color timed, work should be done in the core color-corrected image. Spill suppression should only be performed on the edges if necessary.

In extreme cases of spill where the image is compromised beyond a process's reach, a skilled artist can synthetically re-create the bad channel by blending the other channels together and then reintroducing this result into the original RGB file. It is not easy, but it can be done.

Several packages are available that handle edge spill quite well. Most of them use 3D color algorithms to isolate and replace the spill with the color that is appearing behind it. This will not work if further post-processing is required, since it will not allow the use of the process's composite option.

Degraining Running Footage/Still Images

Adding grain to CG images was discussed in *CG Compositing* in Chapter 7. When dealing with shot images, it never hurts to run a low-level degraining or blurring pass on an image prior to extracting. The extraction might lose a little detail but the result could be worth the loss. However, the original image should be used for the subject in the composite and not the processed one. In extreme cases, re-creation of the image in areas of fine detail (i.e., a sailing ship's rigging) may be necessary by tracking in a still image. This tracked piece can be a big time-saver and should be on the list of possible solutions to try. A clean degrained image can be created if there are several frames to work with. By aligning them, adding them together, and doing some math, a very clean and degrained image can be obtained (i.e., for 10 added images simply multiply by 0.1). Remember to add grain back into the final composite to match the surrounding images.

Starting the Composite

It is always beneficial to have access to the individual layers that go into a composite. Current tools may make it difficult to get in and really alter the pieces that go into the composite, but this is an individual decision that needs to be made at the artist's level.

Generally speaking, today's screen composites are rarely simple "A over B" processes—and sometimes it appears that the entire alphabet is now involved. This alphabet includes such things as relighting the foreground (FG) element in CG (to simulate outdoors), adding interactive light modulation (sun/shadows), plate flashing, edge warp/spill, edge blending, and chromatic edge work, to name a few. It is also critical that any surrounding live-action shots, or reference images shot at the time of filming, be closely analyzed. Since the ultimate goal of the shot is to cut seamlessly into the movie, all of the tricks and techniques at hand—unorthodox or otherwise—might be needed to achieve this result.

Relighting

Relighting can be rather tricky at times, but it can be worth the effort if the element is not appropriately lit. If an element was shot indoors, but is supposed to be outdoors, one solution is to add contrast to the element to simulate the outdoor look. Another option is to isolate the highlights and boost their values and modulate them if the scene can justify this.

Modulate Lighting

Sometimes adding some light/dark modulation to an element will add a little extra life to the image. By using either generated or practical smoke/dust elements a color correction can be run through this matte and achieve a nice and simple interactive lighting effect. In extreme cases (i.e., traveling through a jungle), a more heavy-handed approach can be added to simulate pools of light and shadows.

Plate Flashing/Spill (Standard and Multiweighted)

This technique is one that should not only be used for CGI elements but should also be applied to live-action elements as well. The color spill that was removed from the live-action element is similar to what needs to be added back to bring the element to life. A good visual example is what is seen in a dark room looking at a bright window; the bloom/flash that is spilling into the room is an extreme example of what must be replicated.

A good way to simulate this is by taking the background plate, applying a large blur, and then adding a small percentage back over the FG element (aka, plate flash).

The effect can be improved by performing a secondary, multiweighted plate flash that adds more flash based on the background's hotter areas. This can be accomplished by pulling a high-contrast luminance matte that isolates the hot spots. A Sobel matte[61] is then created of the subject matter, and then the high-contrast matte is placed into the Sobel matte. The resulting matte is composited with the background plate into it. Next, apply a large blur to this image and then screen, or plus it, back over the extraction (compositing order: BG, Extraction, Edge Sobel comp). This should be handled very delicately and can easily be controlled by adding a comp multiplier and adjusting the earlier parameter values.

Edge Wrap

Edge wrap is an element integration technique that is meant to simulate what would happen to a foreground element that was photographed in the real plate environment (i.e., the background bleeding and wrapping over it). This is one compositing technique that must be used correctly, because it can easily be applied incorrectly and overdone. The simplistic approach is to create a Sobel matte from the extraction or CGI element and use this matte to drive the edge wrap. It is very similar to the plate flash/spill technique but more contained along the edge of the element that is being composited. The saying "less is more" really does apply here. The "snail trail" look of a soft even line around the entire element is to be avoided. Using the above-mentioned multiweighted trick can reduce this problem.

---

[61] A Sobel matte is a discrete differentiation operator, computing an approximation of the gradient of the image intensity function. In simplified words, it uses an edge detection algorithm to create an outline around the edge.

Edge Blending

This is more relevant to CGI elements, but external edge blending is something that can help add that final 5% to push the element into the composite. As with edge wrap, this technique simulates the light scattering and edge softening/blending that is seen when analyzing photographic images. Hard edges on extractions are one of the keys that will give away a screened composite; this technique can help to eliminate this issue.

Using a tighter Sobel matte than the edge wrap, a side composite is created where the element is placed over the background (BG). It is then blurred, regrained, and placed into the Sobel matte. Next, add a percentage of this edge element back over the main portion of the composite. A similar trick can be used to add internal edge blending to CGI renders (utilizing a normals or Fresnel render pass) in order to lessen their hard lines.

Compositing Screen Elements in Stereoscopic 3D

The recent rebirth of stereoscopic movies has added a new twist to compositing. Since the requirements are to create two identical composites, some issues can cause breaks in the convergence. One such issue is specular highlights and reflections. These will need to be isolated and conformed to match in the left and right channels to eliminate the problem. Packages such as Nuke may be configured to create left and right composite trees in tandem with the capability to split the composite tree into a left/right branch and rejoin it after the corrections. Certain fractal/noise-based operators create issues as well. It is not without its issues, but with the advent of new compositing packages, the process is not nearly as complicated and cumbersome as in the past. With some work, even elements that were shot without a 3D camera can be converted into passable 3D elements.

Rotoscoping

Brief History

In 1917 Max Fleischer patented the technique of rotoscoping after inventing and using it on his 1915 series, *Out of the Ink Well*. The method involved using a movie projector to project a single frame onto a surface. The projected image(s) were then traced by hand onto paper and rephotographed frame by frame.

Early visual effects artists used a variation of this method to create their mattes as well. This process involved an animation camera focused on a special table. The camera was loaded with already processed footage. By installing a light behind the camera, it was converted into a projector that would project a single image down onto the pin-registered camera bed, where the artist would pencil trace the image onto a peg-registered[62] sheet of paper. This pencil work was rephotographed frame by frame and tested for its integrity against the original. If additional work was needed they would go back and readjust the pencil drawings. After final buy-off was received, the images were then transferred and inked onto peg-registered animation cells and rephotographed onto high-contrast black-and-white film.

In today's visual effects rotoscoping process, digital footage is loaded into a rotoscoping software package and the artists use splines[63] to trace the required articulated mattes. Dependent on the roto software, the splines can be converted into matte images and read into the compositing package. In some cases the compositing software can import the roto spline files directly and allow their editing.

Rotoscope Approaches and Techniques

The best way to begin the task of rotoscoping is to review and study the footage of the subject to be articulated. Things to look for: Can any of the roto be done procedurally (i.e., stabilize the plate and use the inverted data to apply the motion to a single frame)? Will any sections require frame-by-frame hand articulation? Can fine hair detail be extracted using luminance matting?

After the plate has been analyzed, select the frame that has the most complex edge to use as the starting point. One big shape is not the ideal method; rather several smaller key shapes are the preferred approach. This allows each shape to be keyframed independently. In most cases, this is needed especially when major motion is involved (i.e., like a running person) and frame-by-frame keying is required.

Sometimes the most difficult task can come from the need to rotoscope a person who appears to be motionless. Film weave and small movements are always occurring in this situation. Prestabilizing the plate to remove this is helpful, but if that is not a possibility, begin by hand articulating key frames as far apart as possible—then go back and refine as needed. For example, key the spline on 16's,[64] then refine on 8's, and if needed, continue on 4's, then 2's, and if absolutely necessary, on 1's. To avoid matte chatter, floating, or popping, the fewer key frames used the smoother and better the mattes will look. Key frames that are divisible by 2 will allow for a more mathematically even keying (i.e., 32, 16, 8, 4, 2). Using odd, or random, key frames makes final refinement more difficult and inconsistent.

---

[62] Peg-registered paper: special animation paper with registration holes that fit over pegs on an animation stand to ensure line-up.

[63] A series of points connected by a line or curve.

[64] "On 16's" is a common animation phrase meaning use every 16th frame. For example, traditional cell animation is done on 2's, meaning that the image changes every 2nd frame.

Some applications provide automated forms of rotoscoping and can be utilized with varying results. But most rotoscoping is still done by hand and is the unsung hero of the visual effects industry. Every day new techniques are being developed and refined as technology advances. Some newer packages utilize 3D layout data to help automate some of the process.

Using the Articulated Mattes

Once the mattes are complete they can either be converted to black-and-white images on disk or imported into the compositing package. If they can be imported in a native format that allows editing of the splines from within the compositing package, it can speed up slight alterations that might need to be done. Otherwise, it is usually best to edit them in their native package and reimport them.

Processing the Articulated Mattes

The addition of blur to articulated mattes is a standard and necessary practice. An unprocessed matte is rarely used in a shot due to the fact that the resultant image would be too sharp and strobe. If the splines contain vector data for motion blur, they should be switched on for the best results. In addition, post-processing the matted edges by adding some dithering, or randomizing, in the composite will provide a more natural and organic look to spline-based mattes. Depending on the software package, some roto will need to be done to the center of the live-action blur. Other roto tools allow the artist to grow or shrink selected areas of the mattes edges with a built-in fall-off. This can be useful when one side of the matte needs to be softer for extensive motion blur.

Garbage Mattes

Garbage mattes[65] are simpler roto mattes that do not follow a detailed edge but merely serve to isolate a specific area. These are usually used to isolate areas for color correction and can be combined with specific keys to apply the key only in specific areas (hair on a head, etc.). Their use usually requires a very large blur since they are not tightly articulated.

Digital Painting and Plate Reconstruction

Motion Blur Correction with Paint

"When in doubt, paint it out" has been a saying since the migration to digital compositing. At times hand painting can be a good solution for fixing extraction issues. However, the time needed

---

[65] A garbage matte is a simple shape that is placed around the subject to be matted to isolate it.

to fix an extraction should be weighed against how much time is saved by painting away the problem on the final composite.

Cloning and the smudge/drag tool are suggested methods for adding motion blur back to elements shot on a BS/GS. There are even situations when actual hand painting of mattes is still done for motion blur, but for the most part, paint on the final comp is the preferred method.

Plate Reconstruction

The lines become blurred when discussing the plate reconstruction aspect of the visual effects workflow. Each facility may treat it differently. Plate reconstruction can be classified under such areas of responsibility as rotoscoping, compositing, or even layout. Most of the techniques are utilized across several disciplines. A good solid 3D or 2D track solve is very helpful in the process. Once this has been created, a paint package that can read this data is a truly powerful tool that will allow an artist to automate the track, paint, and cloning process.

A first approach should try a fully procedural process in a composite package. It is an excellent introduction to compositing for the junior artist as well. The use of clean plates (shot on location or painted to be clean) is the backbone of plate reconstruction. If one is on location during the shoot, gather as many reference images as possible (see the *Plate Stitching* section below).

After clean frames are obtained, or created (remember to de-grain), the next step is to utilize the tracking data. The data should provide the necessary track to split the clean frame into the moving scene with soft splits and/or articulated mattes, adding the final part of the equation. Running grain should be added to the re-constructed image area, closely matching the existing footage.

If the procedural approach does not solve the problem, moving to a procedural hand-painting method is the next step. By using a track paint solution, the amount of flutter/chatter that could be introduced with a frame-by-frame painting approach can be reduced. In the end, frame-by-frame painting might be the only solution. Keep it simple as it is easy to paint a single frame, but in motion, things can go horribly wrong. This type of painting work requires extreme patience and talent and is not something to be approached lightly.

Rig Removal

Off-the-shelf packages exist that are made to automate the process of rig removal, and at times they work quite well. If not, other methods, like those mentioned in the plate reconstruction section, may be utilized. A standard wire removal technique involves generating a matte for the wire and filling that area with the directly adjacent pixel data. This may cause ghosting at times and should be reviewed closely.

Plate Stitching

Plate stitching is a powerful way to generate new backgrounds, or clean plates, and is used in digital matte paintings as well. At times the original plate shot might be too problematic to work for the final effects shot for any number of reasons. A total reconstruction might be the only option. Hopefully frames can be isolated to help re-create the plate.

Any location images may be very handy and should always be a consideration. The HDRI[66] images are very easy to capture and usually do not require the assistance of the film crew. However, the multiple frames from a film camera, if on a dolly or stabilized arm, will allow an artist to frame average and degrain the image producing a high-quality source image. HDRI frames will likely contain some form of digital noise/grain, but shooting a few frames with the camera mounted on a tripod and a remote shutter release will allow the same degraining capabilities.

Several applications exist that will stitch these images together. Each works with different algorithms, so other packages should be explored if the first package fails. Recent projects have utilized proprietary software that uses running footage (captured from six synchronized running cameras) to create virtual backgrounds to travel through. The VES's (Visual Effects Society) award-winning shot from *War of the Worlds* (2005), where the actors are fleeing down the freeway in a van, is an example of this technique. The stitching for these require complicated 3D tracking and motion solving and image re-projection, but the flexibility it affords is priceless.

Scene Tracking

3D Layout

Layout, also referred to as *matchmoving,* is the building block in today's modern CGI shot production. With its origins in CG feature animation, the 3D layout team creates the scene and camera that will be the foundation for a fully CG shot. Almost every shot, be it a 2D screen shot or a massively complex 3D shot, can and does utilize a properly solved 3D scene. The process may sound relatively simple in the following paragraphs. However, the required user knowledge of lenses, cameras, field of view, image distortion, and numerous other factors make this a very challenging and complicated discipline.

---

[66] High-dynamic-range images, or HDRI, are a series of photographs taken that cover the entire range of stops. They are usually used to re-create the set in CG, allowing the set to be relit in post.

Methods and Data Acquisition

Most of the tracking packages are based on a pattern recognition algorithm that was developed in the late 1980s and published at SIGGRAPH. This is a reference-based system that does subpixel matching using a fast Fourier transform (FFT) on a pixel-by-pixel basis. It is usually based on multiple individually defined search patterns. This data is then translated into 3D special coordinates. This allows the shot to be re-created accurately in the computer. At this point, the layout scene can be passed on to an animator who can correctly place the CGI character in the proper spatial location. This 3D scene and animation can also be loaded into compositing packages for accurate tracking and placement of practical elements.

Utilizing the Data

Almost all of the professional software packages today allow for the importation of 3D scenes (or 2D corner pin/track point data). This data allows the artist to correctly add elements in 3D space that tracks along with the plate (i.e., adding smoke, steam, explosions, etc.) and may be attached to CGI elements as well. The most powerful systems allow for the repositioning of elements in 3D space, which opens the door to the world of 2.5D and, ultimately, 3D compositing. This flexibility eliminates the need to move back and forth between the separate packages, thus saving time. Currently software is in development that combines all of this into one package and will ultimately bridge the gap between all of the disciplines. Specialization is one method that has been proven over time to facilitate and move large volumes of work through a facility. The right tool for the right job is still the most efficient use of resources at this time.

MATTE PAINTINGS/CREATIVE ENVIRONMENTS
Craig Barron, Deak Ferrand, John Knoll, Robert Stromberg

Matte Paintings: Art of the Digital Realm

> *A matte shot is designed to be on quickly, to be part of the picture. You are not creating a pretty painting—you are making a part of an integral piece of film. It should serve the purpose of carrying the transition between the scene before and the scene after; in other words, be part of it. It is not put there to run for 10 minutes, so that you can study it to see if it's a painting. It just serves a purpose, so that the whole picture can be a successful entity in itself.*
>
> —**Matthew Yuricich**

Figure 6.50 Matthew Yuricich in his studio, working on a matte painting for *Ben-Hur* (1959). (Image courtesy of Matthew Yuricich.)

What Is a Matte Painting?

Although matte shots are one of the oldest visual effects techniques in film, the reason for having a matte painting has basically not changed over the years. Filmmaking is telling stories and stories take place in settings that must be depicted visually. Sometimes these settings exist in reality, and the filmmaker can travel to that location to shoot, but in many cases the setting must be fabricated in some way. Very early on, matte painting became an important tool to create settings in a cost-effective and efficient manner. Matte paintings help tell stories that would be impossible without them for technical, logistical, and budgetary reasons.

Matte painting has been and always will be a vital ingredient in expanding the scope of filmmakers' visions, regardless of technology. It is a necessary element in the filmmaker's toolbox. Matte paintings transport the audience to past eras or take them deep into the future to discover new and exciting worlds. They make it possible for filmmakers to keep production costs down and to give scale and importance to settings. Matte paintings are needed so viewers can see clearly. They are needed to tell viewers where they are.

Matte Painting Pioneers and History

It is generally accepted that Norman Dawn is the pioneer who first used glass-matte trickery, such as his visual "repair" work on the historic but dilapidated churches seen in the 1907 film, *California Missions*. The aptly named Dawn ushered in matte

Figure 6.51 A matte-painting-on-glass setup used by director Norman Dawn on location in Tasmania for the silent film *For the Term of His Natural Life* (1927). (Image courtesy of Professor Raymond Fielding.)

painting as a new cinematic art form, mentoring artists who subsequently produced thousands of matte paintings throughout four decades. Dawn has been strangely overlooked, perhaps because the matte painting effect itself has always been designed to be invisible.

Even with today's technology, one cannot assume that creating a matte painting is any easier or automatic. Whether using paint or pixels, matte painters have always had the same creative problems at hand. The great artists and pioneers from Norman Dawn to Albert Whitlock have paved the way for a new generation of young talent. Armed with only a piece of glass and a paintbrush, these early explorers of visual effects were given the same set of creative issues that today's artists face and yet they were successful using only the simple tools available to them. What this conveys is that it doesn't matter what is used—what matters is how it is used. It is and always will be the artist and not the machinery that determines a successful shot.

A simple example would be the addition of a second story to a one-story building. Rather than spend the money with the art department to build a two-story building, just build the first floor and add on the second floor with a matte painting. By understanding this basic concept, adding a matte painting to a shot has the potential for being the answer to numerous creative production problems.

Figure 6.52A To add height to an existing set of buildings, digital wireframes were applied to this shot in *The Truman Show* (1998). (Image courtesy of Paramount Pictures © Paramount Pictures Corp. All rights reserved.)

Figure 6.52B The final cityscape, combined with live-action footage in the foreground, was completed at Matte World Digital by Brett Northcutt. (Image courtesy of Paramount Pictures © Paramount Pictures Corp. All rights reserved.)

A very important consideration in order to fully utilize matte paintings is the skill of the matte artist. He or she must be able to "paint" (using paints, digital technology, or both) a painting that replicates photographic reality perfectly. Not *almost* perfectly but *perfectly*! This is no easy task and anything less than 100% is failure. So taking into regard the cliché of "failure is not an option," there are few tasks as demanding as doing a matte shot. It is a fine line since one cannot do "better than reality" and anything less than reality is obvious to the viewer. Only perfection goes unnoticed.

The need for perfection was not always required in the early days of cinema. Sets were obvious, overacting was sometimes needed for silent films, and even hand-cranked cameras made movement unreal. So miniatures and matte paintings were often recognized by the viewer but still easily accepted as part of the film. However, as filmmaking became more sophisticated, so did the audience and today's best films look and feel real.

Visualizing the Matte Painting Shot in Pre-Production

In recent years matte paintings and overall environment designs have become essential parts of pre-production. Understanding the film world that is about to be created is crucial for budgets and general production costs. How much needs to be built? What does this world look like? More and more the artist's importance comes to light.

Now more than ever, films are made or not made based on costs. A good artist working with a production designer and director can be a pivotal factor in whether a film ever gets made. A matte painter who creates his or her own concepts can save time and money for production by knowing the technical requirements needed, not only for the complexity of the shot, but also for the amount of set that has to be built. This becomes very apparent in set extensions where the matte line is defined by what will not be physically built. The film's producer will find that the ideas and research required for a good concept is priceless. When the concept is right, the matte painting becomes very easy to execute.

On-Set Supervision for Matte Painting Shots

The matte painter should always be on set whenever a live-action plate is photographed for a matte shot. Advice and guidance to the director may be required in order to ensure that a final shot will be correct and within budget. Planning is key. Understanding the story point of the shot is perhaps the most important consideration. Why is the shot in the film? How will it advance the narrative? Where should the viewer look while the shot is on the screen? These questions severely complicate the process. Only by creative collaboration with the filmmakers and by hard work can matte shots become a welcome addition to a film.

A matte artist should have a multitude of skills. He or she should have a basic understanding of cameras, lenses, lighting, and composition. Stages of today are filled with blue or green screens. The matte artist can be extremely helpful in composing shots to give the filmmakers an understanding of what will eventually be added. Highly refined illustrations have become a critical element on set.

The set is a battleground where every minute costs a lot of money, so extreme awareness is required when stepping in as the on-set matte painting supervisor. Most likely an on-set matte painter will work under a VFX Supervisor hired by the studio whose job is to deal with any technical issues pertaining to visual effects. Almost any camera move that can be imagined can be used in conjunction with a matte painting. All that's needed is time and money. The on-set matte painter should be able to give the director a solution for creating his vision of the shot while keeping it on or under budget.

Some of the factors to consider when choosing a matte painting technique on set are cost, levels of interactivity between performers and their environment, and the level of realism in the production design. Is it cheaper to build a set physically for principal photography or later in post-production? Depending on the design and surfacing complexity, it could go either way. For example, a short sequence featuring complex articulated machinery would almost certainly be less expensive to create in post-production. On the other hand, having significantly fewer effects shots in post can sometimes pay for money invested in a set for a lengthy sequence.

How extensively do the performers interact with the environment, both from a lighting and physical interaction standpoint? While many types of interactions can be faked in post, they increase the complexity for everyone involved, especially for the actors. Nothing looks more realistic than photography of a real object. Depending on the skill of the artists involved and the post-production budget, sets created in post will range anywhere from perfectly realistic to significantly less so. What level of stylization is acceptable to the production? It is frequently difficult to light the actors for their intended environment and to light the process screen for good extractability at the same time. Usually this ends up being a compromise and may result in plates where it is extremely difficult to achieve perfect realism.

Very often the answer to these trade-offs is to strive for the best of both worlds by building a partial set with extensions to be made in post. This allows full interactivity both from physical contact and interactive lighting and shadows. It also frees the director of photography from the dual constraints of lighting the set for look, as well as the technical requirements of lighting a process screen for extractability. Portions of the set that will be seen infrequently, or would be prohibitively expensive to construct, can be made in post using less expensive techniques.

How much set is it smart to build? This division is usually determined during discussions with the director and production designer. One fundamental difference between physical sets and post-production set extensions is that once a physical set has been constructed, the production can shoot as much material on that set as desired without incurring additional cost. But every shot of a set extension will require labor to be expended, making longer sequences with more shots more expensive than shorter sequences. This trade-off is usually factored in to the decision so that some portion of the sequence can be played mostly or entirely on set once a scene shifts to dialog exchange.

Figure 6.53A In *Star Trek IV: The Voyage Home* (1986), ILM's matte department filmed extras on an airport runway.
(Image courtesy of Paramount Pictures © Paramount Pictures Corp. All rights reserved.)

Figure 6.53B For the final shot, Chris Evans' matte painting of Star Fleet Command Headquarters was composited with the live-action element.
(Image courtesy of Paramount Pictures © Paramount Pictures Corp. All rights reserved.)

Very often on a set-extension shot, the Director of Photography will have the tendency to frame according to what he can physically see. That becomes a problem when the shot requires the addition of a castle on a hill in the background, and the framing is focused on the beautiful street merchants and buildings in the foreground, cutting off almost completely the top portion needed to insert the castle. *Repo* is the word, but sometimes the action in the foreground will prevent that. An on-set matte painter can show the film crew the concept and even use a grease pencil to draw directly onto the video monitor.

The days of the static establishing shot are almost gone. The majority of shots now use a camera on a moving dolly or a boom arm. This is not so much a problem now that software allows for changing perspectives within matte shots. Creating reference points for tracking software makes these moves possible within a shot.

The on-set matte painter can accomplish tracking by placing little crosses everywhere, or colored spheres, some lighted, on set. But placement of all of that hardware takes time, something there isn't much of during production. And the amount of work in post, digitally removing all of these trackers, translates into more time. Today, most 3D tracking software doesn't need much on-set placement to track a shot. Some architectural elements in frame will be enough to give perfect tracking. Some matte painters don't use trackers and prefer to let the crew shoot clean, as long as there are enough tracking elements in the shot. This allows the production designer and the crew to work faster, saving costs.

Basic Skills and Tricks of the Trade

The matte painter must master all of the basic skills that are required in fine art and create elaborate environments, while keeping costs down. A large portion of digital matte painters could not compete in matching the skills of a traditional matte painter of the optical era. Now, even with the ease of use of Photoshop and the photo-montage approach that most matte painters use, some basic knowledge of fine art is still required for a successful matte painting.

Good composition requires a mastering of perspective. This should be a natural skill where an artist can extend any plate by following vanishing points and finding the horizon line. Three-point perspective is required, even the ability to bend lines to match the lens distortion. Again, in the digital age, the use of 3D software can help with mapping correct perspective for complex shots. This often saves time during production.

Composition is the first thing that will make the difference between a total failure and a flowing shot. Composition is the very subtle craft of creating a pleasant balance of elements that will ultimately harmonize a painting and at the same time allow the audience to focus on a chosen element without being forceful. If a matte painting isn't working, most of the time it's because of bad composition.

There are two ways to prepare for composition. The first one is to use a black-pencil line without any shading, like a drawing. The other is to block the color by volume without ever outlining anything. The latter should be used over the former because the harmony of a good composition is also achieved with tones and colors.

Figure 6.54A Albert Whitlock's matte painting of a mountaintop holy city.

Figure 6.54B The final shot with live action in the foreground. Whitlock centered the city to make it a prominent feature in a shot for *The Man Who Would Be King* (1975). (© 1975, renewed 2003 Columbia Pictures Industries, Inc. All rights reserved. Courtesy of Columbia Pictures. *THE MAN WHO WOULD BE KING* © Devon Company. Licensed by: Warner Bros. Entertainment Inc. All rights reserved.)

The only way to create volume is to have light. The artist needs to understand how light reacts, bounces, and affects other objects. The live-action plate to be matched has all this information, especially when shot outdoors. There is no excuse for mismatched light when the reference is right in front of the artist's eyes. At this point only the light and shadows should be the focus; forget about texture and details. This will come after. No amount of details can save a badly lit matte painting.

At this stage, the work will look real, even without the details. It's quite amazing how the brain will process the information. What is not working can be seen right away. This will be much harder to do after details are added. Remember that a matte painter is matching a live-action plate that is degraded by the amount of information that it can record, its grain, and its depth of field. The quality of the optics plays a large part as well. There's no need to waste time adding details where they are not needed.

Considerations for Interior Scenes

Interiors are usually dominated by indirect light. When rendering interior scenes using computer graphics, the most realistic results are obtained by systems that can efficiently handle multibounce radiosity calculations.

Figure 6.55A The fictional New Orleans train station in *The Curious Case of Benjamin Button* (2008) was shot on a sound stage with a minimally constructed set.

Figure 6.55B Matte World Digital completed the 3D environment using physics-based lighting, seen from dozens of camera angles throughout the film. (Images courtesy of Paramount Pictures. *THE CURIOUS CASE OF BENJAMIN BUTTON* © Paramount Pictures Corporation and Warner Bros. Entertainment Inc. All rights reserved.)

Considerations for Exterior Scenes

Exterior scenes are usually dominated by the need to synthesize natural phenomena, such as terrain of varying types, the sky, clouds, water, and plants. This is such a complex task for computer graphics that a number of specialized products have come to market specifically to create these effects.

Two-Dimensional Flat Extensions

When the camera is fixed in position, the simplest extension technique is often the use of a 2D image. This image could originate from a variety of sources, including a painted image, still photos of existing sets or locations, miniatures, and computer-generated models. This is often the best choice for low-budget projects and one-offs because it is very direct and requires very little setup.

Camera Projection Techniques

One way to get the most bang for the buck is CG camera projection. By creating a single matte painting and dissecting it into layers, the matte artist can project separate elements onto simple geometry in the computer. This allows the artist to achieve the sense of dimensionality without a tedious model build and long render times. It also allows the art to dictate the look of the shot and keep in play a single vision.

The technique of CG camera projection is very simple. It basically allows any painting to stick on a given geometry through the lens of the virtual camera. Some camera moves will increase the amount of work needed to complete the work. Any shift in perspective in a camera move will introduce parallax. What was hidden at one point in the shot will be revealed later on.

A dolly moving sideways creates a lot more work than a vertical boom. In a dolly shot, everything, from foreground to background, will reveal a hidden side. On the other hand, a boom up or down will only show 100% of all the elements at its top position, thus making it very easy to paint since the camera will move to hide what is behind the objects.

Miniatures and Computer-Generated Sets

Miniatures and computer graphics are widely used to extend sets. Miniatures have been used for this purpose since the early 1900s because of their relative simplicity and high level of realism. Both miniatures and computer graphics have advantages over 2D techniques in that generating additional views and altering lighting are small incremental costs, while 2D images must be created anew.

Integrating partial miniature models in a matte painting is a great way to ensure realism. One can also use very crude models to understand the interaction of the light on a given subject. The value of using miniatures becomes very clear when dealing with very specific lighting scenarios on midground objects. The cost of building a miniature has very little impact on the budget as long as it can be used for several shots. Shooting the miniature for an outdoor scene is very rewarding since the sun is the main light source.

It is essential for the orientation of the sun to be matched to the plate, and that the elevation and angle are the same, as well as the field of view. It is also important to keep the image sharp by utilizing good depth of field, which is achieved by using small-aperture settings (such as $f16$ or $f22$) on the lens. The setup must always be photographed on a tripod, and the exposures must be bracketed, even in raw mode. This will give the greatest range to play with to match the plate.

A miniature that is not highly detailed may become more effective after the matte artist adds necessary detailing in the

Figure 6.56A This miniature of Nockmaar Castle was created by Paul Huston for *Willow* (1988). (*Willow*™ & © 1988 Lucasfilm Ltd. All rights reserved. Used under authorization.)

Figure 6.56B Chris Evans painted the dark sky for the final composite. (*Willow*™ & © 1988 Lucasfilm Ltd. All rights reserved. Used under authorization.)

painting. Atmospheric perspective may also be required by reducing contrast in the miniature and the painting. Another good thing about miniatures, when dealing with projection matte paintings, is that all of the hidden sides of the projection can be photographed and patched without having to repaint. Camera projection has become the main tool of the matte painter who in the past decade had to compete with the rise of 3D environments and complex radiosity algorithms that allow filmmakers to move their camera freely in a synthetic landscape. Only with the development of projection tools in 3D packages was the matte painter able to stay in the forefront of today's demands for such shots.

Computer graphics have one large advantage over miniatures when working on large sequences within a short post period. The advantage is that once the asset has been created, any number of artists can use it to create shots simultaneously, while miniature elements must be photographed one at a time and may require a longer post.

Figure 6.57A Projection matte painting techniques were used to create the Bureau for Paranormal Research and Defense (BPRD) building for *Hellboy 2* (2008). The projected matte painting only covers a specific camera move. Different angles will reveal texture smearing as seen in Figure 6.57B. Painting by Deak Ferrand for Hatch FX. (Image courtesy of *Hellboy* © 2008 Universal Studios Licensing, LLLP. All rights reserved.)

Figure 6.57B A top view of the building shows that the projection falls apart when the camera is moved off its set path. Painting by Deak Ferrand for Hatch FX. (Image courtesy of © 2008 Universal Studios Licensing, LLLP. All rights reserved.)

Finding the Best Frame

A time-saving tool when dealing with projection matte painting is the ability to find the *best frame*. The best frame is the moment when the camera shows most of the sides that have to be painted. There will always be such a frame—it just needs to be found. That frame will become the main painting, with all the layers needed. That painting will be projected at that specific frame and will cover the entire view.

After that initial setup comes the task of patching. Patching is like filling gaps on a cracked wall. Any time in the sequence before or after the best frame, one will see two things happen. First, the sides of objects that were previously hidden will be revealed. Second, the horizontal plane will be stretched. That is when the work begins. The artist must find a frame that shows the unprojected elements and then render it; then bring it back in Photoshop to paint over any gaps on separate layers. The layers must be saved with the corresponding alpha channel, before going back to the 3D software. At that frame, the patches are re-projected on the same objects that have the main projection, but this time using the alpha channel to reveal only the area

Figure 6.58A Live-action footage of the Las Vegas strip for *Casino* (1995). (Image courtesy of *Casino* © 1995 Universal Studios Licensing, LLLP. All rights reserved.)

Figure 6.58B Matte World Digital topped the buildings using radiosity software to create the realistic bounce-light reflections of the 1970s-era strip. (Image courtesy of *Casino* © 1995 Universal Studios Licensing, LLLP. All rights reserved.)

needed. Three passes might be necessary, or 20 sets of patches on 20 different frames might be necessary. It depends on the complexity of the shot.

Another trick for lowering the number of patches needed on the perimeter of the image is to render the 3D layout with a wider lens and render it at a higher resolution. Then in Photoshop, the live-action portion is replaced in the exact position of the original view. The artist can then paint with this wider angle and project the painting this way. After this is done, the camera is reset to the original lens. Now there exists a projection that covers far beyond the camera view on all sides, allowing the artist to skip the patching of the sky and background hills.

Digital painting has made it easy to merge imagery from photographic sources, greatly improving realism, while saving vast amounts of time. Layers have made it easy to try out new ideas without committing to a particular path and to easily create multiple versions of a painting. Digital compositing means that tasks like creating invisible blends between paintings and live action, and matching color across the split, have become relatively effortless and can now be taken for granted. The artist is free to focus on aesthetics.

Re-Projected Photo Survey

When the set to be extended consists of repeated elements, like a long corridor, for example, an extremely effective way to create extensions is to photograph the set pieces to be replicated and then build low-detail polygonal geometry to match. The artist projects the photography onto the CG model and renders as needed. This technique is very powerful and flexible and can be used anywhere a set, miniature, or location exists that can be photographed.

This technique was used extensively in *Transformers* (2007) to extend city-street plates shot on the Universal Studios backlot to make them appear to have been shot in downtown Los Angeles. Carefully photographed stills were gathered at the actual Los Angeles location, and these stills were projected onto geometry to replace skylines and extend streets off into the distance.

The objective of re-projecting photographs onto geometry is to be able to render them from a different camera position and have the result look somewhat correct. The geometry is essentially being used to perform a perspective-correct image warp. To reduce labor, it is desirable to avoid building every detail in the object to be re-projected, so generally the minimum amount of geometric detail is built to satisfy the desired illusion. This means that the results are most accurate when the synthetic camera is near the center of projection and becomes less accurate as the synthetic camera moves farther from the center of projection. For this reason it is desirable to photograph the re-projection subject from a perspective relatively close to that needed in the final film.

Because rough geometry must be built to match the re-projection subject, the photo survey should include additional photography to assist that process via image-based modeling techniques. Some basic measurements of a handful of objects in the scene can greatly assist the accuracy of the modeling process.

The Need for Creative Compositing

Part of being a good matte artist is seeing things that others don't. This is something that comes from within and is hard to teach. It's a basic understanding of the surrounding world. Why does the light do that? What happens if atmosphere is added? What happens when it's windy? These are just a few of the thousands of questions a matte artist asks him- or herself, starting as a child growing into an adult. It's looking at the world and trying to understand it while others just walk by.

Having "an eye" cannot be taught. An artist is either blessed with it or not. It is the ability to step back and spot what is wrong in a painting or a finished shot, to self-criticize the work. This is important when trying to figure out why shots don't work: the slightest difference in color, brightness, or softness—there are hundreds of reasons why a shot isn't working. A skilled matte artist can usually zero in on the problem quickly. This can be a tremendous value in times of pressure and frustration.

A great matte painting doesn't always ensure a successful shot. As the artist hands her work over for compositing, many things can go wrong. The need for a compositor with an artistic sense is crucial in taking the shot the full distance. Compositing is an extension of the process of making the painting look alive. A good matte painter needs something essential to successfully create a painting—the eye. It's also applicable to the compositor.

A skilled compositor can make or break the final product. It is also critical for the matte artist to understand how the shot cuts into the film. This means having an understanding of the flow of the shots that precede it and the ones that follow it. There should be a relationship within the entire sequence. Having an edit of at least three shots before and after the matte painting helps make sure that continuity is kept. It's important to know the film. Is it meant to be absolutely real? Is there room for dramatic interpretation?

The matte artist needs to know when to simplify and when to push the drama. Not every sky is perfectly composed. Not every tree is perfectly arranged to fit a frame. There are imperfections everywhere and this should be reflected in the work. Otherwise the audience will know that they are being fooled.

7

DIGITAL ELEMENT CREATION

DIGITAL MODELING
Kevin Hudson

Overview: The Importance of Modeling

The pipeline for digital asset creation begins with digital modeling. It is the birthplace for a digital asset, and it is here that the basic aesthetic form and technology are laid. If they are not done well, this is the place where most problems for the future pipeline begin. Modeling is as important to the creation of an asset as the foundation is to the construction of a house. If the model is solid, all of the other crafts from rigging to painting to color and lighting can be done with far greater ease.

Types of Modeling

Digital modeling can be broken up into four types: character, prop, hard surface/mechanical, and environmental.

Character Modeling

Character modeling assets are assets that will need to move in some fashion. For the most part, they can be classified as actors. These would easily include such models as a cuddly Stuart, from *Stuart Little* (1999), the hyperrealistic Dr. Manhattan from *Watchmen* (2009), the stylized characters from *The ChubbChubbs* (2002), or digital stand-ins for background people such as panicking or stampeding crowds from any number of action films.

Character modeling calls on the true sculptural talent of the modeler. In recent years, software that more and more resembles a sculpting experience has evolved. This type of software includes Zbrush, Freeform 3D, 3D-Coat, and Mudbox.

The VES Handbook of Visual Effects. DOI: 10.1016/B978-0-240-81242-7.00007-7

Figure 7.1 *Stuart Little* (1999) is just one example of a digital character asset. (*STUART LITTLE* © 1999 Global Entertainment Productions GmbH & Co. Medien KG and SPE German Finance Co. Inc. All rights reserved. Courtesy of Columbia Pictures.)

Prop Modeling

Prop models tend to be items that do not necessarily move on their own accord. They are handled or acted on by characters. This does not mean that they will not need to be rigged for movement to some degree, but they are often rigged to a much lesser degree than a character model.

Props are still incredibly important assets and can be either soft or mechanical. Often digital props are re-creations of real-world counterparts. In that case, gathering quality reference is vital to the success of re-creating these assets. Whenever possible, the real-world item should be made available to the modeler. Because this is often not practical, getting good photo reference with measurements is the next best thing.

Hard Surface/Mechanical Modeling

Hard surface modeling has been broken out as its own distinct type of modeling. Cars, trains, helicopters, and highly designed technical items fall into this category.

Environmental Modeling

At a certain point, the line blurs between what separates a prop from an environment. In the case of the train in *The Polar Express* (2004), it functions as a very complicated prop or hard surface model. But it is also a model that characters walk through and perform within. This is where it enters the realm of environmental modeling.

Figure 7.2 A motorcycle is a classic example of a hard surface/mechanical model. (Image © 2007 Sony Pictures Imageworks Inc. All rights reserved.)

Believable versus Real

In motion picture storytelling, it is more important to be believable than it is to be real. Since the software used for modeling has its roots in mechanical engineering, it is all too seductive to get caught up in attempting to make something mechanically real. Production budgets are built around what it will take for modelers to assist in the creation of something that is believable and helps to tell the story. Many people who come out of an industrial design background tend to overengineer their models yet learn that the requirements, though certainly high, are not as precise as might be needed in something that would actually be built.

Model Data Types

The three main data types for models are polygons, NURBS, and subdivision surfaces. Another emerging type is voxel technology.

Polygons: Part 1

The first data type used for entertainment purposes was the polygon data type. A polygon is a basic piece of geometry defined by three points or vertices—a triangular face. A model is made by assembling many of these triangles until a more complicated form is created. Originally, polygons were textured using a series of texture projection techniques.

If multiple planar projections were to be used, an alpha channel would be created to fade off one projection and fade in

Figure 7.3 Meeper is an example of a multi-patch NURBS Model. (Image © 2002 Sony Pictures Imageworks Inc. All rights reserved.)

another. This technique had tremendous inherent limitations and obstacles. Chief among them was stretching of the texture as it approached areas where the normal of the surface would move toward being parallel with the projection plane.

NURBS

The second data type emerged out of the design industry and it solved many of the texture projection issues. NURBS (Non-Uniform Rational B-Spline) have texture coordinates (UVs) already associated with the geometry. A NURBS plane is essentially a mathematically defined surface that uses a B-spline[1] algorithm to generate a *patch*. A model built-in NURBS is a series of these patches quilted together. An average character model may be made up of hundreds of these NURBS patches.

---

[1] B-spline: a generalization of a Bézier curve.

Although using NURBS patches solved many texturing issues, it introduced considerable file management overhead. For each NURBS patch, a unique texture map was created. This meant that for color alone there were hundreds of texture maps to paint and manage throughout a production. Adding bump and specular texture maps would multiply the count by 3.

Polygons: Part 2

Polygons became popular again when techniques emerged to manipulate the UV structure of polygons. Modelers would unwrap an object in UV space and modify the UVs to avoid the stretching pitfalls of the traditional texture projection techniques. This technique of creating a UV layout allowed for superior texturing.

At this time, polygons also began using a tessellation[2] technique whereby the polygonal geometry would be subdivided and smoothed at render time. This allowed the polygonal geometry to function more like NURBS with a control "cage" model, and the tessellated, or subdivided "limit," surface derived from it. Though different from a true subdivision surface, it is often referred to as such.

Subdivision Surfaces

A true subdivision surface is different from tessellated polygons, though it is common to hear tessellated polygons called a *subdivision surface*. This is a data type that is probably going to be retired in the near future because it never found acceptance and tools were never developed to support it.

Voxels

In the not too distant future, modeling may be done using volumetric pixels (voxels). This is most similar to clay in that the model is made up of actual volumetric material. All of the models described above are merely exterior shells. Since voxels are geometry independent, they will provide the most freedom to the modeler. They will allow modelers to easily cut and paste portions of a model, without having to think about how to tie the faces into the model geometrically. It is very exciting technology and has made its way into visualization and medical communities.

Development of Models

The three basic routes for the development of digital models are free-form digital sculpting, 2D reference material, and scanned dimensional information.

---

[2] Tessellation or tiling of the plane: a collection of plane figures that fills the plane with no overlaps and no gaps. One may also speak of tessellations of the parts of a plane or of other surfaces. Generalizations to higher dimensions are also possible.

Free-Form Digital Sculpting

In free-form sculpting, the digital modeler functions as a concept artist/designer and interacts directly with the Director, Production Designer, and/or VFX Supervisor. There has been a recent rise of the independent digital artist as celebrity designer who can deliver a *design sculpt*. In addition, several software tools have come into use lately for doing digital sculpting: Freeform 3D, Zbrush, Mudbox, and 3D-Coat.

Freeform 3D is the oldest and most expensive. It relies on the use of a haptic arm[3] stylus and attempts to emulate a sculpting experience by use of a force-feedback interface. This system uses voxels, and topologically frees up the artist. The completed voxel model will need to be sampled and tessellated into polygons in order to export it to another package for further use.

Zbrush is probably the most common digital sculpting tool in use today. It works with polygonal data, so it does have some topological limitations, but it requires no special interface or graphics hardware, making it a very cost-effective digital sculpting solution.

Mudbox is very similar to Zbrush, but provides some very cool open GL[4] preview technology. As a result, however, a higher end workstation, OpenGL card, is required.

3D-Coat is a new software package that may emerge as the first voxel modeler accessible to the masses.

With each of these technologies, the design phase should be viewed as linked but still separate from the creation of the production model. In particular, since voxels are not supported in a production pipeline, they need to be resurfaced into some form of polygonal or NURBS data. Many people build a polygonal cage on top of the design model using GSI, Topogun, or CySlice software, but most of the common modeling software packages (Maya, 3D Max, Softimage, or Modo) will work for remeshing the design model into a more production-friendly polygonal layout.

From 2D Imagery

This is very similar to free-form, but it involves the creation of orthographic[5] imagery (either photographic or illustrative), which is then loaded into the sculpting or modeling software as background image planes over which the model is built. Even when using the Freeform approach, it can be advantageous to do some work in 2D before proceeding to 3D.

---

[3] Haptic arm: a force-feedback system. One manufacturer is Sensable Technologies (www.sensable.com).
[4] OpenGL (Open Graphics Library): a standard specification defining a cross-language, cross-platform API for writing applications that produce 2D and 3D computer graphics.
[5] Orthographic: representing a 3D object in two dimensions.

When imagery contains perspective, as in photographic reference, it is important to record lens/location information so that matchmoved cameras may be replicated inside the modeling software to approximate the real-life camera. The more the camera approximates an orthographic view of the subject, the more the modeling process can be streamlined.

From Scanned 3D Information

Scanning requires the preexistence of a 3D object. It can be anything from a digital maquette to a skyscraper. It is still common to employ a traditional sculptor to build a maquette for a character prior to going into 3D. In this case, the maquette is scanned using a laser or photographic system.

Laser scanners are the standard of scanning systems. They use a laser light projected onto the surface of an object or actor. The 3D contours of the subject are recorded and sampled into polygons. The most common laser scanning systems come from a company called Cyberware. There are several companies in the Los Angeles area, most with portable laser scanning systems: Gentle Giant, Icon Studios, Cyber F/X, XYZ/RGB, and Nexus Digital Studios, to name a few.

With systems becoming smaller and less expensive, it isn't outside the realm of possibility for artists to purchase a scanner. Next Engine makes an affordable desktop scanner that sells for around $2,500.

Photographic-based scanning is less intrusive, requiring less equipment, time, and setup than the larger laser-based systems. Though the data is lower in resolution, the simplicity and speed of acquisition can be advantageous. Most photographic-based scanning uses a *structured light* approach whereby a grid of light is projected onto a subject from the camera. It is recorded and a 3D impression of the object is created. The limitation of this system is the resolution of the camera. Some photographic-based scanning systems are now using feature recognition to eliminate the need for the structured light pass. As digital resolution becomes finer, they may one day eliminate the need for laser-based scanners altogether. Realscan 3D, Eyetronics, XYZ/RGB, and Mimic Studios are examples of companies that do photographic-based scanning.

Lidar scanning is generally used for large-scale scanning such as entire buildings. The only limitation in these situations is accessibility to scanning locations. Lidar scanning is done from a nodal point, with laser beams cast outward from that location. The more locations from which the scanner can cast beams, the more complete the acquisition of the subject will be. In the case of capturing a building, the ability to cast beams from every side of the building and capture the roof may not be practical. In this case, the data will have holes, and modeling will need to extrapolate. As a result, it is important to capture as much photographic reference of the location to use in addition to the lidar scanning.

Processing the scan data in these situations is best performed by the company that performed the acquisition because the quantity of data can be enormous. A company that has pioneered the use of lidar data for entertainment purposes is Lidar Services Inc. out of Seattle. Gentle Giant is also now providing larger scale lidar scanning.

Figure 7.4 Lidar, survey, and photogrammetric data are often used to build accurate building and cityscape models for *Spider-Man*™ *3.* (Image © 2007 Sony Pictures Imageworks Inc. All rights reserved.)

Photogrammetric Data

Photogrammetry is not a replacement for lidar data, which generates a tremendous amount of information, but for some simpler objects photogrammetry may be an option. It requires less complicated equipment and is less time consuming on location. It does, however, require more post-processing and the use of specific software. PhotoModeler is probably the most common photogrammetric modeling package.

Modeling for a Production Pipeline

When creating or building a model, it is very important to take into account the needs of the major downstream partners: texture painting, character setup, cloth simulation and color and lighting.

Texture Painting Needs

With modeling and texturing tools becoming more and more artist friendly, it is not uncommon these days for a modeler to also do texture painting. Modelers and texture painters communicate through the UV layout. If it is done well, the texture painters will be able to paint on the model with little distortion. It is not uncommon for texture painters to request alternate poses of a model to better facilitate painting.

Character Setup Needs

The Character Setup team will want the least amount of resolution possible to define a surface while still providing enough points to manipulate and define the structure of the model. While specific point counts are arbitrary and difficult to nail down, control meshes, which are delivered to Character Setup, are often in the range of 8000 to 16,000 faces. It is not uncommon for modeling to support two meshes: the lower resolution control mesh, which in turn drives the higher resolution render mesh.

Cloth Simulation Needs

The Cloth Simulation team has needs similar to those of Character Setup. However, they have a few additional requirements. Simulated cloth needs data that can be easily converted into spring meshes. This requires a more grid like (almost NURBS-like) layout. This is not to say that the hero cloth model needs to be completely built in this fashion, but at the very least, the basic layout of the clothing model needs to have a layout that is more grid like.

It is not uncommon for modeling to provide two products for clothing items as well: the basic cloth simulation model, which is the model discussed above, and a more detailed final hero cloth model, which is the model to be rendered. This version would contain additional details such as pockets, buttons, zippers, etc. It will also have the more subtle sculpted details such as seams and buttonholes. It may even contain an inner as well as outer surface to provide thickness. It is important that the hero cloth model not deviate too greatly in shape from the simulation model that is used to drive it. Close collaboration between modeling and the Cloth Simulation team is essential. It is very common to make adjustments to both models throughout production.

Color and Lighting

The Color and Lighting team will want enough resolution to make sure that the main details are clear and built out—relying too much on displacement and a variety of bump mapping techniques only makes their job more time consuming.

Client Servicing Approach

Modelers need to take a client servicing approach in meeting the needs of these different and often opposing groups. Collaboration and cooperation are essential to fostering this sort of team synergy and can be just as challenging as creating a great digital sculpture.

Engineering Aspects for Polygons

The reintroduction of polygons as the main data type of choice for motion picture production use has freed up the modeler from the NURBS-centric UV structure. It has cleared the way for more organic polygonal layouts and allowed artists to more accurately register the use of space in both 3D and UV.

When modeling objects, one of the most important things to keep in mind is edge flow. This is true for both NURBS and polygons, but because polygons can be so free-form, some sense of organization needs to be in place. One of the first recognized strategies uses a technique called *edge loops*. Edge loops simply attempt to describe the shape of the object using a series of concentric rings. What edge looping did was instill a basic modeling strategy and order on otherwise free-form meshes. It creates a mesh that is visibly ordered and would allow Character Setup to better set up their skin weights and falloffs. Edge looping is similar to NURBS, while still allowing some of the free-form advantages of working in polygons.

UV editing opened the door for texturing to have customized UV layouts. These layouts could be made any number of ways, and efficiencies could be introduced into the UV layout that might make the texture artist's job easier.

Engineering Aspects for NURBS

Although NURBS are not as common as they once were, they are still used exclusively in some facilities around the globe. Sometimes they are still the best way to build certain objects. Some basic guidelines for working with NURBS include proper NURBS parameterization and proper maintenance of continuity between the different NURBS patches.

Proper NURBS parameterization entails having uniform parameterization between spans. This doesn't necessarily mean that the points are all equidistant from each other, but rather that the tension between the points is fairly even. A general guideline would be to strive toward a patch with squares that are, for the most part, square. The best mesh is one with even distribution of point resolution that approaches being square.

Achieving proper continuity between NURBS patches is still an art in itself. Most packages that support NURBS have some form of patch stitching. There are several types of continuity: C1 continuity means that points on the edge of a NURBS patch are merely coincident, whereas G2 continuity means that the patches not only line up but also that there is no visible seam or discontinuity between them.

RIGGING AND ANIMATION RIGGING
Steve Preeg

Rigging: What Is It?

Rigging can be simply expressed as a process that allows motion to be added to static meshes or objects. This is not to be confused with actually moving an object because that is left to animation. Rather, rigging is what allows animators to do their job. These rigs can be made up of many aspects such as bones, deformers, expressions, and processes external to the application in which the rig is built. Rigging is considered a relatively technical process, and riggers are often required to have some scripting and/ or programming skills. Python, Perl, C++, and MEL are some of the more desirable languages for a rigger to know.

In general, rigging can be broken into two distinct types: animation rigging and deformation rigging. Each of those types may be further broken down into subcategories such as body rigging, facial rigging, and noncharacter rigging.

Animation Rigging

Animation or puppet rigging is creating a rig specifically to be animated interactively. An animation rig is rarely intended to be renderable but instead a means to get animation onto a full deformation rig, which will be covered later.

It is not uncommon to have multiple controls for the same object in an animation rig, allowing animators to decide the best way to animate a particular object. The additional control structures do, however, need to be balanced with the need for speed and interactivity. Since these rigs may never be rendered and speed is critical, the quality of deformations on these rigs can be quite crude. In fact, geometry is oftentimes simply parented to nodes giving rigid deformations instead of heavier skinning or clustering.

A character rig for animation may come in many flavors and the control structures vary depending on the workflow of the animators themselves. However, most character rigs have certain standard parts.

The ability to switch between inverse kinematics (IK) and forward kinematics (FK) is probably the most common need in a character animation rig. Inverse kinematics happen when a target position for a joint chain is animated. For example, the animator may want the foot to be in a particular place and does not care, as much, how the leg has to bend to get there. Forward kinematics is where the control for a rotation value on each joint is discreetly given. For example, first the hip is rotated and then the knee and ankle to get a new foot position. Switching between these two types of controls and matching the resulting positions when switching are common practices. Another example: As a character is walking, IK may be desirable to lock the feet down at each step. Then, if the character jumps and does a flip, it may be desirable to switch to FK. This way the foot targets do not need

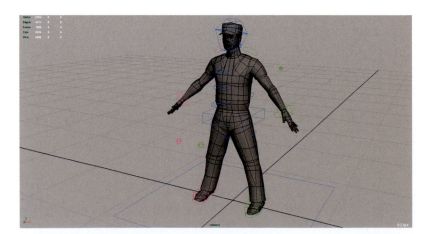

Figure 7.5 Example of an animation rig. (Image courtesy of Digital Domain Productions, Inc.)

to be animated during the flip. Only the rotation of the hips and knees need be rotated. Making sure that the position of the leg/feet at the point of transition is critical.

Motion capture integration is another common need for an animation rig to accommodate. Motion capture is, by its nature, an FK set of motion. It also tends to have data for every joint of every frame. This can be very difficult for an animator to modify, both on a single frame and temporally. In addition, it is difficult to animate "on top of" motion capture; in other words, adding to the motion rather than replacing it. For these reasons it is often desirable to convert the motion capture from its initial FK form onto the control structure of the rig itself. The process itself is application specific and therefore not covered here but should be part of the planning if motion capture is to be used.

Local versus global control, and the ability to switch between them, is another commonly requested feature of a character animation rig. To better understand this concept, imagine animating a character with IK that needs to walk up to, and go up, an escalator. While the character is walking up to the escalator, the feet may need to be in global space. In other words, it does not matter what the torso of the character does as the feet stay locked in world space wherever the foot is placed. Once the character gets on the escalator, some ambient motion needs to be added. But having to keyframe the feet to always stay on the escalator may be difficult, especially if the animation of the escalator changes. At this point it may be easier to have the IK controls in the space of the pelvis. This way, the artist can not only move the body as a whole with the escalator, but can also have the character move around on the step that he is riding on by moving the IK controls relative to, or as a child of, the pelvis motion.

Control structures for character rigging are as varied as the characters themselves. One may need bones to be able to squash and stretch cartoony characters, while another may need to be anatomically correct for realistic body motion. Regardless of the specifics, there are some basic rules to follow.

The controls should be easily seen and accessed by the animators. Color coding controls can be an effective way to distinguish parts, or even sides, of a character. More control is not necessarily better; it can cause confusion when animators are trying to refine animation if there are too many nodes with animation data on them. Speed is critical. If an animator can scrub through a scene in real time, the artist can make many creative animation revisions in short order before rendering the scene out. A sense of timing can be determined without having to play back images or a movie file. Animators should feel that the rig is allowing them to use their talents to animate; anything that slows down that creative process should be avoided.

Facial rigging for animation could be counted as character rigging for animation, but it has specific needs that warrant separate discussion. Motion capture for the face is quite different from motion capture for the body. Various methods are used for facial capture ranging from frame-by-frame dense reconstruction, to marker points on the face, to video analysis. Whichever method is chosen, the integration to the rig is tricky to say the least.

In contrast to body motion capture, where one can explicitly measure, for example, the rotation of an elbow joint, nothing is quite as straightforward in the face. The face may be approached as phonemes, muscles, expressions, etc. A common starting point is Dr. Paul Ekman's system, which is described in his book *Facial Action Coding System (FACS)* (Ekman and Friesen, 1978). This system essentially breaks facial motions down into component movements based on individual muscles in the face. Although it is a common starting point, it is generally understood that it needs to be expanded from its academic version. Once a system like FACS has been chosen, the process of mapping motion capture data to corresponding FACS shapes is a substantial problem.

As with body animation rigs, control structures that are easy to understand, and not overly abundant, can increase the speed as well as the quality of the animation. Unlike body animation rigs, facial rigs can become slow, because it is imperative to see final quality deformations in the animation rig. It is common to see final mesh resolutions and render-ready data in a facial animation rig. The reason is simple: That level of detail is needed to make quality facial animation. Seeing exactly when the lips touch, for example, is critical for lip sync. Dynamic simulations run after animation can add believability. However, care must be taken to leave the critical parts of the face that animation has spent fine-tuning, such as the lips and eyes, unchanged.

Noncharacter rigging, or elements of characters that are mechanical, represents another area of rigging. Examples of this type of rigging would be vehicle suspensions, tank treads, etc.

Control structures for noncharacter rigging change dramatically depending on the level of detail and importance of the action in the shot. For example, there may be a close-up of a complicated linkage in some sort of transformation where animators would need control over the speed and movement of a large number of pieces. Alternatively, there could be a panel opening on a tank far from the camera that merely requires a simple rotation. Clearly the control structure would be different in these two cases. Keeping the control as simple as possible for the needs of the shot can save a lot of time and effort.

Part of keeping the control structures simple for noncharacter rigging is automating ancillary motion. For instance, an opening hatch may need dozens of screws that are turning. The turning of these screws can be automatically driven by a single parameter that opens the hatch. Many mechanical systems are designed to work in films. Taking advantage of systems that only work one way can be a huge benefit to animation. Pistons, flaps, and springs are all good candidates for automated rigging. Often it is desirable to have overrides on these types of controls, which is relatively easy to integrate most of the time.

Animation rigs are often designed not only to deliver animation to a renderable rig but also to prepare for simulations. A tank tread, for example, may have animation controls to move the individual tread pieces around the base of the tank, but a simulation may be run to add vibration and undulating motion, suggesting slack in the treads. Extra values or attributes can be passed to the simulation software based on the animation rig and its motion. Velocity, direction of travel, etc., are values that may enhance the quality of the simulation. Whether these simulations are run by the rigging department or passed off to a dynamics group, preparation for simulation can be a valuable tool supplied by rigging.

Deformation Rigging

Riggers often spend the majority of their time on deformation rigging. The goal of the deformation rig is to take the animation data from the animation rig and deform the final renderable mesh as dictated by the needs of the show. The quality here can vary greatly from far-away digital doubles to hero characters that need to have the feeling of skin sliding over muscles or animated displacement maps.

The first step is to *accept* data from the animation rig. This is done in many ways including constraining the deformation rig to the animation rig, or having an equivalent set of nodes or joints in both the animation rig and deformation rig. The second example allows the

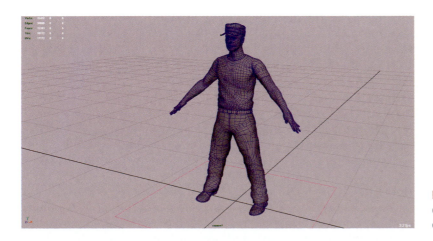

Figure 7.6 Example of a deformation rig. (Image courtesy of Digital Domain Productions, Inc.)

animation to be exported off the animation rig and directly applied to a matching set of objects, or nodes, in the deformation rig. Facial animation may be converted directly, vertex by vertex, or through matching nodes. There are many ways to convert animation data to deformation rigs. These are frequently application specific, so no detailed descriptions are provided here.

There are many different types of deformers and, of course, their names and exact capabilities are application specific. In general they may be grouped into a few different types. One type is linear deformers. This is the simplest and most predictable of all the deformers. However, they are often blamed for deformations looking CG. In general, that is more a misuse of them than a problem with linear deformations themselves. They also do offer some good advantages—for instance, they are extremely predictable. Through simple mathematical calculations they may be reversed and broken down into individual components when multiple linear deformers are affecting a single point. In addition, linear deformers tend to be very fast. Compared to deformation rigs, which might become slow, this can be a huge advantage.

Nonlinear deformers are another common type of deformer used in character rigging. These deformers may be tricky to implement and often have somewhat unpredictable results. For example, a deformer that bulges a surface based on a spherical-shaped object coming into contact with vertices may end up distorting the mesh significantly by allowing the vertices to slide over the spherical shape rather than push them out along their original normals. Nonlinear deformers often lack the control level to change the behavior to a directable level.

Other typically nonlinear deformers that deserve mention are muscle systems, which come in many varieties. They can be dynamic or nondynamic. They may have volume preservation, with stretch and slide attributes, etc. In general one can imagine implementing a muscle system on a character by imitating real-life muscle shapes and attachments and then binding the surface mesh to them. In practice, however, that rarely works. The algorithms used in most muscle systems do not behave the way a real muscle affects real skin. Therefore, the effort to accurately simulate an entire character's muscle structure will not give accurate skin motion. Instead, most muscle systems are implemented using anatomically correct muscle placement as a guide for placement and behavior. Then, contrary to real muscle systems, extra muscles are placed or attachments adjusted until the skin moves in a desirable way. Some muscle systems also allow post-deformation adjustments at the vertex level. This can save huge amounts of time when trying to fix a muscle's contribution to a skin.

Muscle systems, when used correctly, supply certain advantages such as simulated skin sliding or bulging, based on compression of a muscle and its associated volume conservation. In general, the amount of time it takes to rig a character with a full muscle system, compared to standard skinning methods, is much longer. Therefore, the quality of deformation and range of motion that a character is required to do in the project may determine whether or not to build a full muscle rig. As computers get faster and new algorithms are implemented for muscle systems, they could become a more standard rigging tool for the future. However, at this time there is still a need for the simpler rigging solutions in many cases.

Regardless of the method, or methods, finally chosen to rig a character, there is often a need to clean up what the rig generated. Dynamic simulations can be run and smoothing algorithms can help remove pinches or spikes in the deformations. In cases where vertex-by-vertex accuracy is required, as is often the case in facial animation, shot modeling may be considered.

Shot modeling is a phase of production in which a rigging artist adjusts a model specifically for a shot instead of rolling global changes back into a rig to have it affect other shots as well. Shot modeling, though powerful in terms of the level of control per vertex it allows, does have its problems. Shot modeling is dependent on the animation, so if the animation changes, the shot modeling needs to be readdressed. Shot modeling is also time consuming and, as the name suggests, is only useful for that one shot. Post-deformation cleanup, in any form, can be a huge time-saver over refining a rig for months to make sure it stands up in any and all shots.

Noncharacter deformation rigging is usually less time consuming and may have more of an impact on rendering and lighting optimization than on the deformations themselves. It is often more efficient to distinguish between deforming and nondeforming geometry and represent nondeforming geometry in static caches on disk, which can then simply have a transform applied at render time. Many current renderers support this functionality, so the deformation rigger should be aware of when it may be used. As with character deformation rigs, passing animation data can be done in the same ways, and ancillary motion can be driven automatically as in the animation rigs.

Last, there is often the need to prepare deformation rigs to go through a postprocess such as simulation. Again, this can be done on geometry caches, live rigs, etc. Sometimes these simulations are multiple rigs that are dependent on an earlier piece being simulated first; for example, a cloth simulation for clothes hanging on a drying line may need a simulation of the clothesline first. That is a simple case, and it is not uncommon to have many levels of dependencies.

Reference

Ekman, P., & Friesen, W. (1978). *Facial action coding system: a technique for the measurement of facial movement.* Palo Alto, CA: Consulting Psychologists Press.

TEXTURING AND SURFACING
Ron Woodall

The Importance of Texture Painting

The texture artist, along with the modeler, is at the head of the production line. Being able to successfully render and bring a shot to completion depends a great deal on the texture work being complete.

In the world of computer graphics, the texture artist can serve many roles: makeup artist, scenic painter, costume designer, model painter, or all of the above on any given project. These mind-sets can be quite different depending on the type of model that is being painted. If a machine is being painted versus a creature, or a set versus a human, the surfacing approach and methodology are different for each.

Hard Surface Models

When painting a vehicle the texture artist has to think about its direction of travel and how that might bias dirt toward one side versus another. Where is the model most likely going to have scratches or damage due to wear and tear? Generally, ground and air transport have the most damage to their finish coats on their leading edges because those are the surfaces most often hit by bugs, rocks, dirt, or any other thing that may be in the vehicle's path of travel.

Thought also must be given to individual parts of a machine. Where would it get hot and discolored or show cracked paint from the exhaust? Where are the joints that may leak oil? Where would dirt most likely collect? Where then, would rainwater flow over the surface and wash dirt away? There are many things to consider when making a very unreal object look real. One of the most important things a texture artist provides to CG work is imperfection. By nature, computer-generated models tend to be too perfect looking and symmetrical. Generally, the human eye is quick at splitting masses in half and spotting symmetry, so providing asymmetry to a model is a good thing.

If the model to be textured exists as a real vehicle or a practical on-set model, the job is somewhat easier. These real things can be photographed to provide reference and, in some cases, texture source. These practical set pieces, therefore, need to be thoroughly documented. If the texture artist cannot be on set to document these objects, a list should be prepared of every view that is needed. Evenly lit, shadow-free photos that may only need some minor touch-ups to remove highlights can be applied directly to a model to move very quickly toward a finished paint job. However, if a spaceship, for instance, only exists as a piece of artwork, then much thought needs to be given to the previously mentioned aging factors in order to create a paint job that looks believable.

For a model that is entirely fictitious with no on-set counterpart, a photographic source is still the best reference. Photographs of oil stains, dirty cars, the back of a garbage truck, etc., can provide the artist with believable detail to add to the work. There are also many free websites or sites that for a small annual or monthly fee provide a cornucopia of high-resolution texture sources. Painting every detail from scratch is commendable, but very foolish, because it will most certainly take more time. Wherever possible, the use of some combination of painting and using source material is highly recommended.

With the constantly shrinking schedules of today's production world, finding every possible way to get to a great end look quickly should be the goal of every texture artist.

Scale is another major factor in believability, especially with large-scale models. Having a human model in the same scale as the subject model is useful. Use the human model placed in various positions next to the subject model to create a clear sense of scale for paintwork. This practice helps immediately show existing scale problems. For instance, if surface scratches on an object need to be one-eighth of an inch wide in reality, and the scratches that have been painted are much larger, it will be readily apparent.

It is also important to do test rendering with bump and displacement maps. They are first set to whatever height is appropriate for the scale of the model chosen by the texture artist. As an example measurement ratio, 1 unit equals 1 foot. Keeping this in mind, initial bump and displacement heights for normal-sized models can be set to 0.02075 and 0.083, respectively. Knowing that details are being created with a maximum depth or height of 0.25 inch in bump and 1 inch in displacement makes the process of creating these maps happen more easily.

Certain camps believe that modeling every little detail is the only way to achieve realistic results. The majority of texture artists argues that this methodology is not only foolish, but also wrong. For example, if a modeler chooses to create a row of rivets on a surface, he or she will use algorithms that instance and place the rivets. This will create a perfect row of details, which normally is not desired. Creating imperfect fine details via bump or displacement is a much faster process. It's also much easier to achieve synchronicity of maps for dirt, oil, and other effects with these details. If all of the small detail is modeled, the only way to get dirt in around it is to paint it in 3D. Faux details by nature are 2D and, therefore, can be painted in the various effects without having to interact with the model at all. Moreover, an incredible amount of time is also saved; creating UV layouts and texture assignments for tons of little details is not necessary.

Creature Models

Painting creatures provides an artist with a whole new list of concerns. Creatures can require thought about their age, their skin condition, how they move, and many other factors. Where is the skin most likely to have wrinkles from repetitive expansion and contraction? Where is the creature most likely to have dry skin or calluses from contact with the ground? What does the creature eat and how might that stain skin or fur if it has any? What is the creature's native environment? Is it dirty? What color is the dirt? Where is the creature going to collect dirt? On its belly? Does it sleep on one side? Maybe one side is dirtier than another. This all may sound absurd, but small details such as these must be considered in order to foster believability in something entirely fanciful.

Like the hard surface model, if a texture artist is matching a real animal or a puppet from on set, the importance of a complete, thorough, and properly lit set of reference photographs of these practical creatures cannot be underestimated. The minimal time and money spent on gathering great photographic reference pales in comparison to the money that may be spent chasing and correcting textures painted from horrible reference. If an artist starts with improper reference photography, it can take forever to reach a point where the creature looks correct. If the artist has no other choice than to start with improperly gathered reference, additional relative imagery must be gathered from online sources. The artist could also take a field trip to the zoo or local pet store to take reference photography.

Types of Geometry: Their Problems and Benefits

Polygons

Polygonal modeling was once viewed as the dusty forgotten forefather geometry type but has come back around to being the preferred geometry type for productions. A whole host of robust UV layout software packages and options are available within modeling packages that really allow the user to achieve great texture setup with polygons.

Being able to easily texture polygons makes them very appealing to use since polygons are less data intensive and give way to faster render and interaction times. Visually complex parts comprised of one object can be made using polygons. This is a huge plus for most rendering packages. Being able to combine

50 objects into one and still get good texture layout makes polygonal modeling the way of the foreseeable future. The only major downside to polygons is that they shade too perfectly and therefore do not look real. More texture work has to be put into the flat areas and edges of polygons to give them a real level of imperfection.

Catmull-Clark Surfaces

The Catmull-Clark surface is the city cousin of the polygonal surface. Created by Edwin Catmull and Jim Clark, Catmull-Clark surfaces are primarily used for creature modeling or hard surface objects that require compound curved shapes. Catmull-Clark surfaces are used to render complex organic objects from light polygonal proxy objects. A Catmull-Clark is automatically made when a subdividing scheme is applied to a polygonal mesh. A six-sided cube, after one level of subdivision, becomes an icosikaitetragon having 24 sides and appears more like a sphere.

While staying light in interaction preview mode, subdivision surfaces can become very visually complex with a quick keystroke that applies the subdivision scheme. Most Catmull-Clarke meshes are rendered at subdivision level 3. Because this geometry type is ever in flux, so is the UV layout for it. The layout for a Catmull-Clark object looks different in preview mode versus subdivision level 3. It's important to make sure that any part designated to render as subdivision be painted as such. If a surface is painted in polygonal mode and rendered as subdivision, all of the corners where the UV layout have been cut will show gaps in the paint over the entire model.

It may be difficult to make UV layout cuts in areas with only a few control vertices. Often when cutting in these light areas, the paint gets weird and stretchy. Adding another edge to the left and right of the cut edge usually fixes the stretching problem. More often than not, UV layout work is far more difficult on subdivision models than it is when working on polygons.

Splines and NURBS

B-splines and NURBS are somewhat extinct in production today. The one place they are still used is modeling. The painfully missed benefit of spline-based geometry is ready-made UV coordinates. By nature, spline surfaces have a UV layout the instant they are created. Sometimes the layout needs modification, or multiple surfaces need to be stitched together and assigned to a single texture but at least there is a starting point. Splines are easy to set up for painting, but very data intensive. Spline models almost always take much more information to describe a surface than a polygonal or subdivision model of the same subject.

Prepping the Model to Be Painted

UV Layout

Before painting can begin the model has to be prepped to receive paint. This is done most often by creating UV layouts. A UV layout is a 2D representation of points and edges defining texture allocation that correspond to the 3D control vertices and face edges of a model. The UV layout determines how much texture resolution each polygonal face will receive once textures are applied. Generally, texture artists prefer to create their own UV layouts. Most automatic layouts tend to be highly inefficient with regard to optimal usage of texture space. They make for poor memory usage during real-time interactions.

Longer render times are also an unwanted side effect of poor layout and map assignment. Automatic layouts also tend to be extremely visually incoherent. Often in these layouts, parts in proximity on a model tend to have no relationship to one another in 2D layout space. Painting in 2D is easier if parts are laid out in a thoughtful way with UV orientation closely matching that of the geometry and with neighboring model parts near each other in UV space. Painting in 2D is more efficient because the resolution is one to one and interaction with the model is not a factor. Using automatic layouts and painting solely in 3D can create models that have far too many giant resolution textures with overly soft paint mapped into them.

Projection Mapping

Projection mapping is a tried-and-true method of applying texture to a model. Because of the brute force nature of applying textures via projection mapping, this method only works well for hard surface models.

Projection mapping has many merits. Because each pixel of the texture is being projected on an infinite line through any geometry associated with the projector, the information stored in the texture file to describe this mapping is far lighter than a model mapped entirely via UV layout. With UV layout, every single control vertex in the model has multiple coordinate numbers associated with it to describe the vertex location within the UV layout. This can result in many thousands of lines of information just to map one piece of geometry. Most projection coordinate information equates out to less than a dozen lines of information in the texture file. Using projection maps wherever possible results in lighter files. Lighter files equal faster loading, interaction, and render times. Using projectors also eliminates the time needed to create UV layout for the parts being projected.

Because the paint is being blasted through the model from a single axis, any surfaces perpendicular to the projection plane will have streaked paint. If a surface tilts away from, or toward, the projector at a shallow enough angle, a projection map will usually still work well. Once surface pitch out of parallel with the projector approaches around 80 degrees, the paint starts to stretch too much. In cases where this occurs, those surfaces should be removed from the projector and placed in a projector that is closer to parallel with the problem area. The other option is to UV map the parts that do not work well with projections. Because of it strengths and limitations, projection mapping is best suited for models that don't need to stand up to close scrutiny or models that need to go into the rendering pipeline quickly.

Camera Mapping

Camera mapping is very similar to projection mapping with the exception that the paint can be mapped from a camera having any field of view up to, and beyond, 180 degrees. Because the paint can be mapped from a nonorthographic view, camera mapping is ideally suited for adding detail to paint on a shot-specific basis. Models that have limited close-up screen time can be painted solely via camera mapping. For instance, a model that is seen closely in only three shots could be painted from the three shot cameras and most certainly take less time to complete than painting a model that has to stand up to scrutiny from every possible angle.

Volumetric Mapping

With volumetric mapping the texture is described in 3D, instead of 2D, with images being applied to the surface. Because this method of mapping requires no assigning of images or creation of UVs it may very well be the fastest way to get going on a paint job.

In its simplest form, volume mapping only requires the artist to select the model or parts of the model and assign a pixel density value to the selected volume. In a matter of seconds, a model can be ready to paint from any angle without fear of pixel stretching or resolution variation from surface to surface. However, because there are no 2D images, all changes great and small have to be done solely in 3D. With UV mapping or projection mapping, paint versions or changes can be made by simply referencing an alternate version of an original texture. With volume mapping this is impossible since any one given part of the model is part of the whole texture volume. There is no easy way to remove only a portion of the model from the volume and modify the paint of just that portion.

Texture Creation

Texture from Source

When matching to an existing prop, set, or costume, the reference photos should be lit as perfectly and evenly as possible so that they can be used as source texture with a small amount of cleanup. It is also very helpful to ask for painted swatches from the set painters, as well as fabric swatches from the costume department. If any fabrics have a pattern, be sure to ask for a swatch large enough to cover the repeat of the pattern. Actual painted card and fabric swatches are great because they can be easily turned into textures via a flatbed scanner.

Pure Painting

Purely painting textures doesn't happen all that often (perhaps more often in digital animated features than for live-action films). Even then, using source texture where possible is wise because painting every last little detail is time consuming and may in the end not look as real as some combination of painting and source material.

Finding or Making Source Texture

The best weapon for a texture artist is an extensive, organized source library. In addition to whatever source or reference may come from location, gathering personal source texture is a great practice. Keep a camera on hand for the great textures that pop up in everyday life. If a certain texture is needed for a project, but can't be found, make it! Just a half hour outside with India ink and printer paper can result in a wealth of scannable splatters, drips, and stains for use on models.

Diffuse Maps

When creating diffuse maps from scratch, the paint values should be created as the surface would appear in shadowless light. In some rare situations a bit of stage painting can help model details read better. Generally though, diffuse color maps should be free of highlight and shadow.

Small, faux-painted details, such as holes in a surface that do not require an accompanying opacity map, can be painted as zero black to help cheat them as an area that light is entering into but not returning from. These details should also be painted zero black in the specularity map.

The extreme values of light and dark in color maps should be no lighter than 80% and no darker than 20%. This helps to prevent the paint from looking too illustrative and provides some range for a technical director (lighting artist) to push the values up or down in the materials where needed.

Bump Maps

Bump maps are most easily equated with topographical maps in real life. With topographical maps certain colors represent a range of altitudes. Red might represent sea level, orange 1000 feet above sea level, and so on. With bump maps instead of colors, the height change on the model surface is described in values of gray. Most often middle or 50% gray is the pivot point. Any value less than middle gray will read as an indentation, and any value above middle gray will read as a protrusion.

Bump mapping is merely a method of making a simple surface look more complex by modifying the surface normal. The height of a bump map in the material should be rather shallow. Since bump maps don't really change the surface topology, if the height value is much more than one-quarter of an inch, the trick gives itself away. Looking at the middle of the model, the bump map may provide great believable detail, but around the edges of the model there is a perfectly smooth profile. This instantly reveals that the surface detail is merely a cheat. Details that need to have more than a quarter-inch of relief off the surface should either be modeled or added via displacement maps.

Displacement Maps

Like bump maps, displacement maps are described with a range of gray values. Displacement maps are used to actually change the surface detail. If the pivot point in the material is middle gray, anywhere the paint is lighter or darker than middle gray, the paint will get converted to micropolygons pushing out of, or into, the surface of the model.

The result of paint displacement is an actual geometry change. Unlike bump, displaced details will read when the surfaces are in profile or edge on. Displacement mapping takes far longer to calculate at render time; therefore prudent use of displacement is advised. A model with every square inch of surface area displaced will certainly take far longer to render than one with efficient use of bump and displacement.

Specularity Maps

Specularity maps are used to control the specular reflectivity of a model. Typically these maps should have a full range of values from white to black all over, with white representing the most specularity and black presenting none.

More complicated uses of specularity maps involve setting up the material to behave like two or more materials based on a range of values in the map. For instance, 0% to 33% gray has a spec model of tire rubber, 33% to 66% like brushed aluminum, and 66% to 100% has the specularity of chrome. This way of painting helps create more believable faux details on the surface of a single mesh object because of the obvious material changes. On a single mesh object one could paint a rubber gasket surrounded by chromed fastener heads in the displacement and diffuse pass. By painting the same details in the specularity map, each within the appropriate range of gray, the details will have very divergent material looks from the base material of brushed aluminum.

Material Designation Maps

Material designation maps or area maps are another way to create the look of many material types within a single mesh object. Area maps are usually solid white on black maps, with no range of grays in between. Black represents the base material, and white represents the areas where it is desired to switch to an alternate material. By using area maps one can reserve the full range of the specularity map solely for attenuating the specularity and use one or more area maps to switch to various other material types.

The benefit of using area maps is that multiple material switches can be separated cleanly into individual area maps. This separation makes it easy to change how much of any one given material is being used without accidently changing any others.

Luminance Maps

Luminance maps can be used to create faux lighting such as many pools of light on a surface, backlit windows, or hundreds of point lights. Where it may be too render intensive to have many actual lights being calculated for every frame, luminance maps can be used. These maps can be painted or more effectively rendered with real lights and baked into texture maps. Luminance maps should be solid black everywhere except where the surface is being lit or is supposed to be a faux light source.

Various Other Map-Driven Effects

Many other separated maps can be used to add interest to a model; dirt, oil, and rust maps, just to name a few. These maps are essentially the same as area maps since dirt, oil, and rust all have their own material properties.

These maps should be painted pure white on black. White represents dirt or whatever effect is being created, and black is the base material. These additional effects should be set up in the material to use a procedural color map or a single color. Since the percentage of surface area typically covered by dirt, oil, or rust is so small, it doesn't warrant the efficiency hit of an additional full-color map for each effect on every part of the model.

Help from Procedural Textures

Procedural textures are computer-generated images that are based on user-created code. Using mathematical algorithms to create real-looking materials like wood, stone, metal, or any surface that has a random pattern of texture, the true strength of procedural textures is infinite resolution. Use of procedural maps can allow the camera to travel from far away to within a sixteenth of an inch above the surface of a model without losing textural detail. On the whole, procedural color maps still tend to look fake, but procedural bump and displacement can be quite convincing.

Another strength of procedural maps is their efficiency during interactivity and during render time. Because no images are being stored on disk to create the look of the procedural texture, none is called up at render time or when a model is loaded and worked on. Procedural maps are a great way to add an extra high level of detail to surfaces at a relatively very low cost.

Film Look

Most visual effects facilities receive lookup tables (LUTs) from a facility that is color timing the entire film. LUTs can be used to preview on a monitor or digital projector how an image will be reproduced on the final film print. It is important to periodically check how rendered paint jobs look with a film look applied. This helps ensure that the film look is not shifting values or colors so much that things appear to be broken.

Always painting with the film look on is a bad idea, however, unless the reference images for the model being painted have been pre-processed to have the film look baked in. The other exception is when the model being painted has no real-life counterpart on set. In this case, there is no harm in painting with the film look on, since there is nothing real to match.

Texture Painting in Production

It is very important to keep a production on schedule. With that goal in mind, creating a cursory paint job in the course of a day or two that can be handed off to the look development artist gives that artist something to start building material work on. Most average paint jobs take around 2 to 6 weeks to complete. Making look development artists wait this long is foolish, since that artist can make paint work quite a bit easier with great material work.

It is also very important to keep in regular contact with supervisors and art directors multiple times a day. Any time a personal benchmark is reached, a test render of the paint should be sent to the VFX Supervisor, the Paint Supervisor, and the Art Director for input. Making a habit of touching base often will ensure that the work stays on the right track.

Other important points of focus include understanding real-world material behavior and understanding how textures affect materials. Understanding the physics of how and why solid plastic responds to light differently from cast iron will help in the creation of better textures. Also understanding expected gamma settings and pivot point defaults for the various texture map types will help make work go faster and easier. A good solid understanding of how all the various painted maps affect the materials to which they are assigned is imperative to prevent making more work than is necessary.

Making self-created backups is another important mode of working during production. Mistakes happen to everyone. Creating iterated master files, like Photoshop files that contain all of the layers unflattened, makes it easier regain lost paint or make corrections and resave from the master file later in the production schedule.

Some facilities have an automated nightly backup system, but relying solely on this type of system cannot be done. While a restore can take hours, it takes mere minutes to find one's own organized master files. Naming the master files with the same naming convention as the textures they represent with the exception of extension and iteration number makes a quick workflow. For example, finding /car/images/master/Rlite_C.3.psd and saving a copy of it to /car/images/color/Rlite_C.tif is easy because the two locations are close together, and the names differ by only one character and the file extension.

Model Editing

It is important for painters to understand what modelers do to foster better communication between the two disciplines. Learning at least the basics of modeling skills helps a painter to better convey any needs to a modeler more easily. At the bare minimum learn enough about modeling to be able to converse intelligently with a modeler about problems.

Conclusion

Texture mapping is every bit as important as any other part of the pipeline. Often overlooked in the end, without texture maps from a skilled artist, most CG would inevitably fall far short of looking believable. Imagine a world covered in glossy smooth gray plastic and one will begin to understand the importance of good textures.

DIGITAL HAIR/FUR
Armin Bruderlin, Francois Chardavoine

Generating convincing digital hair/fur requires dedicated solutions to a number of problems. First, it is not feasible to independently model and animate all of the huge number of hair fibers. Real humans have between 100,000 and 150,000 hair strands, and a full fur coat on an animal can have millions of individual strands, often consisting of a dense undercoat and a layer of longer hair called *guard hair*.

The solution in computer graphics is to only model and animate a relatively small number of *control* hairs (often also called *guide* or *key* hairs), and interpolate the final hair strands from these control hairs. The actual number of control hairs varies slightly depending on the system used but typically amounts to hundreds for a human head or thousands for a fully furred creature. Figure 7.7 shows the hair of two characters from *The Polar Express* (2004), a girl with approximately 120,000 hair strands and a wolf with more than 2.1 million hairs.

A second problem is that real hair interacts with light in many intricate ways. Special hair shaders or rendering methods utilizing opacity maps, deep shadow maps, or even ray tracing are therefore necessary to account for effects such as reflection, opacity, self-shadowing, or radiosity. Visual aliasing can also be an issue due to the thin structure of the hair.[6]

Another problem that can arise is the intersection of hairs with other objects, usually between hairs and the underlying surface, such as clothes or the skin. For practical purposes, hair/hair intersections between neighboring hairs are usually ignored, because they do not result in visual artifacts.

In almost all cases other than for very short animal fur, hair is not static during a shot but moves and breaks up as a result of the motion of the underlying skin and muscles, as well as due to external influences, such as wind and water. Often, dynamic simulation techniques are applied to the control hairs in order to obtain a realistic and natural motion of the hair. In the case of fully furred creatures with more than 1000 control hairs, this approach can be computationally expensive, especially if collisions are also handled as an integral part of the simulation.

Finally, for short hair or fur, some special purely rendering techniques have been introduced that create the illusion of hair while sidestepping the definition and calculation of explicit control and final hair geometry. These techniques address the

---

[6] This is especially true in the case when applying regular shadow maps instead of deep shadow maps and when using ray-trace renderers.

Figure 7.7 Examples of digital human hair and animal fur. (Image © 2004 Sony Pictures Imageworks Inc. All rights reserved.)

anisotropic[7] surface characteristics of a fur coat and can result in convincing medium to distant short hair or fur shots but can lack close-up hair detail and don't provide a means for animating hairs.[8]

The next subsection introduces a generic hair/fur pipeline and explains how a specific hairstyle for a character is typically achieved during look development and then applied during shots.

---

[7] An anisotropic surface changes in appearance as it is rotated about its geometric normal. An example is brushed aluminum.

[8] See Bruderlin (2004), Goldman (1997), Kajiya and Kay (1989), Marschner, Jenson, Cammarano, Worley, and Hanrahan (2003), Perlin (1989) and Ward, et al. (2007) at the end of this section for more detail.

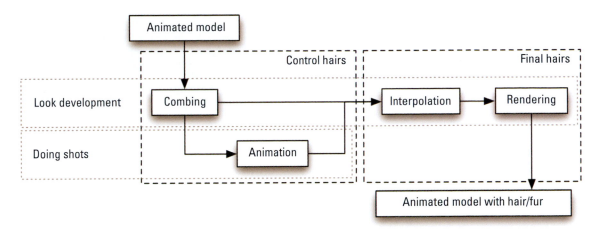

Hair Generation Process

Figure 7.8 shows a diagram of a basic hair generation pipeline. The input is the geometry of a static or animated character, and the output is the rendered hair for that character. The hair or fur is generated in a series of stages, from combing (modeling) and animating of the control hairs to interpolating (generating) and rendering of the final hairs or fur coat.

In a production environment, this process is often divided into look development and shot work. During look development, the hair is styled, and geometric and rendering parameters are dialed in to match the appearance the client has in mind as closely as possible. During shots, the main focus is hair animation.

Look Development

The Hair Team starts out with the static geometry of a character in a reference pose provided by the modeling department. One obvious potential problem to resolve immediately is to make sure that the hair system used can handle the format of the geometric model, which most likely is either of a polygonal mesh type, a subdivision surface, or a set of connected NURBS[9] patches.

With the character geometry available, placing and combing control hairs are the next steps. Control hairs are usually modeled as parametric curves such as NURBS curves. Some systems require a control hair on every vertex of the mesh defining the character, whereas others allow the user to freely place them anywhere on the character. The latter can reduce the overall number required since it makes the number of control hairs independent

---

[9] Non-Uniform Rational B-Spline.

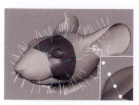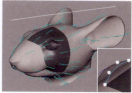

Figure 7.9 *Left:* Uncombed/combed control hairs. *Right:* Rendered final hairs. (Image © 1999 Sony Pictures Imageworks Inc. All rights reserved.)

of the model: Larger numbers of hairs need only be placed in areas of the body where detailed control and shaping are needed (such as the face). Keeping the number of control hairs low makes the whole hair generation process more efficient and interactive, because fewer hairs need to be combed and used in the calculations of the final hairs.

Figure 7.9 illustrates a set of uncombed and combed control hairs from *Stuart Little* (1999). One such control hair with four control points is enlarged in the lower right corners. Similar to the number of control hairs, the number of control points per hair also has an effect on performance.

When control hairs are initially placed on a character, they point in a default direction, usually along the normal of the surface at the hair follicle locations. Combing is the process of shaping the control hairs to match a desired hairstyle. This can be one of the most time-consuming stages in the whole hair generation process. Having a set of powerful combing tools is essential here.[10] For short hair or fur, painting tools are often utilized to interactively brush certain hair shape parameters, such as hair direction or bend over the character's surface.

Interpolation is the process of generating the final hairs from the control hairs. One or more control hairs influence each final hair. The exact algorithm of interpolation depends on the hair system used, but the most popular approaches are barycentric coordinates, where the shape of a final hair is determined by its surrounding control hairs (requiring a triangulation of those control hairs or one per vertex of the mesh) or weighted fall-off based on the distance of a final hair to its closest control hairs.

The interpolation step requires an overall density value to be specified that translates into the actual number of final hairs generated. Frequently, feature maps (as textures) are also painted over the body to more precisely specify what the hair will look like on various parts of the body. For example, a density map can provide fine control over how much hair is placed in different parts of the body. In the extreme case, where the density map is black, no final hairs will appear; where it is white, the full user-defined

[10] For examples and further discussion, see the *General Issues and Solutions* subsection that follows.

density value applies. Maps can be applied to any other hair parameter as well, such as length or width.

It is also helpful during the combing process to see the final hairs at the same time when combing the control hairs, and most systems provide a lower quality render of the final hairs at interactive rates. This is shown in Figure 7.10, an early comb of Doc Ock in *Spider-Man 2* (2004), where the control hairs are in green, and only 15% of the final hairs are drawn to maintain real-time combing.

The hair/fur is then rendered for client feedback or approval, usually on a turntable, with a traditional three-point lighting setup to bring out realistic shadows and depth. During this phase, a Lighter typically tweaks many of the parameters of a dedicated hair shader like color, opacity, etc., until the hair looks right.

Look development is an iterative process in which the hairstyle and appearance are refined step by step until they are satisfactory and match what the client wants. Once approved, shot work can start and a whole new set of challenges arises with respect to hair when the character is animated.

Figure 7.10 Control and final hairs during combing. (Image © 2004 Sony Pictures Imageworks Inc. All rights reserved.)

Shot Work

Animators don't usually directly interact with the hair. When they start working on a shot that includes a furry or haired character, it doesn't have any hair yet. It is therefore helpful to have some sort of visual reference as to where the hair would be to help them animate as if the hair were present. This can be in the form of a general outline of how far out the hair would be compared to the body surface, such as a transparent hair volume, or it might be a fast preview of what the final hair look will be. This is important because it limits the number of corrections that need to be done once hair is applied.

As described earlier, the hair appearance is decided in the look development phase. This includes where all the hairs are on the body and their shape and orientation. When an animator creates a performance for a character in a shot, the hair follows along with the body, and remains stuck to the body surface in the same positions it had in the reference pose. This provides what is known as *static hair*; even though the hair follows along with the body, the hair itself is not animated. If all that is needed is motionless hair on an animated body, then hair work for the shot is done.

Usually, hair motion and dynamics are an important part of making a shot look realistic and can contribute to the character's performance. Hair motion can be:

- *Caused by the character's animation:* If the character folds an arm, the hair should squash together instead of going through the arm.
- *Caused by interaction with other objects:* If the character is holding something, walking on the ground, or hitting an object, in all cases the hair should be properly pushed away by the object instead of going through it.
- *Full dynamics simulation:* Short hair may have a bouncy motion (and take a few frames to settle), whereas long hair will flow with the movement and trail behind.

These situations are usually handled by applying some sort of dynamics solver to the control hairs, so that they react in a physically realistic way, while moving through space or colliding with objects. The final rendered hairs then inherit all of the motion applied to the control hairs.

Third-party hair software packages provide dynamics systems, but some facilities also have proprietary solvers. There are many published methods of simulating hair dynamics (superhelix, articulated rigid-body chains), but the most widely used are mass spring systems, much like in cloth simulations. Whereas these methods provide solutions for physically correct motion, animating hair for motion pictures also has a creative or artistic component: The hair needs to move according to the vision of the movie director. Therefore, the results of dynamic hair simulations are often blended with other solutions (hand animated, hair rigs, static hair) to achieve the final motion.

General Issues and Solutions

Combing

As mentioned earlier, combing can be an elaborate task during look development, especially for long human hair and complex hairstyles. It is therefore crucial for a hair artist to have access to a set of flexible combing tools. Even for a commercially available system like Maya Hair, additional custom tools can be developed to facilitate the shaping of control hairs. For example, to make it easy to create curls or form clumps between neighboring hairs as shown in Figure 7.11, left, the user selected a group of control hairs and then precisely shaped the desired clump profile to specify how those hairs should bunch together.

A fill-volume tool can quickly fill an enclosed surface with randomly placed control hairs. The hair volumes created by modelers to describe the rough hair look of a character can be used to actually generate the control hairs needed by the hair artist. An example is shown in Figure 7.11, right, where braids were simply modeled as cylindrical surfaces by a modeler and then filled with hair. Figure 7.12 illustrates intricate the human hairstyles of two characters from *Beowulf* (2007).

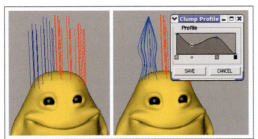

Figure 7.11 *Left:* Clumping tool with a user-customizable profile. *Right:* Combing braids (from left-to-right: three braided cylinders, control hairs generated by tool, final rendered hairs). (Image © 2007 Sony Pictures Imageworks Inc. All rights reserved.)

Figure 7.12 Final comb examples, illustrating the intricate human hairstyles of two digital characters from *Beowulf* (2007). (Image courtesy of Sony Pictures Imageworks Inc. and Paramount Pictures. *BEOWULF* © Shangri-La Entertainment, LLC, and Paramount Pictures Corporation. Licensed by Warner Bros. Entertainment Inc. All rights reserved.)

Render Times and Optimizations

One difference between short hair/animal fur and long human-like hair is the difference in combing needs. Another is render times and memory requirements. Whereas a frame of high-quality human head hair can be rendered from minutes to under an hour depending on hair length and image resolution, rendering the millions of individual hair strands of fully furred creatures can take several hours per frame using several gigabytes of computer memory, especially with motion blur and when close up to the camera.

Optimizations applied at render time can therefore be very effective. One example is *view frustum culling*, in which hair outside the current view is not generated and rendered, which is very useful if most of the character is off-screen. If the hair follicle location at the base of the hair on the skin is used to decide whether to cull the hair or not, a safety margin needs to be added, because (long) hair with follicles outside the view frustum may still have their tips visible in the frame. The same holds true for *backface culling* methods, which do not render hair on parts of the character facing away from the camera.

Another optimization technique is *level of detail* (LOD) applied to the hair, where different preset densities of hairs are generated and rendered for a character depending on the distance from camera. Varying hair opacity to fade out hair strands as they move between levels helps to avoid flickering. Some studios have also developed more continuous techniques, which smoothly cull individual hair strands based on their size and speed.

A feature of many hair systems is the ability to have multiple hair layers. Examples are an undercoat of dense, short hair and an overcoat of longer sparse hair for an animal fur coat or more general base, stray, or fuzz layers. Each layer can have its own set of control hairs, or share them, but apply different stylistic parameters. Using layers can ease and speed up the development of a complex hair or fur style by breaking it up into simpler components, which are then combined at render time.

Procedural Hair Effects

After or during the interpolation step (in Figure 7.8), when the shapes of the final hairs are calculated from the control hairs, special procedural techniques can be applied so that each final hair looks unique in one way or another. Examples are a wave effect to apply possibly random waviness to the strands, a wind effect to blow wind through the hairs, or clumping, where neighboring final hairs are grouped together in clusters. Feature maps can also be painted on the model to vary these effects over the body. The power of these effects lies in the fact that they are independent of the control hairs and provide a finer granularity than the control hairs ever could. An example is shown in Figure 7.13 for a wave and wind effect, which changes the final hairs without changing the control hairs (shown in green).

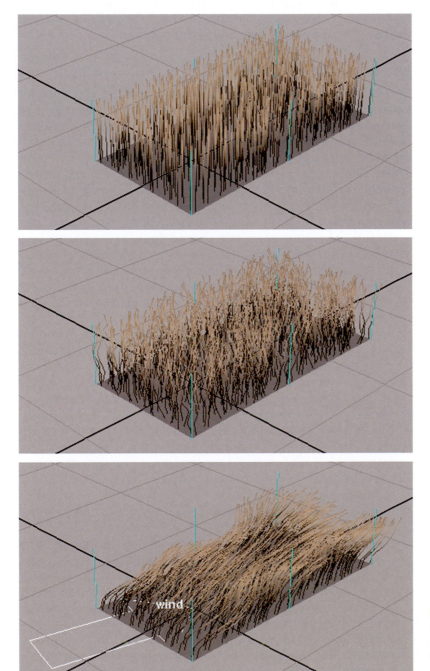

Figure 7.13 *Top:* No effect. *Middle:* Wave. *Bottom:* Wind. (Image © 2007 Sony Pictures Imageworks Inc. All rights reserved.)

Time and Cost: What the Moviemaker Needs to Know

Generating digital hair is both complex and time consuming. It is important to understand what aspects of hair combing and animation can potentially drive up the cost of a character or a shot. The level of quality needed for a project will greatly influence the cost: It is quite easy to get 85% of the way to the desired look, but the last 15% is likely to take exponentially longer.

What Makes a Hairstyle Expensive?

Depending on the level of detail and refinement that is needed for a particular character, hair look development can take anywhere from a few days to a few months. This includes not only making sure the hair appearance satisfies the client but also anticipating what the interactions and the movement of the hair will be in a shot. The most obvious cost is measured by how much time is spent by the artist getting the hair to look as expected. However, external factors often come into play. Here are a few things to keep in mind:

- Decide what the character should look like before starting to comb CG hair. This should be done through reference photography or artwork and be approved by the client. Hair photos for live-action movies, detailed art sketches, or maquettes with "hair engravings" for CG features are all good candidates.
- Some iterations will be needed once the digital hair of a character is seen for the first time, but these should only be for corrective tweaks, not major artistic direction. Going back and forth over sketches or photos beforehand will be orders of magnitude cheaper and faster than combing and rendering fully furred characters, only to see that work thrown away. This is why creating photoreal digital doubles of actors is often very fast, regardless of the complexity of the hairstyle, because a strict reference must be matched and very little flexibility given to supervisors or clients to stray and experiment during the combing stage.
- Make sure that things are changing as little as possible beneath the hair artist's feet. This includes modifying the model that the hair is grown on (which may cause parts of the hair to be recombed or feature textures to be redone).
- Regarding the model, it is critical to properly account for hair volume when modeling fully furred creatures. Early in production on *Stuart Little* (1999) the artists had little experience with how the fur coat would change the appearance of the character. It took several cycles back and forth between the Hair Team and the modeling department and eventually resulted in a considerably skinnier model, which

Figure 7.14 *Left:* Reference photography. *Right:* Digital double. (Image © 2007 Sony Pictures Imageworks Inc. All rights reserved.)

had about the same volumetric appearance with the fur as the initial model without fur. If the extra volume a fur layer adds can be anticipated during modeling, money is saved, because every time the model changes, the hair is potentially affected to the point at which some or most of the work has to be redone. The only consistently reliable solution is to always create an anatomically correct furless model. This may look strange but will produce the desired result when fur is added and will behave much more realistically when in motion.

Be mindful of aspects that will increase the render times, such as the number of hairs and their transparency: The longer the render time, the less time an artist has to address comments in between renders. Try to keep hair counts as low as possible.

What Interactions/Shot Situations Are Problematic (and Drive Up the Cost)?

A hairstyle often consists of millions of final hair strands that an artist can't control directly because they are all generated procedurally at interpolation time. This means any detailed interaction with the final hairs in a shot can spell trouble. If anything is looking incorrect, the artist can't go in and manually adjust the final hairs to look right. What may appear to be minor adjustments to a shot can mean days of extra work in the hair department. This can include characters interacting with the hair (a hand touching

Figure 7.15 *G-FORCE* characters equipped with accessories. (Image courtesy of Sony Pictures Imageworks Inc. © 2009 Disney Enterprises, Inc. All rights reserved.)

Figure 7.16 Wet beaver transitioning to dry. (Image from *THE CHRONICLES OF NARNIA: THE LION, THE WITCH AND THE WARDROBE.* © 2005 Disney Enterprises, Inc. and Walden Media, LLC. All rights reserved.)

or stroking fur) or thin objects that move through the hair (like backpack straps or accessories that slide on a furry character's body, as shown in Figure 7.15).

Transitioning between hair styles within the same shot can also be an issue. Depending on the hair system used, it may not always be easy or possible to blend from one hair look to another if they are very different. A typical example is going from dry to wet hair, or the opposite, which can happen when a creature gets splashed, falls into water, and shakes itself to dry off. Figure 7.16 shows a digital beaver from *The Chronicles of Narnia: The Lion, the Witch and the Wardrobe* (2005).

In some of these problematic cases, one can get away with imperfections simply because the character is moving fast and motion blur will hide things. It is critical to be aware of these situations from the start, at the look development phase: If one knows ahead of time which situations a character will encounter, a hair artist can better strategize how to comb a character. For instance, more control hairs might be placed in areas that require detailed interactions. Control hairs can always be added later for a specific shot, but they may change the overall look of the character approved by the client, requiring extra time to be spent just getting back the original look.

Summary

The process and pipeline for generating digital hair for a motion picture have been explained earlier and some of the issues that can arise and possible solutions for them discussed.

Several commercial hair software packages are available, including Softimage XSI Hair and Maya Hair[11] or Shave and a Haircut.[12] Many of the effects and animation studios also have their own proprietary hair pipelines (see Bruderlin (2004) for an example), which makes it possible for these companies to quickly change or add to the functionality of their systems when a new movie requires it.

For a general and technical survey paper on various approaches and problems related to digital hair modeling, animation, and rendering, see the article by Ward, et al. (2007).

For more technical detail on issues and solutions to shading hair to make it look like real hair, see the articles by Kajiya and Kay (1989) and Marschner, et al. (2003). Examples of generating hair without explicit geometry include Jim Kajiya's volumetric texture maps called *texels* (Kajiya and Kay), Dan Goldman's fake fur probabilistic lighting model (Goldman, 1997), and Ken Perlin's procedural texture approach referred to as *hypertextures* (Perlin, 1989).

References

Bruderlin, A. (2004). Production hair/fur pipeline at imageworks, in photorealistic hair modeling, animation, and rendering, ACM SIGGRAPH Course No. 9. *Computer Graphics.*

Goldman, D. B. (1997). Fake fur rendering, ACM SIGGRAPH Proceedings. *Computer Graphics*, 127–134.

Kajiya, J. T., & Kay, T. L. (1989). Rendering fur with three dimensional textures, ACM SIGGRAPH Proceedings. *Computer Graphics*, 23(3), 271–280.

Marschner, S. R., Jenson, H. W., Cammarano, M., Worley, S., & Hanrahan, P. (2003). Light scattering from human hair fiber. *ACM Transactions on Graphics (TOG)*, 22(3), 780–791.

Perlin, K. (1989). Hypertextures (ACM SIGGRAPH Proceedings). *Computer Graphics, 23*(3), 253–262.

Ward, K., Bertails, F., Kim, T., Marschner, S. R., Cani, M., & Lin, M. C. (2007). A survey on hair modeling: styling, simulation, and rendering. *IEEE Transactions on Visualization and Computer Graphics*, 13(2), 213–234.

---

[11] See www.autodesk.com.
[12] See www.joealter.com.

DIGITAL FEATHERS
Armin Bruderlin, Francois Chardavoine

Digital feathers in movies are not as common as hair or fur, and although there are several commercially available systems to generate hair, only proprietary solutions are available for feathers. This means a studio must always develop its own solutions. These can vary based on the level of quality required and the potential for reuse on future shows.

Computer-generated feathery characters have appeared in animated movies and shorts such as *For the Birds*[13] (2000) and, more recently, *One Pair*[14] (2008). An example of digital birds in a live-action movie is shown in Figure 7.17, Margalo and Falcon from *Stuart Little 2* (2002). A few research papers have also been published on the subject of digital feathers (Streit, 2003; Chen, Xu, Guo, & Shum, 2002).

The generation process is similar to hair in that the final instanced geometry (here, feathers) is created from a few modeled key shapes. In fact, these same instancing and interpolation techniques can be more generally applied to the scales of fish, quills of porcupines, spines or scales of dragons, a field of grass, or even a forest of trees. For instance, a hair/fur system, as described in the previous section, was used to generate the grass and flowers in the animated movie *Open Season* (2006).

One of the main differences between creating feathery and furry creatures is that an individual feather is a more complex 3D structure than a single hair strand. The former has distinct

Figure 7.17 Margalo and Falcon from *Stuart Little 2*. (*Stuart Little 2* © 2002 Columbia Pictures Industries, Inc. All rights reserved. Courtesy of Columbia Pictures.)

[13] See www.pixar.com/shorts/ftb/index.html.
[14] See www.olm.co.jp/en/olm/2008/05/one_pair.html.

components of widely varying shapes, whereas the latter can simply be modeled as a curve and rendered as a ribbon or tube with changeable width and transparency.

Morphology of Real Feathers

For a good explanation of the anatomy of a feather, please see Section 2 of Streit's Ph.D. thesis (Streit, 2003). That section also discusses different types of feathers such as down and contour and flight feathers, as well as feather coats and follicle distribution for real birds.

For practical purposes, a feather consists of three main sections: a shaft or quill, a left vane, and a right vane, as illustrated in Figure 7.18. The shaft is essentially a cylindrical tube with varying radius along its length. The vanes of a real feather consist of a series of branches fused together called *barbs*, which can have abrupt curvature changes and may contain splits. For flight feathers, barbs are locked together by branches called *barbules* with tiny hooks named *barbicels*. In some feather types, the tip and/or base of the vanes may be populated with down hairs.

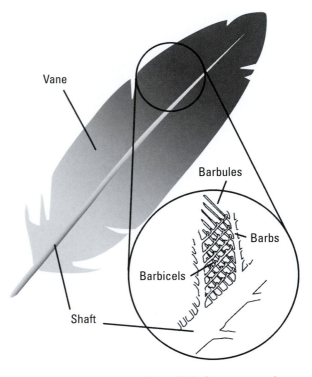

Figure 7.18 Components of a typical flight feather. (Image © 2010 Sony Pictures Imageworks Inc. All rights reserved.)

Modeling Digital Feathers

The simplest feather geometry is a *plate* feather, a flat surface with a detailed texture applied. This geometry is fast and easy to implement but may not hold up for close-up or high-quality projects because the feathers may look unnaturally flat. Another option is to model and render the feather vanes as hundreds of hair strands representing the barbs, which will appear much more realistic by producing the desired anisotropic[15] look. This is shown in Figure 7.19 where both left and right vanes were defined by hundreds of side-by-side hair strands. If a studio has an existing hair system, it may be able to benefit directly from all of its features when generating the feather vanes as hair. Going beyond the resolution of the barbs (i.e., down to the barbicels) is overkill even when modeling realistic-looking digital feathers.

---

[15] An anisotropic surface changes in appearance as it is rotated about its geometric normal. An example is brushed aluminum.

A set of feathers of different shapes, sizes, and styles can be manually premodeled for a given character. An alternative is a procedural generation module. Based on high-level parameters such as shaft length, vane width, breaking up vanes, etc., a feather is automatically generated by the system. Figure 7.20 shows two procedurally generated feathers, one with default values on the left and one with non-default values on the right for vane splitting and base/tip down hair generation.

Generating digital feathery creatures in a production environment brings up a lot of the same issues that were discussed in the previous section on hair with respect to modeling, animating, and rendering. The next subsections will take a brief look at some of the similarities and differences that feathers exhibit compared to hair.

Similarities between Hair and Feathers

The necessity of modeling a feathery character in a slightly skinny or shrunken appearance is somewhat more important than for an animal with short fur because feathers usually add more volume. On *Stuart Little 2* (2002), the modeling department didn't want to change Margalo drastically after she was approved for look (without feathers). As a result, the feathers ended up having to be combed very close to the body. This caused all kinds of problems (more problems than it should have) during animation, where feathers interpenetrated very easily with each other and the underlying skin.

Grooming a feathered character means shaping thousands of feathers in a cohesive pattern and flow over the geometry created by the modeler, in order to match the look the client desires. It would be painfully time consuming for an artist to individually position, orient, and shape every single feather, so instancing systems have been designed that are fairly identical to most hair systems.

The artist will manually place a few pre-modeled or procedurally generated *guide* feathers (or *key* feathers) on the character, and then instruct the system to automatically fill the blanks in between, smoothly interpolating the shape of the guide feathers among all of the instanced feathers. This can happen as an interactive process or on the fly at render time. A quick preview system may be implemented to get a better idea of the final look before the character is fully rendered.

Procedural effects can then be applied at render time to add randomness to the final feathers similar to the process used for hair (waviness, clumping of barbs) or even animation (such as procedural wind flowing through the feathers).

Differences between Hair and Feathers

Individual hair follicles are often lost in the forest of the millions of almost identical siblings that cover a character's body. Feathers, on the other hand, have a distinct structure defined by the vanes and the central shaft, and there are usually a lot less of them (in the thousands). This makes every feather stand out a lot more.

To make matters worse, while having hairs intersect with each other is almost never a problem, any feather-to-feather interpenetration is quite obvious unless the feathers have a very fluffy or downy appearance that makes them look more like hair. Thus, the artist must not only take care to lay the feathers down without their going through each other when grooming the static reference pose, but interpenetrations will also need to be avoided when the character is animating in shots. Feathers that are entirely procedural (and generated at render time) will need an automated mechanism to prevent these penetrations, since the artist cannot directly interact with them (other than through the few guide feathers).

Some form of feather interpenetration solver should therefore be an essential component of a practical feather system. On one end of the spectrum, a full-blown dynamics system with collision "detection and response" can be employed. This fixes feathers going through each other during animation. However, it can be very computationally expensive, complicated to implement, and bound to not work robustly in many cases.

A simpler and often more feasible solution is trying to "prevent" collisions between feathers. The main idea is that if the initial reference pose is groomed such that it does not have any interpenetrating feathers, their relative positions with respect to the skin and each other can be maintained during animation, thus avoiding penetrations.

One way to accomplish this is by calculating for each vertex of each feather the closest point on the skin surface and the distance to that point in the reference pose. These distances are then preserved during animation, so the feathers all move as a whole exactly like the model's surface. This may work in some situations, but the feathers will squash and stretch with the skin in a way that often looks unrealistic. An alternative solution allows the feathers to slide on the surface by only maintaining the distance while recalculating the closest point on the skin surface at each frame during an animation. This effect is shown in Figure 7.21 on the right side, which produces much better results than with no collision prevention applied on the left.

Whatever solution is adopted for the penetration problem, situations invariably come up when the result is not satisfactory or needs to be changed for artistic purposes. At that point, it becomes necessary for the artist to interact directly with individual feathers. Three options are possible, and anyone designing a feather system should consider one or more of these:

- Be able to provide corrective hints, usually in the form of extra guide feathers to change the shapes or motions of the final instanced feathers.
- Be able to un-instantiate problematic feathers. When a render isn't satisfactory, the artist can decide to extract certain feathers from the instancing system and bring them directly into the animation software to modify or animate them as needed and then export them back to the rendering system.
- Be able to deal with all of the feathers as geometry that the user can interact with in the animation package. If the system is properly designed for speed and memory usage, this is the most flexible solution. The full power of the software package is available to correct any problems. Rigs can be built, dynamic solver applied, and the worst offending feathers can

Figure 7.21 Feathers with (*left*) and without (*right*) interpenetration. (Image © 2002 Sony Pictures Imageworks Inc. All rights reserved.)

simply be plucked if needed. Of course, care must be taken not to have the system grind to a halt when thousands of feathers are needed.

Finally, whereas hair usually moves in a subtle or passive way driven by the motion of the character and external forces such as gravity and wind, some feathers are often actively animated as part of a character's performance. This is especially true for the bigger flight feathers toward the tip of the wings, which are frequently used as "fingers" for gesturing (see Margalo's wings in Figure 7.17) or interacting with objects. Such potentially rigged and individually animated feathers can cause extra strain on the interpenetration solver.

References

Chen, Y., Xu, Y., Guo, B., & Shum, H.-Y. (2002). Modeling and rendering of realistic feathers, ACM SIGGRAPH Proceedings. *Computer Graphics*, 630–636.

Streit, L. M. (2003). *Modeling of feather coat morphogenesis for computer graphics*, Ph.D. thesis. Canada: University of British Columbia. www.cs.ubc.ca/labs/imager/th/2003/Streit2004/Streit2004.pdf.

DYNAMICS AND SIMULATION
Judith Crow

Dynamics and simulation techniques are a core component of digital effects. Broadly speaking, they are an attempt to replicate real-world physical characteristics in the digital realm such that realistic behavior and interactions may be achieved by letting the software calculate appropriate results without requiring key-framed animation.

It may be that practical costs are prohibitive (where multiple models may be required to allow for reshoots), don't offer the desired level of control or directability, or that a new generation of supervisors is just more comfortable with digital technology than with traditional practical effects. Whatever the reasons, since the early 1990s practical effects have increasingly become displaced by digital equivalents to the extent that simulations of complex interactions of objects with fluids and fire are now commonplace. Where *Dante's Peak* (1997) uses simple particle systems to digitally enhance models and miniatures together with live-action plates, *2012* (2009) simulates the wholesale destruction of an entire digital city.

While simulation techniques are most commonly associated with destruction and mayhem and encompass fracturing and deforming objects, explosions, fire, smoke, and liquids, they are also used to clothe characters, style and move their hair, and move muscles under their skin. It can be expected that realistic

Figure 7.22 *Dante's Peak* (1997) uses digital effects to enhance practical effects provided by models and miniatures. (Image © 1997 Universal Studios Licensing, LLLP. All rights reserved. Courtesy of Universal Studios.)

Figure 7.23 The 2009 movie *2012* digitally simulates destruction on a huge scale. (*2012* © 2009 Columbia Pictures Industries, Inc. All rights reserved. Courtesy of Columbia Pictures.)

complex interactions may be achieved more readily via simulation than by keyframing.

How Is a Simulation Created?

Generally speaking, a simulation starts with a 3D computer model to which various physical characteristics are assigned, such as mass, density, elasticity, glue strength, and so on as appropriate to the type of object to be simulated. Forces such as gravity and wind are applied and one or more *solvers* (sets of equations) are run for each successive frame to compute the resulting changes for each of the objects in the simulation. For example, a cloth solver and a rigid-body solver may be run together so that a curtain (cloth) may be seen to both deform over the surface of a lampshade (a rigid body) while at the same time push against and move the lampshade.

Often simulations are determined by setting useful initial conditions from which the resulting animation will be derived with little or no further direction from the artist. Any control the artist has comes from varying those initial conditions and rerunning the simulation until the desired results are obtained. However, there is a growing trend toward the use of tools that allow for greater directability—both before and after running the simulation. It is expected that both a faster turnaround (with fewer iterations needed) and greater control over the outcome may be achieved.

When Is Simulation Appropriate?

A number of factors may dictate whether simulation is appropriate for a production:

- Does the production schedule allow for a shot development period? Simulations do not typically deliver results out-of-the-box, but instead require development time.
- Are appropriate resources available? It is still the case that this is highly skilled work, often requiring custom software development and always needing substantial hardware support in the form of fast multiprocessor machines with large amounts of RAM and disk space.
- Can the effort be amortized over a number of shots? A one-off shot can probably be handled with judicious use of traditionally animated components, practical elements, and simpler particle systems, whereas a longer sequence will lack coherency without a simulated foundation.

After examining the scope of work, dynamics and simulation will be appropriate in the following scenarios:

Definitely Appropriate

- Highly realistic natural phenomena are required.
- Detailed and complex animation of liquids and gases is required.
- Complex interaction is required among large numbers of objects too great to animate by hand.
- Large numbers of shots of cloth or hair animation, especially non-hero shots, are required.

Possibly Appropriate

- A small number of hero objects with complex interaction are required.
- Elements for stereoscopic pairs cannot be cheated, such as volumes.

Probably Not Appropriate

- Extensive art direction is expected.
- Short turnaround on a small number of shots is desired.

Tricks and Cheats

Note that running simulations is a laborious and time-consuming process. Every time changes are made, the simulation has to be run again in its entirety, because each frame's results are dependent on those of the previous frame. Adding additional complexity in terms of numbers of objects and the amount of detail tends to have an exponential effect on the time taken to rerun the simulation. A number of strategies can be used to alleviate these problems:

- Once the gross motion is right, much of the smaller detail can be added in the shaders. Rerendering will generally be a great deal faster than rerunning a simulation.
- Detailed final geometry can be substituted for low-resolution stand-in geometry. In a rigid-body simulation, approximations of the chunks can be run through the simulation and then replaced for rendering.
- Particles can be rendered as sprites[16] with detail coming from the texture maps or procedural shaders applied to the sprites.
- Low-resolution simulations can be layered to produce complexity. For example, a particle fluid can be run with fewer particles to get the overall motion right and then rerun with subtly different initial conditions. When the results of the various iterations are added together, there will be enough detail to generate a suitably smooth surface.
- Keyframed animation can provide the starting conditions and, if necessary, override the results coming out of the simulation so specific hero elements can be directed into place with precision.

Important Considerations

Running simulations can consume considerable amounts of time, memory, and storage so it is important to consider a number of strategies to increase efficiency:

- *Size simulations appropriately.* Look at running simulations on a scale that elicits useful information in a time frame that fits the artist's schedule and makes the best use of downtime. Consider what can be learned in an hour, a day, or overnight.
- *If possible, increase the number of iterations.* Can a simulation be simplified or split into parts such that more iterations can be run and the results be used to inform the final, detailed simulations?

---

[16] Sprite: a 2D/3D image or animation that is integrated into a larger scene. In 3D graphics, it is a technique whereby flat images are seamlessly integrated into complicated 3D scenes.

- *Look at ways to manage large datasets.* Simulations can usually be cached to disk and restarted partway through. Time spent simulating will be traded against a greater need for data storage. Some kinds of simulations scale better than others—lower resolution geometry may produce adequate interaction and can be substituted with high-resolution geometry at render time.
- *Plan for data exchange.* Simulations do not live in a void. The source models will be coming from somewhere—quite possibly another 3D package—and the output of the simulation will have to be shaded and rendered or used in some way to drive other geometry.

Planning and Preparation

Simulations benefit from careful planning. Here are some considerations to keep in mind:

- Learn from previsualization. Don't build more complexity than is necessary. Put detail only where it is needed.
- Because shots rarely begin with no action under way, preroll has to be considered. How much action will need to have played out before the shot starts? Can an animator provide convincing initial conditions instead of having to run an expensive simulation for several seconds of run-up?
- It is critical to work at a real-world scale and with correct physical characteristics. Make sure the scene represents the true size of objects and use accurate references for settings such as gravity, density, and friction.
- Always think about how much post-processing the simulation data can add without needing to rerun a simulation. Additional motion can be layered. Detailed geometry can be substituted. Smaller surface detail can be provided during rendering.

Software Solutions: A Broad Overview of Current Options

The earliest implementations have come from academia or are proprietary systems built by some of the larger facilities. Notable early examples are Arete's Renderworld ocean surface simulator [*Waterworld* (1995) and *Titanic* (1997)], ILM's ocean swells for *A Perfect Storm* (2000) and their ongoing collaboration with Stanford University on Physbam; PDI/Dreamworks' cloth and hair simulation for *Shrek* (2001); and Digital Domain's flooding water for *Lord of the Rings* (2002).

Increasingly, third-party applications are available. Some stand-alone or plug-in options specialize in specific types of solvers. Next Limit's RealFlow offers stand-alone fluids and rigid-body dynamics (RBD). Syflex specializes in cloth, whereas Afterworks' FumeFX offers a gaseous fluids plug-in.

Yet others provide a more generalized and integrated environment for dynamics and support multiple solvers. Side Effects' Houdini software uses dynamic operators (DOPs) that provide a wide range of microsolvers for combining RBD, fluids (liquids and gases), cloth, and wire, while also providing a framework for users to add their own solvers. Autodesk Maya's Dynamics includes RBD, fire, liquids, and cloth, while Softimage offers PhysX, a highly optimized RBD solution. Even Blender, a free open-source application, now offers some dynamics capabilities.

Other open-source projects of interest are the Open Dynamics Engine (ODE) and Bullet Collision Detection and Physics library, both of which are finding their way into high-end applications. Often first developed for use in games engines, these specialized solvers are able to provide a surprising level of sophistication in real time and are of increasing interest to filmmakers who are willing to trade some accuracy for vastly increased computational speed.

PARTICLES
Craig Zerouni

What Are Particle Systems?

It would be reasonable to describe particles as the starting point for all computer simulations. They were among the first techniques to be explored as computer graphics evolved into digital visual effects. So what are they and how are they used?

Particles are locations in space. Since space is thought of in terms of X (left to right), Y (up and down), and Z (in and out), each particle is made up of at least an (x, y, z) triplet. Next, *attributes* are added to the particle. Attributes can be anything: color, direction, mass, etc. Typically, particles have at least a direction, a speed, and a life span. Depending on what they are representing, they may also carry attributes for mass, repulsion, attraction, color, or any other information that is necessary later to realize a particular effect.

The Next Step

Particles are sometimes used just as they are, as a way to put a dot of color in a certain location. But for the most part, they are used as a placeholder for something else. Once some particles are moving around, much more complex geometry can be added to those locations later to achieve a flock of birds or a swarm of bees. Or

Figure 7.24 Particles are locations in 3D space. These have motion and other characteristics assigned to them. (Image courtesy of Ryan Bowden.)

very simple geometry can be attached to them, with a complex image painted onto it. In other words, a 2D card could be attached to each particle, and then the card can carry a painting of almost anything—including a bee or a bird. Depending on the shot, that may be all that is needed to achieve a truly fantastic image.

Particles in Motion

The key thing about particles is that they move. Typically, they begin with some kind of speed and direction (carried as a velocity vector), and then, for each frame, their position is a combination of their own internal motivation and external forces. External forces are mathematical simulations of common phenomena like gravity, wind, and especially *turbulence*. Turbulence applied to particles gives them a whirling, swirling quality and is how everything from jet wash to torpedo bubbles to sandstorms is created. Turbulence is a fundamental concept in simulations—it's not randomness but a kind of structured unpredictability. Turbulence is what is seen when a drop of dye is dispersed into a glass of water.

To move the particles, the basic idea is simple: For every frame, each particle is moved along its direction vector, by its speed, subject to the wind, the turbulence, the gravity, and whatever else is affecting it, such as the proximity of other particles. It's often the case that particles attract and/or repel each other, so this also affects their final position for each frame.

Often, adjusting positions at every frame isn't good enough, especially if accurate motion blur is desired, so the positions are calculated several times in each frame, and then geometry is created along the path during the frame (that is, during the time the shutter is open in the computer's "camera").

The Birth of Particles

Particles are born, not made. They can be birthed as the result of some other action, such as one piece of geometry hitting another. This would typically create the puff of dust generated from one piece of a building collapsing on another. Particles can also be born continuously from locations. Think of a stream of bubbles coming up from the bottom of a glass. They have to be born someplace—at some location in space. The starting locations of the particles can be defined by bringing in geometry, such as the back end of the torpedo that is going to stream bubbles. Or the initial positions could be defined mathematically, such as "supply a 1000 points that are randomly distributed inside a sphere of a particular size."

Then the attributes are added. Typically, the attributes are calculated as random numbers within a particular range, rather than entered by hand. So an effects artist would instruct the particle system to do the mathematical equivalent of "pick a speed for each particle that is randomly distributed between 50 and 75 miles per hour."

Often, the particle positions and initial velocities are calculated based on some other event—for example, to generate concrete fragments from a bullet hit. In a case like this, the location of the particles is determined by where the bullet hits, and the initial velocities are calculated based on the angle at which the bullet hits the surface. After that, the particles go off on their own, subject to gravity, wind, etc.

Creating Effects

So far, several examples have been explained of ways in which particles can be used: They can generate fragments from a bullet hit or other explosion, they can give the swarming motion to schools of fish or clouds of insects, they can carry the structure of smoke and fluid simulations, and they are great at creating the framework for explosions and fire.

In the case of explosion or fire the particles are not rendered directly. Instead, they are usually replaced at render time by some kind of geometry or sometimes just an equation that renders something smoky or flame colored. In a fire simulation, for example, the color of the particles would vary with their height, so that the flame would be white at the bottom, moving through red and orange and then blue as it got near the tips. Flame particles typically have a short life span as well, so that the flame flickers

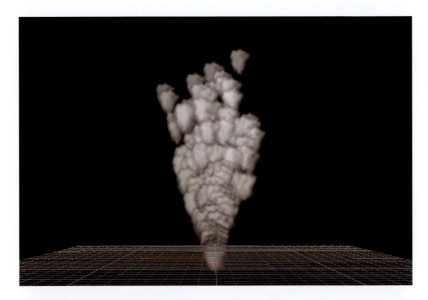

Figure 7.25 Simple two-dimensional cards with images on them (sprites) can be attached to the particles. Often, this is good enough. (Image courtesy of Ryan Bowden.)

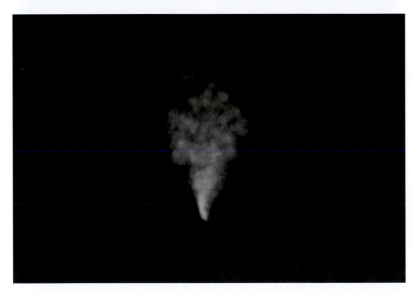

Figure 7.26 Smoke created by having the shader render a volume of smoke centered at each particle. These overlap and combine in visually satisfying ways. (Image courtesy of Ryan Bowden.)

out at the top. Then each particle would contribute some color and opacity to its surrounding area, and the result would blend together to look (and act) like flames.

It's also possible to treat the particles as loosely attached points, and then at each frame connect them together into a solid. Because this kind of solid has points with positions that are not fixed in their distance from each other, this gives the artist one way of doing what is called *soft body dynamics*. If the artist wants to drop a blob of stiff Jell-O onto a table, this is one way to do it.

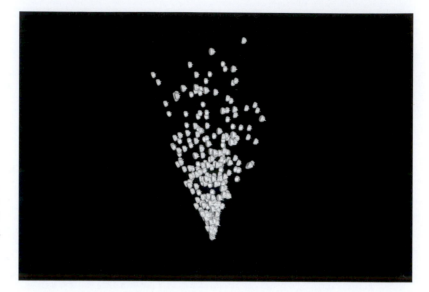

Figure 7.27 Geometry can be attached to each flying particle to generate scenes that appear visually complicated. These are teapots, but they could be bees, or jet fighters, or even people moving across a landscape. (Image courtesy of Ryan Bowden.)

As another alternative, the points can interact with other kinds of simulations. If particles are added to an RBD simulation, they can bounce off hard surfaces. For example, an effects artist could set up a simulation to pour a million ball bearings down some stairs this way—or do a lot of other related things.

All of these techniques are just the entry points to a world of different techniques and solutions that particle systems can be a part of. Because these systems are relatively simple to compute and visualize, they are often the starting point for much more visually complex effects. Readers who want to dig deeper into this technique can consult industry texts such as Cinefex and the ACM SIGGRAPH proceedings.

RIGID-BODY DYNAMICS
Craig Zerouni

Rigid-body dynamics (RBD) are physics simulations in which the objects being simulated do not change shape. That is to say, they are made of stiff, unyielding material, like blocks or ball bearings. In an RBD simulation, it's still possible for objects to fracture into a number of smaller pieces—but when that happens, those pieces are thought of as new objects in the simulation, replacing the original single object. At any given time, all of the objects are thought of as rigid.

RBD simulations are being used more and more to simulate various kinds of destruction, although that's not their only use.

How Rigid-Body Dynamics Are Created

All of these simulations begin with 3D computer models of the objects to be simulated. These can be as simple as a cube or as complex as a jet fighter.

Each object is assigned physical characteristics, such as mass, density, friction, bounce, etc. Since these are being used to create effects, often the desire is to start with reality, and then go farther. An object's mass will need to be animated over time, for example. Or the friction of the object will need to be different at different locations along its surface.

Next, forces are defined in the virtual world: gravity and wind, for starters. But again, because this is for effects, rather than science, the rules can be altered to help solve a particular problem. Gravity does not have to pull down, for example, but can pull sideways. Gravity can be very strong, or very weak, or very strong on some objects and very weak on others. Forces can also be created that help the artist create effects, such as a generic force that starts strong and then very quickly fades out—an explosion, in other words.

Constraints can also be defined. Constraints impose limits on the motion of the objects. For example, one object can be constrained to another, so that where one goes, the other must follow. Types of motion can also be constrained. A door hinge, for example, is a constraint in which the door object is only allowed to rotate, not translate (move). So if the door is hit by another object, or by some forces, it can swing open and shut, but that's all it can do.

After all of the geometry has been defined—the physical characteristics, the forces, and the constraints—the computer takes over. The basic idea is actually quite simple: For each frame, move each object according to the forces that affect it and its own physical characteristics. See if it hits any pieces. If not, the simulation is done. If it does hit something, compute the rebound for this piece and also for the piece it hit. Then repeat for each object.

But because each collision may create other collisions, this generally means going back through all of the objects multiple times per frame. It gets worse, because in order to get any kind of accuracy, doing these updates only once per frame isn't enough—it generally requires anywhere from 2 to 10 subframe increments to get something reasonable. That can slow the simulation down quite a bit, especially when many objects have to be added.

Potential Problems

Apart from speed, there are other issues. One of these is stability. In real life, once an object settles onto the ground, it stays there and stays still. In RBD simulations, this can be a problem, because the calculations for deciding whether an object is on, or above, or penetrating into another object (or the ground) may not be completely precise. This can generate instability, where pieces vibrate against each other rather than stop, because at each frame the relationship comes out slightly differently.

There are also issues with accuracy, where points or edges of one piece may penetrate the face of another, because there is not enough detail for the software to realize there is an intersection. Frequently, this problem is solved by increasing the density of the object mesh. However, that makes the simulation slower still.

An effects artist can also have problems in situations where objects begin inside other objects or are moving so fast that within a single frame time they end up inside another object. Since, according to the rules of RBD simulations, objects are not allowed to be inside other objects, if this happens the results can be unpredictable—and, predictably, the results are not the ones desired.

Other Issues

Because one main use of this technique is to get realistic destruction, it would be beneficial if the simulation broke down (fractured) the geometry as it went in a natural way. But that's generally beyond the capabilities of today's software (though there are systems that can do this in some controlled situations). That means that in order to get an object to crumble into smaller pieces as it collides with other objects, those smaller pieces have to be modeled in advance and then glued together (mathematically speaking) to create the whole original object.

Then the simulation can decide if the forces on the object are strong enough to make the glue break, so that the subobjects fly apart. Although this works well, it means a lot more work up-front. It also forces an artist to decide where the breaks will occur and what they will look like. Of course, this can also be a benefit, since it allows the fracturing to be art directed.

Some facilities have now developed fracturing tools that will do the pre-breaking automatically. It still has to happen before the simulation, rather than as part of it, but at least it doesn't require a modeler to slave over each piece. Future generations of simulation software will undoubtedly not have this restriction and will do the destruction during the simulation itself.

Another issue is that the geometry in these simulations is generally first converted to something called a *level set* (sometimes called a *signed distance field*). This is a volumetric representation of an object, rather than a boundary representation. This means that it represents the object as a lot of little cubes, which are fast to compute collisions with. The downside of this is that in order to accurately model complex shapes, a *lot* of little cubes can be required. That means more calculations are necessary and, thus, slower simulations.

Also, the more objects in a scene, the longer the calculations take. This makes it hard to scale up to really complicated simulations.

Finally, RBD simulations try to model actual physics. But actual physics is generally only the start of what the director wants to see happen. Typically, people want the simulation to look realistic, while simultaneously being able to control how certain hero pieces behave, where they end up in frame (or out of it), etc. Most systems allow this kind of secondary control, but it adds yet more setup time to the simulation process.

Tricks for Getting It Done

Given all of these ways in which creating an RBD simulation can start to stretch a schedule, there are several ways to try to shrink it back. One of these is to pre-calculate the simulation and bake out the geometry frame by frame. This is a slow process, but hopefully it will be done a small number of times. This better prepares the simulation such that the resultant geometry can be brought into a lighting pipeline for repeated lighting and shading takes.

Another technique is to simulate in layers. This means simulating the larger, lower detail pieces first and then baking out that geometry and locking off their motion. Then they are fed back into the simulation as objects that other smaller objects react to (bounce off of), but these larger objects are not affected by the smaller objects. Having these passive objects makes a simulation calculate more quickly. Then the simulation can be repeated with still smaller objects. This can generate a lot of geometry data on disk, but it also allows an incremental approach to simulations.

Lately, some effects facilities have integrated game engines into their pipelines. These are designed to work interactively for game play, and while they can't do that with the complexity of modern effects shots, they can speed the process up quite a bit. Generally they are able to work with proxy objects and generate transforms that describe the motion of the objects in the shot. Then those transforms are applied to the actual detailed geometry, a process that is much, much faster than a simulation.

DIGITAL LIGHTING
Andrew Whitehurst

Light in Reality and in Computer Graphics

The product of simulated illumination and the reflectance of the surfaces in a scene determine the color of every pixel representing part of an object (a spaceship, for example) in computer-generated imagery (CGI). The software that performs these calculations is called a *renderer* and thus the process of generating the images is known as *rendering*.

When considering how light may hit a surface it is not sufficient to simulate sources of light alone. Light may bounce from one surface to another before hitting the eyes and thus the effect of this illumination should also be considered. Further, the surfaces of translucent objects may be illuminated by light that has passed through the volume of the object behind the surface. Until recently many of these effects have been prohibitively costly to render. The earliest uses of computer graphics in film visual effects limited themselves to simulations of light interacting with hard surfaces, because these are the simplest and quickest algorithms to calculate. As computers have become faster and cheaper, it has become possible to render more complex surfaces (fur or skin, for example) in a timely manner. The history of computer graphics (CG), especially in visual effects, can be seen in terms of a continual improvement in the physical accuracy and complexity of the rendering algorithms facilitated by exponential improvements in the speed of computers over time.

Once a ray of light, whatever its origin, hits a surface, it may be reflected or partially absorbed: The incident illumination is turned into radiant illumination by its interaction with the surface. Throughout the history of CG, algorithms of varying complexity have attempted to describe these surface effects. Some algorithms are mathematical models that create a pleasing image but are not derived from any physical understanding of real surfaces. Other algorithms are based on accurate measurement of actual materials. Many of these mathematical models of reflectance are designed to describe a particular surface effect, for example, the reflection of a light source in a shiny plastic surface (called *specular reflection*) or the matte surface of dry cement (*diffuse response*). Often these simpler models will be combined on one surface to create a more visually compelling appearance (e.g., a matte surface summed with a shiny layer).

Two of the earliest shading models in CG are Lambert shading, which models smooth matte surfaces, and Phong lighting, which describes shiny highlights that might be observed on a plastic object. Lambert's model describes how the amount of light hitting a surface decreases if the surface area facing the light is smaller. At a completely glancing angle, the amount of light hitting the surface will be zero, and therefore dark, whereas a surface perpendicular to the incident light will receive the maximum amount of possible illumination and will be brighter. The brightness fall-off across a curved surface, like a sphere, will be smooth and is a reasonable description of a simple matte surface. Mathematically, Lambert shading can be described by computing the dot product of the normalized light direction vector with

Figure 7.28 A CG render of an object shaded with Lambert diffuse lighting (*left*) and Phong lighting (*right*). (Image courtesy of Andrew Whitehurst.)

another vector that describes the direction in which the surface is facing at the point being shaded, also known as the surface normal. This is a very fast computational model, which has contributed to its popularity and longevity in visual effects rendering.

Phong lighting takes this idea of describing the amount of reflected illumination using the light direction and the surface normal one step farther. Bui Tuong Phong noticed that on some shiny objects the reflection of light sources could be seen as a bright highlight with soft edges. Mathematically this effect could be expressed as $\cos(R \cdot L)^{\text{roughness}}$ where R is the normalized reflected vector of the light direction after bouncing off the surface being shaded, L is the normalized vector describing the light direction, and roughness describes how broad and soft the highlight should be.

Case Study of Reality Compared with Simple CG Simulation

Consider a white light shining on to a red plastic object. In reality, the red paint on the plastic is made up of small particles of pigment suspended in a clear medium. The white light hits the surface of the object. Some of the light is immediately reflected off the surface medium. This is the shiny specular highlight one sees, and it retains the color of the light rays hitting it, white in this instance. The rest of the light will enter the paint medium and bounce around among the pigment particles, which absorb the non-red wavelengths of the light and reflect the rest. This light, now red in color, will re-emerge out of the surface. The angle at which the ray emerges from the surface will be determined by the microscopic shape of the pigment in the paint; therefore rays of light that enter parallel may be scattered and emerge on very different paths because of this microscopically rough surface. This is why a matte surface looks different from a mirror-like one: The light rays hitting it scatter in many directions.

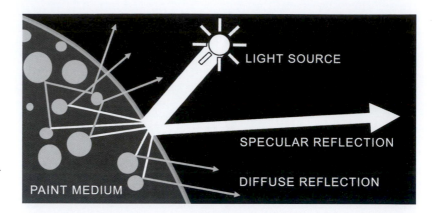

Figure 7.29 A cross section through a plastic paint-like surface. (Image Courtesy of Andrew Whitehurst.)

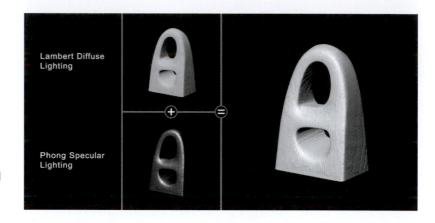

Figure 7.30 A simple plastic surface can be rendered by summing the results of Lambertian diffuse lighting and Phong lighting. (Image Courtesy of Andrew Whitehurst.)

To model this effect in CGI, the fastest method would be to use a matte mathematical reflectance model (Lambertian diffuse, for example) to simulate the light that enters the surface and bounces around among the red pigment particles and then add another model to this that computes the specular highlight (Phong).

Over time modifications and enhancements have been added to these models that increase the range of shading options available to CG artists. For example, it has been observed that many diffuse surfaces are very rough, and light hitting these surfaces often bounces back in the direction from which it came (retroreflection). In these cases, the brightness of the reflectance is not so simply related to the angle of the surface compared with the light, as described by Lambertian shading. The moon is a good real-world example of this. It is lit by the sun and looks almost flat, not spherical. In 1994 Michael Oren and Shree K. Nayar described a mathematical model to account for this, and Oren-Nayar shading is now a popular alternative to Lambertian diffuse in production.

Another example of the increasing sophistication of empirical shading models is the implementation of Fresnel equations, which describe how much light is reflected or transmitted given the angle of the surface to the light source and the viewer. In many materials, glazed pottery for example, light glancing off the surface is much more likely to be reflected, whereas light hitting the surface dead-on has a greater chance of being absorbed. Objects such as these appear shinier at glancing angles on their surface, and the specular models can be adjusted to take this observation into account.

Visual Sophistication through Texture Mapping

One of the most popular methods of disguising the simplicity of the majority of shading models used in CGI is to paint maps to modify the terms of these shading algorithms. For example, a piece of old varnished wood may have areas where the lacquer has worn away, exposing the matte wood grain. A map might be painted where areas covered by varnish were white and dull areas were black. The renderer could then look up this map and multiply the specular term of the surface by the returned value so an area that is deemed to be dull wood (returning a value of zero from the map) would have a specular component of zero. Maps may be painted for a wide variety of effects, for example, the pattern of a surface, the glossiness of a reflection, the roughness of a surface, and so on. Texture maps are the most common method used to add visual complexity to a rendered object.

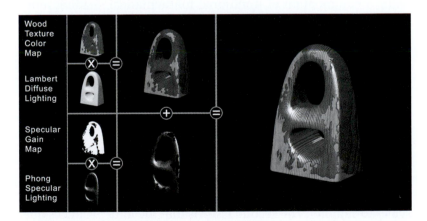

Figure 7.31 Visual complexity can be added to simple shading models through the use of texture maps. (Image courtesy of Andrew Whitehurst.)

Physically Derived Shading Models

The ever-increasing speed of CPUs has made it possible to implement more complex shading models, many of which are modeled on physically measured phenomena unlike mathematically derived shading algorithms like Lambertian diffuse. Examples of these models include Cook-Torrance, a popular model for describing highly specular metallic surfaces, and Ward's anisotropic model, which enables surfaces to be described whose reflectance varies with surface direction, for example, a vinyl record or a spun aluminum kettle.

The next step toward more accurate simulation of surface lighting effects came when researchers began to measure the reflectance of real materials and then apply this data directly in CG rendering. A common example of a material for which this approach is desirable is cloth. Because different cloths vary in the size of the threads that comprise them, what those threads are made of, how they are woven, and what techniques were used to dye them, it is difficult to craft an empirical mathematical model that works well in all cases. Indeed, the complexity of a cloth surface is such that it is problematic to create a simple mathematical shader that works for even one specific instance. One solution to this that has been implemented is to use data acquired from a reflectometer to describe the cloth surface.

A reflectometer is a device that measures the surface reflectance of materials and can be used to output a dataset that describes how the surface responds given every possible combination of light angle, surface normal, and viewing angle. This data can be used directly to instruct the renderer about how reflective a digital representation of a surface is under CG lighting. Renders using this methodology are often highly realistic, exhibiting subtle lighting responses that would be extremely difficult to create using a combination of traditional mathematical shading models. The term for quantitatively describing a surface's response to light is its *bidirectional reflectance distribution function* (BRDF). Traditional CG shading models such as Lambert and Phong are also BRDFs, but the term is most commonly used in visual effects to describe the measurement of an actual surface and the direct use of that data in rendering.

The use of measured surfaces does have some practical production downsides. First, one must have access to a real example of the surface that is to be copied. This is straightforward for a piece of cloth, but more difficult for surfaces that are impractical to move (a historic monument, for example) or for which there is no real instance to measure (there are no real dragon scales to sample). The second issue is that the data produces one, fixed response, which may not tally with the look that the director wants for a particular shot. One major benefit of the empirical mathematical models is that, through adjusting the terms of the equations, modulating their responses with texture maps, and so on, it is possible to modify a surface's appearance from an artistically driven perspective. The advantage of this is that if the director decides that a surface must be a little shinier and the reflections a little glossier (blurrier) in a particular shot, those changes are easy to implement with the more traditional shading models. A measured BRDF is unable to accommodate this.

Beneath the Surface

Thus far, several methods for describing how light behaves when it hits the surface of an object have been examined. This works well for many objects, such as concrete, metal, and wood, but it does a poor job of describing the visual qualities of objects that allow light to enter through the surface, penetrate into the object deeply, scatter, and re-emerge. This effect is called *subsurface scattering*.

Consider two objects, one made of wood, the other of marble. If both objects were strongly backlit, the wood surface would appear very dark. The marble, on the other hand, would show the effects of light scattering through its volume and this contributes greatly to a marble-like appearance.

Many other surfaces exhibit extensive subsurface scattering contributions to their appearance (e.g., milk, skin, and wax). Traditional surface shading models and measured BRDFs cannot account for this visual quality because they measure only light interaction that occurs at the surface. Developments in measuring the amount of light that scatters within a surface by pointing a laser at a scattering medium, for example, a cube of marble, and photographing the patch of light that is produced by the laser

Figure 7.32 Subsurface scattering effects are a significant component to consider when simulating materials like marble. (Image courtesy of Andrew Whitehurst.)

light bouncing around within the surface before re-emerging, have enabled scientists to create functions that describe the subsurface behavior of many materials, from fruit to human skin. These models, when combined with the surface reflection contribution, enable improved visual realism in rendering.

Goals of Lighting in Visual Effects

The goal of all visual effects is to enable the viewer to suspend disbelief and watch a story unfold without having the technical aspects of the film's creation draw attention to themselves. To achieve this using computer graphics, models must be created with sufficient detail that they are indistinguishable from what would occur in reality, they must be animated with such a level of precision and care that every movement feels natural and believable, and they must be lit in a manner that seamlessly blends the CG into the live-action plate.

While shooting, the Director of Photography (DP) will have made many decisions about how the film is to be lit and photographed to determine what emotional effect the lighting should have on the audience. In many cases the job of the digital lighting artist working on photographed plates is to mimic the on-set lighting as perfectly as possible by either using on-set lighting data directly or by placing CG lights within the scene to match the on-set lighting rig. It is clear that in order for digital lighting artists to be able to perform this task, they need excellent reference photography of the lighting conditions on set. Such reference allows the confident placement, coloration, and intensity adjustment of lights to ensure a precise match with the plate.

Equally as important as ensuring that the lighting matches, it is necessary to craft surface shaders (the code that describes the surface behavior: Lambert, Phong, etc.) that accurately mimic the real-life counterparts to these digital creations. Even if the digital lighting is crafted to match reality accurately, if the surfaces that the digital lights strike do not respond in the same way as they would in reality, the match between the photographed plate and the digital object in the finished render will be poor. Lights and surface shading must work together. This process of balancing shaders, maps, and lighting until they match the reference is called *look development*, often shortened to *look-dev*.

An example of a situation that demonstrates this need for precision would be a shot where an actor on set is required to deliver a performance and then do something it is not safe or possible for her to do practically. Here it is common practice to construct a *digital double*, a CG version of the actor. Shaders and texture maps will be crafted that mimic the response of her skin, clothing, and hair while on-set lighting is also copied.

The filmed plate will consist of the first part of the shot where the performance is delivered after which a compositor will paint the real actor out of the plate (using a clean plate if one exists). An animator will duplicate the last few frames of the real performance using the digital double before then animating the impossible feat. The few frames of overlap between the real performance and the digital one allow the compositor to blend the real and CG performances more easily than if the transition took place over a single frame.

The finished animation is then lit by the lighting artist so that the match with the real footage is as close as possible, especially around the frames where the real and animated performances overlap. If the lighting reference and look development have been done well, the digital element should match the plate almost perfectly. The compositor should then be able to craft a seamless blend between the actor and the digital double.

In addition to creating the digital element itself, the lighting artist will also have to create interaction elements for real objects in the plate. Consider the digital double example again. If her feet are seen, it is almost certain that she is casting shadows on the ground. Once the real actor and her shadow have been painted out, it is not sufficient to replace just the performer—her shadow must also be rendered. Reflections in shiny, on-set objects may also need to be digitally crafted and composited. For this reason, in addition to having a digital representation of the actor, it is necessary to have correctly proportioned models of the environment in which the action occurs. If the surface on which the real actor stands is flat, it may be possible to use a simple plane in CG to catch the digital double's shadow. The more complex the environment, the more important it is to have survey data or a laser scan of the set.

There are often instances when replicating on-set lighting is not sufficient to take a shot to completion. Although a DP will often set a general lighting rig for a scene, extra lights for each setup are often added to improve the visual impact of every shot. Clearly the DP cannot set up these extra lights for an object or character to be added later in CG, so these additional per-shot lights will have to be positioned by the digital lighting artist. Occasionally, the DP will still be able to assist in this process and offer feedback to the lighting artist though it is more usual for the DP's intentions to be overseen by the VFX Supervisor of the project during post-production. It is clear that good lighting artists must have not only a finely honed technical understanding of visual effects lighting technology but also a keen artistic sense to enable them to match the aesthetic style developed by the DP.

A good foundation in art theory and practice can help a digital lighting artist gain and improve this visual literacy: the ability to understand what effects the DP is seeking to create through lighting and the facility to produce sympathetic lighting within the digital realm. An understanding of the lighting techniques employed by the great masters of painting, photography, and cinematography can greatly assist in the acquisition of these visual skills. Areas that the digital lighting artist should take time to study would be techniques of lighting design, color theory, composition, staging, and basic film grammar.

Additionally, knowledge of art history has benefits for the lighting artist. First, it fosters a mental repository of great images from which inspiration can be drawn when lighting shots. Second, when discussing matters of aesthetics with directors and VFX Supervisors, the ability to refer to a piece of art as a common frame of reference is invaluable. Discussions of artistic matters inherently lack the cold rigor of a technical briefing. For this reason it is common for all creative departments on a film to reference painting, photography, and the work of other filmmakers. If digital lighting artists are to make a full contribution to these conversations, then they will need to understand the same lexicon of terms and references.

Work Flow for Successful Creative Digital Lighting

While there are many intangibles in the aesthetics of lighting, it is possible to develop working practices that can help ensure high-quality lighting. The first step is to recognize which lighting effects should be achieved in 3D and which should be left to the composite. As a rule of thumb all effects that occur once light hits a camera lens should be done in the composite, which means that lens flares, blooms, halation, chromatic aberration of the lens, and the film's grain pattern should not be rendered. Often depth of field and lens defocus effects (bokeh) will also be left out of the 3D render. The 3D artist should aim to supply the compositor with a render that, when composited directly over the background, already feels as if it is part of the plate. The compositor will finesse this blend and can correct minor discrepancies between CG and the real footage but the best results are achieved when the render already matches the real material.

The process of matching a real scene's lighting has become dramatically easier since the adoption of high-dynamic-range (HDR) image-based lighting (IBL). This will be discussed in detail later in the chapter. IBL is a technology that enables accurate on-set measurement of lighting conditions to be recorded and then used to illuminate the CG objects directly. Thus the correct application of HDR IBL will produce a render that, if the look development has been done well, will feel like it belongs in the plate.

However, as noted earlier, the placement of extra digital lights is often required to match the mood of other shots in the sequence.

When placing extra lights it is good practice to place them one at a time and adjust each until it provides the result sought before placing another light. By adopting this approach the artist limits the number of variables from one test render to the next, enabling a better judgment to be made regarding the next step in the creative lighting process. If an artist places all of the lights he thinks he will need at once and launches a render, it can be difficult to detect which light, or combination of lights, is responsible for any undesired effects seen in that test render. By adopting an iterative approach and adjusting one light per test render, the effect of each light is clear to the artist and he will maintain a clearer understanding of the shot.

Another technique that helps to ensure high-quality lighting is producing test renders over the plate into which the CG is eventually to be composited. Most render viewing software defaults to rendering the image over a black background. This is useful for checking edge artifacts but gives a poor representation of the finished shot. The human eye sees every color relative to the colors that surround it. By judging a render against black, the artist will not see subtle variations in color and how well the CG fits into the photographed element. It is usually possible to load a background image into a render viewer and for the reasons outlined above it is good practice to do so when testing lighting.

The majority of films that utilize digital visual effects now go through a creative grading process at the end of the post-production pipeline. This stage results in the production of a *digital intermediate* and the process itself is now generally referred to as *DI*. The DI involves creatively changing color and contrast in filmed footage to create the finished look that the Director and DP designed. The artists who specialize in this process are often required to modify the photographed plate considerably by introducing shifts in color, contrast, and saturation. This process can exaggerate small differences between colors so it is clear that the CG rendered by the digital lighting artist must match the plate so that it reacts in the same way as the plate itself to any changes applied in the DI.

Because most production facilities now use a floating point pipeline to enable greater color fidelity and flexibility, it is possible for lighting artists to examine their work under a variety of extreme grading situations. A good and simple test is to use compositing software to view the CG layered over the background at two exposure stops above and then two stops below the exposure level of the scan. This will enable the artist to see whether the colors in the shadows and the highlights of the CG are sympathetic to those in the photography. At normal levels of exposure the highlights may be blown out to white on a monitor and the shadows can appear black. This is merely a limit of the viewing technology: They do in fact have color information, and by raising and lowering the exposure in a test composite, it is possible to see whether these too match the plate. If they do not, and the final composite were to be heavily graded, these differences between the CG and the plate could become very apparent and break the realism of the shot.

The Technologies of Lights in Computer Graphics

Several methods are used to simulate illumination in computer graphics, some being more physically accurate than others. As noted earlier, the primary limiting factor in terms of which technologies are used in digital visual effects is generally the speed of the computers rendering the frames. Until recently it has only been possible to use the most basic and, therefore, fastest lighting methods.

The three main types of lighting technologies used in visual effects are direct lighting; IBL, often in conjunction with ambient occlusion; and physically based rendering. There is some overlap between these methods but generally they represent a progression toward more accurate lighting simulations at the expense of longer render times.

Direct Lighting: Source to Surface to Camera

The simplest light source that can be described in CG is a point light. A point light is an infinitely small dot that outputs light intensity in all directions. It is a simple matter for the renderer to compute the light direction by creating a vector from the surface point being shaded to the point light source itself. From there it is possible to perform the calculations for the diffuse and specular models being employed by the surface shader.

The point light may be made more sophisticated by enabling it to observe the inverse square law of illumination fall-off. This law describes how if light falls on two surfaces, one twice as far from the light source as the other, the farther point will receive only one-quarter of the illumination that hit the nearer point.

The next direct light source to consider is the spotlight. This is probably the most commonly used light source in computer graphics. A spotlight consists of a single point of illumination, but rather than radiate out in all directions like a point light, the spotlight's illumination is contained by a cone with the source of illumination at the point. The size of the cone may be varied, enabling narrower or broader areas of light to be described.

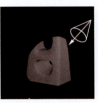

Figure 7.33 Four direct CG light sources (*from left to right*): point light, spot light, parallel light, and area light. (Image courtesy of Andrew Whitehurst.)

In addition to implementing the inverse square law, spotlights may also be engineered to have a fall-off across the section of the light cone. This produces a softer edge to the circular pool of light on the surface. Spotlights are used more often than point lights because the ability to adjust the size of the cone and the fall-off affords the lighting artist more options in controlling which parts of a model receive illumination and which do not.

A third form of CG light is the parallel ray or solar light. These lights are so named because the light that they generate is described only by direction: It does not emanate from a single point; hence the rays of light from it are parallel. This type of light is most often used to simulate the rays of the sun because, even though the sun is a finite-sized light source, it is sufficiently distant from the earth (roughly 150 million kilometers) that its rays are almost parallel, and this is certainly a good enough approximation for visual effects purposes.

The fourth type of direct illumination is area light. This is a light source whose origin is not an infinitely small point but is instead a piece of geometry, usually planar. Algorithms that compute area lights typically do so by considering points on the surface of the geometry as a set of points or spotlights and computing the effect of an area light as the sum of all of these small light samples. It follows, therefore, that the more samples the light considers in simulating the area effect, the better the quality of the finished result at the expense of longer render times.

Negative Lights

All of the lights described above emit an intensity of illumination. This is used by the surface shader to return a value for the reflectance of the object. Because many of these models are mathematically derived, it is possible to put values into these lighting equations that could not occur in reality but can have visually interesting results. One common trick is to use a negative light. By supplying a negative value to the intensity of the light a proportionately negative amount of reflectance will be returned by the surface shader. In other words this will make the surface appear darker. Negative lights are most commonly used to reduce excessively bright areas in a render when an artist does not want to adjust the settings of the other light sources in the scene.

Negative lights are a handy trick but they must be used with caution. As more visual effects use lighting techniques based on physically accurate models of illumination, laws of physics such as the conservation of energy become important in producing realistic renders. Negative lights do not obey these laws and can therefore produce undesirable results in physically based renders.

Reflections

The directional light sources examined so far in this chapter are used for diffuse illumination of surfaces and specular reflection. Specular reflections are the reflections of the light sources themselves. It is often necessary for other objects within a scene also to be reflected in a surface. These reflections can be computed via two main methods.

One method is to use ray tracing. In this technique the surface shader will fire a ray along the reflection vector of the point currently being shaded. If that ray hits nothing, it will return black; there is nothing to reflect. If the ray does intersect another surface, the surface shader for that point is computed and the reflected color of that surface is returned as the color of the reflection. This produces very accurate reflections but is expensive to compute, because it must be calculated for every reflective surface point on every frame, even if the reflection remains unchanging throughout the shot.

Because of this inefficiency another technique for simulating reflections is commonly used. This is a reflection map– or environment map–based reflection. These maps differ in the means of their creation but are referenced in the same way once they have been made.

To create a reflection map, the renderer pre-computes a set of six maps, each of which is a render of the scene from an arbitrary point, and each is aligned so that the six renders can be stitched together to make a cube that represents a complete view

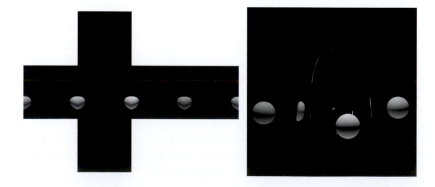

Figure 7.34 A reflection map rendered in the cross format and a render computed using lookups to this map. (Image courtesy of Andrew Whitehurst.)

of the scene from that arbitrary point. These maps are usually "unwrapped" so they appear as T-shaped or cross-shaped. When computing the final render, the reflective surface shader, rather than firing rays, uses the reflection direction vector to compute which part of the pre-rendered map represents that direction and returns the value in the map as the reflection color.

Environment maps are computed by rendering a single map of the scene in the panoramic latitude-longitude format (often shortened to *lat-long*), a format that is akin to the commonly used Mercator projection maps of the Earth's surface, which show areas near the poles as being disproportionately large compared with the equator.

Photographed Reflections

In addition to rendering reflections of other digital objects, photography can also be used to generate reflection maps. This is especially useful in visual effects where a digital object often needs to be incorporated into a real environment. If possible, reference photographs should be taken on set to provide material for these reflection maps. These photographs may be taken using either a chrome sphere or as two sets of images, 180 degrees apart, photographed using a fish-eye lens on the camera. From this data an environment map can be constructed that will create plausible reflections of the set in a CG object.

Figure 7.35 A photographic reflection map in the latitude-longitude format. The image on the right is a render computed using this map for reflection calculations. (Uffizi Gallery Light Probe Image ©1999 courtesy of Paul Debevec, www .debevec.org/probes.)

When considering reflective surfaces that are glossy rather than mirror-like in their reflectivity, an extra property of map-based reflections comes to the fore. To compute blurry reflections with ray tracing, multiple samples must be rendered by randomly offsetting the ray direction around the reflection vector and calculating the average returned reflectance. These blurry reflections will be very accurate but they are also very expensive to render. If maps are being used for reflection it is a simple matter to convolve (blur) the map being used for the reflection to get a result that is often visually indistinguishable from the vastly more costly ray-traced method.

Shadows

Shadowing in CG may also be divided into ray-traced and map-based approaches. A shadow map is an image rendered from the point of view of the light source. In a spotlight shadow map the frustum of the view matches the cone angle of the light. Each pixel in this image represents a value for the depth of the first object seen by the light. During the main render each surface point rendered computes the distance to the light source that may illuminate it and compares this value against a lookup to the shadow map. If the number is greater than the lookup, it means that an object occludes the surface's view of the light and thus it is in shadow. Otherwise the light's illumination effect is calculated for the shaded point.

Shadow maps are prone to several artifacts, such as a blocky appearance, caused by a shadow map of insufficient resolution. Surface self-occlusion problems are also caused when the value returned by the map is very similar to the distance computed by the render and rounding errors can result in dark aliasing patterns. Blocky maps can be improved by rendering a higher resolution map or performing multiple, jittered lookups on the map to produce a blurred shadow. Self-occlusion artifacts are fixed by adding a small offset to the value returned by the map. This is referred to as a *depth-map bias parameter* and must be a value large enough to remove the artifacts from the render but not so large that shadows no longer appear to be connected to the surfaces casting them.

Shadow maps may be rendered for point lights by computing six images, each with a 90-degree field of view that covers all directions from the light. Solar lights may render axonometric projection-based shadow maps to maintain the parallelism of the light rays.

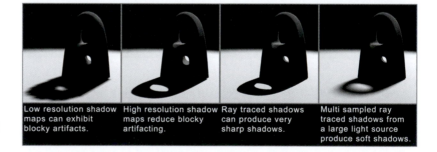

Low resolution shadow maps can exhibit blocky artifacts.
High resolution shadow maps reduce blocky artifacting.
Ray traced shadows can produce very sharp shadows.
Multi sampled ray traced shadows from a large light source produce soft shadows.

Figure 7.36 Comparison of different shadow calculation technologies. (Image courtesy of Andrew Whitehurst.)

A simple ray-traced shadow is computed by each surface shading point attempting to fire a ray at the light source. If the ray hits another surface en route, then the point shooting the ray must be in shadow from that light source. This process creates very accurate but sharp shadows. Softer shadows may be rendered by assuming that the light source has an area and shooting several rays from the shaded point at different parts of the light's surface and averaging the number of ray hits or misses to compute the amount of shadow on the surface. A larger light source will yield softer shadows, but more ray samples will be needed to create a noiseless, smooth result.

Image-Based Lighting

In visual effects, the lighting artist is often called on to illuminate a digital object so that it blends into a photographed background. To do this, the on-set lighting must be meticulously copied. While it is possible to position direct lights to mimic the position, color, and intensity of every real light source on the set, this is laborious and, assuming that infinitely small sourced spot or point lights are used, does not take into account the different areas of light, perhaps coming from an on-set soft box, for example.

Already mentioned is the fact that by taking reference photographs on set with a fish-eye lens or mirrored ball, maps can be created that can then be used to create realistic reflections of real objects on digital surfaces, thus aiding integration between the CG and the photographed plate. These same maps may also be used for diffuse lighting calculations by convolving the images greatly to create a blurred map that approximates how a diffuse surface would react to the scene lighting. For this diffuse reflection, the surface shader looks up a value from the map based on its surface normal, not the reflection vector that is used in the reflection lookup. The diffuse reflection map lookup result is then multiplied by any maps or colors that the surface has in exactly the same way as the reflectance of a direct CG light would be computed.

Although it is not always absolutely necessary to do so, HDR environment maps should be used, because these will provide a much more accurate, and realistic, representation of the lighting on set. Light sources are often extremely bright, so an image with a higher dynamic range will capture the range of light intensities and colors more accurately. This enables more photorealistic renders.

Rendering Occlusion

The use of maps for reflection or diffuse lookups is subject to an inherent problem: Map-based lookups do not take into account any objects that might occlude the path of a ray fired off the surface, and these objects would prevent at least some of the environmental light from illuminating the surface. To account for this visible effect, two prerender passes are computed that simulate the effect of this occlusion. The diffuse environment map lookup is attenuated by an ambient occlusion render and the reflection map lookup by a reflection occlusion render.

Ambient Occlusion

An ambient occlusion render is one in which every visible shaded point fires a series of rays in a hemisphere around the surface normal. The number of rays that hit another surface is divided by the total rays fired. This value represents how occluded the surface is: A value of zero would represent a surface that is not occluded at all, whereas a value of one represents a point that is in total shadow. It is common practice to invert this map so that zero (black) represents complete occlusion and one (white) is not occluded. The reasoning behind this is that it is more easily understandable for artists working with the image and it enables the diffuse lookup to the environment map in the beauty render to be multiplied by this inverted ambient occlusion map to produce a realistic rendering of the effect that the environment's illumination would have on the surface.

Reflection Occlusion

Reflection occlusion renders are produced in a manner similar to that of ambient occlusion and for the same reason: to prevent areas of a CG surface that would not reflect any of the environment from doing so. While ambient occlusion uses surface normal-based hemispherical sampling, the reflection occlusion process samples across a cone centered around the reflection vector. Larger cone angles create occlusion for blurrier reflections, a brushed metal surface, for example. A cone angle of zero (i.e., firing rays down the reflection vector only) will yield

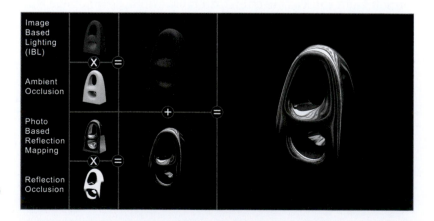

Figure 7.37 Render produced using simple IBL with ambient and reflection occlusion. (Image courtesy of Andrew Whitehurst.)

perfectly sharp reflection occlusion, which would be ideal for simulating a mirrored surface. It is important when computing reflection occlusion to choose an appropriate cone angle for the surface material being rendered.

Average Light Direction Vectors: *Bent Normals*

Attenuating a convolved environment map lookup with an ambient occlusion render adds considerable realism to the lighting of diffuse digital objects. However, it does not accurately represent the direction from which the majority of the light striking a surface came.

Consider rendering the inside of a cave using IBL and ambient occlusion. The normals of the cave floor will be pointing up and the environment map lookup for these normals will return illumination values for the sky. In reality, however, the floor would not be lit by the sky above the cave because the cave ceiling occludes it. Instead the cave floor would be lit by light entering through the mouth of the cave and hitting the surface at an oblique angle.

An additional pre-rendered pass, computed at the same time as the ambient occlusion, can help correct this anomaly. For each ray that does not strike a surface in the ambient occlusion render, a record is made of its direction vector. After all ray samples have been completed, the recorded lighting vectors are averaged. Thus, not only is there data representing how much ambient light strikes the surface, but also from what direction most of it came. This vector, which is the average light direction vector, is stored for use in the main render along with ambient occlusion data.

The reason this data is colloquially referred to as *bent normals* is due to the way the data is applied. When computing the diffuse reflection of an object, the surface normal is not used for the environment map lookup. Instead, the normal direction is chosen from the pre-rendered data, so the normal is bent to face another direction, one that better represents the direction of the main lighting contribution to that point. In the cave example the bent normal would point toward the mouth of the cave.

Creating Light Sources from Environment Maps

Simple lookups to pre-convolved environment maps coupled with occlusion can create very realistic renders efficiently. However, there are many desirable lighting qualities that this simple technique cannot reproduce. For example, an environment map with areas of high-intensity lighting will not cast appropriate shadows on the digital model. Each surface point will receive appropriate illumination, but the effect of the interaction of digital surfaces on one another when lit by IBL will not be accurately modeled. Several techniques are available for simulating these effects and these vary in complexity, accuracy, and computational efficiency.

One method is to create many direct light sources (usually solar or parallel ray lights), which can be arrayed around the digital model. The color and intensity of these lights are derived from the environment map. Provided each of these lights is shadow casting, a reasonable representation of the lighting interaction effects is possible.

Many algorithms are available to assist in determining the optimum number and position of these direct light sources. An example of this would be to use the median cut algorithm to sample the environment map, recursively dividing the map into areas of equal illumination intensity. Some areas will be larger than others but each will be assigned one direct light source, located at the light intensity emission centroid for that area of the map. This technique has the benefit of placing more light sources in areas of greater lighting importance. The process of locating limited numbers of light samples to maximize the rendering efficiency is called *importance sampling*.

A further development of this concept would be to use ray-tracing techniques to perform lighting lookups on light samples from the maps.

Not only do these techniques afford improved realism in the illumination of the objects themselves, they also enable more sophisticated lighting interaction with other surfaces. For example, some of the more sophisticated IBL approaches, like importance sampled lighting, can enable more accurate shadows to be cast on the digital representations of the set, thus facilitating better integration between the digital model and the plate photography.

Physically Based Rendering

Most lighting algorithms, especially those that are efficient to render and have thus proved popular at visual effects houses, are based around the interaction of each point on a surface and the light sources in the scene. In its simplest form each shaded point is utterly unaffected by the presence or surface properties of any other object. The ability to create realistic renders with this lighting pipeline is highly limited. The introduction of shadows on direct light sources is an improvement, because occluded objects no longer receive illumination from lights that could not "see" them. Ambient occlusion performs the same function for IBL sources. With these technologies a surface is aware of the physicality of other objects in the scene but does not take into account the surface properties of those objects. In reality, a blue painted wall standing on a white floor in bright sunlight will produce a blue area of illumination on the white floor. The sunlight hits the wall, and some of the reflected blue light will strike the floor before being reflected once more. Some of that reflected light would strike the retinas, enabling one to see the phenomenon.

The most obvious way of computing this effect is, for every pixel rendered, to trace rays through the scene, detecting and accounting for every surface interaction until a light source is hit. From the intensity value of the light source, one can work back through the sequence of ray hits to compute the ray's effect on the intensity of the light until the ray returns to the camera where a color value for the pixel can be produced. Because diffuse surfaces scatter light that hits them in many possible directions, it is necessary to perform this sampling approach many times for each pixel to produce a render that is free from noise artifacts. Because of the high number of samples required, this technique, although highly accurate, is very time consuming to compute. This approach to rendering is called *path tracing*.

A less precise but computationally faster evolution of path tracing is to make the assumption that the changes in reflectance over a diffuse surface being hit with light are usually quite gradual. (Think of a matte plastic ball being lit by a single light source.) To leverage this observation, rays must be fired into the scene, and the irradiance (reflected color) of each surface point hit en route to the light source is stored in a cache. Although the sampling may be sparse, it is possible to interpolate between the values stored in the cache, so that renders that appear noise free may be computed with considerably fewer samples than were required in the path tracing approach.

Irradiance caches may also have additional processing performed on them to calculate subsurface scattering because the cache contains a representation of the objects in the scene and their surface irradiance values. This additional cache is then referred to by the renderer to obtain a value for the subsurface scattering at any point in the scene.

Irradiance cache–based approaches work well for complex diffuse lighting calculations but sophisticated specular effects such as caustics cannot be reproduced. To simulate such phenomena, a different rendering technique, known as *photon mapping*, is used. Photon mapping is a two-stage process. The first pass is the production of the photon map itself for the scene. The second pass is the main render that uses the data contained in the photon map to improve the speed of its computation.

To produce a photon map, particles of light are fired from light sources in the scene. Whenever a particle encounters a surface, its direction vector and the location of the point hit are stored in the photon map. From there, by taking into account the reflectance

Figure 7.38 A render produced using an irradiance cache shows the indirect bounce light from the spotlight illuminating the wall on the other objects in the scene. (Image courtesy of Andrew Whitehurst.)

properties of the surface, the particle may be absorbed by the surface or reflected back into the scene to continue until it hits another surface when the calculation is performed again. A third option for the particle is that it is transmitted through the surface. This could happen in the case of a material like glass. Subsurface scattering effects may also be computed with photon maps.

The main render uses the photon maps to help compute the soft indirect lighting by providing the ray-tracing algorithm with pre-computed information about how light has been reflected in the scene. Photons that were refracted through participatory media (like glass) onto a solid surface can be used to render caustic effects. Specular reflection and direct illumination are usually ray traced in a traditional manner.

Volumetric Lighting Effects

Rendered representations of light encountering volumetric media such as smoke, cloud, or fog cannot be calculated using any of the techniques outlined above. This is because all of the previous approaches have relied only on performing rendering calculations when a light ray hits a surface. A smoke cloud has no surface; it is a volume.

To render these types of objects, a technique known as *ray marching* must be used. In previous forms of ray tracing discussed

Figure 7.39 Volumetric lighting effects visible in a render of a smoke-like volume. (Image rendered using Double Negative's DNB renderer, courtesy of Double Negative Limited.)

in this section, the ray only becomes interesting when it hits a surface; otherwise it passes unaffected through the scene. With ray marching the ray's condition and its interaction with the scene are sampled at uniform steps along its path. If, for example, the ray were passing through fog, each step along its march would return the amount by which it has illuminated an area of fog. The cumulative effect of all of these samples can be accounted for in the color of the final rendered pixel.

Ray marching is computationally very intensive, and rendering software engineered to perform the more common solid surface rendering is often not optimized to perform ray-marching calculations. For this reason it is not unusual for a special case renderer to be used by visual effects facilities to render volumetric effects, while a more traditional renderer is utilized for the other solid objects. These two renders are then combined in the composite.

Conclusion

Digital lighting and rendering technologies are continuing to evolve. Academic conferences such as SIGGRAPH and Eurographics present new papers every year that offer new techniques and insights into reproducing the effects of light's interaction with the world. Many of these ideas are then incorporated into the software used to produce visual effects.

As machines become faster, techniques that were once only theoretically feasible become practically useful—initially for the companies with large rendering farms and eventually for everybody. The many different approaches to simulating lighting with computers is, in part, the ongoing story of the advancement of computer power harnessed by ever more sophisticated algorithms. The techniques may continually change, but there is always the need for artists with good visual skills to utilize these tools to produce the believable visual effects that today's cinema-going audiences expect.

SHADER BASICS
Derek Spears

What Are Shaders?

Shading is the part of the rendering pipeline that gives each sample on a surface a value. In the design of a rendering system, the shading system, also called the *shading machinery*, is called into play once the renderer discovers visible surfaces at each pixel on the rendered image. The shader is then invoked for the point on that surface corresponding to that pixel. How and why this surface is found is unimportant to the shader.

Ray tracing and global illumination are ways to intersect surfaces and define how much light gets to them. What happens with that information on the surfaces is the responsibility of the shader. What the shader is concerned with is how to color, or shade, the object. A shader, as will be seen later, may also alter the object's geometry. When applied to a CG object, a shader and all of its associated settings that define the look of an object are often referred to as a *material*. The focus of this section is shading in a software context. Hardware shading (which is done on dedicated graphics cards instead of a computer's CPU) is rapidly becoming more powerful and is conceptually similar to the constructs described here.

Shaders can not only modify the color of an object, they can also change the shape of an object. Surface shaders deal primarily with color. Displacement/bump shaders alter the appearance of the geometry of the surface. They provide a way for the lighting artist to add visual detail to a CG object without adding complexity and weight to the model.

Implementation of shaders can either be via an application interface, such as might be seen in Maya or Houdini, or via a software programming interface such as might be found in Renderman. (Houdini and other packages also offer a programming interface.) The advantage of an application interface is ease of use. Nontechnical artists can quickly assemble the look of a material via a graphical user interface. However, they are constrained by the tools that are presented. Software interfaces allow more technical users to write program functions that describe mathematically how to shade an object. The package that allows a developer to write code for a shader is often referred to as a *software development kit* (SDK). SDKs allow for greater flexibility and implementation of features that might not be allowed by a user interface (UI). This construct is very similar to that of a software plug-in.

Shading Models

The most basic building block of a shader is its shading model. The shading model describes how the object responds to light at the most basic level, whether it is matte or shiny, or if the reflections are dependent on more than just the viewing angles. Much research has been done on shading models, and many of the earlier models are approximations of how light reacts with a surface rather than being mathematically or physically correct. Lighting models, such as Lambert lighting, simulate only the diffuse, or nonreflective, aspects of a surface. The Phong and Blinn lighting models allow for specular highlights to imply a shiny surface. Other more advanced models, such as Cook-Torrance, attempt to more accurately model reflectance. In fact, many of the earlier models can be expressed within the framework of the Cook-Torrance model.

More complex shading models might involve ray tracing of actual reflected light to simulate mirrored surfaces. In addition to using contributions from lights, the shader could ask for the reflected light from another object at a given angle. For more realistic lighting, the shader could model the diffuse reflection of light via a global illumination scheme (i.e., modeling the way in which a red wall spills light onto a white wall). Physically based rendering models try to accurately compute how light is transmitted and reflected through the scene. Given an appropriate rendering infrastructure, the shader could implement these shading models in a similar fashion, as described above.

Bump and Displacement

Color is not the only aspect of a surface available to the shader. Surfaces can be perturbed, or displaced, by shaders. Displacement can be thought of as bumps on the surface of the object. Rather than modeling extremely high levels of detail, CG objects often have bump and displacement shaders added in order to increase the level of detail without increasing the model complexity.

Bump mapping, the simplest method, does not actually alter the geometry, but instead alters the normal (or, more simply, the apparent direction in which the surface faces) of the surface to make the surface *appear* displaced. This is a shading illusion; the surface geometry has not actually been changed. A grayscale texture map representing desired detail is used to perturb that normal.

An easy way to visualize what is happening is to consider this bump map to be a height field or elevation map. Much like a topological map in the real world, colors represent altitude. In this case, black would represent the level of the original geometry and white would represent a maximum new height. The bump shader looks at this map and computes a new normal based on how high the bump map raises the point. This is based on the slope of the new surface whose height would have been raised by the bump map. The normal at the current point on the geometry is then added to this new normal, which no longer corresponds to the geometry. Since the lighting calculations are entirely based upon the normal for the surface, the surface now appears bumpy.

This process has the advantage of being simple to compute; the disadvantage is that since the surface has not actually been changed, the edges will still remain the same, and the bump detail is not there (see Figure 7.40a) Normal mapping is an extension of bump mapping, whereby instead of using a single-channel gray image, a 3-channel image is used to completely re-define the normal direction instead of just moving the apparent height of the point up and down.

Displacement mapping goes one step farther. Using the same height field texture map, instead of just altering the normal, the displacement shader will actually move, or displace, each point on the object being shaded along its normal using the height field as an amount. The advantage of true displacement is that the geometry is actually altered, whereas before the bump map left the object's original edges unaltered. The displacement shader will create new detail. Also, the displaced geometry can cast

Figure 7.40 (A) A surface with no bump mapping applied. (B) The bump map, with black representing no change and white representing the highest amount of bump value. (C) The surfaces are rendered with the bump map applied. (Image courtesy of Derek Spears.)

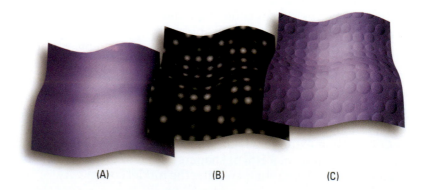

(A)   (B)   (C)

(A)   (B)

Figure 7.41 (A) Bump shading is used. (B) Displacement Shading. With displacement, the profile has detail due to the geometry being moved as opposed to the smooth edge of the bump shader (see inset). Also, note the shadows cast by the displaced ridges in the lower right of the image that are absent in the bump shader. (Image courtesy of Derek Spears.)

shadows, unlike the bump shader, which only shadows using the original unaltered geometry. All of this comes at a price. The renderer has to do significant computations to understand the visibility for this new displaced geometry, leading to higher render times. Also because, in effect, the shader is actually creating more geometry, it will lead to higher memory usage.

Map-Based Shaders

Once the shading model has been established, adding texture is a way in which detail is added. Adding texture to an object is analogous to painting an object in the physical world. The added complication is understanding how to apply a flat, 2D image (or texture) to 3D object. This process of transforming the 2D image space to 3D object space is known as *mapping*. To differentiate between the object and the image, the texture's X and Y coordinates in the image are referred to as u and v, which prevents confusion between the objects X and Y. This is analogous to u and v in parameterized surfaces, and in fact, the same u and v parameterization is often used for the texture coordinates.

Surface parameterization is a method of defining surfaces. Instead of defining a surface traditionally whereby each vertex coordinate is specified, a parametric surface is defined by a mathematical equation. The values for the X, Y, and Z coordinates are determined by a function whose parameters are u and v. A surface defined by these parameters is called a *parametric surface*. The values of u and v typically range from 0 to 1. Assume Fx, Fy, and Fz are equations whose variables are u and v. Hence, each coordinate X, Y, and Z is defined by solving those equations. This is a simplification; for something such as a Bezier surface, there would be a set of control points that help define these equations.

$$X = F_x(u,v)$$

$$Y = F_y(u,v)$$

$$Z = F_z(u,v)$$

For polygonal objects that have no parameterization, some type of parameterization must be created for the surface. That is, for every vertex that has an X,Y,Z coordinate, a u,v coordinate needs to be supplied that will tell the shader what part of the image should correspond to this part of the surface. This process is referred to as *UV mapping*. In Figure 7.42, a 3D surface is shown with its coordinates X, Y, Z and a corresponding u,v. To determine interior UV coordinates, the values would be interpreted from the neighbors. For instance, a value halfway between $u = 0$ and $u = 1$ would have a value of 0.5.

UV mapping can happen in several ways. The simplest way is to use a projection map. A projection map is analogous to projecting a slide onto a screen (or a shaped object for that matter). This is the basis of the 2.5D projection map described in the next section of this chapter, *3D Compositing*. The basic types of projection maps are planar, cylindrical, spherical, and camera.

In planar mapping, the coordinates are projected orthographically out from a plane along the normal direction (similar to a slide projector onto a screen). In cylindrical mapping, the coordinates are projected from a cylinder inward. Similarly, spherical mapping projects the coordinates inward from a sphere. Camera mapping is similar to planar mapping, but instead of projecting orthographically

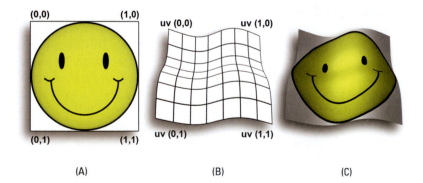

(A) (B) (C)

Figure 7.42 (A) A texture map can be thought of as going from 0 to 1 in the horizontal or vertical direction. (B) The u,v texture coordinates are assigned as shown on the surface geometry. Each vertex will have its own coordinate; only the corners are shown for clarity. (C) The final rendered image has the texture map from part (A) applied to the geometry using the u,v coordinates in part (B). (Image courtesy of Derek Spears.)

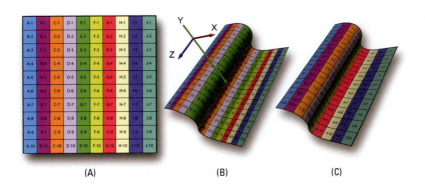

Figure 7.43 (A) A texture is projected using two different methods. (B) The *u,v* coordinates are using a planar projection in the *Y*-axis. Note the stretching of the green texture and the repetition of the C, D, and E rows. (C) The texture has been projected using a more complex unwrapping scheme, which yields better results. (Image courtesy of Derek Spears.)

from a plane (where the projection lines are parallel), the coordinates are projected along a camera frustum[17] and diverge.

The choice of which method to use largely depends on the shape of the object that is being mapped. Flatter objects respond well to planar mapping, tube-like objects to cylindrical, etc. The advantage of projection mapping is its simplicity. However, it becomes limited because of the difficulty of dealing with surfaces that don't line up with the projection. The less perpendicular a surface is to the projection, the more texture stretching can occur. Also, surfaces that overlap with respect to the projection source will have the same *u,v* coordinates, leading to repeated textures.

The solutions to these problems lie in either breaking up the object into smaller, less problematic objects, or groups, or using a more sophisticated mapping method. Surface relaxing and unwrapping methods can deal with these more complex shapes and unwrap them to a flat shape. This flattened shape can then be easily be projected into a *u,v* space. The methodology, although mathematically complex, is analogous to smoothing out a wrinkled sheet of paper in order to make it lay flat.

Now that the surface has *u,v* space, it is possible to apply an image to the surface. As the shader is called for any given point on the surface, the corresponding *u,v* coordinates for that point are available to the shader and it can then look up the corresponding pixel in the texture map. Texture maps can then be used to control all aspects of the material's appearance, such as the material's color or the color of the specular highlight. Maps can even be used to control noncolor parameters, such as the roughness component in the Phong shading model.

---

[17] The camera, or view frustrum, is the pyramid-shaped volume defined by the camera at its apex. The edges are defined by points running from the eye through the four corners of the visible edges of the visible area. Objects inside the volume are visible to the camera or viewer, while objects outside are not. Since it is easily defined mathematically, the view frustrum is often used to cull out unseen objects in order to improve render efficiency.

Procedural Shaders

Texture maps place a tremendous amount of design power in the hands of the CG artists, but there are times when painted maps are not sufficient. Maps are typically static images. It is possible to apply an animated set of maps to a shader, but that requires either painting many different maps or having another piece of software render a sequence of images. Rather than have an external program generate a map, it is easier to just move that code into the shader. This code-driven creation of the texture map within the shader is referred to as a *procedural shader*. Procedural shaders are often used to add noisy detail that is easier to compute than to paint. Additionally, procedural shaders offer the added benefit of being resolution independent. A painted texture map exists at a certain resolution. For example, suppose an artist had a scene where a camera was zooming in to a painting on a wall where the painting was a texture painted at 1024×1024. Once the camera got to the point where the rendered image was 1024×1024, getting closer to the image would not give more detail; the image would only get softer and softer. With a procedural shader, if the camera gets close to the texture, additional detail in the shader can be computed to fill in the detail, providing the possibility of adapting to varying resolution requirements.

A common use of procedural shaders is to produce noise patterns. One example of a procedural noise function is the Perlin noise function developed by Ken Perlin. The Perlin noise function allows for the quick computation of noise of a known frequency and amplitude based on a 3D point in space. The function itself might look simplistic in its appearance, but by layering increasing frequencies of the noise function, it is possible to create realistic and interesting noise patterns. These noise functions can either take the u, v space of the surface as an input (2D shaders) or the X, Y, Z coordinates of the surface as an input (3D shaders). Many different types of noise functions exist that can be layered together to create useful textures.

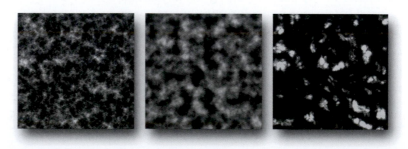

Figure 7.44 Different types of procedural noise patterns. (Image courtesy of Derek Spears.)

Shader Design

With a basic understanding of how shaders work, let's take a quick look at how they are used in readily available animation packages. In Maya, the interface is streamlined to allow the user to layer up components to build a shader. This model is common across other packages as well. The user first chooses a shading model (such as Blinn or Lambert). Then, all of the different components of that shading model, such as diffuse color, specular color, roughness, etc., can be attached to procedural shaders or texture maps. In turn, all these shaders can have each of their parameters attached to another shader.

For example, the diffuse color from the Phong shader could be attached to a texture map. The base color of that texture map could then be attached to a noise shader in order to modulate the texture map with noise. In this way, it is possible to build up complex shaders with the combinations of simpler shaders.

Another approach to shader design is used in the Houdini animation system. Instead of using a list of functions and attaching parameters in a list, Houdini also allows the user to connect the

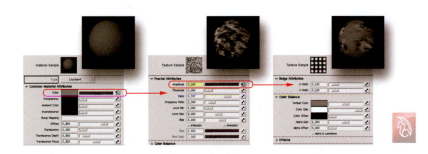

Figure 7.45 In Maya, each parameter can have another shader, or material, as an input. The color in the Lambert shader is linked to a noise field. The amplitude of the noise is linked to a grid with bulges, which produces a shader with noisy sections only in the white areas of the grid. (Image courtesy of Derek Spears.)

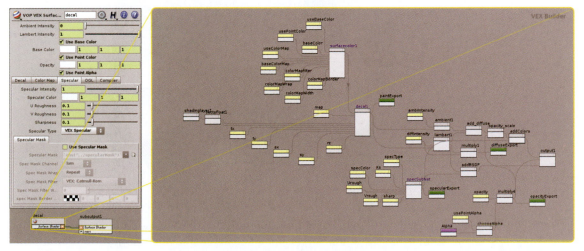

Figure 7.46 Houdini's node-based shader system. (Image courtesy of Derek Spears.)

shader function in a flowchart-style view. This is analogous to a node-based compositor. It has the advantage of being more powerful but at the expense of being somewhat more complicated.

Most artists will find the graphical interface sufficient for most tasks, but some problems go beyond what a prepackaged shader can provide. In this case, many renderers provide an interface for writing custom shaders. These shaders can take the form of compiled C code, such as Mental Ray, or a higher level language that has its own special compiler, such as Renderman. These frameworks allow for low-level access to the renderer. The programmer can then create new shading models or implement shaders with functionality completely outside the scope of original program.

Antialiasing Considerations

Antialiasing in shaders is slightly different from antialiasing in rendering. The latter might be referred to as *edge antialiasing*. When a render samples a surface, it must do so enough times to smoothly determine where the surface is and isn't. With too few samples, jaggy edges are apparent. This is often referred to as pixel samples. However, depending on the implementation of the renderer, it is possible that, no matter how high the pixel samples are, the shader will only get called once per pixel. This may seem fine conceptually but can give rise to shading artifacts, as will be seen.

Imagine a shader that renders a black-and-white grid on a surface. It could either be a texture map or a procedural shader. If the renderer only samples the shader once per pixel, it will only ever get a black or white pixel. No antialiasing will take place because the shader only returns either black or white, inside or outside the grid, as seen in Figure 7.47. Two steps can be taken

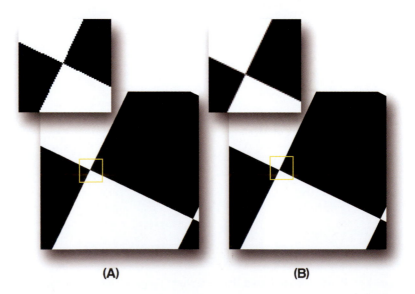

Figure 7.47 (A) No antialiasing results in jaggy image edges in the shader. (B) Correct shader sampling results in smother, correctly aliased edges. (Image courtesy of Derek Spears.)

(A)   (B)

to help minimize this. First, the shader can be sampled multiple times per pixel. Although a pixel seems like an infinitely small area, the pixel actually is a square, the corners of which define an area on the screen. If the shader is sampled multiple times within this area in a random pattern, the average of these values can generate an antialiased pixel for us, much in the same way edge antialiasing works. The control for this is referred to as the shading rate. Second, in designing a shader, it is important to minimize methodologies that give rise to aliasing. For instance, functions that access textures should do so in ways that adequately filter the image. The shader should appropriately filter procedural functions that generate noise or other images.

This has only been a very high-level look at shading. Each individual rendering package will approach the problem in a slightly different fashion. The focus here is to provide the reader with a basic understanding of how shaders can be implemented for any given rendering scheme.

3D COMPOSITING
Derek Spears

Color Representation

To fully understand how compositing works in a digital world, it is important to understand some of the basics of color representation. Color is a complex topic and the details are much broader than can be covered in this chapter. However, some basics are necessary in order to give a framework to the understanding of how and why some of the esoteric elements of compositing work.

The primary ways in which imagery is represented fall into two camps: linear or logarithmic (log). These are not color spaces per se, but are ways in which one chose to store data. CG imagery is typically stored in linear space. That is to say, there is a linear relationship between the value and the brightness of the pixel. In the real world, this is all a bit more complex; a linear gradient does not appear linear on a monitor. Human eyes and display devices have a more logarithmic response. To view a linear ramp as perceptually linear it is necessary to take into the account the response of the monitor/viewing device. This is where expressions like 2.2 gamma[18] (or 1.8 for Mac) come into play. Math operations in linear space are straightforward, that is, multiplying a value by 2 doubles its value and, therefore, makes it appear twice as bright—thus the desire to work in a linear world and for nonlinear devices to do the machinations to make linear imagery appear correct.

---

[18] Gamma: a log compensation to correct the viewing of linear data (an image file) on a nonlinear viewing device (a monitor).

Log encoding is typically used as storage for scanned film imagery. The reason has to do with the dynamic range of film. The Cineon file format was originally built with the intention of capturing 10 stops of film exposure using 10 bits. The data is effectively compressed using a log encoding. By using a log function, large changes in exposure value can be expressed with a smaller range of numbers.

Instead of having a large linear range, in log the same amount of brightness data may be represented by a much smaller range of numbers. Since larger numbers require more bits, log allows one to compress the large exposure range of film into a smaller format. Log scaling also more correctly models the response of film. In Cineon log encoding, each 90 code values corresponds to one stop of film. In linear space, the number of values varies depending on the brightness of the image. However, log tends to be impractical for CG compositing because it can give rise to artifacts in compositing CG images that are typically represented in linear space. Because of this, there exists a need to expand the film representation into a usable linear range, which is discussed next.

Bit Depth and Dynamic Range

Having log data and a CG image with which to composite, the next step is to define the mechanisms to relate the two. In linear space there are several choices. These choices revolve around how big the numbers to be used are. These formats are often referred to by the size of the number being used, for instance, 8 or 16 bit.

The 8-bit format, which has been used historically in CG because of its compact size, stores data between 0 and 255. It does not give a lot of range and does not get used much outside of standard-definition video. Two major problems exist with this space. First, the lack of precision (the low number of values represented) does not allow for a lot of choice in color values. Although using 8 bits for red (R), green (G), and blue (B) provides 256 shades per channel, and 16 million possible colors, problems occur when gradients try to be represented. For example, assume a smooth gray gradient from a dark gray (value 65) to a medium gray (value 125) over 500 pixels is desired. Because 500 pixels can only be covered with 60 possible values,[19] some areas are going to be represented with the same value. This is referred to as *banding* and is a very undesirable artifact. Some modern video formats also allow for 10- and 12-bit linear images, which, although they have a larger range of numbers, still have a more limited dynamic range than is desirable.

---

[19] The values of the colors subtracted from each other: 125 − 65 = 60.

Figure 7.48 An example of banding due to low bit depth. *Left:* A gradient having a large number of values over a large area. *Right:* A small number of values represented over a large area. Having a higher bit depth would help eliminate the banding by allowing more values to be represented. (Image courtesy of Derek Spears.)

Moving up from 8 bits, the 16-bit format provides values between 0 and 65,535. Just by doubling the bit size there is now 256 times more range with which to work. This helps address the banding problem; however, just expanding the log values into this linear space is not the answer. Since most of the image data lies between black and what is perceived as white, it is desirable to have the most precision in this range. From this need to specify a visible range of values comes the concept of a *white point* and *black point*. The white point is the value that is perceived as white. Values much brighter than perceived white can exist. For instance, in a photo, a white sign and the sun may appear to be the same value of white. In reality, the sun is orders of magnitude brighter. Preserving these relative brightness values, or *high dynamic range,* is critical as will be seen later. So with well-defined 16-bit space, there is an allowance for the headroom to store those extra-bright white values.

The Cineon spec is a 10-bit log number, with perceivable black defined as 95 and perceivable white defined to be 685. With 8-bit, there is not much workable space so 95 to 685 *log* is expanded into 0 to 255 *linear.* With 16-bit linear, there is much more precision available, so it becomes easier to preserve those bright overexposed values in the Cineon file. A common mapping is to map 0 to 685 in log space to 0 to 4095 in 16-bit linear for the Cineon log function. Then the values from 689 to 1023 in Cineon (1023 is the maximum value in 10 bit) map to 4096 to 65,535. This mapping is not quite as intuitive as the simple 8-bit mapping, but there is a lot more precision, and the overexposed bright parts of the film are preserved.

To use the example with the sun and the sign, the sign could be represented with a value of 4095 in 16-bit linear, and the sun could have a much brighter value, say, 40,950. This would make the sun 10 times brighter than the white sign. On the monitor, they both would appear bright white. However, if the compositor chose to darken the image, the sign would become less white with the sun staying white—that relationship would be preserved.

So 16 bits gives a workable space with a little manipulation. There is still some loss in precision and although 16 bits seems like a lot, there are still possible issues with banding. The next step up is *floating point*. Instead of calling an arbitrary number such as 4096 white, a more mathematically suitable number such as 1.0 becomes white. Everything brighter than white can be represented by a number greater than 1.0. And since fractional numbers, like 0.986, can be represented, there is virtually unlimited precision to circumvent the banding problem. (In reality, there is a limit to precision, but that limit is reasonably high and unlikely to be reached. For computer representation of fractions, refer to the IEEE floating point standard.)

So, log 0 to 685 values are expanded into 0.0 to 1.0, and 686 to 1023 expands into 1.0 to 13.0. Now this provides a usable linear space with good precision and overexposure capability. Formats can be represented as 16-, 32-, or 64-bit floating point, either having the same or 2× or 4× the storage requirements of a 16-bit integer. However, computation typically needs to happen in at least 32 bits, so the memory footprint used in computation will be higher. However, the benefits in computational precision far outweigh the negatives.

Mattes

Traditionally, when a matte is *pulled*[20] by a keyer, that matte is multiplied against the foreground. The background has the inverse of the matte removed from it, and then the foreground is added. This can be more clearly represented by the following formula:

$$\text{Result} = Fg * (A) + Bg * (1 - A)$$

where *Fg* is the foreground, *Bg* is the background, and *A* is the alpha, or matte.

In CG mattes, the matte can be more appropriately thought of as the percentage coverage of a pixel. Obviously, a jaggy line is not desirable, so in order to antialias the line, the edge pixels have their intensity reduced based on the percentage of the pixel they cover. If the line covers 50% of the pixel, then the pixel brightness is reduced by 50%, or multiplied by 0.5. That percentage of coverage is then stored in the matte. For pixels entirely inside or outside of that line, their coverage values are 1 or 0, respectively. Because that coverage is already multiplied into the edge pixels, CG mattes are referred to as *premultiplied*. This is important because the

[20] The term *pulling a matte* refers to the act of generating a matte from a green or blue screen. This is typically done using a keyer, either a hardware device (as used in live television for placing the maps behind the weatherperson) or an effect in a composite that would generate that matte. Keyers also typically provide services to reduce green/blue spill.

compositing equation is changed accordingly. No longer should the matte be multiplied to the *Fg* CG. It now looks like this:

$$Result = Fg + Bg * (1 - A)$$

This operation is often referred to as an *over*.

The biggest practical side effect of premultiplied images is that a compositor must be very careful when doing color correction. Because the matte is already multiplied in, color corrections not only affect the image but also the relation to the matte as well as the edges and in transparency. If a gamma correction is applied to a CG image, the antialiasing quality at the edges could be adversely affected, and because the CG image is no longer being multiplied (or, more simply, held out) by the matte in the composite, anything done outside the CG image in the black area of the matte will then be added to the entire image (see Figure 7.49).

The solution to these issues is to un-premultiply the image, do the color correction, and then multiply them back together. When an image is un-premultiplied, the areas that are outside (or in the black area) of the mask will usually become strangely colored. Those areas are undefined due to dividing by zero, resulting in random values. The actual values here are not important. When the images are premultiplied back, those areas will get multiplied by zero again and go back to black.

Compositing CG

In the most ideal case, a CG artist lighting a shot would hand a compositor the perfect CG image that just comps directly into the shot, leaving the compositor very little to do. However, in visual effects, as in real life, there are never really any ideal cases. There might be smoke in the shot, or the film might be grainy, or the lighting in the CG might not quite match the shot. All of these problems can be handled in the composite.

CG renders tend to be long and the process not very interactive. Getting iterations of varying light intensities or the color of specular

(A)   (B)   (C)   (D)

Figure 7.49 (A) The CG image to be composited. (B) The CG image composited over a background with no color correction. (C) The same image composited with a color correction respecting premultiplication. Note how the background image is not affected. (D) The same color correction without paying attention to premultiplication. Note how the background image is affected. (Image courtesy of Derek Spears.)

highlights takes long iterations. Computers evolve and become faster, but the problems grow to consume the available resources. So, although in the past it might have taken 1 hour to render a simple CG object, now it takes 1 hour to render a CG object with proper global illumination and ray-traced, motion-blurred reflections. Conversely, compositing is comparatively cheap. It is much easier and faster to explore different lighting levels and looks in the composite than it is in the render. The issue then becomes how to get the right pieces to do it.

Enter multiple lighting layers. While artists can deliver large monolithic CG elements with all of the light, diffuse, and specular values balanced in, there is more recently a trend toward taking care of these balance issues in the composite. This is not to say that multiple-layer lighting is done exclusively throughout the industry, but it is becoming a viable option used in many pipelines.

Each setting in a shader for a CG object that might be adjusted can be broken out into a separate layer. Since the effects of these layers are combined in simple, associative mathematical ways, combining these layers is just as easily done in the composite using the same math. For example, specular or reflective highlights are typically an add operation in the shader, so it is very easy to break out the specular layers as a separate element to the compositor that can be combined with an add node. This can be extended to just about any value that a lighter would control in a shader. Diffuse, specular, reflectivity, and ambient occlusion are just a few layers that are typically broken out.

Lighting is not replaced by this layered approach. There are still many things that need to be taken care of in the lighting setup. Special shading effects that require knowledge about the 3D environment, like refraction, bump/displacement mapping, anisotropic reflection, and light fall-off, will have to be adjusted by the lighter. Shading layers are not the only things broken out. Each individual light or groups of lights are typically broken out as well to give the compositor the ability to rebalance key-to-fill ratios, and alter the light colors in order to more closely match the environment. The ubiquitous gray and chrome spheres are often used against CG render images of those spheres to check those light balances.

All of these layers can give rise to massive organizational problems. Rather than rendering out each of the layers as separate files, modern image formats allow for arbitrary numbers of channels. Whereas artists were once limited to R, G, B, and A in a Cineon image, now TIFF, EXR, and other proprietary image formats allow for all of the rendered lighting layers to be stored in the same file, making all the passes much more portable. This is often referred to as *deep rasters*.

Some rendering options may even be handled more efficiently in the composite. Motion blur tends to be expensive in the render, and invariably, unless the quality settings are turned up high enough, there are artifacts. When those settings are turned up, the render time grows explosively. However, it is possible to closely emulate proper 3D motion blur in the composite, and that typically equates to large savings in render time for small losses in the correctness of the blur.

To use composite-based blur, the render needs to be able to generate a vector for each pixel describing the direction and amount of blur in screen space. This 2D vector can then be used by the compositor within a specialized node to blur the image along the vector in screen space. Although an effective method, problems may arise when a semi-transparent object with motion blur overlies another object. The resulting vectors are then poorly defined because it is hard to associate which object the blur is meant to apply to. The objects could be moving in opposite directions but there is only one set of motion vectors.

Just simply placing a CG object in the scene is not necessarily going to make a convincing shot. Usually a CG creature that is being composited is touching or interacting with an object in the scene. Making that integration work is often what sells the shot. Cast shadows will be provided, as mattes, for the compositor to darken the scene. Care must be taken while darkening the scene with a shadow matte not to darken below the latent shadow value of the scene. Additionally, contact shadows may be provided. Contact shadows are small shadows at the contact points between the CG object and the scene. These provide subtle darkening to aid in grounding the object. Additionally, CG renders are often too sharp, making it necessary for the compositor to mimic the natural softness of the photographed plate. Even in fully CG shots, it is worthwhile to add some blur to better match surrounding live-action footage.

One of the key areas for making CG imagery fit into existing photography is matching black levels. Atmospheric haze and smoke are just some of the plate considerations the compositor will have to deal with. Responsibility lands on the compositor to lift, or lower, the blacks of the CG element to match the blacks of the scene. Often, photographic elements will have a color cast in the blacks that needs to be matched as well.

Perceptually, it is hard to judge the accuracy of these black level matches when they are dark, so a common compositing technique is to view the final composite at different brightness and gamma levels to ensure the black levels track. Although black levels are important, that does not make white levels unimportant. When a shot is worked on in the composite, a choice has to be made before the shot is started about what the color grading will be. This does not mean that this is where it is going to land when it is balanced for the film. The shot could be printed brighter, darker, contrast added or removed, and/or be pushed into a completely different color. If that shot is printed darker, it is going to uncover white level mismatches. For example, if the CG artist has created a CG car at night with headlights, and those headlights are only at a value of 1.2, while real headlights in the scene are at a value of 3.0, the shot will look fine in dailies or on the monitor—because of the limited dynamic range of these display devices, both of those values might appear to be white—but when the colorist prints the shot down two stops, what appeared to be a white headlight is going to appear gray. It is important to pull the final composite down in brightness to check (and measure) the highs, not just the darks. Along the same line of thinking, while the shot is pulled brighter and darker, moving the shot around in color can also be a good check to ensure the CG in the shot tracks correctly through other possible grading choices.

Live-action photography also has grain or noise. Compositing formulas exist that model the exact structure of film grain via mathematical and statistical functions. More empirical methods involve scanning different exposed film stocks to use to comp in film grain. Grain is defined by both size and density and this varies with each color channel, especially in film. In film, three layers of color-sensitive dyes are sandwiched together, red being at the front, green in the middle, and blue at the back. Since light has to pass through the other two layers to reach the blue record, it needs to have larger grain structure to compensate for less light reaching it. Although digitally acquired images have no film grain per se, there will still be some noise present in the sensor that needs to be matched. The amount of grain may change with the exposure. Underexposed areas have more prominent grain structure than overexposed areas. So it is important, when grain matching, to look not only at each individual channel, but to look at different areas of brightness. Whatever grain addition method is chosen, it should not be constant. It also needs to vary from frame to frame.

With CG images, the compositor has the luxury of much more information per pixel than just color or matte. Depth information may also be rendered, giving the compositor the ability to perform depth compositing. A typical encoding scheme might be 0 (black) for objects at the camera plane and 1 (white) for objects at maximum distance. With integer numbers, near and far distances need to be defined at render time. With floating point, the far distance can effectively be infinity (with expected loss of precision at great distances). Using these depth values, it is then possible to accurately composite CG objects in correct depth relation to each other.

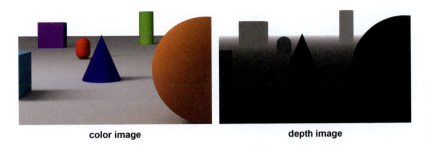

color image   depth image

Figure 7.50 Example of a depth image (*right*) corresponding to a rendered CG image (*left*). (Image courtesy of Derek Spears.)

Depth compositing is not without problems. Motion blur and antialiasing are two particular cases in which depth compositing has problems. In the case of antialiasing, unlike a matte, a depth matte represents distance from camera, not coverage. If an artist attempts to antialias a depth matte, the result will change depth values at the edges. Different depth values will then be introduced at these edges, creating depth inconsistencies. Likewise, motion blur may cause similar problems.

2.5D Compositing

Increasingly, elements in a scene are created with something referred to as *two-and-a-half-D* (2.5D). This 2.5D is used to create the appearance of a complex 3D environment with a much simpler and faster 2D toolset. Currently, most modern compositing packages include 3D tools. Cameras, as well as lights, can be defined and introduced in the compositing package. Simple geometry may be either imported or built. Even animation data can be brought in, such as the tracked CG camera for a shot. With these tools it is possible to create backgrounds and other effects within the compositing environment.

One of the most common uses of 2.5D is for projected matte paintings. Instead of modeling a highly detailed scene, a simple model of the scene is created that represents the outline and basic relief. This geometry is typically very low in resolution—on the order of a few hundred polygons. Instead of texturing and developing shaders, a matte painter would then paint a fully rendered environment onto this scene. All light and shading information is painted into this image—no actual CG lighting takes place. The matte painter's image will then be projected from the CG camera onto the modeled terrain. Given the low poly count and the power of modern graphics cards, this setup can be previewed in real time in the compositing package. Often cracks will be revealed as the background moves, uncovering areas unseen by the camera projection. The matte painter will go back in and fill those gaps so that they may be re-projected onto the painting from another camera position. Because the terrain has been modeled with relief, the image exhibits parallax, giving the appearance of a complex 3D surface. Minute detail is not modeled, because the viewer is provided with enough detail in the texture to believe the result.

Using the same tools it is also possible to take an existing plate and create a new move on it. Using a simple model of the terrain again and a 3D track of the camera, the original photography can be projected onto the geometry. That image will now appear to be locked to the geometry as if it were a still texture just like the matte painting example above.

For moving footage, instead of a static image, the sequence is projected from the moving camera per frame from the camera track. Once projected the artist can create a new camera with an entirely new move. If the new move is significantly different from the original plate, unprojected areas in the geometry may be uncovered. Just as above, a matte painter can go in and fill those areas with detail because the projected texture is locked to the geometry. Still plates can be given full 3D camera moves, and existing moves can be changed. The uses for 2.5D continue to grow because it is becoming a common method for constructing digital backgrounds.

CROWD GENERATION AND SIMULATION TECHNIQUES
John Knoll

Live-Action Replication

The earliest and simplest technique for generating large crowds with a limited number of extras is to shoot multiple passes with the group moved about to fill the needed area. The separate plates can then be composited to create the illusion of a larger crowd. For example, this technique was used to assemble the large crowd around the Washington Mall in *Forrest Gump* (1994).

This technique is easiest to execute when the camera is stationary and motion is limited to pan/tilt; it becomes progressively more difficult as additional axes of motion are added. Particularly complicated multiple-axis camera moves may require motion control to repeat moves, especially where unambiguous perspective cues are present.

Usually groups of extras are arranged to minimize visual overlap per pass to reduce the matting complexity in the composite, especially if it is not practical to use process screens to provide an extractable edge. For example, it is usually a much easier compositing task to arrange extras in left, middle, and right groups as opposed to foreground, midground, and background groups.

Sprites

Another technique is to photograph smaller groups of extras in front of a process screen (or computer animate the extras, for that matter) and then use them to texture cards that are distributed throughout a scene with time offsets. This is inexpensive to create and render but limits camera motion. Such a system was used for cheering crowds in the Pod Race arena in *Star Wars Episode One: The Phantom Menace* (1999).

Computer-Generated Crowds

With the advent of commercial software tools like Massive,[21] it has become increasingly popular to create large crowds using computer graphics. Computer-generated crowds offer numerous advantages over comping together groups of live-action extras:
- Crowd size is unlimited (to a large extent).
- Plate photography can proceed more quickly because it is not necessary to shoot multiple plates or coordinate and move groups of extras.
- Behavior can be more complex and free because it is not necessary for one to police layering issues at the boundaries of the groups.
- Camera motion is not limited in any way.
- Anything that can be represented with computer graphics can be part of the crowd, such as alien creatures or a herd of elephants.
- Action can include events that are extremely dangerous or impractical to shoot.

Modeling for Replication

When building characters for computer-generated crowds, it is not practical to build each member of the crowd individually. A small finite number of individual models are usually built with some mechanism to generate variations of each. In this way one can populate an entire crowd with a limited number of specific models and variations of those models.

Variation

To minimize the number of unique models to be constructed, it is usually a good idea to have a method for creating variations of

[21] Please refer to the Massive Software website for more information (www.massivesoftware.com).

each to provide sufficient visual diversity to the crowd. Four primary techniques are typically used to create variations:

- Shader parameters such as brightness, hue, etc., may be randomly varied per individual.
- Characters can be modeled with multiple wardrobe and prop types, such as different coats and hats, for example. These props and multiple wardrobes may be turned off and on in combination to make a large number of individuals.
- A number of different textures may be prepared per model to give them different looks.
- Different body types (fat, thin, long/short torso, etc.) may be sculpted onto the same base mesh as vertex position deltas or *morph maps*. These can be dialed in randomly per individual. Simple scale variation is also often employed to provide additional individuality.

Mesh Density

Because a large number of instances of each model will have to be processed to make each resulting frame, it is important to keep the geometric complexity of the source models as low as is practical. Some systems alleviate this issue by automatically switching between multiple levels of model complexity based on screen size. This means that very lightweight (and fast to process and render) models are used in the far distance, and more detailed models are used closer to the camera where that detail is needed because it will be visible to the audience.

Animation Cycles for Replication

Most crowd control systems require the characters to have a library of predefined animations to cover their expected behaviors. Exceptions to this are where simple parametric biped and quadruped locomotion models are sufficient.

An effective but limited method to provide motion complexity in a crowd is to have one or more long motion cycles that can be applied to each character with random time offsets.

A much more flexible but complex method involves having a library of different motion types (running, walking, fighting, etc.) and a mechanism to make transitions between them. The ability to assemble strings of motion in nearly arbitrary order (usually called a *motion graph*) allows characters to be directed to respond appropriately to their surroundings and is very powerful when coupled with an artificial intelligence system.

Motion Capture

Because humans or domesticated animals are the most common members of computer-generated crowds, the most direct method to create sufficient realistic motion is via motion capture. (Please refer to Chapter 4 for more information about motion capture.)

Keyframe Animation

When the characters, vehicles, or objects that make up the crowd are inconvenient or impossible to motion capture, traditional keyframe[22] animation can be provided.

Dynamic Motion Synthesis

Endorphin[23] is an example of a system with an understanding of biped locomotion and ranges of motion that can generate realistic movement without example input. Its built-in physics model allows it to realistically simulate dangerous stunts like long falls or tripping down stairs. Endorphin also is able to mix synthetic motion with motion capture or keyframe animation, allowing users to begin with provided motion and then transition into simulation.

Behaviors and Crowd Control

A crowd control system manages the size and behavior of a generated crowd. Two methods are commonly employed to do this, particles and artificial intelligence.

Particles

Members of a crowd can be treated as particles. In its simplest form, particles are generated across a surface and are used to instance model variations driven by random time offsets in long animation cycles. Such a system was employed to create background battle action in the Droid/Gunga battle at the end of *Star Wars Episode One: The Phantom Menace* (1999).

---

[22] Keyframe animation utilizes a *key frame,* that is, a drawing that defines the starting and ending points of any smooth transition. They are called *frames* because their position in time is measured in frames on a strip of film. A sequence of key frames defines *which* movement the spectator will see, whereas the position of the key frames on the film, video, or animation defines the timing of the movement. Because only two or three key frames over the span of a second do not create the illusion of movement, the remaining frames are filled with inbetweens (Wikipedia, http://en.wikipedia.org/wiki/Key_frame).
[23] An animation tool from NaturalMotion Ltd.

A slightly more complex and flexible version of this is to have a particle system directly control the positions and movements of the characters. The particles have rules to constrain their motion, for example, avoid collisions with barriers or other characters or move away from repellers and toward attractors. Appropriate offsets into animation cycles are chosen based on the particle's position along a path. Such a system was employed to generate crowds gathering before and dispersing after the Pod Race in *Star Wars Episode One: The Phantom Menace* (1999), as well as in the Geonosis Arena in *Star Wars Episode Two: Attack of the Clones* (2002).

Artificial Intelligence

A more powerful system employed by Massive is to have an artificial intelligence (AI) system control the behavior of the crowd. Massive users construct a "brain"—basically a parametric behavior decision tree that controls how characters respond to their surroundings and other characters. The brain then drives a motion graph to calculate detailed character motion. This system was developed for the battle scenes in the *Lord of the Rings* trilogy (2001–2003) and has been commercialized to great success. Massive-generated crowds can be seen in numerous films and television shows.

Note that live-action photographed crowds and computer-generated crowds can be, and often are, used in combination to improve realism. Usually live-action photography is used in the foreground with computer-generated characters added to create background action.

CG PROSTHETICS AND ACTOR ENHANCEMENTS
John Knoll

It has become increasingly common in recent years to employ digital techniques to create effects that change the look of an actor that in previous years was solely the province of makeup. These techniques are employed where makeup is insufficient or incapable of the task. Some examples of this might be the removal of limbs on a wounded soldier or adding an effect to a creature to allow it to change or grow during a shot. The "Two Face" effect in *The Dark Knight* (2008) is a particularly good example because the effect creates negative spaces—subtracting from the actor's face—to create a burned away appearance. Makeup can only be additive by its nature.

Examples where a director chose to use visual effects rather than rely on traditional makeup include *Gran Torino* (2008), where a teardrop was added to an actor, and *Invictus* (2009), where the ability to precisely control the bruising on the players could be done in post. This reduced some of the set time but more importantly allowed the order of shots to change in editorial and permitted the director of both movies, Clint Eastwood, to precisely determine the amount required for telling the story.

On-Set Tracking and Capture Considerations

Tracking and lighting are the two most important areas to focus on when shooting material that will receive this treatment. Relatively minor investments in gathering good data on set can vastly reduce the effort, and therefore the cost, required to get good results in post.

Eye Enhancements

The use of contacts lenses to change the color of an actor's eyes or to completely change the look of the eyes is a common makeup approach. However, with the advent of advanced digital tracking, productions may choose to do these as visual effects to avoid issues for the actors, especially the full-eye contacts that can be troublesome to wear. A color change requires isolation of the area and a selection of the existing iris color. A full eye replacement is more complicated and requires tracking a 3D CG eye and rotoscoping for the eyelids.

3D Techniques

As in any 3D work, the camera position(s) must be known, and the usual set survey and matchmoving techniques apply here.

All 3D enhancement techniques require deriving a model of the surface in question, which could be deforming during the shot, as a first step. If the subject to be tracked does not already possess satisfactory trackable detail, additional tracking marks should be added sufficient to the task. For enhancements that are fixed to the skull, common tracking spots are the cheekbones, forehead, nose, and ears. Deforming surfaces such as the area around an actor's mouth are especially difficult and require additional marks. A minimum of three reference points always need to be visible to provide a 3D plane to work with. Due to the complexity of body parts and deformations, multiple points may be required to lock on with the accuracy required.

If tracking markers are not available, then the shot may require tracking of any specific natural features as well as a certain amount of manual tracking. Having a 3D scan of the real body part certainly makes this easier.

Additional views of the subject from one or more witness cameras[24] can be immensely helpful in improving the accuracy of the solution by further constraining the position of points through triangulation. A sync relationship between the taking camera and the witness cameras must be known, and the witness camera footage is easiest to use if the frame rates and shutter open times are synchronized. This is not a strict requirement since frame rate and shutter phase adjustments can be made using optical flow retiming tools if necessary, and unsynched witness cameras are better than none at all.

Because these CG enhancements are often blended with the original photography, the lighting match must be as accurate as possible. Image-based lighting techniques are useful here because of their ability to faithfully reproduce complex light fields with relatively little effort. Good texture reference of the skin to be matched is also very helpful. Images that show diffuse color should include a gray card for calibration. Images that show the specular reflectivity and bump level will help when it comes time to texture the CG asset.

2D Techniques

Cosmetic Wrinkle and Blemish Removal

Cosmetic skin cleanup, such as the removal of acne blemishes, wrinkles, or tattoos, while usually faster and somewhat less expensive to handle on set with makeup, has become a common part of post-production. These removals generally do not require special on-set consideration. They are done in the 2D realm and are handled much the same way as other wire and rig removals:

- An offset brush clones nearby texture to hide the artifact.
- A matte is produced of the offending area, and a procedural fill tool blends across it.
- A still-painted patch is made and tracked over the offending area.

One company that specializes in this type of work is Lola Visual Effects where they have developed special wrinkle removal tools.

2.5D Techniques

Optical flow techniques can be used to make painted artwork track to a performer even when the performer is moving in complex ways, such as while an actor is talking, for example.

---

[24]Witness camera: video camera used to record the same scene from a slightly different position or angle. See more details in the *On-Set Animation Capture: Witness Cam* section in Chapter 3.

Silhouette Changes

Geometric distortion tools can be used to alter the silhouette of a performer or change the proportions of different parts of a body or face. These techniques have been used for years in advertising with still photos and are now being applied to running footage for similar reasons. Recent commercials have featured enlarged heads on bodies as well as enlarged eyes where only a portion of the original image is scaled. In *Star Wars Episode One: The Phantom Menace* (1999), a key shot is when the Sith kicks one of the Jedi off a platform. Because this stunt kick did not make physical contact, the image of the foot was distorted and manipulated to make the visual connection it required.

Re-Projection

3D techniques can help to provide stable coordinate systems for animation. For example, a 3D model of a performer can be matchmoved to follow a performance, the photographed plate can then be projected onto the matched model, and shape changes can be applied to the model. This technique produces results that have a closer match to the correct perspective than a simple 2D method and create a more convincing result.

3D PRODUCTS, SYSTEMS, AND SOFTWARE
Richard Kidd

Digital Element Creation Process

In the early days of digital visual effects, most computer programs used were proprietary software that had been developed in house. Although visual effects studios still use proprietary software for specialized tasks, most of these studios also use off-the-shelf software for general 3D work, including modeling, rigging, texturing, animation, lighting, and rendering. To see how these tasks fall into place in the post-production workflow, see Figure 7.51. The process and workflows mentioned in the following paragraphs are also discussed in greater detail in other chapters of this handbook. Please consult the contents for the specific chapters.

A 3D computer model is a mathematical representation of any 3D object. The 3D software used varies from studio to studio, depending on their operating system platform and pipeline. The major 3D graphics software packages used in visual effects are discussed in the next subsection.

Rigging is the process that replicates a skeletal system for the purposes of animating. Rigging is used primarily with 3D character models but may be used in noncharacter models.

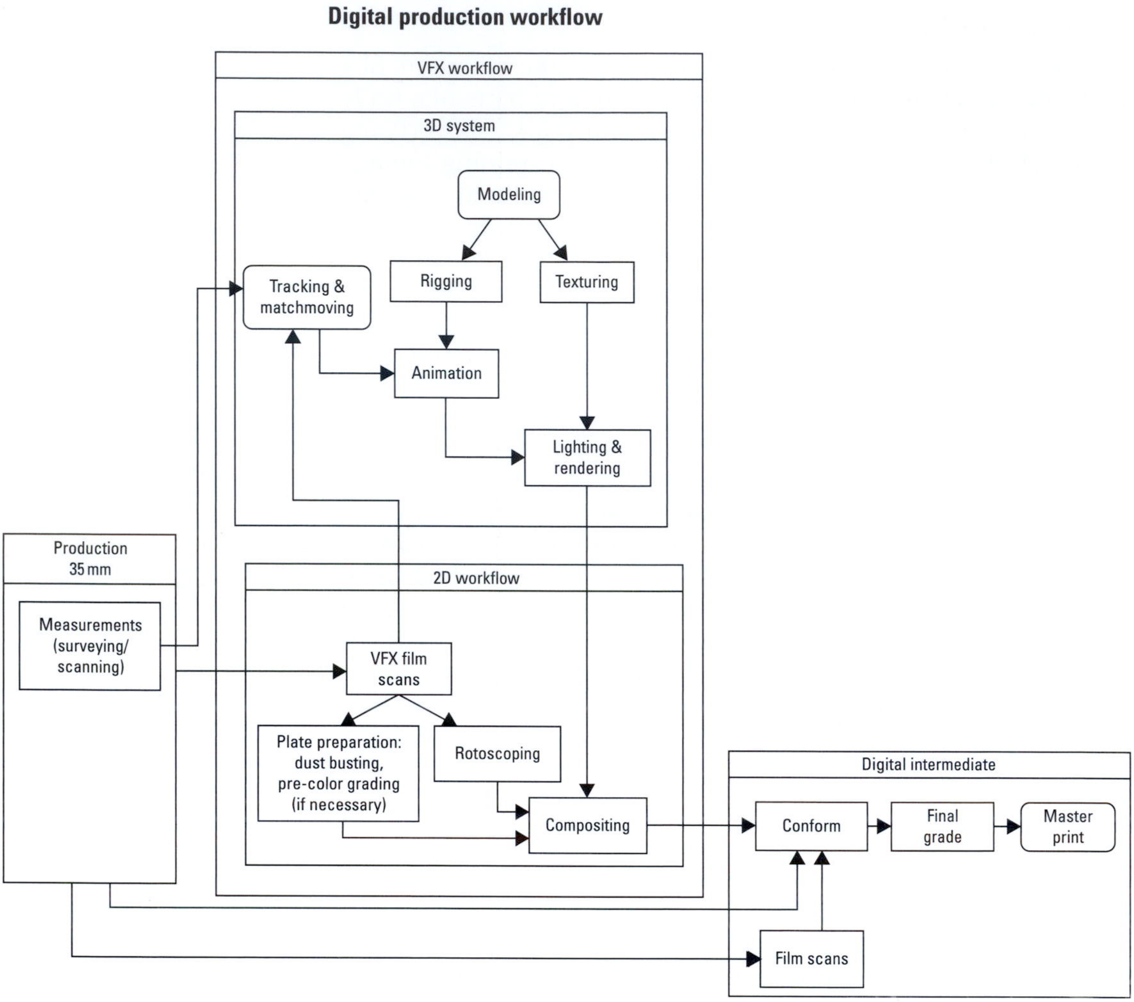

Digital production workflow

Figure 7.51 An overview of the digital production workflow. (Image courtesy of Richard Kidd.)

While the rigging process is under way, textures are created in a 2D paint and editing application, such as Adobe Photoshop. These textures are then applied to the 3D model within the 3D graphics software using UV coordinates or projection methods.

The next process is to animate the 3D computer model if necessary. Animation describes how a 3D object moves through space and/or deforms over a period of time. Various methods can be used to animate a 3D computer model including keyframing, inverse or forward kinematics, motion capture, and simulations. Several of these techniques can be used in combination with one another.

Lighting in 3D graphics software follows the same principles of real-world lighting. It helps to emphasize or highlight objects in a scene or may be used to push them back with the use of shadows created by the lights. Likewise, lights can be used to convey a certain mood or evoke an emotion or intended response from the viewer.

Once the lighting process is complete, the 3D objects that make up a scene are rendered. Rendering refers to generating a 2D image from the 3D objects that have been created within the 3D graphics software. The rendering, or drawing of the 2D image, is done with a renderer that is included with the 3D graphics software, like Maya's Software Renderer, or through a stand-alone renderer like Pixar's Renderman. When creating the 2D image the renderer takes into account the textures, lights, and relative position to other objects. Rendering is usually done in layers, also called *passes*, in order to be manipulated in the compositing stage.

3D Graphics Software

As the visual effects industry has grown and matured, so have the 3D packages in use today. The current versions of 3D software are the result of many revisions and updates and in some cases of mergers and acquisitions of companies that blended together multiple 3D packages. The packages discussed next are the ones used most often in today's 3D workflow.

Houdini

Houdini, version 10 at the time of this writing (early 2010), is a 3D graphics software package with a node-based workflow for modeling, texturing, animation, character rigging, lighting, and particles. This graphics software also includes the ability to perform dynamics simulations such as fluid, rigid-body, wire, and cloth simulations. Rendering is supported through the internal renderer, Mantra, as well as support for third-party rendering. Houdini also provides built-in compositing and Python scripting support.

Although used in all applications of 3D, including character animation, Houdini is best known for its procedural systems. It excels at procedural-based modeling, particle systems, and dynamics. It also gives free unlimited Renderman-compliant rendering through its Mantra renderer.

Houdini is available in noncommercial and commercial versions. The noncommercial versions are Houdini Apprentice and Houdini Apprentice HD. Both of these noncommercial versions have all of the features available in the full commercial version but with minor limitations including a noncommercial file format and maximum resolution limitations. Houdini Apprentice has a max render resolution of 720×576. Meanwhile Houdini Apprentice HD has a max render resolution of 1920×1080.

Additionally, Houdini Apprentice has a small watermark while Houdini Apprentice HD does not.

The commercial versions of Houdini are Escape and Master. Houdini Escape features modeling, animation, character, lighting, rendering, compositing, scripting, and third-party rendering and has no limitation on rendering resolution. Houdini Master includes all of the features found in Houdini Escape but also includes particles, fluid dynamics, rigid-body dynamics, cloth dynamics, and wire dynamics and has no limitation on rendering resolution.

Maya

Autodesk Maya started off as a combination of three different 3D software packages used in the early 1990s. It is now considered one of the top 3D modeling, animation, and rendering packages used in the digital industry today.

At the time of this writing, the current version of the 3D software package is Autodesk Maya 2010 (which coincidently is the first release to unify the Maya Complete and Maya Unlimited versions from previous years). Maya 2010 includes traditional modeling, rigging, animation, texturing, lighting, and rendering modules. It also includes the Maya Nucleus dynamic simulation framework, which includes two fully integrated Nucleus modules: Maya nCloth and Maya nParticles. In addition, the graphics software features Maya Fluid Effects, Maya Hair, and Maya Fur. This version also brings Maya Composite, advanced matchmoving capabilities, five additional Mental Ray for Maya batch-rendering nodes, and a software network render queue manager.

Maya's strengths lie in its advanced modeling tools and customization. The intuitive polygon workflow includes a host of selection and editing tools. Furthermore, the ability to transfer polygon attributes from one mesh to another, regardless of their separation in space or size differences, gives computer modelers extra flexibility. Another reason Maya is widely used is its ability to be customized. This has made it easier for companies to tailor the software for their specific needs and internal proprietary pipeline.

Softimage

Softimage Creative Environment was developed by Softimage Corporation and released for Silicon Graphics workstations at SIGGRAPH in 1988. At that time it was fast and highly regarded for its animation capabilities and was first used for advanced character animation.

In the past decade Softimage was being developed by Softimage, Co., a subsidiary of Avid technology, and was known as

Softimage|XSI. At the end of 2008 Autodesk acquired the Softimage brand and 3D animation assets from Avid. Soon after, Softimage|XSI was rebranded as Autodesk Softimage.

Softimage is currently available as Autodesk Softimage 2010. This 3D software package includes modules for 3D modeling, animation, rendering, and compositing. Softimage made its mark as an animation tool, and today still offers very strong animation capabilities. Animators have access to the following tools: Animation Mixer, Animation Layering, Audio Syncing tools, F-Curve editor, Dopesheet, Shape Manager, and Motor. The animation layering, for example, allows animators to interactively, and nondestructively, add key frames on top of existing key frames. Furthermore, Softimage's F-Curve editor is a powerful tool that allows animators to edit high-density curves from motion capture data using a simplified sculpting tool. The Face Robot toolset, a solution for rigging and animating 3D facial expressions quickly and easily, is also now available.

Softimage is also available as Autodesk Softimage Advanced 2010. This version has all of the features mentioned above but also includes five Softimage batch-rendering licenses and crowd simulation software called Softimage Behavior.

Autodesk Softimage incorporates a node-based workflow called ICE (Interactive Creative Environment), which is an open platform that allows the artist to extend the capabilities of Softimage quickly.

3D Studio Max

3D Studio Max is a full-fledged 3D graphics program that includes tools for 3D modeling, texturing, rigging, animation, and rendering. Historically, 3D Studio Max has been used extensively for video game development. It has a long history of being developed for the Microsoft Windows platform and is currently available only for Windows operating systems. It is now known as Autodesk 3ds Max, and the current version is Autodesk 3ds Max 2010. This 3D package is also used for television, film, web, and multimedia work.

New features in Autodesk 3ds Max 2010 include PFlow Advanced, a Graphite Modeling toolset, Containers, and xView Mesh Analyzer. The PFlow Advanced feature is a particle flow toolkit that builds additional functionality into the previous version. The Graphite Modeling toolset allows modelers to create models quickly with 100 new advanced polygonal modeling and freeform design tools. Containers allow users to collect multiple objects in a complex scene into a single container to be treated as a single element. Another new feature, xView Mesh Analyzer, allows users to view meshes for common errors such as overlapping UVs, duplicate faces, and isolated vertices.

3D Tracking

In the early days of visual effects, most 3D camera tracking was done by eye using manual techniques. As time went on tracking software applications were developed in house at various visual effects facilities. As digital visual effects grew, commercial applications began to be sold. 3D Equalizer was one of the early tracking packages to be widely used in visual effects. Additionally MatchMover Pro was extensively used but was acquired by Autodesk and is now a part of Maya 2010. Today the primary tracking packages are Syntheyes, Boujou, and PFTrack.

Syntheyes

Syntheyes is matchmoving software, developed by Russ Andersson, that made its commercial debut in late 2003. It offered features such as object tracking, lens distortion handling, and light solving. Its early success came not only because of its production-ready toolset but because its price was significantly lower than that of the competition and accessible to freelancers and small and large visual effects facilities.

Since its initial release Syntheyes has had a number of major re-releases, each time adding novel features such as mesh building (2005), special greenscreen analysis (2006), 3D stabilization (2007), and camera holds (2008).

One of Syntheyes' strengths is that it has always been a technical leader. It has been available on 64-bit platforms starting since 2005. Furthermore, multithread and core support has been incorporated in Syntheyes for years as an aid to performance, as has the utilization of CPU features such as MMX and SSE2. The main advantage to moving to full 64-bit operation is the ability to address more than 4 GB of RAM. This enables the artist to store longer HD and film shots with the ability to see tracking data over the clip playing in RAM-based playback.

Syntheyes allows users to create their own customized scripts for exporting that allow the user to export to approximately 25 different industry applications.

Boujou

The primary product of the company, 2d3 Ltd., Boujou, is used by many film and video post-production companies to generate 3D tracking data used in the creation of visual effects.

Boujou's process involves calibrating the camera's internal parameters, such as focal length and film back dimensions, as well as its motion in 3D space. The algorithm that drives Boujou looks at hundreds, if not thousands, of distinctive points that appear in areas of high contrast or high texture. Tracking the motion of these feature points in two dimensions through a sequence of images allows their 2D trajectories to be computed.

The resulting structure, or point cloud, generated from the tracked features enables the 3D movement of the camera to be inferred. The quality of the camera solution is dependent on the quality of the 2D feature tracks it uses in the calibration process. One should also note that the points that are tracked within the image sequence are identified through intensity and not color. Therefore, this algorithm applies to sequences of color, mono-chrome, and thermal imagery.

PFTrack

PFTrack, developed by the Pixel Farm, is a comprehensive image analysis tool with both camera reconstruction and object track-ing. PFTrack, in addition to camera tracking, may also be used for image-based modeling and automatic Z-depth extraction. PFTrack version 5 is the ninth major version and now supports stereo cameras.

Reference frames may also be loaded to assist with tracking difficult shots. Camera focal length information may be imported via a simple XML data format, and depth and optical flow data can be exported as OpenEXR image sequences.

Other GUI improvements include better access to feature tracking buttons, additional feature-track filtering tools, and improvements to the F-Curve editing tools. Integrated Z-depth extraction tools assign depth data to sequences for exporting as a gray map. The program is now fully 64 bit on all platforms includ-ing PC, Linux, Mac-Intel, and PowerPC.

Special Effects

Within the 3D workflow it is sometimes necessary to create cer-tain 3D effects that require specialized effects software products. These include Massive, Mental Ray, Photorealistic Renderman, Photoshop, BodyPaint 3D, and Enzo 3D Paint, among others.

Massive

Massive is a stand-alone 3D package specifically developed to gen-erate crowd simulations. It was originally developed by Stephen Regelous in Wellington, New Zealand, to be used on Peter Jackson's *Lord of the Rings* trilogy (2001–2003).

Massive Prime is used for authoring, directing, and rendering custom autonomous agents for animation and visual effects. It is made up of a node-based interface and allows artists to inter-actively create AI-enabled agents. An agent is simply a 3D char-acter brought into Massive, which gives a performance based on control key frames or motion capture clips, called *actions*. It includes tools for agent authoring, scene setup, agent control and direction, agent technology, rendering, and integration. The agent authoring is done through a brain editor, which is a node-based interface that allows an artist to interactively create an AI-enabled agent without programming.

Massive Prime also integrates with Maya by allowing an artist to import skeletons and motion. It has the ability to import XSI skeletons and motion and be customized through code using the C/C++ API as well as Python scripting.

Massive Jet is a streamlined version of Massive Prime. Massive Jet is designed to make AI-driven animation available to less technical animation and visual effects professionals.

Additionally, prebuilt *ready-to-run agents* are available for purchase. These agents have performances built into their AI and simply need to be added to the scene and tweaked accordingly. Available agents include Locomotion Agent, Stadium Agent, Ambient Agent, Mayhem Agent, and Combat Sword Agent.

Massive Software provides an educational package, called Learning Massive Software, which is an education bundle that includes 10 licenses of Massive Prime; 12 months of upgrades and support; the educational versions of Ambient, Locomotion, and Stadium Agents; and comprehensive courseware.

Rendering

Once the modeling, animation, texturing, and lighting are done, a 2D image is generated from the 3D scene. This process is called *rendering*. The rendering process is performed by a renderer, which is either a module in the 3D graphics program or a stand-alone application designed to generate the 2D images. The renderer calculates a 2D image using a certain type of algorithm, or procedure (i.e., ray tracing, radiosity, etc.). Two of the most widely used renderers in the digital industry are discussed next.

Mental Ray

Mental Ray is a production-quality rendering application developed by Mental Images in Berlin, Germany, and is available both as an integrated render engine for Maya and SoftImage, as well as a stand-alone render engine.

As the name implies, it supports ray tracing to generate images. Ray tracing mimics the natural flow of light rays. This is done by tracing the path of the light ray from the camera back to the light source. Mental Ray's feature set is comparable to that of Photorealistic Renderman. Global illumination was a feature found in Mental Ray long before it was implemented in Renderman. Global illumination takes into account all illumination, both indirect and direct, that occurs in a 3D scene. Nvidia acquired Mental Images in December 2007.

Some notable films that have used Mental Ray are *Hulk* (2003), *The Day After Tomorrow* (2004), and *Poseidon* (2006).

Photorealistic Renderman

Photorealistic Renderman, or PRMan for short, is a proprietary photorealistic renderer that primarily uses the REYES algorithm but is also capable of doing ray tracing and global illumination. Loren Carpenter and Robert Cook at Lucasfilm's Computer Graphics Research Group developed the REYES rendering algorithm in the mid-1980s. It was first used in 1982 to render images for the Genesis effect sequence in the feature film *Star Trek II: The Wrath of Khan* (1982). REYES is an acronym that stands for Renders Everything You Ever Saw. This algorithm was designed with a number to handle complex and diverse models, handle complex shaders, make use of minimal ray tracing so as to have fast speeds, and have unsurpassed image quality and flexibility for customization.

REYES achieves several effects that are deemed necessary for feature-film-quality rendering: smooth curved surfaces, surface texturing, motion blur, and depth of field.

PRMan is used to render all of Pixar Animation Studios' in-house 3D animated movies. It is available as a commercial product as part of a bundle called Renderman Pro Server. In addition, Renderman for Maya is a full version of PRMan that is designed to be completely integrated with Maya 3D graphics software.

Texturing

In 3D workflow, it is necessary to apply textures to the 3D models in order to render a production-ready asset. This texture application is done in the 3D package. However, before a texture can be applied, it must be created. The primary program used in the creation of textures is Adobe Photoshop. Two other specialty pieces of software that allow for the creation of textures and their application in one step are BodyPaint 3D and Enzo 3D Paint.

Photoshop

Adobe Photoshop is 2D image-editing software that is used throughout various stages of post-production and was developed by John and Thomas Knoll.

Artists can use Adobe Photoshop to create 2D imagery from scratch using a combination of paintbrushes and filters. Artists can also create imagery by editing existing images or photographs to create textures that will be applied to the surface of a 3D computer model within the 3D graphics software. The 3D computer models are then lit and rendered.

BodyPaint 3D

Maxon's BodyPaint 3D software is texture creation software. It differs from other texture creation software because it allows artists to paint detailed textures directly onto 3D computer models. Similar to Adobe Photoshop, it has a workflow that contains layers, filters, and tablet support. With the included renderer, called RayBrush, artists can view the result of their texture painting in real time as a rendered image.

In addition, this software package has traditional UV editing tools normally found inside 3D software packages. For example, there are three automatic UV unwrapping algorithms to help in painting across seams. The software includes free plugins to exchange models and textures with popular 3D software packages.

Enzo 3D Paint

Enzo 3D Paint, by Electric Iris, is a paint system that is fully integrated into Adobe Photoshop. Enzo is not a stand-alone software package, but rather a set of plug-ins that turns Adobe Photoshop into a 3D paint program. Similar to BodyPaint 3D, artists can move around in a 3D viewer and paint textures directly on a 3D computer model. The user can also paint a flat traditional 2D texture if they choose. The workflow allows for 2D and 3D layers.

8

INTERACTIVE GAMES

FILMS VERSUS GAMES
Habib Zargarpour

In a very short time the games industry has become as big as the film industry in terms of revenue, and many people are transitioning from working in one industry to the other. There have been numerous discussions about the convergence of films and games but it is important to understand what the differences are and what they have in common. Understanding these differences and commonalities can help the transition from one to the other. There are many types of games and for the most part in this section third-person and first-person games will be compared with films, though many of the same points also apply to other types of games.

Basic Differences

The most important difference between films and games is that, in games, the viewer clearly controls the camera and/or its movement. A theatrical film is linear and is watched passively; the viewer does not have control of its progression (except for simple linear operations like pause and rewind). Games are generally nonlinear, meaning that they will be slightly different every time. Even games that have linear levels can be different each time because of the freedom of movement the viewer/player has and the accumulation of all of the random factors, such as artificial intelligence (AI)-driven character movements or other players' actions. Films are more predictable to make because the various steps of creation, from script to storyboard to previs to final shot process for the entire film, will end up as expected—in general. Games have so many unknowns and variables that typically the final result is quite different from the original concept. Everything is refined to enhance the fun factor and is in a constant state of flux and fine-tuning until the very last second.

The VES Handbook of Visual Effects. DOI: 10.1016/B978-0-240-81242-7.00008-9

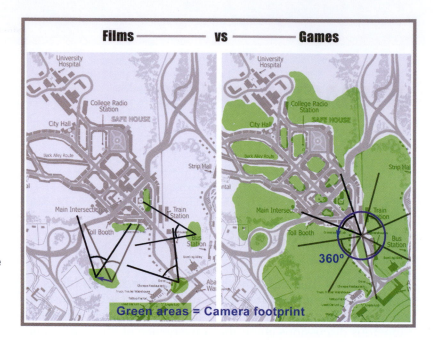

Figure 8.1 Diagram showing the controlled and limited film camera views of an environment (*left*), compared with the free-roaming camera in a game (*right*). Green areas represent where the camera can be placed. (Image courtesy of Habib Zargarpour.)

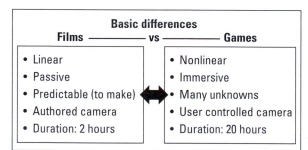

Figure 8.2 A simple chart showing the basic differences between the two media. (Image courtesy of Habib Zargarpour.)

The duration is also another difference; whereas an average film is 1.5 hours long, the average game can provide 20 hours of entertainment if played until the end. It is not uncommon to have some games take as long as 40 to 60 hours to complete.

Most Important Aspect

The core of a good film is a good script.[1] Everything else follows from that. Without a strong script as the foundation, it is very difficult to produce a viable movie; hence, it is the most important aspect of a film. The most important aspect of a game is the gameplay. This is the most pertinent distinction between the two media. The gameplay is what is done within the game and it is the key to advancement: shooting bad guys, solving puzzles, traversing mazes, etc. If this gameplay, sometimes referred to as the *core mechanics* of the game, is not enjoyable, then the game is doomed to fail. All other aspects such as the main story or premise, the character designs, the environment, and the look of the game are incidental to this core and will need to be designed to support it. Early rough prototyping is a good way to determine if the gameplay is fun cost effectively.

[1] A good script in this context is described as a good story as detailed by the script.

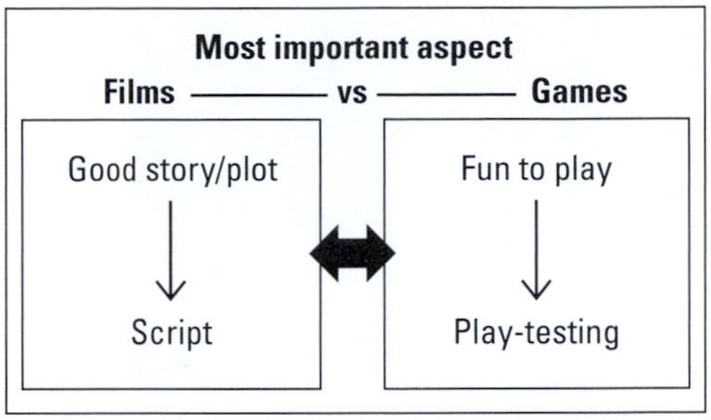

The difference between games and films is that although game prototyping is the most cost-effective way to determine if the gameplay is engaging, it is much more expensive and requires more people and resources than reading a script. A script can be read in a few hours to determine whether it would make a good film, but the gameplay is difficult to imagine and has to be proven via play-testing. While a large number of scripts are written that may or may not ever be made into a film, the process to determine which script to put into production is relatively inexpensive. A game, on the other hand, requires a full commitment from the start and is usually adjusted until it meets the criteria for fun.

Figure 8.3 Each medium has its own fundamental criteria for success. These criteria are used to weigh and prioritize each component that goes into the project. (Image courtesy of Habib Zargarpour.)

Narrative Storytelling

Both mediums provide for narrative storytelling. It is at the core of filmmaking and can be a strong component of a game as well. The immersive visceral nature of games makes them a good narrative medium. Of course some games don't necessarily have to have a plot, for example, *Pong* or *Tetris*, but most games take advantage of this opportunity to involve the player more by having a story. Stories are used to add mystery or define a premise and compel the player to keep advancing through the game to find out more. Games such as *Mass Effect*[2] (2007), *Half-Life 2*[3] (2006), *Bioshock*[4] (2007), *Resident Evil 5*[5] (2009), or *Uncharted 2: Among Thieves*[6] (2009) are good examples of this.

In many games players essentially create their own story as they progress, and navigating through an environment can

[2] *Mass Effect* (2007) is an action role-playing game developed by BioWare for the Xbox 360 and then ported to Microsoft Windows by Demiurge Studios. The Xbox 360 edition was released worldwide in November 2007, published by Microsoft Game Studios. The Windows edition was released on May 28, 2008, published by Electronic Arts.

[3] *Half-Life 2* (2006) is a science fiction first-person shooter computer game and the sequel to the highly acclaimed *Half-Life*. It was developed by Valve Corporation and was released on November 16, 2004.

[4] *Bioshock* (2007) is a first-person shooter video game developed by 2K Boston/2K Australia—previously known as Irrational Games—designed by Ken Levine. It was released for the Windows operating system and Xbox 360 video game console on August 21, 2007, in North America.

[5] *Resident Evil 5* (2009), known in Japan as *Biohazard 5*, is a third-person shooter survival horror video game developed and published by Capcom. The game is the seventh installment in the *Resident Evil* survival horror series and was released on March 5, 2009, in Japan and on March 13, 2009, in North America and Europe.

[6] *Uncharted 2: Among Thieves* (2009) is an action-adventure video game developed by Naughty Dog and published by Sony Computer Entertainment for the PlayStation 3. It is the sequel to the 2007 game *Uncharted: Drake's Fortune*. It was released in October 2009 and has been named by Metacritic as the most critically acclaimed game of 2009.

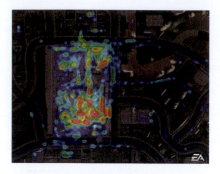

Figure 8.4 Example "Heat Map" showing where players fell the most, superimposed over a top view map of the third-person game *Skate* (2007). (Image courtesy of Electronic Arts.)

generate its own narrative. Many environments[7] become treasure hunts and provide drama and clues as to where to go next. The freedom of movement means that the experience can be very different each time. This adds to the complexity of designing and testing games. There are helpful development tools that can track the movement of hundreds of testers and report back as to where players went and where they got lost. For example, Figure 8.4 shows where players tripped or fell in the skateboarding game *Skate* (2007), and this information is then used to improve the design of the environment and the players' progression.

Differences in Limitations

Thanks to the rapid advances made in real-time graphics technology, CG models made for games can be as complex as ones made for film. The difference is how that asset is processed to fit into the game. When creating digital films, or films with visual effects, there are virtually unlimited resources to render or create a single frame—within budget and time constraints. Some shots can take up to 9 months of work, with frames taking anywhere from 1 to 20 hours, or more, to generate; the process is repeated until the shot is finaled. If physical simulations are needed, those can take several weeks to generate on powerful multicore towers. The data is then rendered for the shot.

The constraints are much more stringent for game makers. Because the game is interactive and has to respond immediately to the player's actions, the frames need to be rendered in real time.[8] The slightest delay will cause players to overcorrect their actions—which results in reducing the fun factor! Figure 8.5 shows the relative memory of various game consoles. All the content needs to fit into those memory limits, including world geometry, textures, characters, animation, music, sound effects, game logic, and the physics software. Additional content can be streamed from the disk or hard drive if the console has one. Streaming the content allows the game environments to be larger than would fit into memory all at once, and only the sections that are viewable by the player are loaded at any one time. Personal computers (PCs) are similar; while they have more memory and hard disk space than a console, the slowest PCs still have to be able to run the game smoothly.

---

[7] The design, art direction, and lighting are key ingredients to the creation of a successful world to support the fiction.
[8] The loose definition of *real time* is anything that is faster than 30 frames per second; any speed lower than this and the game will feel sluggish or unresponsive.

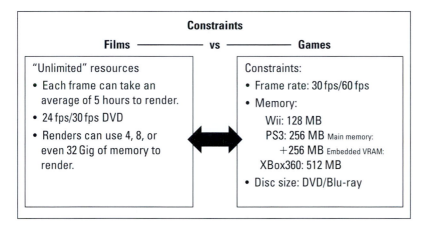

Figure 8.5 Comparison of the constraints for creating pre-rendered images versus real-time ones. A game engine cannot take longer than 1/30 second (33 milliseconds) to render each frame. (Image courtesy of Electronic Arts.)

The content of a film is simply composed of frames, so it has a fixed size on disk depending on the compression used. However, the data for a game is all in pieces. Imagine rendering a digital feature on the fly: all of the original geometry and textures, lighting information, and animation needed to re-create the shot. This is what games have to do. Some games can have between 10,000 and 20,000 individual animations that have to be dynamically loaded depending on the action taking place. The sheer complexity of handling that much data makes the real-time rendering even more challenging.

Cost of Iterations and Changes during Production

If a visual effects shot has been completed for a film, it is very expensive to make changes. The shot would most likely have to be reanimated or simulated, rerendered, composited, and refilmed out. In a game a change can be made on the last day, even as late as when the master disk is being made, and that change will automatically propagate throughout the entire game. For example, if the texture on the main character is changed, then wherever that character appears in the game it will have the new texture. This is also a dangerous aspect of game creation because things can break at the last minute and propagate throughout the game. The data is accessed on the fly and for the most part there are no pre-rendered scenes. Where there are pre-rendered cinematics, the cost of changing them would be similar to the film process. Figure 8.6 summarizes these differences.

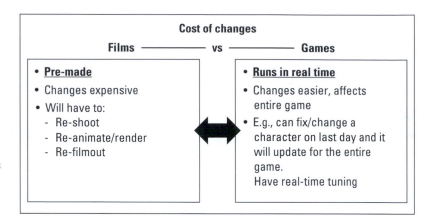

Figure 8.6 Comparison of the differences in the cost of making changes to the content later in production. Making changes to gameplay is generally costlier than content for games. (Image courtesy of Habib Zargarpour.)

Category Types

Films are categorized by their genre such as action, adventure, comedy, drama, and so forth. Games are categorized by the point of view of the player: "first person" or "third person," or types that are referred to with their acronyms (see summary in Figure 8.7):

- **FPS** (first-person shooter): The game camera is from the point of view of the player.
- **Third-person shooter**[9]: The player sees his or her avatar in the game and the camera trails behind.
- **RTS** (real-time strategy): Camera is high above overlooking a section of land.
- **RPG** (role-playing game): Third person.
- **MMO** (massive multiplayer online)
- **Sports**: These can have high cameras overlooking the field (e.g., soccer) or first person (boxing).
- **2D**: Side-scrolling action adventure (a Mario game) or puzzle.
- **Sim**: simulation, such as Flight Simulator or Driving Simulator.

Of course, some of the film genres can apply to games, such as horror or science fiction, depending on the setting, action/adventure, or crime/gangster based on a story or plot.

Format Types

The film format that is most commonly used is 35mm film but with various aspect ratios: 1:1.85, 1:2.35, some IMAX, and most recently, digital format for theaters equipped with digital projectors. On a console, the game output format will match whatever TV standard is used in the country where the console is sold: NTSC/HDTV in North America and PAL/HDTV in Europe. Aspect

---

[9] These are not called TPS, just third-person shooters!

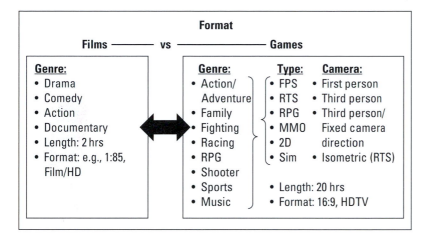

Figure 8.7 Example formats and genres in each media. (Image courtesy of Electronic Arts.)

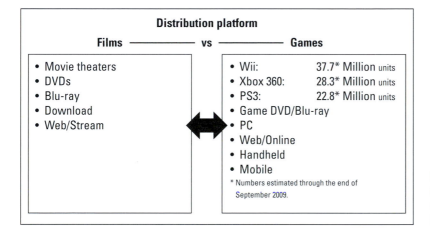

Figure 8.8 Various distribution and platform formats for each media. (Image courtesy of Electronic Arts.)

ratios of 4:3 for standard definition and 16:9 for HD are the most common. On PCs the game will simply play on whatever type of monitor is connected to the computer. Online games can fit within a web browser. Many games are formatted for mobile/handheld devices such as cell phones and the Nintendo DS or Sony PSP.

Most companies try to release their games on as many of the platforms as possible with the exception of first-party games. A *first-party game* is one that is made, or commissioned, by the company that also owns the platform; for example, Microsoft created the Xbox 360, Sony owns the PlayStation 3 (PS3), and Nintendo owns the Wii. Each company will try to create dedicated games that are only released on their own consoles as a way to attract consumers to purchase their hardware and accessories. Games made by other companies are called *third-party games*. Figure 8.8 shows the rough distribution ratios between various consoles.

Transmedia Production Design Techniques

One field that is converging among the various media is production design for the environments. Whether the design is for a film, digital feature, game, web, theater, or real architecture (designing real buildings), the principles and tools/techniques are very similar.[10]

Before designing an environment certain questions need to be answered about the requirements and constraints. These questions are answered differently depending on which of the following media are involved:

1. *Real architecture (for real buildings):*
   a. Designed for a first-person experience.
   b. Depending on the type of building, generally strive for beauty, awe, scale, comfort, and harmony.
   c. Some are designed to look good from the road while driving (car-chitecture[11]).
2. *Environments for films:*
   a. Entirely dependent on the type of film: replicating reality, historic, science fiction, time piece, comedy.
   b. Completely camera dependent: areas not seen from the camera do not need to be built.
   c. Sometimes the set or real environment is extended in post-production and not built in its entirety.
   d. Set pieces may be cheated around on a shot-by-shot basis to make them look good. This applies if the sets are miniatures or digital.
3. *Environments for digital features:*
   a. Similar to film but generally there is less modification of sets between shots in a scene due to the volume of shots to be generated.
   b. Since all of the environments are digital, there is full freedom to design the environment to enhance the story.
4. *Environments for games:*
   a. Creating environments for games is very similar to those of digital features. The level of detail may be more simplified but the environments have to be designed and built as continuous pieces. (Refer to Figure 8.9.)
   b. In many ways there is more similarity to #1: real architecture. (Refer to Figure 8.10.)
   c. Because the viewer is interactively traversing through the environment, the set pieces cannot be moved or cheated on a shot-by-shot basis because there are no shots.
   d. Similar to films, completely camera dependent: Areas not seen from the camera do not need to be built. If the player

---

[10] A more in-depth discussion on this topic may be found at www.5dconference.com.
[11] See the book *Carchitecture: When the Car and the City Collide* by Jonathan Bell.

does not need to go inside a building, the interiors will not need to be built. Similarly, rooftops or backs of buildings would not need to be built if not visible. In films the extras off camera need not continue to act, and in games the AI characters don't need to be drawn.

e. A good game environment is designed to draw the players through to the key places with the use of lighting and object placement while using landmarks to keep them from getting lost or disoriented. (Refer to Figure 8.11.)

Prototyping or previs is an area where all of these media have the most similarity. They use the same tools to create simple geometry and animation and to block in the environments to quickly find out if the designs would work. There are even cases where architects use game engines to preview walking around their building designs and verify their work before the buildings are made.

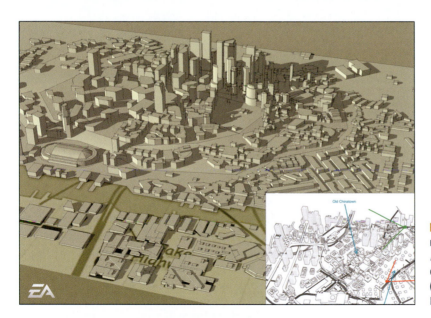

Figure 8.9 City planning for the racing game *Need for Speed Most Wanted* (2006) based on custom-designed roads. (Concept art by Aaron Kambeitz. Image courtesy of Electronic Arts.)

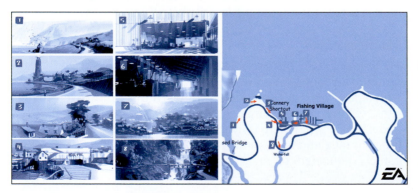

Figure 8.10 Design criteria for environments in a game can be very similar to those for real architecture. Seen here are the key vistas along a coastal drive for the racing game *Need for Speed Most Wanted* (2006). (Concept art by Aaron Kambeitz. Image courtesy of Electronic Arts.)

Figure 8.11 Screenshot from the FPS game *Medal of Honor Airborne* (2008). In a shooter game the environment is designed to provide areas of cover or "affordances" to the player. (Image courtesy of Electronic Arts.)

Figure 8.12 Example of post effects showing the visual filters both on and off. These post effects need to be processed over each frame within the 33-millisecond time limit. Screenshot from the game *Need for Speed Most Wanted* (2006). (Image courtesy of Electronic Arts.)

Digital Intermediate and Post Effects

Films can be processed through a digital intermediate (DI) process, in which all of the color correction can take place and a specific look may be applied to the movie. Games don't have this luxury but do have the option of real-time post-processing. In such a process real-time compositing techniques such as bloom, desaturation, contrast, color correction, and many other effects can be applied. These effects or *visual filters* may be applied to every frame as it is rendered while still maintaining the 30 fps required as a limitation for how intricate they can get.

Machinima Films

Machinima is the term used when a game engine is used to make a film. The footage is rendered in real time but then recorded, edited, and scored. There are examples of this on the web at such sites as http://machinima.com and *Red vs. Blue* (2003) (www .redvsblue.com), where they use the *Halo* game engine to record their footage and apply audio and editing in post. There are now games dedicated to creating Machinima such as Lionshead's

Figure 8.13 Screenshot from the racing game *Need for Speed SHIFT* (2009) shows the advancements in real-time rendering in full HD resolution. (Image courtesy of Electronic Arts.)

The Movies Game. A few film projects have been put online that can be remixed by anyone so they can create their own versions. One such site to see and do this is http://modfilms.com.

Convergence

Much has been said about the convergence of film and games. While no one is thinking that films will become interactive, there is no question that each field is influencing the other. Games are becoming more cinematic, and many of the tools, artists, and programmers working in either field are converging because they both use similar computer graphic techniques. Shaders, once the exclusive domain of offline renderers, are now commonly used in real-time game engines, and advances such as faster graphics cards are in turn helping speed up the visual effects process. The CG medium is helping the two to share their creative crews.

GAMES AND PLATFORMS
Henry LaBounta

Video games are still a relatively new form of entertainment. Competition drives constant innovation in many areas including gameplay, interactivity, technology, graphics, and storytelling. Major game consoles are released approximately every 5 years, which creates a regular pace of innovation and reinvention in the industry. The game market has grown rapidly, with game sales exceeding movie sales in America in 2005. The cost of making games has also risen as more advanced hardware requires more complex engineering. Consumers now expect massive open world game environments in

HD that require more art content. Popular game franchises dominate the market with multiple sequels. Many games are released on multiple platforms, each of which has different graphics, memory, and performance requirements. Game hardware choices also affect the audience that will be reached. A hardcore gamer may be more likely to have PS3 or Xbox 360 than a Wii, for example.

There are many differences and similarities between the game industry and film industry. Unlike the film industry there is no clear, established process of using tools like screenplays and storyboards to previs games. What makes an interactive experience fun is hard to define and requires extensive interactive play testing. Game teams are usually small compared to a film crew, and some positions cover many areas. For example, an Art Director may be involved in doing everything from production design to visual effects supervision, character design, and animation direction and may also be the Director of Photography for the game. Most major game companies also own the products they create, so unlike visual effects contractors it is more like working on staff at a film studio. The computer graphics technology used in games is similar to digital visual effects work, but the hardware rendering all happens in real time.

Game Types

1. *Role-playing games, aka RPG:* In these games the players explore a large open-ended world and develop their character's skills, attributes, and equipment through the course of an epic narrative.
2. *Action games:* These games often feature physical skill challenges that require quick response time and hand–eye coordination (aka twitch-based games). Players face increasingly difficult challenges and opponents as they progress through the game. The goal is usually to achieve some objective or reach some destination without dying. Many games will also allow the player to score points as a measure of how well they are playing. Many additional types of games also fall under the action umbrella:
   a. *First-person shooter games (FPS):* In these shooting games the camera is in the player's point of view (POV), showing the characters' arms and weapon on the bottom of the screen. A popular variation of the FPS is the third-person shooter, in which the camera looks forward over the player-character's shoulder.
   b. *Fighting games:* In these games the player controls a character who is in combat with one or more other characters. Players must master defensive and offensive moves as well as combinations of moves to beat the opponent.

   c. *Platform games (aka Platformer):* From *Donkey Kong* to *Super Mario Brothers,* Nintendo popularized this category. These games started with 2D side-scrolling games where the image scrolled by as the player avoided obstacles while jumping from one platform to another. These and other types of games became more dimensional by using an isometric perspective, aka 2.5D in the 1980s and 1990s. Modern 3D platform games still focus on the core activity of jumping from place to place to reach a destination.

   d. *Action/adventure games:* These are a combination of action and adventure games that deliver both fast-paced action and story elements.

3. *Sports games:* These games present a simulation of a real-life sport where the gameplayer takes on the role of a sports player, a whole team, or even a team manager or owner of a team. They can be played single player against the game AI or multiplayer offline or online. Many use a high camera angle that shows enough of the playing field to be able to pass the ball.

4. *Alternative sports games:* Unlike stadium team sports games, these games feature activities such as snowboarding and skateboarding.

5. *Puzzle games:* Classic games such as *Tetris* spawned a variety of puzzle games that usually involve spatial problem solving within an abstract rule set. Many other types of games also include puzzle-solving challenges.

6. *Racing games:* These range from an arcade experience to more authentic simulation (or sim) driving games. Some include story elements and happen in an open world environment while others are more track based. Generally the player can choose between a third-person camera and a first-person bumper cam or sometimes a cockpit interior camera.

7. *Real-time strategy games (RTS):* These are war-themed games where the player builds and controls an entire army. The player generally looks down on a landscape and builds assets to support an army that a player controls to fight against the AI or other players. These games are also popular online where sometimes up to eight players are participating. Player stats are persistent and often world ranked.

8. *Massively multiplayer online games (MMO or MMOG):* MMO games allow thousands of players to play together in a large, open-ended world. These are typically PC games and, recently, also console games that require an Internet connection to play. These games sometimes use a subscription model, such as *World of Warcraft*, which currently has 11 million subscribers. Many types of games can be MMOs including sports and FPS games.

9. *Serious games:* These are games that aren't focused solely on entertainment. Some of these games are:
    a. training games,
    b. educational games, and
    c. scientific games.
10. *Virtual worlds:* These are generally PC games where many players interact with each other in either a fantasy or more realistic world. Often players can communicate with each other with text or voice. These are very social games and players trade in a virtual economy.
11. *Adventure games:* These types of games are narrative heavy. The player explores the environment and completes problem-solving and puzzle challenges in order to progress through the story. These games rarely include combat or action elements.

Game Platforms

The following is a snapshot of the primary game devices for 2009. Currently, there are no announcements of any new major consoles coming out soon. However, new game platforms are constantly coming out, especially for handheld devices such as cell phones. Online capability has been one of the big developments in the current seventh generation of game consoles. This allows players to both play with friends as well as anyone else who is online. Online also allows players to easily download entire games, content, mini-games, additional post-launch game content, and patches. The online capability has changed some game markets already and will likely change others. In Korea, for example, many games are "free to play" (F2P) meaning the game can be downloaded and played for free. Game companies then sell additional game items through "micro transactions," allowing the player to stand out from the crowd or making the game easier and more convenient to play. Most items cost very little but for successful games they can all add up and some more expensive items are available for hardcore players.

At the 2009 Game Developers Conference (GDC), Reardon Studios announced a new microconsole called *OnLive*. This set-top box allows users to play any game without owning the game hardware necessary for them by streaming the game video to a TV, Mac, or PC. The controller input is sent to their servers for the computing, which then sends the video results back to the player.

The following is a snapshot of the primary game devices as of December 2009:

1. Wii, released in 2006 by Nintendo, has been a huge hit. It uses an innovative controller that combines pointing and orientation.

Players often stand up and swing their arms in full gestures to control the game. Unlike the Xbox 360 and PS3, high-end graphics performance is not a focus for this console.

2. PlayStation 3 (PS3), released in 2006 by Sony, follows the very successful PS2 and PlayStation. The wireless controller is similar to the PS2 controller, but it also has a six-axis orientation control. This console features a Blu-ray DVD player and free online access for players with an Internet connection via the PlayStation Network. The hardware includes a 7 SPU (CPU) cell microprocessor and NVIDIA RSX graphics GPU with 2×256 MB of memory.

3. Xbox 360, released by Microsoft in 2005, was a follow-up to the original Xbox. Xbox Live is a subscription-based service, which allows players with an Internet connection to play online as well as download new content. The controller is very similar to the original Xbox but is wireless. The hardware includes a triple-core, IBM-designed Xenon CPU and ATI GPU for graphics processing with 512 MB of memory.

4. PlayStation 2 (PS2), released in 2000 by Sony, has been the best-selling console to date with more than 140 million units sold. The hardware features a 64-bit, 290-MHz CPU with 32 MB of memory, two vector units (VUs), and a 147-MHz GPU.

5. PC games, unlike console games, operate on a personal computer. Computer games have been around since the 1960s and have evolved by pushing the graphics capability of the latest PC hardware. They are dependent on the PC hardware and operating system, which can be configured in countless ways, so many offer the ability to adjust the graphic quality to accommodate older hardware. The keyboard and a mouse are the basic input devices for many PC games and a wide variety of peripherals including joysticks, gamepads, and steering wheels may be used for specific types of games.

6. Sony PSP (PlayStation Portable), widely released in 2005, is a handheld gaming console offering a wide variety of multimedia capabilities. It uses a UMD optical disk media format and can connect with PlayStation consoles as well as the Internet. While graphics capabilities are limited in handheld consoles, they are still impressive for the screen size. The upcoming PSP Go replaces the UMD drive with internal flash-based memory, allowing games to be distributed online.

7. Nintendo DS, released in 2005, is a dual-screen handheld gaming console. The bottom screen is a touchscreen that users can use either with a stylus or their fingers for input.

8. iPhone, which is Apple's smartphone with gaming capability, has grown rapidly since its launch in 2007. The multimedia smartphone offers a large touchscreen and a three-axis accelerometer, which senses the orientation of the phone. Due to the

lack of conventional game pad buttons on the iPhone, designing interactive controls requires a different approach.

Film and game convergence has been a hot topic for a number of years. It is already happening with games based on films, and films based on games—both with varying degrees of success. On average, console games can take anywhere from 1 to 3 years to create. In the past, there has generally been little to no collaboration between game developers and film production and visual effects studios. Further convergence will come from early collaboration that will likely yield better and more cost-effective games.

Just as great films start with great scripts, great games start with great gameplay. In making a successful game it is easy to focus on the visual aspects, which are also important, but can never replace the need for great gameplay. Some key questions to answer early on include "What is the player doing?" and "Is that fun and rewarding?" This will also help determine not only what type of game it is but which console it should be developed for.

There are many ways to learn more about games including conferences, magazines, and websites. The two main conferences are the Game Developers Conference (GDC) and the Electronic Entertainment Expo (E3). GDC focuses on the art and craft of game creation, whereas E3 focuses more on the business side with developers and publishers exhibiting their games. Additionally, many schools have courses on game development.

WHAT ARE GAME ENGINES AND HOW DO THEY FUNCTION?
Matt Whiting, Jeff Lander

A game engine is a software system or series of modular software components designed to be used for the creation of video games. The engine serves to abstract the details of interfacing with game hardware or several game hardware platforms in order to allow the game creators to focus their time on making the actual gameplay code and logic that define the game. Game engines exist in a variety of levels of complexity and features. While a game developer may develop game engine technology for use on a project, engines are often acquired by license from a commercial engine creator for a fee, or occasionally a royalty, from the game maker. However, the definition of a *game engine* is generally accepted to refer to technology capable of creating complex consumer-quality game experiences in console and PC game titles seen in stores. These are usually, but not exclusively, engines for the creation of 3D games. These types of projects require a great deal of technology to create.

Though the name *game engine* is often mistakenly used for software development kits (SDKs) such as DirectX, OpenGL, or Havok Physics, within the industry these are not considered game engines. SDKs such as these do provide abstraction from the game hardware. However, they only provide a portion of what is needed to create a game, such as a rendering library or physics system. To qualify as a game engine, a software package would have to provide a much more complete solution for game creation. Systems typically covered by a game engine include many low-level modules for rendering, physics, controller input, sound, and artificial intelligence components such as pathfinding, animation, file access, memory management, and network support. Many of these components can be licensed from a software provider, and these individually licensed components are commonly known as *middleware*. Though many game engine creators provide much of this functionality directly, some game engines are created from or supplemented by the inclusion of additional pieces of middleware.

Working with a Game Engine

Game engines at best provide an easy-to-use method for content creators and game makers to get their ideas and assets into a playable game. This is often called the *game production pipeline*. By providing as much of the technical low-level capabilities as the engine's modular components, the game makers can focus on what makes their game different and special.

This means different things to different people, and a variety of game engine technology is available to suit those needs. For a team with strong artistic capability and design vision, but lacking the engineering talent to make a game from scratch, a game engine can provide the program backbone for these artists to express their ideas. Likewise, if the team is engineering savvy and capable of creating the game foundation, they can instead focus on programming innovations to take their game much farther than they could without it. By providing the basic pipeline and game infrastructure, the team can save a great deal of time.

The game engine at the basic level allows artists to create the art and bring it into the game world. Then designers and programmers manipulate the logic to create the game. The engine then allows the developers to package and distribute the game on their target platforms.

Usually someone who uses a game engine has an expectation that this engine will provide a minimum set of tools. The minimum set of tools provides a pipeline that will allow them to take their raw game assets, such as textures, 3D models, and sounds, and bring them into the game world to play. This pipeline can consist of many individual tools and steps, or it can be an all-encompassing game engine editor and playback environment.

The engine must allow the programmers or designers some method for defining and modifying the logic systems that create the game experience itself. This can take the form of writing computer code, scripts, manipulating visual logic controls, or a broad mix of these.

Technical Knowledge and Software

To use a game engine effectively, developers need the skills required to make a game. They need content creators capable of making art and sounds to comprise the game experience. This can, of course, take a number of forms such as 2D pictures, 3D models, videos, audio clips, etc. Many types of software are available to help with this aspect of game creation. High-end 3D modeling and animation packages such as Maya and 2D art creation tools such as Photoshop are commonly used and are required to create a quality game experience. Even if the developer is just going to reuse content from an existing game for the project, he or she must have some knowledge of art creation tools, if only to make the small changes needed in any game project.

For the creation of the game logic, having computer programming knowledge and expertise is usually, though not always, required. Any modification to the game rules or logic systems will mean changing some code or scripts. Most high-end game engines work in the C programming language, although there are exceptions. Many projects employ game design experts who, while not always programmers, are skilled in the art of making games that are fun to play. This knowledge is incredibly valuable to any project.

Similarities among Software Packages

Game engines are similar to 3D computer graphics programs in that they usually work in the 3D world with objects and the manipulation of time and space. However, game engines are specifically designed to organize large game worlds in an efficient manner with complex logic and are able to present this content back at interactive rates. 3D CG programs, as well as 2D paint programs, are generally termed *digital content creation* (DCC) tools. These tools are very efficient at the creation of content for game projects. The focus on user interface for the creators means that they are easy for skilled artists to use. However, their focus is not on the efficient organization and playback of interactive game experiences. It is true that some of the 3D content tools have many elements of a game engine, such as scripting languages and asset organization. However, these tools are not suited to dealing with the amount of logic and data that must be manipulated for a modern game experience.

One particularly blurry line is the concept of the game engine level editor. The *level editor* is the tool in many game projects that allows the game creator to lay out the world objects in space for the play of the actual level. DCC tools can be quite well suited to this task since they have nice, consistent user interfaces specifically designed for 3D object manipulation. These interface systems are very difficult to re-create in a custom tool. However, the DCC tools are often not well suited to the specific needs of individual game environments. They also may buckle under the shear amount of data needed for a modern game level. But for many applications, a DCC tool performs this task well.

CG Applications and Game Engines

Game engines generally receive the game content via export from a DCC tool. This can be done via common content output formats such as TGA files or OBJ models. But often, the complexity of game engines requires custom export formats from the DCC tools. Most game engines need to modify this exported data to be optimally formatted for the target platforms. This step can be done at the export stage, the import stage into the game engine, or as the content is packaged up to play the game.

One of the main things a game engine provides the game developer is the pipeline that brings artistic content from the DCC packages into the game.

Common Game Engines

Many game engines are available in a large variety of categories. These engines all serve specific needs and provide different advantages and disadvantages to the developers. Many lists of game engines exist, but Wikipedia provides a fairly detailed list with links to the engine providers (http://en.wikipedia.org/wiki/List_of_game_engines).

Professional developers are concerned with game engines that provide a great deal of features, appropriate for the desired game, an efficient game creation pipeline, and support for the target platforms (PC, game consoles, etc.).

The most common game engines at the professional level, at this time, include:

Epic Games' Unreal Engine	www.unrealtechnology.com
Garage Games' Torque	www.garagegames.com
Emergent Game Technologies' Gamebryo	www.emergent.net
Valve Corporation's Source Engine	http://source.valvesoftware.com
Crytek's Cryengine	www.crytek.com
id Software's idTech5	www.idsoftware.com
Adobe Flash	www.flash.com

This list is by no means comprehensive and many mid-to high-end game engines exist, including many low-cost to no-cost and open-source solutions.

WHAT ARE THE PRODUCTION STEPS IN CREATING A GAME?
Neil Eskuri

The first major step in creating a game is deciding what kind of game is being created. This sounds obvious, but there are many types of games and platforms. They include first-person shooter, racing, sports, and role-playing games among others (see the earlier sections on games). And they are played on many different types of platforms—each one having its own requirements, limitations, and considerations. These platforms include consoles, handheld units, and PCs. Establishing the idea and platform is crucial to how the game will be developed and produced regardless of the size of the game publishing company.

The idea for a game can be anything one's imagination can conjure up. However, important questions need to be addressed before moving forward:

* *What is the object of the game?* i.e., conquer the world, build a family, win the championship
* *What is the type of game?* first-person shooter, simulation, arcade
* *What is the setting?* fictional environment, stadium, spaceship, etc.
* *What platform is it being created for?* Xbox, PS3, PC, PSP, iPhone, DS, Wii, etc.

The idea should have at least one full thread, from beginning to end, that can be built on for overall development. This will provide a solid basis on which developers can add more facets to gameplay.

It is difficult, if not impossible, to outline how to come up with an idea. That is the seed of the creative process and often the product of inspiration and passion. In this concept phase all blue-sky ideas are brought together and innovative exploration occurs. An extremely useful goal is to create a one-line description of the game that defines what it is about. If people are confused about the game after hearing this description, or elevator pitch, then more thought should go into the overall idea before the big pitch.

Marketing to an Audience

Another important question in game creation is "What is the target audience for the game?" Often, it is not considered until well into pre-production, or even production, which may cause a delay and major reconsideration as to what is going to be produced. A game idea should be pitched to a marketing group that understands the gaming industry and will help with positioning the game to a particular market. This group will usually have ideas about tailoring the concept, visuals, or gameplay to the specific audience targeted. This is a crucial step in focusing the game's market and can be a useful tool in scheduling the overall production.

The gaming industry operates in a fast-changing landscape of cultural tastes. Understanding how the game idea fits within, or even creates, cultural tastes will be a large benefit to its success.

The game's target audience can be better defined after it has been prototyped. However, an idea of the target audience should be determined well before pre-production and certainly before production begins.

Object of Game—Prototypes

Prototyping the game idea will help give clarity to the myriad of possibilities any game at this stage has. The object of the game will be one of the first prototypes created. This can take the shape of a storyboard, a board game, a timeline, or a rough computer model or simulation. The prototypes should be as concise and simple as possible to illustrate just one or two points of the game's objective. The more complex a prototype is, the more difficult it will be to answer the basic questions it *should* have been designed to answer. Dozens, if not hundreds, of prototypes will need to be created and designed to fully flesh out all of the concepts and gameplay ideas and questions. These prototypes must be completed before pre-production begins in order to create an efficient and useful pipeline for production.

Things to consider when creating a prototype:
- What is the main flow of the game?
- Find the fun early—if the prototype is not fun, the game won't be either.

- How will the game end?
- How do players/characters interact?
- How many players/characters are in the game?
- Can the user create any personal assets?
- Are there rewards/setbacks? If so, what are they?
- Can the game be incorporated into a specific culture?
- Prove out any "science projects"—if there will be something that has not been created before, push that feature to a state where it can be confidently accomplished. Additionally, evaluate the time it will take to produce this feature at a level of quality necessary to ship the game.
- Test memory constraints. These prototypes are an excellent method for understanding benchmarks for pipeline, performance, and memory.
- Keep prototypes as simple as possible. Do not try to solve multiple issues with a single prototype. As an example, a "stickman," as opposed to a fully skinned character, may be sufficient to solve gameplay questions. The more that is put into a prototype, the longer it will take to come to a conclusion on the feature. It is easy to fall into the trap of putting too much into a prototype.

As specifics are established they can begin to be incorporated with each other. This will give more clarity on the complexity of the game and the dependencies with other gameplay ideas.

Prototypes will be created throughout the game's production cycle, but these initial prototypes are for establishing a foundation for the game and its natural complexity. Above all, *the game must be fun and compelling*. These early prototypes help to determine what makes the game fun and the reason people cannot live without the game idea.

Visuals

Before the game can be completely set up for success it must have a visual style. Prototypes or concepts need to be visually created to illustrate the different elements of the game and should support the ideas and theme of the game. Visual exploration will generally require a great deal of iteration. Explore as many ideas as possible with concept art and different combinations of elements. Real-world reference is a good guide but may not be applicable to the game idea. The better defined the original game idea is, the better the visuals will be.

Questions to explore with the visual team:
- What are the environments in which the game will be played?
- What do those environments look like?
- What do the characters, if any, look like?
- What specific details are particular to the gameplay or visual look?

- What props/accessories are there and what do they look like?
- Are there any specific physical properties of the environment? Gravity? Air? Wind?
- What screens are needed and what is their style?
- What visual effects are needed?
- What cameras and camera moves are required?
- What gameplay moments need illustration?
- Is there a single image that defines the game? Is there a visual style that resonates with the target audience?

A visual target may be achieved by a quick video using real-world video and photographs. This helps to show how the game might look in motion, even though it is not being controlled by a user, and will give an emotional element in presenting the game to executives.

Animation prototypes are also important in illustrating the motion of characters, graphics, cameras, and visual effects. Again reference is important to show the type of motion during gameplay. Animation prototypes do not need to be fully fleshed out productions, but they should clearly illustrate how things move. The sooner either real-world examples can be found or characters and/or objects can be animated, the better. Along with clear game ideas and visuals, motion exploration gives an immediate sense of what the game will ultimately be.

Along with the visuals, audio should be prototyped as well. The music, voices, and sound effects add a great deal of dynamics to a game and underscore the overall experience for the player(s).

Game Document

The game document is a clear and concise explanation of the overall game, what the object of the game is, and its target audience. It should include descriptions of the visuals and audio direction in as much detail as possible. The cast of characters and locations along with what screens are required for the front end and navigation throughout the game should be detailed as well. In short, all of the work done to lay out the game should be incorporated into this document. This will become the blueprint for all that follows. The areas of focus should include:

- gameplay (flow, levels, AI, animation),
- visuals (environments, characters, effects),
- front-end (screen menus, overlays, game information for user),
- dynasty/story mode,
- presentation (cameras, overlays, cinematics, or noninteractive sequences),
- audio,
- online,
- platforms (Xbox, PlayStation, Wii, PC, etc.),

- marketing (demos, ad sales, exposure, etc.), and
- pipeline (software, hardware, asset management, support).

Budget

Determining the cost to create the game can be a tricky endeavor because no matter how much has been planned, things will always change. Keep that in mind when a budget is being developed. The game document is a very good tool to help establish cost. In general, the more complex the game is, the more expensive it will be to produce.

Software engineers, artists, and technical artists can give valuable estimates to determine what it will take to deliver different features and assets required for production. Game producers will use the game document to break down specific tasks required to develop a game and their dependencies on other game areas. With this information a schedule may be created to provide an understanding of the overall scope of production and give a more accurate idea of people, time, and resources needed to create the game, that is, the cost of the game.

The budget should include an overall schedule of production. This includes pre-production, production, finaling, and manufacturing.

The Team

A team of producers, software engineers, artists, management, and marketing personnel comes together to bring a game to life.

In general, a production team will consist of producers (line producers, assistants, and associates), game designers, art director(s), computer graphic supervisor(s), development directors and managers, software engineers (technical directors and game area leads), artists and animators, sound artists, and marketing and production support personnel.

Of course, the exact number of individuals for each of these roles will depend on the type of game, its platform, and complexity. Several models can be used to organize a team. The entire team can be brought together in one studio or portions of the game can be outsourced. Larger game studios sometimes create central teams for more efficiency in creating assets and organizing data.

In conjunction with the main team, other groups required to complete the game are:
- quality assurance,
- publishing,
- studio operations,
- finance,
- localization (if the game will be distributed in other countries),

- human resources,
- information technology,
- legal/business affairs,
- mastering,
- media services, and
- marketing.

Pipeline

The actual pipeline is determined by what studio creates the game or the personal experiences of the team that comes together for production. Each game production pipeline has different software and hardware needs. The game document and information from the technical team and information technology (IT) department will be extremely valuable in determining the makeup of the pipeline. Things to consider when designing a pipeline are:

- software,
- hardware,
- asset management (versioning, backup, support),
- outsourcing,
- communication,
- iteration, and
- flexibility.

A good pipeline allows the production team flexibility in its use. Different parts of production should be able to add functionality, for quicker development, anywhere along the line without slowing down the process.

Phases of Development

Games are similar to most other types of production. There are phases of pre-production, production, finaling, post-production, and manufacturing—with checkpoints within each phase.

Pre-Production

Pre-production is where the final design for the game is established. Additional brainstorming is done with producers and game designers to flesh out all of the features of gameplay, visual look, and schedule. Additional prototyping on the features is created to prove out ideas and discover what technology is required for the pipeline and infrastructure. All major technical challenges should be addressed in this phase.

In pre-production, a plan is established for the production's capacity, and estimates for a realistic and well-considered production schedule are put in place. Every game is different and the length of time for pre-production will differ in each case. For most games this period can be 1 to 6 months. However, for a brand new type of game it can be as much as 2 years or more.

For a successful pre-production, milestones should be established to ensure the production team will be moving in the right direction and in a timely manner. Some milestones are:

- design review = overall game design with major and minor features,
- business review = budget and financial, and
- development review = detailed game design, schedule, technical plan.

One technique for development is known as *agile development* or *scrums*. This technique creates small groups who are empowered to solve problems, make fast decisions, and develop quick prototypes to determine what works and what does not work. These groups can remove traditional roadblocks in development and involve the entire team.

Production

Production is when the main aspects of the game are built. All of the pieces begin to come together during production. Not all of the pieces are fully tuned to work together at this point, but adequate time should be scheduled for several iterations to bring the game features to a working state. Overall game flow is established and visual themes and assets are incorporated. As with pre-production, production should have specific milestones to keep things on track. These milestones are:

- *Milestone reviews and tuning:* Regular reviews and tuning time are established to adjust schedule, assess risk, and check quality of features and assets.
- *Game reviews:* Demo the game with key features and review with marketing and publishing in preparation for completion.
- *Alpha review:* Review game with an eye of entering the finaling phase. What are the key areas of focus?

The duration for production can be 3 to 15 months or more, depending on the game.

Finaling

Finaling is the process where all the features and functionality of the game come together and the finish line is crossed. Finite milestones are established to ensure the game hits its schedule. Generally these are referred to as:

- *Alpha:* All features are complete. They may have bugs, but the main components are finished.
- *Dev Beta:* This is the first fully functional version of the game with zero bugs. Very little tuning is still to be done.
- *Beta:* All assets and features are final and incorporated. This version should have zero bugs for 2 days. For online games there can be "Open Beta" and "Closed Beta" for testing the game with select groups or the public at large.

- *Final:* The game is completely approved internally and by the first party, the platform on which the game will be delivered (Xbox, PlayStation, Wii, etc.).
- *First-party approval:* Ready for manufacturing and positioning all assets for output to manufacturer. PC games don't have a first-party approval.

As with other phases of production, the length of time for finaling will vary. However, for most games, this phase lasts from 9 to 12 weeks.

Marketing

Marketing should be an ongoing endeavor to ensure that the game is exposed to the chosen target audience. Because things can change during all phases of production, marketing should be kept closely in the loop of where the game is going. Working with the marketing team is a big key to the success of any game. Marketing is responsible for positioning the game in the marketplace for optimal results. If the game is not marketed, no matter how groundbreaking or great it is, it is destined for failure.

Post-Production

Post-production in the gaming world is quite different from that of the film and television world. In gaming, post-production is when the game's cycle is reviewed and a determination made about what works and what does not work—a post-mortem period. This is the time to evaluate the process and work on any corrective actions and plans for the next cycle or new game. During this time, it is a good idea to look at the resources for the next cycle and re-energize the team for the next upcoming cycle or game idea. Look at this time as planting the seeds for the future of the game or company, because the cycle usually begins anew in 3 to 6 weeks.

Manufacturing

Manufacturing is production of the actual disk and packaging. The development team has completed the game and it is now moving toward shipping and its scheduled "street date." The time frame is dependent on the platform(s) for the game—usually about 5 to 10 weeks from mass production and shipping.

Conclusion

Once the project is completed and shipped, it is a good idea to bring the team together and evaluate the overall cycle and conduct a post mortem. This is a perfect opportunity to discuss the process to determine what aspects of production went well and what aspects need some adjustment. The information learned may be extremely valuable in setting up the next game, its pipeline, resources, and future game teams.

GAME CINEMATIC SEQUENCES
Richard Winn Taylor II

Noninteractive Scenes

Noninteractive scene (NIS) sequences, sometimes referred to as *cut-scenes*, are at their core linear sequences that lack interactivity. They briefly take away the player's control and force them to watch a pre-rendered sequence created with CG animation or live action. By using NIS scenes the game designers are able to convey the storyline or the structure of the game. Cut-scenes are used throughout the game to advance the story or inform the player of new challenges. Many games have a closing sequence to conclude the storyline and to reward the player for successfully completing the game.

Replay Sequences

Many games show a sequence of scenes edited together at the completion of a game level or at the end of the game. These sequences show the players' actions through a variety of shots. Replay sequences are most commonly found in sports action games, racing games, and social games. In some games the players can build their own replay sequence by selecting the shots and editing them together. These replay sequences are often posted online.

Pre-Rendering

Pre-rendering is one of the two methods of creating NIS scenes in games. Pre-rendered scenes are created using traditional film, video, and computer graphic production techniques. Generally the scenes are created at 1920×1080 HD at 4:2:2. After the final DI color correction, the scenes are then downsized to 1280×720 using a video codec. Commonly used codecs include AMV, AVS, Bink, Dirac, Indeo, Pixlet, Real Video, RT Video, Sheer Video, Smacker, Theora, VC-1, VP6, and WMV. The NIS scenes need to be compressed so they use as little space as possible on the DVDs that load and play the game on game consoles or onto the PC. PC games use a dual-layered DVD, and the NIS scenes are burned onto the second layer. They generally use about 4 GB of disk space. Console games use a variety of DVDs depending on the manufacturer. For example, the Xbox 360 uses the HDVD, the Sony PS3 uses the Blu-ray, and the Nintendo Wii has its own unique DVD.

There are several aspects to the pre-rendered approach that should be considered because they significantly impact the budget. If the gaming company does not have a dedicated in-house group to create the scenes, then the shots are subcontracted to an independent production company that works in Maya, Max, or Lightwave. In many cases the models and texture maps created for the game are not of sufficient resolution to work in the cinematic sequences and therefore the subcontractor must build all new models. Obviously good preparation by the game company in scripting and boarding the scenes and good communications between the companies are essential.

Pre-rendered sequences play a major role in the marketing of a game. They are incorporated into trailers that are posted online at major gaming sites and on the home page of the game. They are often shown on television and at gaming conferences around the world.

Localization

Games designed for a worldwide audience require that all of the names seen throughout the game and in the user interface (UI) be translated to other languages. This poses a significant logistical challenge in that it entails roughly 10 different composites of each scene.

Game Engine–Rendered NIS Scenes

The second technique for creating NIS scenes is to render them in real time using the game engine (see the earlier section on game engines). The engine is programmed to play a scene using the in-game camera, lighting, environments, characters, animation, physics, and effects. This approach has two advantages: First, the scenes are identical in their resolution and style to the imagery in the game and, second, they require very little disk space. The downside is that the game company must put together a dedicated team of artists and engineers who are familiar with the game engine's camera, lighting, and animation tools to create these scenes.

The Design and Production Process

The creation of pre-rendered cut-scene sequences is parallel to the design and production of animated and live-action films. Game design is the controlling factor in the production of any game, just as the script is the backbone of any film. Until the game designers have defined the storyline and gameplay, there can be no production. Once the game design document is complete, the cinematic director breaks down the script and creates storyboards and proof-of-concept tests. Once the boards are approved, the project is competitively bid to outside production companies. Most bids include a previs step in creating the scenes. Once the job is awarded, the approval process is similar to most film projects. The final scenes are delivered as targa files. The game company's in-house post-production team conforms the targa files to the codec and works with engineering to integrate the scenes into the game.

The processes used in creating the images for games are similar in most respects to the technology used in film production. The difference of course is that the images in games are rendered in real time by a game engine. Many effects studios are now experimenting with game engines as a means of lowering costs by expediting visual effects production. It is apparent that the collaboration between gaming and the film and television industry will continue to grow in the years to come.

9

COMPLETE ANIMATION

WHAT IS AN ANIMATION PROJECT?
Stephan Vladimir Bugaj

Full Animation versus Visual Effects

In contemporary filmmaking, the line between an animation project and a visual effects project has become blurred. At one time distinctions could more reasonably be made. Visual effects could be described as animation done in support of live-action plates, whereas full animation could be described as an artificial, created world; or, put another way, visual effects is primarily about environments and noncharacter dynamics, whereas full animation is primarily about character dynamics. But consider, for example, the *Star Wars* prequels. Those films have animated characters in nearly all of the shots and essentially all of the environments and noncharacter dynamics are also created digitally. A film like James Cameron's *Avatar* (2009) takes this idea even farther. These films are basically photorealistic animated films, with live-action plates created in support of the animation. However, a simple definition falls short of the meaning:

- A *full animation* project can simply be defined as a project that has absolutely no live-action component whatsoever.

This distinction separates the output of Pixar, Dreamworks, and similar animation companies from what ILM, Weta, and similar visual effects facilities generally produce. But this is a formal distinction more than a functional one. Blue Sky's film *Robots* (2005) is 100% CG, whereas Pixar's *WALL-E* (2008) is 99% CG (there are a few live-action shots), but both are universally regarded as animated features. James Cameron's *Avatar* (2009) is perhaps 90% CG and Michael Bay's *Transformers* (2007) is 75% CG (approximately). Both are considered live-action (albeit VFX-heavy) features. But 75% CG versus 100% CG is not a very substantial difference in terms of CG footage on screen when it comes to doing the actual production work, considering that a

The VES Handbook of Visual Effects. DOI: 10.1016/B978-0-240-81242-7.00009-0

full CG feature is often shorter than a visual effects–driven feature, such as the 98-minute length of *WALL-E* (2008) compared to the 144-minute runtime for *Transformers* (2007). Of course, there are differences between the two. In cases where the CG work amounts to less than 100% of the project, a live-action set still exists, but the post-production difference for the animators, TDs, editors, compositors, etc. isn't so great.

As the distinction becomes blurred, an effort must be made to define an animation project's *functionality*. One such attempt is:

- An animation project is one in which stylization, not realism, is the foremost visual concern.

This distinction has two problems. One is that it would incorrectly categorize a photoreal animated film like *Final Fantasy: The Spirits Within* (2001) as a live-action or hybrid project, and it ignores the fact that some live-action films have stylization as their foremost visual concern (the *Matrix* films, for example). Another possible candidate for a workable definition is:

- An animation project is one in which the animated footage is the primary focus, and any live-action footage (if any) is subordinate to it artistically.

WALL-E (2008) is a clear example of a film where this distinction works. *Who Framed Roger Rabbit* (1988) is a little less clear. And the *Star Wars* prequels are less clear still. However, a good case could be made that all of those are animated projects with live-action plates created in support of a synthetic world and the animated characters that populate it. However, the *Star Wars* prequels may not fit the definition—because it is unclear whether the live-action footage was truly subordinate or not. Refining the above definition to try to avoid defining exactly what the filmmakers' *intentions* in this area really were leads to a definition that seems to make the most sense as a *functional* definition:

- An animation project is one that uses an animation pipeline rather than a visual effects pipeline.

Even this distinction is becoming blurred as the needs of the two pipelines converge. But to make a distinction within the current state of the art, one needs to roughly define what an animation pipeline is and after that refine and elucidate on that definition. This is not a difference one can see just by watching the film, which is the point—unless one accepts stylization as the differentiator and, in turn, accepts some full-animation projects, such as *Beowulf* (2007) or *Final Fantasy: The Spirits Within* (2001), as being virtual live action. The primary difference is one that can't necessarily be seen. To establish this pipeline-based differentiation, consider this definition of the distinction between live-action and animation pipelines:

- An animation pipeline is one in which shots are defined in the animation system, and live-action footage (if any) is integrated into the animation system footage either using 2D compositing or as animated textures on a 3D scene object.

- A visual effects pipeline is one in which shots are defined by the digitized live-action footage, and animation is integrated into said footage.

In a visual effects pipeline, the most important thing *procedurally* is the live-action footage. Each shot starts with the live-action framing and movement, and the pipeline is built on the necessity of conforming the visual effects to this source live-action footage. With this definition it becomes more about how the film was actually made, rather than what the intention was. If the starting point for all shots was the live-action footage, it is primarily a live-action project even if the results are highly stylized such as *Sin City* (2005) or *300* (2006). If the footage (and camera definitions) originates in the animation system, it is primarily an animation project. So since the *Star Wars* prequels could have been either one, the pipeline approach used defines whether it was an animated project or a live-action project.

An alternate distinction could be that animated films are made up primarily of animated footage, and live-action films are made up primarily of photographic plates. This distinction becomes muddied by films like *Dinosaurs* (1991), which has all-CG characters composited into live-action backgrounds, and *Spy Kids 3D: Game Over* (2003), which is all live-action characters composited into mostly CG backgrounds. The distinction can be refined further to consider whether the *characters* are primarily CG or live action—but then *Star Wars Episodes I–III* (1999, 2002, 2005) reveal the problem with that definition: Those films used extensive CG backgrounds and included large numbers of CG characters interacting with live-action characters.

Taking the "Where does the pipeline originate?" definition to its logical conclusion presents problems: Is a rotoscoped film like *A Scanner Darkly* (2006) live action? If camera moves originate in a previsualization system, does that make the film animated? The latter is clearly not the case. Even if the previs camera setups are fed into a camera control system, the finishing pipeline would still be live-action plate based. The former is a more interesting film theory question, but in terms of a practical distinction a film like *A Scanner Darkly* (2006) is a live-action film. For the purposes of pipeline distinction, this is because the on-set, photographic process was primary in plate acquisition. From a film theoretic perspective, it is also because live-action performance was primary over keyframe animated or puppeteered performances.

This distinction is not very helpful for film theorists or awards voters, but for visual effects and animation professionals it is one of the only distinctions left that makes much sense. And even that is a fading distinction. Advances in CG technology and the growing popularity of hyper-unrealistic spectacle films draw the two previously distinct disciplines closer and closer together every day. As organizations like VES and SIGGRAPH, and artists moving between companies, continue to spread ideas around visual effects, animation, and games facilities, even the pipeline distinctions will start to blur. Before too long, there will be no de facto visual or procedural difference whatsoever between a full animation project and a mostly CG project with live-action plates. Because of this narrowing gap, understanding animation projects has already become important for essentially anyone in this business. Tools, techniques, and pipelines that were previously restricted to the specialized domain of full animation have been moving into the visual effects world for some time now.

DIFFERENCE BETWEEN VISUAL EFFECTS AND ANIMATION

Rob Bredow

Visual effects and animation have a lot of similarities and some significant differences. Visual effects are only a part of a film and are used to augment the live action. Animation, however, is its own world. The animation studio has complete control over everything in the scene and creates the entire movie from scratch.

Visual effects are typically added to live-action photography in post-production and are integrated with the live action. Even shots that are 100% virtual in a visual effects show are typically locked to the design and execution of the surrounding live action. Additionally, some of the animation within visual effects is not directly viewed (roto-motion for matching an actor or object for interaction, casting shadows, etc.). Also, some animation within visual effects is necessary to match live-action motion to animation such as a stunt double who switches during the shot from a stuntperson to an animated double.

In animation, it's all about creating a virtual world in which the story can be told. With no live-action elements to photograph, the art direction is not limited to any real-world elements. The camera can be dictated by the characters' performance or virtual set blocking requirements since there is no live-action plate to match. In addition, nothing is ever gotten for free. Every prop, set, sky character, and lighting element needs to be designed and built in the style of the film and assembled correctly for every shot.

Production Pipelines

A good place to start breaking down the differences between live-action visual effects and animation is by examining the respective shot post-production pipelines.

Although Figure 9.1 is a simplification of film production environments, it provides a useful reference. With the exception of the layout department, the overlap between live-action visual effects and fully computer-generated animation is significant. In particular, as live-action visual effects become more prevalent throughout film productions and include regularly replacing sets and characters for an entire film, the distinction between the two types of projects is blurred even further.

This section compares the differences and similarities between the two classes of work, starting from the beginning production stages and working through final delivery.

Production

One of the early production differences between visual effects and animation is the approach to budgeting and bidding the project. In both cases, there is usually a set budget to be spent and always a desire to achieve as much volume of work and visual complexity as possible.

In the case of visual effects, this is usually accomplished during post-production as shots are identified, bid, and awarded to the visual effects facility. This process often involves multiple production facilities competing for the work, and costs are controlled by finding the most efficient facilities and minimizing the complexity requirements on a shot-by-shot basis.

In animation, the entire production is commonly awarded to a single production facility (which may or may not be owned by the production company) and an overall budget is set from the start for accomplishing all of the computer graphics animation for the film. The delivery specifications usually include the length of the film and the number of characters, sets, and other metrics that are used to broadly measure the complexity of the movie. From that point on, the production moves forward with careful monitoring of the complexity of the film both in terms of the characters, sets, and props and the complexity of the individual shots to ensure it fits into the original bucket. Overages are usually limited to the addition of major components or schedule delays.

The production of a CG feature can naturally be broken down into two phases:
1. Pre-production: building of all the assets
2. Production: creating the shots

Pre-Production

The building of all of the assets is a substantial part of the creation for both visual effects work and a CG feature film. The pre-production step includes designing, modeling, texturing,

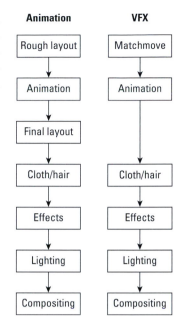

Figure 9.1 A simplified production pipeline comparing animation and visual effects productions. (Image courtesy of Rob Bredow.)

materials, and lighting as well as building the animation rigs for the characters and setting the style of the animation for the film. Depending on complexity, pre-production accounts for 20% to 35% of an animated film's budget and can use approximately half of the production schedule.

The design is driven by the art department whose members primarily design the characters, environments, and props with 2D drawings and sketches for the quickest iterations. Hundreds of designs are attempted while defining the look of the picture and creating all of the assets for the film. Some approved designs will be simple sketches from a single angle, while others may require precise drafting of all of the spatial details that will be used to inform the later departments.

Often the process of designing key characters and environments is continued into the 3D modeling phase where the creative team will explore the 3D interpretation of the model. Early in the process, it's common to encounter significant setbacks during the translation of the 2D drawings to the 3D world. The setbacks may require design changes to satisfy the creative requirements of the show.

Also, the production models of characters and environments have significant technical requirements:

1. being modeled in a median position or T-pose so that the character can be rigged efficiently,
2. certain topologies or layouts to meet rigging, texturing, and rendering needs,
3. specific resolution in various areas of deformation to allow for posing, and
4. the model may need to be generated at multiple levels of detail if hundreds of copies of the model will be seen in the same shot.

For this reason, if the exploration of the 3D model has a significant creative aspect, it's common to create a scratch 3D model that doesn't meet the technical requirements for production but can be used to explore the style of the film. Once the scratch model has been approved, the creation of the final model is primarily concerned with the technical exercise of adjusting the model to meet the production requirements.

Once the model has been approved, the process of adding the textures and materials can begin in tandem with the rigging of the character for animation.

For textures and materials, there are many similarities between live-action visual effects and animation. The basic process of laying out textures to paint the objects and assigning the correct materials for the various parts of the models is the same. The differences are primarily dictated by the style of the animated film. While some animation will adhere to photorealistic principles in terms of the behavior of light, reflection, and other material characteristics, an animated film will often make intentional variations away from pure realism for creative impact. Translating the artistic vision from the 2D artwork to the 3D world in a way that achieves the artistic goals, which maintains consistency and lighting control for later production, is collaboration between the art department and the computer graphics supervisor. It is very common during the early phase of pre-production to view characters, sets, and props on turntables in various lighting conditions. As time progresses, it's common to create test shots that combine environments, characters, and props under various lights for the sole purpose of testing the artistic and technical assumptions.

Simultaneously, the character riggers work with the lead animators to build the characters with their control systems, skin deformations, and facial rigs. Again, in this area many of the tools are very similar to visual effects production in terms of their primary functionality. And once again, the differences are primarily driven by the stylistic needs of the film. For highly expressive cartoony animation styles, great care is required to allow extreme ranges for the facial and body animations, which might include the ability to pull the corners of the mouth all the way up around the ears or bend an arm like a noodle to achieve a pose. These artistic choices are generally quite simple to draw in 2D animation, but in 3D animation they require careful attention to ensure that the animator is provided with the correct set of controls, that the model has the correct flexibility, and that the textures do not overly stretch or become otherwise compromised in the deformation process.

Once the preliminary rigs are in place, the character animation leads begin their testing, putting the characters through their paces. This accomplishes two goals:

1. It tests the range of motion provided by the riggers for the characters to ensure it's sufficient for the character's role in the movie.
2. It begins to explore the animation style for the character and get early feedback from the directors on the performance.

The collaboration between the character riggers and the animation testing continues throughout the pre-production process, while the entire cast of characters is built up to meet the standards of the production.

Production

Pre-production is rarely completed, but there is a slow transition as the first sequences are turned over into production and the members of the pre-production teams begin to assume their new production roles on shots. It's common that new environments, props, and even characters are created as sequences are entering production so the two production phases may overlap very significantly.

Layout

The job of the layout department is to translate the storyboards into the 3D animation world. This consists of establishing the position of the camera along with its lens, the basic blocking of the characters, and the dressing of the sets. The layout artists perform much the same role as the camera operator on a live-action set but do not generally include lighting. (*Wall-E*, released in 2008, was a notable exception where Pixar first experimented with more sophisticated lighting in layout to help set the mood of the shots early in production.) When completed, the layout department delivers a 3D scene for each shot that includes the characters, the set, and the camera ready for animation.

The final camera work is approved in a stage called *final layout* after the animation is completed. It's also common for there to be interaction between animation and the layout teams for shots with dynamic cameras because each department needs to react to the other's work.

In most visual effects work, the closest analogy to the animation layout department is matchmove. In the matchmove department, the live-action photography is precisely matched with a virtual camera and set for every frame of the shot. This generates the camera and environment in which the visual effects work can take place. It is common practice in visual effects work to modify the live-action photography to accommodate the creative requirements of the scene—a task handled by matchmovers, plate-mungers, or the animation department depending on the production. Additionally, some visual effects facilities have embraced the idea of a hybrid layout/matchmove department for complicated CG environments for live-action films.

Animation

The differences in the animation department between visual effects work and animation depend almost entirely on the subject matter and the style of the animated film. Some animated films desire a high level of realism, and for those the same animation principles that guide live-action visual effects work are applicable to animation. Animated films can rely on the same technology options as well, including rigging techniques, deformation methods, use or nonuse of motion capture or video reference, and many other similarities.

However, most often the desire of the filmmakers is to establish a unique look and style for the animation of the movie. This often requires the technologies and animators to adopt new techniques to either emulate a particular look from a 2D animation technique or simply create something new that is well suited to the 3D animation world.

Animation teams for animated films are larger than the average visual effects film and often include dozens of experienced character animators. Animation quotas tend to be based on feet of footage per week, whereas visual effects animation quotas are usually tracked by shot count.

Cloth and Hair

The cloth and hair departments have more similarities than differences when comparing visual effects and animation. Both types of work require refined techniques for grooming, costuming, and manipulating the simulations to achieve the desired look for the picture.

Since animated films require every costume and hair simulation to be animated for every character in every shot of the film, complexity of cloth and hair can have a significant impact on the cost of the film. Simplification strategies include using shorter hairstyles, tighter fitting clothes that can be attached directly to the skin, and other techniques that avoid having to run simulations for every element in every shot. Modern simulation techniques, however, are better at solving clothing and hair issues and require less frequent artist intervention, which can make previously costly costumes and hairstyles more efficient.

Effects Animation

Effects animation is another discipline that is heavily influenced by style when comparing visual effects and animation. Animated films can require completely photorealistic effects animation to complement a detailed style that can be leveraged off traditional visual effects animation techniques. However, animated films can also provide their own set of nonphotorealistic choices for anything from the patterns created in breaking glass all the way to smoke billowing off a fire.

One of the biggest challenges in effects animation for an animated feature is the nonphysical dynamics requested of simulations. Oftentimes, stylized character animation will create movements that move extremely quickly from frame to frame and have a tendency to break systems that expect movement to be based loosely in reality. In these cases, the motion needs to be isolated to get the desired look from an otherwise physical simulation.

In general, a talented effects artist will use similar techniques to control a simulation or create an effect whether it's for a live-action film or an animated feature.

Lighting and Compositing

For lighting and compositing tasks, there are some significant differences. In addition to the obvious requirements that visual effects work must approach photorealism and animation can be created in any style imaginable, there are other important distinctions.

When dealing with animation, the entire scene is lit using 3D tools and there is no requirement to match the lighting to a live-action plate. Because of this flexibility, most studios rely on an art department consisting of one to three painters during production to establish the lighting style of the sequences throughout the movie with loosely painted thumbnails for each important scene. These thumbnail references (referred to as *lighting keys*) are then referenced by the lead lighters for the sequence and help provide a consistent visual style for the movie.

In addition, it's much easier to leverage from key lighting in an animated movie. Key lighting is the process of lighting several key shots in a sequence to establish both the creative look and the technical procedures used to achieve that look. The most experienced lighters are generally given the key lighting responsibilities and help establish the look and workflow for the other artists on the film. Once the key lighting is established, the rest of the lighting team can reference those lighting rigs when creating the rest of the shots. Lighting adjustments are made for each shot just as in live-action photography, but the key lighting rig gives a starting point and encourages consistency and efficiency.

In visual effects work, key lighting can still be used for sequences with a lot of CG elements, but since the requirement is the match against live-action photography, there are more shot-by-shot adjustments so the payoff for key lighting work is reduced.

Compositing for animation is generally a more straightforward technique than for visual effects work. Generally speaking, all elements are CG rendered and therefore come with clean mattes and possibly even extra control passes to adjust the lighting during the compositing phase. Unlike live-action photography where these elements are filmed with strict physical constraints and can never be perfectly registered, in animation the various elements and mattes can fit together perfectly. In addition, complicated techniques for pulling mattes from blue or green screens and other live-action techniques are simply not required.

However, compositing serves a very useful purpose in animation work. Some facilities prefer to use a composite-heavy workflow where many individual passes are rendered out per character and then the final look is dialed in during the compositing phase. This has the advantage of avoiding long rerendering times and providing fast feedback to the artist who balances the various lights and elements to create the final look. One disadvantage of this technique is that these compositing scripts generally require a lot of adjustment from one shot to another so shot-to-shot efficiencies may be reduced. In addition, some techniques that are easy to use in a compositing package can create looks that don't follow any photographic rules, which can result in visual artifacts if not used carefully.

Among artists and supervisors, there are strong opinions about whether it's better to dial in the final look in the 3D lighting package or during the 2D compositing phase, and both techniques can create top-quality imagery. Generally speaking, the longer the render times and the more limited the access to computer processing power, the more appealing the 2D-centric workflow. On the flip side, if the film has a style that can be achieved mostly in 3D lighting and there is sufficient rendering power to iterate on the lighting side, the improved artist efficiency and consistency between shots can be a very significant factor.

In addition to dialing in the look of the lighting, compositing is always required when special-purpose renderers are used to achieve various effects. For example, some looks require volumetric smoke elements to be rendered by stand-alone renderers that are tuned to create images efficiently. In those cases, the compositor will combine the smoke elements with the other rendered elements in the compositing package in much the same way they would approach a live-action visual effects composite. Once again, the advantage of the all-CG elements is in the perfect registration of the matte elements, which gives the compositor the ability to make a clean composite in less time.

A SURVEY AND HISTORY OF ANIMATION TECHNIQUES
Frank Gladstone

If, by definition, animation is instilling motion where none exists, then motion picture animation is just a bit over 100 years old. The first animated film to which a date can be fixed is J. Stewart Blackton's simple but very clever "trickfilm," *Humorous Phases of Funny Faces* (1906).

If, however, one's definition of animation is instilling personality where none exists, the starting point might be Winsor McCay's *Gertie the Dinosaur* (1914). That film was designed to be part of McCay's vaudeville act[1] and featured Gertie, an animated dinosaur who expressed a range of human emotions when prompted by her real-life creator, McCay, who appeared in person, syncing his actions and comments with the character (foreshadowing the live-action/animation combinations that are so familiar today). Gertie was, by turns, shy, mischievous, scared, sad, and content—personality traits now referred to as *character animation*, creating, as pioneering Disney animators Frank Thomas and Ollie Johnston so beautifully put it, "the illusion of life."

This serves to focus on the two very basic and interrelated definitions of animation, which are the core of the art form: animation as *motion* and, more importantly, animation as *emotion*.

All forms of animation rely on preparing a series of still images in a sequential order that, when displayed in a continuous manner at a predetermined speed, gives the viewer the sense that the images are moving of their own volition. Today, there are three basic approaches to achieving animation: traditional or 2D animation, stop-motion animation (also called stop-frame animation), and CG (computer-generated) or 3D animation. Within each of these disciplines are subdisciplines and crossovers.

Traditional Animation

Traditional animation is sometimes referred to as *2D animation* or *cel animation*, named for the celluloid sheets or, cels, on which the individual animation elements were transferred before being photographed onto film. Generally, traditional animation is drawn, with characters, props, effects, and environments first committed to paper. Next, all objects that will appear to move in the final film are traced to cels, painted with opaque colors on the reverse side of the inked line,[2] and assembled in the sequential order that was determined during the animation process. Each setup is a layered sandwich of cels over background art, often with foreground art as well, positioned beneath the animation camera and photographed one frame at a time. This setup is then replaced by the next one, and the next, and so on, until the entire scene is completed.

Cel animation can be a tedious process, because each step has to be planned, timed, and animated, with a drawing (and often several drawings) created for every frame of film. Because of this,

---

[1] McCay was also an important newspaper cartoonist for W.R. Hearst's *New York Journal American*.

[2] Called *ink and paint*.

from the earliest days, storyboards have been employed to help plan out the story and pacing of each sequence before actual animation occurs. (In fact, storyboards were first developed for animation.) From the storyboard, a story reel, in early days referred to as a Leica[3] reel, is created by photographing the storyboard panels and editing them according to a rough estimate of scene length, often employing a temporary soundtrack as well. Story reels, sometimes called *animatics*, are designed to help time the sequences and test out the film's cinematic nature as well as set the tone for the voice acting and animated performances to come. Story reels and the information they provide are the precursor to the previsualization techniques used today in visual effects and CG animation. Similar to previs (in fact, previsualization footage is frequently referred to as an animatic), these reels are the guide for the creation of layouts: backgrounds, foregrounds, camera, character and object placement, and the paths of action within each scene.

Eventually, from the story reels and the voice tracks, exposure sheets[4] are developed. These are usually broken down by scene and give the length of the individual shot. The dialogue is carefully and extensively noted as it is translated into units of linguistic sound (i.e., phonemes), so that the animator can provide lip-sync for the characters. Other specific sound cues, camera movements, and action directions may be entered as well. From this information the animator knows how many frames he or she will have to work with and what will happen in the scene. As animation is completed, it is noted on the exposure sheets.

Animation is either drawn "straight ahead" or by using "key poses." *Straight ahead* means that the animator begins at the start of an action and then proceeds directly to the next drawing and each succeeding one in sequential order. *Key posing* means the animator determines the main segments, or top points of an action, and draws these points as keys. He or she will also determine the number of drawings between each key and how close or far apart those drawings will be in relation to one another. Usually, the animator will provide a chart to show the number and spacing of the drawings between the keys. The most mid-positioned drawing is called the *breakdown* and the ones between the breakdown and keys are called the *in-betweens*. Assistant animators will tie down and complete the animator's rough keys, making sure the drawings are consistent with the character (i.e., on model) and that all details are accounted for. Breakdown artists and in-betweeners will fill in and finish the additional drawings. This operation is commonly referred to as *cleanup*.

---

[3] Leica was the brand of lenses used on the animation cameras that photographed storyboards in the earliest Disney days.
[4] Also called *x-sheets* or *dope sheets*.

Effects animation depicts things that are not characters: objects, props, natural phenomena, and the like. Atmospheric effects are often stylized, providing a kind of enhanced reality that is more in relationship to the tone and subtext of the story. Effects are often animated straight ahead.

Most feature quality animation is designed to work on *ones* or *twos*. This refers to how many frames are photographed of each sequential setup prior to being replaced with the next setup in the sequence. Because motion picture film is projected at 24 fps, ones require 24 separate drawings to achieve 1 second of movement per character or object, while twos, meaning each cel or frame is photographed twice, require 12 drawings per second. Of course, animation cels can be held if a character or an object is at rest, cutting down on the number of drawings that must be animated and prepared per second of film time.

Two terms are often misused in describing animation: *full* animation and *limited* animation. Full animation means that movements and emotions are thoroughly articulated and rendered. Full animation is almost always done on ones or twos (except for held drawings) and often has more than one character moving in the same shot. In full animation, a preponderance of complicated effects is usually at work and nearly all action happens on screen. Limited animation means that movement and emotions are stylized, and oftentimes only one element, or even a part of one element, is moving on screen. Effects are formulaic and much of the action happens off screen.

Limited animation began in the very early days and then took a back seat as people became used to higher theatrical quality. It was reinvented and refined when animation began to be produced specifically for television, accommodating that medium's need for higher volume and lower production costs.

Additionally, while full animation takes little heed of the number of drawings, usually producing as many as deemed necessary to create the desired effect or mood, limited animation does not have that luxury. Instead, it must rely on clever design, isolated facial elements and body parts (so that some movement can happen while other elements hold still), emphasis on layouts and backgrounds, abbreviated and formulaic movements, repeated action (cycles), re-used animation, cel level manipulation, and camera tricks. All of these devices are employed, in any number of combinations, in order to cut down on artwork.

This does not mean that all full animation is good and all limited animation is bad. In fact, sometimes full animation can be overarticulated, or *spongy*, or be so naturalistic that it almost appears creepy. Conversely, in the hands of a good designer and with careful cinematics, limited animation can be quite compelling and often its uncomplicated approach enhances a story rather than detracting from it. In short, the old adage "less is more" also can apply to animation. This is nowhere more apparent than in the often subtle and beautiful limited animation techniques found in much of *anime*, the influential Japanese-inspired animation methodology that has become popular with audiences worldwide.

Confusion arises from these two terms when incorrect interpretation is used, especially when the term *full animation* is used to mean that the shot, scene, or sequence is made up entirely of animated elements, and *limited animation* is used to mean a shot, scene, or sequence which has some animated and some live-action elements. Although this may accurately describe the *construction of a scene*, it mixes definitions that have been used for decades to describe the *style of animation*.

For example, when Jessica Rabbit comes out to do her opening song in *Who Framed Roger Rabbit* (1988), all of the shots are made up of live-action and animated elements, but the actual animation of Jessica and the other cartoon characters is heavily articulated, full animation. Conversely, when Fred Flintstone is talking to Wilma in any episode of *The Flintstones* (1960–1966), every component of each shot is made up entirely of drawn elements but the animation style is decidedly limited.

Remember, in animation terms, *full* means more articulated and complex animation and *limited* means more stylized and less intricate animation. The terms do *not* refer specifically to the combining of live-action and animated elements.

Finally, one more term first applied to traditional animation more than 90 years ago that is still in use today is *rotoscoping*. Invented by the Fleischer Brothers around 1917, the rotoscope was originally designed to allow an animator to trace live-action footage, frame by frame, onto paper, as a method of animating characters. Thus, rotoscoping is the forerunner of today's motion capture technology.[5] The rotoscope was also used as a reference guide for placing animated characters or objects into an otherwise live-action scene and the term is still used to describe the techniques needed for placement of animated elements into live environments (plates).

Stop-Motion

The second approach to animation is *stop-motion*. This technique is probably as old as traditional drawn animation[6] and is most definitely the first attempt to give a 3D look to animated film. That is because stop-motion, by its very nature, *is* 3D. It is

---

[5] Also referred to as *MoCap* or *performance capture*.

[6] Stop-motion may even be older than 2D, but there are no confirmed dates to prove that.

achieved by photographing actual objects one frame at a time and moving the objects in a sequential pattern, between frames, so that when projected at a continuous and predetermined speed, the objects appear to move.

Early on, these stop-motion objects were simply items from everyday life, but soon more complex characters evolved, allowing for personality animation. Movement of these characters was achieved by either manipulation of articulated puppets or by object replacement. Many times, animation was achieved by a combination of both methods.

Articulation is best described as an object, usually a figurine, that possesses some sort of internal structure that facilitates the object being placed in a fixed and stable position, in which it will remain until photographed, and then adjusted into a sequential fixed position for the next photograph and so on until the movement is completed.

Replacement is the term used to describe the process of replacing one object with another between frames in order to achieve movement. For example, a replacement model would have perhaps 18 or 24 separate sets of legs, each in a graduated walking position. Each set would be replaced in turn, between frames, to provide the walking effect. (Alternatively, an articulated model would have just one set of flexible legs that could be positioned in all of the various motions to create a walking effect.) Although extremely time consuming to create, replacement animation allows for easily repeatable and reusable actions and can be more efficient for some kinds of movement during the actual animation process.

A good example of mixed use of articulated and replacement techniques would be the Jack Skellington character from *The Nightmare Before Christmas* (1993). Jack's body was completely articulated, using ball-and-socket and lever-style joints to achieve all of the complicated body movement and choreography the screenplay calls for. Jack's lip-sync and expressions, however, were done with a wide range of replacement heads, notched to fit consistently onto the body and sculpted with mouths and other facial features in various positions so that the animators, by switching out a predetermined continuum of heads between frames, could make Jack both talk and emote appropriately.

The technique of stop-motion demands that all animation be done straight ahead. There is no practical way to position a stop-motion model or puppet for key frames and then go back to put in the in-between motions. In fact, before the days of video playback, there was no way to even preview what a stop-motion animator had shot. Animators simply had to continue their work straight ahead, assisted only by small appliances on the set—called *surface gauges*—that acted as simple reference marks to indicate where their models had been in the previous frame. Today, using frame-by-frame video playback, stop-motion animators can look at the frames they have completed as they set up each new position, which is a great help in keeping the animation consistent and error free.

Stop-motion environments are basically miniature practical sets, often built in forced perspective if added depth is needed. (Often, characters will be scaled in forced perspective as well.) Sets are lit in the same way a live-action set would be, with care taken to keep the light temperatures low, because the lights will be on not for minutes but hours while the animation is achieved. Additionally, sets usually have some way to tie down or fix the feet or base of the animated puppets, keeping them stable when in their various, often off-balanced positions. Another improvement resulting from today's technology allows animators to use external rigs that are visible to the camera to balance or support characters. These rigs can then be removed or painted out of the shot using CG image repair technologies (Photoshop, After Effects, etc.).

Traditionally, moving camera shots in stop-motion required complicated rail systems and human-driven, very precise movement along that rail. Today, computer-controlled camera cranes (motion control) can make smoother and repeated setups possible. Currently, most stop-motion is photographed using lightweight digital still cameras and lenses that send the images directly to computers for storage, so camera moves have become even more flexible and practical.

Since the 1920s, stop-motion has also been used to add fantastic characters into live-action films. This was achieved by animating the characters so that their motions would be in sync when optically matched with previously photographed live-action plates. The most famous of these films is undoubtedly Willis O'Brien's masterpiece, *King Kong* (1933).

O'Brien's protégé, Ray Harryhausen, took his mentor's techniques a step farther, both by giving his animated characters more subtle emotional depth and by perfecting a beamsplitting, rear screen/front screen projection technique, making it possible to join his complex stop-motion creatures more convincingly with live-action actors and backgrounds, resulting in such memorable work as the skeleton fight in *Jason and the Argonauts* (1963).

Today, these kinds of "monster in the real world" visuals are achieved exclusively with CG-animated imagery, because stop-motion's relatively long production schedules and specifically its dream-like movements, which always contrasted somewhat with the live-action plates, are not able to satisfy modern tastes for reality.[7]

Computer Graphic Technology

The third common approach to animation is the use of computer graphic technology. This method of making animated images has more in common with its traditional 2D and stop-motion animation forebears than might seem obvious at first glance.

First, character animation in CG can be compared to the process of moving a virtual stop-motion puppet in that the 3D model has a basic, though usually much more heavily articulated, virtual armature, controlled by the animator who moves the character into key positions—generally referred to as *key frames*. Similar to traditional 2D work, the animator can make decisions about the number, speed, and placement of in-between positions, which can then be generated by the computer.

In fact, most of the activities involved in CG animation production can be directly related to similar activities on the more traditional animation production pipeline. For instance, once story and production designs are determined—much the same process for all types of animated films—CG proceeds with the modeling of characters and rigging of their armatures with appropriate movable parts and controls. These activities are directly correlated to developing model sheets and drawing formulas for 2D animation and construction of puppets for stop-motion.

As stated earlier, story reels, animatics, and layout development are the precursors to previsualization in CG. (Previs is sometimes referred to as *rough layout*.) Virtual sets are constructed and lit in CG, using the same artistic considerations and patterns that are common to stop-motion practical sets or layout design in 2D.

CG effects animation, especially of natural phenomena and atmosphere, often involves the ability to program particle systems, which drive the effects and, like traditional approaches, are most often stylized and animated in a computer-generated version of straight-ahead animation.

In traditional 2D work, cels are inked and painted (done digitally nowadays) and backgrounds are completed with great attention being paid to the lighting, color, and atmosphere of the sequence. In CG, characters and environments are surfaced or

---

[7] Stop-motion models, being shot one still frame at a time, have no blurred elements, as do moving objects when filmed in real time, thereby giving the animated characters a sort of staccato effect to their movements when compared to the live-action plates in which they are positioned.

textured and lit with the same considerations, though CG offers a much broader and more flexible variety of surfaces and lighting applications. Finally, when all elements are accounted for, they are composited into a harmonious image—analogous to cel set-ups that are positioned and photographed in 2D—but the digital age offers an unlimited number of levels to be composited, whereas the older technology was only able to afford six or seven layers to work with before the density of the overlaid cels began to "milk out" the image being photographed.

Camera motion within CG's virtual sets is unlimited, in contrast to the restricted movement afforded by traditional technologies. The early attempts at depth in cel animation involved either a diorama-like arrangement or a multilevel photography apparatus called a *multiplane camera*. These kinds of shots were very time consuming and expensive to produce. The fact that CG technology allows as many digital levels as necessary and that each level has the ability to be moved and adjusted independently now makes multiplane effects possible in any scene. Combined with the virtual moving camera, depth has become a much more usable tool in CG animation than it ever was with the traditional technologies.

Finally, all elements in CG animation's virtual world have to be rendered into the images that their digital information represents. This process is actually begun at the very start of animation production, in rough form, and continues throughout the production process in increasingly more polished versions until the final render and output—sometimes referred to as *film-out*. The need to differentiate, render, and record the production images as they progress throughout the production process drives the technical aspects of the animation pipeline. So, for all intents and purposes, *pipeline* has come to mean both the production process and the hardware and software needed to cope with the demands of that process. Most often, it is necessary to determine the technical requirements of specific productions before actual animation begins to ensure that the pipeline is robust enough to deal with the myriad demands of each stage of the process and can cope with the huge amounts of digital information that will be required to render images throughout the production—up to and including the final images.

To this point, the discussion has been focused on CG animation created within and for a virtual 3D world. There is also the creation of CG animation from live-action reference. Motion capture, like its rotoscope predecessor, involves recording the actual movements of humans or animals. Information about the coordinates of these digitally recorded movements is noted in the computer and that information is then used to manipulate the rigs of animated figures.

Finally, it should also be noted that there are increasing improvements and uses for 2D CG technology; that is, 2D stylized animated images using computer tools. There are many ways to do this, from animating in classic 3D fashion and then "toonshading" the images to create a flat or painterly look, to using software applications such as Flash that allow traditionally drawn images that are scanned into the system to be combined and manipulated in a kind of computer version of limited animation.

In the final analysis, by whatever means animated images have been created—stop-motion, traditional 2D, CG technology, or some combination of techniques—the important thing has always been the ability to use these tools to achieve a believable performance, creating not only movement but also honest and identifiable emotion out of the whole cloth of an artist's imagination.

CONSIDERATIONS FOR A FULL CG-ANIMATED FEATURE PIPELINE
Stephan Vladimir Bugaj

The most substantial consideration in developing a pipeline for feature animation is the realization that an entire world must be created from whole cloth and usually a complex, visually stylized one at that. This implies certain artistic, technical, and production management requirements. All elements of the world must be internally consistent, without any photographic plates to provide context (and when dealing with a stylized world various new problems arise such as how to stylize physically based simulations into *cartoon physics*). Since the world must be created from nothing, feature animation requires a pipeline that addresses every step of image generation from production design, to camera layout, to effects, to final composite.

A feature animation studio needs:
- sufficient artist resources to do the work,
- large amounts of computer power and storage for the many technical assets that will be developed, and
- a production management system that can keep track of many assets across many departments, often working in parallel, and over the long time to delivery that is necessary for producing top-quality feature animation (typically 2 to 5 years for an A-list animated feature).

For those familiar with other animation pipelines, it is important to consider the differences between hand-drawn pipelines and CG animation pipelines. Whether the drawing is done on paper or a digital tablet, hand-drawn animation deals almost entirely with image assets (image layers that compose into frames in the film). Drawn animation requires a system for managing collections of image files, organized into something along these lines: style guides and reference keys (including pencil tests), background plates by sequence; if used, reusable element libraries (walk cycles, facial gestures and phonemes, visual effects elements, etc.) and photographic plates to be rotoscoped. Images in this pipeline basically move from storyboard artists, to layout artists, to background pencilers, to background inkers, to keyframe pencilers, to in-betweeners, to inkers, and finally on to the final assembly (either photography on an animation stand or digital compositing of the plates).

A CG animation pipeline, on the other hand, is more technically complex and is broken down into more departments. These departments are often doing parallel work rather than working in a strictly linear pipeline, and the ability to break down assets into elements relevant to separate, parallel tasks is very important, as is reusability. Reusable components, such as character articulation rigs, shaders and texturers, procedural models, and so on, are created by technical artists and reused throughout the film. CG feature animation pipelines seem similar to a visual effects pipeline in that there are CG modelers, shading/texturing artists, character animators, lighters, effects animators, simulation technical artists, and shot finaling departments such as rendering and compositing. However, because there are no photographic source plates, scanning/input and matchmove are not the starting point of an animation pipeline; rather camera layout in the 3D system and blocking animation are the starting points. In animation the CG artists are responsible for *all* of the acting and cinematography, as opposed to starting from material already acquired on set.

Because animation involves the creation of the entire film, the production pipeline is based around sequences, starting with camera layout and ending with final render, and reel deadlines drive the sequence delivery dates (reels being literally all the sequences that are contiguous on a standard reel of 35mm film). In all filmmaking, a shot is action that takes place during one location and at one point in time.

Sequences are collections of shots that are conceptually related by their role in the story. Everyone is at least roughly familiar with the idea of sequences from DVD chapters, but in animation they are explicitly used to organize production. Assignments are based on sequence delivery deadlines, and sequence deliveries build into a *reel lock* in which a full reel of the film is fed from final render (meaning the approved CG render prior to color grading) into post-production and ultimately edited in to the reel, color graded, and approved for film-out.

Pre-production (particularly storyboard creation and animatics editing) are also heavily sequence based, and that means production design tends to also deliver based on sequences (with the exception of designs for primary characters—a variance that character modeling, rigging, and shading also share because the primary characters appear in too many sequences to be sequence-driven deliverables). Environments (sets/locations) and master lighting rigs are developed for sequences, except for certain key multi-sequence environments, and this work is then inherited by all shots in a given sequence.

Task completion is tracked at the asset level, which blocks all shot-level completions until the assets in a given shot are finaled. Layered on top, shot-level task completion is tracked for the shot work itself, and that blocks sequence completion. A sequence is blocked against completion until all shots in that sequence, and by extension all assets in those shots, are completed. Sequences and reels are reviewed in-context to ensure continuity, both during in-production checkpoints and after finaling. At any point, fixes may be opened on assets or shots that block delivery of the sequence (and therefore its reel) to post-production, and these also must be tracked in the production management system.

CG Feature Animation Pipeline

Storyboard Animatics and Previs

The entire film is boarded and edited into animatics reels. Because changing animation is so expensive, board artists and editors work closely with the director, head of story, and screenwriter to develop the animated film to a nearly finished edit before production begins in earnest. Previs is a full CG extension of the animatics process, where boards are replaced by CG models, and is sometimes used in animation in the same way that it's used in visual effects: to mock up the environment, camera, and action in 3D prior to deciding on final shot designs.

Production Design and Look Development

Because there are no plates, the creation of production designs as a starting point for creating the visual world is utterly essential in animation. There is no opportunity to find interesting people, places, and things in the real world to film. Look development is the process of taking sample sequence(s) and pushing them through the entire pipeline (all the way to film-out) in order to find the right way to translate the production designs into a CG look.

Layout and Set Dressing

In animation, layout does the camera portion of cinematography. Layout artists determine framing and camera moves using virtual cameras that have frame aspect ratios, different focal lengths, aperture/depth of field (DOF), and even virtual dolly, crane, and other jib controls. Layout artists also block in rough environments and character animation, using whatever models are available at the time. Set dressers take the rough layout stand-ins and dress in the real finished environment models for each sequence.

Modeling, Texturing, and Articulation (Rigging)

Environments and character models are digitally sculpted and textured, and characters and other animated models are articulated. In large feature animation pipelines, this may constitute as many as eight departments (one each of modeling, shading, texture painting, and rigging for characters and environments).

Character Animation, Character Simulation, and Crowds

Voice recordings are made, and characters are keyframe animated based on the reading (or motion capture data is acquired and finessed). This is the acting phase of animated filmmaking. Clothing, hair, and any procedural animation elements that are driven by the animation key frames are also done at this time. Shot simulation department(s) may finesse the final simulations, but the setup departments for cloth, hair, and procedurals provide the animators with stand-ins so they can see rough simulations in real time. Crowd animation is usually achieved by a separate department, consisting of animators who create libraries of crowd movements, and technical artists who use procedural systems to control the location, grouping, and movement of the crowds.

Lighting and Compositing

The virtual scene is lit, completing the cinematographic look with light and shadow. Although this stage of the pipeline is easy to describe, it is often a very precise and time-consuming process, because in an animation pipeline there is no natural lighting to modify and enhance. Additionally, in animation, decomposition of shots into layers of elements, and subsequent compositing, is usually done in the lighting department.

Effects Animation and Simulation

Effects artists in animation do nearly everything that effects artists do for live action, using all of the same simulation, effects animation, and compositing techniques, and yet this is only one stage of the CG animation pipeline. And because animation has no real world plates, even easily photographed elements such as a burning match, a car tire kicking up dust, or a person drinking a glass of water must be laboriously constructed.

Shot Finaling, Rendering, and Cleanup

Shot finaling departments are responsible for cleanup of the scene construction, layering, and compositing, as well as optimization to meet render time goals, and post-render paint/roto cleanup if necessary.

Post-Production

Most animation studios do most, if not all, of their post-production in house. Editing has been going on throughout the production process. In post-production, a final edit is created and then the film goes through color grading, sound design, sound editing, final sound mix, and finally film-out (which includes one or both of literally filming out duplication masters on an Arri laser or similar device, or packaging them up for digital cinema delivery).

To create a feature animation, a studio needs artists who can do all of those things. Notice that this includes things like cinematography (both camera and lighting), editing, and acting (character animators) that aren't normally considered essential by shops accustomed to work other than CG feature animation. This means a different staffing and artist development strategy, and a comprehensive filmmaking approach to managing the studio.

Production Management

Production management is another key part of feature animation. Most CG animation shops spend a lot of time on general asset development before a single shot is ever finaled. Character rigs, shaders, garments and wigs, effects and procedural animation rigs, and so on, are all laboriously tested—not just technically, but in look development tests as well. This means that a good percentage of the 2 to 5 years spent creating an animated feature involves everything being in an unfinished state. This situation requires both the right attitude on the part of the producers and a robust production tracking system necessary to keep track of the many assets, and the many intricate interdependencies among assets, and between sequences, shots, and assets. A feature animation production tracking system needs to:

- Track different departmental checkpoints for each kind of asset and shot. A shot or asset needs to clear multiple departments, each of which may have many task checkpoints. These are likely to be interleaved as departments hand work back and forth in order to support iterative refinement.
- Track interdependencies between technical assets such as geometry, articulation rigs, and shaders, which may be built up using multiple levels of reusable assets. An example would

be a sequence shading materials palette that depends on a show-wide materials palette, which in turn depends on a show-wide shading template library, which references a studio-wide shading template library that's built upon a shading language function library.

- Track dependencies between shots and assets, sequences and shots, and reels and sequences.
- Have a system of notes and fixes through which production management can, based on notes given by the director or other lead staff, block clearance of (or even "un-final") a shot or asset relative to a given departmental checkpoint—and therefore all assets, shots, sequences, and reels that depend on it.

Technical Considerations

Technical considerations are also important. CG animation requires different software from cel animation, and although the base packages are often very similar to what is used in the visual effects world, the exact configurations and usage thereof are determined by the fact that a single shop is going to do production design, animatics, previs, creation of every element in every shot, and much of the post-production. Feature CG teams also tend to be larger, placing an added technical infrastructure and budgetary burden on the studio as compared to a live-action film of a similar scope.

Technical considerations for CG feature animation include the following:

- The need for end-to-end software pipeline integration that allows assets and shots to be made up of assets comprised of many components, starting with images and clips created by production design and story, and carrying through into production where many associated 3D assets will be created, which then get rendered out to images that feed into post-production. Add tracking software to keep track of it all.
- A fast, high-capacity network. CG animation moves around a lot of large assets, and parallel iterative refinement means this is done quite frequently.
- A large render farm. Because every element seen in the frame must be generated, animation films are often rendering enormous scenes. Even though the scenes are usually broken up into smaller parts to reduce the load on individual render farm machines, a lot of powerful machines are needed to compute all of the scene data. Farms with several thousands of nodes are not unheard of.
- A large image storage farm. Since there is no photo imagery for reference, all the work of previous departments (and multiple iterations thereof) acts as reference materials for the

departments farther downstream. Therefore, huge numbers of image assets are kept online.

- A large model and shot storage farm. To allow for version control and other safe work practices, multiple revisions of every file for every shot and asset made must be kept. Since that's everything in the film, that adds up quickly.
- A sophisticated backup system. All of this data need to be backed up, and in a way that does not interfere with ongoing work. The backup system must not only be of sufficient capacity, it also needs to be highly optimized.

While many of these considerations, technical and otherwise, also apply to highly effects-heavy live-action films such as the *Pirates of the Caribbean* series (2003, 2006, 2007) or *Lord of the Rings* series (2001, 2002, 2003), this is because those films operate at a scale where they come close to the staffing, management, and technical requirements of an animated feature. However, even in those cases, the existence of photographic plates means that certain elements of production on the CG side are omitted, such as camera staging and editing, while others are reduced, such as acting and lighting. When developing a full CG feature pipeline, the main thing to consider is that no matter how experienced a studio may be with some substantial portion of the filmmaking pipeline, with full animation there is nothing to fall back on and it is necessary to become capable in every aspect of filmmaking.

MANAGING AN ANIMATED FILM
Don Hahn

Film Management and Personal Style

The experience of managing an animated film can vary depending on the technique used for the film. CG production and motion capture usually present more technology challenges than do stop-motion and 2D animation. But the approach to management is essentially the same no matter what technique or medium is used.

To begin this section on the management of an animated film, a discussion of personal style is in order. Each producer has a personal bag of tricks that he or she brings to a project. Some are known as *creative* producers; others come from a business or finance background. This personal background will have as much to do with the management approach on a film as almost any other factor.

The producer on an animated film is a coach, psychotherapist, and cheerleader all wrapped into one. Producers have an important creative role in helping the directors tell the story by building a strong team of collaborators on each film. There is also an equal responsibility to the studio to deliver the film on time and on budget.

Budgets and schedules aside for a moment, the producer's number one priority is to assemble and maintain a world-class team and create a movie of lasting quality. What do producers need to do to successfully manage an animated film? The answer is deceptively simple: They hire the best people that can be found and then do exactly what those people tell them to do!

Building Brain Trusts

A priority for any project manager is to make sure there is a brain trust of experts in place as a support network. Strong brain trusts must be assembled in three areas:

1. *Administration:* consisting of a human resources head, a lawyer, a production finance person, and a technology lead.
2. *Production:* The top managers of the film who evaluate the project, set goals, and then help the team attain them.
3. *Creative:* A group of trusted story artists who will tell the truth about the movie and where it needs to go. A brain trust of writers and story people can help navigate story problems as they happen. At Disney/Pixar the story brain trust includes directors from other projects who can come in with completely fresh eyes and give notes on a project. This is a secret weapon that far too many studios ignore. The producer/manager needs to create that atmosphere of creative debate in a way that will "plus" the movie with frequent notes and debate.

These three groups of people—administration, production, and creative—are the safety net. No single individual has the expertise that these people will bring to the table on a regular basis to solve the problems that come up during the course of the production.

Business Affairs

The business affairs person on the film consults on employee contracts, liaises with labor relations, and negotiates contracts for key talent including producers, directors, composers, and songwriters. Voice talent deals need special attention: Is the talent expected to make personal appearances for the film? How many recording sessions are guaranteed in the contract? What, if any, bonuses do they get on the back end of the film? The guidance and counsel provided by a business affairs associate bring essential order to the filmmaking process.

Production Finance

The schedule and budget are living and breathing documents. It is important to remember that animation is not a traditional assembly-line activity; it is more like sports. A team can prepare, train, and recruit the best players and set a game plan, but it has no control over the variables of the game. The team does have control over how quickly it can react to changes in the game, but it can be prepared and conditioned to adjust to the new conditions and still play at top level.

The weekly monitoring of each department will paint a picture of how the team is playing. Some departments are never a problem and others, usually departments that are prone to creative changes, can be chaotic. The success of these departments in the crunch goes back to the original casting of the players and their experience with the stress and fluidity of production.

There is a mythology in production that for a film to be properly managed, it has to hit quotas, budget, and schedule as originally planned. The truth about successful production management is all about adapting to change. Again, the key here is *preparedness*. Expect and train for change. Expect chaos and moments of indecision, and then train the management team how to react to the change; accessing, listening, planning, and refocusing attention are the goals.

Human Resources

The term *human resources* (HR) has expanded to include many diverse areas of traditional personnel department functions. The HR staff establishes compensation guidelines for the production and can provide valuable third-person counseling to individual crew members outside the pressures of production.

A key part of human resources management is performance evaluation. If regular performance reviews are in place, the company will have the chance to coach employees and guide them to better performance. In the case of high-performing crew members, it is an opportunity to provide reinforcement, and even bonuses or salary adjustments as a reward.

Animated film production is a marathon and it is normal to have some staff turnover. Regular performance evaluation keeps an open channel of communication with the employees and offers the producer and production management staff a way to coach and counsel people throughout the long production period while constantly keeping the crew performing at the highest level.

Recruitment and training often fall to the HR department. Productions need to staff up at a moment's notice and rely on HR to provide an up-to-date contact list of potential crew members. Production should guide HR as to specific future needs and provide a clear *artist loading* schedule on a film. At the same time HR needs an active connection to the industry, labor unions, and schools to help supply the demand for strong people. Most forward-thinking studios have strong long-term relationships with potential talent and encourage artists to upload their portfolios to the studio website.

If the film is a union project, HR also needs a strong connection with labor unions. Strong and frequent communication with the union rep or shop steward will speed communication when a labor problem arises.

Last, HR often takes on the overall task of training and development. Training on an animated film needs to be focused and production specific. A producer or production manager should let the HR department know about necessary training goals and problems. It is better for the production to put forward the training priorities that will directly benefit the movie than to let HR administer the program.

Building the Core Creative Team

Assume a concept for a film exists and now it is time to build a creative team to execute that concept. Take time in the process now to evaluate the scope and scale of the concept and take stock: Can the story be executed for the money budgeted? What new technologies will be needed to execute the film? What key talent can be identified now to start the production?

The director is the first crucial hire. He or she has three responsibilities:
1. to articulate the vision and the story clearly to the crew,
2. to give candid critiques, and
3. to rally the crew and build morale around that vision.

The storytelling aspects of directing are obvious: Work with a writer and the story team to bring the film to life on reels. For a producer, the key ingredient is to foster collaboration between the director and all of the direct artistic leads such as art directors, editors, and animators. It is the director's vision—but the team has to be on board with that vision. It doesn't mean that the story must be negotiated with the team, but the team does need to be heard and the content needs to be debated. If the story isn't debated early and with candor, it will get debated in the reviews when the movie opens. It is better to have those creative discussions early, using the process to build a better, stronger, more coherent team with which to work.

It is not surprising that morale building is included here as one of the director's duties. The core team, and eventually the entire production crew, has to sustain the director's vision over a period of years. And that team must believe where the director is taking them. There will always be frustration, debate, and disagreement on any film, but if the team can agree on supporting the director's vision of the film, the process and result will be stronger.

Writing and Visual Development

Simply put, the script is a road map for a movie and the point of departure for any film project. In animation, it is a fluid document that changes as ideas grow and develop. Animation is a visual medium, so the writers work closely with storyboard artists, visual development artists, and the director to create characters, dialogue, and situations that work well visually. It is a highly collaborative team effort that makes a story work. Animation writers need to be in the room and working around the table with visual artists to launch the movie properly. The script and visual development art are important management tools to evaluate the artistic scope and scale of the movie and aid in early planning.

Storyboarding and Reels

The storyboarding process developed by the Walt Disney Studios in the 1930s was a creative breakthrough and remains the biggest management tool around for animation. As the original script is boarded, story artists supply a blueprint for the film that can be used not only to judge story progress but also to refine the budget and schedule for the film.

The move from script to storyboard is always a bumpy one. Animation is a visual medium and the story has to mature in a visual way. The boards are an incredibly inexpensive way to workshop the story before production starts. The storyboards allow creative heads to refine and remake the film in a visual way that will translate better to the final product. It is the least expensive and most effective way to introduce quality into a film.

By investing a few more weeks or months of story time into refining the storyboards, two things happen: A better story can be told in visual terms, and everyone will gain a better indication of the exact scope and scale of the film, which results in more accurate budgeting and scheduling.

Research, Training, and Development

The management team can work wonders in the research phase of a film. Once the central creative team is together, it is crucial to give them immersion training in the topic and world of the film. For some this means a field trip to the location of the film: *The Lion King* (1994) staffers traveled to Africa. The *Cars* (2006) crew took a trip on Route 66.

Producers can also bring in lecturers, experts, and entertainers to inspire and inform the staff and typically a reference library of films and books is organized for the crew. These early steps to immerse the crew in the film's subject will pay dividends time and again.

There is a team-building aspect to this phase as well. As the team travels, visits museums, or works in long lecture sessions together, the team members get a chance to hear each other's thoughts and test them against their own. It can be a much-needed early bonding experience.

Sometimes production management abdicates staff training to the human resources department. That should never happen. Dictate to the HR crew exactly what the needs are and let them help raise the level of training that will specifically benefit the movie.

Working with a Studio

The management team on a film has to "manage up" to the studio as well as down to the below-the-line crew.

Relationship building is the key here. No executive likes to be an outsider to the creation of a film he or she is charged with overseeing. There are times when it may be best to filter the kinds of information that flows to the studio, but the best course of action is to keep the studio very close, particularly in the early development of the project.

The early crucial decisions of story, scope, scale, artistic leadership, voice casting, and budget are all shared decisions. That is not to say that the studio is directing the film, but they are certainly commissioning the film and as such need to be a party to the creation of the project.

Each studio is somewhat different, but studios usually contain a very small core team of players who are collaborators. The studio head needs to be involved in key creative and financial decisions.

The studio executives in charge of production, finance, marketing, consumer products, and business affairs are the next line of important relationships. These relationships are important alliances for the management on an animated film. If the relationships have been built properly with these people, and if they are kept up on the status of the film, these people become a safety net when things go wrong. Once again any producer of an animated film worth his salt knows to look at these people—finance, marketing, business affairs, production, consumer products—as part of his or her brain trust. They are not bosses as much as they are partners, and by the very nature of having commissioned a film, they have a vested interest in having it succeed.

Completion Bonds

Most independently financed films, including many that are distributed by the major studios, require a completion bond.[8] A *completion bond* or *completion guaranty* is a written contract

---

[8] If the film is produced and fully financed by any of the major Hollywood studios, it is most likely self-guaranteed.

that guarantees a motion picture will be finished and delivered on schedule and within budget.

The production usually secures a completion bond for the benefit of the bank and film financiers. In general, it assures them that the producers will complete and deliver the film in keeping with the screenplay, budget, and production schedule that the bank or financiers approved.

If the production of the film is abandoned, the completion guarantor will fully repay the bank and financiers. As more and more independent animated films appear, the completion bond is an important component of the film that provides assurance to the investors. It is not to be overlooked.

Managing Expectations

Managing expectations during the making of the film can keep the crew focused during a long and often grueling production period. For example, most early screenings of a film are horrible. On *Who Framed Roger Rabbit* (1988), an early audience preview screening was held where more than half of the audience walked out. Other films that failed horribly in their early versions include *Toy Story* (1995), *Beauty and the Beast* (1991), *Aladdin* (1992), and even *Bambi* (1942).

The crew and the studio need to understand that animation is one long intense process and early misfires are common. It is a need for concern, but not a need for panic. Bring in the creative brain trust and be candid and brutal about the film's faults. Then dive back in.

Managing the buzz from a bad screening is crucial. As a manager, it is important to deflect panic and get people on the crew focused on the tasks ahead to make the film better. The movie should not be shown to anyone outside the core team of filmmakers led creatively by the director until there have been multiple screenings to improve the film.

Managing expectations is the key. Yes, the film will have to be shared with the crew and the studio, but the setup to the screening is as important as anything in these early days of the project. Remind people that this is "a rough sketch" or "a very rough pass on this sequence." Anything to prepare the audience for the state of the film will help temper unneeded notes and critiques.

On the other hand, always solicit notes from the crew after a screening. It does two things: It produces a handful of genuinely useful notes from fresh eyes that haven't seen the film before, and at the same time a sense of trust and team is built that is so important as the film goes into the production crunch period.

Facilities and Environment

The physical environment can help or hinder the production. Two examples: Some of the brightest and best animated films have been made in open-plan warehouse environments. The advantage of open plan is that it fosters immediate communication and a sense of team. One of the problems with the old animation building on the Disney lot is that it had separate wings with each artist having a private office. This hindered communication and it actually became much more formal. Memos and meetings took over where casual conversation once worked. The layout of the facility made it very hard to get the crew together in a common space where meetings or casual communications could take place.

Staffing Up for Production

Clearly the work of building a crew into a team is the most important job in managing a project. Alfred Hitchcock said that most of his work was done by the time he had cast his movie; his words can easily apply to casting the team for a production. Hire the brightest and smartest people, and then allow them to do what they do best. The success of a production is based purely on the team of people cast to create the film.

A number of approaches can be used to cast the team. Keep in mind that it is not a party—everyone doesn't have to get along all the time, but there does need to be respect among the team players. Producers who cast their movies based on low labor cost usually get what they paid for—and in the end sometimes end up paying a great deal more than they should have to get an acceptable product. Remember: Cast the film with the best talent that can be afforded. Look for these crucial skills: the individual's expertise, management skill, candor, and the ability to push the team to a higher level.

The team is only as good as the weakest member. Hire only "A" players who are not afraid to be surrounded by other "A" players and the team will have the potential to work at a very high level.

Production Management 101

Managing a project starts with thoughtful analysis of the scope and scale of the project, followed by a detailed breakdown of the project into smaller manageable tasks. The next step is to plan and commit people and money to work on those tasks, and finally to monitor the completion of each task on a regular basis. In short:
- Analyze the job.
- Break it down into component departments and weeks.

- Commit people and money to do it.
- Monitor the progress until finished.

At the core of all this is the trust and belief that the crew can maintain the schedule. Two criteria should be balanced:

1. The project has to be delivered on time and budget.
2. The project must live up to the highest creative potential possible.

There are no shortcuts to streamline production or they would have been used many times over.

Chaos and problems are the currency of an animated film production. The first step is to recognize that problems are a constant. The next step is to identify the problems and fix them quickly and meaningfully. Work with the artistic team to spot problems early.

A regular problem that shows up early is the lack of inventory. Each department relies on a regular flow of work to keep their people busy and to supply the next department with work. When early story changes happen, or departments fail early in the flow of work, the pipeline flow dries up and the crew sits without work. It is an incredibly common problem and also very fixable. It is better to send shots down through the pipeline to warm up the team and get them working. Some managers wait until everything is perfect before they will okay work for production. But it is far better to send off a few dozen shots, even if they have to be redone, just to test out the systems and see some early results.

Early shots are never pretty, but they serve to test the pipeline and the crew and get both ready for the real work crunch coming.

Once work does flow to the crew, do not stop it or let it up. Inventory feeds the studio and it cannot dry up. Regular approvals to send work into production are necessary at regular reliable intervals to feed the production monster.

A manager's job is to serve the creative process and provide the team with a trustworthy plan to complete the project. If the team trusts the plan, and if they trust the manager's ability to constantly revisit that plan in an effective way, then compliance with the production plan, budget, and schedule is a given. If the crew doesn't have faith in the manager's planning abilities, or his or her ability to recognize faults and repair them, the manager will always be chasing their trust—and it is a very hard thing to regain once it is lost. Never, ever, lose the trust of the crew. Admit mistakes, ask for help, but always solicit a mutual trust and respect between artist and management.

Reliable data tracking is the other basic prerequisite to strong management. Production finance will usually provide productivity reports and financial cost-to-date reports to help manage the problem. Accurate up-to-date information can help the manager anticipate problems and stop them before they get worse.

Using Subcontractors

It is likely that the production of a film will include some work to be done by subcontractors outside of the studio environment. For the most part, the deal with subcontractors is a standard negotiation. It is prudent to get three bids. See samples of their work, and get references from others who have hired them. Part of the deal with a subcontractor will be to set goals and benchmarks for delivery. These expectations should be clearly set out in advance in the contract and then managed during the production process.

Work done through a subcontractor should be assigned with careful documentation along with expectations for completion. In some cases if the amount of work is significant, it merits a remote manager to monitor the progress of the production. Receipt of work from the subcontractor should be carefully documented and weekly cost reports should be built in to the weekly production reports.

The Production Brain Trust

Just as there is a brain trust for the administrative team and a story brain trust for the creative team, there is also a brain trust for the production team. This is the engine room of the film. The key players here are the:
- Associate Producer,
- Production Manager,
- Department Head, and
- Production Department Manager (and team).

The Associate Producer has three things to worry about: people, time, and money. Associate Producers are always solving problems that sound like they come from some nightmarish math test. For example: If an animator can complete 4 seconds of film per week and the film is 90 minutes long and has to be animated in 52 weeks, how many animators will be needed to complete the film on time?

The *mathematical* answer is 26, but the *real answer* depends on how many characters there are per second; how experienced the animators are; how many holidays, sick days, and vacation days fall in that year; how much overtime the budget allows; how many versions are required before the scene gets approved; and how many computer crashes will take place during that 52 weeks. The art of producing and managing an animated movie has to allow for false starts, changes, and animation that doesn't work the first time around.

Being a Production Manager (PM) for an animated film is like being the mayor of a small city full of filmmakers. The PM works closely with the producers to set goals for each week and manage the daily flow of work. Each department will need director time, sweatbox critique sessions need to be scheduled, and regular production meetings need to be scheduled in order to keep information flowing between departments.

Film crews are organized by department, and each department has a department head who is a senior artist or technician who manages the artistic or technical goals of a particular department. Most importantly, the department head keeps watch over the quality level of the work—be it animation, modeling, or visual effects.

The department runs like a small business. A PDM (some studios call them Assistant Production Managers or Production Co-Coordinators) runs the department's business. PDMs report to the production manager and work as a team, collaborating with other PDMs. They all manage the production each week. Then there are armies of tireless production secretaries, production assistants, and administrative staff who do everything from typing scripts and memos to arranging for catering during the production crunch, answering phones, booking travel, scheduling massages for tired artists, making coffee, running errands, and generally helping to move the production ahead.

Encouraging Iteration: Managing Change

Another aspect of fostering the creative environment is the art of critique. It is the secret weapon, the advantage that animation has over other movie techniques. Creating an atmosphere where opinion is not only tolerated but also welcomed and fostered is the goal. At every level, foster an openness to discuss and express feelings on story, animation, design, and nearly every aspect of the film.

The director and producer have to be particularly tolerant and welcoming to this culture or it won't happen. The creative leads on the show have to be willing to take the time to listen to dozens of ideas, some of them awful and some useful, in order to get the film to a higher level. This group critique culture builds a tremendous amount of ownership between the filmmakers and the product if done right. Everyone's pride grows when they feel that they have been heard or, at least, included in the process. The director will still have to go back to his or her office and sort through the notes and the final product is, at its best, a single vision, but the culture of honest debate and creative critique is crucial for films to reach their highest level.

This is an intimidating process for production management who want to hit deadlines. Soliciting changes is completely counterintuitive to achieving this. But the job is to deliver the highest quality film on budget and on schedule. If there is no cultural permission to be critical, then there is no incentive for the artists to contribute at their fullest level and they treat the project as nothing more than work for hire. Always driving to inflexibly hit numbers shows that there was no contingency for change and the message that schedule trumps quality is sent out. Neither of these things is good.

Technology

A producer needs a close partnership with a technology lead. This is a person who is constantly trying out new software packages and testing new commercially available tools. Each film is different, so if a project needs a particular tool that doesn't exist, a software engineer can create a custom tool for that production.

For the movie *Monsters, Inc.* (2001) one of the main characters, Sully, needed to be completely covered in fur from head to toe. At the time, no off-the-shelf software was available to do this. So the software crew wrote tools to grow and groom fur on a computer-generated character. They also created other tools and procedures to manipulate that fur in just about any way that an artist might need. It was a huge breakthrough and the film's success proved the value of the software and technology team's efforts.

The software team doesn't develop their tools in a vacuum. The close and equal collaboration of technical and artistic filmmakers produces the best circumstances for quality and yields the best software tools to fit the needs of the story. Always remember that everybody tells the story—everybody—even the software developer. The technology lead also plays a crucial part in keeping the equipment current and running and scheduling upgrades and maintenance.

Post

The editor, who has nurtured the film every step of the way, still has important work to do during the post-production processes when most of the film crew is long gone. Editors have been on the movie from the start, building the earliest story reels and working through dozens of iterations of the film during production. Now the editor presides over final sweatbox sessions and starts to collaborate with music and sound editors to get all of the sound and picture elements to the final sound mixing stage on schedule and with the highest quality.

It is worth pointing out that an editor's most important job on the film is, simply, editing. When a crew spends years on a project, they sometimes lose perspective. At this final step of a film's production, a good editor can look at the film with a fresh eye and cut scenes or whole sequences that are too lengthy or that no longer fit the structure of the film.

Managing the Event

A more global view should be taken of managing an animated film to include the *event* of the film. This means an awareness of consumer products, games, premieres, and events surrounding the release of the film. Consumer products department(s) will need key art and character art for toys and puzzles. The marketing department will need images from the film. Publicity will need access to the key talent of the film. Screen credits and final legal issues need to be resolved. DVD bonus material will need to be shot. Record albums are produced, finished, and shipped; theme park tie-ins and promotional partner relationships are launched.

It comes down to one simple issue: Part of the job is to sell the sellers. A good management team is always feeding the ancillary business groups that will create the toys and products that support and market the film. It is mutually beneficial to have the filmmakers create some of the art for these products and to at least have a discussion with the marketers about how the film will be presented to the public. At this point, the sellers will not only need art, but they can also benefit from the team's enthusiasm for and understanding of the story. Thus, they should be given clear information on what makes this film spectacular and unique.

Audience Previews

There were 11 previews of *The Lion King* (1994); each time the story or the pacing of the film was changed. There is nothing magical about this process and it is a huge advantage that animation has over live-action films: the opportunity to animate new scenes and make changes to existing animation weeks before the film opens. Again, managing change is the key. In the early planning of the project, plan for these previews and embrace them as an important tool to the filmmaking process. The preview is not for marketing. They will learn from it, yes, but it is really done so that the film can get down to size and to be raised to its final level of quality. Learn to use previews.

Eventually, persistence of vision leads to the moment of truth: opening night, when the lights go down and the finished movie is shared with the general public for the first time. An animated film is the ultimate paradox. On one hand, it takes years of work and millions of hours of passion and labor to produce. On the other hand, the audience needs to completely forget all of the technology, craft, and hard work that are poured into a film and simply sit back and enjoy the illusion.

THE PRODUCTION PROCESS: AN ANIMATOR'S PERSPECTIVE

Lyndon Barrois

Working on CG-Animated Content in Live-Action Features

This section provides a general introduction to the world of combining character animation—the process of giving life and personality to inanimate objects to convey a believable performance—with live action.

Planning the Process

Many aspects are involved in the mixing of character-animated media with live-action plate photography. Certain guidelines are adhered to for proper execution. Even though it is an aesthetic medium, where in many cases the process and decisions are made off the cuff, there are still rules that apply to completing a project. Breaking down a script is by far the most important aspect of the field (and is covered in *Overview* and *Breaking Down a Script* in Chapter 2). A breakdown is simply the process of taking the script and dissecting it page by page, line by line. It focuses on the stage direction, dialogue, and character situations. It pays strict attention to the number of characters, scenes, and most importantly shots in which the characters appear or are involved in the story. When these things are determined, the characters can then go into a design phase. In a 3D spatial world, a character's design is a crucial aspect of its performance on a 2D surface plane. It has to be designed in a way that is fitting to the story and to its nature.

Case Study 1: Avatar *(2009),* Iron Man *(2008),* Matrix Revolutions *(2003)*

The main characters in these films require an actual human character to be placed into a large, robot-like mechanism that has to be driven by that person to fight in a war. The production is allowed a very liberal budget (every filmmaker's dream). The sequence has to be compelling and convincing. The desire is for the audience to feel the experience along with the actor. An experienced visual effects team may use an array of complex devices, including motion-based rigs, motion-controlled camera photography, and B and C witness cams. Using the script and breakdown as cues, the sequences are designed by using many tools and work flows: storyboards, previs, character design, character builds, motion tests, plate photography, and slap-compositing.

Once the sequence has been boarded and the characters rigged and built, motion tests begin. The specific use of this data should be twofold: first, to figure out how a behemoth human-driven artillery robot moves and performs; and second, to take the digital animation curves and feed that data into a three-piston motion-based rig on set to have the animation actually move the human driver according to the required performance of a specific shot.

To accomplish this, a rig is constructed for the actors to actually ride in the animation so as to sell the performance of the actor in the scene to an audience. The practically built driver's seat for the actors is set on a three-piston gimbal that rotates in the X- and Y-axis to replicate east/west movement and tilts in the Z-axis to translate falling. To give the illusion of traveling in Z space, the A camera is attached to a motion-controlled camera rig that trucks toward and away from the seat and also pans and tilts for additional compelling angles. For compositing purposes on set and later through the pipeline, the pistons and the entire backdrop are covered in chroma-key greenscreen material and paint.

The raw video footage is then slap-composited onto the animation via QuickTime and on-set editing software for proof of concept. When all looks convincing, the shots are taken back for cleanup animation and tracking and then sent through the production pipeline for effects animation, final lighting, and compositing. When the mix is complete with gunfire, explosions, tracer fire, dying enemy combatants, and thundering debris, mayhem and magic are captured on film!

Case Study 2: Alvin & the Chipmunks *(2007)*, G-Force *(2009)*

The main characters in these films are either chipmunks or guinea pigs. Therefore, the first question that must be answered is whether the rodent will be a realistic character or a stylized version. The characters' design is determined based on what they have to do in the story; that is, do they just do the normal things that these animals do or are they doing things out of the ordinary realm of their nature? These scripts called for the animal to do the latter and, therefore, they had to be designed in a way that can achieve the desired performance.

A team of character designers is assembled to accomplish this crucial first task. The breakdown, storyboards, and/or 3D previsualization are generated for staging and blocking of the sequences and shots, and the character is designed based on its physical capabilities and what it has to do in those shots.

A common misconception is that in CG a character can do anything—which in essence is true. But the larger question is

"Is it pleasing to the eye?" Strict attention is paid to its anatomy and skeletal makeup, as well as scale and proportion to its environment and real actors. Maquettes[9] are usually generated in a series of action poses to convey a character's performance and to allow the director and visual effects team to view the character from all angles. Then 3D models are built in the computer to the exact specifications of the maquettes. However, these models are not built in the action poses, but rather a default T-pose, which is a standing with arms spread pose, to determine its physical makeup. In this phase the characters are scrutinized from every angle via *turnarounds* (where the character is placed on a turntable in an animation file and rotated 360 degrees).

Next, the process of rigging, or assigning animatable controls to the character's body parts, face, and extremities, begins. From there the character goes into the hands of character animators, who do a series of motion tests to determine how effectively a character moves in space. Questions of how does it walk, run, jump, push, pull, etc., are all taken into consideration. Hours of footage of the real animal are studied to determine these aspects. (In the case of nonexisting creatures such as dinosaurs, real-life animal references are chosen for their relative nature to their predecessors—bears, ostriches, rhinoceroses, giraffes, alligators, etc., may be studied). Another useful reference tool is actually studying the footage of the character's voice-over actor, for annunciation, facial expressions, and mannerisms, if the character is required to talk.

In many cases, certain actions of a character aren't specifically spelled out in a script; therefore the character should always be designed to perform any task that it should realistically be able to do. A common misconception is that cheats are a necessary tactic when integrating CG characters into real-world environments. A character's physical integrity must be maintained from all angles, not just from the main camera angle. This is especially crucial when sending animation through the pipeline. Violated poses, those that involve interpenetration of body and limbs, hyperextending of extremities, and improper connections with ground planes and space relationships, are always sent back to be corrected—even when a performance is deemed final.

Production

Shooting Footage

Once a script is broken down and all of the considerations discussed above have been made, the shooting phase begins. When a character is to be added into a scene, on-set supervision is a

---

[9]Very detailed physical sculptures.

must. Painstaking attention to detail must be maintained to sell a compelling and believable live-action performance. This involves interaction between the character(s) and the actors in terms of conversation, physical contact, sets, and props. For conversation, connecting eye lines is the key step to selling a performance. An audience has to believe that the actor is interacting with his or her animated costar. Timing and cadence of dialogue, touching, and disturbance of props are all taken into consideration.

If the character is CG, full-scale 2D cutouts or 3D prosthetics (or stuffies) of the character are generally used as a physical reference on the set. When these aren't available to a production, a rod with a marker on it is used for the actor to focus his or her eye line when delivering lines or emotional responses. The shooting takes place in the usual manner with A, B, and C cameras, or witness cameras for coverage and proper tracking data. The tracking data (i.e., lens, distance of camera to character, measurements of the physical environment being shot, etc.) are all crucial to the integration process. This determines that the character is integrated into the proper camera space with the actor or environment. If these aspects are recorded improperly, the integration suffers and results in a fake look. Eye lines are off, the character is out of proportion, the character slides around the plate (footage), the lighting and compositing are improper, and the integration falls apart. This can also lead to gross budget overruns in an effort to "fix it in post."

In many cases, clean plates[10] are filmed for the purposes of aiding the compositing process. If an animated character covers a spot through body movement or dialogue, the displaced footage needs to be replaced or covered. This also holds true when props are disturbed by a character's interaction with them and whether those props have to employ CG replicas or not.

For interaction with a CG or 2D character, the same tracking principles are employed. In the case of stop-motion characters, however, stricter attention to detail is a must and plate preparation has the extra component of employing motion-control methods of shooting. By its nature, stop-motion photography is a live-action process using the time-lapse or pixelation[11] method. The footage is generally shot in a series of passes. If it involves a live actor or two, that person or persons are shot with all of the performance considerations in mind, and another clean pass is shot to time for integration of the stop-motion animator to work within that same framework. Usually that animation will take place on a greenscreen stage to the exact specifications of the live-action

---

[10] Camera takes done without the actors.
[11] Pixelation is the single-framed photographic manipulation of live subjects via timed exposures or hand-maneuvered processes.

shoot. That performance will then be composited into the footage with the actor. If the stop-motion performance doesn't involve the actor but rather a solo animated performance and a camera move is involved, that camera is a motion control rig, timed and staged specifically for the length of the shot. The animator steps in with the puppet or puppets, gets the desired performance, and backs away. That shot is then recorded again in-camera either in real time or as single-frame passes for clean compositing.

Tracking Footage Properly

Tracking is the process of locking the relationship of character, environment, and props frame by frame in a 2D plane and conveying that in 3D space. It most often involves very complex camera moves. An experienced eye can immediately spot when a track is off—as can the audience members, though they may not be able to verbalize it. Therefore, it is always crucial to check the track first before proceeding with any blocking or performance work. If tracks are off, they need to be corrected before any meaningful work can proceed. In a complex show with hundreds of shots, truncated schedules, or both, these things sometimes unintentionally slide through the cracks. Therefore, having good communication and a good rapport with the tracking team is crucial. The size of a character or object should never be altered to fake a track. Once that footage is properly digitized and placed into the computer with all of the data gathered on set, the 3D environment is generated to exact scale and specifications. These include ground planes, wall to ceiling spaces, furniture, etc. For convincing character integration, proper tracking is a must to ensure correct lighting, shadows, and reflections with regard to a character and its environment.

Working with Riggers

One of the most important aspects of character development is the relationship with the character rigging team. The character rigging team's involvement stretches from the aspects of the actual character animation, to technical effects animation relating to the character, to software and associated technical issues that may arise as that character flows through the integration pipeline. Muscle simulations, cloth, fur, and water interaction are some elements normally created by the effects animation team, but they also work in combination with the rigging department. If a character requires special tools to squash or stretch, distinct facial blend shapes for lip syncing dialogue, cloth interaction due to its costume, hair and fur behavior, and water interaction, these requirements are partly or wholly shepherded by the rigging team (depending on a particular studio's pipeline structure).

It is crucial for riggers and animators to work hand in hand from the very beginning to form an understanding of how the characters move. For instance, designing creatures with six-jointed legs or 16 tentacles is no small task and has no room for assumptions and guesswork. It takes a full team effort and special rigging requests are almost always made during production that need to be addressed in a quick manner. Therefore, as with the matchmovers, riggers are an animator's best friends.

Working with an Animation Team

Every character animator is different, and a comprehensive animation team brings an array of skill sets to every show. Whether it's a small or large team, camaraderie and cohesion go a long way during increasingly tedious production schedules. Since all animators operate at different levels, depending on experience grade or work methods, it is important to cast shots and scenes accordingly within a show. For instance, some animators are better at subtle acting and emotional performance, whereas others may excel at executing broad action. During the course of production, every animator eventually must become familiar with every character in a show because that person may be called on in an instant to deliver a performance for a character he or she hasn't been previously assigned. The goal is always to have everyone eventually work on an even keel. But until then, a well-balanced casting effort ensures performance continuity across an entire film.

Character and Environment Interaction

Very strict considerations need to be made for a character's interaction in his/her/its environment and with props. First, the overall timing of the shot(s) needs to be examined. Is it a 5-, 8-, or 10-second action or sequence? Does it happen in one long take or a series of shots? What angles are most suitable for staging the action of the character—wide, medium, or tight close-ups? These questions are usually answered in the storyboard or previs phase, but more often than not, liberties are taken on set as the project and story evolve during the shooting phase.

Also taken into consideration is the characters' effect on the objects or props they interact with. In the case of a chipmunk on a couch, there may be little or no compression or impression on the couch from the animal's weight—depending on the object's surface. But if the action calls for that chipmunk to leap from the couch to a table, then considerations would be made for the couch pillow to react to the force of the leap as well as the object on which the chipmunk lands. For example, when it lands does it move papers, trinkets, or keys? Does it knock over a vase and flowers? These props would be rigged practically on set, based on the timing of the move, or replaced digitally.

Suppose the chipmunk then leaps onto a bed. Then the cloth interaction, whether on a large or small scale, is an important detail of the action depending on how the cloth has to behave due to the character's effect on it. These are very budget-conscious decisions. The same is true if there is a dinosaur, a gorilla, or behemoth killer robots rampaging through a forest, desert, or city. Admittedly, the stakes are higher at a much larger scale, but the same considerations as in the examples above are at play. How does the rampaging character affect the trees, sand, or concrete and glass edifices? How does that character move through the scene based on its physical size in relation to real-world physics? What needs to be timed and affected practically by the use of pyrotechnics, wind machines, etc.? Which scenes need digital props and enhancements? Again, these are script breakdown and budgetary determinations. But all are also defined by character integration into the live-action footage.

Animating to Dialogue and Sound Cues

Another important aspect in the integration process is animating characters to dialogue or voice tracks. In most cases, the voice actor is recorded during the principal photography phase, and those voice tracks are handed over to the animators. This is also a useful step in the character development stage, because it helps define a character's personality and movements based on cadence, pronunciation, and inflection. An actor's delivery is different in every take and those selected takes are what defines the character's personality.

In some cases, even when a track is laid down and animation begins, ADR[12] sessions are required in which an actor will actually look at the performance of the animation in progress for a better performance match. And then there are the more extreme cases in which a voice or voices are recast while the animation is in progress, in which case that animation may or may not be affected. In CG character animation, the execution of dialogue points back to the character's design—this time focusing on facial expression. Therefore the process used for animation phonemes, or sculpted syllabic mouth shapes, will be determined very early on. Is it "real" or is it stylized (cartoony)? Does it involve one rig or a series of rigged facial morphing targets or blend shapes? In the instance of sound cues, it all comes down to the ancient question

---

[12] ADR: automated dialogue replacement, which is basically a process in which a performer replaces his or her previously recorded dialogue by respeaking the lines in sync to picture or by recording new dialogue in sync to picture.

of which came first, the chicken or the egg—does the animation drive the cue or vice versa? If a sound effects design pass is in progress, animators will often be given the unedited scratch tracks for timing cues. However, in most cases the animation does in fact determine where the sound cues will edit, and in those instances, the sound designers are given either director-approved finals or close to final animation footage.

Importance of Seeing Characters Projected and with Textures

Another very important step in combining 3D characters into a 2D image plane is seeing how the character performs with textures or lighting cues in reference to its environment in a scene. Many things in a character's performance that are judged in quick-shade mode or low-resolution hardware textures are more or less apparent when a character is seen in its proper fully rendered lighting. Therefore the prelighting phase, or defining the character's look in terms of color and surface texture, is a vital part of the production process. Some things may be pushed too extreme; others may not be exaggerated enough. These aspects are made evident by proper lighting. And since that phase is so memory intensive in terms of rendering time and disk space, the sooner it takes place the better.

This also holds true when it comes to the dailies process. Seeing the character projected on screen in sequence on a regular basis is an immeasurably important tool in the live-action integration process. It helps to answer all of the issues involving weight, proportion, and timing, as well as lighting and compositing, that are less evident even on a 24-inch desk monitor.

Conclusion

As stated at the beginning of this section, the steps laid out here serve only as a general overview to integrating character- animated visual effects within live-action projects. It is a constantly evolving process and therefore the practitioners of the medium are always in a state of learning or developing the advancements and inventions. Artists and technicians are working tirelessly toward improving the efficiency of the craft in all aspects and areas to enable the imaginations of filmmakers to broaden the entertainment experience and bring a better product to increasingly demanding audiences.

10

OTHER WORKFLOW CONSIDERATIONS

VIRTUAL STUDIO TECHNOLOGY
Dan Novy

Virtual studio is a term that describes a loose collection of technologies used to achieve real-time mixing of live-action foreground elements with a chosen background—real or created inside a computer. The technology is used currently for newscasting, entertainment news shows, and children's broadcasting. It is a way of creating much grander backgrounds than can physically be built on the budget available. Additionally, it has been used on film sets to help the director and director of photography (DP) set the shots for scenes that will take place in a virtual background. Regardless of the system used, all virtual studios capture, process, mix, and render the final output in a similar manner.

Initially, the foreground element—a live actor, puppet, and the like—must be captured against an environment capable of being keyed in real time. Often a set that has some general set pieces painted chroma blue or green is used, similar to the screens or environments used for visual effects bluescreen compositing (see the *Greenscreen and Bluescreen Photograpgy* section in Chapter 3 and the *Compositing of Live-Action Elements* section in Chapter 6). The obvious difference concerning the virtual studio is that the keying, or creation of an alpha matte, must occur in real time. Unlike software-based compositing, specialized hardware from various vendors is capable of keying and outputting the video stream at the chosen frame rate.

The second necessity of the virtual studio is real-time camera tracking and positioning, sometimes known as *matchmoving*. The virtual camera created within the CG world must synchronize its position, orientation, and lens with the camera used to capture the foreground element—again in real time. Several systems are available that use various methods, including inertial tracking, infrared beacons similar to motion capture systems, tracking

The VES Handbook of Visual Effects. DOI: 10.1016/B978-0-240-81242-7.00010-7

markers, or camera encoding *hot heads*[1] capable of outputting the cameras' orientation and/or position. Most solutions will employ a mixture of these approaches. (See Chapter 4 for further explanations of these technologies.)

Once a matchmoved and keyed foreground element has been captured and processed, it must be mixed, again in real time, with the chosen background environment. This background can either be photographic, captured from another location, or as in most cases, created in a 3D animation package. Unlike software compositing, the elements must be mixed and rendered in real time, for which several hardware-based solutions exist or can be constructed. Once mixed, the output stream can be broadcast live or saved to an offline storage medium. It is important to note that the matched movement of the created background to the foreground photographed elements is automated once the system has been set up and calibrated.

After the initial cost of creating the capture environment, including camera matchmoving, keying, and the specialized hardware necessary for real-time mixing, has been expended, the cost of the virtual studio can be kept low by having only to construct new and varied environments in 3D space—without the time and construction costs associated with real-world set design and building. The space and system can be repurposed for multiple shows or projects without incurring additional costs.

ANALYSIS OF A PRODUCTION WORKFLOW
Stephan Vladimir Bugaj

What is a workflow? Creation of a production workflow starts with analysis and design. To do the analysis, it is important to have an understanding of what a workflow is. A *workflow* is a specific set of procedures and deliverables that defines a goal. The overarching workflow is the total production workflow. The goal is make a movie, and that necessitates a set of procedures that results in the deliverable: the film. Beneath that is a series of departmental workflows, beneath which are artist workflows, and beneath which are task workflows.

A workflow defines a procedure, or series of operations, through which a task is performed and a deliverable produced. In defining a workflow, the task is the goal-oriented view of the work, and the deliverable is the resulting definition. Operations

---

[1] Hot head: A computer-assisted camera-mount head that can either record the pan and tilt of an operated camera or use previously recorded pan/tilt information that is then played back to drive the camera head mount in a manner that replicates the pan/tilt moves. As the equipment improves, more axes are becoming recordable and capable of being played back to drive the camera.

are defined to achieve that goal. A good workflow definition is end to end and defines what the artists need to do to receive the input deliverables, perform each step of the workflow, and hand off the output deliverables.

How granular to make each operation in the definition is an art more than a science, and it requires communication among people in the organization. A level of granularity that most artists and managers agree makes sense is a good starting point. Workflows defined at a whole studio level will then be partitioned and turned into department-specific workflows, which will eventually become tool specifications and user documentation, through iterative refinement. But a good workflow definition makes these subsequent steps tractable.

In practice, a comfortable level of detail is usually one that defines steps involving context switching by the artist, not detailed operations of a tool. For example, the task "lay out UVs" could be defined as a number of small operations about how to operate a particular UV layout tool, but for the purposes of defining a studio workflow that would be counterproductive. In defining the modeling or shading workflow, there may be more steps in the workflow than just "lay out UVs." The steps might be something more like "lay out UVs, check with grid renders, name the UV maps according to spec, etc." than the very low-level, step-by-step details of how to do it.

This definition process often results in a workflow definition that has subdeliverables (such as status updates in a tracking database), in addition to the primary deliverable. Many operation steps could be viewed as stand-alone workflows in theory, but in practice it may be irrelevant or overwhelming to do so. Studio-level production workflows should define the process at a level of detail that is general enough to be understandable by everyone and also define major deliverables. Department-level (and specializations within departments) workflow definitions are more detailed, but should still be high enough level to look more like a to-do list than a how-to manual.

Example: A Simple Department-Level Workflow for Shading

- Receive art from production design.
- Receive geometry from modeling.
- Validate geometry:
  - Single-rooted hierarchy.
  - No disconnected edges.
  - Out-facing normals.
- Lay out UVs:
  - Use multiple maps to maintain detail as needed.
- Set up projection paint cameras and passes.
- Set up tumble paint passes.

- Mark the model as "ready to shade" in the tracking DB.
- Develop shader:
  - Assign materials from library.
  - Test-render initial setup.
  - Refine shader to hit target artwork.
  - Dial-in basic look:
    - Develop new shader library code if needed.
    - Apply textures from texture library.
    - Create new textures if needed.
    - Paint additional detail.
  - Mark the model as "ready for review" in the tracking DB.
  - Show in review.
- Obtain review approval.
- Mark the model as "shaded" in the tracking DB.
- Install new textures into the texture library.
- Install new shader library code into the code repository.
- Contact downstream department(s) and deliver model.

Notice that even this simple shading pipeline example defines five delivery points prior to the master deliverable: three database entries, and two optional installs if newly shared materials are created. It assumes that the artists know their jobs and don't micromanage their steps. Yet, it is at a level of detail that when purchasing or developing a toolset to facilitate this workflow, important details are specified: Model validation scripts need to check specific issues, the model data format must support multiple UVs, both tumble and projection paint systems are needed, etc. As the workflow is implemented, each step will turn into a well-defined procedure, but such implementation details are not needed in the workflow design. For example, how the UVs are laid out doesn't matter, as long as the model has valid UVs. Over the lifetime of a studio, these workflow requirements will evolve, and so will the tools.

From Workflow to Pipeline

A *pipeline* is an implementation of a workflow specification. The term comes from computing, where it means a set of serial processes, with the output of one process being the input of the subsequent process. A production pipeline is not generally perfectly serial because real workflows usually have branches and iterative loops, but the idea is valid: A pipeline is the set of procedures that need to be taken in order to create and hand off deliverables.

The creation of a pipeline from a workflow specification is a matter of selecting and/or developing tools, and procedures for using them, that implement the workflow. A pipeline is, therefore, a workflow specification plus a set of tools that are to be used to achieve the goals defined therein. To create a pipeline, the high-level workflow specification needs to be turned into system requirements, which can also be considered a low-level workflow specification. So requirements analysis gives workflow specification and requirements, design provides a detailed plan for creating the pipeline, and the implementation of that design provides the pipeline itself.

Requirements Analysis

Requirements analysis is a systems engineering term for the process of determining the conditions that a system needs to meet and the goals users must be able to achieve by using it. The process involves taking into account the potentially conflicting needs of multiple sets of users and beneficiaries (the people who receive the deliverables from the system).

A valid requirement is one that can be defined in a testable way, is relatable to a system goal, and is defined at a level of detail sufficient for system design. A set of requirements for systems implementation will start with a high-level workflow specification and, through iterative refinement, be turned into requirement specifications for implementation.

Formalized requirements analysis is the subject of dense books and can be very complex. That level of detail is not discussed here, but rather enough details will be provided such that requirements for the studio workflow can still be developed. What any requirements document needs is the following:
- a definition of the goal to be achieved, and the primary deliverable(s) to be produced;
- identification of the stakeholders (users and beneficiaries);
- a workflow specification overview of the process at a high level;
- for each step in the workflow:
  - a high-level definition of the task (the scenario),
  - input requirements, meaning a definition of the data, if any, that is present to be operated on at the start of the step defined by the requirement,
  - functional requirements, meaning a description of what must be done in this step, at a level of detail sufficient to implement it,
  - usability requirements, meaning both user interface design and performance expectations,
  - output requirements, meaning a definition of the data to be output and passed-on to the next step;
- life cycle expectations (e.g., how long the system will be used, which impacts how much funding is spent on it).

Developing a set of requirements, if done right, can save a lot of time and money during the design and implementation stages. To do it right, it needs to be kept simple. Only requirements that an organization can actually achieve, based on what is right for its size, should be specified. The size of the organization often determines whether a system that supplies the requirements is purchased, or whether they are implemented in house. The number of people in the meetings, the number of meetings, and the length of time dedicated to the process also must scale with size. But that doesn't mean details should be minimized. The requirements document must spell out everything system implementers need to take into account in order to design and build a system that will meet the needs of the staff.

A sufficiently simple, yet usable requirement might look something like this UV layout example:

- *Definition:* UV layout is the creation of a well-defined 2D texture space that has point-to-point correspondence with the 3D mesh.
- *Users:* Modeling or surfacing TDs.
- *Beneficiaries:* Surfacing TDs and texture painters.
- *Process overview:* Take a 3D mesh, start with an automatic mapping, and refine by hand until the grid test render looks good.
- *Scenario:* Automatic mapping.
  - *Input:* A mesh with no existing UV layout.
  - *Functional:* Choice of several mapping techniques including cubic, spherical, and cylindrical projections, pelt-mapping (automated slicing of a 3D mesh into a 2D projection), and projection from any camera.
  - *Usability:* Each technique should produce some result for even a naïve user without parameter tuning. Parameter tuning to produce a better result should be in a user interface (UI) that looks similar for each technique, with parameters that do the same thing having the same name and UI position. Selection of cut edges for pelt-mapping should be automatic, with a user override that uses the standard edge selection tool of the host application. Results should be displayed on a gridded 2D plane immediately. Any parameter tuning that will cause the mapping to take more than a couple of seconds should cause the UI to alert the user and ask if he or she wants to continue.
  - *Output:* A UV map in the data format required by the texturing system. The map should be editable with the hand-editing tools specified in the next requirement.
- *Scenario:* Refinement tools.
  - *Input:* An automatically generated UV map.
  - … and so on.

Formal object modeling language isn't always necessary. Requirements simply need to state what needs to be done, by whom, and to what effect. If it wasn't an example, the pelt-mapping system would likely be spelled out in detail in a subordinate requirement, because it is a complex component, and the mapping and refinement tools might be broken out into one scenario per technique—but otherwise the requirements don't necessarily need to be much more complex than the example. Systems and UI designers will take this information and turn them into designs for the developers, or if off-the-shelf solutions are to be purchased, then there will be a set of requirements and designs that can be discussed in detail with potential vendors. Stakeholders should be included in refining the requirements and designs because implementation details may cause changes, but that is an expected part of the process. If attention to detail and perseverance are used during this phase, however, there will be less frustration during implementation.

From Artistic Requirements into Technical Specs

Artistic requirements need to be translated into technical specifications. What that means to the workflow specification and requirements analysis and design process is that a definition is needed of the processes in terms of both an artistic goal and technical necessities. Supervisors make this translation with respect to a director's vision all the time, taking an artistic desire and turning it into a technical plan, and the need is not much different when it comes to defining a studio workflow for in-house artists to turn their interpretations of the director's and production designer's visions into finished assets ready for delivery to the customer.

Focusing on the artistic goal is essential. The ultimate goal is making images, not building systems or writing software. Technical and usability requirements should be designed to make achieving artistic goals as simple as possible. Reducing complexity wherever possible is key. Artists want to focus on their task, not on the pipeline, and a studio can achieve very good results if their systems requirements create packages that make complex simulations, shading, and so on into flexible yet easy-to-use tools for the artists.

Part of the translation process is that artists will frequently state things in terms of what they already know. During the requirements analysis process, it is important to understand that when someone states their view about how the system needs to function, the task is to translate that view into what the system needs to achieve. Further, the developer needs to isolate what aspects of the application the user has specified are considered positive to that user, and what are merely tolerated, and then build the requirements based on that information. If the artists use an existing tool, and they are given one that has all that tool's benefits and fewer of its deficiencies, they have been helped to progress and evolve.

For example, if the artists state that they must have the Roadkill tool or else their job cannot be done, it is important to understand that what they need is a pelt-mapping UV layout tool and to translate that into a requirement for a pelt-mapping tool. This inevitably takes into account other artists' requirements and, therefore, may or may not be best implemented by using the Roadkill application specifically. The artistic goal is "get the best UV layout possible onto a highly complex geometry, with the least amount of time spent doing by-hand layout," not "run Roadkill." Time needs to be spent talking to the artists about both the specs of their deliverables and their working habits in order to glean this information. This is time well spent.

The technical specifications then developed from these artistic requirements must focus primarily on the goal (in the example, a good UV layout) and how to achieve it, rather than on implementation details (such as what particular pelting algorithms will be used and what kind of data representation those internal computations will act on). What needs to be gleaned from an artistic requirement is a technical requirement that states the artistic goal, defines what the technical deliverable is that embodies that artistic goal, and spells out both how the artists will work within the system to achieve the goal (process and UI) and what the system is doing (at a high level) to allow them to do so.

Balancing Individual versus Group Requirements

When designing a production workflow, it is often necessary to balance individual artists' requirements and preferences with what is needed for the entire team to operate smoothly. Artists may come to the studio accustomed to a personalized workflow that doesn't integrate well with a larger group project. Disorganization, or an organizational system that only makes sense to the individual, is often the hallmark of this situation. Many artists will attempt to cling to their personal system, even though it will not serve them well in a group environment.

Solving this problem is as much a people management issue as a requirements analysis one. Faced with a workflow that requires storing data on a server in well-defined locations organized by project and shot, and which requires good hygiene in terms of naming objects and parameters, some will complain about "wasting time" on these requirements that "don't show up on screen." The solution is not to allow artists to deliver incomplete and poorly organized work to downstream departments, dumping additional work onto other artists. Requirements must be carefully considered to minimize the number of steps artists must take to accomplish their individual tasks, balanced against maximizing the amount of necessary data that is delivered to other artists and managers downstream. And management needs to convince the artists that this will be the case and that their workflow will contain no unnecessary steps.

To achieve this balance, it is useful to look at what benefits come from a personalized workflow and try to replicate them as much as possible in the studio workflow. Individual artists perceive the following as major benefits of their individual workflows:

- Knows where all the files are located
- Knows what all the objects and parameters in the file(s) are named
- Doesn't need to waste time handing off data to other artists
- Doesn't need to waste time learning anything new

The first two are easily replicated in a studio workflow by creating a system of well-defined locations for data that is organized by production, scene, shot, and task, and by developing standards for scene graph organization, including naming of objects and parameters. The latter two are necessary parts of working in a large organization, and what needs to be done is to structure the workflow into departments that maximize the amount of work an individual can accomplish according to the skills of the artists, balanced against being able to work in parallel as much as possible.

To best facilitate working in parallel, decomposition of conceptual assets such as models and shots into files that represent tasks, not just tools, is essential. This allows artists whose work is independent to work at the same time and those who are dependent on each other to iteratively refine in parallel (one artist checkpoints, the other begins work and takes it as far as he or she can until the previous artist updates his or her work—and so on). For example, even if the entire system is based in Maya, splitting a shot into a environment.ma file, characters.ma file, lights.ma file, and fx.ma file and referencing them into the shot .ma file already allows for four people to work simultaneously, as opposed to only one. Once the set is roughed in, and characters given blocking animation, the lighters and visual effects artists can begin their work and make refinements as the environments and characters teams refine their work. Within each department task the workflow may resemble an individualized workflow, in that the artist works solo until delivering the appropriate file into

the system for other artists to work from, but between departments it is essential to do the following:
- Specify well-defined asset locations.
  - Use a file structure that represents logical workflow assets such as models and shots, not just file formats.
  - Use well-defined naming conventions and structures inside each tool.
  - Make delivery of files into the proper global location in the system easy, so the artist doesn't waste time on handoffs.
- Facilitate working in parallel.
  - Decompose logical assets into files/sets of files that are relevant to workflow departments, not just separated by the tool that reads and writes the file.
  - Allow artists to work locally, without being impacted by others' changes, until they reconcile with the global asset system.
- Keep the individual artist workflow intimate.
  - Build on well-known tools (or replicate wherever possible well-known tool concepts if the tool is being built in house).
  - Specify scripts and plug-ins that interface with the asset system within the primary tools, so checkouts, check-ins, and handoffs are well integrated into the artists' existing workflows.

Another requirement in getting individual artists to work efficiently in a group is good communications tools and techniques. Even with the best standards and systems, there will be cases where artists simply need to talk to each other and agree on how something new and different will fit into the system. It is not difficult to add new asset types into a well-defined structure, provided that flexibility is a part of the requirements. However, the mechanisms must be in place for artists and tool builders/maintainers to communicate about these evolving requirements during a production. Requirements that certain data about assets such as shots and models be deployed in human-readable formats can help not only with emergency production hacks, but also in enabling communications about the assets. Designing communication tools into the system, such as a task and fixes allocation and tracking system, notifications about changes to which one can subscribe, and a chat system, is also helpful.

Ultimately, if the studio workflow is sufficiently well defined; is easily understandable; facilitates parallel workflows, iteration, and communication; and can be flexed when needed, artists will not miss working in an individualized workflow for very long.

Service Bureau versus In-House Requirements

A studio that operates as a service bureau, such as a visual effects house providing effects for production companies, has certain requirements that a shop that is either doing feature animation or is an in-house visual effects provider at a large studio does not. All of the general principles and goals of performing the requirements analysis apply, but the external partners must be taken into account as stakeholders in the analysis.

Service bureaus need to be able to input data from third parties, and output it in a readable format as well. File interchange formats are discussed in detail later in this chapter, but an added general principle of analysis for a service bureau is that the input and output points of the pipeline must be specified. If all that is imported are plates from live-action shoots, then what image format(s) will be accepted depends on the needs of the clients. However, if digital scene files, edits, composites, etc., must also be input from other studios, the requirements for each variant of each of these types of inputs must be specified. Output requirements are similar: The downstream clients' needs must be analyzed and what image and data will be delivered must be determined.

Formats designed specifically for interchange, such as the Autodesk cross-package interoperability format filmbox (.fbx), make the implementation task easier, but the requirements analysis cannot be considered complete based on the decision to use .fbx. Issues such as potentially different plug-ins, shading libraries, etc., make the interchange process complex. Both requirements for ways to check and validate this data and also data delivery checklists to share with vendors and clients on both ends of the workflow must be able to be specified.

Because of facilities' desires to protect IP in the form of plug-ins, libraries, etc., there can be some difficulties when data other than image plates needs to be shared—but given the frequency with which multiple facilities work on a single show, being able to provide a comprehensible and comprehensive list of requested data to the other party and depending on the facility being able to check its validity and have mechanisms to deal with missing data (even if it means re-creating it within the facility) are essential. The requirements analysis must reflect these issues.

While a more formal treatment of requirements analysis can result in more deliverables, at the end of the analysis the minimum set of deliverables that can get the workflow development project going consists of the following:

- a high-level workflow overview that explains the entire end-to-end workflow in an understandable manner and allows everyone involved to know the overarching goals of the system;
- a requirements specification for each department workflow, including interchange with the departments before and after it in the workflow; and

- a requirements specification for each task within the department, including the interchange with either other artists or other components of a single-artist process.

At a minimum, each requirement should contain the information detailed earlier in this section: definition, users, overview, scenario, input, functionality, usability, and output. The requirements should be collected into a single volume of workflow requirements that, taken as a whole, define the end-to-end workflow of the studio. Whereas the detailed implementation designs of the systems may get a lot more complex, the requirements analysis documents should be kept as simple as possible while still fully describing the requisite features.

These deliverables are passed along to the following:

- *Stakeholders:* for review, and iterative refinement alongside the analysis team.
- *Designers:* as the input to their workflow design process.
- *Implementers:* as a guideline for understanding the design documents, because the requirements provide a concise, goal-oriented description of each step that can be obscured within a thorough design packet.
- *Users:* as a conceptual-level user's guide to understanding what the system is expected to do for them, which they can refer back to when communicating to the development team any problems they run into with a tool or procedure not delivering on its promise.

Over the years, as studios grow, develop new techniques and tools, and change the workflow to accommodate new ideas, these documents can be revised in order to help readers understand how the changes integrate with, or replace, previous parts of the workflow. It helps with understanding the scope and impact of changes before they're made, and serves as an ongoing guide to check tools and procedures against to make sure they're functioning as required.

DESIGN OF A PRODUCTION WORKFLOW
Dan Rosen

The genesis of tools and user documentation should allow for solid communication and reasonable speed in executing tasks. It is critical for the tools and documentation to be intuitive and user friendly. The design of a workflow comes not only from analysis but also experience. Keeping the design of a workflow open enough to easily integrate changes is an art unto itself. Taking in feedback and continued review of the workflow should spawn upgrades to the process, and continued revisions of the workflow should make it easier to work faster and concentrate on the creative tasks at hand.

From Analysis to Design

Taking a page from the history of architecture, design is inherently about form following function. The form of a workflow should help optimize time spent on creating images and reduce time spent on redundant tasks. An artist may need to seek information about a client note, on-set camera data, or publish an image for supervisor review. A producer may need to input a schedule and track artists' progress. The workflow should be designed to allow different departments to input data, read data, and contain tools to create and review images, all with an intuitive ease of use.

The design of the workflow should respect the majority of users. Whether supervisors, artists, or production staff, a common language must be spoken. Ultimately all people in the organization should have a basic understanding of each department's workflow. In many cases departments share some of the same tools when viewing and tracking data and images. It is important to design a workflow with the entire organization in mind and further break down departmental workflows that can all plug in together.

Speaking the same language can be achieved through experience and time spent with the same people working side by side, but the workflow can and should allow for integrating new people into the team as well as new goals and tasks. There is a common language in computer science that tends to apply to visual effects and, more and more, to everyone who has used a computer.

Change and growth of the workflow may also be tailored to new standards formed every day. Taking another creative tact, design is much like writing, where good writing is rewriting. A workflow will continue to grow. If the design and architecture are good, then it will adapt to scale and contingencies.

The main function defined during analysis, that is, to make a movie, may be broken down into overall workflow, departmental workflow, and, finally, artist workflow. It comes down to relatively basic to-do lists that anyone can understand.

The end goal of deliverables is the tangible result of the efforts put into workflow design. Ultimately the workflow, or to-do list, is designed and executed via functional tools, documentation, and training. Examples might include:

- customized artist applications and plug-ins;
- a database with viewing and entry interfaces to track visual reference, assets, tasks, status, schedule, internal notes, client comments, etc.;
- tools within artist applications to search, replace, and add assets to the workflow tied into the database;
- tools within artist applications to utilize a shot/sequence-specific setups and/or company-wide macros or plug-ins to

achieve a consistent look, technique, color-space, file-format, etc., tied into the database;

- flip-book applications to view visual references, individual elements, shots, or even surrounding shots in editorial context;
- documentation through web or other digital formats, including images and video; and
- training in a formal classroom setting, or in smaller breakdown meetings/turnovers, or even one-on-one interactions.

It has become increasingly easy to use open source and off-the-shelf software to design the workflow. Even a relatively small visual effects studio can create a database that acts as the backbone of tracking data and assets and also contains documentation and training materials. It is also entirely possible to use off-the-shelf software, in combination with smaller scripts and applications, to manipulate those tools to interact with a database and integrate the company's workflow into the artist staff's and production staff's day-to-day tasks.

Regardless of whether the workflow design is created from entirely customized software or off-the-shelf software, speaking the same language becomes very important. Software user-interface (UI) designs are standardized in terms of key commands and processes. It has become a given that most people use computers and schools are training with particular software and methodologies that can lead to these standards. This allows for new artists and production staff to pick up a tool and have a better chance of finding the correct menu, button, or hot key. An easy example is cut-and-paste; the use of the "Control + C" and "Control + V" keys to cut and paste are almost universal in all applications and tools. A more complex common UI control may be using the arrow keys to forward frame by frame, or the "F" key to frame or fit the image or selection within the main UI window. Even more complex are the UI standards for 3D movement including things like "Option + Left-Click" to orbit or "Option + Middle-Click" to pan.

In Western culture, books are read left to right and top to bottom. Therefore, the layout, size, and legibility of menus, shelves, trays, buttons, drop-downs, pop-ups, etc., are all important considerations when designing any UI. Intuitiveness in software cannot be underestimated, and the better it is the more productive the staff will be. A well-designed workflow and pipeline means that everyone can understand the workflow and its tools and find it user friendly.

Workflow tools can enhance every part of the overall processes. The goal is to continually improve communication and increase speed and efficiency while ushering images through the workflow. The tools should remain as transparent as possible. This may be achieved by keeping the tools intuitive and integrating changes seamlessly.

Designing to Scale

Designing the workflow to scale goes back to understanding the main objective, in this example, to make a movie. Even though the workflow has been considered hierarchically (per departmental workflows, artist workflows, and task workflows), the design of the overall workflow should reflect the bigger picture. In an organization that respects openness, it is important for all members to understand the bigger picture.

It is common to break down the task of making a movie, or any narrative project, from the greater whole to sequences and then individual shots. Designing a workflow around the components of the project makes the end goal of delivering individual, final images scalable. In most cases many departments contribute to particular sequences and shots. Therefore, a sequence and its subsequent shots are at the highest level of organization.

The most common directory structures for visual effects and animation are broken down by show > sequence > shot. From there, the effect can then be broken into task or department, for example, modeling, rigging, texturing, effects, lighting, or compositing. Regardless of the task, however, the association of each asset or element is its place in a shot or sequence and therefore in the project.

The process of making a movie or project grows and shrinks based on directorial and editorial decisions. This has a direct impact on the workflow and all of the tools. The tools have to account for adding or omitting shots and sequences. It is also important to account for directorial and artistic changes that directly impact the workflow. For instance, a workflow to create fully 3D environments may be switched to matte-painted backgrounds for artistic, casting staff, render power, or even budgetary reasons. The workflow has to be able to adapt to bringing the new matte-painted backgrounds into shots with the correct camera move and be integrated into the scene with the rest of its elements in a whole new way.

Whether painting a background, animating a character, or tracking the status of an asset, the workflow comes back to a given shot in a sequence in the greater whole, the movie. Each task down the pipeline of a given shot has to keep the input assets up-to-date and contribute new output of assets and data back into the pipeline. The workflow tools should be designed to make the information for each user easy to obtain and update.

Designing for Contingencies

A big part of production is to anticipate problems. Designing for contingencies reduces the chance of having to change the basic architecture of the workflow. Growing a visual effects or animation studio for many years will bring a level of sophistication to workflow, but it is also important, if not an art, to know when to adapt to new formats and methodologies versus holding on to well-formed standards. Migrating and testing new components of workflow as well as phasing out components are extremely sensitive tasks. Tools should allow for legacy operations, especially when updates are pushed out in the middle of an active production. Following up by weaning from the old to the new tools requires interdepartmental sign-off. The workflow should allow for the systematic implementation of change.

Redundancies can provide multiple checks to assets being pushed through the pipeline. It is possible to have tools that can check and validate assets in the most basic sense, but this may also come down to reviewing assets throughout the workflow followed by earmarking a database with those findings.

Making images for a film is an iterative process, so it is extremely important to track versions of each part of the workflow down to the asset level. Naming conventions and asset tracking are important internally and possibly even more so when collaborating with other vendors and delivering images for digital intermediate or directly for film-out. Designing a workflow for contingencies in naming and versioning assets is extremely important. It is also ideal to have the tools make this part of the process as transparent as possible to artists and production staff while retaining solid methods.

A real-world example of a naming convention will show how it reflects its place in the bigger hierarchy, possibly a brief description and a version delimited by something such as an underscore:

- <shot>_<role>_<description>_<version>
- dr0010_fx_debris_v001.1001.exr
- dr0010_fx_debris_v001.ma

Here the asset is defined by an abbreviation of the scene in the project and four padded shot numbers, followed by an abbreviation of the department or role that created it, then a brief description, and finally a three-padded version number. Any person in the organization should be able to quickly, and generally, understand what this asset is associated with. The shot name is a unique moniker to the sequence and the show assigned specifically by visual effects. The department or role that creates effects (debris, rain, sparks, etc.) may be called *fx*. A brief description says as much as possible about what the asset is in a concise manner. And finally the version tracks iterations created by the artist.

The naming convention example shows that the EXR (.exr) image asset is named directly from the Maya (.ma) scene itself to help tie the relationship of the two assets together. Tools and software can also track associations of what images were generated from what scenes as well as by whom it was rendered, on what date, from which particular approved camera, and so on. These tools and software can also set up the initial scene itself and the naming of the various passes and images that it will render. It is also possible to embed metadata within assets to link associations with the rest of the workflow. This embedded data may tie in to a database and provide information to the user through workflow tools.

The naming convention can get extremely complex given all of the data that *could* be included with it, but it is practical to keep the naming convention to a reasonable length and maximize tools that track and associate assets. If a client's desired naming conventions require variations from the internal conventions, then it is possible to build tools that can rename assets and even alter formats upon delivery. It is important to keep internal naming conventions and formats stable.

The client might request the script scene number, but may not be concerned with the department that created it, nor the description. It would be most common to deliver a final composite shot, in this example, so the department and description are not as important at this point in the process. The scene number comes from the script itself and relates any given shot to the entire project chronologically. This is particularly helpful for the director, editorial, digital intermediate, and anyone who has to place a given shot within the bigger picture. Here is an example of a client-delivery naming convention; the added script scene number, stripped down version of the naming, two-padded versioning, and DPX file format:

* <scene>_<shot>_<version>
* 119_DR0010_v01.1001.dpx

It is a good idea not to rely solely on databases. It is important to validate that the data is also reflected on disk. This can be achieved through tools that validate image sequences, sizes, bit depth, etc., but nothing can replace some real human interaction. In traditional cel animation there are checkers whose sole job is to thumb through drawings and dope sheets to ensure that all of the drawings that are expected to be there are in fact present and numbered, etc., before going off to the next part of the workflow. Most facilities create a specific component of the workflow for both the input/output (IO) and editorial departments. The tools built for these departments should allow for the aforementioned image validation as well as delivery and notifications.

One should be able to easily add a great number of image formats and file types within the conceptual types so that new tools are easy to deploy rapidly. For instance, scanning film to the Cineon file format, in a standard Kodak logarithmic color space, at a resolution of 2048 × 1556 pixels can be considered a standard of sorts, but there are many variations closely related and a great number of high-definition (HD) color spaces, file formats, and resolutions continue to be developed. There are also 4k and IMAX resolutions to consider because this is a current trend for stereoscopic films. This is a great example of the potential impact on workflows that may have been initiated before this trend and now need adaptation to change the process. The workflow has to allow for change, whether setting up matchmove cameras, validating film-backs, or converting color space into traditional and new formats.

Design Deliverables

As a result of analysis and design, the ultimate goal is to release functioning tools and training with accurate and useful documentation.

These tools must be tested and deemed functioning through basic alpha and beta software testing methodologies. These tools must also be maintained through versioning based on bug fixes, integrating user comments, and change based on new standards and formats.

Training is extremely valuable. Some smaller companies may not have the time and money to spend on formal classroom training. However, informal training can still be effective. Some facilities use mentoring as a means of on-the-job training. A new hire may be assigned a more experienced mentor to guide him or her through the initial tasks and experience with the workflow. Other means of informal training can come from smaller, breakdown meetings where learning happens on the job. It is also probable that a tip or trick that one person finds may prove incredibly useful and be shared via e-mail, chat rooms, or even hallway conversations. No matter how perfect the analysis and design, real-world use is the best form of testing and even training. Learning on real tasks is how the majority of people not only learn but also retain information. If those findings can make their way back into the formal workflow, then the process grows.

Documentation is extremely useful to allow users to reference components of the workflow. All people learn and retain in different ways. Keeping accurate, easy-to-find and -read documentation can be critical to the workflow. Many forms of digital documents are available to achieve this goal; simple HTML, more complex web code such as PHP with SQL databasing, Wiki, snapshot images and video, etc. Upkeep of documentation is integral to the release and maintenance of any components of the workflow.

Solid design of the tools and documentation of the workflow should continually increase communication and speed of redundant tasks. It can also contribute to avoiding mistakes, making better looking images, increasing continuity, and maximizing the potential of everyone in the organization.

DEPLOYING A PRODUCTION WORKFLOW
Stephan Vladimir Bugaj

From Design to Implementation

Moving from design to implementation is a matter of planning, budgeting, testing, and then deployment. All analysis and design will now take shape in the form of a pipeline: a workflow, and the hardware and software that implement it. A number of decisions must be made in this phase, but if a studio has done a good job of developing specifications and design documents and has the resources to build a system that meets the requirements, whatever gets deployed should be well suited to its needs and sufficiently flexible to grow with the studio. This is necessary to avoid being stuck in a situation where tool selection dictates the capabilities of the studio, rather than vice versa.

To meet the requirements, the implementers must deal with the following during each step of development:

- Can the studio afford to purchase or build the planned component and, if not, is there an affordable alternative that does all of the essential work? If not, revisit the requirements and design and see if it's possible to modify the requirements to meet the budget.
  - Account for time. Money is not the only factor here, it is also necessary to ask how long will this take to deploy, and is that acceptable?
  - Account for hidden resource costs such as CPU usage, disk space, and so on through testing.
  - Account for support staff costs.
- Does the component the studio is about to purchase or build meet the requirements?
  - Does its functionality meet the functional specifications? If not, unless there is absolutely no other choice due to resource constraints, choose a different implementation.
  - Does it follow the design exactly and, if not, is the variation either an acceptable shortfall or a gain? If it is possible to accept the variation, make sure that change is reflected in the requirements and design so others are made aware of it.
  - Is this component sufficiently extensible/flexible that it can grow with the studio?
  - Can the artists use it efficiently and effectively?

Implementation should attempt to stick to the requirements and design specifications as closely as possible. Whenever variations must be made, the best solution is to make amendments to the design and requirements documentation to reflect the original goal, the modification, and the reason for it. This not only gives users an understanding of how their system works, but also allows future growth projects to revisit these issues. Often what was an insurmountable obstacle at one point becomes easy to achieve a few years later. If the studio maintains the planning documents even after implementation, it is possible to proactively stay on top of changing technologies and artists' needs while saving a lot of time and money over the long run.

To Build or Purchase?

One very important question that comes up when implementing a workflow is when to build and when to purchase—and what to purchase when buying. Cost analyses performed when making these decisions seem to inevitably fall short of reality, mainly because support costs are often ignored, as is the reality that even with commercial software all but the smallest shops will still need to do some custom development.

In some areas the off-the-shelf solutions, such as modeling, compositing, editing, and 3D paint, shader development, and simulation, are so robust that the thought of building one is ridiculous except for the largest studios with the resources to push the cutting edge of technology. Full 3D packages such as Maya, 3ds Max, Softimage XSI, and Houdini; sculpt and paint tools like Mudbox and Zbrush; and compositing software like Nuke, Fusion, and Shake also have the advantage that artists will arrive already knowing how to use them. Familiarity and low start-up costs make it inevitable that one or more commercial 3D, paint, editing, and compositing packages will play a critical role in any pipeline—this is true even at the large studios where tens of millions of R&D dollars are spent annually.

Some of the larger commercial packages have dozens of programmers constantly working to improve them to give them the edge against competing packages. An in-house solution may be quickly eclipsed by a commercial package, unless the studio can afford a Pixar or ILM sized R&D team of more than a hundred people. Lacking the ability to compete with the commercial developers in terms of scale, a studio that chooses in-house development may be stuck with an outdated system or the expense of switching. Training artists on a custom package comes with significant cost and time factors, which the likes of Pixar or ILM can easily absorb, but which may not be viable for a smaller studio. In-house software requires all new employees to take training classes. Existing packages have an existing user base, and are also are taught in schools and through numerous books. Even with all of their resources, industry leaders like Pixar and ILM still use a mixture of in-house and off-the-shelf packages.

Two major reasons in-house development continues is the drive for innovation and the fact that few of the off-the-shelf packages were developed with a simultaneous multiuser workflow in mind. Their facilities for file referencing are often buggy, and none of them natively supports the idea of a shot being composed of a large number of components. Instead, most of the commercial packages were written for single-user workflows where all data for a shot exists in a single file. Getting these packages to function correctly in a custom production workflow where multiple artists are doing different things on and to a shot or model in parallel can be tricky—and it requires building. Even midsize shops will find it necessary to do some R&D in order to facilitate a true multiuser, multidepartment workflow that facilitates simultaneous work on an asset by more than one user at a time. Whether this development is done entirely in house or based on a commercial package, it is important that end-user artists be very involved in development because software engineers may try to solve nonexistent problems and miss important ones.

None of the commercial packages encapsulates an entire production workflow optimally, even after installing a number of third-party plug-ins. Furthermore, none of the existing data interchange formats, even .fbx, natively supports all possible production data. Even if studios that don't intend to develop in-house plug-ins, shader library code, simulation engines, or other proprietary asset generation codes, they will still need one or more programmers. Glue code[2] will need to be written to move data around the pipeline, including interfacing with an asset tracking database. It's necessary to account for in-house development and support when building a production pipeline, regardless of what grand promises vendors may make.

Because no single package is sufficiently good at every part of a full CG pipeline, end-to-end modeling through film-out pipelines is generally based entirely on commercial packages linked together with glue code to facilitate data passing and management—except for large studios, with large R&D budgets. A willingness to undertake this development makes a studio more able to choose which package to use for which parts of the pipeline based on its relative strengths—even within the 3D portion of the pipeline; for example, modeling and animation in 3ds Max, effects through rendering in Houdini, and compositing in Nuke. Even single-person shops are likely to end up working with more than one package, unless that shop only provides service in a single part of the production pipeline (such as a compositing-only operation).

Once a studio moves beyond the basics, the necessity of writing plug-ins, custom shading libraries and templates, better articulation components, and other code that does more than

---

[2] Glue code is code that ties different parts of the pipeline together, whether it is data interchange between programs that write different file formats or interprocess control of one piece of the pipeline by another.

just move data around between packages and talk to databases quickly becomes obvious. For example, no unmodified commercial package provides a particularly robust lighting tool. Commercial packages provide a lot of value, but they all need expert users and developers customizing and extending them in order to achieve their full potential. Knowing when to build and when to purchase is a matter of analyzing the production needs and deciding when to put money toward purchasing components versus when to hire talented R&D people to take the system to the next level. However, any studio that attempts to deploy a multiuser pipeline with support for parallel tasking and asset tracking without a good developer on staff will quickly find itself in trouble.

Platforms, Packages, and Other Religions

During deployment, it is likely that employees will voice strong opinions about hardware and operating system platforms, production software packages, programming languages, and so on. Sometimes, these opinions can border on the fanatical. However, when deploying any system it is necessary to take into account the requirements, the full life-cycle costs, and the usability of the system. Full life-cycle costs include not only development and deployment costs, but also the support costs involved in administering the systems, including core IT infrastructure in addition to application maintenance. What is best is relative to the particulars of a given studio and is something that is affordable, sufficiently familiar to the artists (and/or that they can learn quickly), and, most importantly, meets the specified requirements.

Proponents of Linux point to its low entry cost and flexibility, whereas proponents of Windows tout its familiarity and availability of commercial packages. Both sides say that the other system requires a great deal of system administration maintenance to perform reliably and optimally—and both are correct. In a production situation, hiring expert systems administrators is far more important than deciding which platform is chosen. No platform (not even OSX) is so reliable and so optimized out of the box that it can be expected to perform perfectly without support. Depending on what the requirements are, Linux, OSX, Windows, or a combination thereof may be what is needed. Each has strengths and weaknesses. OSX has a plethora of both commercial and free software available on it and supports symlinks and a full shell environment (both important to large, TD[3]-heavy

---

[3] A Technical Director (TD) in a feature animation facility may also be called a Technical Artist or Technical Animator, and his or her responsibilities include production disciplines such as Surfacing, Simulation, Articulation, etc. However, a Technical Director in a visual effects facility is usually a lighting artist or developmental lighting artist.

workflows), but is not as cheap, flexible, or tunable (or as efficient out of the box) as Linux. Windows lacks many of those virtues, but on the other hand is familiar to more users, and a lot of software packages are available for it. No platform is better in all situations than the other.

Packages are amenable to similar comparisons. For example, Houdini is fantastic for simulation, effects, shading, and rendering, and it is amazingly customizable and extensible; Modo is a wonderful modeler; and XSI has industry leading animation tools. On the other hand, Max and Maya are decent across the board and are also very familiar to many users. However, none of these packages fully implements an entire production pipeline optimally, even though many of them implement large portions of the pipeline. Perhaps in future revisions one of the major packages will provide a complete pipeline solution out of the box.

Any combination of platform(s) and package(s) can serve as a solid foundation for a pipeline given the right people developing for and using them. Again, requirements and costs will dictate which one or more of these packages are deployed. While a strong team is the most important asset at any studio, their platform religion should not necessarily dictate deployment choices. Artist input is critical in any such decision, but the big picture of end-to-end pipeline development must also be kept in mind. Making a solid requirements analysis and design plan, and showing people that the choices being considered will meet those needs, can convince even the biggest platform zealots that it is reasonable to develop a system that may not be entirely (or at all) based on their favorite toolkit.

Test Now, Save Later

Testing during development is essential. Software engineering calls for unit tests (functioning of a single component) and white box (internal structure) and black box (input/output correctness) tests, which are indeed crucial to successful deployment of build-it-yourself components. However, target users should test all aspects of a system—in-house or off-the-shelf. Creating interim checkpoints and deliverables will facilitate discovery of problems early, before they become very costly. Regardless of the number of formal tests or design and code reviews employed, ultimately the only way to know if an implementation is meeting the specified requirements is to let the users say whether or not it is.

Interim user checkpoints should include the following:
- requirements and design reviews, where the users comment on the in-progress analysis and design;
- feature checkpoints, where advanced users test the core functionality, even if the user interface (UI) is not necessarily up to par;

- component checkpoints, where a feature and its associated UI elements are tested, even when the rest of the system isn't ready;
- alpha testing, where advanced users, using realistic data, test the earliest stages of a full system;
- beta testing, where a candidate for release is tested by a broad group of users, including its integration into whatever part of the pipeline has already been deployed.

Testing is often seen as an impediment to deployment, a speed bump in a timely delivery. However, testing copiously early in the development and deployment phase will reduce the long-term costs associated with fixing errors (both in the system and those a broken system creates in production assets) and the lost production time associated with a faulty system.

Development Deliverables

The end game of the beta testing phase of development and deployment is preparing for rollout and getting buy-in from the artists, managers, etc., who will be using the system in production. A system should not be released into production until most of the users are happy with its functionality and usability. Doing so otherwise is a waste of time and money. It is never cost effective to support and repair a system that decreases efficiency rather than increases it. This situation also leads to mistrust and resentment on the part of the production artists, making the ongoing job of the workflow team much more difficult.

In preparation for rollout, a beta should be promoted to a release candidate and a final round of comments solicited. All of the formal tests should be run on the release candidate. While this process comes from software engineering, it also applies to off-the-shelf solutions as well. Test the suitability of all software to meet the requirements and to reliably produce correct data and a viable user experience before deploying it.

Buy-in refers to getting enough users to approve of the release candidate as a sufficient tool for doing their job that they are willing to put it into production. Note that, by this point, a rollout plan needs to be in place. The rollout plan should provide for minimal downtime for the target users. This includes arranging to translate any data that needs format changes to work in the new version of the tool before the switch is made. Immediate follow-up with users and ongoing support should also be part of the rollout plan. Typically this is heavy in the first few days and ramps down to normal afterward.

During this final phase of development, the following occurs:
- A release candidate is approved.
- After release candidate approval, provide users with a rollout plan, guide, and instructions. The rollout plan should include

clear instructions for users on how to get immediate follow-up support as well as the ongoing support plans for the system.

- After rollout plan approval, but before the actual rollout, update any data, protocols, documentation, and so on that may be affected by the new or updated system.
- Install the new system on the users' computers.
- Test the installations on a sufficient number of users' computers in order to be confident the rollout has been generally successful.
- Provide immediate follow-up support in the form of a team that proactively circulates among the users (at least contacting them by e-mail, if nothing else) and offers assistance with, and solicits feedback on, the new system.
- Provide an ongoing user support apparatus.

These general principles of deployment will help create robust production workflow systems, regardless of which parts of the system are purchased and which are built. By taking the time to do all of the analysis, design, planning, and testing suggested herein, a studio will save time and money and have a more effective production pipeline. Return on this investment comes more quickly than people often think because the impact of a well-conceived, well-documented, and well-developed system on employee morale and efficiency is substantial. When a system is deployed that is reliable and meets its requirements from the onset, the support burden is reduced. This allows the studio to spend more time and money producing great visual effects and/or animation work and the workflow software team to spend more time developing ahead of the curve with advanced features rather than combating the effects of rushed, haphazard pipeline development.

INFRASTRUCTURE
Dan Novy

Infrastructure topologies among visual effects facilities are as varied as the number of facilities themselves. Using a best practices approach reveals a few simple paradigms. Facilities are designed along standard TCP/IP switching laid out in a client/server relationship, much as any large enterprise class computing operation would be. In general, a large, centralized data center for storage and computation is connected to branched, managed, or unmanaged workgroup switches. Artists, developers, and administrators have access to a unified data structure, with user and group permissions determining access and editing rights. As with other enterprise class computing systems, visual effects computing requires high-availability (HA) servers and networks. HA servers are defined as redundant, status-aware servers and software monitoring systems deployed to ensure that users have absolute access to the data structure regardless of power, network, or hardware issues. HA servers may be mirrored or clustered similar to RAID storage systems and are capable of load balancing as well as fail-over operations—in which backup servers come online without administrative intervention should the main server become inaccessible.

In addition to HA data service, facilities must deploy a robust backup system, timed incrementally, located locally, and ideally remotely as well, as part of a designed and tested disaster recovery system. Real-time backups are generally achieved through the clustering action of the HA servers, but incremental backups, done on a timed schedule, such as hourly, half day, daily, and nightly, should also be deployed. This allows the restoration of data down to the block level in all situations from a simple ill-timed file write or corrupted file system up to, and including, facility destruction.

Current enterprise class computing networking is a mix of gigabit or 10-gigabit over CAT6 or CAT6a, Fibre Channel, PCI Express, Serial ATA, or InfiniBand. Depending on the topology, switching is either hierarchical as with Ethernet or switched fabric.

Several visual effects facility–specific characteristics that explain network deployment and administration for enterprise class computing follow. Note, however, that this is not a comprehensive examination, nor is one possible, because each facility provides its own unique challenges and requirements.

1. *Ingestion.* Ingestion is defined as the place and process by which background plate material, scanned elements, or other digital assets enter the facility, are ideally logged, and become available to administration and artists for use. Pure animation, creating all of its own elements internally, would still benefit from a planned ingestion process because the artists may be receiving materials from other animation facilities. The hardware involved may vary from tape media to portable hard drive enclosures employing IEEE 1394 or USB buses to high-density optical media.

2. *Delivery.* Delivery is defined as the point and the process when anything from daily iterations to final shots leave the facility to be critiqued or scanned to film or made ready for final distribution. Again, media vary according to speed, time, and cost.

3. *Archiving.* Regardless of the facilities' individual choice of media for ingestion and delivery, once a shot has been finaled, it is usually the contractual obligation of the facility to archive all elements and digital assets used in the production of the shot. Archiving is a continually growing and changing concern as data sets become larger and new storage mediums evolve.

TRACKING ASSETS
Stephan Vladimir Bugaj

What Is Task and Asset Tracking?

Once a production team grows beyond one or two people, or clients become involved, some form of production tracking becomes essential. Both internal facility producers and outside clients need incremental updates on progress. They also need to be able to pull up elements from their production (for verification, legal clearance, reuse, etc.) at a moment's notice. Without some kind of production tracking, it is difficult to ascertain if the project is staying on time and on budget—until it is too late. When jobs do go over bid, production tracking can help determine why. Although this is not the most interesting or glamorous aspect of production, it is crucial to the viability of all productions.

Task planning and tracking are the processes of breaking down a job into tasks, estimating how long each task will take, and then tracking the progress to make sure the project is staying on time and on budget. For producers, planning information turns into bids and budgets. Tracking is then essential to see how the bid will be adhered to and will aid the production to take corrective measures before it gets out of hand. Production department heads can use tracking data not only to see how their own team is doing but also to see how their predecessor departments are doing in terms of delivering work to their team.

Each task in the pipeline should roughly equate to the work done by one artist at each stage in the pipeline. Often there will be more than one task per department, depending on artist specialization, such as separate technical shading and texture painting tasks within the texturing department. The primary asset associated with a task is generally either a shot or a model. Dealing with assets below the model or shot level for task planning and tracking is generally more expensive and time consuming than it is worth (and almost always incorrect). It is necessary to track these at the asset tracking level, but for task management it is only crucial to associate the task with a specific shot, model, or other reusable model-like object, such as an articulation rig, script, lighting rig, etc., that isn't specific to a single shot or model.

Tasks that may need to be tracked in a production are as follows:

- Production design (either per model or per shot):
  - model design illustrations,
  - shader callouts and material reference paintings and photos,
  - dressing plans and sketches, and
  - lighting keys and references.

- Modeling, rigging, and shading (per model):
  - base geometry sculpt,
  - articulation and procedurals,
  - shader definitions and binding, and
  - texture painting and/or detailing sculpt in a tool like Mudbox.
- Layout and set dressing (per shot):
  - camera definition (framing and motion) and
  - set dressing.
- Animation and simulation (per shot):
  - animation (usually tracked separately for character animation and visual effects animation departments, and often split up per character or visual effects element in the shot) and
  - simulation (usually tracked separately for character cloth and hair and visual effects simulation departments).
- Lighting, rendering, and compositing (per shot):
  - master lighting rig definitions are tracked separately, more like models are tracked, as they're reused across shots,
  - shot lighting,
  - rendering, and
  - final composite.

This may seem straightforward, and in many ways it is. One hitch is that often each task needs multiple task *stages* or *phases* to support parallel iterative refinement, so artists may work from rough to fine. For example, animation might have blocking, key, and polish stages, whereas modeling might have rough, sculpted, and detailed stages. Given preliminary data from animation, a lighting team knows to start master shot lighting after blocking is finished and a shading team knows to start basic shading after a rough sculpt is completed.

Two other elements to task track are *global assets* and *fix requests*. Global assets are things like scripts and plug-ins that are not specific to a model or shot. These still need to be tracked and generally can be tracked in the same system as models. After all, models are somewhat like global assets except that they appear on-camera. This means models (and model-like assets such as lighting rigs and articulation rigs) can be associated with one or more shots for the purpose of knowing when to release shots into further stages of production based on model dependencies—their main difference from other global assets.

Fix requests are reports back to a department that has already marked the asset as finished. This is done per stage, so a fix can be generated against the model and, whether it is in the rough, sculpted, or detailed stage at the time of the request, should get flagged in the tracking system for fixes. This is both a communication system between departments and a way for producers to track problems with assets that may be holding up crucial footage.

When associating assets with tasks, usually a top-level file (such as a Maya .ma file) or a virtual asset[4] is used to stand in for the potentially many on-disk assets. So, to associate modeling, rigging, and shading tasks with a model, they are tied to the record of the model's scene file in the primary package or to the virtual definition of that model. All of the other files would be indirectly associated through their association with the model in the asset tracking system, but their state wouldn't directly matter to the task. When tracking assets and tasks at a lower level, it is still not recommended to track down to the lowest file levels. Geometry might be tracked through a Maya or 3ds Max file and shading through a main Slim palette or through database definitions of "model, geometry" and "model, shading"—but associating every file reference in those top-level files directly with the task would be overkill and potentially misleading, particularly given shared resources that may be referenced. It is too inflexible to validate completion of a task this way and leads to people checking in bogus files just to clear the validation checkpoint and declare the task done when they may legitimately have completed the task without all of the required files being accounted for (or they may have needed too many files), since even the same tasks vary in complexity quite a bit.

Asset tracking, on the other hand, requires only that files be associated with one or more models, shots, or other global assets. These associations are either by inclusion or by reference. *By inclusion* means that a file is part of the definition of that asset. It is stored in a directory structure rooted at the directory that defines the asset by virtue of its being a key field in a database definition and/or containing the top-level defining file of that asset. *By reference* means the file is part of the definition of one or more assets—and it is referenced into the asset through a referencing/ linking system. References are generally tracked at the level of other assets, not individual files, in order to make the asset-tracking task tenable. Actual file-level tracking may be used as well, but highly technical artists and developers in extreme troubleshooting situations only refer to that complex relationship.

An example of which assets might need to be tracked can be seen in this definition of what subassets comprise a model's surface (or surfacing or texturing or shading) asset:

• Surface definition:
  • root shader definitions and parameter values (Slim palette or otherwise):
    – referenced definitions (external palettes),

---

[4] A database definition of an asset that is not actually a file on disk.

- library shaders (these aren't always tracked as part of the model-level definition, but could be, by reference),
- direct-read texture images read in by the definitions or referenced definitions,
- projection or tumble paint[5] definitions file (if external to the package scene file), and
- projection or tumble paint texture images.

In practice, this surface definition could range anywhere from a couple of files, for a purely procedural single shader on a simple model, to hundreds of files, mostly textures, for surfacing a very complex hero model. Tracking the database definition and/or the top-level asset file helps manage the complexity and tracks assets by what they are conceptually (surfacing) rather than by defining an assumed required set of files that may in practice vary in quantity and composition for *every single distinct instance* of the asset type.

Purchased, built, or both, a system ideally should provide:

- Task tracking:
  - Stages of completion to support parallel iterative refinement.
  - A system for managing fixes as a special type of task.
- Revision control at the asset level (similar to release packages in software revision management):
  - Asset-level revision control is generally not for every file check in but rather on user request. This process should version *all* of the files in the asset at once, marking all the current file versions as part of this new asset version.
  - *Publication* (aka release) of a new version of the asset is the process of taking the source files and installing them for use in the scene/shot editing environment. This should be a user-specified step and only be done when the artists feel the asset in the unpublished (source) area is ready to go live.
- Revision control at the individual file level:
  - Artists check in and out of these files (or subassets that are collections of individual files, but not a full asset) to allow for simultaneous multiuser work.
  - File versions are kept for debugging purposes, but only file versions associated with a published asset version are relevant to the asset-level revision control system.
  - Associations are created between file versions and tool versions to try to avoid editing a file with an incompatible version of the tool.

---

[5] Tumble paint is a term of art used to distinguish 3D paint systems that allow direct painting on the mesh, such as Mudbox or Zbrush, as different from systems that use projection cameras to place textures on a model.

- References into frame storage (and a way to version frame sequences, which will have to be set up in a render management system and then reflected in the tracking system):
  - A system for maintaining old versions of frames for comparison, preferably with information about what versions of the assets created those frames.
- Associations between tasks and conceptual/top-level assets:
  - Multiple associations, so a task/fix can be related to one or more assets—this is especially useful for associating a model fix with one or more shots that are held up waiting for that fix.
- A GUI that shows information about tasks and assets, provides a viewer for seeing associated renders, and provides handlers to open the asset into the appropriate tool from the tracking system.

Commercial Task and Asset Tracking Systems

Task planning and tracking are generally thought to be well understood, and many in production management use generic tools such as Microsoft Project for doing this. Although Project, or a similar tool, may be used successfully for broad-outline planning of a production, it is not well suited to production task tracking. Live-action budgeting and on-set production management tools from vendors such as Entertainment Partners and Jungle Software also are not perfectly suited to tracking production tasks in a visual effects or animation studio (although a VFX Supervisor on set may want to keep his or her own visual effects camera logs with traditional camera report specialty software or a spreadsheet).

Until recently, digital production studios were not the target market for any off-the-shelf production tracking software due to their being more of a niche industry within the film production market. Recently products such as Shotgun and VFX Showrunner have emerged, with the former targeted at animation houses and larger visual effects facilities and the latter more to boutique facilities. Either a piece of commercial software like this must match any given studio's production process exactly, right out of the box, or it will need to be tailored to fit. Fortunately, most of the off-the-shelf software has some degree of built-in configurability in terms of defining departments, tasks, and stages in the pipeline. But, for a very customized, large, and/or complex pipeline, the package of choice also needs to support scripting and/or plug-ins so that it can be expanded later without relying on the vendor to do so (and charge for it). Even if the pipeline is reasonably straightforward, it may still become necessary at some point to customize the task-tracking tool with regard to associating tasks with data in the asset tracking system. The facilities for doing that in the various commercial task-tracking packages range in quality from fair to nonexistent, so there should be a plan from the start to do some customization.

Asset tracking, or digital asset management (DAM), deals with the actual asset files themselves. The artists use this capability more than management, and successful asset tracking systems contain elements of revision control systems, media databases, and bug tracking systems. Canto Cumulus and Avid Alienbrain are two major commercial digital asset management systems. Both are highly customizable, and this is essential in a DAM package because it is necessary to be able to store every kind of file asset in the system that needs to be versioned and associated with a model, shot, or other global asset and also able to be viewed/loaded.

Storing rendered frames and final composites can become very data intensive. While most DAMs handle image file formats natively and some now even support OpenEXR and other high-end formats, how they do this can make a big difference in performance. Scalability testing is recommended before purchasing a commercial system and storing rendered frames in it, and a high-speed network attached storage (NAS) system like NetApp or BlueArc is crucial. Large shops with huge render farms generally write frames directly to the NAS via a specialized render management system, like Pixar's Alfred or an in-house tool, and only associate references to image sequences with the shots rather than trying to cram all of the image data into a DAM system that may not be able to handle it. The necessity of specialized in-house or high-end commercial tiff sequence playback tools to review uncompressed, color-managed 1, 2, 3, and/or 4k tiff sequences at 24 fps, due to the insufficiency of most movie file formats—which are generally both compressed and not frame accurate—is another reason why a lot of studios do not check the frames directly into their DAM system but use references instead. The slowdowns are just too great as most, if not all, DAMs cannot handle either the huge render farm loads or the playback speed requirements.

Building Task and Asset Tracking Systems

As with 2D and 3D production pipeline software in general, a studio will inevitably wind up developing at least some customizations to a commercial system, if not creating one from scratch. Once a studio workflow reaches a certain level of complexity, native capabilities of off-the-shelf systems are exceeded and it becomes essential to either extend it (if it is sufficiently flexible) or replace it with a custom system. Building a custom system can proceed from the starting point of a commercial system special-ized for production purposes or generic tools like a commercial (or freeware) relational or object-oriented database system and revision control system.

Revision control systems and databases, from simple ones like RCS and MySQL to more sophisticated commercial systems like Perforce and Oracle, can also serve as the basis for a task and asset tracking system. Because the off-the-shelf market did not really serve the animation and visual effects communities for so many years, many studios use in-house asset and task track-ing systems built on a relational database and a revision control system (with either proprietary GUIs in Qt, Tk, or wXwidgets or Web front ends for viewing tabular data, filling out forms, brows-ing assets by rendered image, and other front-end functions of a task and asset tracking system). As with commercial DAM sys-tems, storing frame image data in a RDBMS[6] like Oracle, MySQL, or Postgres is not a particularly good idea. A system for writing frames to a NAS and referencing them via the database is much more efficient.

Building a system from scratch can be expensive, but if a com-mercial system like Shotgun isn't sufficient, it becomes necessary to do some development to expand on it and create the complete asset tracking system that meets requirements. In addition to the fact that it is inherently suited to a particular production work-flow, a big advantage of planning to build a custom system from the onset, even if it's based on a commercial system as a starting point, is that combined task tracking and asset tracking can be designed into the system from the beginning.

An example of a high-level design of a combined asset and task tracking system is as follows:

- Task definitions:
  - name of task.
  - type of task (such as build or fix or a more complex type system if desired).
  - designated department.
  - task stage:
    - stage completion (such as unassigned, assigned, in progress, omitted, and completed).
  - assigned artist.
  - key (conceptual) asset(s) (model, shot, other global asset):
    - associated on-disk asset(s), such as the top-level file associated with the conceptual asset, such as a Maya, 3ds Max, Houdini or XSI scene file (note that for shot-related tasks, it's also necessary to have paths to the ren-dered clips in the frame storage area) and

---

[6] Relational database management systems.

- – icon, which is just a thumbnail of a canonical "what is this" image such as a model render or a key frame from a shot, that is used in the UI to visually represent the asset(s) with which the task is associated.
  - bid.
  - due date.
  - requester (who asked for this task to be done, in case the artist has follow-up questions).
  - downstream department (who is expecting this task to be finished in order to get their work done).
- Asset definition:
  - name of asset.
  - type of asset (usually a multilevel-type system):
    - – distinguish between time-based assets like shots and sequences, "physical" (renders out as an image) assets like models, and "virtual" (doesn't directly produce pixels) assets like light rigs, articulation rigs, and scripts,
    - – within models, generally a model-type system is used to specify characters, props, architecture, vehicles, etc., as determined by the production, and
    - – within shots, it may be necessary to specify shot types to distinguish full cg from plate-integrated shots or to specify shots that need a special post process, etc.
  - status (in the production, or omitted—do not remove all traces of deleted assets from the production in case someone changes his or her mind and it's necessary to revive them later),
  - files:
    - – included files: root directory that the files are stored within—this is usually thought of as *the asset* on disk; a complete list of all checked-in files associated with that asset, in a revision control system that is either part of the DAM system or hooked up to it and
    - – referenced assets: references to only the conceptual asset and, depending on the design of the database and the code that references it, possibly also the top-level scene or other definition file.

Some information necessary to comprehensive production management can only be determined by looking in both places (*query joins,* in database parlance). For example, knowing if an asset is done requires querying the tasks associated with the asset and seeing that all workflow tasks are marked as completed (including fix tasks associated with that asset)—and doing this for all referenced assets as well.

It is likely that if the workflow is complex, or the facility large, the deployed system will be one that combines off-the-shelf production-oriented software, like Shotgun and Alienbrain, with customizations (including custom front-ends), links to a render management system and NAS frame storage system, and perhaps also an RDBMS like Oracle and general file revision system like Perforce. This is because no one system is completely suited to the complexity of real-world production management when using a sophisticated digital workflow with many artists working on many disparate tasks and, sometimes, for many clients, all at once. All of this information then needs to come together into a unified view of the state of the production and to output final renders at the end.

SCENE ASSEMBLY
Stephan Vladimir Bugaj

3D Scene Assembly

In order for articulation and shading artists to work on the same character at the same time, some means of breaking up a single model into components and then reassembling it later is necessary. A similar asset break-down strategy applies to all areas of the pipeline, for example, a lighter and an animator working on the same shot at the same time. Most commercial software packages have mechanisms for referencing and importing scene data, and with some file formats, automatic merges are also possible.

Decomposition of a model into components can take the form of separating definitions of different tasks into different files, such as putting shader definition and binding information into separate files that can be version controlled (and locked for editing) separately from the model geometry file. For example, Pixar's Renderman Artist Tools comes with a system called Slim, hosted in Maya, which has this capability. The software package's native file referencing and importing system can also be used to provide this functionality for other components that need to be worked on in parallel—especially reusable components like articulation rigs and *greeblies.*[7]

A model might be broken down into the following components that get stored in separate files and thus need reassembly:
- Geometric mesh data:
    - Background objects and characters may simply be referenced-in or imported-in collections of reusable components such as robot or car parts or creature heads, arms, legs, and torsos.
    - Hero models may start off by referencing-in geometry from a library of reusable components as a starting point.

---

[7] Greeblies is used here to mean small reusable model geometry components and comes from the term used by ILM to describe an assortment of detail pieces from kit-bashed commercial plastic model kits used on production models.

- Articulation rig:
  - Rigs can be built up from component rig parts.
- Texturing information:
  - Shader definitions/templates
  - Shader parameter values (set in instances of the templates)
  - Shader bindings
  - Projection or tumble paint camera definitions
  - Textures
- Procedurals (articulation or shading components that initiate automatically based on scene data, such as frame number).

A number of artists need to work on these components separately and at the same time, especially at large studios where specialization in areas like modeling, texturing, and articulation becomes necessary. Having a single artist work on all of these components in a single model file isn't tenable because it extends the timeline necessary to accomplish the work.

Final scenes, by their nature, require even more decomposition. Each scene is made up of a number of models. To maintain consistency (and artist sanity) it is necessary to build and test any models that appear in more than one shot in scene files that exclusively have the model definition data. These test scenes should be completely neutral with regard to lighting and animation. They are usually self-contained without any reference to actual shots in the film. Furthermore, to facilitate the parallel pipelines, which are necessary to get major production jobs done on time and on budget, breaking apart the work on the scenes themselves is often essential as it collapses the timeline.

Scenes may be broken down most naturally into the following components:

- Matchmove or animation camera layout (including initial dressing of stand-in 3D objects and simple blocking animation of dummy characters or fx stand-ins).
- Set dressing, which is the placement of the noncharacter objects in the scene. Shot dressing may start with one or more scene/sequence/location level sets that get imported or referenced in and then adjusted for the shot.
- Animation (keyframed or MoCap) and simulation, and herein the separation is usually made between these two types of time-varying data and between character and visual effects workflows.
  - Multiple files of parameter values may be referenced or imported during final scene assembly, because it can be highly beneficial to break apart animation data into separately managed files. An animator references in another's work to animate against, but only changes his or her own character or visual effects animation.

- Because of the differing data demands, file formats and workflows of different simulation engines for visual effects, cloth and hair, additional files also need to be managed.
- Crowd animation often results in additional files to manage, not only because of the additional characters but also because systems like Massive require their own data.
- Lighting. As with set dressing, lighting shots often start with referenced or imported sequence-level setups.

All of these things need to come together in order to form a final scene that can then be rendered and composited into the final plate. The data management challenge is to keep track of all of these files as being part of a particular scene or model, using the approaches discussed in the tracking assets section. By knowing what must come together, one can determine when assembly can occur.

Data that is not stored directly in a package scene format usually comes with a developer-supplied workflow for translating that data back into scene data within the primary package. This happens either directly as data in the package or as directives in the scene file that get passed to the renderer, such as by associating a Renderman RIB archive with the scene.

Data that is not native to the package, such as various kinds of simulation, crowd animation, shading, and similar data that may be kept separately from the primary scene file, is assembled back in by either writing the data into the native scene format or by adding to the scene format a callback that runs at render time to output the special data into a format the renderer understands. Some developers do a better job of this than others. Therefore, this is one area in which studios and visual effects facilities invest a lot of in-house development.

Revision control is important with both 2D and 3D scene assembly. It is necessary to ensure that the most current relevant version of the asset is being assembled into the scene. This is especially important on the 3D side where there are many complicated compound assets. An asset tracking system that allows for revision control, labeling of revisions, locking a particular scene (2D or 3D) to a revision label, and annotation of versions is essential. Scenes, and their components, should also be associated with versions of the tools because it is sometimes the case that tool upgrades break older versions of their data files and may require time-consuming fixes by the artists.

The scene assembly process must be fed by a coherent, comprehensive revision management system that will allow the artists to trust that they are using the most appropriate version of the assets. Consider the importance of this when there may be hundreds or even thousands of assets in any given scene. The system itself must default to the most current agreed-on version of the asset and only vary from that upon request from an artist who has a particular need in a particular scene. Otherwise, the complexity encountered during scene assembly will quickly become overwhelming, and a large amount of time and money will be lost dealing with an easily avoidable problem.

Once all off-board scene and model data have been accounted for in the format of the primary 3D package, there is the issue of final model and scene assembly through referencing, importing, or merging. Each of these techniques has advantages and disadvantages. Merging, which is the taking of two files in the package format and combining them, has all the disadvantages of importing. At the same time, it is much more complex. No common packages support doing a merge natively and it is therefore usually done using an in-house or third-party purchased plug-in or script. It is generally only used if the package of choice simply does not support either referencing or importing—a very uncommon situation with modern 3D software. In some cases, if a package only supports referencing, merging may be developed if an import rather than reference is required.

Importing, as a way to assemble a shot or model, is easy in that it is well supported in popular packages such as Maya. The resulting scene or model file is independent of other files. An import takes the data from the external file, such as an articulation rig or some greeblie geometry and writes that data locally into the scene file. Once the import is complete, the component(s) from the external file are now defined in the local scene file and no dependency on the other file is maintained. While this is a simple and reliable solution for small, fast jobs such as TV commercials, it quickly becomes untenable when trying to create large, long-term projects.

On the other hand, referencing, which involves a situation where the final scene or model file will contain data that is loaded from other files, is ideal for larger shops working on larger projects. Referencing (sometimes also called *linking,* such as in 3ds Max) does not break the connection between the file the reference was created *in* and the file the reference was created *to*. This means that any changes in the referenc*ed* file get reflected in the referenc*ing* file—generally upon reload (few, if any, 3D systems implement in-memory live referencing).

The big advantage of referencing is parallel iterative refinement. Because referencing allows for changes to propagate into all scenes or models that reference the changed subasset, artists can create and check in rough versions of their work, which allows the artists that depend on it to begin their own work. In this way, whole teams may work from rough to fine in parallel. For example, layout creates cameras, rough sets, and blocking; at the same time, set dressers and animators may create rough dressing and blocking animation. From there, lighters may join in by creating the master scene and/or rough shot lighting while the animators and dressers refine their work.

The challenge is that the changes may create unforeseen side effects in the referencing files. Systems for testing change integration and version control over the referenced assets are essential. Scene assembly from references, imports, or merges is as much about data management and developing good practices around testing and communicating changes as it is any technical considerations. The artistic and artist management challenge is to get the decomposition of tasks correct and, thus, definitions of what is referenced and what is local to the model or scene, based on workflow requirements. This greatly depends on the size and budget of the facility and how the skill sets of the artists break down, accounting for any plans to change this breakdown based on training and hiring. The variations on suggestions above, and elsewhere in this chapter, are relatively common within the industry.

Referencing is an essential part of a simultaneous multiuser workflow and large studios thrive on it. Without referencing, large studios could not have teams of sometimes as many as a dozen people working on a single model or shot simultaneously—a crucial part of a large-scale production pipeline. One reason that smaller studios tend to be less fond of referencing is that many 3D packages have limitations and/or problems with their referencing systems. This leads to many hours spent on debugging referencing-related problems and/or writing in-house systems to repair, extend, or bypass the referencing system in the commercial package. Vendors have been improving this ability in their tools for a few years now, however, such that referencing may be worth another look even at the smaller facilities.

2D Scene Assembly (Compositing)

Assembly of a scene in 2D requires a number of input plates that are then put together utilizing the compositing software. Creation of the input plates and management of that data are tied into the rest of the workflow—including 3D scene assembly. Plates come from one of three sources: original camera plates (and/or portions thereof isolated by keying or roto shapes), 2D animation and matte paint layers, and from renders of 3D scene data.

3D scene assembly choices result in 2D plates that feed into the final comp. Usually, the entire 3D scene rendered into a single plate is not what is needed. Creating multiple plates may be done using renderer arbitrary output variables (AOVs) from a single scene file or by selectively turning on and off parts of the entire final scene and then rendering them separately. The latter approach can be achieved by separately rendering intermediate scene files that define components of the shot or by using some notion of layering or grouping in the primary 3D package to turn on and off geometry and lights per pass. Alternatively one could write a custom tool that does this process of sending multiple passes of the scene to a renderer separately. Although this approach seems cumbersome at first, it often turns out to be easier to manage than AOVs, which require render passes to be defined at shader definition time rather than on the fly based on the particular needs of a specific project, sequence, or even individual shot.

Setting up the 3D scene to create render passes for compositing depends on the compositing goals and style of the shop. Level of detail and render resource management considerations can also be taken into account: for example, splitting out the background elements of a shot in order to render them with different, cheaper settings than the hero elements. Both approaches require developing a system, within a given toolset, for defining holdout mattes for objects in the 3D scene that are in front of those in the current render or else a lot of hand-rotoing will be required.

If the primary 3D package cannot already do something like this, a good way achieve this holdout is to create a plug-in to a render prep system. This render prep plug-in would discard all objects behind those defined as being in the pass, at each frame, since objects can change relative positions during the scene. Then the objects in front are identified algorithmically based on their Z-depth, a cheap shader is assigned as the material for this holdout pass, and then the holdout objects are rendered. Subsequently, it is necessary to subtract the holdout alphas (which won't always be one with motion blur) from the final image alpha.

Here are some passes that are common in the industry:

- Arbitrary output variables:
  - By lighting component (diffuse, specular, reflection, etc.). Usually used by shops that do a lot of lighting/relighting in the compositing software rather than with virtual 3D light rigs.
  - By shader type, so that shaders are assigned that have been defined in advance to call particular AOV macros.
  - As a render pass system more generally, by creating an in-house system by which a plug-in is used in the shading and render prep system to associate each surface with an AOV macro at scene assembly time rather than at shader definition time. By doing this, AOVs basically function like the system below.
- Layering/grouping/multiple component files:
  - Separating out foreground/midground/background and rendering with different geometric level of detail (LOD),

different renderer LOD and quality parameters, different light rigs, etc., in order to save resources on background elements and prioritize foreground.

- Isolating particular characters, environment elements, or visual effects elements that require specific, separate image treatments in the compositing phase.
- Isolating elements (such as gigantic simulations) that are so resource intensive that they need to be rendered as a separate pass in order to make it through the renderer.

WORKING ACROSS MULTIPLE FACILITIES
Scott Squires

It is common for large visual effects film projects to be spread over multiple visual effects companies or facilities. This can be due to a factor of schedules, budgets, and specialization. The work is usually broken up by sequences but may in turn be broken up by specific types of visual effects (matte paintings, CG animation, etc.). When possible, it is best to break up the work to minimize the amount of interaction between companies. Overlap of work means that resources and schedules become even more problematic. It can also be very inefficient. This should be reviewed when creating the budget and considering the trade-offs with regard to the number of companies working on the project.

If a shot needs to go through multiple facilities (each facility doing a different CG character, one facility handling the animation and another doing the compositing, etc.), then any change or snag will cause a ripple delay through all of the facilities. If the director makes a change, then the shot may have to go through all of the same stages again. If there's a conflict then there may be a lot of finger pointing about whose problem it is and how to solve it.

Unfortunately there are many circumstances where there will be overlap among facilities. This section provides some guidance on dealing with this overlap. The visual effects field does not have a lot of technical standards since the software and techniques are rapidly evolving. Many facilities use their own proprietary software or pipeline that they wish to keep private. The technical leads from the different facilities will need to discuss the requirements directly and work together to come up with a feasible solution that minimizes some of the risks. Note that this may even happen with previs in the pre-production stage. A production may move to a different location and require a local facility to rework some of the original previs.

If a project is known to have overlap at the pre-production stage, then the visual effects facilities should be notified in the bidding stages so they can plan accordingly. The facilities may have to agree to certain standards of data formats and transferring. They may also have to write specific programs to help import/export from their internal formats to something another facility can use. The pre-production time should be used to test the interchange of test shots to work out any problems before post-production begins.

The easiest interchange is when facilities use the same off-the-shelf software. Note that this also requires the facilities to be using the same version number. Sometimes visual effects facilities may be behind on updating their software because they are working on a large show and don't want to risk having problems with the update. They may also have specialized plug-ins, scripts, and programs that they have created that depend on the version they are currently using.

One facility usually takes the lead for specific models or tasks and the other facility may take the lead on other items. Once the model or look is approved by the director, then the files and other data are provided to the second facility. The first facility provides visual references to the second facility for making comparisons.

Even when using the same software, additional work is likely necessary to make it work in another pipeline. In some cases it may be necessary to duplicate the work from scratch, such as building a model, if it is too problematic to transfer the necessary data into a useful form. This is why any overlap needs to be considered in the budgeting stage.

In some cases it may be a 911 (emergency) project where a facility is not able to accomplish what is needed in the time provided. In this case it can be difficult and costly for other facilities to step in quickly and take on some of the work due to the complexity of interchanging data and a very compressed schedule. As studios reduce post-production time and make creative changes very late in the schedule these situations are happening more and more. In the end the studios pay a very large price for creating this situation and the final quality likely suffers as well. At some point the project may have to be delayed due to this type of situation that in most cases could have been avoided.

Images

Scanning and recording facilities have standard image formats to pass images back and forth to visual effects facilities such as DPX.[8] The facilities should agree on a standard image format that

---

[8] DPX: scanned film file format.

can be used to pass images back and forth. This format may not be used internally but could be used as an exchange format. This could be EXR[9] or other format that maintains the full quality of the image. Image file naming schemes will have to be agreed on along with the issue of color space. A known film clip or standard image is useful to confirm that the color isn't being shifted through the process inadvertently. Images can be passed via high-speed connections or hard drives.

Models

It is common for CG models to need to be used by multiple facilities. Ideally the facilities use the same software, which makes transferring models easier. Many different model formats are available, each with its various pros and cons. Some standard formats are used for prebuilt models but these may be lacking the additional information required for a complex model. Standard formats also exist for the 3D scanning companies but these models lack some of the naming, structure, and metadata features that will be required for production use. Transferring hard surface models is usually easier than transferring creature models that require special skinning or complex fur and hair. In some cases a base model will be transferred that will have to be modified or rebuilt at least in part to work in another facility's pipeline. The model lead from each facility should discuss which format works best for a specific project.

Texturing

There are many ways of using textures. Each facility may have a different means of applying the textures or even a different color space and gamma. The textures from one facility may have to be adjusted in a graphics program or in the shader of a 3D program to obtain a result consistent with another facility.

Animation

Many facilities consider their rigging of the models (animation skeleton system) proprietary. The dynamic simulation may be all done using special in-house proprietary software. The animation may require special plug-ins or scripts to handle procedural animation. The facilities may be using totally different animation software. All of these issues make it difficult to pass pure animation back and forth between facilities. In many cases the animation is rendered out as an image element that another visual

---

[9] EXR: open-source file format for high-resolution images developed by ILM.

effects facility can composite. It may be better to render the different lighting passes separately (specular, ambient lighting, etc.) so the other facility can do a final balance in the composite. This allows finessing the image without having to do a full re-render and sending back the element. In some cases the animation is *baked out*[10] to provide what amounts to a 3D model per frame. This way they can be lit and placed by the second facility.

Compositing

Elements are passed between facilities but typically composite projects are not. Much depends on whether the same compositing software is used at all facilities. If the same software is used, the next issue will be the organization of the elements in terms of file names and directory structures. If it's a complex composite with many elements, it may be faster and easier for the compositor to rebuild the composite rather than reverse engineer the composite done with a different style.

R&D

Research and development is where things become even more difficult. If one facility has developed a specialized software system for creating a specific look, then they may be reluctant to supply the source code or application to a potential competitor. It's possible a nondisclosure agreement can be signed to allow proprietary information and data to be shared. In some cases, other facilities will have to try to re-create the finished look from scratch. The production VFX Supervisor and Producer will need to discuss this in pre-production with the facilities involved.

Summary

Interchanging shots and data among facilities can be difficult. This always incurs additional costs and time, so it is recommended that the number of facilities whose work overlaps be minimized. When possible, break the work into separate sequences or types of shots to minimize interaction. In all cases take this into account in the planning stages and be sure to determine (and test) a workflow and interchange process between facilities before post-production begins.

---

[10] Bake out: to output in a format that is fixed. In this case the model is no longer animatable but exists essentially as a 3D model for each frame.

ACKNOWLEDGMENTS

Special Thanks

Margaret Adamic (Disney Publishing Worldwide)
Paul Bloch (Rogers and Cowan–Shangri-La Entertainment)
Doug Cooper (Wiki Technical Director)
Trinh Dang (Associate Manager, Clip Licensing Department,
Twentieth Century Fox Film Corporation)
Margarita Diaz (Executive Director, Clip & Image Licensing,
Sony Pictures Entertainment)
Sarah Garcia (Contract Administrative Assistant, Business
Affairs, Lucasfilm Ltd.)
Julie S. Heath (Executive Director, Clip & Still Licensing,
Warner Bros. Entertainment Inc.)
Ryan C. Likes (Executive Vice President, The Halcyon Company)
Roni Lubliner (Universal Studios Media Licensing)
Susie Oh (Vice President Business & Legal Affairs, Sony
Pictures Digital Production Inc.)
Brian Palagallo (Film Clip Licensing, Paramount Digital
Entertainment)
Miles Perkins (ILM)
Stephen Strauss (Attorney)
Martha Winterhalter (American Society of Cinematographers)

The Entire Handbook Committee and all of the fantastic
writers who contributed their talent and time to this book

Thanks

Tom Boland
Bennett Cain
Buf Compagnie
Digital Domain Productions, Inc.
Electronic Arts
Harrison Ellenshaw (Consultant)
Tom Fletcher
Beth Franco (Marleah Leslie & Associates PR)
Robert S. Getman, Esq.
Gradient Effects, LLC
Steve Katz
Laika, Inc.
New Deal Studios
RealD

Don Shay, Publisher, Cinefex
Fred Specktor (Creative Artists Agency)
Summit Entertainment, LLC
Technicolor Creative Services
Ultimatte Corporation

Eric Roth (VES)
Brent Armstrong (VES)
Colleen Kelly Bromley (VES)

Personal Thanks

Scott Squires
Toni Pace Carstensen
Kevin Rafferty
Linda and Valerie Squires
Dick Carstensen
Elisabeth, Jonathan, and Oliver Okun

CHARTS AND FORMULAS

Miniatures

(From *The Photography of Miniature Effects—High-Speed Photography* in Chapter 3.)

Formula to determine proper frame rate for scale being used:

$$(\sqrt{m}) \times (r) = f$$

where
m = miniature's scale
r = base frame rate
f = new frame rate.

Example: 1:4 scale at 24 fps = $(\sqrt{4}) \times (24) = (2) \times (24) = 48$ fps

Formula to determine proper actual speed of a scaled object at a scaled frame rate:

$$(rs/m) = (b)$$
$$(b) \times (r) = (as)$$

where
rs = real object speed
m = miniature's scale
b = base speed
r = frame rate factor
as = actual speed for filming.

Examples: 36 mph × 1:6 scale car = 8.8 feet per second
8.8 feet per second × 2.5 normal frame rate = 22 feet per second

The VES Handbook of Visual Effects. DOI: 10.1016/B978-0-240-81242-7.00011-2

Camera and Lens Chart
(From *Digital Cinematography* in Chapter 3.)

Table A.1. Lens Focal Length Equivalency Chart

35mm Equivalent	2/3-Inch Equivalent	1/3-Inch Equivalent	Vertical Angle	Horizontal Angle
12.5mm	5mm	2.72mm	66.0°	87.0°
17.5mm	7mm	3.8mm	51.0°	69.6°
25mm	10mm	5.4mm	37.0°	52.0°
35mm	14mm	7.6mm	26.8°	38.4°
50mm	20mm	10.8mm	18.8°	27.0°
70mm	28mm	15.2mm	13.4°	19.4°
100mm	40mm	21.6mm	9.6°	13.8°
175mm	70mm	38.1mm	5.4°	7.8°

Pixel Resolution
(From *4K + Systems Theory Basics for Motion Picture Imaging* in Chapter 6.)

Table A.2 Number of Film Pixels per Height and Width

Format	Width × Height (SMPTE/ISO Camera Gate)	Pixels
Super 16mm	12.35mm × 7.42mm	2058 × 1237 pixels
Super 35mm	24.92mm × 18.67mm	4153 × 3112 pixels
65mm	52.48mm × 23.01mm	8746 × 3835 pixels

Table A.3 Required Scanning Pixels

Format	Width	Pixels	Scanning Resolution/Digital Acquisition	Final Image Size
Super 16mm	12.35mm	2058 pixels	3k	2k
Super 35mm	24.92mm	4153 pixels	6k	4k

Mattes

(From *3D Compositing* in Chapter 7.)

$$\text{Result} = Fg^*(A) + Bg^*(1 - A)$$

where *Fg* is the foreground, *Bg* is the background, and *A* is the alpha, or matte.

Premultiplied

$$\text{Result} = Fg + Bg^*(1 - A)$$

This operation is often referred to as an *over*.

Camera and Lens Formulas

(From *American Cinematographer Manual*.[1])

For these variables:

O = object size
D = distance from object to camera lens
F = focal length
A = aperture size

$$\frac{O}{A} = \frac{D}{F}$$

$$\text{Distance} = \frac{\text{object size} \times \text{focal length}}{\text{aperture size}}$$

$$\text{Object size} = \frac{\text{distance} \times \text{aperture size}}{\text{focal length}}$$

$$\text{Focal length} = \frac{\text{distance} \times \text{aperture size}}{\text{object size}}$$

$$\text{Aperture size} = \frac{\text{focal length} \times \text{object size}}{\text{distance}}$$

35mm film full frame sound aperture: 0.866 inch × 0.630 inch
35mm film full frame aperture: 0.980 inch × 0.735 inch
(See the *American Cinematographer Manual* for other film formats.)

---

[1] Reproduced by permission of the American Society of Cinematographers.

Lens Angle

$$\text{Tangent } \tfrac{1}{2} \text{ viewing angle} = \frac{\tfrac{1}{2}A}{F}$$

where
A = aperture size (width or height)
F = focal length in same units.

For anamorphic:

$$\text{Tangent } \tfrac{1}{2} \text{ viewing angle} = \frac{\tfrac{1}{2}A \times \text{squeeze ratio}}{F}$$

Depth of Field

$$D_N: \text{camera to near limit} = \frac{H \times S}{H + (S - F)}$$

$$D_F: \text{camera to far limit} = \frac{H \times S}{H - (S - F)}$$

where
H = hyperfocal distance
F = focal length of lens
S = distance from camera to object,

$$\text{Total depth} = D_F - D_N$$

Hyperfocal Distance

$$H = \frac{F^2}{f \times Cc}$$

where
H = hyperfocal distance
F = focal length of lens
f = f-stop
Cc = circle of confusion, where 35mm camera Cc = 0.002 inch (0.0508mm).

Right Triangles

Right triangles are useful for calculating sizes and distances and for laying out 2D objects.

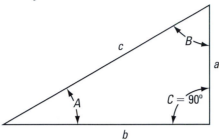

Known sides and angles	Unknown sides and angles			Area
a and b	$c = \sqrt{a^2 + b^2}$	$A = \arctan\dfrac{a}{b}$	$B = \arctan\dfrac{b}{a}$	$\dfrac{a \times b}{2}$
a and c	$b = \sqrt{c^2 - a^2}$	$A = \arcsin\dfrac{a}{c}$	$B = \arccos\dfrac{a}{c}$	$\dfrac{a \times \sqrt{c^2 - a^2}}{2}$
b and c	$a = \sqrt{c^2 - b^2}$	$A = \arccos\dfrac{b}{c}$	$B = \arcsin\dfrac{b}{c}$	$\dfrac{b \times \sqrt{c^2 - b^2}}{2}$
a and $\angle A$	$b = \dfrac{a}{\tan A}$	$c = \dfrac{a}{\sin A}$	$B = 90° - A$	$\dfrac{a^2}{2 \times \tan A}$
a and $\angle B$	$b = a \times \tan B$	$c = \dfrac{a}{\cos B}$	$A = 90° - B$	$\dfrac{a^2 \times \tan B}{2}$
b and $\angle A$	$a = b \times \tan A$	$c = \dfrac{b}{\cos A}$	$B = 90° - A$	$\dfrac{b^2 \times \tan A}{2}$
b and $\angle B$	$a = \dfrac{b}{\tan B}$	$c = \dfrac{b}{\sin B}$	$A = 90° - B$	$\dfrac{b^2}{2 \times \tan B}$
c and $\angle A$	$a = c \times \sin A$	$b = c \times \cos A$	$B = 90° - A$	$\dfrac{c^2 \sin A \cos A}{2}$
c and $\angle B$	$a = c \times \cos B$	$b = c \times \sin B$	$A = 90° - B$	$\dfrac{c^2 \cos B \sin B}{2}$

Figure A.1 Right triangle formulas. (© Carr Lane Manufacturing Co. All rights reserved. Compliments of Carr Lane Mfg. Co., www.carrLane.com)

Compositing Blends Modes

(Based on http://dunnbypaul.net/blends. Used with permission from Paul Dunn.)

These are approximate formulas. Pixel values are considered to be 0–1 and results are scaled to this range. Use 255 for 8-bit and 65535 for 16-bit.

The values p1 and p2 represent two corresponding pixels, and *pixel* represents the final. Values are computed on red, green, and blue channels separately.

Multiply: pixel = p1 * p2

Screen: pixel = 1 − (1 − p1) * (1 − p2)

Darker: if (p1 < p2) pixel = p1
        if (p2 < p1) pixel = p2

Lighter: if (p1 > p2) pixel = p1
        if (p2 > p1) pixel = p2

Difference: pixel = |p1 − p2|

Negation: pixel = 1 − |1 − p1 − p2|

Exclusion: pixel = ½ − 2 × (p1 − ½) × (p2 − ½)

Color Burn: pixel = 1 − (1 − p1)/p2

Linear Burn: pixel = p1 + p2 − 1

Color Dodge: pixel = p1/(1 − p2)

Linear Dodge: pixel = p1 + p2

Overlay: if (p1 > ½) pixel = 1 − (1 − 2 × (p1 − ½)) × (1 − p2)
        if (p1 <= ½) pixel = (2 × p1) × p2

Soft Light: if (p2 > ½) pixel = 1 − (1 − p1) × (1 − (p2 − ½))
        if (p2 <= ½) pixel = p1 × (p2 + ½)

Hard Light: if (p2 > ½) pixel = 1 − (1 − p1) × (1 − 2 × (p2 − ½))
        if (p2 <= ½) pixel = p1 × (2 × p2)

Vivid Light: if (p2 > ½) pixel = 1 − (1 − p1)/(2 × (p2 − ½))
        if (p2 <= ½) pixel = p1/(1 − 2 × p2)

Linear Light: if (p2 > ½) pixel = p1 + 2 × (p2 − ½)
        if (p2 <= ½) pixel = p1 + 2 × p2 − 1

Pin Light: if (p2 > ½) pixel = max (p1, 2 × (p2 − ½))
        if (p2 <= ½) pixel = min (p1, 2 × p2))

CREDITS/TITLES TO BE SUBMITTED IN ACCORDANCE WITH VES GUIDELINES

Production

Senior Visual Effects Supervisor	Visual Effects Production Assistant
Visual Effects Supervisor	Visual Effects Accountant
Senior Animation Supervisor	Visual Effects Plate Supervisor
Additional Visual Effects Supervisor	Visual Effects Plate Producer
Visual Effects Co-Supervisor	Visual Effects Editor
Visual Effects Associate Supervisor	Visual Effects Assistant Editor
Animation Director	Visual Effects Previs Lead
Animation Supervisor	Visual Effects Previs Artist
Senior Visual Effects Producer	Visual Effects Previs Editor
Visual Effects Producer	Visual Effects Previs Sound Editor
Visual Effects Associate Producer	Visual Effects Data Coordinator
Visual Effects Production Supervisor	Visual Effects Data Assistant
Visual Effects Coordinator	Visual Effects Vendor Coordinator
Visual Effects Assistant Coordinator	Visual Effects Consultant
Visual Effects Production Associate	

Facility

	[Production]
Senior Visual Effects Supervisor	CG Supervisor
Visual Effects Supervisor	Compositing Supervisor
Additional Visual Effects Supervisor	Senior Visual Effects Art Director
Co-Visual Effects Supervisor	Visual Effects Art Director
Visual Effects Associate Supervisor	Concept Artist
Visual Effects Plate Supervisor	Storyboard Artist
Visual Effects Consultant	Visual Effects Editor
Senior Animation Supervisor	Assistant Visual Effects Editor
Animation Supervisor	Projectionist
Senior Visual Effects Producer	Color Grading Artist
Visual Effects Producer	Color Grading Supervisor
Visual Effects Executive Producer	Previs Supervisor

The VES Handbook of Visual Effects. DOI: 10.1016/B978-0-240-81242-7.00012-0

Visual Effects Associate Producer	Previs Artist
Visual Effects Coordinator	I/O Supervisor
Production Associate	I/O Operator
Production Supervisor	I/O Neg Cutter
Visual Effects Production Manager	I/O Coordinator
Visual Effects Plate Producer	Scan/Record Technician
Visual Effects Plate Coordinator	Still Photographer
3D Stereoscopic Supervisor	

Facility	[Digital Unit]
CG Sequence Supervisor	Lead Texture Artist
Digital Production Supervisor	Senior Texture Artist
Animation Supervisor	Junior Texture Artist
Animation Producer	Motion Capture Supervisor
Animation Production Manager	Motion Capture Producer
Animation Coordinator	Motion Capture Engineer
Technical Animation Supervisor	Motion Capture Technician
Technical Animation Lead	Dustbuster
Digital Effects Producer	Lead TD
Digital Effects Production Manager	TD
Digital Effects Coordinator	Assistant TD
Character Setup Supervisor	Lighting Supervisor
Character Setup Lead	Lighting Lead
Character Rigging Supervisor	Lighting Artist
Character Rigging Artist	FX Animator
Rigging Supervisor	Character Animation Lead
Rigging Artist	Character Animator
Look Development Supervisor	Animation Lead
Look Development Lead	Animator
Compositing Sequence Supervisor	Layout Supervisor
Compositing Lead	Layout Artist
Compositor	Modeling Supervisor
Matte Supervisor	Modeling Lead
Matte Painter	Modeler
Matte Artist	Simulation Supervisor
Matte Painting Supervisor	Simulation Lead
Lead Digital Matte Painter	Simulation Artist
Senior Digital Matte Painter	Matchmove Supervisor
Digital Matte Painter	Matchmove Lead
R&D Supervisor	Matchmove Artist
R&D Artist	Rotoscope Supervisor
Senior Technical Developer	Rotoscope Lead
Software Development Supervisor	Rotoscope Artist
Software Developer	Digital Artist
Systems Manager	CG Artist

Systems Coordinator
Systems Engineer
Integrators
Pipeline Supervisor
Pipeline Engineer
Shading Supervisor
Shading Artist
Texture Paint Supervisor
Texture Lead
Texture Painter
Texture Paint Artist

Paint Supervisor
Paint Lead
Paint Artist
Digital Paint Lead
Plate Restoration Supervisor
Plate Restoration Lead
Plate Restoration Artist
Technical Associate
Technical Assistant
Render Coordinator

Motion/Performance Capture Unit

Motion Capture Line Producer
Motion Capture Supervisor
Motion Capture Producer
Motion Capture Systems Technician
Motion Capture Systems Engineer
Motion Capture Systems Operator
Motion Capture Real Time Operator

Motion Capture Camera Operator
Motion Capture Pipeline TD
Motion Capture Pipeline Engineer
Motion Capture Stage Manager
Motion Capture Coordinator
Motion Capture Assistant
Motion Capture Production Assistant

VFX Physical Production Unit

Visual Effects Director of Photography
Visual Effects Photographer
Visual Effects Camera Operator
Visual Effects 1st Assistant Camera
Visual Effects Survey Supervisor
Visual Effects Surveyor

Visual Effects Data Capture
Visual Effects 2nd Assistant Camera
Visual Effects Camera Loader
Digital Camera Engineer
Digital Camera Assistant

Special Effects Unit

Senior Special Effects Supervisor
Special Effects Supervisor
Senior Special Effects Coordinator
Special Effects Coordinator
Special Effects Technician
Pyrotechnic Supervisor
Pyrotechnic Technician
Head Special Effects Electronic Engineer
Special Effects Electronic Engineer

Special Effects Best Boy
Senior Special Effects Stage Technician
Special Effects Stage Technician
Senior Special Effects Rigger
Special Effects Rigger
Senior Special Effects Workshop Technician
Special Effects Workshop Technician
Head Special Effects Maintenance Engineer
Special Effects Maintenance Engineer

Special Effects Unit

Special Effects Electronic Technician
Head Special Effects Stage Technician

Head Special Effects Machinist
Special Effects Machinist

Motion Control Unit

Motion Control Supervisor
Motion Control Producer
Motion Control Cameraman
Motion Control Operator

Motion Control Camera Assistant
Motion Control Previs
Motion Control Technician
Motion Control Crane Operator

Models/Miniatures Unit

Models/Miniatures Director of Photography
Models/Miniatures Producer
Models/Miniatures Gaffer
Models/Miniatures Coordinator
Models/Miniatures Sr. Camera Operator
Models/Miniatures Camera Operator
Models/Miniatures 1st Assistant Camera
Models/Miniatures 2nd Assistant Camera
Models/Miniatures Camera Loader
Models/Miniatures Technical Apprentice
Digital Camera Engineer
Digital Camera Assistant
Models/Miniatures Stagehand
Models/Miniatures Production Manager
Modelshop Supervisor
Models/Miniatures Effects Supervisor

Models/Miniatures Supervisor
Senior Modelmaker
Chief Modelmaker
Modelmaker
Models/Miniatures Sculptor
Senior Plasterer
Senior Painter
Graphic Artist
Creature Supervisor
Senior Creature Tech
Creature Tech
Supervising Mechanical Engineer
Mechanical Engineer
Chief Scenic Artist
Scenic Artist
Assistant Scenic Artist

Stop Motion Unit

Head Stop Motion Animator
Stop Motion Animator
Stop Motion Assistant Animator
Stop Motion Puppet Coordinator
Stop Motion Puppet Wrangler
Stop Motion Junior Puppet Wrangler
Stop Motion Lead Armature Engineer
Stop Motion Armature Engineer
Stop Motion Character Fabricator

Stop Motion Lead Sculptor
Stop Motion Sculptor
Stop Motion Lead Model Rigger
Stop Motion Model Rigger
Stop Motion Lead Mold/Mould Maker
Stop Motion Mold/Mould Maker
Stop Motion Camera Manager
Stop Motion Camera Operator
Stop Motion Assistant Camera

Animatronics Unit

Animatronics Supervisor
Animatronics Coordinator
Animatronics Designer
Animatronics Mechanical Supervisor
Animatronics Technician
Animatronics Control Systems Designer

Animatronics Foam Latex Technician
Animatronics Mold/Mould Makers
Animatronics Sculptor
Animatronics Seamstress
Animatronics Hair/Fur Technician

Questions regarding these guidelines can be addressed by calling the VES at 818-981-7861.

GLOSSARY

This glossary is intended to be a practical guide to words commonly used in the visual effects field. It includes not only well-defined technical terms but also a number of colloquialisms that are often used within the industry. The visual effects industry is still a fairly new, volatile field. As such, any attempt to define the terminology that is in use within this discipline risks rapid obsolescence. What's more, many terms used in the visual effects world can be rather ambiguous, or at least very context dependent. This is due in no small part to the fact that visual effects is a mesh of so many different disciplines. Terms from the fields of traditional animation, computer animation, image processing, photography, computer science (both hardware and software), art, special effects, visual effects, electronics, optics, physics, film, television, video games, and multimedia have all become part of the visual effects lexicon. We have attempted to give some idea of how multiple-definition terms might be interpreted depending on the situation in which they are used.

You will find that many entries will need to resort to the use of other visual effects terms in their definitions. In most cases, if there is a word within a given definition that is also defined elsewhere in this glossary, that word is printed in bold. The exceptions to this rule are those words (such as *digital* or *color*) that are used so often that it would be cumbersome to note their every occurrence.

The majority of this Glossary was provided by Ron Brinkman.

Words from the Stereoscopic Glossary (provided by Lenny Lipton) have been added with a designation of "(stereo)" at the beginning of the entry.

A

Academy aperture: A specific 35mm film framing.

Academy leader: The standardized length of film attached by the lab at the head and tail of **release prints** that meets the standards specified by the **Academy of Motion Picture Arts and**

The VES Handbook of Visual Effects. DOI: 10.1016/B978-0-240-81242-7.00013-2

Sciences (**AMPAS**). The leader contains a countdown running from 8 to a single frame of 2, which is accompanied by a pop on the soundtrack.

Academy of Motion Picture Arts and Sciences (AMPAS): The professional organization that includes branches for almost every area of filmmaking and encourages continued artistic and technical research and development in the industry.

accommodation: The focusing of the eyes—or more properly, the ability of the eyes' lenses to change shape in order to focus.

accommodation/vergence relationship: The learned relationship established through early experience between the focusing of the eyes and verging of the eyes when looking at a particular object point in the visual world. This is also commonly called the *accommodation/convergence relationship* (or the *convergence/accommodation relationship*).

ACM: Abbreviation for **Association for Computing Machinery.**

ACM SIGGRAPH: See **SIGGRAPH.**

acquisition format: A term used to describe the film format used to **capture** images. For example, **Cinemascope** and **Super 35** are often used to capture images when the desired delivery format is **2.35:1** (often referred to as **2.35 format**).

active region: The portion of a video signal that is used for actual image information, as opposed to blanking, closed captioning, time code, etc.

AD: Assistant Director.

ADR: Abbreviation for *automated dialogue replacement*. A process in which a performer replaces his or her previously recorded dialogue by respeaking the lines in sync to picture or by recording new dialogue in sync to picture.

affine: Any linear **geometric transformation** including pan, rotate, scale, and shear.

AIFF: Abbreviation for *Audio Interchange File Format*. A standard **file format** for storing audio data.

AIM: Refers to a value measured in the Laboratory Aim Density (**LAD**) printing control method. By exposing a **LAD** patch, the value of the exposure of that piece of film can be determined. Kodak publishes suggested density tolerances for each type of film in the duplicating and print system.

algorithm: A procedure or set of instructions for solving a problem or accomplishing a particular goal.

aliasing: An artifact that is due to limited **resolution.**

alpha channel: The portion of a four-channel image that is used to store transparency information.

ambient light: For **computer graphics** (CG), a directionless light source that uniformly distributes light in all directions, illuminating objects equally regardless of their surface orientation. CG ambient lighting is used as an inexpensive way to simulate the indirect illumination that occurs in the real world when light bounces off of other objects in the environment.

ambient occlusion: A CG shading method that uses a type of **global illumination** to better compute self-shadowing of objects. Often used in compositing as part of a **multiple-pass rendering** workflow.

American Cinematographer Manual: A manual, published by the **American Society of Cinematographers,** that is considered to be the industry Bible for **cinematographers** and anyone else involved in the field.

American Society of Cinematographers (ASC): The nonprofit organization dedicated to the continued advancement of the art of cinematography through technical and artistic growth. See also **British Society of Cinematographers (BSC), Canadian Society of Cinematographers (CSC).**

anaglyph: A **stereoscopic image** that requires the use of **anaglyph glasses** to view properly.

anaglyph: (stereo) Wavelength selection using complementary colored images and color filters to filter or pass the appropriate perspective views to the appropriate eyes.

anaglyph glasses: A type of **3D glasses** that uses two different lens colors, usually red and blue, to control the images that are seen by each eye in a **stereoscopic image.** See also **flicker glasses, polarized glasses.**

analog: Information/data that is continuously variable, without discrete steps or quantization, as opposed to **digital.**

anamorphic: Any distorted image that can be undistorted to restore it to its original format.

anamorphic format: A film format characterized by the fact that the image captured on the negative is horizontally squeezed by the use of a special lens. It is later unsqueezed at projection time by the appropriate amount. For most 35mm feature-film work, the standard anamorphic format produces a 2.35:1 aspect ratio when projected. See **Cinemascope, Panavision.**

anamorphic lens: A lens that changes the width-to-height relationship of the original image. The most common anamorphic camera lenses in film work compress the horizontal axis by 50%. See **Cinemascope.**

animated: Having characteristics that change over time.

animatic: A rough animation that gives some idea about the timing of a sequence. Essentially a moving **storyboard.** See **previs.**

animation: Moving imagery that is created on a frame-by-frame basis. This may be accomplished via the use of computers or with more traditional **cel animation** techniques.

animation rig: CG structure built for the CG model and used by an animator as a type of skeleton to pose the animation model.

animator: A person responsible for producing **animations.**

anisotropic: Having properties (such as color or reflectivity) that differ based on the direction of measurement.

answer print: The first **print** from the lab containing synchronized image and sound and which has had all of the scenes color balanced.

antialiasing: Techniques used to mitigate the artifacts caused by a lack of sufficient **resolution.**

aperture: (1) In a lens, the size of the opening that light passes through (usually given in terms of its *f*-**stop** or *t*-**stop**). (2) In a camera body, the mask opening that defines the area of film that will be exposed on each frame. (3) In a projector, the mask opening that defines the area of the frame that will be projected.

API: Abbreviation for *application programming interface.* An interface implemented by a software program to enable interaction with other software, much in the same way that a user interface facilitates interaction between humans and computers. APIs are implemented by applications, libraries, and operating systems to determine the vocabulary and calling conventions the programmer should employ to use their services. It may include specifications for routines, data structures, object classes, and protocols used to communicate between the consumer and implementer of the API.

apparent motion: The natural ability of the eye to perceive motion in a series of images that are played back quickly enough. See also **persistence of vision.**

articulate matte: A **matte** whose shape changes over time and which is designed to accurately follow the contours of the object to which it corresponds.

artifact: A (usually undesirable) item in an image that is a side effect of the process used to generate or modify that image.

ASA rating: A standard numerical rating for specifying a film's sensitivity to light. ASA refers to the American Standards Association, now known as the American National Standards Institute, or ANSI. Many manufacturers now use their own specific **exposure index** instead. See also **DIN rating, ISO index.**

ASC Manual: See *American Cinematographer Manual.*

ASCII file: See **ASCII.**

ASCII: Abbreviation for *American Standard for Computer Information Interchange.* Pure and simple text file based on an American standard. A very common alphanumeric text interchange format. The term is used colloquially to refer to data that is stored in a text format that does not require a special program to decode and is usually somewhat comprehensible to a human reader.

aspect ratio: A single number that is the result of dividing the width of an image by its height. The units used to measure the width and height are irrelevant, since they will cancel when divided together to give a unitless result. See also **pixel aspect ratio.**

Association for Computing Machinery: An organization, founded in 1947, that is the world's first educational and scientific computing society. **SIGGRAPH** is one of the many special interest groups within the ACM.

atmosphere: A **depth cue** that causes objects to decrease in contrast as they move into the distance.

autostereoscopic: (stereo) Sometimes called *auto-stereo*, which can be confused with a car sound system.

B

background: In a composite, the bottom element over which all others are added. In general, the background makes up the majority of the image.

backing color: The color of the uniform background that is used when shooting an element for **traveling matte** extraction.

BAFTA: Abbreviation for the *British Academy of Film and Television Arts.*

Bake in: Term used to mean that whatever settings, composite layers, color, animation, and so on that have been used, have been permanently set in the shot. For example, "Do not bake in any bad animation or you will never be able to change it."

Baked out: To output in a format that is fixed. In this case the model is no longer able to be animated but exists essentially as a 3D model for each frame.

banding: An artifact that appears in areas of a color gradient where the lack of sufficient color resolution causes noticeable bands instead of a smooth transition. Also known as **contouring**. See also **Mach banding.**

barrel distortion: Distortion of a lens that causes straight lines to bend away from the center of the image.

base: The transparent material (usually cellulose acetate) on which emulsions are applied to make photographic film. Note that a base is generally not completely transparent, but rather has a slight characteristic color that may need to be compensated for when scanning.

batch compositing: A method of compositing that entails the creation of a script or set of instructions that will be executed at a later time, without the need for a **graphical user interface.**

beamsplitter: (stereo) Technically this is a couple of prisms cemented together with a semi-silvered layer to split a light beam into two halves. For the rig used for stereo-cinematography, a thin sheet of glass that is semi-silvered is used in the optical path. Such a device is more properly called a *pellicule* (or *pellicle*).

beauty pass: (1) In **multiple-pass photography,** the pass of the object that contains the most color and detail, as compared with the **matte pass, reflection pass,** or **shadow pass.** Also called the **color pass.** (2) In **multiple-pass rendering,** the **CG element** that contains the most color and detail information. See also **light pass, matte pass, shadow pass,** and **reflection pass.**

Bézier curve: a curved line or path defined by mathematical equations. It was named after Pierre Bézier, a French mathematician and engineer who developed this method of computer drawing in the late 1960s while working for the car manufacturer Renault. The most basic Bézier curve is made up of two end points and control handles attached to each node. The control handles define the shape of the curve on either side of the common node.

BG: Abbreviation for *background.*

bicubic interpolation: A method of **interpolation** based on an average of the 16 nearest neighbors. See also **linear interpolation, bilinear interpolation.**

bilinear interpolation: A method of **interpolation** based on an average of the four nearest neighbors. See also **linear interpolation, bicubic interpolation.**

binocular: (stereo) Two eyes. The term *binocular stereopsis* (two-eyed solid seeing) is used in some psychology books for the depth sense more simply described as stereopsis.

bipack: The process of loading two pieces of film in such a way that they travel through the same movement of the camera at the same time. Sometimes referred to as *sandwiching.*

bit: The basic unit for representing data in a digital environment. A bit can have only one of two values: 0 or 1.

bit depth: A way of specifying the **color resolution** in an image by measuring the number of bits devoted to each **component** of the pixels in the image.

bitmapped image: An image that consists of a rectangular, two-dimensional array of **pixels.** The standard method for representing an image in a digital format.

black point: (1) On a piece of film, the measured density in the area of greatest opacity. (2) In a digital image, the numerical value that corresponds to the darkest area that will be represented when the image is eventually viewed in its final form.

bleach bypass: A general term used to describe a number of film processing techniques offered by various labs, in which the bleaching function done during normal processing is partially or completely skipped as a means of increasing **contrast** and reducing **saturation.** Also called **ENR.**

blue record: The layer of the film that captures blue light.

blue screen: (1) Commonly used as a generic term that refers to **bluescreen photography** or any similar process, which may use other colors as well as blue. (2) Literally, a screen of some sort of blue material that is suspended behind an object for which a **matte** is to be extracted. Ideally, the blue screen appears to the camera as a completely uniform blue field. (Note that in this handbook the standard is to use *blue screen* to designate the screen itself and the term *bluescreen* to designate the process.)

blue spill: Any contamination of the foreground subject by light reflected from the **blue screen** in front of which it is placed. See also **spill, green spill.**

bluescreen photography: The process of photographing an object in front of a blue screen with the intention of extracting a **matte** for that object using various keying and/or color-difference techniques.

bokeh: A photographic term referring to the appearance of point-of-light sources in an out-of-focus area of an image produced by a camera lens using a shallow depth of field.

bounce light: Light that is reflected or bounced off of other objects in a scene before it reaches the subject.

box filter: A specific digital **filter** that is often used when **resampling** a digital image. The box filter is fast but fairly low quality.

British Academy of Film and Television Arts (BAFTA): The British version of the **American Academy of Motion Picture Arts and Sciences (AMPAS).**

British Society of Cinematographers (BSC): The British version of the **American Society of Cinematographers (ASC).** See also **Canadian Society of Cinematographers (CSC).**

B-spline: Simply a generalization of a **Bézier curve.**

burn-in: Photographic double exposure of an element over a previously exposed piece of film.

C

camera aperture: The opening in a camera lens. It is usually referred to in f-stops or t-stops. It allows a specific amount of light to hit the film or sensor, thus resulting in an image.

camera frustum: Basically, what the camera sees. See also **frustum** and **viewing frustum.**

camera mapping: A CG technique in which an image is projected from the **camera** onto a **3D object**. This technique is useful for re-creating a simulation of a 3D environment using 2D photographic elements. Also called *projection mapping.*

Canadian Society of Cinematographers (CSC): The British version of the **American Society of Cinematographers (ASC)**. See also **British Society of Cinematographers (BSC).**

cardboard effect: (stereo) An effect in which a viewer perceives the objects and characters in a 3D composition to be flat (as if on cardboard cutouts). This effect is often the result of using a lens with a long focal length.

CBB: Abbreviation for *could be better*. When a shot has a few minor technical or aesthetic adjustments to be made, but the delivery date is close at hand, this term is used to **final** a shot with the caveat that it will be improved at a later date if time and budget permit.

CC: Abbreviation for *color correction.*

CCD: Abbreviation for *charge-coupled device*, a light-sensitive semiconductor that is often used in scanners and video cameras to capture an image.

cel animation: Animation that is the result of sequences of images drawn on individual clear acetate cels. Many aspects of traditional cel animation are now being supplemented by digital techniques.

center extraction: A term used to describe any process, such as masking or cropping, that is used to extract the centered portion of the original image to produce the final viewing format.

centroid: The geometric center of an object.

CG: Abbreviation for *computer graphics.*

CG feature: Any feature film created entirely with **computer-generated imagery.**

CG Supervisor: Abbreviation for *Computer Graphics Supervisor.* (See the list of VES-approved titles in Appendix B.)

CGI: See **computer-generated imagery.**

channel: For a given image, the subimage that is composed only of the values from a single **component** of each pixel.

characteristic curve: A curve that plots the relationship between light falling on a piece of film and the resulting density of the developed image.

chroma-keying: A **keying** technique that allows one to separate an object from its background based on colors that are unique to either the foreground or background.

chromatic aberration: An image **artifact** that is caused by the fact that different wavelengths of light are bent by slightly different amounts as they pass through a lens. The artifact is usually seen as a color shift along sharply delineated edges in an image.

chromatic resolution: Another term for **color resolution.**

chrominance: The color portion of a video signal, carrying the **hue** and **saturation** values. See also **luminance.**

Cinemascope: An **anamorphic** film format that produces an image with an aspect ratio of 2.35:1. Although Cinemascope (or CinemaScope) was originally a specific process developed by Twentieth Century Fox in the 1950s, it has become a generic term for the 2.35 anamorphic format. The most common lenses used for this purpose today are produced by **Panavision.**

cinematographer: An individual who is experienced in the art of capturing images on camera. The main cinematographer for a film is the **Director of Photography.**

Cineon: A specific image file format used most often in film compositing work.

circle of confusion: The size of the circle to which an idealized point will diverge when the lens is focused at different depths. Used as a way to measure the focus of a lens.

circular polarization: (stereo) A form of polarized light in which the tip of the electric vector of the light ray moves through a corkscrew in space.

clean plate: A **plate** that differs from the primary plate only in that it does not contain the subject(s) in the frame.

clip: A small piece of film, often clipped from a longer shot, that can be used as a reference for color, lighting, etc.

clipping: The process (intentional or otherwise) whereby data above or below a certain threshold is removed or lost. With digital images, this usually translates to colors outside a specific range.

clone: In **digital paint,** a method of copying information from one region of an image to another.

cloud tank: A large water-filled glass enclosure that is used to create clouds and other atmospheric effects. The clouds are usually produced by injecting some opaque liquid (such as white paint) into the water.

CLUT: Abbreviation for *color lookup table.*

CMY: Abbreviation for *cyan, magenta, and yellow,* the three complementary colors, or a method of specifying the colors in an image based on a mix of these three components.

codec: A specific type of compression used on images.

color bars: Standard test patterns used in video to determine the quality of a video signal. Color bars consist of equal-width bars representing black, white, red, green, blue, yellow, cyan, and magenta. These colors are generally represented at 75% of their pure value.

color contamination: A term used to describe a **backing color,** such as **blue screen** or **green screen,** that is contaminated with one of the other primary colors. Color contamination can make the job of **matte extraction** much more difficult.

color correction: Any process that alters the perceived color balance of an image.

color difference method: A compositing technique that utilizes the difference in color between the different channels of an image in order to extract a **matte.** The technique relies on the subject being photographed in front of a uniformly colored background, such as a **blue screen.**

color lookup table: A **lookup table** that is specifically designed to modify color.

color management: A global term used to describe the process of producing consistent color across a range of software and devices.

color resolution: The amount of data allocated for specifying the value of an individual color in an image. See also **bit depth.**

color script: (stereo) Colors used for scene-to-scene and character design to match image depth requirements per script.

color space: Any method for representing the color in an image. Usually based on certain components such as RGB, HSV, etc.

color temperature: A method of specifying color based on an absolute temperature scale, degrees Kelvin (K). The color is equivalent to the color of light that would be emitted if a pure black object were heated to that temperature. Higher color temperatures are more blue; lower temperatures are more red.

color timer or grader: A person who adjusts the scene-to-scene color **continuity** when preparing the final print of a film.

color timing or grading: The color balance of a particular image or scene, or the process of color correcting and balancing that image or scene.

color wedge: A series of images that feature incremental alterations in the color of a certain element (or sometimes the entire frame) for the purpose of choosing a final value for the color of that element.

complementary color: The color that results when the primary color is subtracted from white.

complementary matte: The matte that results when the primary matte is inverted.

component: One of the elements that is used to define the color of a pixel. In most digital images, the pixel color is specified in terms of its red, green, and blue components.

component video: Video signal in which various aspects of color such as luminance and chrominance are maintained separately.

composite video: Video signal in which the color elements are all combined (encoded) into a single signal.

compositing: The manipulated combination of at least two source images to produce an integrated result.

compositing engine: Within a package used for compositing, the code that is responsible for the actual image-processing operations, in contrast to other code that may deal with the user interface, file input/output, etc.

Compositing Supervisor: The individual responsible for the aesthetic and technical supervision of all digital composites created for a project. The Compositing Supervisor leads a team of **compositors**. (See the list of VES-approved titles in Appendix B.)

compositor: A person who creates composites. (See the list of VES-approved titles in Appendix B.)

compression ratio: The ratio of the data sizes between an uncompressed element and its compressed equivalent.

computer-generated imagery (CGI): An image or images created or manipulated with the aid of a computer. Often used to refer specifically to 3D computer animation, although it is really a much broader term.

computer graphics: An image or images created or manipulated with the aid of a computer.

Computer Graphics Supervisor: The person responsible for determining the aesthetic and technical solutions, software selections, and overall **pipeline** for the **3D** work on a project. (See the list of VES-approved titles in Appendix B.)

conform: The process of matching raw, original footage with some edited version of that footage.

conjugate points: (stereo) See **corresponding points.**

contact shadow: A shadow that is cast from one object when it is in direct contact with another object, as opposed to a shadow that is cast on a distant surface.

continuity: The smooth flow of action or events from one shot or scene to the next, without any indication that the different shots/scenes may have been photographed at different times or processed differently.

contouring: An **artifact** that results from not having enough **color resolution** to properly represent a color gradient. See also **Mach banding.**

contrast: The ratio of the brightest tones in an image to the darkest.

control points: The specific points that are interpreted to define the shape of a curve.

convergence: (stereo) The inward rotation of the eyes, in the horizontal direction, producing fusion. The more general term is *vergence*, which includes inward and outward rotation. The term has also been used, confusingly, to describe the movement of left and right image fields or the rotation (toe-in) of camera heads.

conversion: (stereo) Also known as *synthesis*. A process by which a planar image is turned into a stereoscopic image—a flat image into a 3D image.

convolution filter: A matrix of numbers used to control the weighted averaging performed in a **convolve** operation. Sometimes also referred to as a *convolution mask*.

convolution kernel: The group of pixels that will be considered when performing a **convolve** operation. Generally the size of the kernel is the only worry, which is usually a square matrix with an odd number of elements in each dimension. The most common kernel size is 3×3. Occasionally the term is used as a synonym for the **convolution filter.**

convolution mask: See **convolution filter.**

convolve: An image processing operation that involves the specialized averaging of a neighborhood of pixels using a **convolution filter.** Also known as *spatial convolution.*

cool: A nonexact term that is used to describe an image that is biased toward the blue portion of the spectrum.

corresponding points: (stereo) The image points of the left and right fields referring to the same point on the object. The distance between the corresponding points on the projection screen is defined as parallax. Also known as *conjugate* or *homologous points.*

CPU: Abbreviation for *central processing unit,* the computational heart of a computer.

crawling: An undesirable **artifact** characterized by edges that do not remain stable over time.

creature shop: Any facility that creates prosthetics, animatronics, puppets, robotics, and creatures for use in a film.

cropping: The removal (intentionally or otherwise) of part of an image that is outside a specific boundary.

crosstalk: (stereo) Incomplete isolation of the left and right image channels so that one leaks (leakage) or bleeds into the other. Looks like a double exposure. Crosstalk is a physical entity and can be objectively measured, whereas ghosting is a subjective term.

C-scope: Abbreviation for *Cinemascope.*

C-stand: Common three-legged adjustable stand used by the grip department to hold things such as lighting flags.

cukaloris: Panel with irregular holes cut in it to project patterned shadows onto a subject. Also known as a *kukaloris, cuke,* or *cookie.*

cursor: A graphical marker, usually controlled by a device such as a mouse or a tablet pen, that is used to point to a position or object on a computer's display.

curve editor: Any **graphical user interface (GUI)** module that allows the user to create and modify curves.

D

D1 format: A digital **component video** format. D1 is considered to be a nearly lossless format, although it does use **4:2:2 compression.**

D2 format: A digital **composite video** format. D2 is a lower quality than **D1,** but is also significantly less expensive.

D5 format: A digital **component video** format. D5 is considered to be of the same quality as **D1** and also has provisions for storing **HDTV**-format imagery.

dailies: Imagery produced during the previous day's work or a meeting to view this work.

day for night: The process of shooting footage in daylight conditions with the intention of eventually presenting it as a nighttime scene. It may involve a combination of photographic, lighting, and digital post-processing techniques.

dB: Abbreviation for *decibel.*

DCI: Abbreviation for *Digital Cinematography Initiative for Digital Projection.*

decibel (dB): A unit of measurement that expresses a ratio using logarithmic scales to give results related to human perception.

decimation: The process of throwing away unnecessary information when reducing the size of an image.

deinterlace: The process of separating the two **fields** that make up a video image into two distinct images.

densitometer: Instrument used to measure the optical density of a piece of processed film.

density space: A **nonlinear color** representation that is based on the density of developed negative relative to the amount of light that reached it.

depth channel: Another term for the **Z-channel.**

depth cue: Information that helps to determine the distance of an object from the camera.

depth of field (DOF): The depth of field of a specific lens is the range of acceptable focus in front of and behind the primary focus setting. It is a function not only of the specific lens used but also of the distance from the lens to the primary focal plane and of the chosen aperture. Larger apertures will narrow the depth of field; smaller apertures will increase it.

depth of focus: A term that is often improperly used when one wishes to refer to the **depth of field.** Depth of focus is a specific term for the point *behind* the lens (inside the camera body) where a piece of film should be placed so that the image will be properly focused.

depth range: (stereo) A term that applies to stereoscopic images created with cameras. The limits are defined as the range of distances in camera space from the background point, producing maximum acceptable positive parallax, to the foreground point, producing maximum acceptable negative parallax. See also **parallax budget.**

desaturation: A term that describes the removal or loss of color in an image. A completely desaturated image would consist only of shades of gray.

detail generator: An adjustment available on some video cameras that introduces additional **sharpening** into the captured image.

DI: Abbreviation for **digital intermediate.**

difference matte: A **matte** created by subtracting an image in which the subject *is* present from an otherwise identical image in which it is *not* present.

diffusion: An effect, caused by **atmosphere** or special **filters** placed on the lens, that is characterized by a scattering of light, elevated dark areas, and an overall softer look.

digital: A method of representing data via discrete, well-defined samples, as opposed to **analog.**

digital artist: Any artist who creates and manipulates images digitally. The term encompasses both 2D and 3D artists and can be synonymous with the various titles used, such as CG Artist, Technical Director (TD), Compositor, Matte Painter, Character Animator, etc. (See the list of VES-approved titles in Appendix B.)

digital compositing: The digitally manipulated combination of at least two source images to produce an integrated result.

Digital Effects Supervisor: The individual responsible for the creation of all digital effects work required for a production. The DFX Supervisor oversees the work of the **CG Supervisor** and the **Compositing Supervisor** and reports directly to the **Visual Effects Supervisor**. (See the list of VES-approved titles in Appendix B.)

digital intermediate (DI): A high-quality digital version of a film that is used to finalize all color balancing issues.

digitization: The process of sampling any analog subject to produce a digital representation. Within the field of digital compositing, usually refers to the process of converting a video or film source to digital information.

dilation: An image-processing technique that results in brighter areas of the image increasing in size and darker areas decreasing. See also **erosion.**

DIN rating: A standard numerical rating for specifying a film's sensitivity to light. DIN is an abbreviation for *Deutsche Industrie Norm* (German Industry Standard). Many manufacturers now use their own specific **exposure index** instead. See also **ASA rating, ISO index.**

diopter: An auxiliary lens that goes in front of the camera lens to allow for close-up photography.

Dirac filter: Another name for an **impulse filter.**

director: The person with the primary responsibility for overseeing the creative aspects of a project or production.

disparity: (stereo) The distance between conjugate points on overlaid retinae, sometimes called *retinal disparity*. The corresponding term for the display screen is *parallax*.

dissolve: A specific **transition effect** in which one scene gradually fades out at the same time that a second scene fades in. Halfway through a linear dissolve the image will be a 50% mix of both scenes.

dither: A method for representing more colors than would normally be available with a given **palette.** Dithering uses combinations of colored pixels and relies on the fact that the human eye will average them together and interpret the result as a new intermediate color.

D-max: See **maximum density.**

D-min: See **minimum density.**

DOD: Abbreviation for *domain of definition.*

DOF: Abbreviation for *depth of field.*

domain of definition (DOD): A (usually rectangular) region that defines the maximum boundaries of useful information in an image. Generally, everything outside of the DOD will have a value of 0 in all channels of the image. The DOD is usually determined automatically, as opposed to a **region of interest.**

dots per inch (DPI): A common method for measuring spatial resolution in the print industry. The horizontal and vertical scales are assumed to be equal, unless specified otherwise.

double exposure (DX): In the optical world, a double exposure is accomplished by exposing two different images onto a single negative. The result is a mixture of the two images. In the digital world, this effect is accomplished by mathematically averaging the two images.

double framing: The process of duplicating and repeating every frame in an image sequence. The result is a new image sequence that appears to be moving at half the original speed. Also known as *double printing.*

DoP, DP: **Director of Photography.** Also see **cinematographer.**

DPI: Abbreviation for **dots per inch.**

DPX: Abbreviation for *Digital Picture Exchange,* a specific image file format.

drop frame: Video footage in which two frames are dropped every minute except the tenth. It is used to compensate for the fact that time code works at exactly 30 frames per second, but NTSC video runs at only 29.97 **fps.**

dubbing: The process of making a copy of a videotape.

dust busting: The term used to describe the process of removing dirt and scratches from scanned imagery.

DVE: Abbreviation for *digital video effect* that usually refers to any of a number of **geometric transformations** that are typically performed by specialized real-time video equipment. Examples of a DVE move include animated pans, rotations, or flips, as well as various hardware-specific effects such as page turns or customized wipes.

DX: Abbreviation for *double exposure.*

dynamic range: (1) The range of brightness values in a scene or an image, from brightest to darkest, often expressed as a ratio. (2) In a digital image, the total number of different colors in the image.

dynamic resolution: Another term for **color resolution.**

E

ECU: Abbreviation for *extreme close-up.*

edge detection algorithm: An algorithm used to enhance or isolate transition areas, or *edges,* in an image.

edge matte: A specialized **matte** that includes only the outlines or borders of an object.

edge numbers: Sequential numbers printed along the edge of a piece of film (outside of the **perforations**) by the manufacturer to help identify particular frames.

edge quality: A term used to describe the characteristics of the edges of an **element** that has been matted into a scene.

editing: The process of assembling shots and scenes into a final product, making decisions about their length and ordering.

EDL: Abbreviation for *edit decision list,* which is a text file that lists the order and length of each shot in a sequence or movie.

E-fan: Special effects fan commonly used to generate and control a specific volume of air.

effects animation: A term that usually refers to elements that were created via **cel animation** or digital rotoscoping techniques but are not character related. Common examples include sparks, lightning, or smoke.

effects filter: Any of a number of different optical **filters** that can introduce **diffusion, flares,** glows, etc., in front of the camera. Very problematic when shooting **bluescreen** elements.

EI: Abbreviation for **exposure index.**

8-bit image: In the **visual effects** world, this term typically refers to any image containing 8 bits of color information per **channel.**

8mm film: A narrow-gauge film that contains 74 frames per foot.

eight-perf: A nickname for the **VistaVision** film format that comes from the fact that each VistaVision frame has eight **perforations** along each edge.

element: A discrete image or sequence of images that will be added to a composite.

emulsion: The light-sensitive material that is applied to a transparent **base** to create photographic film.

encoder: (1) A piece of video equipment that combines a **component video** signal into a **composite video** signal. (2) A generalized term used to refer to a number of different data capture devices, usually ones that convert measurements into digital data.

ENR: Named for its inventor, Ernesto Novelli Rimo, a former control department operator at Technicolor Rome who designed the technique for Vittorio Storaro, ASC, AIC to use on Warren Beatty's 1981 film *Reds*. ENR is a proprietary color-positive developing technique that utilizes an additional black-and-white developing bath inserted at an appropriate stage of a print's processing in order to retain silver. After the film has been bleached, but prior to the silver being fixed out of the film, this extra bath allows for a controlled amount of silver to be re-developed, adding density in the areas with the most exposure–primarily the blacks. See also **bleach bypass.**

erosion: An image-processing technique that results in darker areas of the image increasing in size and brighter areas decreasing. See also **dilation.**

E-split: See **exposure split.**

Estar film stock: A polyester film base that is much more rugged than an acetate film base. It is thinner and much stronger than acetate. It can damage the moving parts of a camera or projector if it jams, whereas acetate films will just tear. Its durability allows its use for compositing many takes of a scene or for longer wearing **release prints.**

exposure index (EI): A standardized, but manufacturer-specific, numerical rating system for specifying a film's sensitivity to light. Several industry-standard systems are in use, including the **ASA rating,** the **ISO index,** and the **DIN rating.** To make it even more interesting, many manufacturers will specify a rating for both daylight lighting and tungsten lighting.

exposure latitude: Amount of over- or underexposure a given type of film can tolerate and still produce acceptable results.

exposure sheets: Sheets that tell the Oxberry camera, or down-shooter, cameraman in what order to layer and shoot the animation cels and for how many frames per cel, per layer. They do essentially the same thing for the optical printer cameraman: Indicate order of layout, exposure, length, and filtration of the elements to be rephotographed. (In animation also called *x-sheets* or *dope sheets.*)

exposure split: A simple **split-screen** shot in which multiple exposures of a given scene are combined in order to bring areas of widely divergent brightness into the same shot. Also known as an *E-split.*

exposure wedge: A series of images that feature incremental alterations in the exposure (brightness) of a certain element (or sometimes the entire frame) for the purpose of choosing a final value for the exposure of that element.

EXR: See **OpenEXR**.

extrastereoscopic cues: (stereo) Those depth cues appreciated by a person using only one eye. Also called *monocular cues*. They include interposition, geometric perspective, motion parallax, aerial perspective, relative size, shading, and textural gradient.

eye line: Specific direction in which the actor looks. In visual effects, usually a point that is frequently off camera to represent another actor or object.

F

FACS: Abbreviation for *Facial Action Coding System*, a method by which all the possible actions of the human face can be encoded.

fade: Decreasing the brightness of an image over time, eventually resulting in a black image.

fast Fourier transform (FFT): An algorithm for converting an image so that it is represented in terms of the magnitude and phase of the various frequencies that make up the image. Yes, there *is* a regular Fourier transform, but nobody uses it because it's not … fast.

FFT: Abbreviation for *fast Fourier transform*.

FG: Abbreviation for **foreground**.

field: (1) An image composed of either the even or odd scan lines of a video image. Two fields played sequentially will make up a video frame. (2) A unit of measure on a **field chart**.

field chart: A method of dividing an image into a grid so that certain areas of the frame can be specified by grid coordinates.

field dominance: The order in which the fields in an interlaced image are displayed. Essentially, whether the even or the odd field is displayed first for any given frame.

field of view (FOV): The range of a scene that will be captured by a specific camera. FOV is usually measured as the number of horizontal degrees (out of 360), although a vertical field of view is also a valid measurement.

field-sequential: (stereo) In the context of cinema stereoscopy, the rapid alternation of left and right perspective views projected on the screen.

file format: A standardized description of how a piece of data (such as an image) is to be stored.

film gauge: The width of a particular film stock, that is, 16mm, 35mm, etc.

film-out: Term meaning the actual recording of the digital image data onto motion picture film.

film recorder: A device that is capable of transferring digital images to a piece of film negative.

film recording: The process of transferring digital images to a piece of film negative via the use of a **film recorder**.

film speed: A very context-dependent term that may refer to (1) the rate at which film is moving through a camera or a projector (24 frames per second in normal feature-film work) or to (2) the light sensitivity of the film itself. Slow-speed film is less light sensitive; high-speed film is more sensitive.

film weave: Irregular horizontal movement (generally undesirable) of a piece of film as it moves through a camera or projector.

filter: (1) A translucent material that is placed in front of a light or camera to modify the color that is transmitted. Certain of these optical filters may also be designed to introduce specific artifacts, such as **diffusion, flares,** etc. (2) Any of a number of algorithms used within the computer for sampling an image. Different filters can be used when transforming an image and can result in differing amounts of sharpness or artifacts. (3) The process of using either of the aforementioned types of filters.

final: The term given to a composite shot once it is considered complete and has been approved by the appropriate decision makers.

fix it in post: A phrase commonly used when time and/or conditions prohibit the ability to shoot a scene exactly as intended. Rather than delaying the production, a decision is made to shoot as quickly as possible and correct any problems during **post-production,** usually using visual effects techniques.

fixed matte: As opposed to a **traveling matte,** a fixed matte will not change position or shape during the shot.

flare: Any of a number of effects that will show up on an image as the result of a light source shining directly into the lens of a camera.

flashing: An optical process whereby an unprocessed negative is exposed to a small amount of light for the purpose of reducing the contrast or saturation of the scene that will eventually be photographed with that film. In the digital realm, flashing is the application of any number of nonspecific techniques to produce similar results. An image that appears to suffer from some of these characteristics is often referred to as appearing *flashed*.

flat: Another term for low **contrast.**

flat lens: Another term for a **spherical lens.** Sometimes also used as a relative term for measuring the distortion and exposure variance of any lens.

flatbed: A mechanical picture and sound editing machine on which multiple film rolls and audio tracks are loaded separately and lay flatly on a motorized table-like surface, allowing film editors smoother, quieter, and better viewing of the material for the purpose of editing and reviewing the edit. These machines were essentially the last improvements in editing equipment, following the **Movieola,** before nonlinear digital editing machines took over. They are now rarely if ever used. (Sometimes referred to as a KEM.)

flicker glasses: A type of **3D glasses** that use an electronic shutter to block the light reaching each eye independently. By syncing the glasses to the projection device, alternate stereo pairs can be presented to the viewer in a fashion that simulates a stereoscopic scene. See also **anaglyph glasses, polarized glasses.**

flip: A simple geometric transform in which an image is mirrored about the X-axis so that it is now upside-down. This process is different from merely rotating the image 180 degrees.

float: A number defined with **floating point** precision.

floating point: A term used to describe a number in which no fixed number of digits must be used before or after a decimal point to describe a number, meaning that the decimal point can float.

floating windows: (stereo) Invented by Raymond and Nigel Spottiswoode, this is the use of printed vertical bands to create a surround to supplant the physical screen surround. The result is a so-called virtual window that is floating in space to eliminate the screen edge cue conflicts and to extend the parallax budget of the projected image.

flop: A simple geometric transform in which an image is mirrored about the y-axis.

focal length: A measure of the magnification power of a given lens, based on the distance from the center of the lens to the film. Also known as simply the *length* of a lens. A longer focal length will produce greater magnification than a shorter length.

focus: (1) To adjust a lens so that the image it produces is as sharp as possible. (2) The point in space behind a lens where this sharpness occurs.

folding: The process of consolidating discrete mathematical operations into a single function.

forced perspective: A technique used to create the illusion of increased depth in a scene by building more distant objects at a smaller scale than normal.

foreground: Usually the primary element to be added to a composite and placed over the **background.** A composite often has several foreground elements.

format: (1) The size, resolution, aspect ratio, etc., for a given image. (2) The **file format** for a given image. (3) The physical medium (such as film, video, etc.) used to capture or display an image sequence. (4) A multitude of additional variations and subcategories of the first three definitions.

four-perf: A nickname for the standard 35mm film format that refers to the fact that each frame spans four pairs of **perforations.**

four-point track: A type of **2D tracking** in which four points are selected from a sequence of images to extract an approximation of an object's movement relative to the camera. Allows for **corner pinning** techniques.

4:1:1 compression: A method of encoding the data needed to represent an image by sampling **Y (luminance)** for every pixel but removing every other **UV** (**chroma**) pixel in both the horizontal and vertical directions.

4:2:2 compression: A method of encoding the data needed to represent an image by sampling **Y (luminance)** for every pixel but removing every other **UV** (**chroma**) pixel in the horizontal direction.

4:4:4 compression: A method of encoding the data needed to represent an image by sampling **Y (luminance)** and **UV (chroma)** for every pixel in the image.

4k resolution: A general term referring to any digital image containing an X **resolution** of approximately 4096 **pixels.** The actual dimensions of a 2k image depend on the **aspect ratio** of the imagery. A common 4k resolution used in **visual effects** when working with **full-aperture** framing is 4096 × 3112.

FOV: Abbreviation for *field of view.*

fps: Abbreviation for *frames per second*. See also **frame rate.**

fractal compression: A **lossy** compression algorithm that is based on repeated use of scaled and rotated pixel patterns.

frame: A single image that is usually part of a group designed to be viewed as a moving sequence.

frame rate: The rate at which sequences of images are captured or displayed. The frame rate is usually measured in frames per second, or **fps.**

freeze: The process of stopping the action. In digital compositing, this is usually accomplished by repeating the same frame for a duration of time.

freeze frame: A single frame that is held for a duration of time.

fringing: An **artifact** of the matting process in which a foreground element has a noticeable (usually bright) outline.

frustum: Term commonly used in **computer graphics** to describe the 3D region that is visible on the screen (which is formed by a clipped pyramid); in particular, **frustum culling** is a method of hidden surface determination.

frustum culling: Or **view frustum culling** is the process of removing objects that lie completely outside the viewing frustum from the rendering process. Rendering these objects would be a waste of time since they are not directly visible.

***f*-stop:** A measurement of the **aperture** of a lens.

full aperture: A specific 35mm film framing, also known as **camera aperture.**

fusion: (stereo) The combination, by the mind, of the left and right images—seen by the left and right eyes—into a single image.

G

gamma: (1) In film, a measure of the contrast of an image or emulsion, based on the slope of the straight-line portion of the **characteristic curve.** (2) An adjustment applied to a video monitor to compensate for its nonlinear response to a signal. (3) A digital effect used to modify the apparent brightness of an image.

gamut: The range of colors that any given device or format is able to display or represent.

garbage matte: A rough, simple **matte** that isolates unwanted elements from the primary element in an image.

Gaussian blur: A specific method for blurring an image based on a **Gaussian filter.**

Gaussian filter: A specific digital **filter** that is often used when **resampling** an image.

gel: Abbreviation for *gelatin filter,* a flexible colored optical **filter.**

generation loss: The loss of quality of an image due to repeated duplication. Generation loss is significantly reduced and in some cases completely eliminated when dealing with digital images.

geometric transformation: An effect that causes some or all of the pixels in a given image to change their current location. Such effects include **translation, rotation, scaling, warping,** and various specialized distortion effects.

ghosting: (stereo) Term used to describe the perception of **crosstalk.**

GIF: Abbreviation for *Graphics Interchange Format,* a specific image file format.

global illumination: A general term used to describe the modeling of all of the reflected and transmitted light that originates from every surface in a scene.

glue code: Code that ties different parts of the pipeline together, whether it is data interchange between programs that write different file formats or interprocess control of one piece of the pipeline by another.

G-matte: Abbreviation for *garbage matte.*

gobo: See **cukaloris.**

Go-Motion photography: Technique that gives naturalistic motion blur when shooting miniatures. The camera shutter remains open with the motion control rig moving continuously through the shot.

grading: Another term for **color timing,** used primarily in Great Britain.

grain: The individual particles of silver halide in a piece of film that capture an image when exposed to light. Because the distribution and sensitivity of these particles are not uniform, they are perceived (particularly when projected) as causing a noticeable graininess. Different film stocks will have different visual grain characteristics.

graphical user interface (GUI): A **user interface** that utilizes images and other graphical elements to simplify the process of interacting with the software. Also known as the *look and feel* of the software.

gray card: A card (gray) usually designed to reflect about 18% of the light that strikes it; used as a reference for measuring exposure.

grayscale image: A completely **desaturated** image, with no color, only shades of gray.

greeblies: A term for small reusable model geometry components, from the term used by ILM to describe an assortment of detail pieces from kit-bashed commercial plastic model kits used on production models.

green-lit: A project that is approved to proceed into full production with funding.

green record: The layer of the film that captures green light.

green screen: Identical in use and concept to a **blue screen** (only it is green). (Note that in this handbook the standard is to use *green screen* to designate the screen itself and *greenscreen* to designate the process.)

green spill: Any contamination of the foreground subject by light reflected from the **green screen** in front of which it is placed. See also **spill, blue spill.**

guesstimate: A combination of a guess and an estimate that is used to qualify a quick or not particularly accurate budget, time, and technique approach.

GUI: Abbreviation for *graphical user interface.*

H

halation: A blurring or spreading of light around bright areas on a photographic image. Also seen as a glow around a bright object on a monitor or television screen. Most films have an anti-halation backing to keep the light from bouncing around in the camera and adding additional unwanted exposure—or halation.

handles: Extra frames at the beginning and end of a shot that are not intended for use in the final shot but are included in the composite in case the shot's length changes slightly.

haptic arm: A force-feedback system. In computer graphics it sometimes takes the form of a pressure-sensitive stylus to be used with a computer tablet.

HD resolution: A general term referring to any digital image that contains the **spatial resolution** of one of the **HDTV** standards, of which 1920 × 1080 is the most common.

HDR: Abbreviation for *high dynamic range.*

HDRI: Abbreviation for *high dynamic range imaging.*

HDTV: High-definition television. A television standard with significantly greater spatial resolution than standard **NTSC, PAL,** or **SECAM.**

Hermite curve: A specific type of **spline curve** that allows for explicit control over the curve's tangent at every **control point.**

high dynamic range (HDR): Related to imagery or devices that can deal with a larger than normal **dynamic range.**

high dynamic range imaging (HDRI): A technique for capturing the extended tonal range in a scene by shooting multiple pictures at different exposures and combining them into a single image file that can express a greater dynamic range than can be captured with current imaging technology.

high-pass filter: A **spatial filter** that enhances high-frequency detail. It is used as a method for **sharpening** an image.

histogram: A graphical representation of the distribution (usually frequency of occurrence) of a particular characteristic of the pixels in an image.

histogram equalization: An **image-processing** technique that adjusts the contrast in an image so that it fits into a certain range.

histogram sliding: Equivalent to adding a certain number to the values of every pixel in an image.

histogram stretching: Equivalent to multiplying the values of every pixel in an image by a certain amount.

HIT: (stereo) Horizontal image translation. The horizontal shifting of the two image fields to change the value of the parallax of corresponding points. The term *convergence* has been confusingly used to denote this concept.

HLS: Hue, luminance, and **saturation.** A method of specifying the colors in an image based on a mix of these three components.

hold: To stop the action by using the same frame repeatedly.

hold-out matte: A **matte** used to prevent a foreground element from completely obscuring an object in the background plate.

homologous points: (stereo) See **corresponding points.**

hot: A nonexact term for describing an image that is too bright. Completely unrelated to the terms **warm** and **cool.**

hot head: A computer-assisted camera mount head that can either record the pan and tilt of an operated camera or use previously recorded pan/tilt information to play back; that is, to drive the camera head mount to replicate the pan/tilt move. As the equipment improves, more axes are becoming recordable and capable of being played back to drive the camera.

HSB: Hue, saturation, and **brightness.** A method of specifying the colors in an image based on a mix of these three components.

HSI: Hue, saturation, and **intensity.** A method of specifying the colors in an image based on a mix of these three components.

HSL: Hue, saturation, and **lightness.** A method of specifying the colors in an image based on a mix of these three components.

HSV: Hue, saturation, and **value.** A method of specifying the colors in an image based on a mix of these three components.

hue: A specific color from the color spectrum, disregarding its **saturation** or **value.**

Huffman coding: A **lossless** image compression scheme. See also **run-length encoding, JPEG, MPEG.**

I

ICC: Abbreviation for *International Color Consortium.*

ILM: Abbreviation for *Industrial Light & Magic.*

image processing: The use of various tools and algorithms to modify digital images within a computer.

IMAX: A proprietary film capture/projection process that uses an extremely large-format negative.

impulse filter: A specific digital **filter** that is often used when **resampling** a digital image. It is considered to be the lowest quality, highest speed filter in common use. Also known as the **Dirac filter** or the **nearest-neighbor filter.**

in-betweening: The process of **interpolating** between the **key frames** of an animation sequence.

in-camera effects: Visual effects that are accomplished solely during principal photography, involving no additional post-production.

indexed color: A method of storing image data, in which the value of the pixel refers to an entry in a table of available colors instead of a numerical specification of the color itself.

Industrial Light & Magic (ILM): A pioneering visual effects company that was the first to widely use digital compositing in feature-film work.

interactive lighting: Lighting in a scene that changes over time and responds to the activity within the environment.

interaxial distance: (stereo) The distance between camera lenses' axes. See **T.** Also called *interaxial separation.*

interframe coding: The process used in **MPEG** encoding whereby intermediate images in a sequence are defined by their deviation from specific key frames.

interlacing: The technique used to produce video images whereby two alternating **field** images are displayed in rapid sequence so that they appear to produce a complete **frame.**

intermediate: General term used for copies (not necessarily first generation) of the **original negative,** which can be used as the source for duplicate copies. See **interpositive, internegative.**

internal accuracy: The measurement of the precision or **bit depth** that a software package uses to represent and modify image data.

International Color Consortium (ICC): The organization established for the purpose of standardizing **color management** across different platforms.

internegative (IN): Short for **intermediate negative**, a copy made from the **interpositive** through printing and developing.

interocular distance: The spacing between the eyes, usually referring to the human average of about 2.5 inches; an important factor for the production of a **stereoscopic image.**

interocular distance: (stereo) See "**T.**"

interpolation: The process of using certain rules or formulas to derive new data based on a set of existing data. See also **bicubic interpolation, bilinear interpolation, linear interpolation.**

interpositive (IP): Short for **intermediate positive,** a **positive print** made from the **original negative** for use in making **internegatives.** A positive film copy on negative film stock. It is used to protect a negative from overuse. From this interpositive, a duplicate negative may be made, when necessary. IPs usually retain a finer film grain than if the negative were printed to positive film stock and then back to negative film stock.

interpositive film stock: Orange-based motion picture film with a positive image made from the edited camera negative. The orange base provides special color characteristics that allow for more accurate color reproduction than if the IP had a clear base, as in print films.

interpupillary distance: (stereo) The distance between the eyes' axes. See **T.** Also called *interpupillary* or *interocular separation.*

ISO index: A standard numerical rating for specifying a film's sensitivity to light. *ISO* is the abbreviation for International Standards Organization. The **ISO index** actually incorporates both the American **ASA rating** and the European **DIN rating.** Many manufacturers now use their own specific **exposure index** instead. See also **ASA rating, DIN rating.**

J

JPEG: A (typically **lossy**) compression technique or a specific image format that utilizes this technique. *JPEG* is an abbreviation for the Joint Photographic Experts Group.

K

kernel: The group of pixels that will be considered when performing some kind of spatial filtering. See also **convolution kernel.**

key: (1) Another name for a **matte.** (2) The process of extracting a subject from its background by isolating it with its own matte and **compositing** it over a new background.

key code: See **edge numbers.**

keyer: A device or operation used for **matte extraction** or **keying.**

key frame: Any frame in which a particular aspect of an item (its size, location, color, etc.) is specifically defined. The frames that are not key frames will then contain interpolated values.

keyframe animation: The process of creating animation using **key frames.**

keyframing: Another term for **keyframe animation.**

keying: The process of algorithmically extracting an object from its background and combining it with a different background.

Keykode numbers: A specific form of **edge numbers** that was introduced by Kodak.

Keylight: The trade name of a **color difference keyer** developed by the Computer Film Company (CFC).

keystone distortion: A geometric distortion resulting when a rectangular plane is projected or photographed at an angle not perpendicular to the axis of the lens. The result is that the rectangle becomes trapezoidal. Also referred to as *keystoning.*

kukaloris: See **cukaloris.**

L

LAD: Abbreviation for *Laboratory Aim Density* (LAD) printing control method. By exposing a LAD patch, the value of the exposure of that piece of film can be determined. Kodak publishes suggested density tolerances for each type of film in the duplicating and print system.

large-format camera: Any camera designed to use wide-gauge films, such as **65mm film.**

large-format film: Generally refers to any film larger than the standard **35mm film** format.

latent image: The invisible image that exists on an exposed piece of negative that has not yet been developed.

layering operation: A global term referring to any **compositing** operation that integrates one **element** with another element based on their **alpha channels** or **RGB values.**

Leica camera: One of the finest still cameras made. Known for their quiet shutter and for great lenses that have amazing contrast and sharpness.

Leica lenses: The brand of lenses used on the animation cameras that photographed storyboards in the earliest Disney days.

lens artifact: Any **artifact,** such as a **lens flare** or **chromatic aberration,** that appears in an image as a result of the **lens assembly.**

lens assembly: Referring to the set of specially matched lenses that are assembled to form a single lens component in a standard camera lens.

lens flare: An **artifact** of a bright light shining directly into the lens assembly of a camera.

letterboxing: A method for displaying images that preserves the **aspect ratio** of the film as it was originally shot, using black to specify areas outside of the original frame.

light pass: (1) In **multiple-pass photography,** the pass of individual lights striking the subject, such as the **key** or **fill,** for later use in **compositing.** (2) In **multiple-pass rendering,** the **CG element** that represents the effects of a particular **light** striking the **object.** See also **beauty pass, matte pass, reflection pass, shadow pass.**

lighting reference: A **stand-in** object that can be used to judge the lighting in a scene.

linear color space: A **color space** in which the relationship between a pixel's digital value and its visual brightness remains constant (linear) across the full **gamut** of black to white.

linear encoding: A method of converting the colors from the input image to an output image in an evenly distributed, linear way. Also referred to as *linear mapping.* See **linear color space, nonlinear color space.**

linear interpolation: A method of interpolation that is based on the average of the two nearest neighbors. See also **bicubic interpolation, bilinear interpolation.**

linear polarization: (stereo) A form of polarized light in which the tip of the electric vector of the light ray remains confined to a plane.

linear space: See **linear color space.**

locked cut: Term meaning that no more editing will be done on the shot, scene, or project; the edit is 100% complete.

locked-off camera: A camera whose position and lens settings do not change over the duration of the shot.

log space: Abbreviation for *logarithmic color space,* a **nonlinear color space** whose conversion function is similar to the curve produced by the logarithmic equation.

long lens: A relative term, in contrast to a **short lens.** Also known as a **telephoto lens.**

lookup table (LUT): An array of values used to convert data from an input value to a new output value. See also **color lookup table.**

lossless compression: A method of compressing and storing a digital image in such a fashion that the original image can be completely reconstructed without any data loss.

lossy compression: A method of compressing and storing a digital image in such a fashion that it is impossible to perfectly reconstruct the original image.

lowball bid: A very low bid based on extreme best case scenarios.

low-pass filter: A **spatial filter** that removes high-frequency detail. It is used as a method for blurring an image.

luma-keying: A matte-extraction technique that uses the **luminance** values in the image.

luminance: In common usage, synonymous with brightness. In the **HSL** color space, luminance is the weighted average of the red, green, and blue components.

LUT: Abbreviation for **lookup table.**

LZW compression: A **lossless compression** method that finds repeated patterns in blocks of pixels in an image. Variations of LZW compression are used in a number of image file formats, including **GIF** and **TIFF**. *LZW* stands for Lempel-Ziv-Welch.

M

Macbeth chart: An industry standard test chart made up of square color and gray patches.

Mach banding: An optical illusion (named after the physicist Ernst Mach) in which the eye perceives emphasized edges in areas of color transition. This illusion causes the eye to be more sensitive to **contouring** artifacts.

macro: (1) In the digital world, a combination of functions or effects that are grouped together to create a new effect. (2) A specialized lens that is capable of focusing at an extremely close distance to the subject.

mandrel: Form to replicate the volume and basic shape of an object for on-set interaction. The actual image of the object will be added in post-production. An example is a mandrel with the basic shape of a rhino used to smash in a wall that is later replaced with a CG rhino.

maquette: Very detailed physical sculpture of a creature or character.

mask: An image used to selectively restrict or modify certain image-processing operations on another image or the process of doing so.

matchmove: The process of extracting the camera move from a live-action plate in order to duplicate it in a CG environment. A matchmove is often created by hand as opposed to **3D tracking** in which special software is used to help automate the process.

matte: An image used to define or control the transparency of another image. See also **articulate matte, complementary matte, difference matte, edge matte, fixed matte, garbage matte, hold-out matte, rotoscoped matte, static matte, traveling matte.**

matte channel: Another name for the **alpha channel** in a four-channel image.

matte extraction: Any process used to create a **matte.**

matte line: An artifact of the matting process wherein a foreground element has a noticeable outline.

matte painting: A hand-painted image, usually intended to be photorealistic, that is combined with live-action footage.

matte pass: (1) In **multiple-pass photography,** a pass that is lit in some high-contrast fashion so that it can be used as a **matte** during **compositing.** (2) In **multiple-pass rendering,** a separate **render** of the **alpha channel** of one of the objects in the scene for use during compositing. See also **beauty pass, light pass, reflection pass, shadow pass.**

maximum density: The point of exposure at which additional light (on the negative) will no longer affect the resulting image. The definitions of maximum and **minimum density** would be reversed if you were speaking of print (reversal) film instead of negative. Also known as *D-max.*

median filter: A specialized **spatial filter** that removes pixel anomalies by determining the median value in a group of neighboring pixels.

miniaturization: (stereo) Often occurs when a large interaxial separation is used for shots of people at medium distances or for photography of distant objects, like houses or hills. The perception of such images as miniatures is idiosyncratic and varies from person to person.

minimum density: The point of exposure just below the amount needed (on the negative) to start affecting the resulting image. The definitions of minimum and **maximum density** would be reversed if you were speaking of print (reversal) film instead of negative. Also known as *D-min.*

Mitchell filter: A specific digital **filter** that is often used when **resampling** a digital image. The Mitchell filter is particularly well suited to transforming images into a higher resolution than they were originally.

MoCap: Abbreviation for *motion capture.* A technique whereby an individual being's performance is captured and translated for use in driving a CG being's performance. Also known as **performance capture.**

moco: Abbreviation for ***motion control.***

monochrome: An image that contains only a single hue, and the only variation is in the luminance of that hue. Typically, a monochrome image consists only of shades of gray.

monocular cues: (stereo) See **extrastereoscopic cues.**

morphing: A process in which two image sequences are warped (see **warping**) so that key features align as closely as possible and then a selective **dissolve** is applied to transition from the first sequence to the second. The result should be a seamless transformation between the two sequences.

MOS: Term used to mean there is no sync sound recorded for this take. Comes from the early days of filmmaking when the German director would shout out "Mit out Sound!"

motion artifact: A general term describing all forms of image artifacts due to motion, such as **strobing** or **wagon wheeling.**

motion blur: An artifact caused by the fact that a camera's shutter is open for a finite duration as it captures an image. Any object that is moving during that time will appear blurred along the path that it was traveling.

motion control: A method of using computer-controlled mechanisms to drive an object's movement so that it is continuously repeatable.

motion control camera: A camera whose position, orientation, and lens settings are motion controlled.

motion graphics: Animated graphic imagery that is done primarily to achieve a specific visual design rather than to produce photorealistic images.

Movieola: A self-contained mechanical film viewing device. Typically used by film editors, it allowed for rapid stopping, reversing, and vari-speeding of the film (and separate sound strips) for the purpose of editing and/or reviewing the cut. The large green machine had many conveniences built into it over the years, but due to the advent of nonlinear digital editing devices, it is no longer in use.

MPEG: A (typically **lossy**) compression technique specifically designed to deal with sequences of images or the format of the images produced by this technique. *MPEG* is an abbreviation for the Moving Picture Experts Group.

multimedia: A broad categorization that generally refers to some method of displaying information using sound and imagery simultaneously.

multiplane compositing: A technique that simulates a moving camera by automatically translating the different layers in a composite by an amount that is appropriate to their intended distance from this camera. Layers that are intended to appear farther away are moved by a smaller amount than layers that are intended to be nearer, producing a simulated **parallax** effect.

multiple-camera rig: (stereo) A technique commonly used in virtual 3D photography in which more than one stereo camera pair is used to photograph the scene. Individual objects in the scene are assigned to each camera pair with each one using unique stereoscopic parameters. Also describes the collection of camera pairs used to photograph such a scene.

multiple-pass photography: Any filming in which multiple exposures of the same subject are filmed, generally with different lighting setups. If the camera is moving, then it must be motion controlled to ensure accurate alignment between passes. Typical passes might include a **beauty pass, matte pass, reflection pass,** and **shadow pass.**

multiple-pass rendering: A technique in which a 3D object or scene is rendered in a series of separate images, each with different lighting or rendering characteristics. Typical passes might include **color, shadow, reflection, key light, fill light, backlight.** See also **multiple-pass photography.**

multiplexing: (stereo) The technique for placing the two images required for a stereoscopic display within an existing bandwidth.

N

naming conventions: The standardized names that are used within a facility to differentiate the various elements and files that are stored on disk for a project.

ND filter: See **neutral density filter.**

nearest-neighbor filter: Another term for the **impulse filter.**

neutral density filter: An optical **filter** that is designed to reduce the intensity of the light passing through it without affecting the color of the light.

Newton's rings: An artifact, usually seen in optical printing, characterized by circular moiré patterns that appear in the image.

NG: Abbreviation for *no good* (e.g., that take was NG or no good).

nodal point: The point at which light entering a lens converges before it spreads again to form an image at the film plane. A nodal setup allows the camera to pan, tilt, and roll without creating any parallax shift between foreground and background elements.

node view: A view, available in most compositing software, that shows the hierarchical structure of the image-processing operations that will be used to generate a final composite.

nonlinear color space: A **color space** in which the relationship between a pixel's digital value and its visual brightness does not remain constant (linear) across the full **gamut** of black to white.

nonlinear editing: Editing that does not require that the sequence be worked on sequentially.

nonlinear encoding: A method of converting the colors from an input image to an output image in a nonlinear way. See **linear color space, nonlinear color space.**

nonsquare pixel: A pixel whose width is not the same size as its height. The ratio of width to height is measured in terms of a **pixel aspect ratio**.

normalized value: A digital value that has been converted to fall within a specific range. With digital compositing, this is usually the range of 0 to 1.

NTSC: Abbreviation for *National Television Systems Committee.* Refers not only to the committee itself, but also to the standard that they established for color television in the United States and other countries. It carries 525 lines of information, played back at a rate of approximately 30 frames per second (actually 29.97). Due to its unreliable color reproduction ability, the initials are often said to stand for *never the same color* or *never twice the same color*.

NURBs: Abbreviation for *nonuniform rational B-spline.*

O

occlusion: State in which objects, or portions of objects, are not visible because they are blocked by other objects or portions of objects.

off-line compositing: Another term for **batch compositing.**

Omnimax: A proprietary film capture/projection process that uses the same large-format negative as the **IMAX** process but is designed for projection on the interior of a dome-shaped screen.

1:85: Common **aspect ratio** of width to the height of the image.

o-neg: Abbreviation for *original negative.*

one-point track: A type of **2D tracking** in which a single point is selected in a sequence of images to extract an approximation of an object's movement relative to the camera. Tracking a single point only allows for translational movements.

1k resolution: A general term referring to any digital image containing an X resolution of approximately 1024 pixels. The actual dimensions of the 1k image depends on the **aspect ratio** of the imagery.

on-line compositing: A method of compositing that uses a highly interactive hardware/software combination to quickly provide the results of every compositing operation. Distinguished from an **off-line** or **batch compositing** system.

on-set previs: Creates real-time (or near real-time) visualizations on location to help the director, visual effects supervisor, and crew quickly evaluate captured imagery. This includes the use of techniques that can synchronize and composite live photography with 2D or 3D virtual elements for immediate visual feedback. Also see **previs, pitchvis, technical previs,** and **postvis.**

opaque: The characteristic of an image that causes it to fully obscure any image that is behind it. Opaque is the opposite of **transparent.**

OpenEXR: A specific image file format designed for use with high dynamic range imagery.

OpenGL: Abbreviation for *open graphics library*. A standard specification defining a cross-language, cross-platform **API** for writing applications that produce 2D and 3D computer graphics. Programs that use OpenGL can leverage graphics cards to accelerate graphics.

optical compositing: The process of using an optical printer to produce composite imagery.

optical flow analysis: A method for procedurally determining the movement of objects in a sequence of images by examining the movement of smaller blocks of pixels within the image.

optical printer: A device used to combine one or more different film elements and rephotograph them onto a new piece of film.

original negative (o-neg): The first-generation negative that captured the original image directly from the scene. Later duplicates of this negative are known as *intermediate negatives* or **internegatives.**

orthographic: Representing a 3D object in two dimensions.

orthographic view: A view of a 3D scene rendered without any perspective—objects appear to be the same size regardless of their distance from the camera.

overcrank: Running a **camera** at a faster speed than the intended projection rate, resulting in projected footage that appears to move slower than normal. Footage shot at a faster-than-normal rate is said to have been *shot overcranked*. See also **slow motion.**

oversampling: Sampling data at a higher-than-normal resolution in order to mitigate sampling errors or inaccuracies from uncharacteristic data.

P

paint software: A program that allows the artist to "paint" directly onto an image in the computer using a device such as a **tablet** or a mouse.

paintbox: Usually used in the video post-production world as a generic term for a variety of paint and compositing devices.

PAL: Abbreviation for *phase alternation by line*. A standard for color television found in many European, African, and Asian countries. It carries 625 lines of resolution, played back at a rate of 25 frames per second.

palette: The range of colors available for use in any particular application. A system that uses 8 bits per channel would have a palette of more than 16 million colors.

pan and scan: A technique that is used to convert images shot with a **widescreen** film process to a less expansive video format. It generally involves selectively cropping the image to fit into the new frame, arbitrarily choosing what portions of the image are unnecessary.

pan and tile: A technique in which a series of images of a scene are stitched together to create a larger panoramic view of the scene.

Panavision: (1) A manufacturer of motion picture lenses and cameras. (2) The trade name for a specific widescreen process and lenses developed by the Panavision company. It is an anamorphic format that produces an image with a 2.35:1˙aspect ratio. See also **anamorphic format, Cinemascope.**

Pantone Matching System (PMS): A color identification standard used in print work that contains more than 3000 different colors. Many computer graphics programs allow the user to select colors based on their PMS number.

parallax: The perceptual difference in an object's location or spatial relationship when seen from different vantage points.

parallax: (stereo) The distance between conjugate points. It may be measured with a ruler or, given the distance of an observer from the screen, in terms of angular measure. In the latter case the parallax angle directly provides information about disparity.

parallax budget: (stereo) The range of parallax values, from maximum negative to maximum positive, that is within an acceptable range for comfortable viewing.

particle system: A 3D computer graphics technique that is used to create a large number of objects that obey well-defined behavioral rules. Useful not only for controlling multitudes of discrete objects such as asteroids or flocks of birds but also as a tool for creating natural phenomena such as fire or smoke.

pattern matching: Process by which missing image data is synthesized by continuing patterns that are found elsewhere in the image into the missing area. Also can be used for motion tracking.

peg registered: Special animation paper with special holes that fit over animation pegs on an animation stand to ensure proper registration of the paper. Also used with animation cels for the same purpose.

perf: Abbreviation for *perforation.*

perforation: One of the sprocket holes that runs along the edges of a piece of film. They are used to guide the film reliably through the camera. Also called a *perf.*

performance capture: A technique whereby an individual being's performance is captured and translated for use in driving a CG being's performance. Sometimes called **MoCap.**

periscope lens: A lens mounted to a tube that extends out from the camera (typically 20 inches or so) and can photograph objects at a 90-degree angle to the body of the camera. Also known as a *snorkel lens.*

Periwinkle effect: Technique for shooting wet-for-dry using an underwater bluescreen process. Invented by Jeffrey A. Okun and Thomas Boland.

persistence of vision: The characteristic of the human eye that allows it to continue to perceive an image for a fraction of a second after it disappears.

perspective: A term relating to the size and depth relationships of the objects in a scene.

perspective compensation: The use of a 2D **geometric transformation** to correct a 3D discrepancy.

photogrammetry: A method in which textured 3D geometry is created based on the analysis of multiple 2D images taken from different viewpoints.

photorealism: A global term used to describe CG images that cannot be distinguished from objects or scenes in the real world.

picture element: See **pixel.**

pincushion distortion: A type of **lens distortion** in which straight lines are bent inward toward the center of an image. See also **barrel distortion.**

pipeline: A well-defined set of processes for achieving a certain result.

pitchvis: Illustrates the potential of a project before it has been fully funded or greenlit. As part of development, these sequences are conceptual, to be refined or replaced during pre-production. Also see **previs, technical previs, on-set previs,** and **postvis.**

pixel: Originally an abbreviation for *picture element*, although the term *pixel* is generally considered to be an actual word nowadays. A digital image is composed of a rectangular array of individual colored points. Each one of these points is referred to as a pixel.

pixel analyzer: A tool available in most **compositing** and **paint packages** that allows the user to point the mouse over an area of pixels in order to get the specific or average color values for that portion of the image.

pixel aspect ratio: The width of a given pixel divided by its height. A number of image representation methods do not use pixels that have an equivalent width and height. The pixel aspect ratio is independent of a particular image's **aspect ratio**. See also **nonsquare pixels.**

pixelation: An effect caused by displaying a bitmap or a section of a bitmap at such a large size that the individual pixels that make up the image are visible to the eye.

pixelation animation: Stop-motion technique in which live actors are used as a frame-by-frame subject in an animated film by repeatedly posing while one or more frame is taken and changing the pose slightly before the next frame or frames. The actor becomes a kind of living stop-motion puppet.

planar: (stereo) Flat; two dimensional. A planar image is one contained in a 2D space, but not necessarily one that appears flat. It may have all the depth cues except stereopsis.

plano-stereoscopic: (stereo) A stereoscopic projected image that is made up of two planar images.

plate: A piece of original photography that is intended to be used as an **element** in a composite.

playback speed: The rate (usually measured in frames per second) at which a sequence of images is displayed.

polarized glasses: 3D glasses that use polarizing filters to differentiate between the images sent to the right and left eyes in stereo films. See also **flicker glasses, anaglyph glasses.**

post-house: A facility where the **post-production** work takes place.

postmove: Referring to any move added to a plate via image transformations performed in compositing, as opposed to shooting the scene with the desired camera move.

posterization: An effect applied to an image that intentionally causes **banding.**

post-production: Work done once principal photography has been completed.

postvis: Combines digital elements and production photography to validate footage selection, provide placeholder shots for editorial, and refine effects design. Edits incorporating postvis sequences are often shown to test audiences for feedback and to producers and visual effects vendors for planning and budgeting. Also see **previs, pitchvis, technical previs,** and **on-set previs.**

practical effects: Effects that are accomplished live, without any post-production. Practical effects include explosions, artificial rain, and smoke.

precomp: Abbreviation for *preliminary composite.*

preliminary composite: Any intermediate imagery that is produced during the digital compositing process that can be saved and used as a new source element. Also called a *precomp*.

premultiplied image: An image whose red, green, and blue **channels** have been multiplied by a **matte.** Usually this matte is stored as the **alpha channel** of this image.

pre-production: Any planning, testing, or initial design that is done before actual production begins.

previs: Abbreviation for *previsualization*. Previs is a collaborative process that generates preliminary versions of shots or sequences, predominantly using 3D animation tools and a virtual environment. It enables filmmakers to visually explore creative ideas, plan technical solutions, and communicate a shared vision for efficient production. Also see **pitchvis, technical previs, on-set previs,** and **postvis.**

Primatte: A proprietary **chroma-keying** tool that can be used to extract a **matte** from an image shot in front of a uniform backing.

prime lens: A camera lens with a fixed focal length, as opposed to a zoom lens, which has a variable focal length.

print: A positive image that is suitable for viewing directly or for projection. Generally produced from an original or an intermediate negative.

procedural paint: A specialized form of paint software that can actually apply brush strokes and other paint processes over a sequence of images instead of just a single frame. Parameters for these painting effects can usually be animated as well.

processing: (1) The time spent by the computer as it computes any instructions that it has been given. (2) At a photo laboratory, the process of developing and printing a piece of film.

producer: Administrative head of a project. Responsible for budget, schedule, etc. (See the list of VES-approved titles in Appendix B.)

production sense: The near-mythical ability of an experienced digital artist to decide on the proper course of action when creating a visual effects shot.

progressive scan: A method of displaying an image that does not rely on **interlacing.**

projection mapping: See **camera mapping.**

projection speed: The **playback speed** for projected imagery.

proxy: A scaled-down image that is used as a stand-in for a higher resolution original.

pull a matte: The process of creating a **matte** for an object, usually through **keying** techniques.

pulldown: Shorthand for **3:2 pulldown.**

pullup: Shorthand for **3:2 pullup.**

Q

quantization: The process of assigning discrete digital values to samples taken from a continuous analog data set.

quantization artifact: A term generally used to refer to a visually noticeable artifact of the **quantization** process.

quantizing: Colloquial term for a **quantization artifact.**

R

Ramsdell rig: (stereo) First designed by Floyd Ramsdell. A rig that allows two cameras to be arranged in a way that provides the means for taking stereoscopic moving images, by use of a **beamsplitter,** to create an **interocular** separation that is the same distance apart as typical human eyes. See **beamsplitter.**

raster graphics: Image representation using a grid of pixels. **Vector graphics** uses line information to represent images.

raw stock: Unexposed, unprocessed film.

R&D: Abbreviation for *research and development*.

RDBMS: Abbreviation for *relational database management system*.

real time: (1) Displaying a sequence of images at the same speed as they will be viewed in their final form. (2) Computational processing that appears to be nearly instantaneous.

rear projection (RP): A compositing process in which the previously photographed background scene is projected onto a large translucent screen from behind while the foreground action takes place. The composite is thus considered an **in-camera effect**.

record: One of the red, green, or blue color-sensitive layers in a piece of film. Thus, the blue record is equivalent to a digital image's blue **channel**.

red record: The layer of the film that captures red light.

reference spheres: Chrome and neutral gray globes, used on the set to visually record the placement of lights within a scene. CG artists later use the sphere(s) reference as a guide for placing CG lights to help make CG and live-action objects appear to be in the same environment.

reflection pass: In motion control photography is one of a set of passes that include the **beauty pass,** the **matte pass,** and the **shadow pass.** Its purpose is to capture only the light that is reflected on the subject. In the CGI world, it is a separate render output that retains only the reflections for use in compositing.

region of interest (ROI): A (usually rectangular) region that is determined by the user in order to limit certain calculations. See also **domain of definition.**

release print: A print of a movie that will be sent to theaters for display. A release print is several generations removed from the original negative.

render: The process of creating a synthetic image from a 3D data set.

render farm: A group of computers that is set up as a place to submit 2D or 3D processes for noninteractive computation.

render queue: The list of tasks waiting to be processed on a **render farm**.

RenderMan: Specialized **rendering** software offered by Pixar, Inc.

reposition: The process of adjusting the placement of an **element** within the frame. Also referred to as *repo*.

resampling: The process of reading previously sampled data for the purpose of converting or modifying it.

resolution: The amount of data that is used to capture an image. The term is typically used to refer specifically to the **spatial resolution** of a digital image. See also **color resolution, temporal resolution.**

resolution independence: The characteristic of a software package that allows the user to easily work with and move between an arbitrary number of different **resolutions.**

retinal disparity: (stereo) See **disparity.**

RGB: Red, green, and blue. The three primary colors or a method of specifying the colors in an image based on a mix of these three components.

RGBA: Red, green, blue, and alpha, grouped as a single unit.

ride film: A location-based entertainment that features a film whose camera movements are synchronized with some sort of moving seat or platform. Term was first coined by Douglas Trumbull.

rig: (stereo) Dual camera heads in a properly engineered mount used to shoot stereo movies.

ringing: A visual **artifact,** often caused by excessive **sharpening,** that is characterized by overemphasized transitions between bright and dark areas in an image.

RLA: Abbreviation for Run-Length Encoded Version A, a specific image file format. RLA is primarily used by the Wavefront Advanced Visualizer animation package to store output data and to exchange graphical data with other software applications. There are actually three variations of the RLA image file format.

ROI: Abbreviation for *region of interest.* Also used in the financial world as an abbreviation for *return on investment*, something your employer is probably worrying about right now.

rotation: A **geometric transformation** that changes the orientation of an image relative to a certain axis.

rotoscope: Originally the name of a device patented in 1917 by Max Fleischer to aid in **cel animation.** Now used as a general term for the process of creating imagery or mattes on a frame-by-frame basis by hand. Also referred to as a *roto.*

rotoscoped matte: A **matte** created via **rotoscoping** techniques.

rotoscoping: Also known as "Rotoing." The process of hand drawing or tracing mattes around subjects. See **rotoscope.**

RP: Abbreviation for *rear projection.*

RTFM: Abbreviation for *read the manual* (sort of), a suggestion that is often given when someone asks a question instead of taking the time to look it up him- or herself.

run-length encoding: A **lossless** compression scheme that consolidates sequences of identical pixels into a single data representation.

run takes: In-progress versions of a shot, designated by specific numerical take numbers, to serve as a record of the shot's progress at a particular point in its production history.

rushes: Another term for **dailies,** used primarily in Great Britain.

S

sampling: (1) The process of reading a signal at specific time increments. See also **digitization.** (2) The process of reading the color value from a pixel or a group of pixels.

saturation: The brilliance or purity of a given color. The difference between a pastel and a pure color is the amount of saturation.

scaling: A **geometric transformation** that changes the size of an image, usually without changing its location or orientation.

scan line: A single horizontal row of pixels in a digital image.

scanner: A device for digitizing film, print material, etc.

scene: (1) The image captured by a camera. (2) A collection of shots that share a common setting or theme.

scene-referred image: An image that has a direct, well-defined mapping between the colors in the image and the colors in the original scene.

scope: (1) Abbreviation for any *anamorphic* process, such as *Cinemascope, Techniscope, Superscope.* (2) Shorthand for video scope, a **waveform monitor.**

screen left: The left side of the screen or image from the viewpoint of the viewer. Opposite of **screen right.**

screen resolution: The number of horizontal and vertical pixels that a given display device is capable of showing. This should be independent of the resolution that the system is capable of processing.

screen right: The right side of the screen or image from the viewpoint of the viewer. Opposite of **screen left.**

screen space: (stereo) The region appearing to be within the screen or behind the surface of the screen. Images with positive parallax will appear to be in screen space. The boundary between screen and theater space is the plane of the screen and has zero parallax. See **theater space.**

script: A **program** written in a scripting language, including the language used by a compositing package to describe the set of image-processing operations to be applied to a set of images.

SDK: Abbreviation for *software developer's kit.*

SECAM: Officially this is an acronym for *séquentiel couleur à mémoire*, but most English speakers use the translation *sequential color and memory*. SECAM is a standard for color television used in France and a few African and Eastern European nations. It carries 625 lines of resolution, played back at a rate of 25 frames per second.

seed: A number that is fed into a program or algorithm to produce a random number. The same seed will result in the same random numbers and therefore can provide for repeatable iterations.

selection device: (stereo) The hardware used to present the appropriate image to the appropriate eye and to block the unwanted image. For 3D movies the selection device is usually eyewear used in conjunction with a device at the projector, like a polarizing device.

self-illuminated blue screen: See **transmission blue screen.**

sequence: (1) A collection of images designed to be played sequentially. (2) A group of related **scenes** in a film, usually set in the same time and/or location.

server: A computer that is shared over a network by several users.

70mm film: The widest **gauge** film format, featuring twice the width of standard **35mm film.** See also **IMAX.**

SFX: Often used as an abbreviation for **special effects**, although sound effects people will dispute this usage.

shadow pass: In motion control photography is one of a set of passes that include the **beauty pass,** the **matte pass,** and the **reflection pass.** Its purpose is to capture only the shadows cast by the subject. In the CGI world, it is a separate render output that retains only the shadow for use in compositing.

sharpening: The process of applying an algorithm that emphasizes the edges in an image. The result is an image that appears to have increased **sharpness.**

sharpness: The visual sense of the abruptness of an edge.

short lens: A relative term, in contrast to a **long lens.** Also known as a **wide-angle lens.**

shot: An unbroken continuous image **sequence.**

Showscan: A proprietary film capture/projection process that is characterized by a large-format negative and a playback speed of 60 frames per second. Pioneered by Douglas Trumbull.

shutter angle: The part of a motion picture camera that determines how long a given area of film will be exposed to a scene. Most cameras have the ability to adjust their shutter angle. A larger shutter angle will result in increased **motion blur** on moving objects.

shutter speed: The amount of time that a camera will spend capturing an individual image.

SIGGRAPH: The Special Interest Group for Graphics, a subgroup under the **Association for Computing Machinery,** and the major organization for graphics professionals. Also, the annual conference sponsored by this group, which features a large number of courses, seminars, and some really big parties.

silver halide crystals: The silver compounds, usually silver bromide and silver iodide, that are impregnated in the photographic emulsion of film. These compounds, when acted on by actinic rays, are disintegrated, with the formation of metallic silver in a finely divided state. The photographic image results when the film is subjected to processing. They are commonly seen as film grain.

sinc filter: A specific digital **filter** that is often used when **resampling** a digital image. The sinc filter is particularly well suited to transforming images into a lower resolution than they were originally.

16-bit image: In the **visual effects** world, this term typically refers to any image containing 16 bits of color information per **channel.**

16mm film: A film format with a gauge of 16mm that carries only two **perforations** along each frame and contains 40 frames per foot. Because the **captured** image area is significantly smaller than that of **35mm film,** this film format is rarely used for visual effects work. However, 16mm is still occasionally used for documentaries and television commercials.

65mm film: A popular **widescreen** format that contains five **perforations** per frame (hence, the nickname *five-perf*). The 65mm acquisition negative is usually printed onto **70mm film** stock for release.

skinning: See **texture mapping.**

skip frames: A method of speeding up the motion of a sequence of images by removing selected (usually regularly spaced) frames. Also known as *skip printing*.

slate: Information about a particular shot that is placed at the head of the shot, before the actual image begins.

slop comp, slap comp: A very rough initial composite that is usually used to test or visualize basic element relationships.

slow motion: Any technique that is used to slow down the motion of objects in a scene. It may involve filming at a faster speed than the intended projection speed or it may involve some post-processing technique. Also referred to as *slow-mo.*

SLR: Abbreviation for *single-lens reflex camera.*

SMPTE: Abbreviation for *Society of Motion Picture and Television Engineers.*

snorkel lens: See **periscope lens.**

Sobel filter: A specific type of **edge detection** algorithm.

Sobel matte: A discrete differentiation operator, computing an approximation of the gradient of the image intensity function. In simplified words, it uses an edge detection algorithm to create an outline around the edge.

software developer's kit (SDK): A programming interface that accompanies many software packages. It is used to write additional plug-ins and stand-alone programs to extend the capabilities of that software package.

solarization: An effect that is produced when a range of brightness within an image is inverted. Can be used to mimic an optical effect that occurs with extreme overexposure.

spatial aliasing: An **artifact** that is due to limited **spatial resolution.**

spatial convolution: See **convolve.**

spatial filter: A method of sampling and modifying the data in an image by looking at pixel groups.

spatial resolution: A measurement of the amount of data used to capture an image. In a digital image, spatial resolution is usually specified by giving the X and Y dimensions of the image as measured in **pixels.**

special effects: Term for on-set mechanical and in-camera optical effects that are created in front of the camera. Also known as *practical* or *mechanical* effects. The general public tends to use this term to encompass both practical effects and visual effects. Also referred to as *SFX.*

special visual effects: See **visual effects.**

spherical lens: A lens that does not change the apparent width-to-height relationship of the scene being photographed. This is in contrast to an **anamorphic lens.**

spill: Any light in a scene that strikes an object it was not intended to illuminate. See also **blue spill, green spill.**

spill suppression: Any process that removes or neutralizes undesirable **spill** from an object.

spline: A series of points connected by a line or curve. See **spline curve.**

spline curve: A continuous smooth curve defined by a certain number of **control points**. See **spline.**

splinter unit: A part of the production crew that is tasked with going off on their own to film or capture specific shots or plates.

split diopter: A split **diopter** is an auxiliary lens—half lens and half plain glass—that goes in front of the camera lens so only half of the scene is focused for close-ups.

split-screen: A basic composite in which two elements are combined using a simple matte with little or no articulation.

sprite: General term for a (usually small) 2D element that is animated within a larger scene. Often used in conjunction with a **particle system.**

square pixel: A **pixel** with equal X and Y dimensions.

squeezed image: An image that has been **anamorphically** compressed.

sRGB: A standard RGB color space created cooperatively by HP and Microsoft in 1996 for use on monitors, printers, and the Internet.

stabilization: The process of removing bounce or jitter from a sequence of images.

staircasing: A **spatial aliasing artifact** in which a line or edge appears jagged, like the profile of a staircase, instead of smooth. Also called *stairstepping.*

stand-in: A reference object photographed in a particular scene that can later be used to help match the color and lighting of any new elements that will be added to that scene.

static image: An image that contains no motion.

static matte: Another term for a **fixed matte.**

steadiness: An image sequence in which the individual frames are stable relative to each other and do not suffer from any frame-to-frame jitter or bounce.

steady test: A test to determine if a camera or the imagery shot with that camera is steady.

stereo: (stereo) Short for *stereoscopic.* (If you are trying to learn about multichannel sound, you are in the wrong place.)

stereographer: The individual who is responsible for making sure all shots of a project are properly composed in terms of stereoscopic depth.

stereoplexing: (stereo) Short for *stereoscopic multiplexing.* A means of incorporating information for the left and right perspective views into a single information channel without expansion of the bandwidth.

stereopsis: (stereo) The binocular depth sense—literally, "solid seeing."

stereoscope: (stereo) A device for viewing plano-stereoscopic images. It is usually an optical device with twin viewing systems.

stereoscopic image: Imagery that is designed to send a different image to each observer's left and right eyes, thereby producing a sense of depth.

stereoscopic pair: A pair of images (one for each eye) that comprise a **stereoscopic image.**

stereoscopy: (stereo) The art and science of creating images with the depth sense stereopsis.

stochastic sampling: A random or semirandom sampling of a data set. Used for **antialiasing, motion blur,** etc.

stock: General term for motion picture film, or the specific manufacturer, manufacturer's product code, or rating of that film.

stop: A way of measuring exposure that traces back to the different *f*-**stop** settings available on any given lens. The *f*-stops on a lens are calibrated so that each successive stop will give twice the exposure. Thus, "increase the brightness by one stop" means to double the brightness; "decrease by two stops" would result in one-fourth the original brightness.

stop-motion animation: An animation technique that involves photographing objects or characters a frame at a time, changing the pose or position of the object between each frame. The result, when played back at normal speed, is of a subject or object with motion or "life to it."

storyboard: A sequence of drawings that shows the intended action in a scene. Used as a visualization tool before the scene is shot.

strobing: A rhythmic flicker in a moving image. Often due to a lack of motion blur when dealing with synthetic images.

subpixel: Any technique that works at a resolution of greater than a single pixel; usually accomplished by making slight weighted corrections to several surrounding pixels.

super: Shortened form of **superimpose.**

Super 8mm film: The Super 8 format is a narrow-gauge film that contains one **perforation** along each side and runs 72 frames per foot.

Super 16mm film: A **16mm film** that uses an image area that extends beyond the sound track of normal 16mm film. It is a single-**perforation** film that extends the image area out to where the second row of perforations would normally be. Also called single-perf.

Super 35mm film: The Super 35 format is a 35mm film that uses the **full aperture** of the negative to capture its images. Super 35 can be used for a number of different **formats** that use full-aperture framing, but it is most commonly used for films that are intended to be projected with a 2.35:1 **aspect ratio.** Also referred to as **Super Techniscope,** *Super 1.85,* or *Super 2.35.*

Super Techniscope: Another name for **Super 35.**

superblack: Any brightness level that drops below the normal representation of black for a given image or device. In video, superblack levels may be used for keying.

superimpose: To place one image on top of another, usually with some transparency involved.

Superscope: An early **anamorphic** format that uses the full width of the **35mm film** area and is cropped top and bottom for a

2:1 **aspect ratio** during projection. See also **Cinemascope, Techniscope.**

superwhite: Any brightness level that rises above the normal representation of white for a given image or device.

surface normal: A vector that is perpendicular to a surface at a specific point on the surface. In compositing, **multiple-pass rendering** will often include a surface-normal pass.

surround: (stereo) The vertical and horizontal edges immediately adjacent to the screen.

sync block: A mechanical device used to measure film length. Film is loaded onto a cylinder calibrated at 1 foot per rotation. An attached counter reads and updates the total amount of footage that winds through.

T

"T": (stereo) In stereoscopy, "T" is used to denote the distance between the eyes, called the *interpupillary* or *interocular distance*; "T" is used to denote the distance between stereoscopic camera heads' lens axes and is called the *interaxial.*

tablet: A user-input device that provides a greater amount of control than the traditional computer mouse. Generally used in conjunction with a special pen.

tail slate: Slate information that is recorded at the end of the shot instead of the beginning. Generally only used in live-action photography; the slate information is filmed upside-down, to distinguish it from a normal slate.

take: When a particular shot is photographed multiple times in order to achieve a desired result, each time is referred to as a *take.* This concept extends to digital compositing, where each test that is sent to film or video is usually kept track of with a *take number.*

TARGA: A specific image file format.

Technical Assistant (TA): An individual who is responsible for much of the basic data wrangling within a facility; often handles file backups. (See the list of VES-approved titles in Appendix B.)

Technical Director (TD): An individual responsible for ensuring that the technical aspects of a digital shot are addressed. Generally considered to be a subset of **digital artist** with particular technical skills. (See the list of VES-approved titles in Appendix B.)

technical previs: Incorporates and generates accurate camera, lighting, design, and scene layout information to help define production requirements. This often takes the form of dimensional diagrams that illustrate how particular shots can be accomplished, using real-world terms and measurements. Also see **previs, pitchvis, on-set previs,** and **postvis.**

Techniscope: A system designed to produce 35mm **anamorphic** prints from 35mm negatives using an image area that is approximately half the height of regular 35mm images and a special camera. The negative image area is then stretched to normal height and projected at an **aspect ratio** of **2.35:1**. See also **Cinemascope, Superscope.**

telecine: A device for rapidly converting motion picture film into a video format. A telecine device is much faster than a film **scanner** but will produce lower quality results.

telephoto lens: Any lens that has a longer-than-normal **focal length**. For a 35mm camera, a focal length of 50mm is considered normal, since it reasonably duplicates the magnification of a human eye.

temp comp: Shortened form of **temporary composite.**

temporal: Relating to time or something that changes over time.

temporal aliasing: An **artifact** that is due to limited **temporal resolution.**

temporal filling: Process by which missing image data is replaced from frames elsewhere in a shot where that image area is revealed.

temporal resolution: A measurement of the amount of data used to capture a sequence of images. Temporal resolution is usually specified by giving the number of frames per second used to capture the sequence.

temporary composite: A rough composite produced for a number of different reasons, usually to better judge the spatial and color relationships of the elements in a scene so that they can be modified to produce a **final** composite. Also called a *temp comp*.

10-bit image: In the **visual effects** world, this term typically refers to any image containing 10 bits of color information per **channel**. The most widely used 10-bit image **format** used in **visual effects** work is the **Cineon** file format.

tessellation: A collection of plane figures that fills the plane with no overlaps and no gaps. One may also speak of *tessellations* of the parts of a plane or of other surfaces. Generalizations to higher dimensions are also possible. Tessellations frequently appeared in the art of M. C. Escher. Tessellations are seen throughout art history, from ancient architecture to modern art. Also referred to as *tiling of the plane*.

texture mapping: Process in which an image is overlaid onto a CG object.

TGA: See **TARGA.**

theater space: (stereo) The region appearing to be in front of the screen or out into the audience. Can also be called *audience space*. Images with negative parallax will appear to be in theater space. The boundary between screen and theater space is the plane of the screen and has zero parallax. See **screen space.**

35mm film: The most common film format used in professional moviemaking. Each **frame** contains a gauge of 35mm and four **perforations** (thus its nickname *four-perf*) and there are 16 frames per foot. The sound information usually runs along the left side of the film between the perforations and the image.

32-bit image: In the **visual effects** world, this term typically refers to any image containing 32 bits of color information per **channel**. At this **bit depth** the channels are usually stored with a floating point data representation; hence, a 32 bit-per-channel image is thus also referred to as a **float** image.

3:2 pulldown: Usually synonymous with **2:3 pulldown.**

3:2 pullup: Usually synonymous with **2:3 pullup.**

3D: Shorthand for *three dimensional.* Having characteristics in three different dimensions, most often width, height, and depth.

3D film: (1) A general term referring to a film created entirely with 3D **computer graphics.** (2) Often used as another term for a stereoscopic film.

3D glasses: Specially designed glasses that are worn to view **stereoscopic imagery.** See also **anaglyph glasses, flicker glasses, polarized glasses.**

3D graphics: Computer graphics that involves the creation of three-dimensional models within the computer.

3D motion blur: Motion blur that is calculated for a CG scene as it is rendered, as opposed to applying **2D motion blur** as a postprocess.

3D tracking: Unlike **2D tracking,** 3D tracking is intended to recreate the full 3D movement of the camera that photographed a particular scene (or, less commonly, the full 3D movement of an object in the scene). See also **matchmove.**

three-perf: A technique used to maximize the use of raw film stock in **1.85 formats** so that almost no film is wasted. Most cameras use a four-perf pulldown that creates a lot of unused film between the captured images, whereas a three-perf pulldown positions the captured images closer together.

TIFF: Abbreviation for *tagged image file format,* a specific image file format.

time code: An electronic indexing method used with videotapes. Time code is measured in hours, minutes, seconds, and frames.

timeline graph: A graph that represents the temporal relationships between objects or data.

timing: (1) A general term referring to how a particular event or object moves or evolves over a period of time. (2) See **color timing.**

tracking: The process of determining the movement of objects in a scene (relative to the camera) by analyzing the captured footage of that scene. See **2D tracking, 3D tracking.**

tracking markers: Another term for **witness points.**

transformation: Usually refers to a geometric transformation.

transition effect: A method for moving from one **scene** to the next. See also **wipe, dissolve.**

translation: A **geometric transformation** that refers only to a change in position, without a change in scale or rotation.

translucent: A term that refers to something that is partially **transparent**; usually implies some additional image distortion, such as blurring.

transmission blue screen: A blue screen that has a series of lights behind the translucent blue screen that would illuminate evenly. They are very easy to use but due to their design they are not very flexible or portable.

transparent: The characteristic of an image that allows other images that are behind it to still be partially visible. Transparent is the opposite of **opaque.**

traveling matte: Any **matte** that changes over time, as opposed to a **static matte.**

trucking: Camera movement that is perpendicular to the direction of the camera lens.

_t_-stop: A measurement of the **aperture** of a lens that also takes into account the amount of light lost when passing through the lens elements themselves.

tumble paint: A term of art used to distinguish 3D paint systems that allow direct painting on the mesh, such as Mudbox or Zbrush, as differentiated from systems that use projection cameras to place textures on a model.

turnover: The process of handing over a visual effects shot or edited and locked visual effects sequence to a visual effects facility to begin work.

24p: Video that is shot at 24 frames per second.

2D: Shorthand for _two dimensional_. Containing information in only two dimensions (generally width and height) without any sense of depth.

2D graphics: **Computer graphics** that does not use any 3D information and thus involves no explicit depth information.

2D motion blur: **Motion blur** that is added as a post-process to moving objects in an image.

2D tracking: The process of determining the motion of objects in a scene relative to the camera. The data derived by a 2D track is dependent on the number of points tracked. See **3D tracking, one-point track, two-point track, four-point track.**

2k resolution: A general term referring to any digital image containing an X **resolution** of approximately 2048 **pixels.** The actual dimensions of a 2k image depend on the **aspect ratio** of the imagery. A common 2k resolution used in **visual effects** when working with **full aperture** framing is 2048 × 1556.

two-perf: Nickname for **16mm film** because it carries only two **perforations** for each frame.

two-point track: A type of **2D tracking** in which two points are selected from a **sequence** of images to extract an approximation of an object's movement relative to the camera. Allows for the determination of rotation and scale as well as basic translation. See **one-point track, four-point track.**

2.35 format: Pronounced "two-three-five format," 2.35 is a widely used **aspect ratio** for film. It can also be written as 2.35:1, which means that the image is 2.35 times as wide as it is high. **Cinemascope** and **Super 35** are most commonly used as the acquisition format to acquire this **widescreen** format.

2.5D (2 1/2 D): Pronounced "two-and-a-half D," this is a general term for techniques that use 2D imagery in a 3D environment to give the illusion of a true 3D scene.

2:3 pulldown: Pronounced "two-three pulldown," this is a method for converting 24-fps film to 30-fps video. Also called a *3:2 pulldown* or just *pulldown.*

2:3 pullup: Pronounced as "two-three pullup," this is a method for converting 30-fps video to 24-fps film. Also called a *3:2 pullup* or just *pullup.*

U

Ultimatte: A proprietary tool based on the **color difference method** that can be used to extract a matte from an image shot in front of a uniform backing.

undercrank: Running a camera at a lower speed than the intended projection rate, resulting in projected footage that appears to move faster than normal. Footage shot at a slower-than-normal rate is said to have been shot undercranked.

underscan: The adjustment on a video monitor that increases the viewable height and width of the image area so that the edges of the display can be seen.

unpremultiplied image: An image whose red, green, and blue **channels** have not been multiplied by an alpha channel. Opposite of **premultiplied image.**

unpremultiply: To redivide the **RGB channels** of an image by its own **alpha channel**. See **unpremultiplied image.**

unsharp masking: A particular technique used to **sharpen** an image that involves subtracting a slightly blurred image from the original. Used not only in the digital realm but also as a photographic technique.

user interface: The portion of a computer program that deals specifically with how the user interacts with the software. See also **graphical user interface.**

V

value: In the **HSV** color space, the value equals the maximum of the red, green, and blue components.

vaporware: A product that does not yet exist but is nevertheless being promised for delivery.

vector graphics: Geometrical primitives, such as points, lines, curves, and shapes or polygon(s), that are based on mathematical equations that represent images in computer graphics. Unlike **raster graphics,** which is made up of a grid of pixels, vectors are usually just lines drawn on a screen.

vectorscope: A device used to view the **chrominance** portion of a **video signal**. Radial distance from the center of the display represents **saturation** (chrominance amplitude), and the counterclockwise or clockwise angular distance represents the **hue** (chrominance **phase**). See also **waveform monitor.**

VFX: Abbreviation for **visual effects.**

view frustum culling: The process of removing objects that lie completely outside the **viewing frustum** from the rendering process.

viewing frustum: The region of space in the modeled world that may appear on the screen; it is the field of view of the notional camera. The exact shape of this region varies depending on what kind of camera lens is being simulated, but typically it is a frustum of a rectangular pyramid (hence the name). The planes that cut the frustum perpendicular to the viewing direction are called the *near plane* and the *far plane.* Objects closer to the camera than the near plane or beyond the far plane are not drawn. Often, the far plane is placed infinitely far away from the camera so all objects within the frustum are drawn regardless of their distance from the camera. Also referred to as a *view frustum.*

vignetting: A camera or lens artifact characterized by a darkening of the image in the corners of the frame.

virtual asset: Database definition of asset that is not actually a file on disk.

visible spectrum: The range of colors between ultraviolet and infrared that is visible to the human eye.

VistaVision: A specialized 35mm film format that runs the film through the camera horizontally instead of vertically and is able to capture more than twice the resolution of a standard 35mm frame. Generally only used for **visual effects**

work nowadays. Also known as **eight-perf** and also spelled *Vistavision.*

visual effects (VFX): A broad term that refers to just about anything that cannot be captured using standard photographic techniques. Visual effects can be accomplished **in camera** or via a number of different optical or digital **post-production** processes. Visual effects are a subcategory of **special effects.**

Visual Effects Director of Photography: The individual responsible for photographing any elements that will be used in visual effects production. (See the list of VES-approved titles in Appendix B.)

Visual Effects Producer: The individual responsible for the administrative side of visual effects production. (See the list of VES-approved titles in Appendix B.)

Visual Effects Supervisor: The individual responsible for the creative and technical side of visual effects production. (See the list of VES-approved titles in Appendix B.)

Volume: Term used to describe the motion capture stage. However, unlike *stage*, it implies a 3D space.

W

wagon wheeling: An image **artifact** caused when a rotating object (such as a wheel) appears to be moving at the wrong speed or in the wrong direction relative to the object to which it is attached. This is a **temporal aliasing** artifact.

Waldo: A mechanical input device that has encoders attached to its axes of motion such that any motion of the device will translate to a series of numbers that are read by a computer as locations or rotations in 3D space. Such devices are used to assist in animation of characters, motion-controlled rigs, etc. Named after the Robert A. Heinlein short story *Waldo.*

warm: A nonexact term used to describe an image that is biased toward the red portion of the spectrum.

warping: A geometric, per-pixel distortion of an image, often based on some kind of spline- or grid-based control.

warping engine: Within a package used for compositing, the code that is responsible for any **geometric transformations.**

waveform monitor: A device primarily used to measure the luminance of a video signal with respect to time. Also called a *scope.* See also **vectorscope.**

wavelet: A method of representing an image based on frequency information. Used as the basis for certain compression techniques.

weave: See **film weave.**

wedge: See **color wedge, exposure wedge.**

white balance: The calibration of a camera for accurate color capture or of an image for accurate color display based on specific lighting conditions.

white point: (1) On a piece of film, the measured density in the area of least opacity. (2) In a digital image, the numerical value that corresponds to the brightest area that will be represented when the image is eventually viewed in its final form.

wide-angle lens: Any lens that has a smaller-than-normal **focal length.** For a 35mm camera, a focal length of 50mm is considered normal, since it reasonably duplicates the magnification of a human eye.

widescreen: A generic term that usually refers to any image with an **aspect ratio** greater than 1.33:1.

window: (stereo) The stereo window that corresponds to the screen surround unless floating windows are used.

wipe: A specific **transition effect** in which one scene is horizontally or vertically revealed to replace another scene.

wire removal: A generic term for the process of using digital painting or compositing techniques to remove undesirable wires, rigs, or harnesses that were needed to aid certain stunts or **practical effects.**

witness camera: Cameras used to film or videotape the action from one or more viewpoints that are not the same viewpoints used by the primary production camera. This data is used in the creation of many things, ranging from determining where everything on the set was in three dimensions to providing animation reference.

witness points: Specific objects placed into a scene that can later be analyzed to determine the movement and configuration of the camera that photographed the shot using **tracking** techniques. Also known as *tracking markers.*

working resolution: The resolution of the images that will be produced by any given compositing process.

X

x: An abbreviation used to denote a **frame.** For example, "24x" denotes 24 frames.

x-**axis:** Generally the horizontal axis.

Y

y-**axis:** Generally the vertical axis.

Y-depth image: A specialized image that uses the brightness of each pixel to specify the height of that pixel relative to some reference ground plane. See also **Z-depth image.**

YIQ: A color space used for **NTSC** television, in which the brightness (Y), orange-cyan (I), and green-magenta (Q) components are encoded together.

YUV: A **color space** in which Y represents the **luminance** and U and V represent the **chrominance** of an image or video.

Z

z-axis: The axis perpendicular to the **x-axis** and the **y-axis,** and consequently the axis that is used to represent depth.

Z-buffer: Another term for a **Z-depth image.**

Z-channel: A **Z-depth image** that is integrated with a color image as an additional **channel.**

Z-depth compositing: Compositing images together with the use of a **Z-buffer** to determine their relative depths or distances from the camera.

Z-depth image: A specialized image that uses the brightness of each pixel to specify the relative depth for each pixel in the corresponding RGB image. This depth may be measured relative to some arbitrary fixed point in space or relative to the virtual camera that is being used to capture the scene. Also called a **Z-buffer.**

zoom: (1) In a real camera, the act of increasing the **focal length** of the camera's lens to magnify a portion of the scene. (2) With digital images, the act of increasing the scale of a portion of an image in order to duplicate the effect of a camera zoom.

ZPS: (stereo) Abbreviation for *zero parallax setting,* which is the means used to control screen parallax to place an object in the plane of the screen. ZPS may be controlled by HIT, or toe-in. Refer to the plane of zero parallax or the point of zero parallax (PZP) so achieved. Prior terminology says that left and right images are *converged* when in the plane of the screen. That term should be avoided because it may be confused with the convergence of the eyes and because the word implies rotation of camera heads. Such rotation produces geometric distortion and may be expedient in camera rigs, but it is unforgivable in a CG virtual camera rig.

Z-space: A way of stating where an object is in relation to the camera on one axis—close to near.

INDEX

An *f* following page numbers indicates a figure and *t* indicates a table.